Foreword

This book is the first volume of a running series under the title *International Handbooks on Informati*... eries is edited by Peter Bernus, Jacek I... Shaw. One objective is to give state of ... information systems theory and applica... ternational group of academics and pra... erence source not only for problem solv... ment but also for professional research...

It se... series with a volume covering some basic aspects about information systems. The focus of the first volume is therefore *architectures*. It was decided to have a balanced number of contributions from academia and practitioners. The structure of the material follows a differentiation betweeen modelling languages, tools and methodologics. These are collected into separate parts, allowing the reader of the handbook a better comparison of the contributions.

Information systems are a major component of the entire enterprise and the reader will notice that many contributions could just as easily have been included in another volume of the series which is on enterprise integration. Conversely, some traditionally information systems topics, as organisational analysis and strategic change management methods, will be treated in more depth in the Handbook on Enterprise Integration. The two volumes will complement each other.

The editors of this volume decided to share their work. Peter Bernus and Günter Schmidt put up the framework and arranged most of the chapters. Kai Mertins took care of some contributions presented in parts three and four. We think the result is a representative survey on the most important results on Architectures of Information Systems which are presented by prominent experts. We have to thank not only the contributors for their effort but also various colleagues who helped us by suggesting relevant topics and qualified authors. The editors acknowledge the role of the advisory board members: Andy Bond, Guy Doumeingts, Keith Duddy, Mark Fox, Tom Gruber, Ted Goranson, Rudolf Haggenmüller, Linda Harvey, Matthias Jarke, Jim Melton, Chris Menzel, John Mylopoulos, Elmar J. Sinz, Riitta Smeds, François Vernadat.

One of the challenges was a technical one. We had to compile text and graphics together generated by distributed software systems from all over the world. Jörg Winckler expertly resolved not only this problem with a number of supporters who are too many to name them all. We sincerely thank them for their help and support.

Contents

CHAPTER 1

Architectures of Information Systems

Peter Bernus, Günter Schmidt

This chapter is an introduction into the scope of the Handbook on Architectures of Information Systems. We will point out that this volume gives a comprehensive survey of the most important aspects in this area giving not only a list of available alternatives but providing also a guidance amidst the many proposals.

1 What is an Information System?

During the past three decades the concept of information system and the discipline of information systems underwent an evolution, as witnessed by definitions given by various authors.

Mader and Hagin in 1974 [MH74] defined the information system as the system which provided "... transaction processing and decision support ...". Brookes *et al* [BGJL82] defined it as "... all forms of information collection, storage, retrieval, processing and communication ..." as "... the organization's instrumentation ... informing decision makers of the state of the organization ... including computer based and human implemented systems". Inmon [Inm86] defines "... information systems architecture: [as] the modelling of the data and processes of a company and how that model relates to the business of the company ...". Tatnal *et al* [TDM95] define an information system as "... [a system] comprising hardware, software, people, procedures, and data, integrated with the objective of collecting, storing, processing, transmitting and displaying information" and elaborate further by defining "functional information systems" which support specific business functions, e.g. accounting, human resource management, manufacturing, marketing, etc. and "integrated information systems" which provide information flow across all areas of application. Sandstrom [San88] proposes that the information system "... is a designed tool, the purpose of which is to serve people in active work with information and in an organization. It is an organized construction with subsystems for collecting, processing, storing, retrieving, and distributing information together, influenced by people. It becomes an abstraction of a service function when studied". In [SK92] it is proposed that "... the field is known now as Information Systems. 'Systems' is the operative word, since the field includes not only technologies, but people, processes, and organizational mechanisms as well ...". All of these definitions contribute to our understanding of information systems.

The main requirement that an information system must satisfy is to provide and maintain an integrated information flow throughout the enterprise, so that the right information is available whenever and wherever needed, in the quality and quantity needed. This generic requirement defined different tasks for information systems practitioners in the past. The first focus of information systems research and development emerged from the need of physically enabling the information flow, a level of integration that we call today *physical integration*. As physical integration became reality through the installation of networks and adoption of standards it became possible to concentrate efforts on the *interoperability* of applications, i.e. to enable the various business applications to be combined and interconnected for new tasks, without having to re-design them. Interoperability is not yet achieved in many business areas, but practice of the 1990s brought success in some of them, such as database interoperability. The next challenge after application integration is *business integration*, which is the question how various business functions can be interconnected and efficiently combined through information systems.

An *information system* is a system for collecting, processing, storing, retrieving, and distributing information within the enterprise and between the enterprise and its environment. The information system is a *functionally defined subsystem* of the enterprise, i.e. it is defined through the services it renders. It may be implemented by the enterprise's own resources (automated equipment and humans), but parts of the information system's services may be provided to the enterprise by other enterprises.

2 What is an Information System Architecture?

An architecture is the integrated structural design of a system, its elements and their relationships depending on given system requirements. The notion of an architecture is widely used in the context of buildings and computers. When applied to information systems we follow the definition of Wall [Wal96] and assume that an *architecture* is the abstract plan including the corresponding designing process of the system's structure appropriate to the goals of the system based on design principles and a methodological framework.

Below, we treat the required components of information system architecture according to the Generalized Enterprise Reference Architecture and Methodology (GERAM) [TF97], defining the information system within the context of the enterprise (see Figure 1 for an overview on GERAM). GERA, the Generalized Enterprise Reference Architecture is one component and defines several important ingredients of architectures for any enterprise entity, including the information system.

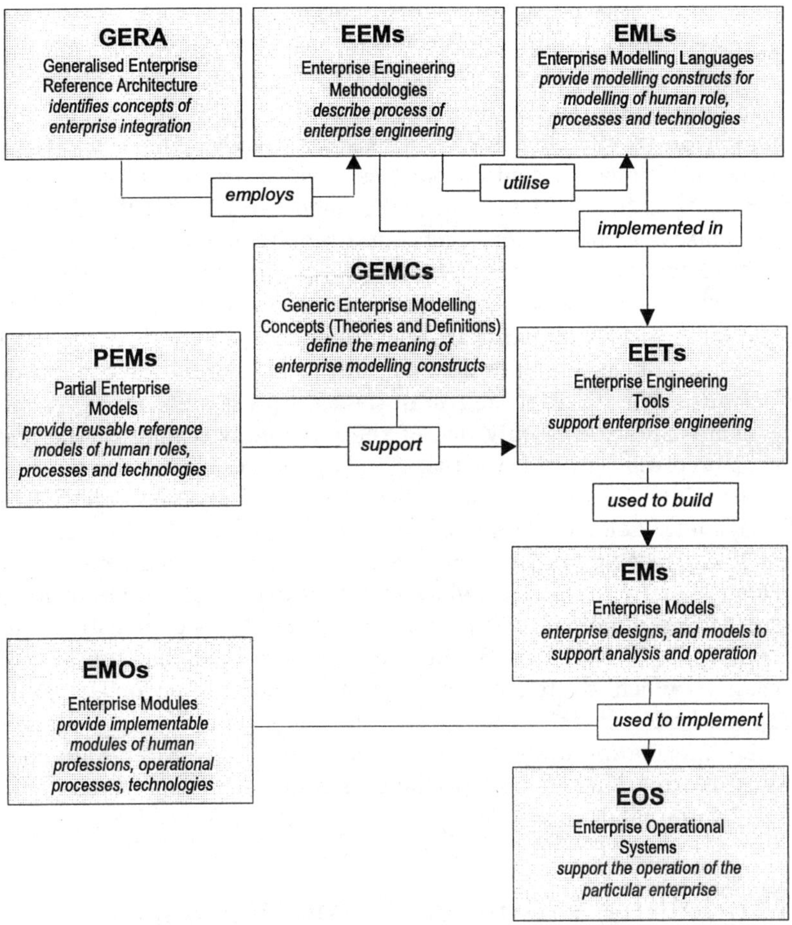

Figure 1: GERAM framework components

Entities involved in the information system's architecture are the enterprise and its products. Both must be considered for the purposes of information systems design, implementation, and operation, especially when more and more systems are designed for virtual enterprises. Thus the information system must support the information flow

- which integrates the value chain, i.e. the business process involved in producing the product(s) and service(s) of the enterprise,
- which integrates the development of the enterprise throughout its entire life.

Both entities, i.e. the enterprise and the product have a life history, which is the history in time of all relevant events, transformations and milestones that happened or are planned to happen to the entity. Life histories are unique and particular, therefore a functional abstraction is used to describe the common functional elements of life histories, called *life-cycle*. The life-cycle model is defined to contain "phases", which are regarded as types of transformation rather than as temporal sequences. E.g. GERA defines the life-cycle phases: identification - concept - requirements - design - detailed design - implementation - operation and decommissioning. For more details about the relationships among life-cycles of enterprise entities see [TF97].

In the early phases the enterprise and its strategies, objectives, mission, vision, values, policies etc. are defined, and at this stage the separation of the information system from the rest of the enterprise is not always possible. Rather, this separation is only one of the possible outcomes of the identification of involved enterprise entities; it happens if the enterprise decides to outsource information system services to an external provider. Consequently (i) methodologies developed for strategic information systems management and strategic management are very similar - both essentially managing change, and (ii) information system considerations are important but not exclusive ingredients in that process. However, if it is demonstrated early in a change process that it is the information system of the enterprise that needs change (which is often the case), then specialized information systems planning methodologies may be utilized. In the ensuing enterprise life-cycle phases the information system becomes more and more a separate component; thus information systems specific design and implementation methods and tools can be made available.

3 Modelling Framework and Views

An architecture has to represent all relevant aspects of a system. These aspects are defined by models representing different system views. They are derived from the goals the system has to fulfil and the constraints defined by the system's environment. The GERA modelling framework describes what models of the enterprise may need to be created and maintained during the enterprise's life history. The following views on information systems are considered essential to be represented by the models of an architecture.

1. *Information, Functions, Co-ordination and Synchronisation.* The major elements of information systems are the data, the functions using or producing the data, and relationships describing how functions relate to data and other functions. The modelling framework therefore needs to represent

   - the structure of data,
   - the structure and behaviour of functions, and
   - the rules for co-ordination and synchronisation (defining the dynamic properties of a system).

   Depending on the actual selection of a modelling language these three views may or may not be separate.

2. *Organization.* Information systems are invariably integrated into organizations. Thus an organizational view needs to describe the relation between the users and the system. It shows how the information system is used by an organization in terms of collecting, processing, storing, retrieving, and distributing information. There are two important issues which have to be covered: (i) the structure of the organization where the information system is used has to be represented, i.e. which department, group, and individual takes over the responsibility for correct usage of the system, and (ii) how the flow of information is organized to meet the requirements of the organization.

3. *Resources.* Resources are used to physically implement and to run the information system. The most important information processing resources are software, hardware, and humans to carry out innovative or otherwise not automated information processing tasks.

Each of these views are represented by models belonging to a life-cycle phase, such as described in Figure 2. Accordingly

- the models of the "management and control" of the enterprise describe the service of the information system traditionally rendered by a management information system.
- the models of the enterprise's "service to the customer" describe the information exchange requirements among the business processes, supporting business transactions with product related information.

The purpose of an information system is derived from the mission of the enterprise which it needs to serve. Requirements level models of the system describe its functionality (necessary tasks) while design level models propose a solution to how these tasks can be performed. Design level models are more detailed and concrete in the phases of detailed design and implementation.

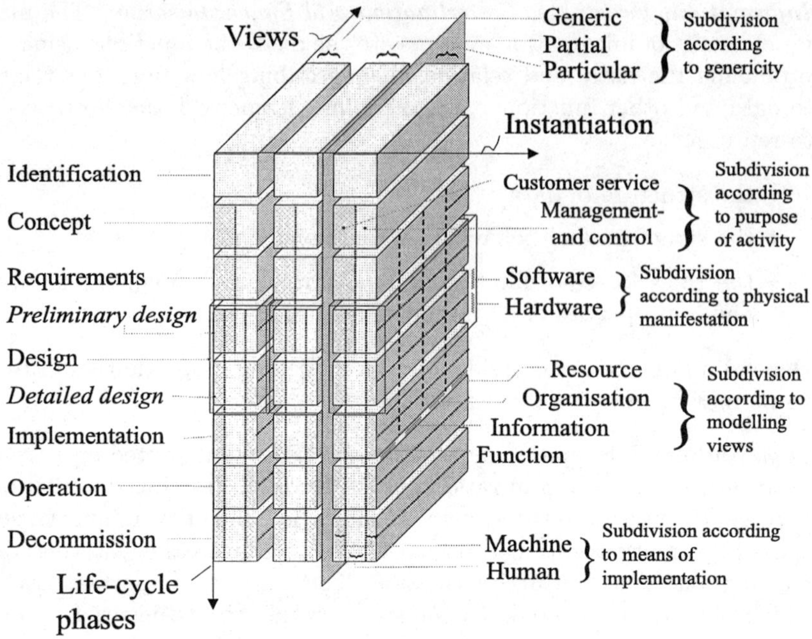

Figure 2: GERA modelling framework

The first part of the handbook describes a representative selection of modelling languages supporting the analysis and the design of information systems, while the third part presents tools which are suitable for model representation and analysis at each of these levels. It is to be noted, that the model categories of GERA are not only meant for information systems representation, but for the modelling of the entire enterprise, and the handbook describes only those languages which are most important from the point of view of the integrated information flow in the enterprise, i.e. information system models. For this reason there is no chapter in this handbook about "languages to describe functional models of technological equipment", "languages to model factory layouts (detailed design level resource models)" or "financial models of the resources". Not that these models would be less important, but because they are beyond the scope of this volume. Even organizational and resource modelling languages are treated less prominently, for exactly the same reason.

3.1 Models and Methodologies

Using the modelling framework and associated tools information systems models are built. An architecture has to guarantee that the mission of the enterprise is taken into account in the process of design, and that the system will support the enterprise in achieving its objectives. The models of the information system should provide sufficient evidence for the designer to believe that this will indeed be the case. From the models the system properties should be derivable and conversely, the models have to be designed so that the system requirements can be fulfilled. The second part describes methodologies for information system construction which are intended to ensure that the system is consistent and supportive of the enterprise mission. We also plan to amalgamate enterprise engineering and information systems engineering methodologies in a forthcoming volume, the Handbook on Enterprise Integration to broaden the scope of methodologically supported change.

Information systems design methodologies should safeguard that basic modelling requirements are met. Among these are the following:

- correctness, integrity, consistency, completeness,
- low level of complexity through modularity,
- clarity and ease of communication,
- adequacy, as a basis for system development,
- provision of a guideline for research.

It would be impossible to design good quality models without relying on suitable reference models. Typical models, or *reference models* of the information system are presented in the fourth part. Such models are also often called "Type 1 Reference Architectures" [BNW96]. Information system architectures are defined for the long term and thus have to cope with continuous change: they must be stable, open, flexible, extendible and should be supported by standards. These properties also ease the re-use of different models, methods and techniques within the same architectural framework.

Reference models may be provided for certain classes of enterprises on certain levels. This property is referred to as granularity in [Sch96]. Thus there exist generic reference models of good practice which are general enough to cover a broad spectrum of applications, while a more specific model may be related to a certain class of enterprise, so that all companies belonging to this class might use the enterprise model as a guideline for more detailed model building. The most specific model refers to a particular enterprise and its information system integrating its business functions.

3.2 Building Blocks of Information Systems

Significant resources of the implementation of the information system are: humans (individuals, groups, and higher level organizational units), and computer software and hardware systems.

From these this handbook treats in its last part some basic *modules*, or product types which are likely to play very significant roles in the building of any information system. The treatment includes a strategic analysis of the direction of information technology in the enterprise, as well as an overview of the latest distributed system technologies, and the requirements and examples for an information integration infrastructure.

Readers familiar with information systems literature will be missing from this handbook a chapter on organizational analysis, agent modelling, or on information system evaluation methods. After all the human organization plays a significant part in the information system, both as user and as producer of information. Hirschheim *et al* [HS88] state that "Organizations are complex social and political entities which defy purely objective analysis. As information systems form part of organizational reality (i.e. the gestalt) they cannot be viewed in isolation.". We therefore plan to treat the social organizational domain of information systems, combining analysis and design, using interpretive approaches in the larger context of enterprise engineering, including it in a forthcoming volume, the Handbook on Enterprise Integration.

References

[BNW96] P. Bernus, L. Nemes, T. J. Williams (eds.), Architectures for Enterprise Integration, Chapman and Hall, 1996

[BGJL82] Brookes, C. H. P., Grouse, Ph. J., Jeffrey, D. R., Lawrence, M. J., Information Systems Design, Prentice Hall, 1982

[HS88] Hirschheim, R., Smithson, S., Critical analysis of is evaluation, in: N. Bjorn-Andersen, G. B. Davis (eds.), Information Systems Assessment: Issues and Challenges, North Holland, 1988, 17-37

[Inm86] Inmon, W. H., Information Systems Architecture: A System Developer's Primer, Prentice Hall, 1986

[MH74] Mader, C. H., Hagin, R., Information Systems: Technology, Economics, Applications, Science Research Associates, 1974

[San88] Sandstrom, G., Pragmatic quality of information systems, in: N. Bjorn-Andersen, G. B. Davis (eds.), Information Systems Assessment: Issues and Challenges, North Holland, 1988, 195-206

[Sch96] Schmidt, G., Informationsmanagement - Modelle, Methoden, Techniken, Springer, 1996

[SK92] Stohr, E. A., Konsynsky, B. R., Information Systems and Decision Processes, IEEE Comp. Soc. Press, 1992

[TDM95] Tatnal, A., Davey, B., Mcconville, D., Information Systems: Design and Implementation, Data Publishing, 1995

[TF97] GERAM Version 1.5, IFIP-IFAC Task Force on Enterprise Integration, 1997

[Wal96] Wall, F., Organisation und betriebliche Informationssysteme, Gabler, 1996

PART ONE

Techniques and Languages for the Description of Information Systems

This part is about those techniques and modelling languages which are typically used to specify and design information systems. A modelling language is a set of constructs for building models of systems, such as an information system. Models can be prepared of a system at various stages of the system life-cycle (e.g. specification, design, implementation), and from various viewpoints (e.g. information, function, resources). Depending on the goal of modelling the selected modelling language should be adequate or competent for the purpose of the modelling task. From the point of view of the user of the language it must be understandable, easy to use, and models developed using the language must be presentable and easy to interpret for the intended audience. From the point of view of the use of the language it must have sufficient expressive power to be able to capture all the information that the required type of model needs to contain. E.g., if the model of the system must be used for calculating the minimum time necessary to perform a process, then a pure functional modelling language which has no notion of time is inadequate [Sch97].

Modelling languages can be described by their syntax and semantics. The syntax of a language defines what are the legal constructs of that language. The most often used form of syntax definition is the Bacus-Naur Form (BNF). The definition of the language's syntax defines all legal constructs of the language, including terminal symbols which have no further structure and expressions, i.e. structures which can be built out of these symbols. The syntax definition of a language is useful for being able to build a parser that will examine an arbitrary expression and accept or reject it as a legal expression of the language. Furthermore, if the expression is legal, then the parser is able to analyse the structure of the expression and present it in the form of a parse tree or of parse trees determining how the expression is built using structure definitions given in the BNF.

The semantics of a language defines the meaning of the expressions written in that language. There are several ways to define the meaning of a language. Denotational semantics is used to define how expressions formed in the given language can be mapped to an interpretation or model which may be a real world or a symbolic system. If the language is mapped to an equivalent representation in a suitably selected logic (mostly first order logic) then the model theory of that logic will be suitable for the definition of the semantics. It is also customary to define a proof theory that allows reasoning about the constructs of the language, in particular proving properties of expressions. The meaning of expressions in the language will then be determined by what possible models are described by those expressions. E.g., the meaning of an Entity Relationship Schema is what is common in all possible implementations of that schema. For further details on denotational semantics refer to [Sch86].

For languages that describe operations the definition of the semantics can be using operational semantics. This can be done, for example, by defining an abstract machine and describing the effect of operations on the state of that abstract machine. Depending on the reason why the operational semantics is developed operations may be described by their pre-conditions and post-conditions i.e. statements that must be true to be able to execute the operation, and statements that will be true after the execution as well as invariants i.e. properties that are not effected by the execution of the operation. Some languages developed for the purpose of specifying the meaning of languages especially programming languages are the Vienna Definition Language [Weg72] and Z [Spi88].

The formal specification of the operational semantics for a language can be used for the unambiguous definition allowing compatible and certifiable implementations of interpreters for the language. However, for any language of appreciable size this is a complex matter and due to the nature of these definitions other more simple definitions of the semantics are also necessary for end users. Users will still wish to verify the models developed in the language, but the verification will use several independent means, such as (i) execution of the models using test examples, (ii) in certain cases formal proofs, (iii) informal means, such as discussions. Even if the formal specification of the language's semantics was used only by the implementors or interpreters and not used by the end users of the language, it will be ensured that the evaluation of these models across different implementations will produce identical results.

Informal specification of the language semantics is usually given by formal presentation of the language syntax accompanied by natural language description of the intended meanings of the constructs (both in case of denotational and operational semantics). This is the approach that authors of this part have taken. The focus is on the question which languages are available to support information modelling and systems description. There is not one language which is equally suited for all purposes; each language has its individual strength to meet specific modelling requirements. Some languages might be applicable for a broad range of applications while others are more specialised and purpose oriented.

A model of an information system must represent all relevant views on the system. These are related to the system's elements and their relationship, i.e. the data and the objects of the application domain, the processes and activities to be carried out, the organizational environment and the communication needs. This part contains three groups of techniques and languages according to their purpose or intended use:

- Data and object modelling languages – intended for the modelling of the information view, i.e. the information that is stored or processed by the information system at various phases of the system life-cycle,
- Activity and process modelling languages – intended for the specification, design, and implementation modelling of the function of the information system,
- Multi view languages – those languages which are suitable for the representation of multiple views of the information system, possibly serving the modelling needs of multiple levels of the system life-cycle.

The choice of languages for information system modelling is so great that to select a few that will get prominent exposition in this book was extremely hard. We intended to provide examples of languages which can cover the life-cycle phases of the information system, from initial specification to implementation and operation.

Some languages are defined together with a modelling method or technique. A modelling method gives guidance for the user regarding how models are best built using the language. For example a modelling method would give specific instructions for information gathering, model building, model quality control etc. Information systems design methodologies would in turn incorporate such modelling methods or techniques as components of the methodology.

This part starts with a contribution by John Mylopoulos. It gives a state of the art survey on information modelling techniques for knowledge representation, data modelling, and requirements analysis. It also offers a comparative framework for information modelling approaches classifying them according to ontologies, abstraction mechanisms, and available tools.

The next three contributions are related to the group of data and object modelling languages. Reiner Anderl, Harald John and Christian Pütter give a description of Express which is a formal modelling language for the specification of static aspects of information representation. Terry Halpin presents

Object-Role Modelling also known as ORM or NIAM. This is a language designed for modelling and querying an information system at the conceptual level. Jim Melton surveys the main features of the database language SQL, in fact SQL2. We did not include SQL3 in this handbook because we felt that the SQL3 standard was still in developing stage and therefore its description would better wait until a next edition.

Although the editors were keen to include contributions on the Entity Relationship (ER) data model, and on the Object Database Management Group's (ODMG) data model, the contributions did not make this edition. The extended ER data model is prevalently used as a requirements and design level data model and is usually followed by a mapping to the relational data model on the detailed design and implementation levels. The ODMG data model serves as the common data model of many objectoriented database management systems. For details of the ER data model the reader is referred to [Elm94, Bat92] and for ODMG to [ODMG97].

The next four contributions belong to the group of activity and process modelling languages. Jean-Marie Proth gives an introduction into the theoretical background of Petri Nets. They are widely used for the evaluation and simulation of discrete event systems. State Transition Diagrams have the same focus and are discussed by Jules Desharnais, Marc Frappier, and Ali Mili. This language has a long tradition being expanded in the recent past to include features to represent hierarchy, timing, and communication. Jintae Lee, Michael Gruninger, Yan Jin, Thomas Malone, Austin Tate and Gregg Yost present PIF, the Process Interchange Format. It is designed to help automatically exchange process descriptions among different process tools using a single interface. Recent developments regarding PIF should be mentioned, especially the likely merger of PIF with the Process Specification Language (PSL) effort currently underway at the US National Institute of Standards (NIST). PSL has the ambitious objective to describe manufacturing processes such that the semantics of the language is axiomatised in form of ontological theories. Günter Schmidt gives a survey on GPN, a language especially developed for planning and scheduling of processes. GPN is mainly used for the optimisation of business processes in terms of time and cost. It directly relates to the framework of scheduling theory. It is possible to build models which match to the application of optimisation algorithms.

The third group is related to multi view languages and contains seven contributions. Christopher Menzel and Richard J. Mayer describe the IDEF family of languages. They cover the syntax and the semantic rules of the three most widely used IDEF0, IDEF1X, and IDEF3. Note that the languages are used in conjunction with a modelling method, thus the authors refer to IDEF0, 1X and 3 as modelling methods, not languages only. The CIMOSA languages are presented by Francois Vernadat. These languages are based on an event driven process model and cover functional, information, resource and organisational aspects of an enterprise and are defined for all life-cycle phases. It is expected that this wide scope approach to modelling would eventually get harmonised with many of the languages less wide in their coverage, or based on the formal definition of the semantics of these modelling languages more and more semantic translators would become available. Manfred A. Jeusfeld, Matthias Jarke, Hans W. Nissen, and Martin Staudt write on ConceptBase. This is a meta data management system intended to support the cooperative development and evolution of information systems with multiple interacting formalisms. ConceptBase, which is the implementation of a version of the Telos specification language, allows its user to extend the basic modelling formalism, because of the ability of the language to specify meta-schemas on arbitrary levels (meta, meta-meta, etc.). In spite of the seemingly higher order nature of the language it has a first order semantics, which is important for efficiency reasons. The next contribution is on Conceptual Graphs (CGs) given by John F. Sowa. These graphs show the logic designed for the visualization of knowledge represented in computer systems. Conceptual graphs can be thought of as a graphical notation for First Order Logic, which determines the expressive power of CGs. In fact CGs have been proposed as graphical representation of KIF (Knowledge Interchange Format) [GF92]. One important application is the possibility to use KIF for the formal specification of the meaning of different modelling languages through the expression of their semantics in form of ontological theories. Guy Doumeingts, Bruno Vallespir, and David Chen describe a language called the GRAI Grid which has been developed for the modelling of the management system of enterprises. As the paper shows management is best described in terms of decisions, thus the name decisional modelling. The uniqueness of this language lies in the fact that it has been developed on the basis of an ontology which has proven correct in systems theory and control system theory. This ontological underpinning, though not fully formalised, gives the language an advantage over other languages in which the user needs to develop a theory of what the best representation of management may be. The approach defines decision centres and their relationships defined by information links and decision frameworks. The Semantic Object Model (SOM) is described by Otto K. Ferstl and Elmar J. Sinz. SOM supports modelling of business systems on multiple levels of the life-cycle, such as planning, analysis, and design. The last contribution of this part is given by Mathias Weske and Gottfried Vossen discussing workflow languages. They survey the requirements, concepts, and usage patterns of such languages which are used in commercial workflow management systems.

Günter Schmidt, Peter Bernus

References

[Bat92] Batini, C., Ceri, S. Navathe, S. B., Conceptual Database Design: An Entity-Relationship Approach, Benjamin Cummings, 1992

[Elm94] Elmashri, N. S., Fundamentals of Database Systems, Benjamin Cummings, 1994

[GF92] Genesereth, M. R., Fikes, R. E., Knowledge Interchange Format, Version 3.0 Reference Manual, Stanford University, Knowledge Systems Laboratory, KSL-92-86, June 1992

[ODMG97] Object Database Standard ODMG 2.0, Edited by R. G. G. Cattell, D. Barry, D. Bartels, M. Berler, J. Eastman, S. Gamerman, D. Jordan, A. Springer, H. Strickland, D. Wade, Morgan Kaufmann, 1997

[Sch86] Schmidt, D., Denotational Semantics, Allyn and Bacon, 1986

[Sch97] Schmidt, G., Prozeßmanagement - Modelle und Methoden, Springer, 1997

[Spi88] Spivey, J. M., Understanding Z : a specification language and its formal semantics, Cambridge University Press, 1988

[Weg72] Wegner, P., The Vienna Definition Language, ACM Computing Surveys 4, 1972, 5-63

CHAPTER 2

Characterizing Information Modeling Techniques

John Mylopoulos

Information modeling is concerned with the construction of symbolic structures which capture the meaning of information and organize it in ways that make it understandable and useful to people. Given that information is becoming a ubiquitous, abundant and precious resource, information modeling is serving as a core technology for information systems engineering. We present a brief history of information modeling techniques in Computer Science and survey such techniques developed within Knowledge Representation (Artificial Intelligence), Data Modeling (Databases), and Requirements Analysis (Software Engineering and Information Systems). The presentation then offers a comparative framework for information modeling proposals which classifies them according to their *ontologies*, i.e., the type of application for which they are intended, the set of *abstraction mechanisms* (or, structuring principles) they support, as well as the *tools* they provide for building, analyzing, and managing application models. Examples of ontologies include static worlds consisting of entities and relationships, or dynamic ones consisting of processes. Generalization, aggregation, and classification are three of the best known abstraction mechanisms, adopted by many information models and used widely in information modeling practice. The final component of the paper uses the comparative framework proposed earlier to assess well known information modeling techniques, both from a user and a designer perspective.

1 Introduction

Information modeling constitutes a cornerstone for information systems engineering and management. To build, operate and maintain an information system, one needs to capture and represent the meaning and inherent structure of a variety of rich and multi-faceted information, including the system's subject matter, its internal structure, its operational environment and its development history. Once captured, the information can be used for communication between people – say, the information system owners, users and developers – but also for building tools which facilitate their management throughout their lifetime.

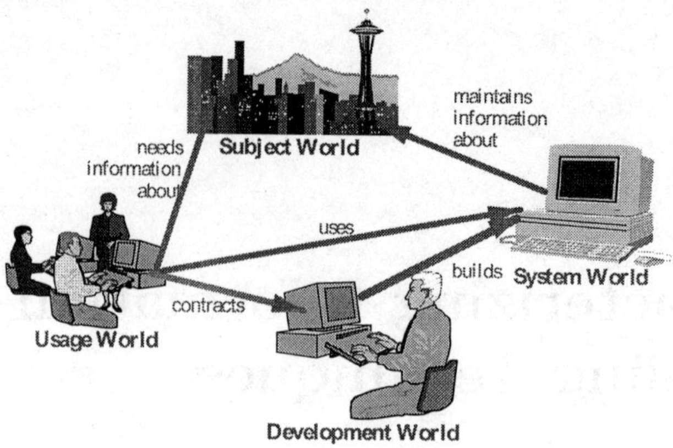

Figure 1: The Four Worlds of Information Systems Engineering

The DAIDA project [JMSV92], whose aim was the development of an environment for building information systems, characterized this information in terms of four "worlds", illustrated in Figure 1. The subject world consists of the subject matter for an information system, i.e., the world about which information is maintained by the system. For instance, the *subject world* for a banking system consists of customers, accounts, transactions, balances, interests rates and the like. The *system world*, on the other hand, describes the information system itself at several layers of implementation detail. These layers may range from a specification of functional requirements for the system, to a conceptual design and an implementation. The *usage world* describes the (organizational) environment within which the system is intended to function and consists of agents, activities, tasks, projects, users, user interfaces (with the system) and the like. Finally, the *development world* describes the process that created the information system, the team of systems analysts and programmers involved, their adopted methodology and schedule, their design decisions and rationale. All of this information is relevant during the initial development of the system but also later on during operation and maintenance. Consequently, all of this information needs to be represented, somehow, in any attempt to offer a comprehensive framework for information systems engineering. This is precisely the task of information modeling.

Information modeling has been practiced within Computer Science since the first data processing applications in the '50s, when record and file structures were used to model and organize information. Since then, there have been literally thousands of proposals for information models, covering many different areas of Computer Science and Information Systems Engineering.

The purpose of this paper is to propose a comparative framework which characterizes information modeling techniques and practice and also to hint

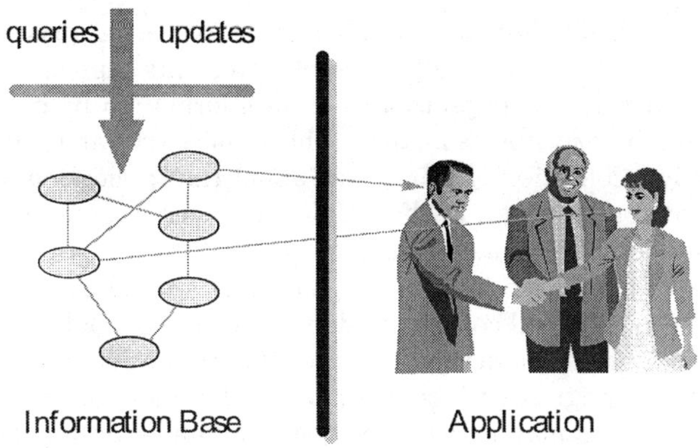

Figure 2: Modeling an application with an information base

at some directions for further research. Section 2 of the paper introduces basic definitions, while section 3 presents a brief (and admittedly biased) history of the field. Section 4 offers a comparative framework for information models in terms of the ontologies and abstraction mechanisms they support, also the tools they offer for modeling, analysis and management. Section 5 assesses particular information modeling techniques, while section 6 summarizes the basic thesis of the paper and suggests directions for further research.

2 Preliminaries

Information modeling involves the construction of computer-based symbol structures which model some part of the real world. We will refer to such symbol structures as *information bases* (generalizing the term from others terms in Computer Science, such as database and knowledge base). Moreover, we shall refer to the part of the real world being modeled by an information base as its *application*. Figure 2 illustrates the fundamental nature of information modeling. Here, the information base is modeling some real-world situation involving several individuals. The atoms out of which one constructs the information base are assumed to denote particular individuals in the application, while the associations within the information base denote real world relationships, such as physical proximity, social interaction, etc. The information base is queried and updated through special-purpose languages, analogously to the way databases are accessed and updated through query and data manipulation languages.

It should be noted that an information base may be developed over a long time period, accumulating details about the application, or changing to remain a faithful model of a changing application. In this regard, it should be thought of as a *repository* that contains *accumulated, disseminated, structured* information, much like human long-term memory, or databases, knowledge bases, etc., rather than a mere collection of statements expressed in some language. Consequently, the organization of an information base should reflect its *contents* and its *use*, not its *history*. This implies that an information base can't be simply a collection of statements about the application, added to the information base over time. Rather, these statements have to be organized according to their subject matter and interrelated according to their content.

As indicated earlier, an information base used during the development of an information system will contain models of one or more of the four worlds of Figure 1. Some of these models may be used during the definition of databases and applications programs which are part of the information system under development. Others may be used for operation and maintenance purposes, e.g., explaining to users how to use the system, or to maintenance personnel how the system works.

What kinds of symbol structures does one use to build up an information base? Analogously to databases, these symbol structures need to adhere to the rules of some information model. The concept of an information model is a direct adaptation of the concept of a data model. So is the following definition.

An *information model*[1] consists of a collection of symbol structure types, whose instances are used to describe an application, a collection of operations which can be applied to any valid symbol structure, and a collection of general integrity rules which define the set of consistent symbol structure states, or changes of states. The *relational model* for databases [Cod70] is an excellent example of an information model. Its basic symbol structure types include `table`, `tuple`, and `domain`. Its associated operations include `add`, `remove`, `update` operations for tuples, and/or `union`, `intersection`, `join`, etc. operations for tables. The relational model supports a single integrity rule: No two tuples within a table can have the same key.

Given this definition, one can define more precisely an *information base* as a symbol structure which is based on an information model and describes a particular application.

Is an information model the same thing as a *language*, or a *notation*? For our purposes, it is not. The information model offers symbol structures for representing information. This information may be communicated to different users of an information base (human or otherwise) through one or more languages. For example, there are several different languages associated with the relational model, of which SQL is the most widely used. In a similar spirit, we see notations as (usually graphical) partial descriptions of the contents of an information base. Again, there may be several notations associated with the same information model, e.g., the graphical notations used for data flow diagrams.

The information models proposed and used over the years have been clas-

---

[1] Adopted from Ted Codd's classic account of data models and databases [Cod82]

sified into three different categories. These, roughly speaking, reflect a historical advance of the state-of-the-art on information modeling away from machine-oriented representations and towards human-oriented models which are more expressive and can cope with more complex application modeling tasks.

Physical information models. Such models employed conventional data structures and other programming constructs to model an application in terms of records, strings, arrays, lists, variable names, B-trees, and the like. The main drawback of such models is that they force on the programmer/modeler two sets of conflicting concerns, one related to computational efficiency, and the other to the quality of the application model. For example, if one chooses to model persons in the application in terms of 8-character strings and structure an information base in terms a B-tree, these choices are driven by efficiency considerations and have nothing to do with the application.

Logical information models. The early '70s saw several proposals for *logical data models* which offered abstract mathematical symbol structures (e.g., sets, arrays, relations) for modeling purposes, hiding the implementation details from the user. The relational and network models for databases are good examples of logical models. Such models free the modeler from implementation concerns, so that she can focus on modeling ones. For instance, once the modeler has chosen the relational model, she can go ahead and use tables to build an information base, without any regard to how these tables are physically implemented. Unfortunately, logical symbol structures are flat and unintuitive as to how they should be used for modeling purposes.

Conceptual information models. Soon after logical information models were proposed, and even before relational technology conquered the database industry, there were new proposals for information models which offered more expressive facilities for modeling applications and structuring information bases. These models (hereafter, *conceptual models*) offer *semantic terms* for modeling an application, such as `Entity`, `Activity`, `Agent` and `Goal`. Moreover, they offer means for organizing information in terms of *abstraction mechanisms* which are often inspired by Cognitive Science [CS88], such as generalization, aggregation and classification. Such models are supposed to model an application more directly and naturally [HM81]. In the sequel, we focus the discussion on conceptual models, since they constitute the state-of-the-art in the field for more than two decades.

3 Brief History

Over the years, there have been thousands of proposals for conceptual models, most defined and used once, within a single research project. We note in this section some of the earliest models that launched fruitful lines of research and influenced the state-of-practice. Interestingly enough, these models were launched independently of each other and in different research areas within Computer Science.

Ross Quillian [Qui68] proposed in his PhD thesis *semantic networks* as convenient directed, labeled graphs for modeling the structure of human memory (1966). Nodes of his semantic network represented concepts (more precisely, word senses). For words with multiple meanings, such as "plant", there would be several nodes, one for each sense of the word, e.g., "plant" as in "industrial plant", "plant" as in "evergreen plant", plant as in "I plant my garden every year", etc. Nodes were related through links representing semantic relationships, such as `isA` ("A bird is a(n) animal", "a shark is a fish"), `has` ("A bird has feathers"), and `eats` ("Sharks eat humans"). Moreover, each concept could have associated attributes, representing properties, such as "Penguins can't fly"(Figure 3).

There are several novel ideas in Quillian's proposal. Firstly, his information base was organized in terms of *concepts* and *associations*. Moreover, generic concepts were organized into an `isA` (or, generalization) hierarchy, supported by attribute inheritance. In addition, his proposal came with a radical computational model termed *spreading activation*. Thus, computation in the information base was carried out by "activating" two concepts and then iteratively spreading the activation to adjacent, semantically related concepts. For example, to discover the meaning of the term "horse food", spreading activation would fire the concepts `horse` and `food` and then spread activations to neighbors, until the two semantic paths

`horse` –`isA`→ `animal` –`eats`→ `food`

`horse` –`isA`→ `animal` –`madeOf`→ `meat` –`isA`→ food

are discovered. These paths correspond to two different interpretations of "horse food", the first amounts to something like "the food that horses eat", while the second to "food made out of horses".

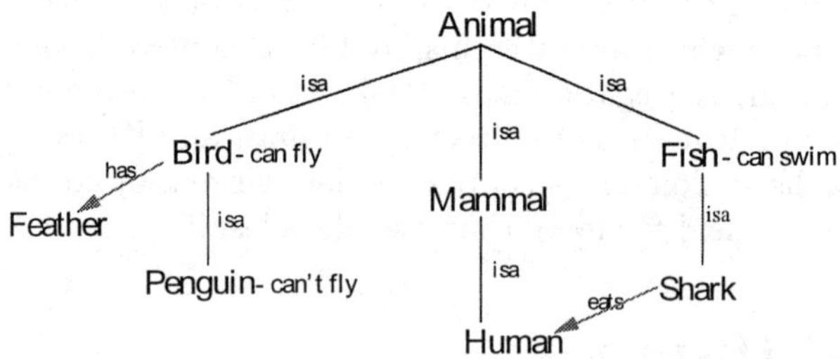

Figure 3: A simple semantic network

Ole-Johan Dahl proposed in 1966 *Simula*, an extension of the programming language ALGOL 60, for simulation applications which require some "world modeling". Simula [DH72] allows the definition of classes which serve as a cross between processes that can be executed and record structures. A class can be instantiated any number of times. Each instance first executes the body of the class and then remains as a passive data structure which can only be operated upon by procedures associated to the class. For example, the class `histo` defined in Figure 4 is supposed to compute frequency histograms for a random variable, i.e., how often the random variable falls within each of $n+1$ intervals $(-, X_1)$, (X_1, X_2), $...(X_n, -)$.
Each histogram will be computed by an instance of the class.

```
histo
     class histo (X,n);array X;integer n;
     begin integer N; integer array T[0;n]
        procedure tabulate (Y); real Y;
             begin integer i; i := 0; ...  end;
        procedure frequency (i); integer i;
             frequency := T[i]/N;
        integer i;
        for i := 0 step 1 until n do
             T[i] := 0; N := 0
        end
    end.
```

Figure 4: A Simula class definition

When the class is instantiated, the array `T` is initialized. Then each instance keeps count of a random variable's readings through use of the procedure `tabulate`, while procedure `frequency` computes the frequency for interval i.

Simula advanced significantly the state-of-the-art in programming languages, and has been credited with the origins of object-oriented programming. Equally importantly, Simula influenced information modeling by recognizing that for some programming tasks, such as simulating a barber shop, one needs to build a model of an application. According to Simula, such models are constructed out of class instances (*objects*, nowadays). These are the basic symbol structures which model elements of the application. Classes themselves define common features of instances and are organized into subclass hierarchies. Class declarations can be inherited by subclasses through some form of (textual, actually) inheritance.

Jean-Raymond Abrial proposed the *semantic model* for databases in 1974 [Abr74], shortly followed by Peter Chen's *entity-relationship model* [2] [Che76].

[2]The model was actually first presented at the First Very Large Databases (VLDB) Conference in 1975.

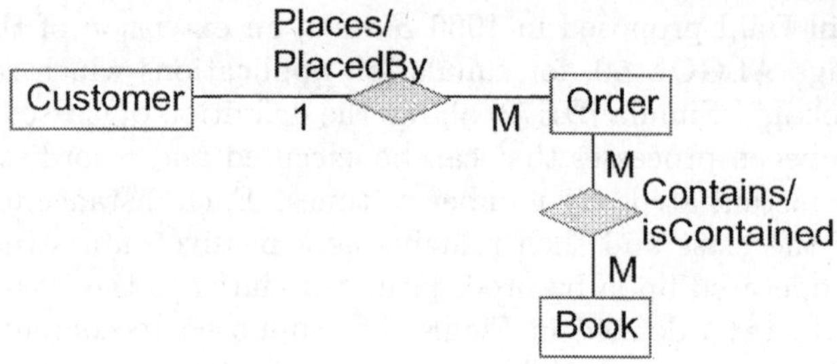

Figure 5: An entity-relationship diagram

Both were intended as advances over logical data models, such as Codd's relational model proposed only a few years earlier.

The entity-relationship diagram of Figure 5 shows entity types `Customer`, `Order` and `Book`, and relationship `Places/PlacedBy`, `Contains/isContained`. Roughly speaking, the diagram represents the fact that "Customers place orders" and "Orders contain books". The `Places` relationship type is one-to-many, meaning that a customer can place many orders but each order can only be placed by a single customer, while `Contains` is a many-to-many relationship type ("an order may contain many books, while a book may be contained in many orders").

Novel features of the entity-relationship model include its built-in types, which constitute *ontological assumptions* about the intended modeling applications. In other words, the entity-relationship model assumes that applications consist of *entities* and *relationships*. This means that this conceptual model is not appropriate for applications which violate these assumptions, e.g., a world of fluids, or ones involving temporal events, state changes, and the like. In addition, Chen's original paper showed elegantly how one could map a schema based on his conceptual model, such as that shown on Figure 5, down to a logical schema. These features made the entity-relationship model an early favorite, perhaps the first conceptual model to be used widely world-wide.

On the other hand, Abrial's semantic model was more akin to object-oriented data models that became popular more than a decade later. His model also offers entities and relations, but includes a procedural component through which one can define procedures for performing four operations on instances of a class and can attach these to classes.

Douglas Ross proposed in the mid-'70s the *Structured Analysis* and *Design Technique* (SADT^{TM}) as a "language for communicating ideas" [RS77, Ros77b]. The technique was used by Softech, a Boston-based software company, in order to specify requirements for software systems.

According to SADT, the world consists of activities and data. Each activity consumes some data, represented through input arrows from left to

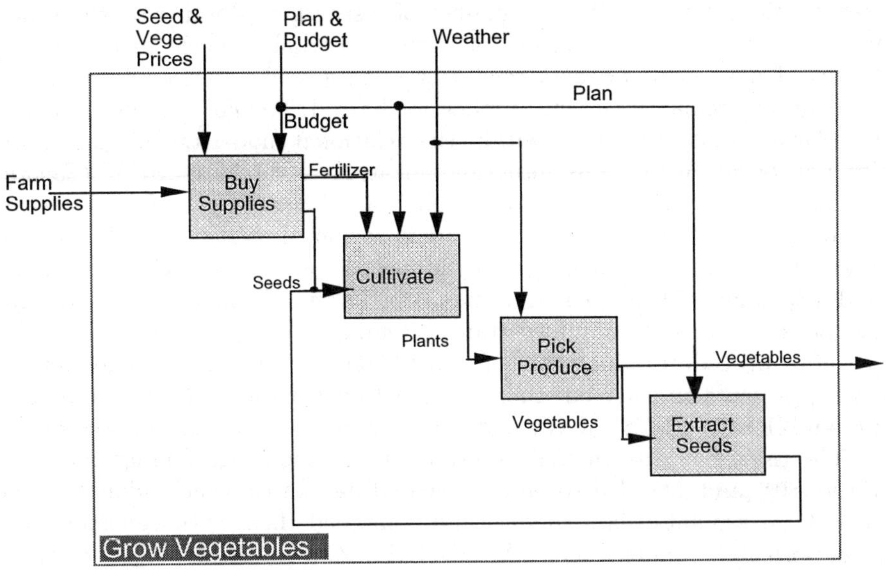

Figure 6: An SADT activity diagram

right, produces some data, represented through output arrows from left to right, and also has some data that control the execution of the activity but are neither consumed nor produced. For instance, the `Buy Supplies` activity of Figure 6 has input arrow `Farm Supplies`, output arrows `Fertilizer` and `Seeds` and control arrows `Prices` and `Plan & Budget`. Each activity may be defined through a diagram such as that shown in Figure 6 in terms of sub-activities. Thus `Growing Vegetables` is defined in terms of the sub-activities `Buy Supplies, Cultivate, Pick Produce` and `Extract Seeds`.

One of the more elegant aspects of the SADT conceptual model is its duality: Data are described in terms of diagrams with input, output and control arrows too, but these now represent activities which can produce, consume or affect the state of a given datum.

Ross' contributions include a conceptual model with some advanced ontological assumptions. Unlike the entity-relationship model, for SADT applications consist of a static and a dynamic part. He also was influential in convincing software engineering researchers and practitioners alike that it pays to have diagrammatic descriptions of how a software system is to fit its intended operational environment. This contributions helped launch Requirements Engineering as an accepted early phase in software development.

After these pioneers, research on conceptual models[3] and modeling broad-

[3]The term "conceptual modelling" was used in the 70s either as a synonym for semantic data modelling or in the technical sense of the ANSI /X3/SPARC report [ANSI75] where it referred to a model that allows the definition of schemata lying between external

ened considerably, both in the number of researchers working on the topic, and in the number of proposals for new conceptual models. In Databases, dozens of new *semantic data models* were proposed, intended to "capture more of the semantics of an application" [Cod79]. For instance, *RM/T* [Cod79] attempts to embed within the relational model the notion of entity and organize relations into generalization hierarchies. *SDM (Semantic Data Model)* [HM81], offers a highly sophisticated set of facilities for modeling entities and supports the organization of conceptual schemata in terms of generalization, aggregation, as well as a grouping mechanism. *Taxis* [MBW80] adopts ideas from semantic networks and Abrial's proposal to organize all components of an information system, even exceptions and exception-handling procedures, in terms of generalization hierarchies (taxonomies). [TL82] presents an early but thorough treatment of data models and modeling, and [HK87, PM88] survey and compare several semantic data models.

The rise of object-oriented programming as the programming paradigm of the '80s (and '90s) led to object-oriented databases, which adopted some ideas from semantic data models and combined them with concepts from object-oriented programming [ABDDMZ89, ZM89]. Early object-oriented data models supported a variety of sophisticated modeling features (e.g., *Gemstone* was based on the information model of Smalltalk), but the trend with recent commercial object-oriented database systems seems to converge towards the information model of popular object-oriented programming languages, such as C++. As such, object-oriented data models seem to be taking a bold step backwards with respect to conceptual modeling. The rise of the internet and the World Wide Web has created tremendous demand for integrating heterogeneous information sources. This has led to an emphasis on *metamodeling* techniques in Databases, where one is modeling the meaning and structure of the contents of different information sources, such as files, databases, digitized pictorial data etc., rather than an application [KS94, Wid95].

Within Artificial Intelligence (AI), semantic network proposals proliferated in the seventies [Fin79], including ones that treated semantic networks as a graph-theoretic notation for logical formulas. During the same period, [Min75] introduced the notion of *frames* as a suitable symbol structure for representing common sense knowledge, such as the concept of a room or an elephant. A frame may contain information about the components of the concept being described, links to similar concepts, as well as procedural information on how the frame can accessed and change over time. Moreover, frame representations focus specifically on capturing common sense knowledge, a problem that still remains largely unresolved for Knowledge Represntation research. Examples of early semantic network and frame-based conceptual models include *KRL* [BW77], *KL-ONE* [Bra79] and *PSN* [LM79].

---

views, defined for different user groups, and internal ones defining one or several physical databases. The term was used more or less in the sense discussed here at the Pingree Park workshop on *Data Abstraction, Databases and Conceptual Modelling*, held in June 1980

Since the early eighties there have been attempts to integrate ingredients from semantic networks, logic and procedural representations. An early example of this trend is *Krypton* [BFL83] and later *terminological languages* such as *CLASSIC* [BBMR89]. A CLASSIC information base consists of two components: a terminological component where terms are described, and an assertional one including assertions about the application. For example, a CLASSIC information base may include a description for the term `Bachelor`, which uses other more primitive terms such as `Married`, `Male`, and `Person`, along with an assertion involving a particular bachelor, for example, `Bachelor(John)`. The '80s also witnessed a growing interest in the study of tradeoffs between the expressiveness and the tractability of knowledge representation techniques [BL85]. Such studies are now serving as major methodological vehicles in Knowledge Representation research. Knowledge Representation is thoroughly presented in [BL85b], reviewed in [Lev86] and overviewed in [KM91].

Requirements Engineering was born around the mid-'70s, partly thanks to Ross and his SADT proposal, partly thanks to others such as [BT76] who established through empirical study that "the rumored 'requirements problems' are a reality". The case for world modeling was articulated eloquently by Michael Jackson [Jac78], whose software development methodology [Jac83] starts with a "model of reality with which [the system] is concerned." The use of conceptual models for information systems engineering was launched by [Sol79], while Bubenko's *Conceptual Information Model*, or CIM [Bub80] is perhaps the first comprehensive proposal for a formal requirements modeling language. Its features include an ontology of entities and events, an assertional sublanguage for specifying constraints, including complex temporal ones. Greenspan's RML (*Requirements Modeling Language*) [GMB82, Gre84, BGM85, GBM86]. Attempts to formalize SADT by using ideas from knowledge representation and semantic data models. The result is a formal requirements language where entities and activities are organized into generalization hierarchies, and which in a number of ways predates object-oriented analysis techniques by several years.

During the same period, the *GIST* specification language [BGW82], developed at ISI over the same period as Taxis, was also based on ideas from knowledge representation and supported modeling the environment; it was influenced by the notion of making the specification executable, and by the desire to support transformational implementation. It has formed the basis of an active research group on the problems of requirements description and elicitation (e.g., [JFH92]). *ERAE* [DHLPR86] was one of the early efforts that explicitly shared with RML the view that requirements modeling is a knowledge representation activity, and had a base in semantic networks and logic. The *KAOS* project constitutes another significant research effort which strives to develop a comprehensive framework for requirements modeling and requirements acquisition methodologies [DFL93]. The language offered for requirements modeling provides facilities for modeling goals, agents, alternatives, events, actions, existence modalities, agent responsibility and other concepts. KAOS relies heavily on a metamodel to provide a self-descriptive and extensible modeling framework. In addition, KAOS offers an explicit methodology for constructing requirements which begins with the acquisition of goal structures and the identification of relevant concepts, and ends with the definition of actions, to be performed by the new system or existing agents in the system's environment.

The state-of-practice in Requirements Engineering was affected by SADT and its successors. *Data flow diagrams* (e.g., [DeM79]) adopt some of the concepts of SADT, but focus on information flow within an organization, as opposed to SADT's all-inclusive modeling framework. The combined use of data flow and entity-relationship diagrams has led to an information system development methodology which still dominates teaching and practice within Information Systems Engineering. Since the late '80s, however, object-oriented analysis techniques [SM88, CY90, RBPEL91, Boo94] have been introduced and are becoming increasingly influential. These techniques offer a more coherent modeling framework than the combined use of data flow and entity-relationship diagrams. The framework adopts features of object-oriented programming languages, semantic data models and requirements languages. A recent proposal, the *Unified Modeling Language* (UML) [UML97] attempts to integrate features of the more pre-eminent models in object-oriented analysis, thereby enhancing reusability.

An early survey of issues in Requirements Engineering appears in [Rom85] and the requirements modeling terrain is surveyed in [Web87]. [TD90] includes a monumental in volume tutorial on Requirements Engineering. Several recent textbooks on the same topic, e.g., [Dav93], touch on modeling and survey a broad range of techniques.

The histories of conceptual modeling within the areas reviewed here did not unfold independently of each other. An influential workshop held at Pingree Park, Colorado in 1980 brought together researchers from Databases, AI, Programming Languages and Software Engineering to discuss conceptual modeling approaches, compare research directions and methodologies [BZ81]. The workshop was followed by a series of other interdisciplinary workshops which reviewed the state-of-the-art in information modeling and related topics ([BMS84, BM86, ST89]). The International Conference on the Entity-Relationship Approach[4], held annually since 1979, has marked progress in research as well as practice on the general topic of conceptual modeling.

Several papers and books provide surveys of the whole field of Conceptual Modeling, or one or more of its constituent areas. [LZ92] includes a fine collection of papers on conceptual modeling, most notably a survey of the field [RC92], while [BBJW97] offers a more recent account. [MB88] surveys the interface between AI and Databases, much of it related to conceptual

[4]Recently renamed *International Conference on Conceptual Modeling*(ER)

modeling. Along a similar path, [Bor90] discusses the similarities and differences between knowledge representation in AI and semantic data models in Databases.

It should be acknowledged that this discussion leaves out other areas where conceptual modeling has been used for some time, most notably Enterprise Modeling (e.g., [Ver84, BN96, Ver96]) and Software Process Modeling (e.g., [MP93]).

4 A Comparative Framework for Conceptual Models

The proliferation of proposals for new conceptual models calls for some form of a comparative framework, so that one can classify new proposals, or evaluate whether a particular candidate is appropriate for a particular information modeling task. This section proposes such a framework structured along three dimensions:

Ontologies. As we saw from the previous section, each conceptual model makes some assumptions about the nature of the applications it is intended to model. Such *ontological assumptions* determine the built-in terms offered by a conceptual model, and therefore its range of applicability.

Abstraction mechanisms. These determine the proposed organization of an information base using a particular conceptual model. This is a fundamental concern for conceptual models because organizations that are natural and intuitive lead to more usable information bases which can be searched effectively and can grow without users losing track of their contents.

Tools. If an information base is to scale up and remain useful for a long time, it needs tools which perform information base operations efficiently, also ones that support analysis of its contents, to give users confidence that they are correct and consistent.

The reader may have noticed that the proposed characterization ignores the methodologies supported by a particular conceptual model. This omission is deliberate. All methodologies that have been proposed, including ones used in practice, are specific to particular *uses* one intends for an information base. For instance, using an information base for requirements engineering, e.g., [CY90], calls for a very different methodology than, say, one used for data modeling [BLN92], or knowledge engineering in AI [HWL83].

4.1 Ontologies

Ontology is a branch of Philosophy concerned with the study of what exists. General ontologies have been proposed since the 18th century, including recent ones such as [Car67] and [Bun77]. For our purposes, an ontology characterizes some aspects of a class of applications. For instance, an ontology for time may characterize the temporal aspect of many applications in terms of points and temporal relations among them. Likewise, an ontology for manufacturing, may consist of (industrial) processes, resources and the like. Research within AI has formalized many interesting ontologies and has developed algorithms for generating inferences from an information base that adopts them (e.g., [VKV89]). Along a very different path, [Wan89, WW90] study the adequacy of information systems to describe applications based on a general ontology, such as that proposed in [Bun77].

Note that a conceptual model offers built-in generic symbol structures, or *terms* for modeling applications. For instance, the entity-relationship model offers two built-in, generic terms: `entity` and `relationship` for modeling applications which are assumed to consist of entities and relationships. The reader should note that comparison of conceptual models on the basis of the terms they offer is highly dependent on problems of synonymy, homonymy etc. In other words, two different models may be appropriate for the same class of applications, but use different terms to talk about them. We'd like to have a framework which deems these conceptual models as being comparable with respect to the intended subject matter. Ontologies help us achieve precisely this objective.

In order to give some structure to a broad and highly multidisciplinary topic, we focus on four rather coarse-grained ontologies, based on a broad survey of conceptual models and the primitive terms they support.

Static Ontology. This encompasses static aspects of an application, by describing what things exist, their attributes and interrelationships. Most conceptual models assume that the world is populated by *entities* which are endowed with a unique and immutable identity, a lifetime, a set of attributes, and relationships to other entities. Basic as this ontology may seem, it is by no means universal. For instance, [Hay85] offers an ontology for material substances where entities (say, a litter of water and a pound of sugar) can be merged resulting in a different entity. Also note that very successful models, such as Statecharts [Har87], don't adopt this ontology, because they are intended for a very different class of applications (real-time systems). Nor is this ontology trivial. For certain applications it is useful to distinguish between different modes of existence for entities, including physical existence, such as that of the author of this paper, abstract existence, such as that of the number 7, non-existence, characteristic of Santa Claus or my canceled trip to Japan, and impossible existence, such as that of the square root of -1 or the proverbial square circle [Hir89].

Spatial information is particularly important for applications which involve the physical world. Such information has been modeled in terms of 2- or 3-dimensional points or larger units, including spheres, cubes, pyramids etc. (for instance [Dav86]). A hard modeling problem for spatial information is its inherently approximate nature, calling for special modeling provisions [TM96].

Dynamic Ontology. Encompasses dynamic aspects of an application in terms of *states, state transitions* and *processes.* Various flavors of finite state machines, Petri nets, and more recent statecharts have been offered since the '60s as appropriate modeling tools for dynamic discrete processes involving a finite number of states and state transitions. Such models are well-known and well-understood and they have been used successfully to describe real-time applications in telecommunications and other fields.

A popular alternative to state transition ontologies is founded on the notion of *process.* A process is a collection of partially ordered steps intended to achieve a particular goal [CKO92]. Processes are executed by agents, human or otherwise. Under different guises, processes have been modeled and studied in several different areas, including software processes (Software Engineering), activities (Requirements Engineering), plans (AI), tasks (CSCW), office procedures (Office Information Systems), and business processes (Management Studies). Depending on their intended use, process models generally focus on "how" or "what" information. Models intended to support the execution of the process focus on the "how", while models intended for analysis (such as consistency checking) focus on the "what".

Temporal information is fundamental to the nature of dynamic worlds. Such information, for example "Maria graduated before her 20th birthdate" can be modeled in terms of points and associated relations. The temporal dimension of events, such as Maria's graduation, can be represented in terms of a single time point (for instantaneous events) or two time points. These points can then be related through relations such as `before`, `after`. [All84] proposes a different ontology for time based on intervals, with thirteen associated relations such as `overlap`, `meet`, `before` and `after`. A related concept is that of causality. Causality imposes existence constraints on events: if event A causes event B and A has been observed, B can be expected as well, possibly with some time delay. Within AI, formal models of causality have been offered as far back as [McC68] and [Rie76].

Intentional Ontology. Encompasses the world of agents, and things agents believe in, want, prove or disprove, and argue about. This ontology includes concepts such as *agent, issue, goal, supports, denies, subgoalOf,* etc. The subject of agents having beliefs and goals and being capable of carrying out actions has been studied extensively in AI, e.g., [MS82] addresses the problem of representing propositional attitudes, such as beliefs, desires and intentions for agents. The importance of the notion of agents, especially for situations involving concurrent actions, has a long tradition in requirements modeling, beginning with the work of Feather [Fea87] and continuing with recent proposals, such as [DFL93].

Modeling the issues which arise during complex decision making is discussed in [CB88]. The application of such a framework to software design, intended to capture the arguments pro and con, and the decisions they result in, has been a fruitful research direction since it was first proposed in [PB88], with notable refinements described in [MYBM91] and [LL91]. For example, [MYBM91] models design rationale in terms of `questions` (Q), `options` (O) and `criteria` (C). Figure 7 shows the structure of a decision space concerning the design of an Automated Teller Machine (ATM). The four questions raised, have associated options. Choice among them will be done by using an associated list of criteria. For example, for the question of what range of services will be offered (by the ATM under design), there are two options, full range and cash only, and two criteria for choosing among them. The cash-only option raises an auxiliary question, whether services can be restricted by having switchable machines, where services can be "masked out", or by having machines which are inherently limited in the services they offer. On a complementary front, [GF95] studies the types of contributions a stakeholder can make to an argumentation structure such as the one shown in Figure 7.

More recently, [Chu93] proposes *softgoals* as a suitable concept for modeling software non-functional requirements, such as software usability, security or user-friendliness. Softgoals are supposed to be ill-defined goals, without a clear-cut definition of when they have been satisfied (hence their name). Nevertheless, they play an important role in many applications and many information system development projects.

Social Ontology. This ontology covers social settings, permanent organizational structures or shifting networks of alliances and inter-dependencies ([Gal73, Min79, Sco87]). Traditionally, this ontology has been characterized in terms of concepts such as *actor, position, role, authority, commitment* etc. [Yu93, YM94, YML96] proposes a novel set of concepts which focus on *strategic dependencies* between actors.

Such a dependency exists when an actor has committed to satisfy a goal or softgoal, carry out a task, or deliver resources to another actor. Using these concepts, one can create organizational models which *do* provide answers to questions such as "why does the manager need the project budget?". Such models can serve as starting points in the analysis of an organizational setting, which precedes any reengineering of business processes, and the subsequent development of software systems.

Figure 8 shows a simple strategic dependency graph between two actors, a (car) owner and a body shop. The dependencies shown on the graph include a goal dependency, "Owner depends on the Body shop to fix the car",

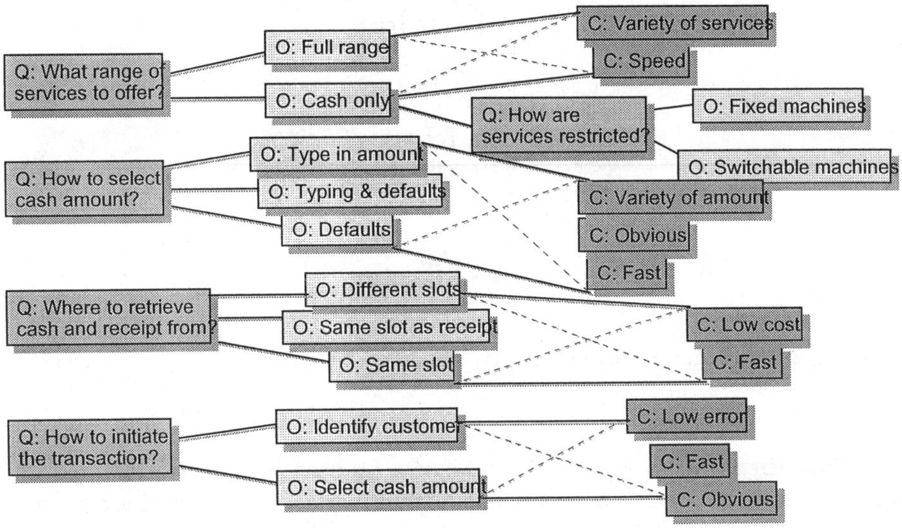

Figure 7: Modeling design rationale in terms of questions, options and criteria [MYBM91]

a resource dependency, "Body shop depends on owner to pay for repairs", and two softgoal dependencies, "Owner depends on Body shop to maximize estimates", while "Body shop depends on Owner to continue business".

4.2 Abstraction Mechanisms

By definition, abstraction involves suppression of (irrelevant) detail. For example, the generic concept of person can be abstracted from those of particular persons (George, Maria, Chryss,...) by suppressing personal details such as each person's age, preferred food, etc., so as to concentrate on commonalities: persons have an address, an age ranging from 0 to 120, etc. Likewise, the concept of employee might be abstracted from those of secretary, teacher, manager and clerk by suppressing particular features of these concepts (teachers teach a subject, managers manage some group of people) and focus on commonalties (all employees have a salary, a position, a job description,...)

Abstraction mechanisms organize the information base and guide its use, making it easier to update or search it. Not surprisingly, abstraction mechanisms have been used in Computer Science even before the advent of conceptual models. For instance, abstraction was used heavily in pioneering programming languages such as ALGOL 60 and LISP. Of course, the source of ideas for suitable abstraction mechanisms has to be grounded in Cognitive Science [CS88]. In the discussion that follows, we list for each abstraction mechanism one reference which surveys the literature (when available).

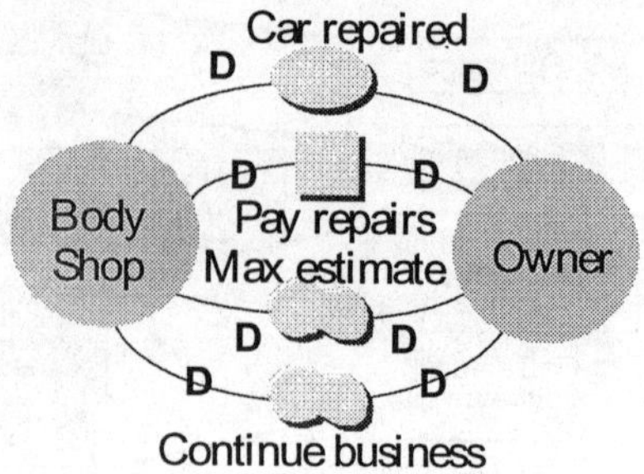

Figure 8: Strategic dependencies between actor

Classification (see [MM92]). This is a fundamental abstraction mechanism for human cognition, and it has proven just as fundamental for conceptual models and information bases. According to this abstraction mechanism, sometimes called *instanceOf*, an atom (entity, relationship, attribute, activity or whatever) within an information base is *classified* under one or more generic atoms (*classes*), thereby making it an instance of these classes. Instances of a class share common properties. For example, all atoms classified under `Person`, have an address and an age, while others classified under `Dog`, possess a master (sometimes) and have four legs.

Classification has been used under a number of guises to support syntactic and semantic consistency. For example, sorts in Logic [Coh89] and types in programming languages are used mostly for syntactic checking. So do tables or relations in the relational model. In semantic networks and object-oriented information models, classification distinguishes between *tokens or objects*, which represent particular individuals in the application, and *types* or *classes* which represent generic concepts.

Besides syntactic and semantic consistency, classification can also lead to more efficient search algorithms for a knowledge base. If, for instance, the system is looking for an object whose student number is `98765432` and it is known that only students have student numbers, then only the set of instances of `Student` must be searched.

Some information models (e.g., Smalltalk) allow classification to be recursive; i.e., classes may (or must) themselves be instances of other classes. In this case the class `Person` might be an instance of the (meta)class `AnimateClass` which has as instances all classes describing animate entities.

In such situations classification may be unconstrained, allowing both a token and a class that it is an instance of to be instances of some common class, or constrained in the sense that there is a linear order of strata (or levels) so that every atom in the information base belongs to a unique level and an atom at level τ can only be an instance of classes at level $\tau + 1$. To allow for classes which have themselves as instances, such as `Class`, the class that has all classes as instances, one needs a special ω level.

Telos [MBJK90] adopts such a stratified classification scheme and uses it to classify not only entities but all atoms in an information base, including attributes and relationships. Figure 9 shows portions of a Telos information base. The entity[5] `EntityClass` is a metaclass at level 2 of the Telos stratosphere (as indicated by its superscript). Its instances include classes `Student`, but also `Person` and `Professor` (the latter `instanceOf` arrows are not shown on the diagram). Likewise, `RelationshipClass` is a binary relationship metaclass relating entity classes to other entity classes.

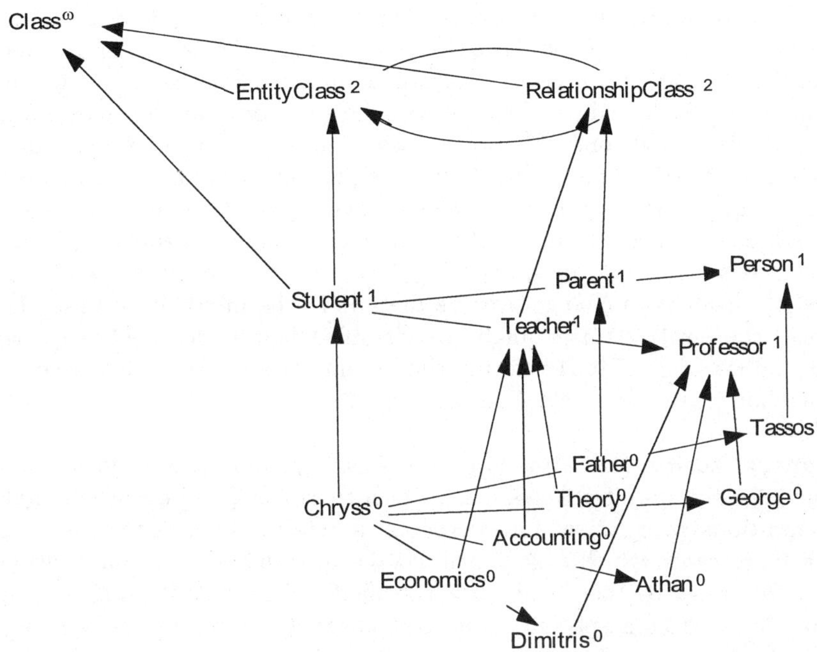

Figure 9: Multi-level classification of entities and relationships in Telo

Going one level down, Student is an instance of `SimpleEntityClass` but also of the ω-class `Class` (which actually, has all classes and metaclasses shown in the figure as instances, thought this is not shown). `Parent` and `Teacher` are relationship classes and instances of `RelationshipClass`. Finally, looking at level 0, `Chryss` is a student and has three teachers and one parent. Note that the four relationships `Chryss` participates in have their own labels (so that one can distinguish between the three teachers of `Chryss`

[5]For consistency, we are using here the terminology introduced earlier in this paper, rather than used the one in [MBJK90]

as her Theory, Economics and Accounting teachers respectively.)

A major advantage of any classification scheme which allows for metaclasses is that it is in a strong sense extensible. If the modeler wants to use the concept of process to the information base of Figure 9, she can do so by adding the metaclass ProcessClass (with associated information, whose nature depends on the information model being used) and then use it the same way EntityClass and RelationshipClass are on Figure 9. This is the essence of metamodeling. For more discussion on this topic, see [JJNS98] in this volume.

Classification mechanisms offered in different conceptual models vary widely as to the features they offer and the overall structure they impose on the information base. In most proposals, classification has only two levels (tokens/type, or instances/class, tuples/relation, etc.) Some proposals treat classes like atoms which need to be classified under metaclasses (see above). In other schemes, including Telos, everything in an information base needs to be classified under one or more classes. Moreover, some schemes allow multiple classifications for an atom, such as placing the token Chryss under classes Student, Employee and HockeyPlayer, even though these classes are unrelated to each other. Lastly, some classification schemes treat classification as an invariant property of each atom, while others allow classifications of an atom to change over its lifetime in the information base. For instance, the entity George might be classified first under Newborn, then Child, Adolescent, Adult during the lifetime of an information base, reflecting changes in the application being modeled.

Generalization (see [Bra83b]). As we have already seen from previous sections, units in an information base which represent generic concepts have been traditionally organized into taxonomies, referred to as *isA*[6] or *generalization hierarchies*, which organize all classes in terms of a partial order relation determined by their generality/specificity. For example, GradStudent may be declared as a specialization of Student ("Every grad student is a student"), which is in turn a specialization of Person ("Every student is a person").

Inheritance is a fundamental ingredient of generalization hierarchies. Inheritance is an inference rule that states that attributes and properties of a class are also attributes and properties of its is-a descendants. Thus the address and age attributes of Person, are inherited by Student and, transitively, by GradStudent. This inheritance may be *strict* in the sense that constraints on attributes and properties can be strengthened but cannot be overridden, or *default*, in which case overriding is allowed. For example, if the

[6] Note that the literature on Conceptual Modeling has generally treated *isA* as a semantic relationship between generic atoms, such as "a shark is a fish", rather than as a relationship between an instance and its class, as in "Clyde is a fish". In AI, some of the frame-based representations used *isA* ambiguously to represent both generalization and classification relationships.

age of persons has been declared to range from 0 to 100 years old, with strict inheritance the age of students can be declared to range from 5 to 80 but not from 5 to 120. Default inheritance, on the other hand, allows students to be 120 years old, though persons were declared to live only up to 100 years, or penguins to not fly though birds were declared to do so.

Generally, the organization of classes/concepts into a generalization hierarchy is left entirely up to the human modeler. An interesting alternative to this practice is offered by terminological logics [BBMR89], where term definitions can be automatically compared to see if one is more general ("subsumes") the other. For instance, the term "patients with age under 64" is subsumed by "patients with age under 70" and is disjoint from "persons with age over 72". Within such conceptual models, generalization hierarchies can be automatically computed, simplifying the task of extending but also searching an information base.

Aggregation (see [Mot93]). This mechanism, also called *partOf*, views objects as aggregates of their components or parts. Thus, a person can be viewed as a (physical) aggregate of a set of body parts – arms, legs, head and the like – or as a (social) aggregate of a name, address, social insurance number etc. Components of an object might themselves be aggregates of yet other simpler components. For example, the address of a person might be declared as the aggregation of a street number, street name, city, etc.

There is psychological evidence that most of the information associated with a concept is of the aggregation variety [MJ76]. Within Computer Science, [KBG89] proposed a formalization of aggregation within his object-oriented data model in order to move away from pointer-type references between objects. In his proposal, components may be *dependent* on the aggregates to which they belong. This means that if an aggregate is removed from the information base, so are its dependent components. Likewise, a component may be *exclusive*, which means that it can only be part of a single aggregate. In addition, aggregation may be strictly hierarchical or recursive. For instance, an employee may be defined as the aggregation of a department, a salary and another employee who serves as the employee's manager. Finally, an atom in the information base may be treated as an aggregate in more than one ways.

Figure 10 models an organization as an aggregate in two complementary ways: as a hierarchical aggregation of different managerial levels (managerial perspective), or as a vertical aggregation of departments serving different functions, such as production and marketing (administrative perspective). The notation used on Figure 10 is adopted from [EKW92] and it depicts aggregations in terms of triangles. Moreover, the allowable (min, max) cardinality of each aggregate is indicated by the two numbers shown next to each aggregation link. In particular, looking at the administrative perspective, an organization may have zero to one finance, production, sales, and administrative departments respectively.

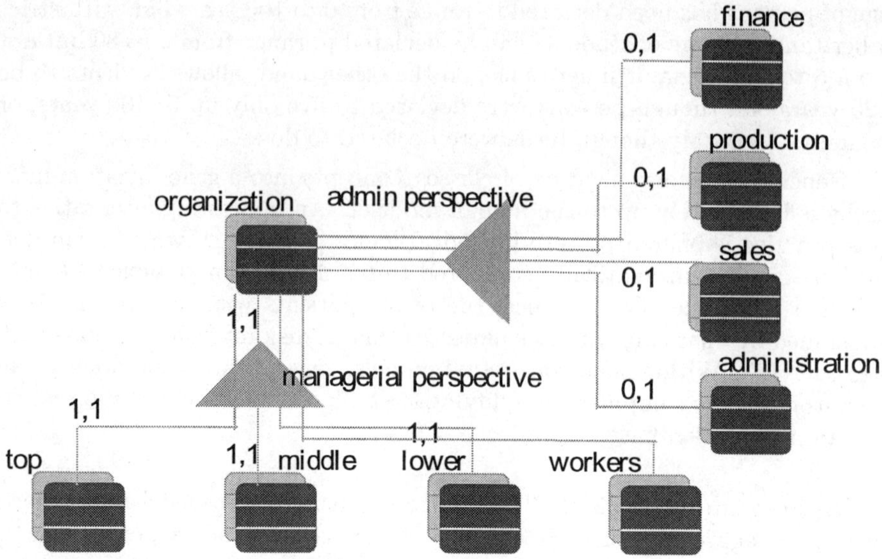

Figure 10: Multiple decompositions of the concept of organization

Contextualization. A problem inherent in any modeling task is that there are often differences of opinion or perception among those gathering, or providing information. Contextualization can be seen as an abstraction mechanism which allows partitioning and packaging of the descriptions being added to an information base. In a situation where one is modeling how patients are admitted into a hospital, this abstraction mechanism allows relative descriptions of the process, i.e., the process according to a particular person, or even a hospital unit, rather than insisting on a description which captures all the viewpoints in one shot.

Various forms of a contextualization mechanism have been used routinely in advanced information system applications [NW94]. Since the early days of AI, *contexts* have found uses in problem solving, as means for representing intermediate states during a search by a problem solver in its quest for a solution [Hew71], in knowledge representation, as representational devices for partitioning a knowledge base [Hen79]. In CAD and Software Engineering, *workspaces, versions* and *configurations* [Kat90] are by now generally accepted notions offering respectively mechanisms for focusing attention, defining system versions and means for defining compatible system components. Database *views* have been traditionally used to present partial, but consistent, viewpoints of the contents of a database to different user groups. More recently, such mechanisms have been adopted for object-oriented databases [SLT91, AB91, Ber92]. Programming language *modules, scopes* and *scope rules* determine which parts of a program state are visible to a particular program segment. *Perspectives*, have been proposed as a structuring mechanism for hypertext bases [PT93]. Most recently, the modeling of relative viewpoints has emerged as a significant research issue in requirements engineering as well as in distributed, heterogeneous databases. [FK92] describes early and influence work on this issue from a Requirements Engineering perspective. Using viewpoints to relativize descriptions in an information base is serving as a mechanism for dealing with inconsistency in requirements specifications [FG93, NKF93, RF94].

Materialization (see [PZMY94]). This abstraction mechanism relates a class, such as `CarModel`, to a more concrete class, such as `Car`. Other examples of materialization include the relationship between a (theatrical) play, say "Hamlet", and particular productions of the play, say the one now playing at the Royal Alexandra theater. These can be further materialized by particular shows of each production, such as the matinee show on October 26, 1997. This is clearly a very useful abstraction mechanism for manufacturing applications, which involve multiple, often indistinguishable entities, of the same type. As argued in [PZMY94], the formal properties of materialization constitute a combination of those of classification and generalization.

Normalization. Special, extraordinary circumstances abound in any application, and considerably complicate its understanding, especially so during early modeling stages. This has led to proposals for a *normal-case* first *abstraction* [Bor85b], where only the common/typical entities, states and events in the application are modeled first, while successive pass(es) deal with the special/exceptional situations and how they are to be treated. This abstraction mechanism is particularly successful if there is some *systematic* way to find the abnormal cases and moreover, there is a way to specify the exceptional circumstances as footnotes/annotations that do not interfere with the first reading. Similarly, it is not uncommon to find examples were generalization leads to over-abstraction (e.g., "all patients are assigned to rooms"), so that a subclass may contradict some aspect of one of its ancestors (e.g., "emergency-room patients may be kept on stretchers in hallways"). [Bor88] analyzes the conflicting desiderata for subclass hierarchies that allow such 'improper specialization', and then suggests a simple language facility to accommodate them, while maintaining the advantages of inheritance, and even subtyping.

Note however that the above papers deal with the issue of exceptions only at the level of (database) programming languages, albeit ones supporting conceptual modeling. The issue of exceptions in specifications has however been considered in [FG93] and [Sch93], among others. It seems interesting to contrast and perhaps combine these approaches.

Parameterization. This is a well known abstraction technique, imported from Mathematics, that has been used with great success in programming and formal specification languages such as Z [Spi89]. Among requirements modeling languages, ERAE and its successors [DDR92] support parameterization to enhance the reusability of requirements. For example, one may define a requirement model with two parameters, `resource` and `consumer`, which includes actions such as `request` and `grant` and constraints such as "a grant will take place for an available resource if there is a waiting consumer". This model can then be instantiated with resource bound to `book` and customer bound to `libraryUser`. Alternatively, the model may be instantiated for a car rental application with different bindings for the two parameters.

4.3 Tools

Computer-based structures, for information modeling or anything else, are useless without tools that facilitate their analysis, design, construction and management. Assessment of a conceptual model needs to take into account the availability of such tools, alongside their expressiveness and support for abstraction mechanisms.

It is interesting to note that successful tools developed in other areas of Computer Science are founded on elaborate theoretical research, produced over many years. For example, compilers in programming languages greatly facilitate programming by performing various forms of syntactic and semantic analysis, also by generating efficient machine-executable code. Likewise, database management systems (DBMS) greatly simplify the task of managing databases, thanks to facilities such as query optimization, transaction processing and error recovery. In both cases, these tools are based on theoretical research, such as formal languages, optimization techniques, query optimization techniques and concurrency control concepts and algorithms.

For this paper, we focus on three basic classes of tools which we consider basic for any technology intended to support the creation and evolution of information bases: *analysis, design* and *management* tools.

4.3.1 Analysis Tools: Verification and Validation

Analysis tools perform various forms of checking on the contents of an information base to establish that they are consistent and accurately reflect the application, thereby giving users confidence that the information base is meaningful and correct. One type of checking, called *verification*, treats an information base as a formal symbol structure which must satisfy syntactic and semantic rules provided by its conceptual model. Verification can take the form of establishing that syntactic rules are obeyed, checking candinality constraints for entity-relationship-like models, or checking semantic consistency of rules and constraints included in the information base.

Verification tools are grounded on the formal definition of a conceptual model. There is little non-trivial analysis one can do for a conceptual model that is only informally defined, such as SADT or data flow diagrams. There is much analysis that can be done (*but*, at great computational cost) for formal, and expressively powerful conceptual models which offer an assertional sublanguage, such as RML or KAOS. In between these extremes we have conceptual models which are formally defined, but offer no assertional sublanguage, and therefore don't need a computationally expensive inference engine. Among many others, various forms of the extended entity-relationship model fit this in- between category.

This discussion points to a great advantage of conceptual models which offer built-in terms that cover the ontology of a particular application over ones that do not, but offer instead general facilities for defining the terms that one needs for a given application: analysis tools based on the former type of conceptual model will generally be much more efficient than analysis tools based on the latter type.

Here is a partial list of different types of analysis that may be offered by a particular information model, depending on the ontologies that it supports:

- Static ontology – cardinality constraints, spatial reasoning
- Dynamic ontology – proving that state invariants defined in terms of assertions are preserved by processes defined in terms of pre/post-conditions; proving termination and liveness properties, temporal reasoning
- Intentional ontology – goal satisfaction algorithms for AND/OR goal graphs, marker-passing algorithms
- Social ontology – means-ends analysis

Whereas verification tools are concerned with the internal consistency of an information base vis-à-vis its conceptual model, *validation* tools check for the consistency of an information base with respect to its application. Clearly, such consistency is critical to the usefulness of an information base. Surprisingly, not much research has been done on this topic. [Pol85] is an example of early work on validating expert system rules (here the information base is capturing expertise in the performance of some task) by examining the performance of the expert system and noting failures, which are then traced back to the use of particular rules. A study on verification and validation techniques for expert systems, with a focus on nuclear industry applications, can be found in [SAIC91].

4.3.2 Design Tools

An information base constitutes an artifact. As such, it needs careful crafting, or design, based on rules which guide the design process. These rules suggest when is an artifact well structured and when it is not. For information modeling, such rules have been proposed for the relational model [Cod72], and they define formally various *normal forms* for relational schemata. Placing a relational schema in these forms eliminates the danger for certain types of anomalies which can occur in the database upon the insertion/removal/update of tuples. To the extend that this work is based on tuple attributes, it also applies to other information models, such as the entity-relationship model, which offer attributes and are relatively unstructured. For more expressive conceptual models, which cover more than the static ontology and support several abstraction mechanisms, the problem of normalization, or alternative means for defining and practicing good information base design, has largely been ignored.

4.3.3 Management Tools

Management tools begin with a good implementation which offers facilities for building, accessing and updating an information base. Beyond a mere implementation, one would like to have an *efficient* implementation which scales up in the sense that primitive operations are relatively unaffected by the size of the information base. In the case of databases, such efficiency is derived from elaborate systems research into physical storage management, caching and indexing techniques.

Query optimization makes it possible to efficiently evaluate queries expressed in a high level, declarative language such as SQL. Experience from databases suggests that having such a facility broadens the class of users for the information base. In addition, concurrency control can increase dramatically the number of transactions that can be executed against an information base per unit time. Also, error recovery can serve as safeguard against system failure, ensuring that the information base can be returned to a consistent state after a crash.

Of course, all these are accepted features of commercial relational DBMS products. Much work has been done on extending the research which makes these features a reality for relational databases to other, more advanced data models, including object-oriented, and multimedia ones. Generally, there are few supported management tools for conceptual models (but, see ConceptBase [JGJSE95], and [JJNS98] in this volume for some work in the right direction). Note also that some research has been done on the subject (e.g., [LNW91, MCPST96]).

5 Assessment of Conceptual Models

The three-dimensional characterization of conceptual models, can now be exploited to assess different conceptual models, to guide the design of new models so that they truly advance the state-of-the-art, also to evaluate and compare candidates for a given information modeling task. We begin the section by offering an admittedly coarse-grained evaluation of some well known conceptual models. We then present some suggestions to those who have to choose among conceptual models, or dare to design new ones.

5.1 Evaluating Conceptual Models

An obvious way to use the framework proposed in the previous section is to evaluate the degree to which different conceptual models cover the four basic ontologies, support the six abstraction mechanisms and offer the three classes of tools. The overall "mark" for a given conceptual model is some combination of the marks it gets with respect to each dimension. Likewise, the overall mark for each dimension is some combination of the partial marks for each component of the dimension.

A disclaimer is in order here. Like any other form of evaluation scheme, this one is highly dependent on the definition of the dimensions we have proposed, and arbitrary with respect to the actual assigned "marks". Nevertheless, we consider it a useful coarse-grain instrument for the assessment of conceptual models, certainly better than no evaluation scheme at all.

Let's use the entity-relationship (ER) model as example to present and illustrate our evaluation scheme. Firstly, the model clearly supports the static ontology. Secondly, the model offers minimal support for the other ontologies in the sense that one can define activities, goals and social dependencies as entities or relationships, but none of the semantics of these terms is embedded in the ER model or the tools it offers. To assign marks, and keep things simple, we will allocate a mark in the range {`excellent, good, OK, so-so, none`}, depending on how well a conceptual model supports each ontology, abstraction mechanism or tool type. In the case of the ER model, its mark for the static ontology might be `good+`, and `so-so` for all other ontologies. Why only `good+`? Well, there is at least one other conceptual model, [HM81], which offers a substantially more elaborate notion of entity than the ER model. In other words, we reserve a perfect mark for the best proposal in the literature in covering a particular ontology, supporting an abstraction mechanism, or offering a set of tools.

Turning to abstraction mechanisms, ER supports a simple form of classification, in the sense that every entity/relationship is an instance of a single entity/relationship type. This is clearly a long way from the sophistication of some of the more recent proposals, so it only gets a `so-so`. Other abstraction mechanisms are supported circumstantially. One can define `isA`, `partOf`, `instanceOf`, etc. as relationships, but the semantics of these are not embedded either in tools, or the ER model itself. Let's give ER, rather generously, `so-so`-marks for all other abstractions.

With regard to tools, there is a variety of tools which perform simple forms of analysis on ER schemata, including normalization tools. Moreover, there are well-accepted techniques for mapping down an ER information base into a relational database. For these reasons, we give ER high marks with respect to the tool dimension, say excellent, excellent, and good+ respectively. A few points have been taken away for management tools because whatever is available was developed specifically for the relational model. Overall then, the ER model gets high marks for its support of the static ontology and the availability of management tools, but can use enhancements in all other areas. Of course, for the time it was proposed, this conceptual model is still a classic.

Relational Model. The model makes no ontological assumptions about the application, so its marks on ontologies are uniformly none. For its support of a simple form of classification (tuples are members of relations) the model gets a so-so, while its score for tools is perfect. Its overall score then is perfect on tools and close to none in other areas. It should be noted, however, that this assessment applies to Codd's original proposal and also the model supported by most commercial DBMS products. The literature abounds with extensions of the model which do offer some form of an ontology, including entities, time, and/or space. Moreover, the model has been extended to support at least aggregation and generalization as far back as '77 [SS77].

Extended Entity-Relationship Model. This is an extension of the entity-relationship model (used, for example, in [BLN92]) which supports reasonably sophisticated forms of generalization and aggregation, plus the simple form of classification found in ER, so we'll give it so-so, good, and good respectively for classification, generalization and aggregation. The marks for supported ontologies don't change, but analysis, design and normalization tools become a bit more problematic because of the presence of the two abstraction mechanisms.

SADT. This model supports, to some extent, both the static and dynamic ontologies, though its marks in both cases are OK. Likewise, with respect to abstraction mechanisms, SADT offers a single structuring mechanism where each box (representing data or activity) can be elaborated into a diagram. This structuring mechanism has no associated semantics, so it can be treated as a rather primitive form of aggregation and lands a mark of OK. Finally, the marks for tools are also OK, since SADT did come with a basic implementation along with some, generally ad hoc, design rules.

The reader may want to apply the evaluation scheme to her favorite conceptual model. Even though crude, the scheme points to the progress that has been made since the mid-'70s. Specifically, pioneering conceptual models such as ER and SADT support one ontology, or less than two, respectively, and offer little in terms of abstraction mechanisms. Conceptual models of the mid-'80s, such as ones embedded in object-oriented databases and requirements languages, support aggregation and generalization and improve on the support of the static and dynamic ontology. Finally, in the mid-'90s we are looking at conceptual models which begin to grapple with the intentional ontology, treat classification with the respect that it deserves and also support various forms of parameterization and modularization (e.g., [DFL93, EKW92]).

5.2 Choosing a Conceptual Model

Suppose then that you are leading a project that has an application modeling component. How could you use the insights of the proposed characterization to select the conceptual schema to be used in your project?

A starting point for the selection process is to consider three alternatives. The first involves adopting an existing generic information base. For example, if you are developing a banking system, there may be an existing collection of defined banking terms available, using some conceptual or even logical information model. Adopting it has the obvious advantage of cutting costs and project time. No wonder reuse of generic information bases has received much attention in AI [LG90, PFPMFGN92], as well as in Requirements Engineering (e.g., [LMV97, MV97]).

A second alternative is to adopt an existing conceptual model and develop your own information base from scratch. This is clearly a preferred alternative only if the first one does not apply. Selection of an existing conceptual model can proceed by identifying the nature of the application to be modeled, i.e., answering the question "what kinds of things will we need to talk about?", or "does the application involve temporal or spatial information?" In addition, one needs to make rough guesses on the size of the information base, i.e., "how many generic and token units?" For a project which will involve a large number of generic terms, abstraction mechanisms are essential. For instance, for a project involving the description of aircraft designs where the number of generic terms may be in the tens of thousands, use of abstraction is unavoidable. For a project which will require the construction of a very large information base, say with billions of instances, management tools are a must.

It is important to keep in mind during the selection process that not all abstraction mechanisms will be equally helpful to any given project. For a project requiring the modeling of few but very complex concepts, aggregation is clearly most helpful and modeling through stepwise decomposition is the most appropriate modeling strategy. If, on the other hand, the modeling task involves many simple but similar concepts, generalization is the abstraction to turn to. Finally, a project involving heavy use of multiple descriptions for one and the same entity, such as multiple versions of the same design or multiple views on the same database, use of contextualization is recommended to organize and rationalize these multiple descriptions.

The last, most time consuming, and least desirable alternative is for your project to develop its own conceptual model. Such an alternative is feasible only for long term projects. Before adopting it, you may want to think twice what is unique about your modeling task, and why it is that none of the existing conceptual models apply. Also to think of the overhead involved in designing and implementing your new conceptual model, before you can actually exploit it.

The moral of this discussion is that not all conceptual models are created equal with regard to their usefulness for your modeling task. The exercise of identifying what is the application like, also what abstractions and tools are most useful can greatly reduce the danger of disappointment later on. Moreover, design of new conceptual models should be avoided at all costs because it is rarely justified when you are trying to model an application, as opposed to furthering the state-of-the-art in conceptual modeling.

6 Conclusions and Directions for Future Research

We have set out to study and characterize information modeling, both in research and practice, in different areas of Computer Science. Our study included a brief summary of the history of the topic, a characterization of conceptual models in terms of three orthogonal dimensions, and the assessment of several conceptual models from the literature.

Clearly, there is much research to be done in information modeling. On conceptual models, the study of new ontologies, and the consolidation of existing ones such as the intentional and social ontologies, will continue. Other abstraction mechanisms will be proposed, formalized and integrated into existing or new conceptual models. The field of Databases will continue to push the limits of database management technology so that it applies to ever more powerful and expressive information models, including conceptual ones. As well, new application areas will need to be explored and methodologies will have to be developed, analogously to the state-of-practice for knowledge engineering in AI, data modeling in Databases, and requirements engineering.

Acknowledgments: I am grateful to many colleagues who helped shape my ideas on the topic of conceptual modeling, most notably Alex Borgida (Rutgers University), Sol Greenspan (GTE Laboratories), Matthias Jarke (Technical University of Aachen), Hector Levesque (University of Toronto), Nicholas Roussopoulos (University of Maryland), and Eric Yu (University of Toronto). Thanks are also due to the editors of the Handbook and the anonymous reviewers for helpful feedback. Funding sources for the research include the Natural Sciences and Engineering Research Council (NSERC) of Canada and the City University of Hong Kong, where the paper was actually prepared.

References

[AB91] Abiteboul, S., Bonner, A., Objects and Views, Proceedings of the ACM SIGMOD International Conference on the Management of Data, 1991, 238 - 247

[Abr74] Abrial, J.-R., Data Semantics, in: Klimbie, Koffeman (eds.), Data Management Systems, North-Holland, 1974

[All84] Allen, J. F., Towards a General Theory of Action and Time, Artificial Intelligence (23), 1984, 123-154

[ANSI75] ANSI/X3/SPARC Study Group on Database Management Systems, Interim Report, FDT 7(2), 1975

[ABDDMZ89] Atkinson, M., Bancilhon, F., DeWitt, D., Dittrich, K., Maier, D., Zdonik, S., The Object-Oriented Database System Manifesto, in: Deductive and Object-oriented Databases, Elsevier Science Publishers, Amsterdam, Netherlands, 1990

[BGW82] Balzer, R., Goldman, N., Wile, D., Operational specifications as a basis for rapid prototyping, in: Proceedings Symposium on Rapid Prototyping, ACM Software Engineering Notes 7(5), 1982, 3-16

[BLN92] Batini, C., Lenzerini, M., Navathe, S., Database Design: An Entity-Relationship Approach, Benjamin Cummings, 1992

[BT76] Bell, T. E., Thayer, T. A., Software Requirements: are they really a problem, in: Proceedings Second International Conference on Software Engineering, 1976, 61-68

[BN96] P. Bernus, L. Nemes, (eds.), Modelling and Methodologis for Enterprise Integration, Chapman, Hill, 1996

[Ber92] Bertino, E., A View Mechanism for Object-Oriented Databases, International Conference on Extending Database Technologies (EDBT'92), Vienna, April 1992, Lecture Notes in Computer Science, 1992

[BW77] Bobrow, D. G., Winograd, T., An Overview of KRL, a Knowledge Representation Language, Cognitive Science 1, 1977, 3-46

[BBJW97] Boman, M., Bubenko, J., Johannesson, P., Wangler, B., Conceptual Modeling, Prentice Hall, 1997

[Boo94] Booch, G., Object-Oriented Analysis and Design, Benjamin-Cummings, 1994

[BGM85] Borgida, A., Greenspan, S., Mylopoulos, J., Knowledge Representation as a Basis for Requirements Specification, IEEE Computer 18(4), April 1985, Reprinted in: Rich, C., Waters,

R., Readings in Artificial Intelligence and Software Engineering, Morgan-Kaufmann, 1987

[Bor85b] Borgida, A., Features of Languages for the Development of Information Systems at the Conceptual Level, IEEE Software 2(1), January 1985

[Bor88] Borgida, A., Modeling Class Hierarchies with Contradictions, Proceedings ACM SIGMOD Conference, 1988, 434-443

[BBMR89] Borgida, A., Brachman, R., McGuiness, D., Resnick, L., CLASSIC/DB: A Structural Data Model for Objects, Proceedings ACM SIGMOD Conference, Portland, 1989

[Bor90] Borgida, A., Knowledge Representation and Semantic Data Modelling: Similarities and Differences, Proceedings Entity-Relationship Conference, Geneva, 1990

[Bra79] Brachman, R. J., On the Epistemological Status of Semantic Networks, in: N. V. Findler (ed.), Associative Networks: Representation and Use of Knowledge by Computers, Academic Press, New York, 1979

[BFL83] Brachman, R. J., Fikes, R. E., Levesque, H. J., Krypton: A Functional Approach to Knowledge Representation, IEEE Computer 16(10), 1983, 67-74

[Bra83b] Brachman, R., What Is-a is and isn't: An Analysis of Taxonomic Links in Semantic Networks, IEEE Computer, 1983

[BL85] Brachman, R. J., Levesque, H. J., A Fundamental Tradeoff in Knowledge Representation and Reasoning (Revised Version), in: [BL85b]

[BL85b] R. J. Brachman, H. J. Levesque, (eds.), Readings in Knowledge Representation, Morgan Kaufmann, Los Altos, CA, 1985, 41-70

[BZ81] M. Brodie, S. Zilles, (eds.), Proceedings of Workshop on Data Abstraction, Databases and Conceptual Modelling, Pingree Park Colorado, Joint SIGART, SIGMOD, SIGPLAN newsletter, 1981

[BMS84] M. Brodie, J. Mylopoulos, J. Schmidt, (eds.), On Conceptual Modelling: Perspectives from Artificial Intelligence, Databases and Programming Languages, Springer-Verlag, 1984

[BM86] M. Brodie, J. Mylopoulos, (eds.), On Knowledge Base Management Systems: Perspectives from Artificial Intelligence and Databases, Springer-Verlag, 1986

[Bub80] Bubenko, J., Information Modeling in the Context of System Development, in: Proceedings IFIP Congress 80, 1980, 395-411

[Bun77] Bunge, M., Treatise on Basic Philosophy: Ontology I – The Furniture of the World, Reidel, 1977

[Car67] Carnap, R., The Logical Structure of the World: Pseudoproblems in Philosophy, University of California Press, 1967

[Che76] Chen, P., The Entity-Relationship Model: Towards a Unified View of Data, ACM Transactions on Database Systems 1(1), 1976

[Chu93] Chung, L., Representing and Using Non-Functional Requirements: A Process-Oriented Approach, Ph.D thesis, Department of Computer Science, U. of Toronto, 1993

[CY90] Coad, P., Yourdon, E., Object-Oriented Analysis, Yourdon Press, Englewood Cliffs, NJ, 1990

[Cod70] Codd, E. F., A Relational Model for Large Shared Data Banks, Communications of the ACM 13, No. 6, 1970, 377-387

[Cod72] Codd, E. F., Further Normalization of the Data Base Relational Model, in: Data Base Systems, Courant Computer Science Symposia Series, Prentice Hall, 1972

[Cod79] Codd, E. F., Extending the Database Relational Model to Capture More Meaning, ACM Transactions on Database Systems 4, No. 4, 1979

[Cod82] Codd, E. F., Relational Database: A Practical Foundation for Productivity, Communications of the ACM, 1982

[Coh89] Cohn, A. G., On the Appearance of Sortal Literals: a Non Substitutional Framework for Hybrid Reasoning, in: Proceedings of the First International Conference on Principles of Knowledge Representation and Reasoning, Toronto, 1989, 55-66

[CS88] Collins, A., Smith, E., Readings in Cognitive Science: A Perspective from Psychology and Artificial Intelligence, Morgan-Kaufmann, 1988

[CB88] Conklin, J., Begeman, M., gIBIS: A Hypertext Tool for Exploratory Policy Discussion, Transactions on Office Information Systems, 6(4), 1988, 281-318

[CKO92] Curtis, B., Kellner, M., Over, J., Process Modelling, Communications of the ACM 35(9), September 1992

[DH72] Dahl, O.-J., Hoare, C., Hierarchical Program Structures, in: O.-J. Dahl, E. Dijkstra, C. Hoare, (eds.), Structured Programming, Academic Press, 1972

[DFL93] Dardenne, A., Fickas, S., Lamsweerde, A. van, Goal Directed Requirements Acquisition, in: Science of Computer Programming, 20, 1993, 3-50

[Dav86] Davis, E., Representing and Acquiring Geographic Knowledge, Pitman, 1986

[Dav93] Davis, A., Software Requirements: Objects, Functions and States, Prentice Hall, 1993

[DeM79] De Marco, T., Structured Analysis and System Specification, Prentice Hall, 1979

[DHLPR86] Dubois, E., Hagelstein, J., Lahou, E., Ponsaert, F., Rifaut, A., A Knowledge Representation Language for Requirements Engineering, Proceedings of the IEEE 74(10), 1986

[DDR92] Dubois, E., Du Bois, P., Rifaut, A., Elaborating, Structuring and Expressing Formal Requirements for Composite Systems, Proceedings Fourth International Conference on Advanced Information Systems Engineering (CAiSE-92), Manchester, 1992

[EKW92] Embley, D., Kurtz, B., Woodfield, S., Object-Oriented Systems Analysis, Yourdon Press, Prentice Hall, 1992

[ESEC93] Proceedings of the Third European Software Engineering Conference, Milan, Italy, Springer-Verlag, 1993

[Fea87] Feather, M., Language Support for the Specification and Derivation of Concurrent Systems, ACM Transactions on Programming Languages 9(2), April 1987, 198-234

[FN88] Fickas, S., Nagarajan, P., Critiquing Software Specifications: a Knowledge-Based Approach, in: IEEE Software, November 1988

[Fin79] N. V. Findler, (ed.), Associative Networks: Representation and Use of Knowledge by Computers, Academic Press, New York, 1979

[FK92] Finkelstein, A., Kramer, J., *et al*, Viewpoints: A Framework for Multiple Perspectives in System Development, International Journal of Software Engineering and Knowledge Engineering, 2(1), World Scientific Publishing, March 1992, 31-57

[FG93] Finkelstein, A., Gabbay, D., *et al*, Inconsistency Handling in Multi-Perspective Specifications, in: [ESEC93], 84-99

[Gal73] Galbraith, J. R., Designing Complex Organizations, Addison Wesley, 1973

[GF95] Gotel, O., Finkelstein, A., Contribution Structures, Proceedings Second IEEE International Symposium on Requirements Engineering, York, England, March 1995

[GMB82] Greenspan, S., Mylopoulos, J., Borgida, A., Capturing More World Knowledge in the Requirements Specification, Proc. 6th Int. Conf. on SE, Tokyo, 1982, Reprinted in: P. Freeman, A. Wasserman (eds.), Tutorial on Software Design Techniques, IEEE Computer Society Press, 1984, also in: Prieto-Diaz, R., Arango, G., Domain Analysis and Software Systems Modeling, IEEE Comp. Sci. Press, 1991

[Gre84] Greenspan, S., Requirements Modeling: A Knowledge Representation Approach to Requirements Definition, Ph.D. thesis, Department of Computer Science, University of Toronto, 1984

[GBM86] Greenspan, S., Borgida, A., Mylopoulos, J., A Requirements Modeling Language and Its Logic, Information Systems 11(1), 1986, 9-23, also appears in: M. Brodie, J. Mylopoulos (eds.), Knowledge Base Management Systems, Springer-Verlag, 1986

[HM81] Hammer, M., McLeod, D., Database Description with SDM: A Semantic Data Model, ACM Transactions on Database Systems, September 1981

[Har87] Harel, D., Statecharts: A Visual Formalism for Complex Systems, Science of Computer Programming 8, 1987

[Hay85] Hayes, P. J., The Second Naive Physics Manifesto, in: J. R. Hobbs, R. C. Moore (eds.), Formal Theories of the Commonsense World, Ablex Publishing Corp., Norwood, N. J., 1985, 1-36

[HWL83] F. Hayes-Roth, D. A. Waterman, D. B. Lenat, (eds.), Building Expert Systems, Addison-Wesley, Reading, MA, 1983

[Hen79] Hendrix, G. G., Encoding Knowledge in Partitioned Networks, in: N. V. Findler (ed.), Associative Networks: Representation and Use of Knowledge by Computers, Academic Press, New York, 1979, 51-92

[Hew71] Hewitt, C., Procedural Embedding of Knowledge in PLANNER, Proceedings International Joint Conference on Artificial Intelligence (IJCAI'71), London, September 1971, 167-182

[Hir89] Hirst, G., Ontological Assumptions in Knowledge Representation, in: Proceedings of the First International Conference on Principles of Knowledge Representation and Reasoning, Toronto, 1989, 157-169

[HK87] Hull, R., King, R., Semantic Database Modelling: Survey, Applications and Research Issues, ACM Computing Surveys 19(3), September 1987

[JCJO92] Jacobson, I., Christerson, M., Jonsson, P., Overgaard, G., Object-Oriented Software Engineering, A Use Case Driven Approach, Addison-Wesley, 1992

[Jac78] Jackson, M., Information Systems: Modeling, Sequencing and Transformation, Proceedings Third International Conference on Software Engineering, 1978, 72-81

[Jac83] Jackson, M., System Development, Prentice Hall, 1983

[JMSV92] Jarke, M., Mylopoulos, J., Schmidt, J., Vassiliou, Y., DAIDA: An Environment for Evolving Information Systems, ACM Transactions on Information Systems 10(1), 1992, 1-50

[JGJSE95] Jarke, M., Gallersdörfer, R., Jeusfeld, M. A., Staudt, M., Eherer, S., ConceptBase - a deductive object base for meta data management, Journal of Intelligent Information Systems, (Special Issue on Advances in Deductive Object-Oriented Databases), Vol. 4, No. 2, 1995, 167-192

[JJNS98] Jeusfeld, M., Jarke, M., Nissen, H., Staudt, M., ConceptBase: Managing Conceptual Models About Information Systems, (this volume)

[JFH92] Johnson, W. L., Feather, M., Harris, D., Representing and Presenting Requirements Knowledge, IEEE Transactions on Software Engineering, October 1992, 853-869

[Kat90] Katz, R. H., Toward a Unified Framework for Version Modeling in Engineering Databases, ACM Computing Surveys 22(4), December 1990, 375-408

[KBG89] Kim, W., Bertino, E., Garza, J. F., Composite Objects Revisited, in: Proceedings Object-Oriented Programming Systems, Languages and Applications (OOPSLA'89), 1989, 337-347

[KS94] W. Klas, A. Sheth, (eds.), Special Issue: Metadata for Digital Data, ACM SIGMOD Record 23(4), December 1994

[KM91] Kramer, B., Mylopoulos, J., A Survey of Knowledge Representation, in: S. Shapiro (ed.), The Encyclopedea of Artificial Intelligence, John Wiley and Sons Inc., 2nd edition, 1991

[LMV97] Lam, W., McDermid, J., Vickers, A., Ten Steps Towards Systematic Requirements Reuse, in: Proceedings Third IEEE International Symposium on Requirements Engineering, Annapolis, January 1997, 6-15

[LL91] Lee, J., Lai, K.-Y., What is Design Rationale?, Human-Computer Interaction 6(3-4), 1991

[LG90] Lenat, D., Guha, R., Building Large Knowledge Based Systems - Representation and Inference in the CYC Project, Addison-Wesley, 1990

[LM79] Levesque, H. J., Mylopoulos, J., A Procedural Semantics for Semantic Networks, in: N. V. Findler (ed.), Associative Networks: Representation and Use of Knowledge by Computers, Academic Press, New York, 1979, 93-120

[Lev86] Levesque, H. J., Knowledge Representation and Reasoning, Annual Review of Computer Science 1, 1986, 255-287

[LNW91] Lockemann, P. C., Nagel, H.-H., Walter, I. M., Databases for Knowledge Bases: An Empirical Study, Data and Knowledge Engineering 7, 1991, 115-154

[LZ92] P. Loucopoulos, R. Zicari, (eds.), Conceptual Modeling, Databases and CASE: An Integrated View of Information System Development, Wiley, 1992

[MS82] Maida, A., Shapiro, S. C., Intensional Concepts in Propositional Semantic Networks, Cognitive Science 6, 1982, 291-330

[MV97] Massonet, P., Lamsweerde, A. van, Analogical Reuse of Requirements frameworks, in: Proceedings Third IEEE International Symposium on Requirements Engineering, Annapolis, January 1997, 17-26

[McC68] McCarthy, J., Programs with Common Sense, in: M. Minsky (ed.), Semantic Information Processing, MIT Press, Cambridge, MA, 1968, 403-418

[MR95] Macfarlane, I., Reilly, I., Requirements Traceability in an Integrated Development Environment, in: Proceedings Second IEEE International Symposium on Requirements Engineering, York, England, March 1995

[MYBM91] MacLean, A., Young, R., Bellotti, V., Moran, T., Questions, Options, Criteria: Elements of Design Space Analysis, Human-Computer Interaction 6(3-4), 1991

[MP93] N. Madhavji, M. H. Penedo, (eds.), Special Section on the Evolution of Software Processes, IEEE Transactions on Software Engineering 19(12), 1993

[MJ76] Miller, G., Johnson-Laird, P., Language and Perception, Harvard University Press, 1976

[Min68] M. Minsky, (ed.), Semantic Information Processing, MIT Press, Cambridge, MA, 1968

[Min75] Minsky, M., A Framework for Representing Knowledge, in: P. Winston (ed.), The Psychology of Computer Vision, the MIT Press, 1975

[Min79] Mintzberg, H., The Structuring of Organizations, Prentice Hall, 1979

[MM92] Motschnig-Pitrik, R., Mylopoulos, J., Classes and Instances, International Journal of Intelligent and Cooperative Systems 1(1), April 1992

[Mot93] Motschnig-Pitrik, R., The Semantics of Parts Versus Aggregates, in: Data/Knowledge Modeling, Proceedings Fifth Conference on Advanced Information Systems Engineering (CAiSE93), Paris, June 1993

[MBW80] Mylopoulos, J., Bernstein, P. A., Wong, H. K. T., A Language Facility for Designing Data-Intensive Applications, ACM Trans.

on Database Systems 5(2), June 1980, reprinted in: S. Zdonik, D. Maier, Readings in Object-Oriented Database Systems, Morgan-Kaufmann, 1989

[MB88] J. Mylopoulos, M. Brodie, (eds.), Readings in Artificial Intelligence and Databases, Morgan-Kaufmann, 1988

[MBJK90] Mylopoulos, J., Borgida, A., Jarke, M., Koubarakis, M., Telos: Representing Knowledge About Information Systems, ACM Transactions on Information Systems, October 1990

[MM95] Mylopoulos, J., Motschnig-Pitrik, R., Partitioning an Information Base Through Contexts, Proceedings Third International Conference on Cooperative Information Systems (CoopIS'95), Vienna, May 1995

[MCPST96] Mylopoulos, J., Chaudhri, V., Plexousakis, D., Shrufi, A., Topaloglou, T., Building Knowledge Base Management Systems, Very Large Databases Journal 5(4), October 1996

[NW94] Norrie, M. C., Wunderli, M., Coordination System Modelling, Proceedings of the Thirteenth International Conference on The Entity Relationship Approach, Manchester, UK, December 1994

[NKF93] Nuseibeh, B., Kramer, J., Finkelstein, A., Expressing the Relationships Between Multiple Views, in: Requirements Specification, Proceedings 15th International Conference on Software Engineering, IEEE Computer Science Press, Baltimore, MD, May 1993, 187-196

[PFPMFGN92] Patil, R., Fikes, R., Patel-Schneider, P., Mckay, D., Finin, T., Gruber, T., Neches, R., The DARPA Knowledge Sharing Effort: Progress Report, Proceedings Third International Conference on Knowledge Representation and Reasoning, Boston, November 1992

[PM88] Peckham, J., Maryanski, F., Semantic Data Models, ACM Computinf Surveys 20(3), September 1988

[PS78] Pfeffer, J., Salancik, G., The External Control of Organizations: A Resource Dependency Perspective, Harper and Row, 1978

[PZMY94] Pirotte, A., Zimanyi, E., Massart, D., Yakusheva, T., Materialization: A Powerful and Ubiquitous Abstraction Pattern, Proceedings Very large Databases Conference (VLDB'94), Santiago Chile, 1994

[Pol85] Politakis, P., Empirical Analysis of Expert Systems, Pitman Publishers, 1985

[PB88] Potts, C., Bruns, G., Recording the Reasons for Design Decisions, in: Proceedings Tenth International Conference on Software Engineering, Singapore, 1988

[PT93] Prevelakis, V., Tsichritzis, D., Perspectives on Software Development Environments, in: Proceedings Fifth Conference on Advanced Information Systems Engineering (CAiSE'93), Paris, France, June 1993, Lecture Notes in Computer Science 685, Springer Verlag, 1993

[Qui68] Quillian, M. R., Semantic Memory, in: M. Minsky (ed.), Semantic Information Processing, MIT Press, Cambridge, MA, 1968, 227-270

[RE93] Proceedings IEEE International Symposium on Requirements Engineering, IEEE Computer Society Press, January 1993

[Rie76] Rieger, C., An Organization of Knowledge for Problem-Solving and Language Comprehension, Artificial Intelligence 7(2), 1976, 89-127

[RF94] Robinson, W., Fickas, S., Supporting Multi-Perspective Requirements Engineering, in: [ICRE94]

[RC92] Rolland, C., Cauvet, C., Trends and Perspectives in Conceptual Modeling, in: [LZ92]

[Rom85] Roman, G.-C., A Taxonomy of Current Issues in Requirements Engineering, IEEE Computer 18(4), April 1985

[RS77] Ross, D. T., Schoman, Structured Analysis for Requirements Definition, in: [TSE77], 6-15

[Ros77b] Ross, D. T., Structured Analysis: A Language for Communicating Ideas, in: [TSE77], 16-34

[RBPEL91] Rumbaugh, J., Blaha, M., Premerlani, W., Eddy, F., Lorensen, W, Object-Oriented Modeling and Design, Prentice Hall, 1991

[SAIC91] Guidelines for Verification and Validation of Expert Systems: Review of Conventional Methods, Science Applications International Corporation, Report to the US Nuclear Regulatory Commission and the Electric Power Research Institute (EPRI), 1991

[SM88] Shlaer, S., Mellor, S., Object-Oriented Systems Analysis, Yourdon, Englewood Cliffs, NJ, 1988

[ST89] J. Schmidt, C. Thanos, (eds.), Foundations of Knowledge Base Management, Springer Verlag, 1989

[Sch93] Schoebbens, P. Y., Exceptions in Algebraic Specifications: On the Meaning of 'but', Science of Computer Programming 20, 1993, 73-111

[SLT91] Scholl, M. H., Laasch, C., Tresch, M., Updateable Views in Object Oriented Databases, Proceedings of the Second International Conference on Deductive and Object-Oriented Database Systems, Munich, December 1991

[Sco87] Scott, W., Organizations: Rational, Natural or Open Systems, Prentice Hall, 2nd edition, 1987

[SM88] Shlaer, S., Mellor, S., Object-Oriented Systems Analysis: Modeling the World in Data, Prentice Hall, 1988

[SS77] Smith, J., Smith, D. C. P., Database Abstractions: Aggregation and Generalization, ACM Transactions on Database Systems 2(2), Jun. 1977, 105-133

[Sol79] Solvberg, A., A Contribution to the Definition of Concepts for Expressing Users Information System Requirements, in: Proceedings International Conference on the E-R Approach to Systems Analysis and Design, December 1979

[Spi89] Spivey, J. M., The Z Notation: A Reference Manual, Prentice Hall, 1989

[TD90] Thayer, R., Dorfman, M., System and Software Requirements Engineering, (two volumes), IEEE Computer Society Press, 1990

[TM96] Topaloglou, T., Mylopoulos, J., Representing Partial Spatial Information in Databases: A Conceptual Modeling Approach, Proceedings Fifteenth International Conference on Conceptual Modeling (ER'96), Cottbus, Germany, October 1996

[TSE77] IEEE Transactions on Software Engineering 3(1), Special Issue on Requirements Analysis, January 1977

[TSE92] IEEE Transactions on Software Engineering, 18(6) & 18(10), Special Issue on Knowledge Representation and Reasoning in Software Development, June & October 1992

[TL82] Tsichritzis, D., Lochovsky, F., Data Models, Prentice Hall, 1982

[UML97] Rational Software Corporation, Unified Modeling Language Resource Centre, http:/www.rational.com/uml, 1997

[Ver84] Vernadat, F., Computer-Integrated Manufacturing: On the Database Aspect, Proceedings of CAD/CAM and Robotics Conference, Toronto, 1984

[Ver96] Vernadat, F., Enterprise Modeling and Integration, Chapman and Hall, 1996

[VKV89] Vilain, M., Kautz, H., van Beek, P., Constraint Propagation Algorithms for Temporal Reasoning: A Revised Report, in: D. Weld, J. De Kleer (eds.), Readings in Qualitative Reasoning About Physical Systems, Morgan Kaufmann, 1989

[Wan89] Wand, Y., A Proposal for a Formal Model of Objects, in: W. Kim, F. Lochovsky (eds.), Object-Oriented Concepts, Databases and Applications, Addison-Wesley, 1989

[WW90] Wand, Y., Weber, R., An Ontological Model of an Information System, IEEE Transactions on Software Engineering 16, 1282-1292

[Web87] Webster, D. E., Mapping the Design Representation Terrain: A Survey, TR-STP-093-87, Microelectronics and Computer Corporation (MCC), Austin, 1987

[Wid95] Widom, J., Research Problems in Data Warehousing, in: Proceedings Fourth Conference on Information and Knowledge Management, November 1995

[Yu93] Yu, E., Modeling Organizations for Information Systems Requirements Engineering, in: [RE93], 34-41

[YM94] Yu, E., Mylopoulos, J., Understanding 'Why' in Software Process Modeling, Analysis and Design, Proceedings Sixteenth International Conference on Software Engineering, Sorrento, 1994

[YML96] Yu, E., Mylopoulos, J., Lesperance, Y., AI Models for Business Process Re-Engineering, IEEE Expert 11(4), August 1996

[ZM89] S. Zdonik, D. Maier, (eds.), Readings in Object-Oriented Databases, Morgan-Kaufmann, 1989

CHAPTER 3

EXPRESS

Reiner Anderl, Harald John, Christian Pütter

The ISO standard 10303-11, also known as EXPRESS, is a formal modelling language for the specification of static aspects of an information model. To this intent EXPRESS provides object oriented constructs, such as specialisation, aggregation and modularization. For the specification of dynamic, behavioural and other non-static aspects of a model, various dialects of EXPRESS have been developed which will be unified in the future ISO standard, EXPRESS edition 2. EXPRESS or one of its dialects is being used in a number of research and industrial projects related to the area of product data technology for the specification of even large scale models such as, for instance, the application protocol development in STEP or the modelling of environmentally sound products.

1 Introduction

EXPRESS is a formal language developed to describe information models. An information model is a formal description of objects, facts and ideas which together form a mapping of part of the 'real world'. An information model also provides an explicit set of interpretation rules [SW94]. EXPRESS has been under development since 1984. The first version was standardised by the International Standardisation Organisation (ISO) in 1994 [ISO94]. Since then EXPRESS (or one of its dialects) have been used in many industrial and research oriented projects. Up to now, one of the main domains EXPRESS is used in is the specification of the integrated product data model of the "Standard for the Exchange of Product Data" (STEP, ISO 10303 [ISO94c]). The formal specification of an information model using EXPRESS has two main advantages:

1. The information model can be algorithmically transformed into a computer accessible representation, e.g. a database schema.
2. The formal specification of the information model usually contains less ambiguity than any model described in natural language.

The problem with formal information models is that they are more difficult for users to read and understand than natural language. In this article we will therefore describe the elements of EXPRESS from a user's point of view. Rather than a formal specification we will use a model defining product structure to explain the syntax and semantics of EXPRESS (Section 2). For a detailed and formal specification of EXPRESS, see [ISO94]. While using EXPRESS some deficits have been encountered. A description of some EXPRESS enhancements which deal with these deficiencies are described in Section 3 focusing on their extensions to the standard. Two large scale examples - the information model for the development of environmentally sound products and the application protocol development process in ISO 10303 - are presented in Section 4. Section 5 discusses the application area of EXPRESS and compares it to public object oriented modelling languages.

2 EXPRESS Language Constructs

In contrast to most modelling languages, EXPRESS contains two different notations. The graphical one - EXPRESS-G - is a subset of the textual notation. The example of a simplified product structure will be used to introduce both notations.

2.1 Aggregation

In EXPRESS the basic element to structure data is the entity type. Entities are used to represent objects of the real world (like assemblies or product components in the following example). Entities do not describe individuals of the real world, but groups of instances which have same properties. Mandatory or optional relations are used to express relationships such as aggregations or associations between entities.

The model in Figure 1 specifies that the entity `product_component` has an attribute `shape` described by entity `geometry`. The entity geometry is not further described. This means that attributes of the real world object geometry are of no importance in the context the model used, but it does not mean a geometry has no properties in general.

Properties of an entity without internal structure like version number, name or mass are described as Simple Types. Depending on the data to be described, seven different kinds of Simple Types may be used:

1. An attribute of type STRING may contain a list of characters defined in the EXPRESS character set. A simple type could be seen as a set. The STRING set is defined as:

$$STRING = \{x \mid x \in ASCII^*\}$$

2. Properties of type INTEGER describe numbers. The INTEGER set is defined as:

$$INTEGER = \{x \mid M < x < N;\ M, N, x \in Z\},$$

where the values of M and N depend on the model's implementation and are not specified in EXPRESS.

3. Rational numbers are represented by properties of type REAL, defined by the set:

$$REAL = \{x \mid M' < x < N';\ M', N', x \in Q'\},$$

where the values of M', N' may also differ among different implementations. Q' is a finite subset of rational numbers.

4. If the type of a property could be in one case of type REAL and of type INTEGER in an other, the set NUMBER is used. NUMBER is specified by:

$$NUMBER = INTEGER \cup REAL$$

Usually the sets NUMBER and REAL are identical, but an implementation may use huge integer arithmetic where $M < M'$ and $N' < N$.

5. As in most formal languages (e.g. programming languages), the BOOLEAN set is defined as:

$$BOOLEAN = \{true,\ false\}.$$

Boolean attributes are often used to indicate whether an entity has a special property or not, so that details of this property do not matter in the given context.

6. The LOGICAL set extends the BOOLEAN set by one value:

$$LOGICAL = \{true,\ false,\ unknown\}.$$

It is used, where attributes could not be determined to be true or false for a given context.

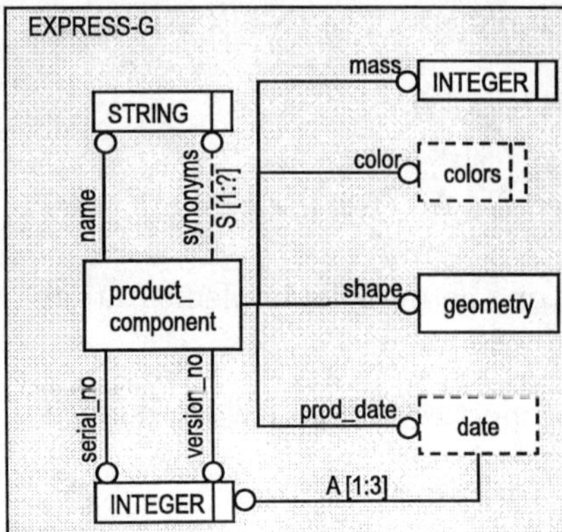

EXPRESS

```
ENTITY geometry;
END_ENTITY;
ENTITY product_component;
  name : STRING;
  synonyms : OPTIONAL SET [1:?] OF
             STRING;
  serial_no: INTEGER;
  version_no : INTEGER;
  color : colors;
  shape : geometry;
  prod_date : date;
  mass : INTEGER;
END_ENTITY;
TYPE colors = ENUMERATION OF
           (red, green, blue);
END_TYPE;
TYPE date = ARRAY [1:3] OF INTEGER;
END_TYPE;
```

Figure 1: Example of a product structure model (1)

7. Attributes of type BINARY are used to describe digital data (e.g. images or sounds). The BINARY set consists of two values:

$$BINARY = \{0, 1\}.$$

In addition to the predefined simple types, users can specify additional sets using either the enumeration or select type. An enumeration is a finite set of ideas called items. An enumeration item must be unique within the enumeration definition. A common example of an enumeration is the set of colours. This set consists of the items red, green, blue and so on. As with simple types, enumerations may be used to describe attributes of entities. The possible value of these attributes is thus constrained by the items of the enumeration.

The set defined by a select type consists of items that have already been specified in the model (such as `connection_type` in Figure 2). At instance level the value of an attribute described by a select type will be an instance of one of the types specified in the set of the select type.

It is possible to define global synonyms for types like entities, enumerations, simple types or select types. These global synonyms are called defined types and are represented in EXPRESS-G using a dashed box (see Figure 1). Defined types are basically used to give more semantic weight to the model. They help to understand the context in which the underlying type is used.

Up to now the relationships between entities and other types discussed, are 1:1 relations. EXPRESS defines collection types which may be used to represent ordered or unordered 1:n relations. A collection can have fixed or varying sizes depending on the specific collection type being used. There are four different collection types defined. Each has a special behaviour and is used for different purposes. The four collection types are:

1. ARRAY. The array collection type represents an ordered, fixed-size collection of elements of the reference type. Its bounds m and n are (possibly negative) integer values. Exactly n-m +1 elements must be stored in the array collection.

2. BAG. A bag represents an unordered collection of elements. Duplicate elements within the bag collection are permitted. A bag may hold any number of elements within the restrictions or is unlimited.

3. LIST. A list constitutes of an ordered collection of elements. The number of elements in the list may be specified if needed. If it is not specified, the list may possibly contain an infinite number of elements.

4. SET. A set is similar to a bag. It contains an unordered collection of elements. The size of the set is also restricted or unlimited. The difference between a set and a bag is that a set may not contain two elements of the same value.

The synonyms of product component may be specified by an unlimited set of strings, where as its construction date would be defined as an array of three elements of type integer (Figure 1). In order to realise m:n relationships between entities, an *inverse relation* can be defined. The inverse relation can have a different name and cardinality. All attributes in an EXPRESS model can be labelled with the keywords OPTIONAL and/or UNIQUE, where UNIQUE means that the values of the attribute must be different among all instances of the type. If an attribute is declared to be OPTIONAL, an instance of the type need not specify a value for this attribute.

2.2 Specialisation

In addition to the ability to structure data using the aggregation relationships described above, EXPRESS provides specialisation mechanisms for entities which differ from any mainstream programming or modelling language.

In general the specialisation (or inheritance) relationship is used to reduce complexity of an information model by constructing type hierarchies. Along a specialisation relation, properties are inherited by more specific entities (subtypes) from more general entities (their supertypes).

As far as the product structure example is concerned, the entities assembly and `product_component` have some attributes in common (e.g. `name`, `version_no` etc.). In order to reduce complexity and prevent redundancy, a supertype of `product_component` and `assembly`, `item` for example, has been introduced which contains the common attributes. Hence, these attributes do not need to be specified explicitly in the subtypes (2). The entity `item`

EXPRESS-G

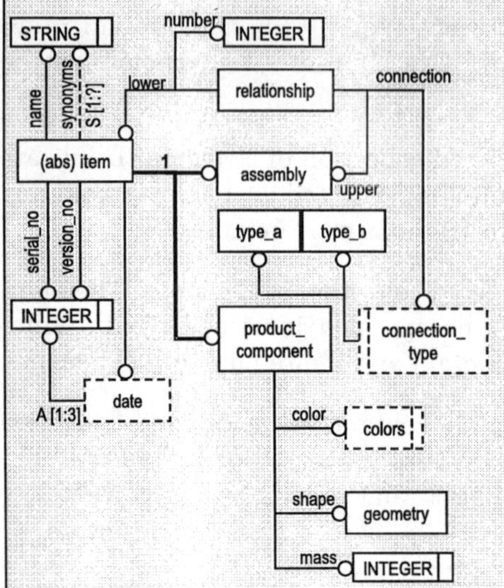

EXPRESS

```
ENTITY geometry;
END_ENTITY;
ENTITY item ABSTACT SUPERTYPE OF
 (ONEOF (assembly,product_component));
  name : STRING;
  synonyms : SET [1:?] OF STRING;
  serial_no: INTEGER;
  version_no : INTEGER;
  prod_date : date;
END_ENTITY;
ENTITY relationship;
  conncetion : connection_type;
  upper : assembly;
  lower : item;
END_ENTITY;
ENTITY assembly SUBTYPE OF (item);
END_ENTITY;
ENTITY product_component SUBTYPE OF
            (item);
  color : colors;
  shape : geometry;
  mass  : INTEGER;
END_ENTITY;
TYPE connection_type = SELECT OF
            (type_a, type_b);
END_TYPE;
TYPE colors = ENUMERATION OF
            (red, green, blue);
END_TYPE;
TYPE date = ARRAY [1:3] OF INEGER;
END_TYPE;
```

Figure 2: Example of a product structure model (2)

must be declared as abstract, since only instances of the entities `assembly` or `product_component` are required to define a particular product structure. Entities declared abstract must not be instantiated. Furthermore an `item` must be either an `assembly` or a `product_component` but not both.

EXPRESS provides different types of specialisation relations. The specialisation relation between `item` and its subtypes is called a `oneof` specialisation (Figure 3b), because there are no real world objects, being assemblies as well as product components.

In addition to this public specialisation relation, which is used in common object oriented languages, EXPRESS provides additional mechanisms which lead to the concept of complex instantiation.

There are two further kinds of specialisation relations. If the subtypes are mutually inclusive the relationship between the subtypes is specified using the and specialisation relation. In this case the instances in the example of Figure 3c must have the properties of entity `A` and entity `B`. Instances of entity `A` or entity `B` are not allowed. The and specialisation relation should only be used in combination with other types of specialisation (e.g. the `oneof` specialisation).

The third type of a specialisation relation is the andor specialisation.

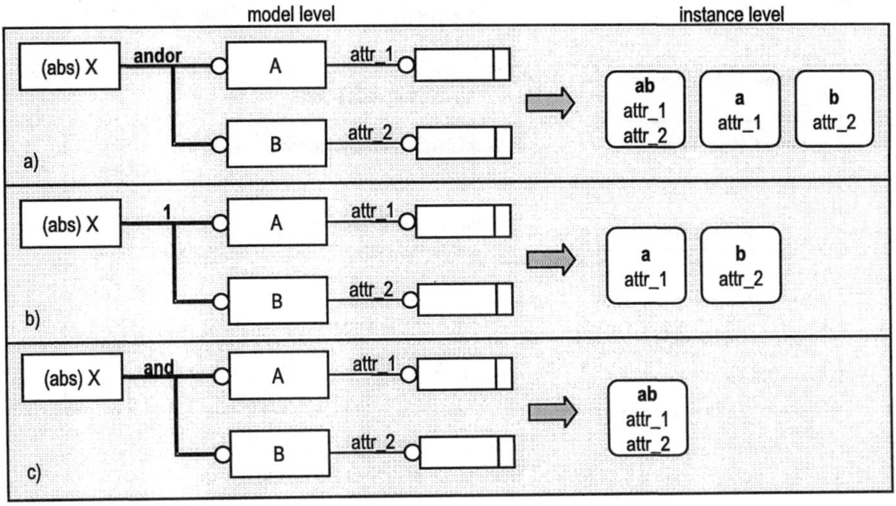

Figure 3: Possible specialisation relationships in EXPRESS

Given the example of Figure 3a, instances which (only) have the properties of entity `A` could exist as well as instances of entity `B` and instances with the properties of both `A` and `B`. The subtypes `A` and `B` are neither mutually exclusive nor mutually inclusive. Instances which contain the attributes of more than one entity are called complex instances. The concept of complex instantiation is difficult to implement using a programming language, which does not support this concept (e.g. C++, Smalltalk or Eiffel). However, Mayer *et al* suggest a solution in [Mai94] where any inheritance hierarchy defined in EXPRESS is automatically transformed to an equivalent common `oneof` hierarchy which can be processed by the compiler of most mainstream programming language.

The solution implies that it must be possible to renounce the special inheritance relation provided by EXPRESS. This - in fact - is the case, but the complexity of the information model may grow substantially.

2.3 Schemas

An information model may consist of hundreds of entities. To control the complexity EXPRESS offers the schema mechanism `schema mechanism`, by which a model can be divided into several isolated parts. Further, EXPRESS allows a schema A to reference elements of schema B using the `reference from` and `use from` constructs. Elements of another schema accessed using `reference from` can only be instantiated as attributes of entities from the importing schema. In contrast, elements imported using `use from` could have an independent existence.

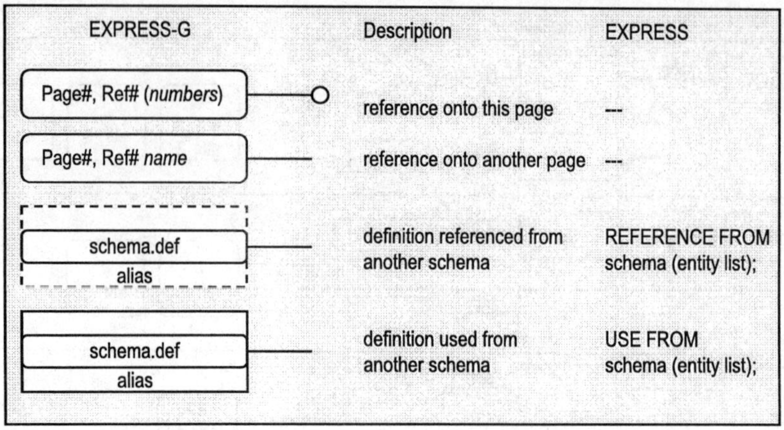

Figure 4: Graphical and lexical notation of schema constructs

Moreover EXPRESS-G offers additional symbols, so-called page references, to distribute a large, single schema over different sheets. Figure 4 summarises the graphical and lexical notation of these constructs.

2.4 Functions and Rules

As mentioned above EXPRESS-G is a subset of EXPRESS. The essential facilities supported by EXPRESS and not included in EXPRESS-G are local and global functions, and local and global rules. Functions and rules will not be specified formally, but explained by extending the product structure example.

2.4.1 Functions

Local functions are included in the definition of an entity using the keyword DERIVED. A local function in EXPRESS consists of an identifier, an attribute name and a single, unconstraint formula. Local functions are used to derive values relevant to the model from a combination of other attributes of the entity concerned. The checksum of an item for example can be defined as:

```
ENTITY item ABSTRACT SUPERTYPE OF
 (oneof (assembly, product_component));
   serial_no : INTEGER;
   version_no : INTEGER;
   ...
  DERIVED
  cs:
```

```
    checksum:=serial_no+version_no mod 9;
END_ENTITY;
```

Global functions are not related to any particular entity or type definition. As in most programming languages, global functions compute a result from given function parameters. Global functions may be used in the formulae of local functions. In the following example, the given function calculates the mass of the assembly entity, which is supposed to be defined as in the product structure example.

```
FUNCTION assembly_mass(a : assembly) : INTEGER;
 relations : LIST [1:?] OF
RELATIONSHIP:=BASE.RELATIONSHIP;
 mass : INTEGER := 0;
 REPEAT i :=1 TO SIZEOF (BASE.RELATIONSHIP);
  IF (relations[i].top=a AND
 TYPEOF (relations[i].lower)=product_component)
  THEN mass:=mass+relations[i].lower.mass
              * relations[i].number;
  END_IF;
  IF (relations[i].top=a AND
    TYPEOF (relations[i].lower)=assembly)
 THEN mass:=mass+assembly_mass(relations[i].lower);
  END_IF;
 END_REPEAT;
 RETURN (mass);
 END_FUNCTION;
```

2.4.2 Rules

Like local functions, local rules are declared within an entity declaration. Local rules constrain the possible values an attribute may take at instance level. A local rule consists of an identifier and a logical formula, which evaluates to true or false. For valid instances all local rules must evaluate to true. For example the version number of an item must be greater or equal to zero. This can be specified by extending the entity item by a local rule as follows:

```
ENTITY item ABSTRACT SUPERTYPE OF
 (oneof (assembly, product_component));
   version_no : INTEGER;
   ...
 WHERE
legal_version : version_no >= 0;
END_ENTITY;
```

In the same way as local rules define constraints for the values of attributes, global rules specify constraints which an instantiation of the whole schema must satisfy. In the product structure example, the frequency with which a assembly or product component in the next level occurs within a super-assembly is given by the attribute number of the entity relationship. Therefore an assembly may not contain duplicate subassemblies or product components. This constraint is defined by the following global rule:

```
#1 RULE assembly_constraint;
#2   indicator : BOOLEAN:= true;
#3   relations : LIST [1:?] of
#4 RELATIONSHIP:= BASE.RELATIONSHIP;
#5   REPEAT i := 1 TO SIZEOF(BASE.RELATIONSHIP);
#6    REPEAT j := 1 TO SIZEOF(BASE.RELATIONSHIP);
#7   if (relations[i].lower = relations[j].lower and
#8            relations[i].upper = relations[j].upper)
#9 THEN indicator:= false;
#10 END_REPEAT;
#11  END_REPEAT;
#12 where assembly_constraint : indicator = true;
#13 END_RULE;
```

The where clause in line #12 indicates the case that schema instantiation satisfies this rule.

The constructs described in this contribution enables the user to specify the static aspects of an information model using a combination of graphical and textual notation.

3 Extensions to Standard

3.1 Shortcomings of EXPRESS

During the use of EXPRESS, especially in the context of STEP, several shortcomings were detected. On the one hand, these shortcomings prevent a complete specification of all properties an information model may contain. On the other hand, there are some aspects, which when modelled using EXPRESS constructs lead to complicated models, difficult to read and understand. One of the main elements missing in EXPRESS is the support for modelling dynamics and behaviour of information. With EXPRESS only a time invariant snapshot of an information model can be described. The ability to specify the change of information is most important for a number of application domains, such as business process reengineering or software development.

Furthermore, EXPRESS is not fully object-oriented (EXPRESS is said to be structural object-oriented). It is not possible to define methods within an entity declaration which are local to the entity and operating on local attributes. In EXPRESS global functions are used to support the restricted local functions. This strategy may cause side effects difficult to control in complex models.

Another disadvantage is the subset relationship between the graphical and lexical notation. It is hence necessary to refer to the lexical notation as well to fully understand the contents of an information model.

Finally, EXPRESS does not support the creation of instance scenarios or the definition of different views of the model for validation and application purposes. With these, the use of an information model in a real application context could be simulated and simplified before being implemented.

Several extensions to the ISO standard have been developed to deal with the shortcomings of EXPRESS described above. Four of these EXPRESS-dialects which are not mutually compatible are described briefly below.

3.2 EXPRESS-X

An information model must be complete and unambiguous. In general, information represented in a model can be a union of requirements of different sources (e.g. application systems). As a result, this information model contains data that is not needed by individual sources. This may cause problems in application systems working with this data. To prevent such problems a view of the model must be defined which only contains the information necessary for the particular application.

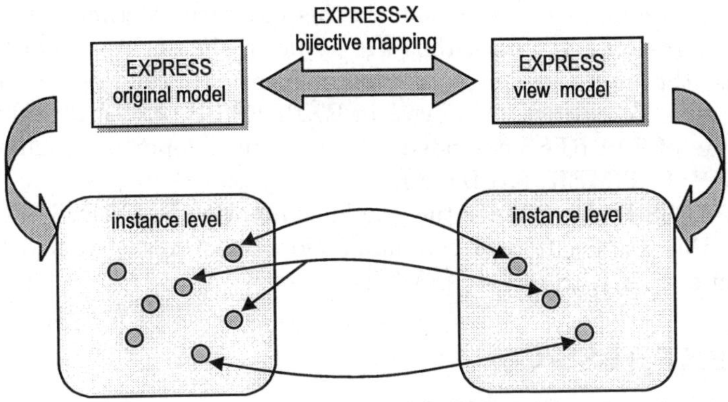

Figure 5: Schema mapping with EXPRESS-X [ISO96b]

The main purpose of EXPRESS-X is to describe such views. EXPRESS-X can be used to define mappings between entities from one EXPRESS schema (e.g. the entire information model) to entities in another schema, a view of the first (Figure 5).

With EXPRESS-X the creation of a view of an EXPRESS model is divided into two phases: materialise and compose. In the materialise phase, the view entities and their attributes that depend on the original entities are defined. In the compose phase, additional attributes which depend on the view entities are created (e.g. an attribute which specifies a relationship between view entities). A particular view of a schema is defined by determining the original EXPRESS schema, the view schema and a mapping schema (defined in EXPRESS-X) which specifies the mapping. The mapping itself is a partial bijection on attribute level. This enables an EXPRESS-X processing application to convert the data back to the original schema. In this way EXPRESS-X combines the capabilities of EXPRESS-M and EXPRESS-V [ISO95, HS96] and is intended to become an ISO standard independent of the existing standard EXPRESS.

Up to now EXPRESS-X does not provide a graphical notation. For a detailed description of EXPRESS-X, see [ISO96b].

3.3 EXPRESS-P

EXPRESS-P is an extension of standard EXPRESS for process modelling and monitoring and is upward compatible with EXPRESS. EXPRESS-P additionally specifies communication structures between processes and their behaviour. Therefore, the concept of dynamic entities is introduced extending the static entity declaration of EXPRESS by a behavioural section. The behavioural section may contain descriptions of interfaces, methods, channels and processes or explicit references to other processes. As attributes, these constructs are inherited from supertypes to subtypes. Interfaces define signals which can be received or sent via this interface. Methods are functions or procedures only visible within the scope of the enclosing entity. Using channels, the user can define the communication structure between interfaces of different entities. A process in EXPRESS-P is a list of statements in the syntax of EXPRESS extended by statements supporting communication (e.g. INPUT, TIMER, KILL etc.).

EXPRESS-P also extends the graphical notation EXPRESS-G with symbols for the visualisation of communication structures. For a detailed description of EXPRESS-P, see [FM94].

3.4 EXPRESS-C

Like EXPRESS-P, EXPRESS-C is an upward compatible extension to EXPRESS, extending EXPRESS with object-oriented and behavioural facilities. The entity declaration is extended by operations using the definition of signatures, pre- and postconditions and algorithms. Pre- and postconditions must be satisfied before and after execution of an algorithm respectively. Operations as well as attributes are inherited along the specialisation hierarchy. They may be overloaded or redefined. Attributes and operations can be labelled by the keyword private, preventing their accessibility from outside the entity's scope. Behavioural aspects of an information model are defined using a declarative event- action paradigm. Events are raised by changing attribute values. If a (Boolean) condition in an event evaluates to true the associated action procedure which is a sequence of statements (possibly raising other events) is executed. Furthermore EXPRESS-C supports the concept of dynamic typing. This concept allows instances to change their types during their lifetime.

The extensions of EXPRESS-C are - in a way - similar to those of EXPRESS-P, because both modelling languages extend EXPRESS by dynamic elements. The main difference is the point of view and therefore the application area. For a detailed description of EXPRESS-C, refer to [ISO94b].

3.5 EXPRESS Edition 2

The shortcomings of EXPRESS described in the previous section are in fact the subject of activities of the ISO SC4 committee to extend and improve the standard. Various dialects are currently being analysed, with the view to the following goals:

- the improvement of the static modelling provided by EXPRESS,
- the upward compatibility to EXPRESS,
- the integration of dynamic and behavioural aspects,
- the extension of the graphical notation, and
- the unification of dialects.

As a first step, the static modelling has been extended by the definition of new data types and user defined operators. The event-action concept of EXPRESS-C has been taken for the modelling of behaviour. EXPRESS-G has been extended by new symbols for the visualisation of the new data types and the behaviour of the model [ISO96]. EXPRESS edition 2 is intended to become an international standard within the next decade.

4 Large Scale Examples

In the area of virtual product development, the requirements of computer applications involved such as CAD, PDM or Database Systems are increasing. In particular the processed data structures have reached a level of complexity where database schemas or file formats can only be specified by formal information models. It has been proven in several industrial and research projects that EXPRESS is a suitable language for modelling even large scale information models and converting the information to computer accessible form. Two of such projects, the application protocol development process and the information model for environmentally sound design are briefly explained below focusing on the use of EXPRESS or an extension of it.

4.1 Application Protocol Development in STEP

STEP (ISO 10303) is a standard for computer accessible representation and exchange of virtual products. It provides a neutral mechanism for the description of product information throughout all life cycle phases (e.g. product planing, manufacturing, usage or recycling) independent of any particular system. STEP is suitable for file exchange as well as for shared product databases [ISO94c]. STEP is a series of standards, rather then one standard, since for each significant type of information exchange a separate application protocol can be developed and standardised. The standard is organised as a series of parts specifying:

- The description method EXPRESS,
- integrated resources, containing basic information models, independent from a particular application area or implementation (i.e. geometry or material data),
- abstract test suites for the verification of each application protocol,
- implementation methods (e.g. for the implementation of a standard data access interface),
- conformance testing methods for the validation of models and their implementation according to the standard, and
- application protocols, defining the use of integrated resources in a particular application context (e.g. core data for automotive mechanical design processes).

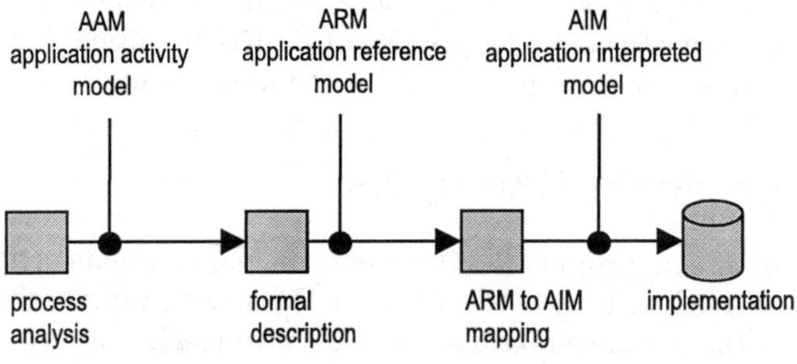

Figure 6: Development process of an application protocol

The development process of an application protocol is the process in which ISO 10303 is extended to be used in a particular application context (i.e. process chain ship building). It is divided into four phases (Figure 6). The first phase aims to define a process model. This process model (in STEP terminology an "application activity model" - AAM) consists of activities creating or using product data. An AAM is defined to restrict and specify the process chain supported by this application protocol. A typical modelling language used for the specification of AAM is IDEF0 [Ros77].

An application reference model (ARM) must be developed on the basis of AAM. The ARM in an information model developed for example in EXPRESS which describes the the product data description requirements of the application area of which the scope is defined in the AAM. The model is specified in the terminology of its application area. Therefore experts of this domain are able to understand and verify the model to ensure its correctness and completeness. ARMs are usually very large information models, containing hundreds of entities, functions or rules. Therefore an ARM is divided into units of functionality which are sets of entities, rules and types concerning the same topic (e.g. 3D geometry). The modelling language for the specification of the ARM is not prescribed by ISO 10303, but up to now EXPRESS has been used.

Further to the ARM specification, an "application interpreted model" (AIM) has to be created. This model defines how elements of the integrated resources have to be used in order to meet the requirements described in the ARM. Therefore these elements have to be used directly, if possible, or by the introduction of subtypes expanding the entities from the integrated resources by additional local rules or attributes. The AIM must be defined with EXPRESS and is used as a basis for implementation.

To derive an application interpreted model from the application reference model mapping rules have to be defined specifying the relationships between ARM and AIM entities. These mapping rules (possibly specified with EXPRESS-X) are used to check correctness and completeness of the AIM.

Finally suggestions for the implementation of the AIM are specified concerning, for instance, the compatibility of a particular implementation with the application protocol and other parts of ISO 10303.

According to the standardisation process defined by ISO, the application protocol has to be reviewed several times by users and domain experts. The development of various application protocols have proven the suitability of EXPRESS for the definition of large information models which have to be analysed by domain experts or users, not familiar with information modelling or even implementation tasks.

4.2 Development of Environmentally Sound Products

The development of environmentally sound products requires efficient access to environmental, technical and economical knowledge of all life cycle phases. Since this complex knowledge is distributed over a variety of sources such as enterprise departments, their co-operation is recommended including early design phases to minimise harmful influences on the environment. Of crucial importance is the sharing of information between the experts involved. The sharing of this information in the design process and its supporting environment requires a suitable information model as a basis.

To create such an information model, application experts from a number of disciplines or areas must work together. The engineers and scientists involved handle information in different ways, resulting in various types of environmental information.

This information is not suitable for direct use by a designer and must be transformed. Furthermore the environmental knowledge is distributed over suppliers or institutions - such as UBA (Umweltbundesamt) [1] - at different locations. Some kind of support for their co-operation is necessary.

EXPRESS is a suitable basis for information modelling of an interdisciplinary group of distributed application experts as well as for the representation of the complex environmental knowledge; however, it has been found that some extensions are necessary.

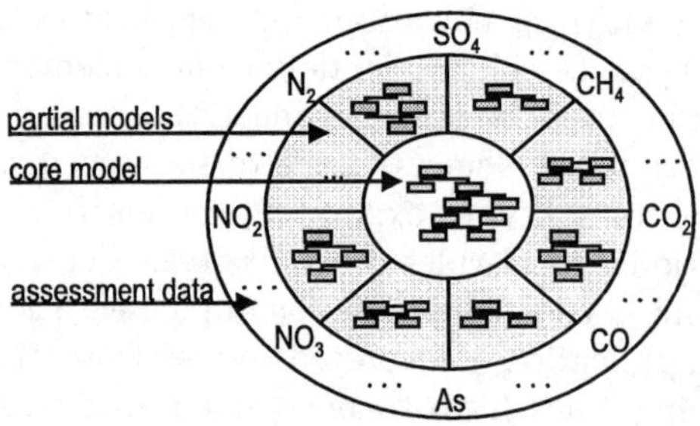

Figure 7: Information model for environmentally sound design

In the research project "SFB 392: Development of Environmentally Sound Products" at Technical University of Darmstadt an information model, an allied database and a design system environment are being developed by an interdisciplinary group of scientists. To allow their co-operation, the information model is partitioned according to the life cycle phases which constitute the domains of the research experts (Figure 7). The core of this information model contains a product data model covering all development phases as developed within ISO 10303. Any partial model representing environmental knowledge refers to this core model to ensure its relevance for design. Based on this architecture an information and assessment system for product models of all design phases enable the designer to decide between product alternatives depending on their technical, economical and environmental properties.

The modelling methodology used is called CO-operative Object Modelling Technique (COOM) and follows principles similar to those in co-operative product modelling [Kre96]. During the development of the information model

[1] Federal Office of the Environment

the interfaces between life cycle functions must be defined, the partial models have to be harmonised and the modellers need a view of the actual model as a whole. Such a concept of co-operative modelling needs to be implemented in terms of an information modelling method as well as with software tools and techniques.

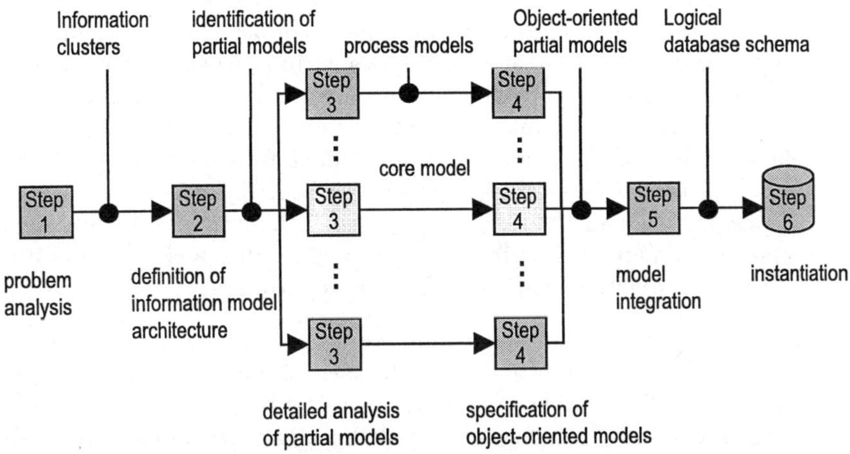

Figure 8: Process Chain 'information modelling' with COOM [ADJP97]

COOM consists of six modelling steps. The first and second steps of this method do not require any modelling task. The application area is analysed (first step) and the architecture of the information model is defined (second step).

The third step aims at the develpment of informal process models which are the result of the detailed analysis of the partial models. In the fourth step a simple graphical, object-oriented modelling language based on EXPRESS-G is used in order to represent the complex information model of the environmental knowledge. Figure 8 shows the whole modelling process. For a detailed description of the modelling methodology, see [ADJP97].

An important aspect for database creation by application experts is a facility which allows direct translation of the object-oriented model into a database structure, which is supported by EXPRESS.

Standard object-oriented modelling languages are too complex to be used by an application expert and cannot be translated directly into database schemas. For this reason a modelling language based on EXPRESS-G is developed for COOM. The language must be capable of presenting all important information at the first glance to allow co-operative work fully graphic representation as in standard object-oriented methods is obligatory. To meet the requirements of complex environmental knowledge, the following graphical modelling constructs are necessary:

- Static Object Modelling. EXPRESS-G is taken as a basis for static modelling. It can be simplified by integrating attributes of simple types into the class symbol as in UML. The reduced number of relations makes the model easier to survey. To avoid complex modelling structures, further redundant types such as fuzzy sets are defined.
- Functional Modelling. To specify functional relations between class attributes there are three different types of functions: Local functions only refer to attributes of simple types within one class and are shown inside the class symbol. They are used e.g. to transform units of process parameters. Complex functions may refer to attributes of other classes especially to derive assessment data from parameters of products and processes. Tables represent measured data as combinations of parameters and their result, because in many cases environmental relations cannot be described with functions. Pre- and post-conditions of complex functions can be defined as constraints.
- Constraint Modelling. Constraints are used to ensure database consistency for both instantiation and automatic or manual change of objects. They are defined by logic statements using Boolean operators. Local constraints limit the range of an attribute value. Complex constraints define dependencies between class attributes of the same type.
- Rule Modelling. The definition of rules is based on object states. An object state specifies values of a restricted group of attributes at a particular time. These states can be divided into conditions and consequences. Conditional states are linked by Boolean operators and refer to attribute values by means of mathematical expressions (e.g. equations). Consequence states express the effect of a rule on the value of object attributes. Rules are important for describing processes during product use that cannot bc specified with functional relations.

Incorporating these aspects into the current ISO 10303 EXPRESS-G diagrams would increase their size. In addition to optimising the graphic representation itself various model views or layers are defined. They can be realised by blanking selected aspects within one diagram.

The approach of modelling technique and graphical language has to be realised with suitable modelling tools. A software tool developed for COOM must support the entire process of modelling to minimise the training period, and provides transitions between modelling steps. Because of the analogy with co-operative product development, computer support for co-operative information modelling can be realised in similar ways. The collaboration support in general is synchronous, asynchronous or limited to document publishing techniques.

The collaboration support for information modelling should include an entire survey of the actual model. For this reason an administration module has to be developed to communicate with a model repository and to control access on the partial models. The administration tool also offers facilities to search for redundant model components and provides information about partial models under modification to ensure consistency. Access to design patterns for information modelling is provided to achieve high quality of the models. Synchronous presentation of model changes will be realised especially to co-ordinate information modelling in early development phases.

The modelling tool environment also includes a compiler to create a database schema directly from the information model which enables a rapid prototyping for model implementation. The object-oriented approach for the conceptual model including dynamic properties of a product suggests an implementation in an object-oriented database system. The compiler developed to support the database schema generation transforms the schema into the Data Definition Language (DDL) of the database (e.g. OQL).

The database is the main component for a design system. Additional systems required for the development of environmentally friendly products are integrated into the design platform:

- parametric 3D-CAD system
- assessment system for ecological properties of products
- knowledge based system to facilitate the designer's task in finding relevant information in the database and
- user interfaces for direct access to the database using a query language

This prototype design environment might serve as an example of a shared database, derived from an information model based on a graphical EXPRESS dialect.

5 Conclusion

EXPRESS is a suitable basis for the development of large scale information models which will be implemented, for instance, as database schemas accessed by different software applications. Comparing EXPRESS to public object-oriented modelling methods or languages like OMT or UML, both advantages and disadvantages of EXPRESS can be identified.

The main disadvantage of the actual standard is the absence of constructs to model time variant dynamics or behaviour yielding incomplete information models. In particular UML provides facilities to graphically represent almost all static, dynamic and behavioural properties a model may have.

The advantage of EXPRESS is that it is easy to learn and to handle (in comparison with UML), even for users not familiar with implementation details of information models. Moreover, there is often only one way to model real world ideas with EXPRESS. This makes it easier for somebody who is not involved in the modelling process to understand the contents of an EXPRESS model.

This features of EXPRESS enables teams consisting of domain experts, users, modelling experts and implementers to develop an information model which is understood and therefore influenced by everyone involved. This information model serves as a suitable basis for the development of data structures accessed by software systems as is the case in STEP.

References

[ADJP97] Anderl, R., Daum, B., John, H., Pütter, C., Co-operative Product Data Modelling in Life Cycle Networks, in: 4th International Seminar on Life Cycle Engineering, Berlin, 1997

[BJR97] Booch, G., Jacobson, I., Rumbaugh, J., Unified Modeling Language - UML Summary Version 1.0, Rational Software, 1997

[FM94] Felser, W., Mueller, W., Extending EXPRESS for Process Modelling and Monitoring, in: Proceedings of the 1994 ASME Computers in Engineering Conference, Minneapolis, MI, September 11-14, 1994

[HS96] Hardwick, M., Spooner, D., EXPRESS-V Reference Manual, Technical Report of the Rensselaer Laboratory for Industrial Information Infrastructure, 1996

[ISO94] ISO TC184/SC4/WG5, EXPRESS Language Reference Manual, ISO 1994

[ISO94b] ISO TC184/SC4/WG5, EXPRESS-C Language Reference Manual, ISO 1994

[ISO94c] ISO TC184/SC4, Overview and fundamental principles, ISO 1994

[ISO95] ISO TC184/SC4/WG5, EXPRESS-M Reference Manual, ISO 1995

[ISO96] ISO TC184/SC4/WG5, Requirements for the second edition of EXPRESS, ISO 1996

[ISO96b] ISO TC184/SC4/WG11, EXPRESS-X Reference Manual, ISO 1996

[Kre96] Kress, H. *et al*, An Open System Environment to Support the Integrated Product Development Process (in German), in: Proceedings of the Conference on Electronic Imaging, Science & Technologies, San Jose, 1996

[Mai94] Maier, M. *et al*, Multiple Class Membership and Supertype Constraint Handling - Concepts and Implementation Aspects, in: Proceedings of the 4th EXPRESS Users Group Conference Greenville, S.C., Oct. 13 - 14, 1994

[Ros77] Ross, D. T., Structured Analysis (SA): A Language for Communicating Ideas, in: IEEE Transactions of Software Engineering, Vol 3, No. 1, 1977

[Rum91] Rumbaugh, J. *et al*, Object-Oriented Modeling and Design, Prentice-Hall, 1991

[SW94] Schenck, D. A., Wilson, P. R., Information Modelling: The EXPRESS Way, Oxford University Press, 1994

CHAPTER 4

ORM/NIAM Object-Role Modeling

Terry Halpin

Object-Role Modeling (ORM) is method for modeling and querying an information system at the conceptual level, and mapping between conceptual and logical (e.g. relational) levels. ORM comes in various flavors, including NIAM (Natural language Information Analysis Method). This contribution provides an overview of ORM, and notes its advantages over Entity Relationship and traditional Object-Oriented modeling.

1 Introduction

1.1 ORM: What is it and Why use it?

Object-Role Modeling (ORM) is primarily a method for modeling and querying an information system at the conceptual level. In Europe, the method is often called NIAM (Natural language Information Analysis Method). Since information systems are typically implemented on a DBMS that is based on some logical data model (e.g. relational, object-relational, hierarchic), ORM includes procedures for mapping between conceptual and logical levels. Although various ORM extensions have been proposed for process and event modeling, the focus of ORM is on data modeling, since the data perspective is the most stable and it provides a formal foundation on which operations can be defined.

For correctness, clarity and adaptability, information systems are best specified first at the conceptual level, using concepts and language which people can readily understand. Analysis and design involves building a formal model of the application area or *universe of discourse* (UoD). To do this properly requires a good understanding of the UoD and a means of specifying this understanding in a clear, unambiguous way. Object-Role Modeling simplifies this process by using natural language, as well as intuitive diagrams that can be populated multiple with examples, and by expressing the information in terms of elementary relationships.

ORM is so-called because it pictures the world in terms of *objects* (entities or values) that play *roles* (parts in relationships). For example, you are now playing the role of reading, and this paper is playing the role of being read. In contrast to other modeling techniques such as Entity-Relationship (ER) and Object-Oriented (OO) approaches, ORM makes no explicit use of *attributes.* For example, instead of using countryborn as an attribute of Person, we use the relationship type *Person* was *born in Country.* This has many important advantages. Firstly, ORM models and queries are more stable (attributes may evolve into entities or relationships). For example, if we decide to later record the population of a country, then our *countryborn* attribute needs to be reformulated as a relationship. Secondly, ORM models may be conveniently populated with multiple instances (attributes make this too awkward). Thirdly, ORM is more uniform (e.g. we dont need a separate notation for applying the same constraint to an attribute rather than a relationship).

ORM is typically more expressive than ER or OO. Its role-based notation makes it easy to specify a wide variety of constraints, and its object types reveal the semantic domains that bind a schema together. One benefit of this is that conceptual queries may now be formulated in terms of schema paths, where moving from one role though an object type to another role amounts to a conceptual join (see later).

Unlike ORM or ER, popular OO models often duplicate information by wrapping facts up into pairs of inverse attributes in different objects. Moreover, OO notations have weak support for constraints (e.g. a constraint might have to be duplicated in different objects, or even ignored). Unfortunately, OO models are less stable than even ER models when the UoD evolves. For such reasons, OO models should be used only for implementation, not for analysis.

Although the detailed picture provided by ORM is desirable in developing and transforming a model, for summary purposes it is useful to hide or compress the display of much of this detail. Various abstraction mechanisms exist for doing this, e.g. [CHP96]. If desired, ER and OO diagrams can also be used for providing compact summaries, and are best developed as views of ORM diagrams. For a simple discussion illustrating the points in this section, see [Hal96].

The rest of this contribution provides a brief history of ORM, summarizes the ORM notation, illustrates the conceptual design and relational mapping procedures, and mentions some recent extensions before concluding.

1.2 A Brief History of ORM

In the 1970s, especially in Europe, substantial research was carried out to provide higher level semantics for modeling information systems. Abrial [Abr74],

Senko [Sen75] and others discussed modeling with binary relationships. In 1973, Falkenberg generalized their work on binary relationships to n-ary relationships and decided that attributes should not be used at the conceptual level because they involved "fuzzy" distinctions and also complicated schema evolution. Later, Falkenberg proposed the fundamental ORM framework, which he called the "object-role model" [Fal76]. This framework allowed n-ary and nested relationships, but depicted roles with arrowed lines. Nijssen [Nij76] adapted this framework by introducing the circle-box notation for objects and roles that has now become standard, and adding a linguistic orientation and design procedure to provide a modeling method called ENALIM (Evolving NAtural Language Information Model) [Nij77]. Nijssen led a group of researchers at Control Data in Belgium who developed the method further, including van Assche who classified object types into lexical object types (LOTs) and non-lexical object types (NOLOTs). Today, LOTs are commonly called "Entity types" and NOLOTs are called "Value types". Kent [Ken77] provided several semantic insights and clarified many conceptual issues.

Meersman added subtypes, and made major contributions to the RIDL query language [Mee82] with Falkenberg and Nijssen. The method was renamed "aN Information Analysis Method" (NIAM) and summarized in a paper by Verheijen and van Bekkum [VB82]. In later years the acronym "NIAM" was given different expansions, and is now known as "Natural language Information Anslysis Method". Two matrix methods for subtypes were developed, one (the role-role matrix) by Vermeir [Ver83] and another by Falkenberg and others.

In the 1980s, Falkenberg and Nijssen worked jointly on the design procedure and moved to the University of Queensland, where the method was further enhanced by various academics. Halpin provided the first full formalization of the method [Hal89], including schema equivalence proofs, and made several refinements and extensions to the method. In 1989, Halpin and Nijssen co-authored a book on the method. A second edition of this book, authored by Halpin, was published in 1995 [Hal95]. Another book on the method, written by Wintraecken, was published in 1990 [Win90].

Many researchers have contributed to the ORM method over the years, and there is no space here to list them all. Today various versions of the method exist, but all adhere to the fundamental object-role framework. Although most ORM proponents favor n-ary relationships, some prefer Binary-Relationship Modeling (BRM), e.g. Shoval [SS93]. Habrias [Hab93] developed an object- oriented version called MOON (Normalized Object-Oriented Method). The Predicator Set Model (PSM) was developed mainly by ter Hofstede, Proper and van der Weide [HPW93], and includes complex object constructors. De Troyer and Meersman [DM95] developed another version with constructors called Natural Object-Relationship Model (NORM). Halpin developed an extended version called Formal ORM (FORM), and with Bloesch and others at InfoModelers Inc. developed an associated query language called ConQuer [BH97]; this work is being extended at Visio Corporation. Van der Lek and others [BZL94] allowed entity types to be treated as nested roles, to produce Fully Communication Oriented NIAM (FCO-NIAM). Embley and others [EKW92] developed Object-oriented Systems Analysis (OSA) which includes an "Object-Relationship Model" component that has much in common with standard ORM, with no use of attributes.

2 Data Modeling in ORM

2.1 Notation

A modeling method includes both a notation and a procedure for using its notation. This subsection discusses notation, and later subsections discuss procedures. Each well defined version of ORM includes a formal, textual specification language for both models and queries, as well as a formal, graphical modeling language. The textual languages are more expressive than the graphical languages, but are mentioned only briefly in this paper. Figure 1 summarizes most of the main symbols used in the graphical language. We now briefly describe each symbol. Examples of these symbols in use are given later.

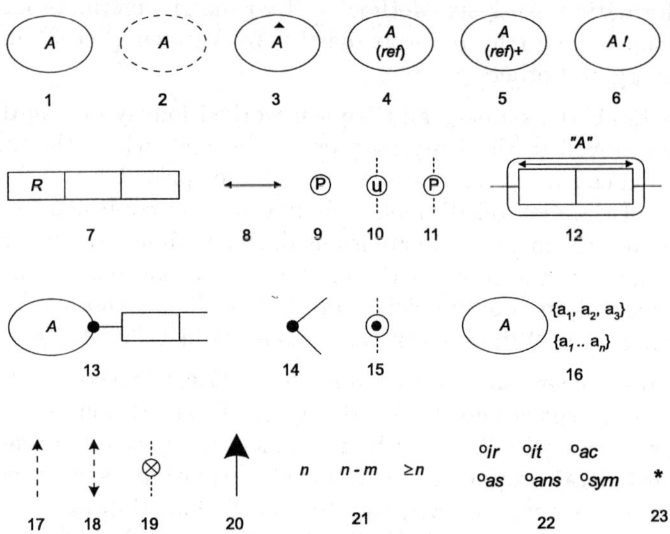

Figure 1: Main ORM symbols

The symbols are numbered for easy reference. An *entity type* is depicted as a named ellipse (symbol 1). A *value type* denotes a lexical object type (e.g. a character string or number) and is usually shown as a named, dotted ellipse (symbol 2). Another notation for value types encloses the value type name in parentheses. Object types that appear more than once in the schema may be tagged with an arrow tip (see symbol 3), that "points" to the existence of another occurrence. Each entity type must have at least one *reference scheme*, which indicates how each instance of the entity type may be mapped via predicates to a combination of one or values. A simple injective (1:1 into) reference scheme maps entities to single values. For example, each country may be identified by a single country code (e.g. USA). In such cases the reference scheme may be abbreviated as in symbol 4 by displaying the *reference mode* in parentheses beside the name of the entity type, e.g. Country(code). The reference mode indicates how values relate to the entities. Symbol 5 shows that a plus sign "+" may be added if the values are numeric. Values are constants with a universally understood denotation, and hence require no reference scheme to be declared.

Although not strictly a conceptual issue, it is normal to require each entity type to have a *primary* reference scheme. Relationship types used for primary reference are then called *reference types*. The other relationship types are known as *fact types*. In symbol 6, an exclamation mark is added to declare that an entity type is *independent*. This means that instances of that type may exist without participating in any facts. By default, this is not the case (i.e. we don't normally introduce an object into the universe unless it takes part in some fact).

Symbol 7 shows a ternary *predicate*, comprised of three *roles*. Each role is depicted as a box, and must be played by exactly one object type. Roles are connected to their players by a line segment (see symbol 13). A predicate is basically a sentence with object holes in it, one for each role. The number of roles is called the *arity* of the predicate. Except for the BRM version, ORM allows predicates of any arity (1 = unary, 2 = binary, 3 = ternary etc.). Predicates are usually treated as ordered, as in predicate logic. In this case, the name of the predicate is written either in or beside the first role box, and if necessary each object hole may be shown as an ellipsis "...". Different readings may be provided so the information may be read in any direction. FORML allows mixfix predicates so objects may be placed at any position in the predicate. For example, the fact type *Room at Time is used for Activity* involves the predicate "*... at ... is used for ...*". Apart from facilitating natural verbalization of n-ary relationships, mixfix predicates allow binary relationships to be verbalized in languages where the verb is not in the infix position (e.g. in Japanese, verbs come at the end). In some versions of ORM, relationship types are given a name, and each role is also given a name, thus making order irrelevant.

Internal uniqueness constraints are depicted as arrow tipped bars (symbol 8), and are placed over one or more roles in a predicate to declare that instances for that role (combination) in the relationship type population must be unique. For example, adding a uniqueness constraint over the first role of *Person was born in Country* declares that each person was born in at most one country. A predicate may have one or more uniqueness constraints, at most one of which may be declared *primary* by adding a "P" (symbol 9). An *external uniqueness constraint* shown as a circled "u" may be applied to two or more roles from different predicates by connecting to them with dotted lines (symbol 10). This indicates that instances of the combination of those roles in the join of those predicates are unique. For example, to say that a state is identified by combining its statecode and country, we add an external uniqueness constraint to the roles played by Statecode and Country in the reference types: *State has Statecode; State is in Country.* To declare an external uniqueness constraint primary, use "P" instead of "u" (symbol 11). An object type may have at most one primary reference constraint.

If we want to talk about a relationship type we may *objectify* it (i.e. make an object out of it) so that it can play roles. Graphically, the objectified predicate is enclosed in either a rounded rectangle (symbol 12) or an ellipse, and named. Objectified predicates are also called *nested* object types. Typically the objectified predicate must have a spanning uniqueness constraint, but 1:1 cases may also be allowed [Hal93].

A mandatory role constraint declares that every instance in the population of the role's object type must play that role. It is usually shown as a black dot (see symbol 13) but a universal quantifier is sometimes used. Mandatory roles are also called *total* roles. A disjunctive mandatory constraint may be applied to two or more roles to indicate that all instances of the object type population must play *at least one* of those roles. This may often be shown by connecting the roles to a black dot on the object type (symbol 14) or in general by connecting the roles by dotted lines to a circled black dot (symbol 15).

To restrict an object type's population to a given list, the relevant values may be listed in braces (symbol 16, top). If the values are ordered, a range may be declared separating the first and last values by ".." (symbol 16, bottom). These constraints are called *value constraints.*

Symbols 17-19 denote *set comparison constraints*, and may only be applied between compatible role sequences (i.e. sequences of one or more roles, where the corresponding roles have the same host object type). A dotted arrow (symbol 17) from one role sequence to another is a *subset constraint*, restricting the population of the first sequence to be a subset of the second. A double- tipped arrow (symbol 18) is an *equality constraint*, indicating the populations must be equal. A circled "X" (symbol 19) is an *exclusion constraint*, indicating the populations are mutually exclusive. Exclusion constraints may be applied between two or more sequences.

A solid arrow (symbol 20) from one object type to another indicates that the first object type is a (proper) *subtype* of the other. For example, Woman is a subtype of Person. Totality (circled black dot) and exclusion (circled

"X") constraints may also be displayed between subtypes, but are implied by other constraints if the subtypes are given formal definitions.

Symbol 21 shows three kinds of *frequency constraint.* Applied to a sequence of one or more roles, these indicate that instances that play those roles must do so exactly n times, between n and m times, or at least n times.

Symbol 22 shows six kinds of *ring constraint*, that may be applied to a pair of roles played by the same host type. These indicate that the binary relation formed by the role population must be irreflexive (ir), intransitive (it), acyclic (ac), asymmetric (as), antisymmetric (ans) or symmetric (sym).

Symbol 23 is an asterisk "*", which may be placed beside a fact type to indicate that it is derivable from other fact types. Not all versions of ORM support all these symbols, and some versions have a few more symbols. InfoModeler, a popular ORM tool, supports all the symbols shown, as will a future release of Visio Professional.

2.2 Conceptual Schema Design Procedure

The information systems life cycle typically involves several stages: feasibility study; requirements analysis; conceptual design of data and operations; logical design; external design; prototyping; internal design and implementation; testing and validation; and maintenance. ORM's *conceptual schema design procedure* (CSDP) focuses on the analysis and design of data. The conceptual schema specifies the information structure of the application: *the types of fact* that are of interest; *constraints* on these; and perhaps *derivation rules* for deriving some facts from others. With large applications, the UoD is divided into convenient modules, the CSDP is applied to each, and the resulting subschemas are integrated into the global conceptual schema.

Table 1 shows the CSDP used in FORM. Although different versions of the CSDP exist, they all agree on the importance of verbalization in terms of elementary facts, population checks, and thorough analysis of business rules. The rest of this section illustrates the basic working of this design procedure by means of an example. Because of space limitations, our treatment is necessarily brief. A much more detailed discussion of the same example can be electronically accessed from [Hal97].

Step	
1.	Transform familiar information examples into elementary facts, and apply quality checks.
2.	Draw the fact types, and apply a population check.
3.	Add uniqueness constraints, and check arity of fact types.
4.	Add mandatory role constraints, and check for logical derivations.
5.	Add value, set comparison and subtyping constraints.
6.	Add other constraints and perform final checks.

Table 1: The conceptual schema design procedure (CSDP)

Step 1 is the most important. Examples of the information required from the system are verbalized in natural language. Such examples are often available in the form of output reports or input forms, perhaps from a current manual version of the required system. If not, the modeler can work with the client to produce examples. To avoid misinterpretation, a UoD expert (a person familiar with the application) should perform or at least check the verbalization. As an aid to this process, the speaker imagines he/she has to convey the information contained in the examples to a friend over the telephone.

For our case study, we consider a fragment of an information system used by a university to maintain details about its academic staff and academic departments. One function of the system is to print an academic staff directory, as exemplified by the report extract shown in Table 2. Part of the modeling task is to clarify the meaning of terms used in such reports. The descriptive narrative provided here would thus normally be derived from a discussion with the UoD expert. The terms "empnr" and "extnr" abbreviate "employee number" and "extension number."

A phone extension may have access to local calls only ("LOC"), national calls ("NAT"), or international calls ("INT") . International access includes national access, which includes local access. In the few cases where different rooms or staff have the same extension, the access level is the same. An academic is either tenured or on contract. Tenure guarantees employment until retirement, while contracts have an expiry date.

Empnr	EmpName	Dept	Room	Phone Extnr	Access	Tenured/ Contract-expiry
715	Adams A	Computer Science	69-301	2345	LOC	01/31/95
720	Brown T	Biochemistry	69-301	9642	LOC	01/31/95
139	Cantor G	Mathematics	62-406	1221	INT	tenured
430	Codd EF	Computer Science	67-301	2911	INT	tenured
503	Hagar TA	Computer Science	69-507	2988	LOC	tenured
651	Jones E	Biochemistry	69-803	5003	LOC	12/31/96
770	Jones E	Mathematics	67-404	1946	LOC	12/31/95
112	Locke J	Philosophy	1-205	6600	INT	tenured
223	Mifune K	Elec.Eng.	50-215A	1111	LOC	tenured
951	Murphy B	Elec.Eng.	45-B19	2301	LOC	01/03/95
333	Russell B	Philosophy	1-206	6600	INT	tenured
654	Wirth N	Computer Science	69-603	4321	INT	tenured

Table 2: Extract from a directory of academic staff

The information contained in this table is to be stated in terms of *elementary facts*. Basically, an elementary fact asserts that a particular object has a property, or that one or more objects participate in a relationship, where that relationship cannot be expressed as a conjunction of simpler (or shorter) facts without introducing new object types [Hal93]. For example, to say that Bill Clinton jogs and is the president of the USA is to assert two elementary facts.

As a first attempt, one might read off the information on the first data row as the six facts f1-f6. Each asserts a binary relationship between two objects. For discussion purposes the *predicate* is shown in **bold** between the noun phrases which identify the objects, and object type names start with a capital letter. Some obvious abbreviations are used ("empnr", "EmpName", "Dept", "extnr"); when read aloud these can be expanded to "employee number", "Employee name", "Department" and "extension number". The second data row contains different instances of these six fact types. Row three, because of its final column, provides an instance f7 of a seventh fact type, a unary.

f1 The Academic with empnr 715 **has** EmpName 'Adams A'.

f2 The Academic with empnr 715 **works for** the Dept named 'Computer Science'.

f3 The Academic with empnr 715 **occupies** the Room with roomnr '69-301'.

f4 The Academic with empnr 715 **uses** the Extension with extnr '2345'.

f5 The Extension with extnr '2345' **provides** the AccessLevel with code 'LOC'. mdy-code '01/31/95'.

f6 The Academic with empnr 715 **is contracted** till the Date with mdy-code '01/31/95'

f7 The Academic with empnr 139 **is tenured**.

Different readings may be provided to allow relationships to be read in different directions. For example, the *inverse* reading of f4 is: The Extension with extnr 2345 is used by the Academic with empnr 715. To save writing, both the normal predicate and its inverse may be included in the same declaration, with the inverse predicate preceded by a slash "/". For example:

f4 The Academic with empnr 715 **uses/is used** by the Extension with extnr 2345.

Predicate names are usually unique in the conceptual schema. In some cases (e.g. "has"), the same name may be used externally for different predicates: internally these have different identifiers.

As a quality check at Step 1, we ensure that objects are well identified. Values are identified by constants (e.g. *Adams A, 715*). *Entities* are "real world" objects that are identified by a definite description (e.g. the Academic with empnr 715). Fact f1 involves a relationship between an entity (a person) and a value (a name is just a character string). Facts f2-f6 specify relationships between entities. Fact f7 states a property (or unary relationship) of an entity.

As a second quality check at Step 1, we use our familiarity with the UoD to see if some facts should be split or recombined (a formal check on this is applied later). For example, suppose facts f1 and f2 were verbalized as: The Academic with empnr 715 and empname 'Adams A' works for the Dept named Computer Science. The presence of the word "and" suggests that this may be split without information loss. The repetition of "Jones E" on different rows of Table 2 shows that academics cannot be identified just by their name. However the uniqueness of *empnr* in the sample population suggests that this suffices for reference. Since the "and-test" is only a heuristic, and sometimes a composite naming scheme is required for identification, the UoD expert is consulted to verify that empnr by itself is sufficient for identification. With this assurance obtained, the composite sentence is now split into f1 and f2.

As an alternative to specifying complete facts one at a time, the reference schemes may be declared up front and then assumed in later facts. For example, suppose we have declared the following: Academic(empnr); EmpName(); Dept(name). The empty parentheses after *EmpName* indicates it is a value type and hence needs no reference scheme. Now facts f1 and f2 may be stated as: Academic 715 has EmpName 'Adams A'; Academic 715 works for Dept 'Computer Science'. Facts f1-f7 are instances of the following fact types:

F1 Academic has EmpName

F2 Academic works for Dept

F3 Academic occupies Room

F4 Academic uses Extension

F5 Extension provides AccessLevel

F6 Academic is contracted till Date

F7 Academic is tenured

Step 2 of the CSDP is to *draw a draft diagram of the fact types and apply a population check* (see Figure 2). As a check, each fact type has been populated with at least one fact, shown as a row of entries in the associated fact table, using the data from rows 1 and 3 of Table 2. The English sentences listed before as facts f1-f7, as well as other facts from row 3, may be read directly off this figure. Though useful for validating the model with the client and for understanding constraints, the sample population is not part of the conceptual schema itself.

Suppose the information system is also required to assist in the production of departmental hand-books. Figure 3 shows an extract from a page of one such handbook. In this university academic staff are classified as professors, senior lecturers or lecturers, and each professor holds a "chair" in a research

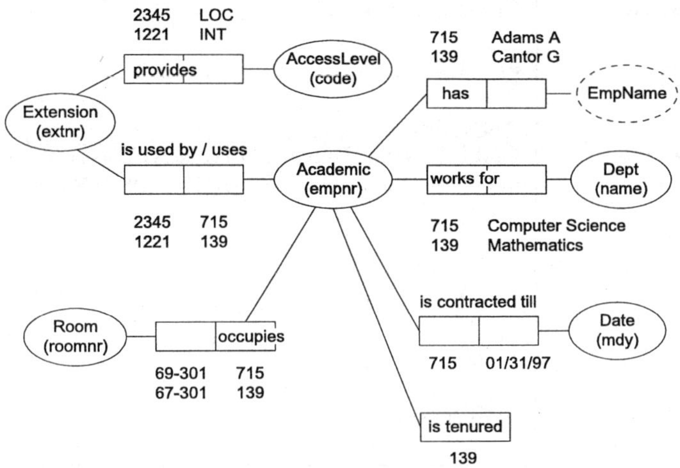

Figure 2: Draft diagram of fact types for Table 2 with sample population

area. To reduce the size of our problem, we have excluded many details which in practice would also be recorded (e.g. office phone and fax). To save space, details are shown here for only four of the 22 academics in that department. The data are, of course, fictitious.

It appears from the handbook example that within a single department, academics may be identified by their name. Let us assume this is verified by the UoD expert. However the complete application requires us to handle all departments in the same information system, and to integrate this subschema with the directory subschema considered earlier. Hence we must replace the academic naming convention used for the handbook example by the global scheme used earlier (i.e. *empnr*).

We use this report to illustrate *Step 3* of the CSDP: *check for entity types that should be combined, and note any arithmetic derivations.* Suppose we verbalized the degree information in terms of the three ternary fact types: *Professor obtained Degree from University; SeniorLecturer obtained Degree from University; Lecturer obtained Degree from University.* The common predicate suggests that the entity types *Professor*, *SeniorLecturer* and *Lecturer* should be collapsed to the single entity type Academic, with this predicate now shown only once. To preserve the original information about who is a professor, senior lecturer or lecturer we introduce the fact type: *Academic has Rank.* Let's use the codes "P," "SL" and "L" for the ranks of professor, senior lecturer and lecturer.

The second aspect of Step 3 is to see if some fact types can be derived from others by arithmetic. Since we now record the rank of academics as well as their departments, we can compute the number in each rank in each

Department:	Computer Science
Home phone of Dept head:	9765432
Chairs	*Professors (5)*
Databases	Codd EF BSc (UQ); PhD (UCLA) (Head of Dept)
Algorithms	Wirth N BSc (UQ); MSc (ANU); DSc (MIT)
...	...
Senior Lecturers (9)	
Hagar TA	BInfTech (UQ); PhD (UQ)
	...
Lecturers (8)	
Adams A	MSc (OXON)
	...

Figure 3: Extract from Handbook of Computer Science Department

department simply by counting. So the fact type *Dept employs academics of Rank in Quantity* is derivable. If desired, derived fact types may be included on a schema diagram if they are marked with an asterisk "*".At any rate, a *derivation rule* must be supplied. This may be written below the diagram (see Figure 4). Here **"iff"** abbreviates "if and only if".

Step 4 of the CSDP is to *add uniqueness constraints and check the arity of the fact types.* For example, we add a uniqueness constraint to the first role of *works for* to ensure that each academic works for at most one department. One simple arity check ensures that each uniqueness constraint on an n-ary spans at least n-1 roles.

Step 5 of the CSDP is to *add mandatory role constraints, and check for logical derivations.* For example, we need a disjunctive mandatory constraint to declare that each academic either is contracted till some date or is tenured. Roles that are not mandatory are *optional.* If an object type plays only one fact role in the global schema, then by default this is mandatory, but a dot is not normally shown.

Suppose that departmental handbooks include a building directory, which lists the names as well as the numbers of buildings. A sample fact might be: Building '67' has Buildingname 'Priestly'. Earlier we identified rooms by a single value. For example "67-301" was used to denote the room in building 67 which has room number "301". Now that buildings are to be talked about in their own right, we replace the simple reference scheme by a composite one which shows the full semantics (see Figure 4). Here *Roomnr* now means just the number (e.g. "301") used to identify the room within its building.

To illustrate nesting, suppose the application also has to deal with reports about teaching commitments, an extract of which is shown in Table 3. Not all academics currently teach. If they do, their teaching in one or more subjects may be evaluated and given a rating. Some teachers serve on course curriculum committees. Here the new fact types may be schematized as shown in Figure 4. The nested object type *Teaching* plays only one role, and this role is optional, so Teaching is an *independent* object type (as shown by the "!").

The second stage of Step 5 is to check for *logical derivations* (i.e. can some fact type be derived from others without the use of arithmetic?). One strategy here is to ask whether there are any relationships (especially functional relationships) which are of interest but which have been omitted so far. Another strategy is to look for transitive patterns of functional dependencies. Suppose that our client confirms that the rank of an academic determines the access level of his/her extension. For example, suppose a current business rule is that professors get international access while lecturers and senior lecturers get local access. This rule might change in time (e.g. senior lecturers might be arguing for national access). To minimize later changes to the schema, we store the rule as data in a table. So it can be updated as required by an authorized user without having to recompile the schema. The relevant rule is shown at the bottom of Figure 4.

Empnr	Emp. name	Subject	Rating	Committees
715	Adams A	CS100		
		CS101	5	
430	Codd EF			
654	Wirth N	CS300		BSc-Hons
				CAL Advisory

Table 3: Extract of report on teaching commitments

In *Step 6* of the CSDP we add *any value, set comparison and subtyping constraints.* One value constraint is that Rankcode is restricted to P,SL,L. In Figure 4, a pair-subset constraint runs from the heads predicate to the works for predicate, indicating that a person who heads a department must work for the same department. The rule that nobody can be tenured and contracted at the same time is captured by an exclusion constraint. Subtyping is determined as follows. Each optional role is inspected: if the role is played only by some well-defined subtype, a subtype node is introduced with this role attached. Subtype links and definitions are added. Figure 4 contains three subtypes: *Teacher; Professor;* and *TeachingProfessor.* In this university, each teacher is audited by another teacher. Moreover, only professors may be department heads, and only teaching professors can serve on curriculum committees (not all universities work this way).

Step 7 of the CSDP adds other constraints and performs final checks. For example, auditing is *irreflexive* (no teacher audits himself/herself). Suppose we also need to record the teaching and research budgets of the departments. We might schematize this using the ternary *Dept has for Activity a budget*

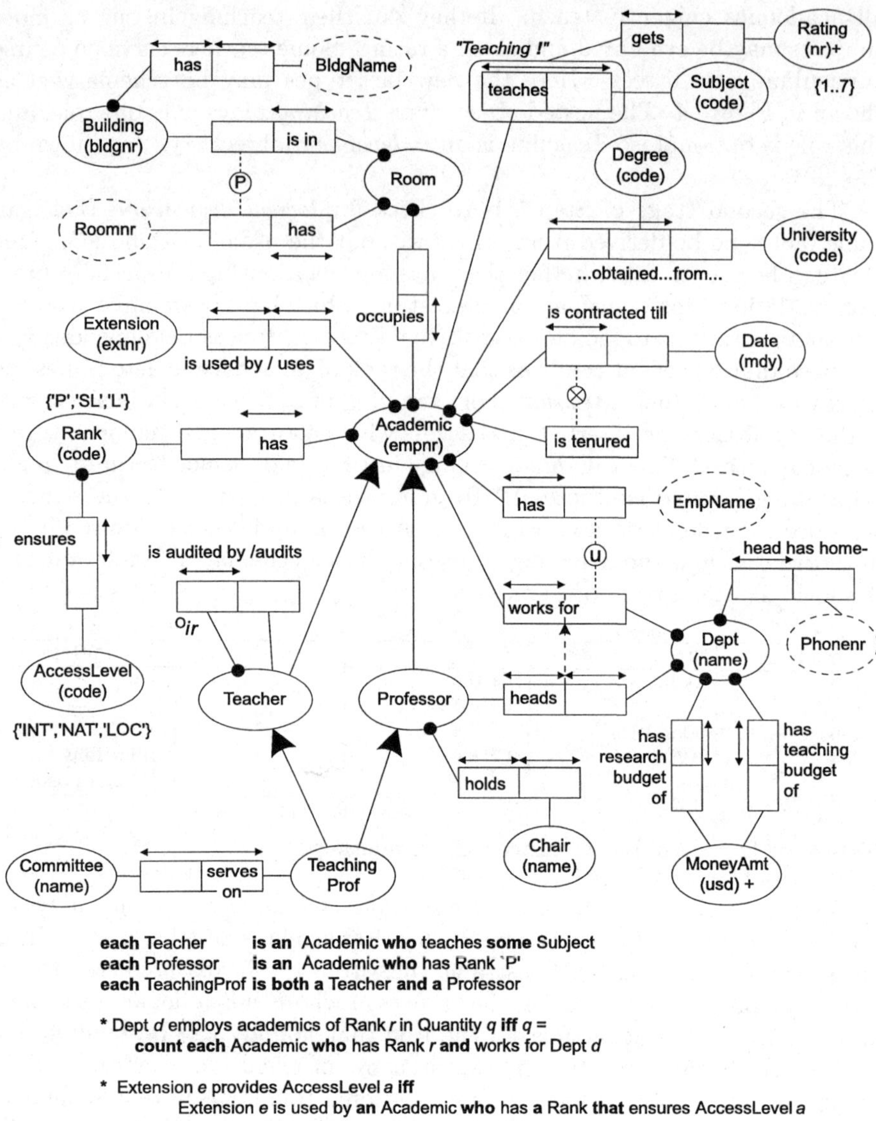

Figure 4: The final conceptual schema

of MoneyAmt, where *Activity* has the value constraint {*Teaching, Research*} and the first role is mandatory and constrained to a *frequency* of 2.

Once the global schema is drafted, and the target DBMS decided, some optimization can often be performed to improve the efficiency of the logical schema obtained by mapping. Assuming the conceptual schema is to be mapped to a relational database schema, the ternary fact type about budgets will map to a separate table all by itself, leading to extra joins for some queries. We can avoid this problem by transforming the ternary into the following two binaries before we map: *Dept has teaching budget of MoneyAmt; Dept has research budget of MoneyAmt.* These binaries have simple keys, and will map to the "main" department table. Another optimization may be performed which moves the home phone information to *Dept* instead of *Professor.* Figure 4 includes these optimizations. Such *conceptual schema transformations* require a rigorous theory of schema equivalence and optimization strategies. For details on such topics (see [Hal95], ch.9, [HP95b] and [DeT93]).

Once the conceptual schema has been specified, the target data model is selected and the mapping is done. For example, the Rmap algorithm [RH93, Hal95] maps our conceptual schema to the relational schema shown in Figure 5 (domains omitted). If the conceptual fact types are elementary (as they should be), then the mapping is guaranteed to be free of redundancy, since each fact type is grouped into only one table, and fact types which map to the same table all have uniqueness constraints based on the same attribute(s). Keys are underlined. If alternate keys exist, the primary key is doubly-underlined. A mandatory role is captured by making its corresponding attribute mandatory in its table (not null is assumed by default), by marking as optional (in square brackets) all optional roles for the same object type which map to the same table, and by running an equality/subset constraint from those mandatory/optional roles which map to another table. The <2,1> in the pair-subset constraint indicates the source pair should be reversed before the comparison. Subtyping is captured by qualified optionals or qualified subset constraints. The word "exists" means "a non-null value exists".

3 Recent Extensions

3.1 Conceptual Queries

Besides information modeling, ORM is also ideal for information querying. The first significant ORM query language was RIDL [Mee82], a hybrid language with both declarative and procedural components. Temporal aspects were added later to form TRIDL. Currently, research is being carried out on at least three ORM query languages: LISA-D [HPW93]; OSM-QL [EWPC96]; and ConQuer [BH96]. Of these ConQuer (CONceptual QUERy) is the only one to be commercially released. A more powerful version, ConQuer-II [BH97], is currently under development at Visio Corporation.

Using ConQuer, an ORM model may be queried directly without prior knowledge of either the conceptual schema or the corresponding relational schema, by dragging object types onto the query pane, selecting predicates

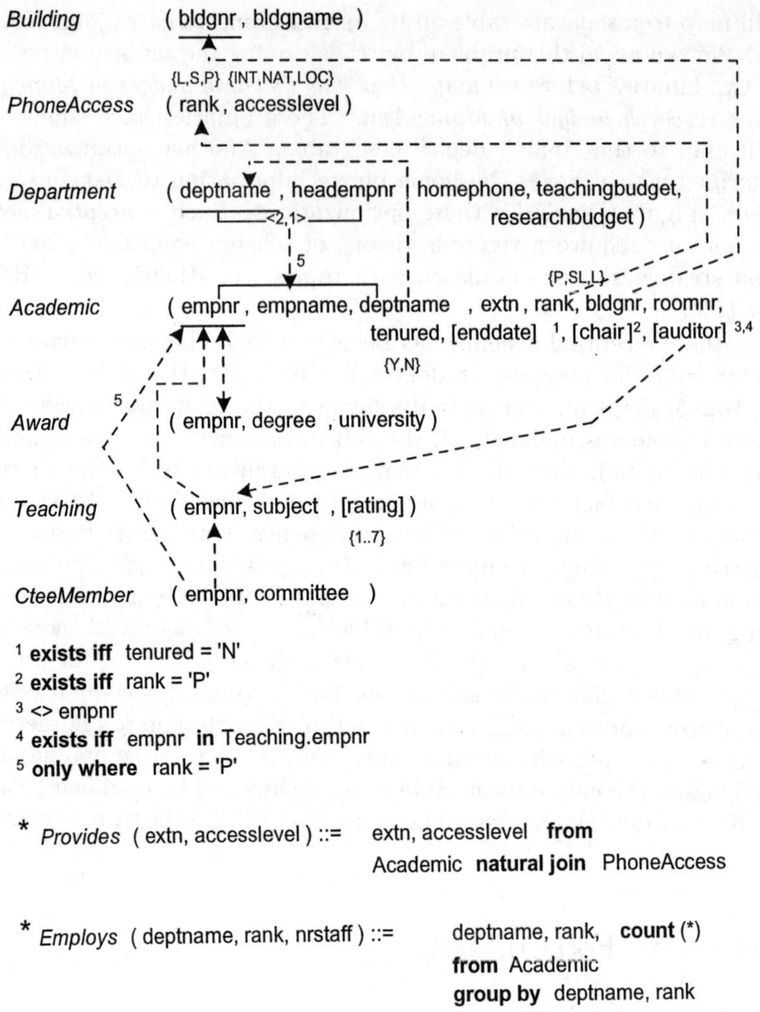

Figure 5: The relational schema mapped from Figure 4

of interest, applying restrictions and functions as desired, and ticking the items to be listed. As a simple example, consider the following English query on our academic database: list the empnr, empname and number of subjects taught for each academic who occupies a room in the Chemistry building and teaches more than two subjects. This may be formulated by drag-and-drop basically as shown in Figure 6.

Notice how easily the conceptual joins are made. A verbalization of the query is automatically generated, as well as SQL code. Formulating queries in terms of objects and predicates is much easier than deciphering the semantics

```
Academic
    ├── is identified by √ Empnr
    ├── has √ Empname
    ├─── occupies Room
    │          └─ is in Building
    │                   └─ has BldgName 'Chemistry'
    └─── teaches Subject
               └─ √ count (Subject) for Academic > 2
```

Figure 6: Query on an academic database

of the relational schema and coding in SQL or QBE. A major benefit of such queries is their semantic stability. For example, ConQuer queries are unaffected by most schema changes (e.g. addition of fact types, or changes to constraints). In contrast, such changes often require the corresponding SQL or ER query to be reformulated, since they depend on attribute structures.

3.2 Other Extensions

Researchers are actively investigating several extensions to the basic ORM framework. These include abstraction mechanisms to allow users to control the amount of detail seen at any given time [CHP96], reverse engineering [SS93, CH94], support for complex objects [HW93, DM95], process-event modeling [Hof93], external schema generation [CH93], schema evolution [Pro94], schema optimization [HP95b] [Bom94], meta-modeling [FO94], null handling [HR92], object-oriented mapping [ME96], unary nesting [BZL94], and empirical research [Eve94].

Although various versions of ORM have added support for complex objects, they differ in their approaches. Currently there seems to be a growing agreement that constructors (e.g. set, bag, sequence) should only be added after a flat ORM model is first developed. There are also different opinions on whether such constructors should be considered part of the conceptual model, or regarded as mapping annotations. Commercial developers of ORM tools are also extending the method. For example, InfoModeler includes extra constructs for mapping to object-relational databases, and extensions of this technology are being incorporated into Visio Professional.

4 Conclusion

This contribution has provided only a brief sketch of the ORM method, emphasizing its fundamental features and touching on some of its advantages. Apart from its sound theoretical basis, the method has been used successfully in many countries, on applications from the small to the very large. The recent emergence of intuitive and powerful ORM tools has led to wider adoption of the method, which is now being successfully taught as early as high school level. Perhaps the greatest strengths of ORM are that it lifts the communication between modeler and client to a level where they can readily understand and validate the application model using simple sentences, and that it has been designed from the ground up to facilitate schema evolution. This second advantage is very relevant to today's business world where change is ongoing.

In an article this brief, several aspects of ORM have necessarily been glossed over. The reader who is interested in pursuing the area further should consult the cited references, which are included at the end of the contribution.

References

[Abr74] Abrial, J. R., Data Semantics, in: J. W. Klimbie, K. L. Koffeman (eds.), Data Base Management, North-Holland, Amsterdam, The Netherlands, 1974, 1-60

[BZL94] Bakema, G. P., Zwart, J. P. C., Lek, H. van der, Fully Communication Oriented NIAM, in: G. M. Nijssen, J. Sharp (eds.), NIAM-ISDM 1994 Conf. Working papers, Albuquerque, NM USA, 1994, 1-35

[BH96] Bloesch, A. C., Halpin, T. A., ConQuer: a conceptual query language, Proc. ER'96: 15th Int. Conf. on conceptual modeling, Springer LNCS, vol. 1157, 1996, 121-133

[BH97] Bloesch, A. C., Halpin, T. A., Conceptual queries using ConQuer-II, in: Proc. ER'97, 16th Int. Conf. on Conceptual modeling, Springer LNCS 1331, 1997, 113-26

[Bom94] Bommell, P. van, Implementation selection for Object-Role models, in: T. A. Halpin, R. M. Meersman (eds.), Proc. First Int. Conf. On Object-Role Modeling (ORM-1), Magnetic Island, Australia, 1994, 103-112

[CH93] Campbell, L., Halpin, T. A., Automated Support for Conceptual to External Mapping, in: S. Brinkkemper, F. Harmsen (eds.), Proc. 4th Workshop on Next Generation CASE Tool, Univ. Twente Memoranda Informatica 93-132, Paris (June), 1993, 35-51

[CH94] Campbell, L., Halpin, T. A., The reverse engineering of relational databases, Proc. 5th Workshop on Next Generation CASE Tools, Utrecht (June), 1994

[CHP96] Campbell, L. J., Halpin, T. A., Proper, H. A., Conceptual Schemas with Abstractions: making flat conceptual schemas more comprehensible, Data and Knowledge Engineering, vol. 20, no. 1, 1996, 39-85

[DeT93] De Troyer, O., On data schema transformations, PhD thesis, University of Tilburg (K. U. B.), Tilburg, The Netherlands, 1993

[DM95] De Troyer, O., Meersman, R., A logic framework for a semantics of object oriented data modeling, OOER'95: Object-Oriented and Entity-Relationship Modeling, Springer LNCS, vol. 1021, 1995, 238-249

[EKW92] Embley, D. W., Kurtz, B. D., Woodfield, S. N., Object-Oriented Systems Analysis, Prentice Hall, Englewood Cliffs, NJ, 1992

[EWPC96] Embley, D. W., Wu, H. A., Pinkston, J. S., Czejdo, B., OSM-QL: a calculus-based graphical query language, Tech. Report, Dept of Comp. Science, Brigham Young Univ., Utah, 1996

[Eve94] Everest, G., Experiences teaching NIAM/OR modeling, NIAM-ISDM 1994 Conf. Working Papers, G. M. Nijssen, J. Sharp (eds.), Albuquerque, NM USA, 1994, 1-26

[Fal76] Falkenberg, E. D., Concepts for modelling information, in: G. M. Nijssen (ed.), Proc. 1976 IFIP Working Conf. on Modelling in Data Base Management Systems, Freudenstadt, Germany, North-Holland Publishing, 1976, 95-109

[FO94] Falkenberg, E. D., Oei, J. L. H., Meta-model hierarchies from an Object-Role Modeling perspective, in: T. A. Halpin, R. M. Meersman (eds.), Proc. First Int. Conf. On Object-Role Modeling (ORM-1), Magnetic Island, Australia, 1994, 218-227

[Hab93] Habrias, H., Normalized Object Oriented Method, in: Encyclopedia of Microcomputers, vol. 12, Marcel Dekker, New York, 1993, 271-285

[Hal89] Halpin, T. A., A Logical Analysis of Information Systems: static aspects of the data-oriented perspective, PhD thesis, University of Queensland, 1989

[Hal93] Halpin, T. A., What is an elementary fact?, in: G. M. Nijssen, J. Sharp (eds.), Proc. First NIAM-ISDM Conf., Utrecht, (Sep), 1993, 11

[Hal95] Halpin, T. A., Conceptual Schema and Relational Database Design, 2nd edn, Prentice Hall Australia, Sydney, 1995

[Hal96] Halpin, T. A., Business Rules and Object-Role Modeling, Database Prog., Design, vol. 9, no. 10, Miller Freeman, San Mateo CA, 1996, 66-72

[Hal97] Halpin, T. A., Object-Role Modeling: an overview, electronic paper available on website http://www.visio.com, 1997

[HP95a] Halpin, T. A., Proper, H. A., Subtyping and polymorphism in Object-Role Modeling, Data and Knowledge Engineering, Elsevier Science, vol. 15, 1995, 251-281

[HP95b] Halpin, T. A., Proper, H. A., Database schema transformation and optimization, OOER95: Object-Oriented and Entity-Relationship Modeling, Springer LNCS, vol. 1021, 1995, 191-203

[HR92] Halpin, T. A., Ritson, P. R., 1992, Fact-Oriented Modelling and Null Values, in: B. Srinivasan, Z. Zeleznikov (eds.), Proc. 3rd Australian Database Conf., World Scientific, Singapore, 1992

[Hof93] Hofstede, A. H. M. ter, Information modelling in data intensive domains, PhD thesis, University of Nijmegen, The Netherlands, 1993

[HPW93] Hofstede, A. H. M. ter, Proper, H. A., Weide, Th. P. van der, Formal definition of a conceptual language for the description and manipulation of information models, Information Systems, vol. 18, no. 7, 1993, 489-523

[HW93] Hofstede, A. H. M. ter, Weide, Th. P. van der, Expressiveness in conceptual data modelling, Data and Knowledge Engineering, vol. 10, no. 1, 1993, 65-100

[Ken77] Kent, W., Entities and relationships in Information, in: G. M. Nijssen (ed.), Proc. 1977 IFIP Working Conf. on Modelling in Data Base Management Systems, Nice, France, North-Holland Publishing, 1977, 67-91

[Mee82] Meersman, R., The RIDL conceptual language, Research report, Int. Centre for Information Analysis Services, Control Data Belgium, Brussels, 1982

[ME96] Mok, W. Y., Embley, D. W., Transforming conceptual model to objectoriented database designs: practicalities, properties and peculiarities, Proc. ER96: 15th Int. Conf. on conceptual modeling, Springer LNCS, vol. 1157, 1996, 309-324

[Nij76] Nijssen, G. M., A gross architecture for the next generation database management systems, in: G. M. Nijssen (ed.), Proc. 1976 IFIP Working Conf. on Modelling in Data Base Management Systems, Freudenstadt, Germany, North-Holland Publishing, 1976, 1-24

[Nij77] Nijssen, G. M., Current issues in conceptual schema concepts, in: G. M. Nijssen (ed.), Proc. 1977 IFIP Working Conf. on Modelling in Data Base Management Systems, Nice, France, North-Holland Publishing, 1977, 31-66

[Pro94] Proper, H. A., A theory of conceptual modelling of evolving application domains, PhD thesis, University of Nijmegen, The Netherlands, 1994

[RH93] Ritson, P. R., Halpin, T. A., Mapping Integrity Constraints to a Relational Schema, Proc. 4th ACIS, Brisbane, (Sep.), 1993, 381-400

[Sen75] Senko, M. E., Information systems: records, relations, sets, entities and things, Information Systems, vol. 1, no. 1, Jan. 1995, Pergamon Press, 1975, 3-13

[SS93] Shoval, P., Shreiber, N., Database reverse engineering: from the relational to the binary relational model, Data and Knowledge Engineering, vol. 10, 1993, 293-315

[VB82] Verheijen, G. M. A., van Bekkum, J., NIAM: an information analysis method, Information systems Design Methodologies: a comparative review, Proc. IFIP WG8.1 Working Conf., Noordwijkerhout, The Netherlands, North Holland Publishing, 1982, 537-590

[Ver83] Vermeir, D., Semantic hierarchies and abstractions in conceptual schemata, Information systems, vol. 8, no. 2, 1983, 117-124

[Win90] Wintraecken, J. J. V. R., 1990, The NIAM Information Analysis Method: Theory and Practice, Kluwer, Deventer, The Netherlands, 1990

CHAPTER 5

Database Language SQL

Jim Melton

SQL, a data sublanguage used to access relational databases, is sometimes described as "English-like" because many of its statements read a bit like English. It is a non-procedural language since complex data operations are formulated by specifying their intended result rather than the method used to obtain that result. Both ANSI and ISO have published three generations of the *de jure* SQL standards. The syntax and semantics of SQL is examined and the conformance requirements are stated; a few components of the language are considered in greater detail and the future of the language is outlined.

1 Introduction

SQL is not a complete programming language, but is a *data sublanguage* used with a *host language* for access to relational databases. Programs written using SQL depend on the host language for input/output and control facilities. The syntax of SQL is sometimes described as "English-like" because many of its statements read a bit like English. SQL is described as a *non-procedural* language, or an *intentional* language because complex data operations are stated by specifying their intended result rather than the method by which that result is to be obtained.[1] This results from SQL's relationship to the relational model of data and has resulted in the fact that much of the research related to SQL implementation is intended to improve the optimization of SQL statement execution. Both ANSI (American National Standards Institute) and ISO (International Organization for Standardization) have published three generations of the *de jure* SQL standard, and a consortium, X/Open, has published an SQL specification that is often said to be a *de facto* standard.

[1] In mathematical logic we would say that SQL describes intensionally the set of tuples (specifies the set through its *intension*, i.e. the properties of the tuples in the set that the user of the language wants to denote, as opposed to the extension of the set, which would be the enumeration of tuples) [Ed].

The relational model gained prominence in 1974 when E.F.Codd published his seminal paper [Cod74] that provided a mathematical foundation for *logical* representation and manipulation of data, independent of *physical* representation, relationships, and other implementation considerations. Shortly afterwards, Don Chamberlin and Raymond Boyce published the first paper on the language that became SQL [CB74]. This paper was based on research prototypes on data languages named SQUARE and SEQUEL, as well as on IBM's research relational database project, called System R. The relational model uses terms like *relation, attribute,* and *tuple* for the concepts that SQL calls *table, column,* and *row.* It should be noted that SQL does not correspond perfectly to the relational model – most significantly in the fact that SQL does not prohibit duplicate rows in a table, although SQL does permit users to restrict their tables to contain only unique rows.

In 1978, the principle standards body in the United States, ANSI, approved a project to develop a standard for a data definition language for network databases and established a new Technical Committee, X3H2, to do the work on that project. In 1986, a complete network database language standard was published as Database Language NDL (ANSI X3.133-1986). However, X3H2 members recognized the importance of the relational model and worked in the background on a derivation of SEQUEL called RDL (many viewed this as an acronym for "Relational Database Language"). After a couple of years of RDL work, X3H2 found the work wasn't reaching closure and accepted an IBM proposal to use IBM's SQL specification. X3H2, in cooperation with a newly-established corresponding ISO group, spent another year refining the SQL specification, which was published in 1986 by ANSI and in early 1987 by ISO [ANSI86, ISO87].

SQL-86 (or SQL-87, depending on one's frame of reference) omitted support for *referential integrity*, but a revised standard, called SQL-89, was published three years later by both ANSI and ISO, with a minimal referential integrity facility [ANSI89, ISO89]. In 1992, a major new version of the language was published [ANSI92, ISO92]. While SQL-86 and SQL-89 did not have adequate features for real applications, SQL-92 contained language features and conformance requirements that would allow significant applications to be built using only standardized language features. The fourth generation of SQL (the project is called "SQL3") is currently being prepared for publication perhaps as early as the end of 1998; it adds significant new facilities to SQL, including support for object orientation, and divides the specification into several parts that can be progressed more or less independently.

2 Requirements Leading to SQL

SQL derived from the need for a database language that, analogous to COBOL, was relatively easy to use and supported the most important features of the relational model of data that was in the 1980s attracting so much attention from large application builders and software vendors. Like the CODASYL-defined language [Coda71] supporting "network database" applications, a relational database language had to be complete, allowing definition and maintenance of a database and its structure, as well as management of its contained data. In addition, it was widely agreed that such a language was required to provide better support for application modeling, including enforcement of business rules, without depending on the database structure. Several languages were developed in support of these requirements. SQL became the most popular of those languages – not necessarily because of inherent technical superiority, but because of that most powerful of forces, the marketplace. SQL was supported and implemented by several marketplace-leading vendors and demanded by several important computer system users: the combination determined the outcome of any competition from other languages.

2.1 Database Definition

Like the relational model itself, SQL's database definition capabilities specify only the logical contents of a database and say nothing about the physical structure. Although virtually every dialect of the SQL language includes facilities for defining certain physical aspects of a database – such as indexes that are used for higher-performance access to some data, or allocation of data storage to physical devices – those facilities vary quite widely from implementor to implementor and are generally viewed as extensions to the language rather than an inherent part of it.

Instead of allocating significant language facilities to physical database design, SQL focuses on the higher abstraction levels of data. The *data definition language* of SQL, called the "schema manipulation language" in the SQL standard, allows database designers to specify the data elements that they wish represented, the data types of those elements, and how those elements are grouped together into "records" of data. Database designers are also able to identify specific rules that the database must follow when applications perform various operations that manipulate the data that it contains. Some versions of SQL, including the emerging next generation of the SQL standard sometimes called SQL3, allow database designers to specify active behaviors that the database system takes when applications perform certain classes of operations on the data.

2.2 Data Manipulation

As important as database design is to successful application creation, the essence of a database management system is the operations that it permits on the data that it is designed to contain. SQL provides four major classes of data manipulation operation: retrieval, insertion, update, and deletion. All operations in an SQL database are performed in the context of a transaction

[GR93] that provides atomicity of groups of operations. The SQL standard, as well as most implementations of the language, allows application writers to determine the degree of isolation that transactions have from the effects of other transactions. Data manipulation operations are, of course, performed in the larger context of an application, which leads to special considerations that are not immediately obvious.

Because of its relationship to the relational model of data, SQL's operations are inherently *set oriented* operations, meaning that a single SQL data manipulation statement specifies both an action to be performed and a rule by which the database system is able to identify – possibly many – data items on which the action is performed. However, SQL is not a complete programming language but is used in conjunction with more traditional programming languages for building applications. Those traditional programming languages do not process data in sets, but one datum at a time. It often happens that SQL and its host language must interact as they manipulate the database data. This leads to one component of what is commonly called the *impedance mismatch* between SQL and other programming languages. SQL provides a construct called a *cursor* to resolve this aspect of impedance mismatch; a cursor identifies a set of data to manipulate, but actually operates on that data one datum at a time.

Since SQL's data types are not identical to those of any single traditional programming language – much less to all such languages – a second component to the impedance mismatch is revealed. As data is transferred between SQL and code written in the host language, there may be a need for some of that data to be converted from one data type to another. In doing so, it is possible that information (e.g., precision) could be lost; application writers must exercise some caution to ensure that data loss possibilities are well understood and actual loss minimized or eliminated. A final component of the impedance mismatch arises from SQL's recognition that not all data is well known at the time that collections of data are created. SQL uses the notion of a *null value* to represent data that is missing, inapplicable, or otherwise unavailable. Traditional programming languages do not have inherent facilities for dealing with those concepts and this leads to difficulties when it is necessary to retrieve data from an SQL database into an application program and that data is null (or, conversely, when data is being stored into an SQL database and the application must notify SQL that the data to be stored is null). This aspect of the impedance mismatch is resolved by exchanging two components for every potentially null datum transferred between SQL and the host language: one component is a sort of flag that identifies whether or not the datum has the null value, and the other – relevant only if the flag indicates that the datum does not have the null value – contains the actual value of the datum.

2.3 Business Rules

Data models that predate the relational model – and the database access facilities, including database languages, that supported those models – typically required that the database be designed in a way that enforced the various rules of the business and its applications in the database structure itself. This approach made database designs very inflexible and difficult to adapt to new business conditions with different rules. The relational model, and SQL, permit and encourage a very different approach, in which the logical structure of a database is independent of the business rules that applications must enforce. Of course, one possible outcome of this change in approach is that each application program might be responsible for enforcing all of the business rules itself. Besides raising the costs of writing applications considerably, this situation would significantly increase the risk that errors in programming could cause many sorts of anomalies in database contents. This is clearly an undesirable result.

To avoid such problems, SQL provides facilities that allow database designers to define business rules within the database itself and to modify or even remove those rules as circumstances require. Because the rules are not instantiated in the database structure, the database design remains quite flexible and can respond readily to business changes – and application programs need not even be aware of the existence of such rules and certainly don't have to be changed as business conditions evolve. Some such rules are called *semantic integrity constraints* because they provide restrictions on data content that enforce the integrity of the meaning of the data. For example, most business entities require that all wages and salaries be greater than zero – employees are rarely required to pay for the privilege of working. Therefore, a meaningful (if trivial) business rule applied to salary data is that values representing such data must be greater than zero.

2.4 Modeling Businesses and Applications

There are other sorts of business rules, however. Many of these govern the relationships between different aspects of business data. For example, it is common to require that business departments be managed by exactly one employee; departments cannot be comfortably managed by two or more employees simultaneously, and it's clearly undesirable to have departments without any management at all. A different sort of business rule called a *referential integrity constraint* allows database designers to place restrictions on certain data to insist that the data reference existing data in other places in the database.

Real business requirements go even further than this. It is often necessary that certain actions performed on data in a database always be accompanied by other actions in order to maintain consistency of data in different places in the database. For example, it is common for a business to require that an increase in capital expenditures for one project in a department be supported by an equal decrease in the capital budget for one or more other projects in the same department. SQL database systems often provide *triggers* that allow a database designer to make the database an active database by prescribing specific actions to be automatically taken by the database management system whenever certain specific actions are taken by an application.

Facilities such as referential (and semantic) integrity constraints and triggers – and others that will be introduced shortly – make it possible for SQL databases to do more than merely model the data associated with an application – SQL permits the modeling of entire applications and businesses.

3 The SQL Language

SQL is a sufficiently large and complex language that no strictly linear treatment of it can be wholly successful. However, a good understanding of the main concepts of SQL provides a foundation on which other aspects of the language can be acquired as needed.

3.1 Principle Concepts

The most fundamental concept of SQL is the table. A *table* is a logical unit of data that has one or more *columns*, each of which has a name and a data type. Data in a table is stored in *rows* that have columns corresponding to those of the table. Each column of a table has a single data type for all rows in that table. (A column in a row is sometimes called a "cell", though the SQL standard does not use or define that term.) Figure 1 illustrates these concepts.

SQL provides a number of data types, broken into the categories of *numeric, string, datetime,* and others. Table 1 shows each category, the further breakdown of those categories, and the specific data types.

All data in an SQL database belongs to one of those data types, even if some data has the null value. The concept of null doesn't have a data type itself, but the cell in which a null is stored always has one of the SQL data types.

In addition to representing data, SQL databases are *self-describing*; that is, besides the tables they contain that hold the application data, they contain tables with *metadata* that describes the tables in the database (and describing the tables containing the metadata). While the SQL standard doesn't define the word "database", it does define the words *catalog* and *schema*. A *catalog* is a named collection of schemas, including the special schema that contains the metadata for all objects in the catalog. A *schema* is a named collection of tables (and their columns), character sets, and other SQL-defined objects. Catalog names *qualify* schema names, allowing multiple schemas with the same name to exist in different catalogs; similarly, schema names qualify the

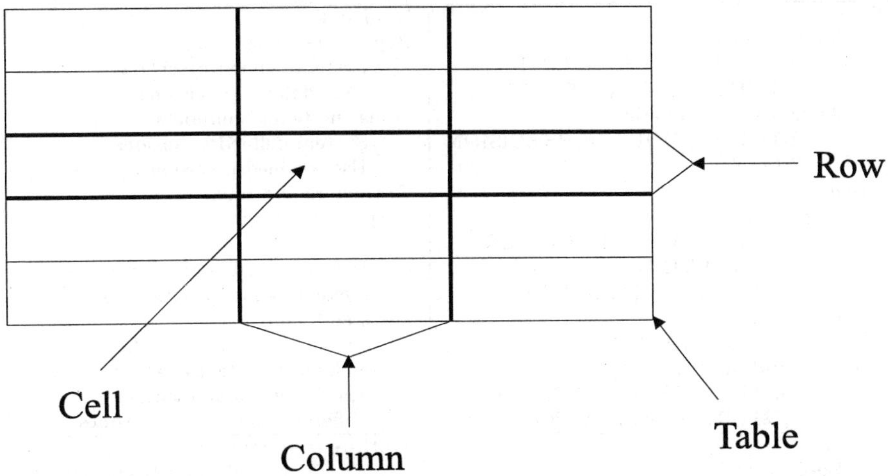

Figure 1: Illustration of *Table* concepts

names of tables and other objects, and table names qualify the names of columns. Qualified names are represented by the various components of the name separated by periods. For example, the name of a table might be

```
CATALOG3.MYSCHEMA.EMPLOYEES
```

Part of the power of SQL lies in the aids that it provides database and application designers. SQL databases can contain *constraints*, including:

- semantic integrity constraints that instruct the database system how to enforce business rules associated with the data stored in the database, and
- referential integrity constraints that tell the database system how to keep its data internally consistent when changes are made by applications.

If an application attempts to violate a semantic integrity constraint (for example, a rule that says "all salaries must be greater than 0"), then it is notified of the error and the statement attempting that violation is not executed. Attempted violations of some referential constraints (e.g., a rule prohibiting elimination of departments having one or more employees) are handled similarly. However, referential constraints can be more sophisticated – a database designer might permit resignation of a project's manager, but require the database to effect resolution of the status of the project. One design could result in the project's automatic deletion, while a second design might assign the project to someone responsible for "orphaned" projects, and

SQL data type	Description
Numeric	Numbers
Exact numeric	Represents values exactly
INTEGER and SMALLINT	System-defined precisions
DECIMAL and NUMERIC	User-defined precisions
Approximate numeric	"Floating point" numbers
REAL and DOUBLE PRECISION	System-defined precisions
FLOAT	User-defined precision
String	Characters and bits
Character string	In specific character sets
CHARACTER, CHARACTER VARYING	User-specified character set
NATIONAL CHARACTER	System-defined character set
Bit string	Zeros and ones
BIT, BIT VARYING	Fixed- or varying-length
Datetime and interval	Chronological, or temporal, data
DATE, TIME, and TIMESTAMP	Specific dates and times
INTERVAL (with precision)	Difference between datetimes
Logical	Truth-related data
Boolean	TRUE, FALSE, and UNKNOWN
User-defined	Extending the database
Abstract Data Type (ADT)	User-defined encapsulated type
Named row type	"Record" or "structure"
Distinct type	Based on an existing type
Object orientation	New paradigm support
Reference type	References to instances of named row type

Table 1: SQL Data Types

a third design leaves the project in an unassigned state pending explicit action at a later time. Each of these designs results in *automatic* resolution without execution of any additional SQL statements by the application.

A related feature, called *triggers*, allows a database designer to force the database system to take certain specific actions whenever certain tables are accessed in specified ways. For example, a trigger could be defined to add a row to a log table whenever changes are made to the salary column of an employee table, or to adjust the budgets for departments whenever new projects are assigned to them. Triggers can be arbitrarily complex and "intelligent" and their actions can cause additional triggers to be invoked.

When rows are created in a table, an application programmer can choose to provide a value for every column in each created row; alternatively, some rows might have an obvious default value. For example, employees might be hired as members of the Staff department often enough that the application assumes that department assignment for new employees if no specific department is provided. SQL allows the database designer to specify a default value for each column in a table; if no default value is specified, then a default of null is implied.

It sometimes happens that database designers find themselves using a particular combination of data type, constraint, and default value frequently (perhaps in various tables). SQL allows the definition of a *domain* [2] to give a name to that combination; the domain name can then be used in place of the data type (and constraint and default value) when defining columns in tables. For example, the name MONEY might be applied to a domain providing a data type of DECIMAL(8,2) – decimal with 8 total digits of precision, two of them after the decimal point – along with a constraint saying that the value must never be negative, and a default value of null. Columns such as SALARY and BUDGET could then be defined to be MONEY, providing a convenient shorthand as well as ensuring consistency of specification.

SQL programmers have several alternatives for using the language. The most widely-used alternative is to *embed* SQL statements into programs written in ordinary third-generation programming languages (3GLs). This technique, called *embedded SQL,* requires the application programmer to write the application in a 3GL (the SQL standard supports Ada, C, COBOL, Fortran, MUMPS, Pascal, and PL/I; SQL implementations often support other languages and standard support is likely for increasingly important languages such as Java). Each embedded SQL statement starts with a distinguished string, such as "EXEC SQL". In a typical SQL implementation, this embedded SQL program is processed by a *preprocessor* that extracts the SQL statements and (conceptually, at least) replaces them with a "call statement" to invoke the (conceptual or literal) *procedure* that the system creates to contain the SQL statement. The SQL statement (contained in that procedure) is then compiled and optimized by the SQL system to prepare it for later execution, while the remaining application program is compiled in the normal way. When the program executes, the optimized SQL statements are executed as specified by the 3GL code.

In some SQL implementations and in the SQL standard, it is possible to write actual SQL procedures (each containing a single SQL statement), collecting related procedures together into a *module.* Called *module language,* this technique permits applications to be written in a more modular fashion – database-related operations are coded in "pure SQL" and processed by an SQL compiler, while other application operations are coded in the appropriate 3GL and processed by that language's compiler. The SQL procedures are invoked through actual "call statements" by the application program. The two techniques are completely isomorphic with one another. In implementations that support both techniques, the choice of which to use is often a matter of taste or of organization policy.

In many applications, such as traditional mainframe applications, the SQL statements to be executed are well-known when the application is written. Embedded (or module language) SQL is appropriate for such applica-

[2]SQL does not follow the mathematical convention here with respect to the use of the term *domain.* Mathematically an SQL attribute (column name) is a function which maps the attribute domain to its range, where the set of possible tuples (rows) are the domain of the this function, and the set of possible values are the *range* of that function. The SQL terminology 'domain' really refers to this range.[Ed].

tions. In other situations, such as *ad hoc* query generators, graphical database browsers, or client-server systems with widely-varying users, the SQL statements that will be executed are often not known until execution time, when the user formulates a question. A technique called *dynamic SQL* allows SQL statements to be formulated at runtime, prepared for execution by the database system, and executed on demand. Dynamic SQL is typically slower than *static SQL* because of its inability to precompile and optimize statements. Of course, the benefits of flexibility often make this a worthwhile cost.

3.2 Basic Data Definition Language (DDL)

Manipulation and management of data in an SQL database depends, of course, on the existence of the database. SQL does not specify how a database itself is created; there are simply too many different reasonable (and commercially-successful) implementation techniques to support standardization of any one or a set of them. Because the SQL standard does not even define the term "database", the closest analog to a database in SQL is the catalog. Catalogs contain schemas, including the schema (called the "Information Schema") that describes all other schemas (and their contained objects) in the catalog. The SQL standard does not provide statements for creating and destroying catalogs, either. It explicitly leaves that to "implementation-defined" means.

However, SQL does provide a CREATE SCHEMA statement that allows users to define new schemas, as well as a DROP SCHEMA statement to allow the destruction of schemas and their contents. Creation of a schema is normally accompanied by the creation of one or more objects within the schema, such as tables; in addition, such objects can be added to schemas already in existence. A schema belongs to a specific authorization identifier (authorization identifiers are the way that SQL identifies and represents users of the database). All objects in a schema ordinarily belong to the owner of the schema and only the owner of a schema is able to define and manage objects in that schema. Some SQL products provide language extensions permitting the owner of a schema to grant other users privileges allowing them to create and otherwise manage objects in that schema. The privilege structure of SQL is covered later.

The SQL statements that create and destroy schemas are:

```
CREATE SCHEMA schema-name...
DROP SCHEMA schema-name
```

The ellipsis (...) represents one or more statements that create schema objects, such as tables or views.

To create or destroy a table, these SQL statements would be used:

```
CREATE TABLE table-name (table-element, ... )
DROP TABLE table-name
```

Each table-element can be a column definition or a table constraint definition.

A column definition specifies the column name and data type, optionally with additional information:

```
column-name data-type
  default-clause
  column-constraint
  collation
```

The column-name must be unique within the table and data-type can be either one of SQL's data types or the name of a domain. The other clauses are optional. Default-clause provides an explicit default for the column and a collation instructs the database system how to sort character string columns. Constraints (column and table constraints) are discussed later.

A *virtual table* is a table that is not persistently stored in the database, but that is generated on demand as the result of a query expression. A *view* is a named virtual table whose definition is stored in the database as part of the metadata. One use of views is to capture complex query expressions once so they can be used by many application programs without the costs and risks of errors that rewriting them for each program entails. Another important use of views is to allow access to some data in some tables without allowing unrestricted access; this subject is discussed along with SQL's privilege model later.

3.3 Basic Data Manipulation Language (DML)

Creation of a database and its contained objects is of course necessary, but the essence of a database management system is the storage, retrieval, and manipulation of the data stored within it. SQL's Data Manipulation Language provides the statements necessary to retrieve information from a database, as well as to insert information into, modify information in, and remove information from a database.

A number of additional SQL statements exist for managing various aspects of the database and the application's use of it; however, those statements are usually not characterized as Data Manipulation Statements.

3.3.1 Retrieving Information from a Database

Arguably, the most basic operation that is performed on an SQL database is the retrieval of information stored in it. Information may be retrieved directly into an application, or it may be retrieved for use strictly within an SQL statement.

The SELECT expression is the foundation for retrieval of SQL information. With a little variation in syntax, the SELECT expression can be used as an SQL statement to retrieve the information into the application or to define a view, as well as in the form of a *subquery* within an SQL statement. The format of a SELECT expression is:

```
SELECT select-list
  FROM table, table...
  WHERE logical-expression
  GROUP BY grouping-columns
  HAVING logical-expression
```

The WHERE, GROUP BY, and HAVING clauses are all optional. The result of the SELECT expression is always a *virtual table*; SQL exhibits *closure* such that operations on tables produce new tables. A SELECT expression is evaluated according to the following rules (effectively, that is; products must provide this effect, but may – and usually do – provide significant optimizations):

1. First, all rows in the table or tables specified in the FROM clause are retrieved; if more than one table is specified, then the Cartesian product of all tables is retrieved, producing new, extended rows. (Two tables with N and M columns and n and m rows have a Cartesian product with $N + M$ columns and nm rows; each row in one table is "matched" with every row from the other table.)

2. The predicates in the WHERE clause (if present) are applied to the rows produced by the preceding step. All rows that do not satisfy the predicate or combination of predicates in the logical-expression (that is, for which the logical expression does not evaluate to *true*) are eliminated from the working set of rows.

3. If a GROUP BY clause is present, then rows are grouped together according to equal values in the column or columns (grouping-columns) identified in that clause.

4. If a HAVING clause is present, then its logical-expression is applied to the groups; all groups for which the logical-expression does not evaluate to *true* are eliminated. (A HAVING clause without a GROUP BY clause effectively makes the result of the WHERE clause a single group.)

5. Finally, the select-list is used to determine the columns produced as the result of the SELECT expression. If groups have been formed by the presence of a GROUP BY clause or a HAVING clause, then the select-list can include only columns used as grouping columns, certain "statistical operations" (sum, average, maximum, and minimum) on other columns, and count operations on the resulting table. These statistical and count operations can be also used without groups having been formed. If no groups have been formed, then any column of the resulting virtual table can be used. In any case, the select-list can

include expressions of various sorts as long as the expressions do not include any columns prohibited by the grouping rules.

It is worth noting that SQL supports several sorts of *joins*, including *inner joins* (in which the result includes only rows that have a match between the two tables being joined) and *outer joins* (in which the result may include rows from one or both tables that have no match in the other table – columns corresponding to those from the table with no match are filled in with nulls).

To form a SELECT *statement*, the target of the retrieved information must be given:

```
SELECT select-list
  INTO target-list
    FROM table, table...
    WHERE logical-expression
    GROUP BY grouping-columns
    HAVING predicates
```

The target-list is a list of host language variables (or, in module language, a list of parameters of the containing procedure); there must be as many targets as there are columns in the select-list, and the data types of each target must match the data type of its corresponding select-list column.

A problem arises if the SELECT statement produces a virtual table containing more than one row. The host language variables into which the columns of the result are retrieved can only accept a single value at a time. If the SELECT statement were to produce multiple rows, then only one of them could be retrieved into the list of targets. This illustrates part of the impedance mismatch between SQL and the host languages. The SELECT statement, then, is really a "single-row SELECT statement". If it produces more than one row, an error is signaled.

The difference between SQL's set-at-a-time semantics and the datum-at-a-time character of the host languages makes it infeasible to write a simple SELECT statement to retrieve more than one row, yet many applications need exactly this capability. SQL resolves this impedance mismatch by providing a device called a *cursor*, which allows the application to identify sets of rows, but to process them one at a time. The set of rows is identified by a *cursor declaration* that specifies the SELECT expression:

```
DECLARE cursor-name CURSOR FOR
  SELECT select-list
  FROM tables
  WHERE logical-expression
```

The cursor declaration is just that – a declaration. It is not executed at all. However, when the application program *opens* the cursor, the SELECT expression is evaluated. Once the cursor has been opened, rows can be *fetched* through the cursor until the last row has been retrieved (signaled by a special status returned to the application program). Finally, the cursor is *closed.*

```
OPEN cursor-name
label:
FETCH FROM cursor-name
  INTO target-list
```

... *3GL statements to process the data* ...

```
  if not end-of-data, then loop to label
CLOSE cursor-name
```

3.3.2 Inserting Information into a Database

However useful it might be to retrieve information from a database, that information must first be somehow placed into the database. SQL's INSERT statement is used to insert information into tables.

The INSERT statement has three alternative formats, allowing information to be inserted using literal values, information retrieved from another table or tables, or merely the default values for each column. The syntax of INSERT is:

```
INSERT INTO table-name (column-name, column-name... )
  data-source
```

The parenthesized list of column-names is optional; if it is not specified, then the system assumes a list containing every column of the table, in the order in which they are defined in the table. The number of column-names and the number of columns in the data-source must be the same and the data types of each corresponding column must match.

If the data-source is a list of literals or host variables, then a single row is inserted into the identified table. If the data-source is a SELECT expression, then many rows might be inserted – one per row of the virtual table resulting from evaluation of the SELECT expression. If data-source is the keywords DEFAULT VALUES, then a single row is inserted in which each column takes on the default value for that column (which, of course, is null if no explicit default value has been defined).

3.3.3 Updating Information in a Database

In addition to retrieving information from a database and inserting new information into it, real applications frequently require that data already in a database be modified. In fact, after retrieval, updating information is probably the most common operation performed on SQL databases.

SQL provides two types of UPDATE statement – one for set-oriented update operations, and a second for cursor-oriented updates. The first, sometimes called a *searched update* because of its self-contained nature of locating and updating rows in tables, exemplifies SQL's set-oriented nature. Using this, an application is able to change many rows of a table with one statement – without the programmer having to write a loop of any sort. The second form of UPDATE is called the *positioned update;* the word "positioned" is used to imply that the statements affect the row on which a cursor is currently positioned. UPDATE statements use the syntax:

```
UPDATE table-name
   SET column-name = update-value,
       column-name = update-value...
 WHERE locator
```

The WHERE clause in the searched UPDATE is optional; if it is omitted, then *all* rows of the table are affected. If WHERE is specified and locator is a logical-expression, then only those rows in the table for which the logical-expression is satisfied are updated. If WHERE is specified and locator is "CURRENT OF cursor-name", then the single row currently identified by the cursor is updated. The update-values can be expressions with a data type suitable for the corresponding column (including scalar subqueries), but they can also be the keyword NULL or the keyword DEFAULT. In the cases of NULL or DEFAULT, the corresponding column in each identified row is set to null or to its default value (which, of course, might itself be null). When an expression is used for an update-value, the expression can use values in the row being updated. For example:

```
UPDATE employees
   SET salary = salary * 1.05
 WHERE dept_id = 'ENG'
```

will give a 5 % raise in salary to every member of the engineering department.

3.3.4 Removing Information from a Database

Of course, not all data that is put into a database remains there forever; some data become obsolete and must be removed, while other insertion operations are wrong and the incorrect rows must be deleted. SQL provides two forms of the DELETE statement, analogous to the two forms of the UPDATE statement, to allow applications to remove data from tables.

The first form, called the *searched delete,* allows applications to remove (possibly many) rows from a table based on criteria specified in the statement, while the second form is called the *positioned delete* and deletes from the identified table only the row on which the specified cursor is positioned. The format of the DELETE statement is:

```
DELETE FROM table-name
  WHERE locator
```

The WHERE clause here, as in the searched UPDATE statement, is optional; if absent, then all rows in the specified table are deleted. As with the two variants of UPDATE, it's possible to delete *all* rows of a table (obviously a DELETE without a WHERE is to be used with discretion!), all rows for which a logical-expression is satisfied, or the one row currently identified by a cursor.

3.4 SQL-86

The 1986/1987 standard for SQL was widely characterized as a "least-common denominator" standard. Its goal was to standardize only those features of SQL that had been widely implemented by the major database system vendors (principally, IBM, Oracle, Informix, Sybase, and Ingres). In fact, although public awareness of this was minimal, SQL-86 had two *levels,* called Level 1 and Level 2. Level 1 was viewed as so minimal that almost any vendor with any sort of database product could conform with a few months work. In fact, Level 1 was rejected by NIST (the National Institute of Standards and Technology) on behalf of the U.S. Federal Government when it adopted FIPS (Federal Information Processing Standard) 127 for use in government agency procurements.

Level 2 was also rather minimalist. For example, all DDL operations in SQL-86 were to be performed in the context of a "schema definition processor" distinct from the SQL language processor, and once a database was created, no changes to its metadata (e.g., addition of tables, addition of columns to tables, etc.) could be performed. There were many concessions made to accommodate the goal of standardizing only that which was already implemented, meaning that no serious applications could be written using *only* standardized SQL language.

The most controversial omission in SQL-86 – which nearly caused it to be rejected by the international standards community – was referential integrity. Progression in ISO was saved only because of a last-minute offer from the United States to work on an *addendum* to SQL-86 specifying referential integrity that could be quickly progressed.

3.5 SQL-89

While development of the referential integrity addendum to SQL-86 was being developed, a number of the more active standardization participants began working on a second addendum that was intended to add a number of significant new features to the language.

As work proceeded on both addenda, it became obvious that the ANSI and ISO processes were sufficiently different that it would be easiest to recast the referential integrity addendum as a replacement standard that could be adopted in identical form by both communities. The delays in making this discovery and restructuring the document itself, coupled with the (by then, significant) distractions of the second addendum, led to a three-year lapse before publication as SQL-89. SQL-89 was virtually identical to SQL-86 other than the addition of basic (restrictive) referential integrity facilities.

However, there were two mechanisms specified in SQL-86 and SQL-89 for coupling SQL with other programming languages. One mechanism, module language, was specified in the *normative* part of the standards, but very few vendors had actually implemented it. The other mechanism, embedded SQL, was specified only in an *informative* annex to the standard! The U.S. Federal Government participants expressed concern that it would serve only to limit the number of vendors competing for Federal procurements if only a few vendors implemented module language and all of the others implemented only the "non-standard" embedded capabilities. To avoid this potential problem, ANSI progressed a second SQL-related standard in 1989, called "Database Language Embedded SQL" [ANSI89b]; ISO did not pursue a corresponding standard.

Besides the technical content, SQL-89 contained the same two levels that SQL-86 contained. NIST issued a revised FIPS 127-1 that combined requirements for SQL-89 and Embedded SQL.

3.6 SQL-92

By 1989, it had become obvious that the proposed second addendum to SQL-86 was going to take significantly longer than originally thought and that the content was going to be quite a bit larger. Both ANSI and ISO decided to transform that addendum into another replacement standard that would be published about three years after SQL-89.

Industry dissatisfaction with the least-common denominator aspect of SQL-89 led to another important decision: to ensure that the new version of the SQL standard contained enough features that realistic applications could be built using only standardized language features. There were, predictably, vastly differing opinions about what such a set of features would be. Intense technical work and negotiations among the representatives of database implementers, large and small customers, government agencies, and even academia continued for three years, culminating in a new SQL specification that took roughly five times as many pages (nearly 600) to present as SQL-89 had taken.

Close analysis of those nearly 600 pages show that the actual language itself grew by a factor of between two and three; the remaining increase in size was due largely to more detailed specification of features (even those from SQL-86) and the inclusion of auxiliary components of the language like definitions of the tables that describe various schema objects (the metadata tables). Nonetheless, the size of the language was sufficiently daunting that participants agreed to divide it into three levels: Entry SQL, Intermediate SQL, and Full SQL. Entry SQL was to be very little more than SQL-89, while Intermediate SQL was to contain roughly half of the new features added to the language; Full SQL, of course, was the entire standard.

NIST released a revised FIPS 127-2 that carefully analyzed the features in SQL-92 and specified a taxonomy of features divided into the three levels specified in the standard. As an aid in guiding the vendors, NIST included a fourth level, called Transitional SQL, that contained roughly half of the features that were standardized in Intermediate SQL. Unfortunately, a great many compromises had to be made in determining the set of features in Transitional and Intermediate SQL in order to acquire enough votes for a majority – and those compromises may have made it unattractive for any vendor to pursue conformance to either level. By early 1997, no vendor had made a formal claim of conformance to Transitional SQL, although most of the features in that level, and even in Intermediate SQL had been implemented by multiple vendors.

3.7 SQL3

Even before SQL-92 was finalized, it was obvious to participants that many good ideas proposed for that version of the standard were either too immature or in insufficient demand to justify delaying publication in order to complete their specification. Instead, a new project for yet another replacement version of the standard was initiated. If SQL-86 had been the first SQL standard, then SQL-89 was not so much the second SQL standard as it was a minor enhancement. The project under which SQL-92 was developed was widely called "SQL2", so it was natural to call the next edition "SQL3", particularly since it was uncertain how long development would take.

A sort of theme quickly developed for SQL3: support for object orientation. Even though a large number of additional, more traditional, features have been proposed for and are included in SQL3, the most energy has been required for the object-oriented aspects of the specification. Among the other features are new data types and predicates, support for recursion, and better support for analytical processing.

Early proposals that specified several different aspects related to the object paradigm were surprisingly contentious and resulted less in stable specifications than in heated debate and competing approaches. Some facilities were quickly endorsed philosophically – although working out the details was still difficult and time-consuming; others proved to be extremely difficult in terms of reaching agreement amongst the principle participants. The most difficult aspect turned out to be the definition of just what an object is! Several different approaches were taken, notably creating a new storage category (in addition to tables) that provided extents for user-defined data type instances, treating rows of tables as instances of user-defined data types with the table's columns equivalent to the instance's attributes, and requiring instances of user-defined data types to be stored in columns of tables whose rows could then be treated as objects with identity. That last approach finally won over enough participants to move forward.

Unfortunately, by the time that decision was reached, the goal of publishing the revision to SQL-92 in three years – by 1995 – was no more than a lost dream. Instead, participants realized that publication even by 1998 would require incredible efforts, especially since other components of SQL3 were by then partitioned into separate documents and progressing to standardization very rapidly (SQL's call-level interface, SQL/CLI, is closely related to the ODBC interface from Microsoft and others and was standardized in 1995; a standard for stored procedures, SQL/PSM, was standardized in 1996).

In late 1996, the first formal ballot was held on the most crucial parts of SQL3. This ballot, as expected, failed, but a large number of comments were submitted from many participants all over the world. Meetings to resolve those comments, limit the feature set of SQL3, and pursue publication no later than late 1998 or early 1999 are currently in progress.

4 Advanced Topics

There are a number of additional aspects of SQL that demand some attention. These range from security and error handling issues, as well as putting business rules in the database, to aspects of object orientation.

4.1 Security

SQL offers the ability to protect data from unauthorized access. Every schema object is covered by one or more *privileges* so that only users (identified by authorization identifiers) having the appropriate privilege are able to use that schema object. Objects containing data, such as tables and views, require that users have the SELECT privilege on the object before they can successfully perform any operation that reveals data values, such as data retrieval; users must have the INSERT privilege on the object in order to create new rows of data, the UPDATE privilege in order to modify data values, and the DELETE privilege in order to delete rows of data. The REFERENCES privilege permits the definition of referential integrity constraints that reference data values stored in a table.

The owner of a schema object automatically gets all possible privileges on that object; when the object is a view, "all possible privileges" is often less than all of the privileges that theoretically might apply to the view, as we'll see shortly. The owner is able to grant privileges to other authorization identifiers by using the GRANT statement, specifying the specific privileges to be granted, the schema object on which privileges are being granted, and the authorization identifiers to which those privileges will be given. If the privileges are granted WITH GRANT OPTION, then the recipients are permitted to grant those privileges to additional users. Privileges are taken away with the REVOKE statement, which requires the same information that was used for the GRANT.

The INSERT privilege can be granted for access to an entire table or only to selected columns of the table, since users might be authorized to insert rows into a table but supply non-default values only for some columns; the same granularity applies to the UPDATE privilege since users might be authorized to change only some columns of a table. Because it is meaningless to attempt to delete only some columns of specified rows, the DELETE privilege can be granted only at table granularity. The SELECT privilege is also limited to table granularity, although there is interest in extending it to column granularity. The REFERENCES privilege is applied at either table or column granularity.

Every SQL statement is executed under the privileges of exactly one authorization identifier. The success of an attempt to execute an SQL statement depends in part on the privileges required by the statement itself and the privileges available to that authorization identifier. If the user on whose behalf an SQL statement execution is attempted does not have all of the privileges required for successful execution of the statement, SQL will inhibit execution of that statement; implementations are sometimes able to determine the presence or absence of required privileges when applications are compiled, but they must always reconfirm the continued existence of those privileges before executing the statement (thus avoiding the situation where a user compiled a program while having the privileges and then runs the program after those privileges are revoked).

Views accomplish two principle functions: assignment of a name to persistent specification of a query expression so applications can avoid recoding that query specification; and provision of a security mechanism that allows users to access data through the view that they are not authorized to access directly in the underlying tables. For example, instead of giving users SELECT privilege on a table that contains salary information for all employees, views can be created that permit users to see only their own salary information, but that allow all users to see office telephone numbers of any employee. In order to create a view that derives its contents from data stored in one or more tables or other views, the definer of the view must have the appropriate privileges on the view. The privileges that the view definer has on those underlying tables and views determines the privileges that the definer gets on the view. If the privileges required for the view's creation are later revoked from the view's definer, the view is automatically destroyed by the system. (Of course, no data is lost since destruction of a view only destroys the persistent query expression.) A view definer might have only SELECT privileges on the tables underlying the view; in this case, the privileges given to the definer would not include UPDATE, DELETE, or INSERT since those privileges are unavailable on the underlying tables.

4.2 Semantic Integrity Constraints and Assertions

SQL supports the creation of business rules at several levels of granularity. Semantic integrity constraints can be applied to entire tables or to individual columns (though SQL automatically transforms column constraints to table-level constraints). Table constraints can apply to individual columns or groups of columns in the table or they can apply to the table as a whole. Table constraints that apply to the entire table might make restrictions on the total number of rows stored in the table. Constraints applying to columns could be used, for example, to prohibit null values being stored in the columns, to require that the columns' values not contain any duplications, or to place restrictions on the values that can be stored in columns.

Another form of semantic integrity constraint, called an *assertion,* can be specified at the schema level and is intended primarily to specify relationships between data stored in more than one table. For example, an assertion might be used to restrict the sum of salaries in a table of employee information plus the sum of capital budgets in a table of department information to some maximum value. Such a constraint could be written as a table constraint, but a decision would have to be made to define the constraint in the context of the employee table or in the context of the department table; to avoid such arbitrary and possibly misleading choices, assertions provide a more appropriate mechanism.

4.3 Referential Integrity Constraints

Many types of data represented in an SQL database have a natural component that serves to uniquely identify each row of data. For instance, employees usually have employee identification numbers and products being sold in a store always have a product code of some sort. While SQL, unlike the relational model, does not prohibit storage of more than one row in a table with all corresponding column values equal, many application benefit from the identification of some such unique value. SQL gives database designers the ability to specify PRIMARY KEY for any column or group of columns that provide such a unique value. SQL requires that the table contain no two rows for which the values stored in the column or columns specified as a PRIMARY KEY are equal; it also requires that the PRIMARY KEY column (or, if more than one column participates in the PRIMARY KEY, the combination of all such columns) not have the null value.

Applications often require that data stored in one table correspond closely with data stored in a different table. For example, if employees are assigned to departments, then the table representing employees must require that the values stored in the departments column all be equal to a value stored in the department identification column of the table representing departments. Such a requirement is called a *foreign key.* SQL allows database designers to specify one or more columns as a FOREIGN KEY that references a specific table; if a FOREIGN KEY specification does not provide the names of the columns in the referenced table, then SQL assumes that the PRIMARY KEY of that table will be used – and, of course, the number and data types of those PRIMARY KEY columns must match the number and data types of the FOREIGN KEY columns. Although a table can have at most one PRIMARY KEY, it can have any number of FOREIGN KEYs, and a given column might participate in more than one FOREIGN KEY.

The simplest kind of FOREIGN KEY reference, which was supported in SQL-89, simply prohibits any value in the referencing columns that do not appear in the referenced columns – applications will encounter an error on any attempt to delete a row from the referenced table that would delete the referenced column values on which some referencing columns depend, as well as on any attempt to add a row to a referencing table with values that depend on values that don't exist in the referenced columns.

SQL-92 added the ability for FOREIGN KEYs to specify the action that a database system can take to correct referential integrity violations. Database designers can specify that deletion of a referenced row automatically causes deletion of referencing rows or that referencing rows have their referencing column values replaced with their default values or with null values. Similarly, they can specify that modification of a referenced column automatically cause referencing rows to be updated so their referencing column values updated to the same new values or replaced with either their default values or the null value. (Of course, replacement of a referencing value with the default value requires that that default value appear as a referenced column value, and replacement with the null value requires that there be no constraint prohibiting null values on the referencing column or columns.)

4.4 Triggers

SQL3 provides the ability for database designers to build into a database the ability for the database to react to changes made by an application in ways other than simply making the specified changes. The database can make additional changes not specified directly by the application, including making changes to completely different tables.

Triggers can be specified to respond to specific application actions, such as insertion, update, or deletion of rows from specific tables (or even updates to specific columns); they can execute any sequence of SQL statements, and can be made to execute once per application statement or once per row affected by such statements.

Triggers are even able to access column values in rows being updated both before the update is applied and after it has been applied, permitting database designers to prohibit certain transitions of data in the database. For example, a trigger could be designed that allows the amount of remaining capital expenditure budget for a project to be decreased but not increased.

4.5 Recursion

Certain classes of applications require the ability to recursively retrieve data from tables. A common example is called the "bill of material" application, in which it is desired to retrieve information about all components required to manufacture some product. Given the part number of the product, the application must locate all subassemblies required to build the product; some of those subassemblies are made of other subassemblies, possibly through several iterations before basic indivisible parts are the only components used.

Constructing such a bill of materials requires recursively retrieving part information, sometimes through a number of levels not well known in advance. Until SQL3 is implemented, the only approaches available to applications are awkward to write and limited to a pre-known number of levels of recursion. SQL3, however, provides inherent recursion capabilities that can be used by applications for bill of material and other analogous requirements (including, for example, genealogy or genetics research). These recursion facilities even allow the definition of views that are inherently recursive, thus removing yet another burden from application writers.

4.6 Abstract Data Types (ADTs)

While SQL's "traditional" data types, such as numbers and character strings, have supported countless applications for years, increasing numbers of applications require the ability to store and manage more complex forms of data, including things like documents, images, and sound. Furthermore, the increasing popularity of object-oriented technology places additional requirements on database systems.

SQL3 responds to these needs with the addition of abstract data types. ADTs allow database designers to define data types that include arbitrarily complex structures and fully encapsulate them so that their components are accessible only through a functional interface (*methods* is the word used in the object-oriented community). Type hierarchies can be defined using ADTs (e.g., employees are a type of person, and managers are a type of employee; while persons may not be assigned to a department, employees might be, and managers typically have some signatory authority that other employees do not). SQL also allows the definition of multiple functions with the same name but with different combinations of parameter definitions; this allows applications to *overload* function names and have the database system decide the most appropriate function of a given name to use based on the parameters that the application provides. While most function resolution is done when applications are compiled, functions having parameters that are abstract data types in a type hierarchy can sometimes only be fully resolved when the application runs, based on the most specific type passed as an argument to the function.

4.7 Reference (REF) Types

ADTs alone do not provide all elements expected for object orientation; they are missing the important characteristic of *identity.* If objects have a unique identity, then applications can reference an object strictly by its identity instead of by the values of attributes of the object: for example, persons with the same height, weight, hair color, and name are still distinct persons having their own unique identities. SQL3 provides a data type called *named row type,* and allows database designers to define tables whose columns are not specified individually (which would give the table an *anonymous row type*), but are taken from a specified named row type. SQL3 also provides a reference type (called a *REF type*) that can be applied to instances of a specified named row type. Thus, a column in a database table can contain references to rows in other database tables that are of that named row type. These references serve the function of object identity while preserving SQL's table and row orientation. By defining a named row type having exactly one column whose data type is some ADT, rows in that table correspond one-to-one with instances of the ADT – REF values identifying rows of that table behave like object identifiers and the ADT instances provide the other behaviors of objects including the method interface.

4.8 Error Handling

Applications written using any programming language may always encounter unexpected conditions and errors; SQL is not an exception to this rule. Execution of SQL statements cause the database system to set a status in a structure called the *diagnostics area.* The status includes a 5-character value called the SQLSTATE resulting from the statement's execution; the SQLSTATE informs the application of the statement's outcome, including successful execution, warnings, or outright exceptions, or whether a statement intending to affect data actually did so.

SQL statements invoked through module language or embedded SQL cause the SQLSTATE value to be returned in a required parameter to the module language procedure or to a host language variable assigned for that purpose. Applications should generally test the SQLSTATE variable after the execution of every SQL statement to ensure its success or other expected outcome before dispatching the next SQL statement. Embedded SQL applications can use a special language facility, the WHENEVER declaration, to cause compiled embedded SQL programs to automatically test the outcome of each SQL statement and branch to a specified target when the specified conditions are met.

Multiple SQL statements can be combined together into *compound statements* when the facilities of SQL/PSM are used by an application. Compound statements allow the specification of *condition handlers* that can take application-specified action when specified exception or other conditions are encountered.

5 Future Evolution

The database industry does not expect that SQL3 will be the end of the development for SQL standards. Indeed, as SQL3 progresses towards formal publication, additional features deemed insufficiently mature and stable (or for which the market requirements have not yet proved sufficiently high) are being developed – at a lower priority – for an anticipated fourth generation of the SQL standard, naturally called "SQL4". The SQL standards community generally anticipates that SQL4 will be published as a *de jure* standard in roughly 2001 or 2002, i.e. three years after SQL3 is published.

Will there be another generation of the SQL standard beyond SQL4? It's difficult to be certain, but as long as relational database systems remain as important to industry and commerce as they are today, evolution of SQL and its standard is probably inevitable.

References

[ANSI86] ANSI, ANSI X3.135-1986, American National Standard for Information Systems – Database Language SQL, American National Standards Institute, 1986

[ANSI89] ANSI, ANSI X3.135-1989, American National Standard for Information Systems – Database Language SQL with Integrity Enhancement, American National Standards Institute, 1989

[ANSI89b] ANSI, ANSI X3.168-1989, American National Standard for Information Systems – Database Language Embedded SQL, American National Standards Institute, 1989

[ANSI92] ANSI, ANSI X3.135-1992, American National Standard for Information Systems – Database Language SQL, American National Standards Institute, 1992

[CB74] Chamberlin, D. D., Boyce, R. F., SEQUEL: A Structured English Query Language, Proceedings of the ACM SIGFIDET Workshop, 1974, 249-264

[CO93] Cannan, S., Otten, G., SQL – The Standard Handbook, McGraw-Hill Book Company, 1993

[Cod74] Codd, E. F., A Relational Model of Data for Large Shared Data Banks, Communications of the ACM (13,6), 1974, 377-387

[Coda71] Data Base Task Group Report to the CODASYL Programming Language Committee, ACM, New York, 1971

[DD93] Date, C. J., Darwen, A Guide to the SQL Standard, Addison-Wesley Publishing Company, 1993

[GR93] Gray, J., Reuter, A., Transaction Processing: Concepts and Techniques, Morgan Kaufmann Publishers, San Mateo, CA, 1993

[MS93] Melton, J., Simon, A. R., Understanding the New SQL: A Complete Guide, Morgan Kauffman Publishers, 1993

[ISO87] ISO, ISO 9075:1987, Database languages – SQL, International Organization for Standardization, 1987

[ISO89] ISO, ISO/IEC 9075:1989, Information technology – Database languages – SQL, International Organization for Standardization, 1989

[ISO92] ISO, ISO/IEC 9075:1992, Information technology – Database languages – SQL, International Organization for Standardization, 1992

[ISO95] ISO, ISO/IEC 9075-3:1995, Information technology – Database languages – SQL – Part 3: Call-Level Interface (SQL/CLI), International Organization for Standardization, 1995

[ISO96] ISO, ISO/IEC 9075-4, Information technology – Database languages – SQL – Part 4: Persistent Stored Modules (SQL/PSM), International Organization for Standardization, 1996

[ISO97a] ISO, ISO/IEC CD 9075-2, Information technology – Database languages – SQL – Part 2: Foundation (SQL/Foundation), International Organization for Standardization, 1997

[ISO97b] ISO, ISO/IEC CD 9075-5, Information technology – Database languages – SQL – Part 5: Host language bindings (SQL/Bindings), International Organization for Standardization, 1997

[XOPN93] X/Open, CAE Specification – Structured Query Language (SQL), X/Open Company Ltd., 1993

CHAPTER 6

Petri Nets

Jean-Marie Proth

The objective of this contribution is to provide the basics of Petri net theory in order to model and evaluate Discrete Event Systems (DES). The first part of the contribution is devoted to the common definitions and properties of Petri nets. Qualitative properties are then introduced. These properties are those who are of importance when manufacturing systems are concerned. Finally, a short introduction of event graphs is proposed; these graphs are of utmost importance to study cyclic DES.

1 Introduction

Discrete Event Systems (DES) such as manufacturing systems or information networks are highly parallel and distributed. They need to be evaluated from a qualitative point of view as well as from a quantitative point of view. The goal of qualitative analysis is, for instance, to verify the absence of deadlocks, the ability to reach some states (reachability) or the ability to return to some pre-defined states (reversibility and home state), to quote only a few.

Quantitative analysis aims at evaluating performance properties (for instance throughput), utilisation properties (for instance lengths of the queues in front of the resources), or responsiveness properties (for instance average time for message transmission). To summarise, quantitative analysis aims at evaluating the efficiency of the system at hand.

Both qualitative and quantitative analyses are used more and more frequently at the preliminary design phase of systems (manufacturing or information networks) since the complexity of these systems increases due to the constraints of the market and the rapid changes of technologies.

We claim that Petri nets, introduced by C.A. Petri in 1962 (see [Pet62]), are the most powerful set of tools which can support the functional specification, as well as the qualitative and the quantitative analysis. In this contribution, we provide the foundations of Petri nets. We deliberately restrict ourselves to simple Petri nets, since these nets have the most powerful analytical properties. More precise information about the use of Petri nets to model and evaluate manufacturing systems is available in [DHPSV93, HP92, Pet81, PX96, Ram74].

2 Basic Definitions

2.1 Petri Nets and Related Definitions

A Petri net is a five-tuple $PN = (P, T, A, W, M_0)$ where:

- $P = (p_1, p_2, \ldots, p_n)$ is a finite set of places. Places are represented by circles.

- $T = (t_1, t_2, \ldots, t_q)$ is a finite set of transitions. Transitions are represented by bars.

- $A \subseteq (P \times T) \cup (T \times P)$ is a finite set of arcs. An arc joins a place to a transition or a transition to a place, but never a transition to a transition or a place to a place.

- $W : A \to (1, 2, 3, \ldots)$ is a weight function attached to the arcs. The weight is represented by an integer located near the arc. If this integer is missing, it is assumed that the weight of the arc is 1.

- $M_0 : P \to (0, 1, 2, \ldots)$ is the initial marking. $M_0(p), p \in P$, is the marking of place p. $M_0(p)$ is the initial number of tokens included in place p. Each token is represented by a bullet.

Note 2.1 *A Petri net is said to be ordinary if all the weights are equal to 1.*

A Petri net is represented in Figure 1. In this Petri net:

- $P = (p_1, p_2, p_3, p_4, p_5)$

- $T = (t_1, t_2, t_3, t_4, t_5)$

- $A = \{(p_1, t_2), (t_2, p_2), (p_2, t_3), (t_2, p_3), (p_3, t_4), (t_4, p_4), (p_3, t_5), (t_1, p_5), (p_5, t_5)\}$

The weights are represented by integer numbers located near the arcs. For instance, $W(p_1, t_2) = 2; W(t_1, p_5) = 1$, since the integer is missing, $W(p_5, t_5) = 4$. The initial marking is $M_0 = [3, 1, 2, 0, 1]$ since $M_0(p_1) = 3, M_0(p_2) = 1, M_0(p_3) = 2, M_0(p_4) = 0, M_0(p_5) = 1$.

We usually denote by:

- $^\circ t$ the set of input places of transition t, that is the set of places p such that $(p, t) \in A$. For instance, $^\circ t_5 = (p_3, p_5)$ in Figure 1.

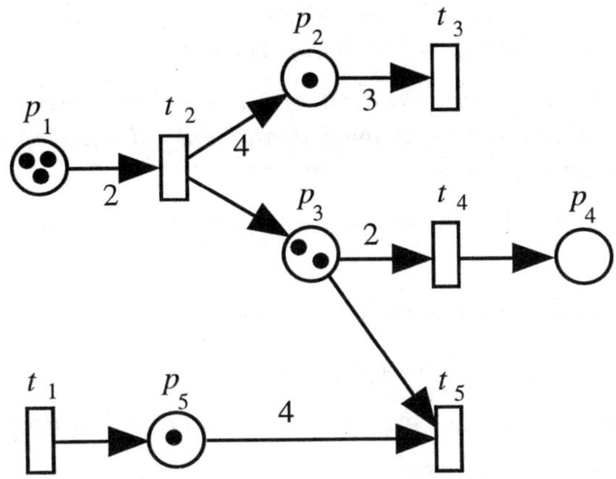

Figure 1: A Petri net

- t° the set of output places of transition t, that is the set of places p such that $(t, p) \in A$. For instance, in Figure 1, $t_2^\circ = (p_2, p_3)$ and $t_3 = \emptyset$, where $\emptyset$ denotes the empty set.
- $^\circ p$ is the set of input transitions of place p, that is the set of transitions t such that $(t, p) \in A$. For instance, in Figure 1, $^\circ p_4 = \{t_4\}, ^\circ p_1 = \emptyset, ^\circ p_2 = \{t_2\}$.
- p° is the set of output transitions of place p, that is the set of transitions t such that $(p, t) \in A$.

If $^\circ t = \emptyset$ (resp. $^\circ p = \emptyset$), then t (resp. p) is called a source transition (resp. source place). If $t^\circ = \emptyset$ (resp. $p^\circ = \emptyset$), then t (resp.p) is called a sink transition (resp. sink place). For instance, in Figure 1:

- p_1 is a source place.
- t_1 is a source transition.
- t_3 and t_5 are sink transitions.
- p_4 is a sink place.

2.2 Dynamics of Petri Nets

A transition t is said to be enabled if, whatever $p \in {}^\circ t$, p contains a number of tokens greater than or equal to $W(p, t)$. If M is the marking of a Petri net, this definition can be formally written as:

t $\in$ T is enabled if and only if, whatever p $\in {}^\circ t$, M(p) $\geq$ W(p,t).

For instance, in Figure 1, t_2 is enabled since $M_0(p_1) > W(p_1, t_2) = 2$, but t_5 is not enabled since $M_0(p_5) = 1 < W(p_5, t_5) = 4$.

Note 2.2 *According to the definition of an ordinary Petri net, a transition t of an ordinary Petri net is enabled if and only if each of its input places contains at least one token.*

If a transition t is enabled, it may or may not be fired. Firing a transition t consists in:

- removing $W(p,t)$ tokens from each $p \in {}^\circ t$
- adding $W(t,p)$ tokens to each $p \in t^\circ$.

For instance, firing t_2 in the Petri net represented in Figure 1 consists in:

- removing two tokens from p_1
- adding four tokens in p_2 and one token in p_3.

After firing t_2, the marking becomes $M = [1, 5, 3, 0, 1]$.

A source transition is always enabled. Firing a source transition consists in adding $W(t,p)$ tokens to each $p \in t^\circ$. A sink transition can be fired if it is enabled. If a sink transition is fired, the tokens are removed from the input places following the usual rule, but no token is added in a place. In Figure 1, firing source transition t_1 once changes M_0 into $M = [3, 1, 2, 0, 2]$. None of the sink transitions being enabled, they cannot be fired.

Let us assume that, starting from the marking M_0 represented in Fig. 1:

- we fire t_1 three times in sequence
- we fire t_5 once
- we fire t_2 once
- we fire t_3 once.

After firing t_1 three times, the marking becomes $M_1 = [3, 1, 2, 0, 4]$. After firing t_5 once, the marking becomes $M_2 = [3, 1, 1, 0, 0]$. After firing t_2 once, the marking becomes $M_3 = [1, 5, 2, 0, 0]$. Finally, after firing t_3 once, the marking becomes $M_4 = [1, 2, 2, 0, 0]$. In this case, we write:

$$M_0 \xrightarrow{\sigma} M_4, \text{ where } \sigma = < t_1, t_1, t_1, t_5, t_2, t_3 >$$

Note that sequence $\sigma_1 = < t_5, t_1, t_1, t_1, t_2, t_3 >$ which is composed of the same set of transitions, is not firable since t_5 cannot be fired first starting from M_0. This remark is of great importance, as we will see in the remaining of this contribution.

Note 2.3 *The set of markings derived from M_0 is denoted by $R(M_0)$. Thus, in the previous example, $M_i \in R(M_0)$ for $i = 1, 2, 3, 4$.*

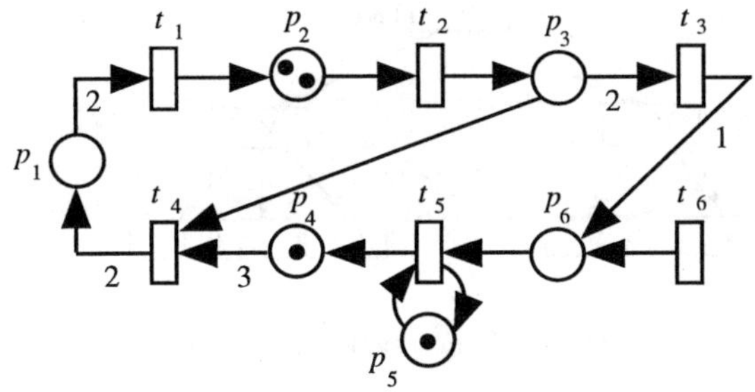

Figure 2: Elementary circuits and self-loops

2.3 Siphons and Traps

We consider the case when the Petri net under consideration is an ordinary Petri net, i.e. a Petri net where all the arcs are weighted to 1. A set $P(s)$ of places is a siphon if any transition $t \in T$ which has an output place in $P(s)$ has at least one input place in $P(s)$. In other words, $P(s)$ is a siphon if $t^\circ \cap P(s) \neq \emptyset$ leads to ${}^\circ t \cap P(s) \neq \emptyset$. Note that we may have, for some transitions t, $t^\circ \cap P(s) = \emptyset$ and ${}^\circ t \cap P(s) \neq \emptyset$. As a result, some siphons may become empty by firing transitions. Thus, a siphon in the Petri net model of a discrete event system, for instance a manufacturing system, may reflect a mistake at the design level.

A set $P(t)$ of places is a trap if each transition which has an input place in $P(t)$ has at least one output place in $P(t)$. Formally, $P(t)$ is a trap if ${}^\circ t \cap P(t) \neq \emptyset$ leads to $t^\circ \cap P(t) \neq \emptyset$. Note that we may have, for some transitions t, ${}^\circ t \cap P(t) = \emptyset$ and, nevertheless, $t^\circ \cap P(t) \neq \emptyset$. A trap which contains tokens will never become empty, but the number of tokens in a trap may increase to infinity: a Petri net model containing a trap may reflect a design mistake.

2.4 Elementary Circuits and Self-Loops

An elementary circuit in a Petri net is a directed path that goes from one place (or transition) back to this place (or transition), and which does not contain more than once any place (or transition). In Figure 2, $\gamma_1 = < t_1, p_2, t_2, p_3, t_4, p_1 >$ and $\gamma_2 =< t_1, p_2, t_2, p_3, t_3, p_6, t_5, p_4, t_4, p_1 >$ are two elementary circuits.

A self-loop is an elementary circuit containing one place and one transition. $\gamma =< t, p >$ is a self-loop if $\{t\} = p^\circ = {}^\circ p$. In figure 2, $\gamma_3 =< t_5, p_5 >$ is a self-loop.

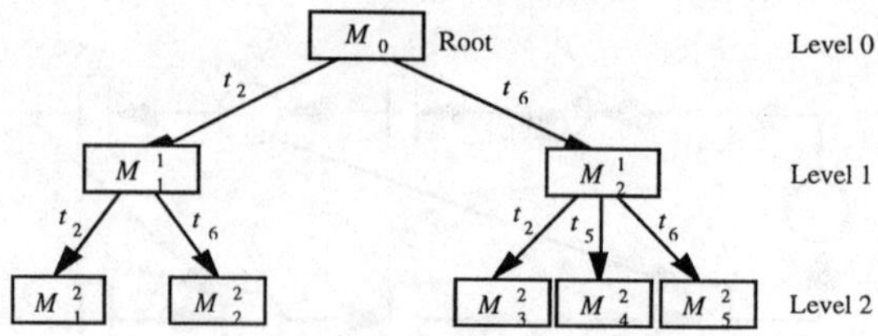

Figure 3: The first three levels of the reachability tree

3 Reachability Tree and Coverability Tree

Let us consider a Petri net $PN = (P, T, A, W, M_0)$. The goal of the reachability tree is to find all the markings which can be reached starting from the initial marking M_0 by firing a sequence of transitions.

To find the reachability tree, we start from the initial marking M_0 which is the root of the tree (level 0). Then we consider all the transitions enabled by M_0 and compute the markings obtained by firing each of these transitions starting from M_0. Each of these new markings represents a node of the reachability tree at level 1. In the example represented in Figure 2, $M_0 = [0, 2, 0, 1, 1, 0]$ and the following transitions can be fired starting from M_0:

- t_2, which leads to marking $M_1^1 = [0, 1, 1, 1, 1, 0]$
- t_6, which leads to marking $M_2^1 = [0, 2, 0, 1, 1, 1]$.

In this case, level 1 of the reachability tree includes two nodes. The next level, level 2, of the reachability tree is obtained by firing all the transitions enabled by M_1^1 and by M_2^1.

Starting from M_1^1, it is possible to fire:

- t_2, which leads to marking $M_1^1 = [0, 0, 2, 1, 1, 0]$
- t_6, which leads to marking $M_2^1 = [0, 1, 1, 1, 1, 1]$.

Starting from M_2^1, it is possible to fire:

- t_2, which leads to marking $M_3^2 = [0, 1, 1, 1, 1, 1]$
- t_5, which leads to marking $M_4^2 = [0, 1, 1, 2, 1, 0]$
- t_6, which leads to marking $M_5^2 = [0, 2, 0, 1, 1, 2]$.

The first three levels of the reachability tree of the Petri net represented in Figure 2 are given in Figure 3.

We obtain the nodes at level 3 by firing all the transitions enabled by the marking which are the nodes at level 2, and so on. When no transition is enabled by a marking, no further node is derived from the node corresponding to the marking. If the markings corresponding to different nodes are the same, we merge these nodes. It is easy to understand that a reachability tree may have an infinite number of levels, and thus an infinite number of nodes. It is the case for the Petri net introduced in Figure 2 since transition t_6 can be fired as many times as we want. As a consequence, the reachability tree is not an efficient tool to analyse the dynamics of most of the Petri nets.

To limit the size of the tree (at the expense of the information provided by the tree), the following decisions were made:

(i) a node is marked "old" if the corresponding marking was already found at another level of the tree, i.e. we do not fire a transition from the corresponding marking anymore,

(ii) if a marking $\tilde{M}$ reached at a given level is such that there exits a marking M corresponding to a node located on the path joining the root to the node corresponding to $\tilde{M}$ which verifies:

- $\tilde{M}(p) \geq M(p), \forall p \in P$
- $\tilde{M}(p*) > M(p*)$, for at least one $p* \in P$

then the marking of $p*$ is denoted by ω, where ω stands for infinity. As a consequence, the marking of $p*$ will remain ω in all the markings derived from $\tilde{M}$, and rule (i) also applies to these markings.

- A node is marked "dead-end" if the corresponding marking does not enable any transition: such a node is a leaf of the tree.
- A node which is neither "dead-end" nor "old" is marked "new". Only the "new" nodes produce nodes at the next level.

The tree obtained by applying the previous rules is called coverability tree. A coverability tree contains less information than a reachability tree, but always remains limited in size. The following conclusions can be drawn from a coverability tree:

- if none of the markings corresponding to the nodes of a coverability tree contains ω, then $R(M_0)$, set of markings reachable from M_0, is finite
- the coverability tree provides the transitions which are never enabled
- when the Petri net under consideration is bounded, the reachability tree provides the same information as the coverability tree.

The algorithm used to obtain the coverability tree is given hereafter.

Coverability tree algorithm

1. Initialisation: one node, reprocessing the initial marking M_0, is assigned to level 0. Let X_0 be this node.
2. For each and every node $\tilde{X}$ marked "new":
   (a) If there exists a node X on the path joining X_0 to $\tilde{X}$ such that the marking corresponding to X is the same as the marking corresponding to $\tilde{X}$, then mark $\tilde{X}$ with "old". $\tilde{X}$ is a leave of the tree.
   (b) If none of the transitions is enabled by the marking corresponding to $\tilde{X}$, then mark $\tilde{X}$ with "dead-end". $\tilde{X}$ is a leave of the tree.
   (c) If at least one transition is enabled by the marking $\tilde{M}$ corresponding to $\tilde{X}$ then, for each enabled transition t:
      i. Compute $\tilde{M}_1$ derived from $\tilde{M}$ by firing t. Let $\tilde{X}_1$ be the node corresponding to $\tilde{M}_1$.
      ii. If, on the path joining X_0 to $\tilde{X}_1$, there exists a node X the marking of which is M and such that $\tilde{M}_1(p) \geq M(p), \forall p \in P$ and $\tilde{M}_1(p) > M(p)$, for at least one $p \in P$, then set $\tilde{M}_1(p) = \omega$ for any p such that $\tilde{M}_1(p) > M(p)$.
      iii. Introduce $\tilde{X}_1$ in the tree, as well as arc $(\tilde{X}, \tilde{X}_1)$, and mark this arc with t.
      iv. If there exists another node of the tree the marking of which is $\tilde{M}_1$, then mark $\tilde{X}_1$ with "old", otherwise, mark $\tilde{X}_1$ with "new".
   (d) Go to 2.

4 Incidence Matrix and State Equation

Let $P = (p_1, p_2, \ldots, p_n)$ (resp. $T = (t_1, t_2, \ldots, t_q)$) be the set of places (resp. transitions) of a Petri net. The incidence matrix of this Petri net is a matrix $A = [a_{ij}], i = 1, \ldots, n; j = 1, \ldots, q$ defined as follows:

$$a_{ij} = \begin{cases} W(t_j, p_i) & \text{if } t_j \in {}^\circ p_i \\ -W(p_i, t_j) & \text{if } t_j \in p_i^\circ \\ 0 & \text{otherwise} \end{cases}$$

where W is the weight function attached to the arcs.

Example 4.1 *We consider the Petri net given in Figure 1. Its incidence matrix is:*

$$A = \begin{bmatrix} 0 & -2 & 0 & 0 & 0 \\ 0 & 4 & -3 & 0 & 0 \\ 0 & 1 & 0 & -2 & -1 \\ 0 & 0 & 0 & 1 & 0 \\ 1 & 0 & 0 & 0 & -4 \end{bmatrix}$$

Note 4.1 *An incidence matrix concerns only pure nets, i.e. nets without self-loop since, if (p_i, t_j) would be a self-loop, a_{ij} should equal simultaneously -1 and $+1$, which is impossible.*

Let us consider an initial marking M_0 of a Petri net, and let σ be a firable sequence of transitions which applies to M_0. The counting vector V_σ of σ is the vector:

$V_\sigma = [v_1, v_2, \ldots, v_q]$ where v_j is the number of times t_j is included in σ.

If M is the marking obtained by firing σ, then:

$$M^t = M_0^t + AV_\sigma^t \tag{1}$$

where t denotes the transpose and A the incidence matrix.

Note 4.2

1. *Relation 1 is the state equation of the Petri net.*
2. *The counting vector V_σ remains unchanged when transitions permute in sequence σ, but a firable sequence σ may become non-firable by permuting its transition. Thus the state equation applies only if we know that σ is firable: it helps us to compute the new marking M when we know the initial marking and the fact that σ is firable.*

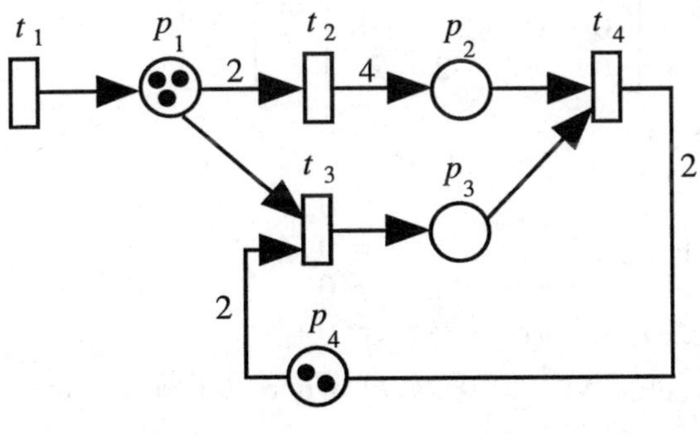

Figure 4: A marked Petri net

Example 4.2 *Let us consider the net represented in Figure 4. The initial marking is* $M_0 = [3, 0, 0, 2]$ *and the incidence matrix is:*

$$A = \begin{bmatrix} 1 & -2 & -1 & 0 \\ 0 & 4 & 0 & -1 \\ 0 & 0 & 1 & -1 \\ 0 & 0 & -2 & 2 \end{bmatrix}$$

Consider the firing sequence $\sigma =< t_2, t_3, t_4 >$. *The corresponding counting vector is* $V_\sigma = [0, 1, 1, 1]$. *It is easy to check that* σ *is firable. Thus, firing* σ *leads to marking* M *which can be computed using state equation 1:*

$$M^t = \begin{bmatrix} 3 \\ 0 \\ 0 \\ 2 \end{bmatrix} + \begin{bmatrix} 1 & -2 & -1 & 0 \\ 0 & 4 & 0 & -1 \\ 0 & 0 & 1 & -1 \\ 0 & 0 & -2 & 2 \end{bmatrix} \begin{bmatrix} 0 \\ 1 \\ 1 \\ 1 \end{bmatrix} = \begin{bmatrix} 3 \\ 0 \\ 0 \\ 2 \end{bmatrix} + \begin{bmatrix} -3 \\ 3 \\ 0 \\ 0 \end{bmatrix} = \begin{bmatrix} 0 \\ 3 \\ 0 \\ 2 \end{bmatrix}$$

Note that $\sigma_1 =< t_4, t_2, t_3 >$, *which is not firable, has the same counting vector as* σ, *and thus would lead to the same making* M *when applying the state equation.*

5 p-Invariants and t-Invariants

5.1 p-Invariants

A vector $X = [x_1, \dots, x_n]$ with non-negative integer components is a p-invariant if $XA = 0$, where A is the incidence matrix of the Petri net (with n rows and q columns) under consideration. For instance, a p-invariant of the Petri net represented in Figure 3 is such that:

$$[x_1, x_2, x_3, x_4] \begin{bmatrix} 1 & -2 & -1 & 0 \\ 0 & 4 & 0 & -1 \\ 0 & 0 & 1 & -1 \\ 0 & 0 & -2 & 2 \end{bmatrix} = \begin{bmatrix} 0 \\ 0 \\ 0 \\ 0 \end{bmatrix}$$

which leads to:

$$\begin{cases} x_1 & & & & = 0 \\ -2x_1 & +4x_2 & & & = 0 \\ -x_1 & & +x_3 & -2x_4 & = 0 \\ & -x_2 & -x_3 & +2x_4 & = 0 \end{cases}$$

Thus any vector $X = [0, 0, 2k, k]$, where k is a non-negative integer, is a p-invariant.

Theorem 5.1 *If* X *is a p-invariant and* M_0 *the initial marking of a Petri net, then* $XM_0^t = XM^t$ *for any* M *reachable from* M_0, *i.e. for any* $M \in R(M_0)$.

For instance, in the previous example:

$$2M(p_3) + M(p_4)$$

is constant whatever M reachable from $M_0 = [3, 0, 0, 2]$.

Definition 5.1 *The set of places which correspond to the strictly positive components of a p-invariant X is called support of X and denoted by $|X|$.*

Definition 5.2 *The support $|X|$ of a p-invariant X is minimal if, whatever the support $|X_1|$ of a p-invariant X_1, $|X| \not\supset |X_1|$, where $\not\supset$ stands for "does not contain".*

Definition 5.3 *A p-invariant X is minimal if there does not exist another p-invariant the components of which are less than or equal to the corresponding components of X.*

Theorem 5.2 *Any p-invariant is a linear combination of minimal p-invariants.*

In the previous example, we have only one minimal p-invariant which is $X^* = [0, 0, 2, 1]$. Thus, any p-invariant X can be written as $X = kX^*$, where k is a positive integer number.

Important properties:

(i) If a p-invariant X of a Petri net is such that all its components are strictly positive, then the Petri net is bounded, i.e. for any place $p \in P$ there exists a positive integer k_p such that $M(p) \leq k_p$ whatever $M \in R(M_0)$.

(ii) If all the components of a p-invariant X of a Petri net are equal to one, then the total number of tokens in the net remains constant for any $M \in R(M_0)$.

5.2 t-Invariants

A vector $Y = [y_1, \cdots, y_q]$ with non-negative integer components is a t-invariant if $AY^t = 0$, where A is the incidence matrix of the Petri net (with n places and q columns) under consideration. For instance, a t-invariant of the Petri net represented in Figure 3 is such that:

$$\begin{bmatrix} 1 & -2 & -1 & 0 \\ 0 & 4 & 0 & -1 \\ 0 & 0 & 1 & -1 \\ 0 & 0 & -2 & 2 \end{bmatrix} [y_1, y_2, y_3, y_4] = \begin{bmatrix} 0 \\ 0 \\ 0 \\ 0 \end{bmatrix}$$

which leads to the system:

$$\begin{cases} y_1 & -2y_2 & -y_3 & & = 0 \\ & 4y_2 & & -y_4 & = 0 \\ & & y_3 & y_4 & = 0 \\ & & -2y_3 & +2y_4 & = 0 \end{cases}$$

Thus: $y_3 = y_4 = 4y_2$, $y_1 = 6y_2$

A t-invariant of this Petri net is $Y = [6, 1, 4, 4]$. Also, any vector $Y = [6k, k, 4k, 4k] = k[6, 1, 4, 4]$, where k is a non-negative integer, is a t-invariant.

Theorem 5.3 *Let σ be a firable sequence and V_σ be the counting vector of σ. Let $M \in R(M_0)$ be the marking reached by firing σ. If V_σ is a t-invariant, then $M = M_0$.*

For instance, let us consider the firing sequence:
$\sigma =< t_1, t_1, t_1, t_1, t_1, t_1, t_3, t_2, t_4, t_3, t_4, t_3, t_4, t_3, t_4 >$, the counting vector of which is $V_\sigma = [6, 1, 4, 4]$. It is easy to verify that σ is firable and that we come back to M_0 after firing σ.

Definition 5.4 *The set of transitions which correspond to the strictly positive components of a t-invariant Y is called support of Y and is denoted by $|Y|$.*

Definition 5.5 *The support $|Y|$ of a t-invariant Y is minimal if, whatever the support $|Y_1|$of a t-invariant Y_1, $|Y| \not\supset |Y_1|$, where $\not\supset$ stands for "does not contain".*

Definition 5.6 *A t-invariant Y is minimal if there does not exist another t-invariant the components of which are less than or equal to the corresponding components of Y.*

Theorem 5.4 *Any t-invariant is a linear combination of minimal t-invariants.*

Since we have only one minimal t-invariant in the previous example, that is $Y^* = [6, 1, 4, 4]$, then any t-invariant Y can be written as $Y = kY^*$, k being a positive integer number.

Property 5.1 *If, in all the minimal t-invariants of a Petri net, the same component is equal to 0, then it is impossible to come back to the initial marking after firing the transition corresponding to this component.*

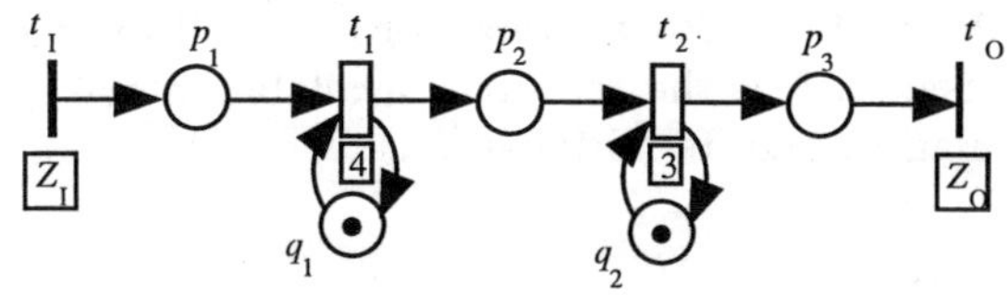

Figure 5: A flow-shop

6 Timed Petri Nets

Two types of timing are used by the researchers working in the Petri net field that is timing of places and timing of transitions. A time associated with a place represents the minimal time a token should remain in this place after its arrival as a result of a firing. In the following of this contribution, we associate times with transitions since, usually, transitions represent operations while places represent buffers.

Let us assume that a time θ is associated with a transition t, and that t is enabled. Firing t at time μ consists in:

- removing $W(p,t)$ tokens from each $p \in {}^{\circ}t$ at time μ
- adding $W(t,p)$ tokens to each $p \in t^{\circ}$ at time $\mu + \theta$.

In the time interval $(\mu, \mu+\theta)$, tokens disappear in the transition: This models the fact that an operation is performed on the components represented by the tokens arriving from the input places of t. The result of this operation is represented by the tokens arriving in the output places of t. Note that the time assigned to a transition may be deterministic or stochastic depending on the kind of operation considered. To illustrate this concept, we present in Figure 5 the model of two machines M_1 and M_2 working in series to manufacture one type of product.

t_1 (resp. t_2) represents the operation performed by M_1 (resp. M_2). The self-loops (q_1, t_1) and (q_2, t_2) are introduced to prevent t_1 and t_2 to be fired more than once at a time, since a machine performs at most one operation at a time. The framed integer numbers are the manufacturing times. The framed variables represent random variables. Z_I is the random variable the values of which represent the time intervals between consecutive arrivals of raw material. Z_0 is the random variable the values of which represent the time intervals between consecutive demands. p_1 (resp. p_2) represent the buffer at the entrance of M_1 (resp. M_2), and p_3 represent the inventory of finished products.

7 Qualitative Properties

In this section, we restrict ourselves to the behavioural properties, which depend on both the structure of the Petri net and the initial marking. In terms of applications, behavioural properties depend on the layout of the system under consideration, the resources available in the system, the way the system is managed, and its initial state.

7.1 Reachability

When studying the dynamics of a Petri net the initial marking of which is M_0, it is often useful to decide if a marking M can be reached from M_0 (i.e. whether $M \in R(M_0)$, or if it cannot be reached from M_0 (i.e. whether $M \notin R(M_0)$). This kind of problem is referred to as reachability problem.

The reachability tree introduced in Section 3 provides the set of reachable markings. Unfortunately, its size may be infinite, except if the Petri net under consideration is bounded, i.e. if the number of tokens in each place is bounded.
The most useful information about reachability is summarised in the following theorems, where M_0 is the initial marking.

Theorem 7.1 *If a Petri net is bounded, then $M \in R(M_0)$ if and only if the reachability tree contains a node marked with M. If a Petri net is unbounded, we have to use the coverability tree, and it is impossible to verify whether $M \in R(M_0)$. It is only possible to verify whether there exists $M^* \in R(M_0)$ such that $M \leq M^*$.*

A more powerful theorem exists in the case of acyclic Petri nets, i.e. Petri nets without cycles.

Theorem 7.2 *For an acyclic Petri net, $M \in R(M_0)$ if and only if the following equation has at least one solution:*

$$M^t = M_0^t + AX^t$$

where A is the incidence matrix, M_0 is the initial marking and the components of the solution vector X are non negative integer numbers.
Furthermore, for each solution X, there exists a firing sequence σ such that:

$$M_0 \xrightarrow{\sigma} M, \text{ and } V_\sigma = X$$

where V_σ is the counting vector of σ.

7.2 Boundedness

A place of a Petri net is bounded if the number of tokens in this place never exceeds an integer value k. Such a Petri net is said to be k-bounded. A Petri net is bounded if all its places are bounded.

Theorem 7.3 *A Petri net is bounded if and only if the markings of the nodes of the coverability tree do not contain the symbol* ω. *The Petri net is k-bounded if and only if the elements of the markings of the nodes never exceed* k. *A Petri net is said to be safe if it is 1-bounded.*

A sufficient (but not necessary) condition for a Petri net to be k-bounded is given by Theorem 7.4.

Theorem 7.4 *A Petri net is bounded if there exists a positive integer k such that, for any vector X the components of which are non-negative integer , the marking M which verifies:*

$$M^t = M_0^t + AX^t$$

is such that $M(p) \leq k, \forall p \in P$.

A is the incidence matrix and M_0 is the initial marking. Note that a marking M obtained as expressed in Theorem 7.4 may be not reachable.

7.3 Liveness and Deadlock

The liveness guarantees that the system the model of which is the Petri net at hand never blocks. It is easy to understand that liveness is of great importance for dynamic systems.

Formally, a transition t is said to be alive if, $\forall M \in R(M_0), \exists M^* \in R(M)$ such that t is enabled for M^*. In other words, whatever the marking M which has been reached from the initial marking M_0, it is always possible to reach a marking M^* from M such that t is enabled for M^*. A Petri net is said to be alive if all its transitions are alive.

A marking $M \in R(M_0)$ is deadlock if none of the transitions of the Petri net is enabled for M. A Petri net is deadlock free if, whatever $M \in R(M_0)$, M is not deadlock.

Theorem 7.5 encapsulates most of the properties related to liveness and deadlock for bounded Petri net. Remember that nodes corresponding to the same marking are merged in a reachability tree.

Theorem 7.5

1. *A bounded Petri net is alive if its reachability tree is such that, from any node, it is possible to find a directed path which contains an arc marked with* $t \in T$, *whatever transition* t.
2. *A bounded Petri net is deadlock free if it does not contain leaves.*

Theorem 7.6 concerns unbounded Petri nets.

Theorem 7.6

1. *Assuming that the nodes corresponding to the same marking are merged in a coverability tree, the first part of Theorem 7.5 holds for unbounded Petri nets by replacing "reachability tree" by "coverability tree".*

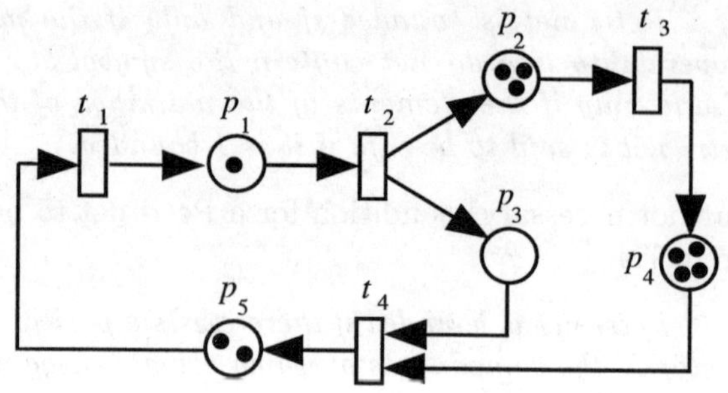

Figure 6: An event graph

2. *Similarly, the second part of Theorem 7.5 holds for unbounded Petri nets by replacing "reachability tree" by "coverability tree".*

7.4 Reversibility and Home State

A Petri net is reversible if $M_0 \in R(M)$ whatever $M \in R(M_0)$. In other words, a Petri net is reversible if it is possible to come back to the initial marking whatever the marking derived from the initial marking by firing a sequence of transitions. A marking M^* is a home state if $M^* \in R(M)$ whatever $M \in R(M_0)$. Theorems 7.7 and 7.8 summarise the conditions to be fulfilled by a Petri net to be reversible or have a home state.

Theorem 7.7 *If a Petri net is bounded:*

1. *it is reversible if and only if its reachability tree is strongly connected*

2. *it has a home state if and only if its reachability trcc has onc and only one strongly connected component without an outgoing arc.*

Theorem 7.8 *If a Petri net has a home state, its coverability tree has one and only one strongly connected component without an outgoing arc.*

8 Event Graphs

8.1 General Properties

An event graph is an elementary Petri net in which the arcs are weighted to one and each place has exactly one input transition and one output transition. Figure 6 presents an event graph the marking of which is $M_0 = [1, 3, 0, 4, 2]$.

The following theorems are of the utmost importance from a practical point of view.

Theorem 8.1 *The number of tokens in an elementary circuit of an event graph is invariant by any sequence of transitions firing. Another way to express the same property is to say that* $X = [x_1, x_2, \ldots, x_n]$ *is a p-invariant if:*

$$x_i = \begin{cases} 1 & \textit{if } p_i \in \gamma \\ 0 & \textit{otherwise} \end{cases}$$

where γ *is an elementary circuit and* n *is the number of places.*

Theorem 8.2 *The vector* $Y = [y_1, y_2, \ldots, y_q]$ *the components of which are all equal to 1 is the unique t-invariant of an event graph having* q *transitions. Another way to express the same property is to say that we come back to the same marking after firing exactly once each of the* q *transitions.*

Theorem 8.3 *An event graph is deadlock free and alive if and only if each elementary circuit contains at least one token.*

For instance, if we assign the initial marking $M_0 = [0, 3, 0, 4, 0]$ to the event graph presented in Figure 6, then the event graph is neither deadlock free nor alive since the elementary circuit $\gamma =< t_1, p_1, t_2, p_3, t_4, p_5 >$ does not contain tokens.

8.2 Deterministic Event Graphs

We call "deterministic event graph" a timed event graph in which times are deterministic. Let γ be an elementary circuit in such a Petri net, $\mu(\gamma)$ the sum of the firing times assigned to the transitions of γ and $M(\gamma)$ the number of tokens in γ. Then $C(\gamma) = \mu(\gamma)/M(\gamma)$ is the cycle time of γ. Since, according to Theorem 6, $M(\gamma)$ is invariant, $C(\gamma)$ is also invariant. In a strongly connected event graph, the quantity $C^* = \max_{\gamma \in \Gamma} C(\gamma)$, where Γ is the set of elementary circuits, is the cycle time of the event graphs. An elementary circuit $\gamma \in \Gamma$ such that $C(\gamma) = C^*$ is called a critical circuit.

Theorem 8.4 *Assuming that a transition fires as soon as it is enabled, the quantity* $1/C^*$ *is the throughput rate of tokens at any point of the event graph. As a consequence, if we want to increase the speed at which tokens evolve in the system, we should add tokens in the critical circuit.*

9 Conclusion

In the previous sections, we provided the basics of Petri nets which are required to model and evaluate DES. Petri nets are particularly convenient to analyse manufacturing systems and information networks since their qualitative properties perfectly reflect the desirable properties of these systems. As a consequence, the analysis of such a system can be decomposed into qualitative analysis, which results in defining if this system is well designed or not, and quantitative analysis, which concerns the management of the system and its evaluation. Event graphs have been introduced since they are very convenient when cyclic systems are concerned.

References

[DHPSV93] DiCesare, F., Harhalakis, G., Proth, J.-M., Silva, M., Vernadat, F., Practice of Petri Nets in Manufacturing, Chapman and Hall, London, UK, 1993

[HP92] Hillion, H. P., Proth, J. M., Mathematical Tools in Production Management, Plenum, Paris, France, 1992

[Pet62] Petri, C. A., Kommunikation mit Automaten, Bonn, Institut für Instrumentelle Mathematik, Schriften des IIM 3, 1962

[Pet81] Peterson, J.L., Petri Nets Theory and Modeling of Systems, Prentice Hall, Englewood Cliffs, NJ, USA, 1981

[PX96] Proth, J.-M., Xie, X.-L., Petri Nets: A Tool for Design and Management of Manufacturing Systems, John Wiley and Sons, Chichester, UK, 1996

[Ram74] Ramchandani, C., Analysis of Asynchronous Concurrent Systems by Timed Petri Nets, Technical Report 120, Project MAC, M.I.T., Cambridge, MA, USA, 1974

CHAPTER 7

State Transition Diagrams

Jules Desharnais, Marc Frappier, Ali Mili

State transition diagrams are a graphic notation that has long been used to represent computing systems. Two basic models of state transition diagrams were introduced simultaneously by G.H. Mealy and E.F. Moore in the mid fifties, and have played a major role in hardware design for a long time. These basic models have been expanded significantly in the recent past to include such features as the ability to represent hierarchy, timing and communication, and have been used to model complex software systems. In this contribution, we discuss the original models of state transition diagrams, their semantic definition and their extensions; then we discuss current application domains and support tools.

1 Introduction

Graphs and graphic notations play a prominent role in the representation and analysis of software specifications and software designs: From data flow diagrams, to entity-relation diagrams, to modular structure diagrams, to Petri Nets, the range of application of graphs is very wide, as it varies with how nodes and arrows are interpreted, and how they are annotated. The purpose of this section is to give a characterization of state transition diagrams; our characterization attempts to be specific enough to exclude all other graphic notations, yet general enough to include all the notations that are typically considered as such diagrams. Basically, a state transition diagram is a graph whose nodes represent states of a system and whose arrows represent transitions between states.

The literature about state transition diagrams is abundant. We have chosen to restrict our presentation to the initial models of state transition diagrams, and to present some of their successors which have retained the attention of both researchers and practitioners. Our presentation starts with the models of Mealy and Moore, who have first studied several fundamental aspects of finite state machines. We then present two extensions which were proposed to deal with more complex concurrent systems using a graphical representation. Finally, we present a brief overview of the integration of state transition diagrams in the practice of software engineering.

2 The Basic Model

In two seminal papers [Mea55, Moo56], Mealy and Moore laid the foundations of finite automata theory. Moore's paper is concerned with the concept of *experimentation* with a finite machine (or finite automaton), that is, with the conclusions that can be drawn about the internal state of such a machine from external experiments. An external experiment consists in the observation of the outputs of the machine after sending it some inputs. Moore proves numerous theorems about the equivalence and the reduction of machines; these theorems have become standard material in textbooks on automata theory (e.g., [DDQ78]). Mealy applied Moore's concepts to the synthesis and reduction of digital circuits (even though [Mea55] was published before [Moo56], Mealy knew about [Moo56]). The finite machines Mealy used were a variant of Moore's machines. Because they suit our purpose better, we introduce them first and present Moore's as a variant.

Definition 2.1 *A* Mealy machine *(or* Mealy automaton*) [DDQ78, Mea55] is a six-tuple*

$$(S, I, O, \delta, \gamma, s_0),$$

where

S *is a finite set of states,*
I *is a finite input alphabet,*
O *is a finite output alphabet,*
$\delta : S \times I \to S$ *is the state transition function,*
$\gamma : S \times I \to O$ *is the output function and*
$s_0 \in S$ *is the initial state.*

Thus, the δ function prescribes what the new state of the machine is after receiving an input and the γ function prescribes what the output is.

As a simple example, consider the state transition diagram of Figure 1. It represents a Mealy machine modeling the behavior of a bounded stack with at most two elements taken from the set $\{a, b\}$. There are seven states (the nodes), labeled with the contents of the stack (ϵ denotes the empty stack). The short arrow indicates that ϵ is the initial state. The input alphabet is $\{\mathsf{push}_a, \mathsf{push}_b, \mathsf{pop}, \mathsf{top}\}$, where

- push_a and push_b represent the actions of pushing an a or a b on the stack, respectively,
- pop represents the action of removing the top element from the stack, and

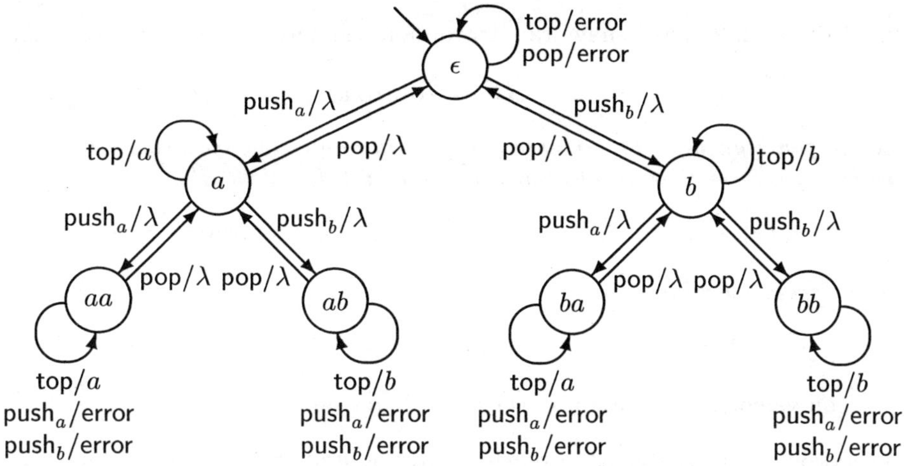

Figure 1: The state transition diagram of a Mealy machine

- top represents the action of returning the top element of the stack.

The output alphabet is $\{a, b, \lambda, \text{error}\}$. The δ and γ functions can be read directly from the diagram: a label x/y, with $x \in I$ and $y \in O$, on a transition from state s to state t corresponds to $\delta(s, x) = t$ and $\gamma(s, x) = y$. Thus, an input push$_b$ in state a results in a transition to state ab and produces an output λ (the symbol λ can be interpreted in a number of ways, including that the output is a *don't-care* value, or a mute message, or the absence of output). Applying the pop and top operations to an empty stack results in an error output; similarly, a push$_a$ or a push$_b$ operation applied to a full stack yields an error output. The loop labeled top/a over state a means that the top operation can be applied repeatedly to the stack containing a as a single element, and that the output of this operation is a.

But what does one define when one draws the state transition diagram of a Mealy machine? A related question is: When do we say that two Mealy machines are equivalent? Once the semantics of Mealy machines is defined, we consider that two machines are (semantically) equivalent if they have the same semantics.

Before giving the definition of semantics, let us introduce the following notations:

τ	the empty sequence,
T^+	the set of non-empty finite sequences of elements of set T,
$T^\star$	the set of finite sequences of elements of set T ($T^\star = T^+ \cup \{\tau\}$).

Concatenation of elements or sequences over T is denoted by juxtaposition.

Definition 2.2 *The* behavioral abstraction *(*semantics*) of a Mealy machine*

$$\Sigma = (S, I, O, \delta, \gamma, s_0)$$

is the function $g_\Sigma : I^+ \to O$ *defined by the following recursive equations, where* $d_\Sigma : I^\star \to S$ *is an auxiliary function,* $x \in I$ *and* $t \in I^\star$*.*

$$d_\Sigma(\tau) = s_0, \qquad d_\Sigma(tx) = \delta(d_\Sigma(t), x), \qquad g_\Sigma(tx) = \gamma(d_\Sigma(t), x).$$

Two Mealy machines

$$\Sigma = (S, I, O, \delta, \gamma, s_0) \text{ and } \Sigma' = (S', I, O, \delta', \gamma', s_0')$$

are equivalent *if and only if* $g_\Sigma(t) = g_{\Sigma'}(t)$ *for all* $t \in I^+$*.*

In words, $d_\Sigma(t)$ is the state reached after submitting the input sequence t to the machine, and $g_\Sigma(t)$ is the last output of the machine. Two machines are equivalent if they have the same last output for the same sequence of inputs. Note that the semantics could also be defined as the following function $g_\Sigma^\star : I^\star \to O^\star$:

$$g_\Sigma^\star(\tau) = \tau, \qquad g_\Sigma^\star(tx) = g_\Sigma^\star(t) g_\Sigma(tx).$$

That is, the semantics is a function from input sequences to output sequences. It is easy to see that $g_\Sigma^\star(t) = g_{\Sigma'}^\star(t)$ for all $t \in I^\star$ if and only if $g_\Sigma(t) = g_{\Sigma'}(t)$ for all $t \in I^+$.

Moore machines are similar to Mealy machines, except that the output function γ is replaced by a function $\gamma' : S \to O$. An output is associated to a state rather than to a transition. Such an output can be viewed as an action to take after reaching a state. Moore machines can be given a semantics similar to that of Mealy machines by defining a function that, when applied to a sequence of inputs, returns the last output (function g_Σ) or the whole sequence of outputs (function $g_\Sigma^\star$) produced by the machine. A Mealy machine Σ and a Moore machine Σ' are *equivalent* (or *similar*) if, for each possible sequence of inputs, the sequence of outputs of Σ' is exactly that of Σ preceded by one arbitrary, but fixed, symbol (the symbol that the Moore machine outputs in its initial state, before any input is submitted to it). It is shown in [DDQ78] that, given a Mealy machine Σ, one can construct a Moore machine Σ' that is similar, and conversely.

3 Extensions to the Basic Model

3.1 Statecharts

When the time comes to use them for the design of large reactive systems, Mealy machines and Moore machines prove to have significant limitations: they provide no natural notion of depth or hierarchy, they are inherently

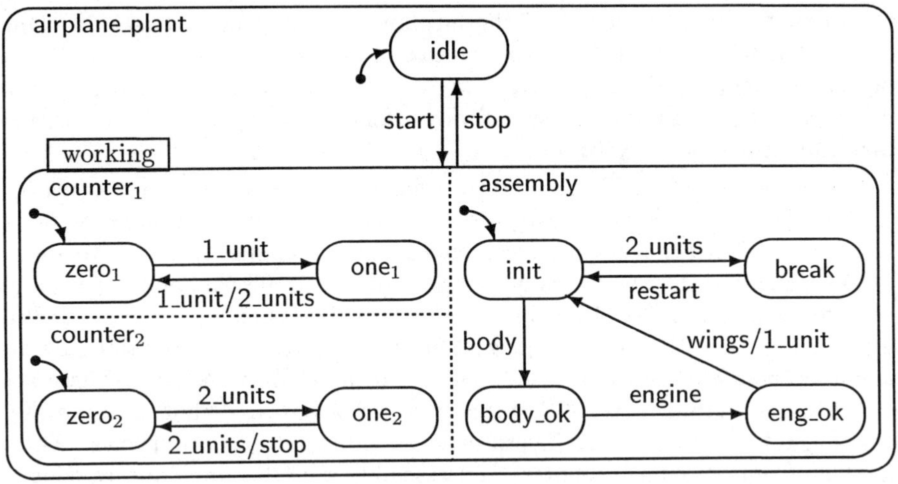

Figure 2: A statechart

sequential in nature and do not cater for concurrency in a natural way, and they are very uneconomical because the number of states needed for the description of a system grows exponentially with a linear increase of the size of the system [Har88].

Statecharts have been designed by Harel [Har87, Har88] to overcome these limitations. Their main features are synthetically described by the formula

$$\begin{aligned} \text{statecharts} &= \text{state transition diagrams} + \text{depth} \\ &\quad + \text{orthogonality} + \text{broadcast communication}. \end{aligned} \tag{2}$$

We will explain and illustrate these features with a grossly simplified example, that of an airplane assembly plant. The informal specification of the module airplane_plant follows; it is done in terms of *events* and *signals*, as is appropriate for the description of a dynamic system. The external signals (inputs) sent to the module are a start signal followed by two sequences of the body, engine and wings signals, in that order. After receiving these signals, the module emits a 2_units signal (output) and waits for a restart signal, followed by two sequences of the body, engine and wings signals, in that order. The module then emits a stop signal and stops. Other output signals may be emitted by the module for synchronization purposes. The statechart of a possible implementation of this specification is given in Figure 2. The decomposition has been chosen for illustration purposes and is not the simplest possible. For instance, two modulo 2 counters are used instead of one modulo 4 counter.

It is not possible to give a short definition of statecharts as we have done for Mealy machines (Def. 2.1), so we will content ourselves with presenting the main features by means of the airplane assembly plant example. One can find a full description of the syntax of statecharts, too lengthy to be presented here, in [HRR92]. Note that the term *statechart* is not a synonym of *state transition diagram*, but specifically refers to the type of state transition diagrams introduced by Harel.

As one can see from Figure 2, a statechart is a set of labeled nodes (states) and labeled arrows (transitions), just like any state transition diagram; however, the organization of these elements is more complex than for Mealy or Moore machines. Conventionally, the label of a node appears on the left hand top corner of the node, either inside, like the label assembly, or appended in a small box, like the label working. Depth (or hierarchy) is obtained by allowing *superstates* containing substates and internal transitions. There are two types of superstates, OR-states and AND-states. What distinguishes them graphically is that AND-states are subdivided by dotted lines. Thus, airplane_plant, $\mathsf{counter}_1$, $\mathsf{counter}_2$ and assembly are OR-states and working is an AND-state. The initial state of a superstate is indicated by a small arrow; for instance, init is the initial state of the assembly superstate (we also say that init is the initial substate of the assembly state).

We now describe informally the semantics of statecharts in an operational manner. Since a state containing substates and transitions can be viewed as a program or a machine, we will sometimes use the expression *execution of a state*, which would be a language misuse if states were unstructured entities.

The execution of a statechart proceeds in discrete time steps. For the moment, assume that the statechart consists only of the assembly node of Figure 2. This node is an OR-state. Its transitions have either the form *event* or *event/signal*. The latter form is just the same as for Mealy machines; the former could be put under the same form by writing it as *event/invisible signal*. An event is a signal that takes no time (so that the body event, for example, may be understood as the end of the assembly of the body of the airplane rather than the assembly itself). The execution of the assembly state consists in following an arrow when the event labeling the arrow occurs. The execution starts from the initial state init. A statechart can be in only one substate of an OR-state. These OR-states correspond to the *state transition diagrams* aspect of Equation 2. The loop body, engine, wings/1_unit depicts the assembly of an airplane from three parts and the emission of the signal 1_unit when done.

The execution of an AND-state consists in executing in parallel the substates of this AND-state. Execution starts with each substate in its initial state. This default behavior can be overridden. For example, the start arrow in Figure 2 could go from the idle node to both the break node and the one_1 node (split arrow); in this case, the execution of the statechart in the working superstate would begin in the combined state (one_1,zero_2,break), zero_2 being used by default.

Table 1 shows the behavior of the statechart of Figure 2 when the external

time	state	external event	internal event
1	idle	start	
2	($zero_1$, $zero_2$, init)	body	
3	($zero_1$, $zero_2$, body_ok)	engine	
4	($zero_1$, $zero_2$, eng_ok)	wings	
	($zero_1$, $zero_2$, init)		1_unit
5	(one_1, $zero_2$, init)	body	
6	(one_1, $zero_2$, body_ok)	engine	
7	(one_1, $zero_2$, eng_ok)	wings	
	(one_1, $zero_2$, init)		1_unit
	($zero_1$, $zero_2$, init)		2_units
8	($zero_1$, one_2, break)	restart	
9	($zero_1$, one_2, init)	body	
10	($zero_1$, one_2, body_ok)	engine	
11	($zero_1$, one_2, eng_ok)	wings	
	($zero_1$, one_2, init)		1_unit
12	(one_1, one_2, init)	body	
13	(one_1, one_2, body_ok)	engine	
14	(one_1, one_2, eng_ok)	wings	
	(one_1, one_2, init)		1_unit
	($zero_1$, one_2, init)		2_units
	($zero_1$, $zero_2$, break)		stop
15	idle		

Table 1: An execution sequence of the airplane_plant statechart

events occur in the order shown. What happens is that after the start signal, the assembly system and the two modulo 2 counters, $counter_1$ and $counter_2$, enter their initial state and start executing. When assembly has received the signals body, engine and wings (note here that signals external to the airplane_plant superstate are visible in the lower levels of the hierarchy), it outputs 1_unit, thus signaling that one airplane is completed.

When $counter_1$ has detected two such signals, it outputs a signal 2_units. This 2_unit signal becomes visible to *all the other nodes*, including nodes outside the airplane_plant node (thus satisfying the requirements concerning this signal); this is the *broadcasting* aspect of Equation 2. Now, all nodes that can react to a given event do so. Thus the signal 2_units increments $counter_2$ and changes the sub-state of assembly to break.

Note how a single signal, here wings (at time 7) provokes a cascade of internal events and transitions. This cascade occurs at the same *micro-instant*, which is indicated in Table 1 by the system being in three different states at the same time. There are other cascades at times 4, 11 and 14. Note how the signal stop emitted by $counter_2$ causes the execution to leave

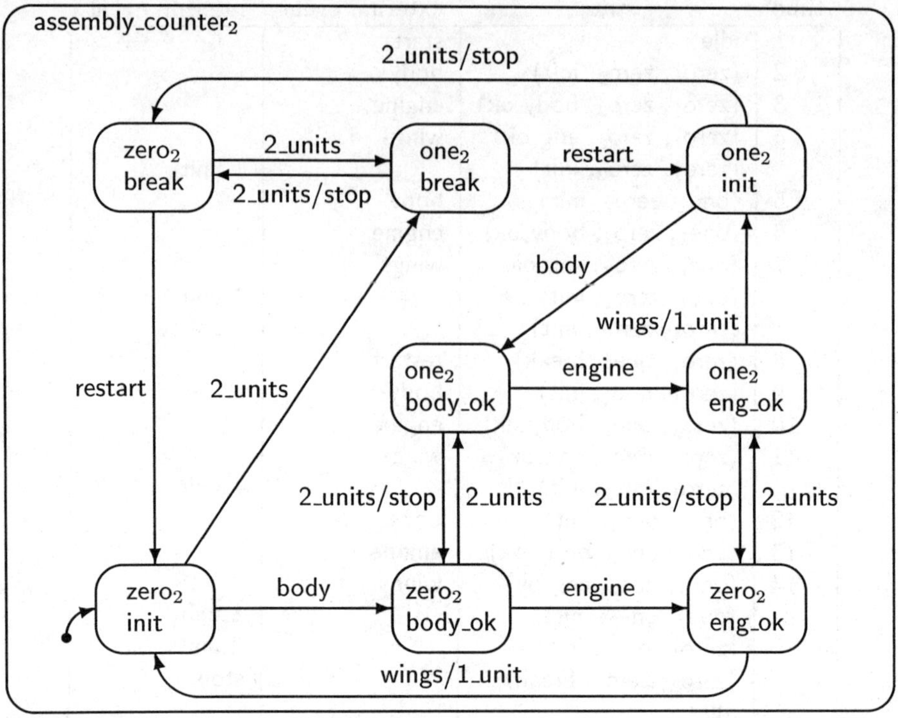

Figure 3: An unorthogonal statechart for counter$_2$ and assembly states

each substate of the working AND-state (because of the arrow labeled stop from the working state to the idle state).

The immediate substates of an AND-state are called *orthogonal* states. Thus, AND-states provide the *orthogonality* aspect of Equation 2. This concept permits a compact description of systems. Removing orthogonality by replacing an AND-state by an equivalent OR-state results in a large increase in the number of nodes (which is the product of the number of states of each substate of the AND-state). For example, an OR-state equivalent to the AND-combination of the two states counter$_2$ and assembly is given in Figure 3. The number of nodes is 8, which is the product of the number of nodes of counter$_2$ and assembly.

Giving a formal semantics to statecharts is not easy, mostly because they have many more features than what we have described here. This has resulted in quite a few variants, which are described in [Bee94]. For material on the semantics of statecharts, we refer the reader to [Bee94, Har87a, HRR92].

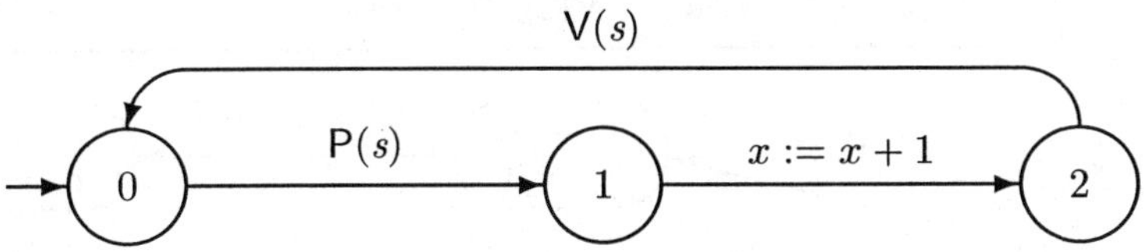

Figure 4: A state transition diagram for the process $\mathcal{P}$

3.2 The Temporal Logic of Actions

Many specification methods are based on a formal language such as predicate logic, temporal logic or the calculus of relations. Whereas these have a very precise semantics, their use for the description of complex systems may lead to formulae that are difficult to understand, thus inhibiting fruitful communications between clients and specifiers. For that reason, it is desirable to have a graphical means to depict some of the properties described by the formulae; moreover, it is desirable that the association between the graphical view and the formula-based view be formal, so that pictures can be used in a precise manner. We present here an example showing how this goal is achieved in the case of the Temporal Logic of Actions (TLA) [Lam94, Lam95].

The example, drawn from [Lam95], uses a *semaphore* to synchronize two concurrent processes. A semaphore is a (programming) variable with value in the set of natural numbers, $\{0, 1, \dots\}$, to which two operations, called P and V, can be applied [Dij68]. Let s be a semaphore. The effect of executing $\mathsf{V}(s)$ is the same as that of executing the assignment $s := s + 1$, except that V is guaranteed to be executed in a single non-interruptible step (an *atomic step*). If $s > 0$, the effect of executing $\mathsf{P}(s)$ is the same as that of executing the assignment $s := s - 1$ atomically. A process $\mathcal{P}$ executing $\mathsf{P}(s)$ when $s = 0$ is blocked until another process executes $\mathsf{V}(s)$, thus incrementing s that can then be decremented by $\mathcal{P}$.

Suppose that x is some critical resource, to be protected from arbitrary access by means of a semaphore s (more precisely, x must be accessed by only one process at a time). To make things simple, assume that a process $\mathcal{P}$ needs to make the assignment $x := x + 1$. Ignoring all operations other than those on x and s, the execution of the process might be represented by the state transition diagram of Figure 4. That is, $\mathcal{P}$ repeatedly loops through the sequence $\mathsf{P}(s); x := x + 1; \mathsf{V}(s)$. Note that if $s = 0$ when the control is in node 0, then $\mathcal{P}$ is blocked and cannot execute $\mathsf{P}(s)$ and access x until $\mathsf{V}(s)$ is executed by another process. Thus, $\mathcal{P}$ requests access to x (the P operation), uses x (the $x := x + 1$ operation) and releases x (the V operation).

In TLA, a *state* is a listing of the values of the relevant variables. For the above process $\mathcal{P}$, these variables are s, x and a *control variable* c indicating the control state (that is, before $\mathsf{P}(s)$, before $x := x + 1$, or before $\mathsf{V}(s)$); we can take $c \in \{0, 1, 2\}$, the set of labels of the nodes of Figure 4.

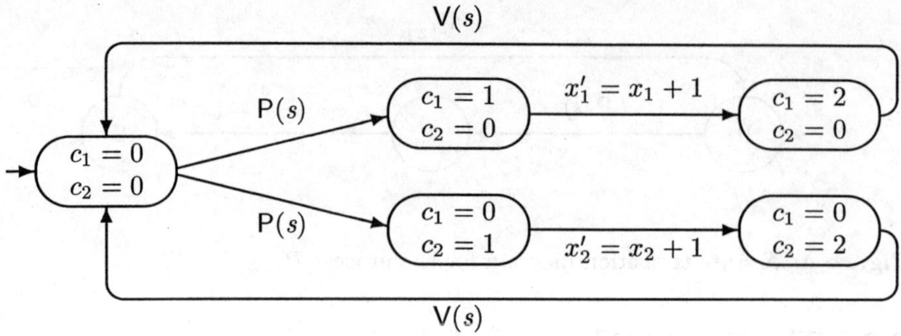

$$
\begin{array}{rcl}
\mathsf{P}(s) & \triangleq & 0 < s \wedge s' = s - 1 \\
\mathsf{V}(s) & \triangleq & s' = s + 1 \\
P_1 & \triangleq & c_1 = 0 \wedge c_2 = 0 \wedge \mathsf{P}(s) \wedge x_1' = x_1 \wedge x_2' = x_2 \wedge c_1' = 1 \wedge c_2' = 0 \\
P_2 & \triangleq & c_1 = 0 \wedge c_2 = 0 \wedge \mathsf{P}(s) \wedge x_1' = x_1 \wedge x_2' = x_2 \wedge c_1' = 0 \wedge c_2' = 1 \\
Q_1 & \triangleq & c_1 = 1 \wedge c_2 = 0 \wedge s' = s \wedge x_1' = x_1 + 1 \wedge x_2' = x_2 \wedge c_1' = 2 \wedge \\
 & & c_2' = 0 \\
Q_2 & \triangleq & c_1 = 0 \wedge c_2 = 1 \wedge s' = s \wedge x_1' = x_1 \wedge x_2' = x_2 + 1 \wedge c_1' = 0 \wedge \\
 & & c_2' = 2 \\
R_1 & \triangleq & c_1 = 2 \wedge c_2 = 0 \wedge \mathsf{V}(s) \wedge x_1' = x_1 \wedge x_2' = x_2 \wedge c_1' = 0 \wedge c_2' = 0 \\
R_2 & \triangleq & c_1 = 0 \wedge c_2 = 2 \wedge \mathsf{V}(s) \wedge x_1' = x_1 \wedge x_2' = x_2 \wedge c_1' = 0 \wedge c_2' = 0 \\
S_1 & \triangleq & P_1 \vee Q_1 \vee R_1 \\
S_2 & \triangleq & P_2 \vee Q_2 \vee R_2 \\
S & \triangleq & S_1 \vee S_2 \\
w & \triangleq & (c_1, c_2, s, x_1, x_2) \\
\Delta & \triangleq & c_1 = 0 \wedge c_2 = 0 \wedge \Box(S \vee w' = w) \\
\mathit{Init} & \triangleq & c_1 = 0 \wedge c_2 = 0 \wedge s = 1 \wedge x_1 = 0 \wedge x_2 = 0 \\
\Psi & \triangleq & \mathit{Init} \wedge \Box(S \vee w' = w) \wedge \mathsf{SF}(\mathcal{P}_1) \wedge \mathsf{SF}(\mathcal{P}_2)
\end{array}
$$

Figure 5: A TLA diagram and specification

Thus, e.g., $c = 0, s = 1, x = 3$ is a state of $\mathcal{P}$; if the order of presentation of the variables (c, s, x) is understood, this state can simply be given as $(0, 1, 3)$. Because $s > 1$, $\mathcal{P}$ can execute the operation $\mathsf{P}(s)$ and change state for the state $c = 1, s = 0, x = 3$. Since a state in TLA is not a vertex in a diagram, we will use the term *node* to refer to vertices in diagrams (while discussing TLA).

We now introduce a TLA formula Ψ specifying a program with two processes $\mathcal{P}_1$ and $\mathcal{P}_2$, similar to the above process $\mathcal{P}$, and running concurrently. Assume that $\mathcal{P}_1$ needs protected access to x_1 in order to increment it, and that $\mathcal{P}_2$ needs protected access to x_2, for the same purpose. Assume also that the synchronization between the two processes must be done using a semaphore s. The specification Ψ is given in Figure 5, with other formulae and a diagram, called a ***predicate-action diagram*** in [Lam95]. We proceed with the explanation of these formulae and diagram.

The variables defining a state of the system are s, x_1, x_2 and two control variables c_1 and c_2, taking their values in the set $\{0, 1, 2\}$; these variables indicate the control state of each process. The diagram of Figure 5 shows how these variables change when the P, V and increment operations are performed. Each node of this diagram is labeled by a predicate over the variables c_1 and c_2 (read the two labels in a node as a conjunction). Note how the predicate $c_1 = 0 \wedge c_2 = 0$, labeling the leftmost node, represents the set of all those states with $c_1 = 0, c_2 = 0$ and s, x_1, x_2 arbitrary. In this example, predicates labeling different nodes are disjoint; the general case is treated in [Lam95]. Each transition is labeled by a predicate defining a relation between the values of the variables before and after the transition. An unprimed variable refers to the value before the transition and a primed variable to the value after. Variables that do not appear in the predicates labeling a transition or the nodes at the origin or destination of this transition are left unchanged (this avoids cluttering the diagram); for example, the transition labeled by $x_1' = x_1 + 1$ leaves x_2 and s unchanged. The fully written predicate corresponding to this transition is

$$Q_1 \triangleq c_1 = 1 \wedge c_2 = 0 \wedge s' = s \wedge x_1' = x_1 + 1 \wedge x_2' = x_2 \wedge c_1' = 2 \wedge c_2' = 0$$

(the symbols $\triangleq$ and $\wedge$ denote equality by definition and conjunction, respectively); this indeed describes the assignment $x_1 := x_1 + 1$. Note how the variables of the destination node are primed (c_1', c_2'). The predicates $P_1, P_2, Q_1, Q_2, R_1, R_2$ of Figure 5 correspond to the six transitions of the diagram given in the same figure (P_1, Q_1, R_1 correspond to process $\mathcal{P}_1$ and P_2, Q_2, R_2 to process $\mathcal{P}_2$). These predicates use auxiliary predicates defining the P and V operations; note how these predicates are much more concise and precise than the informal presentation of the operations given above.

The predicates S_i $(i = 1, 2)$ associated to each process are obtained by taking the disjunction (denoted by $\vee$) of P_i, Q_i and R_i. The predicate $S \triangleq S_1 \vee S_2$ defines the *next step* relation of the diagram (recall that the predicates with primed and unprimed variables relate states before and after a transition). Such relations and diagrams can also be described within a relational, rather than logical, formalism; for instance, they are used in [DKFM97] to give partial descriptions of the interactions between two systems (*scenarios*) and to formalize the integration of such partial descriptions.

Finally, the TLA formula associated to the diagram is

$$\Delta \triangleq c_1 = 0 \wedge c_2 = 0 \wedge \Box(S \vee w' = w).$$

In this formula, $w \triangleq (c_1, c_2, s, x_1, x_2)$ is the list of variables composing a state. The notation $w' = w$ is an abbreviation for

$$c_1' = c_1 \wedge c_2' = c_2 \wedge s' = s \wedge x_1' = x_1 \wedge x_2' = x_2.$$

The symbol $\Box$ is read *always*. To explain the formula of Δ, we need to introduce the notion of *models* of a TLA formula.

The models of a TLA formula are infinite sequences of states $w_0, w_1, w_2, \ldots$ such that w_0 satisfies the formula. The predicate $c_1 = 0 \wedge c_2 = 0$ in Δ specifies that the initial state w_0 must correspond to the initial node of the diagram. The expression $S \vee w' = w$ is true at state w_i if the pair (w_i, w_{i+1}) satisfies the formula $S \vee w' = w$, with the substitution $w \triangleq w_i$ and $w' \triangleq w_{i+1}$. A formula $\Box p$ is true at state w_0 if p is true at state w_0 and at every state that follows it in the sequence. Thus, an infinite sequence that is a model of Δ must be a sequence of states obtainable by starting in a state such that $c_1 = 0 \wedge c_2 = 0$ and taking steps in the diagram of S, with the possibility of repeating a given state (this corresponds to time steps where the system under consideration does not move). Still put differently, a model sequence of Δ is a possible execution of the combination of processes $\mathcal{P}_1$ and $\mathcal{P}_2$, where each process may either take a transition or stay in the same state.

The formula for the specification Ψ is

$$\Psi \triangleq \mathit{Init} \wedge \Box(S \vee w' = w) \wedge \mathsf{SF}(\mathcal{P}_1) \wedge \mathsf{SF}(\mathcal{P}_2).$$

It is similar to Δ, with some additional constraints:

- The predicate *Init* dictates the initial values of s, x_1 and x_2, in addition to those of c_1 and c_2.
- The formula Δ (and the corresponding diagram) allows process $\mathcal{P}_2$ to be stopped forever, with only $\mathcal{P}_1$ executing its loop. To prevent this possibility, the specification Ψ adds the strong fairness conditions $\mathsf{SF}(\mathcal{P}_1)$ and $\mathsf{SF}(\mathcal{P}_2)$, whose explicit formulae we do not present. The condition $\mathsf{SF}(\mathcal{P}_2)$, for instance, says that if $\mathcal{P}_2$ is enabled (can take a transition in the diagram) infinitely often, then it must take a transition infinitely often. Thus, if only $\mathcal{P}_1$ were executing, $\mathcal{P}_2$ would be enabled each time the control passes in the initial node $c_1 = 0 \wedge c_2 = 0$; the fairness condition $\mathsf{SF}(\mathcal{P}_2)$ implies that $\mathcal{P}_2$ would eventually have its turn in the loop. A simple implementation of Ψ could consist in letting $\mathcal{P}_1$ and $\mathcal{P}_2$ execute alternately. The fairness conditions cannot be easily expressed in a diagram and this is why they are left out.

Thus, the diagram and its formula Δ give only a partial view (abstraction) of the whole specification Ψ. One can show (see [Lam95]) that $\Psi \Rightarrow \Delta$.

As a final word, we mention that the diagram given in Figure 5 is only one possible view of Ψ. Depending on the abstraction chosen, other diagrams are possible. Lamport [Lam95] gives another view of the specification Ψ where the nodes of the diagram are labeled by predicates over the semaphore variable s only. Obviously, a diagram of a whole specification may be too complex to be useful, but representing relevant abstractions of a large specification by simple diagrams promotes understanding.

4 Practice of State Transition Diagrams

The use of state transition diagrams has rapidly spread in the software engineering practice in various application domains (e.g., telecommunications, aerospace, defense, transportation, electronics). Several software development approaches (e.g., Unified Modeling Language (UML) [UML97], Real-Time Object-Oriented Modeling (ROOM) [SGW94], Specification and Description Language (SDL) [EHS97]) have adopted state transition diagrams for specifying the behavior of real-time systems or objects. Industrial-strength tools are now supporting the definition of state transition diagrams and the execution of state transition diagrams for validation. Several of these tools use a variant of Harel's statechart notation. In this section, we will provide a brief overview of the integration of state transition diagrams with other elements of these software development approaches and some of the capabilities of these tools.

4.1 Object-Oriented Modeling

Object-oriented approaches to software development use state transition diagrams to illustrate the behavior of objects [Boo94, JCJÖ92, Rum91]. The notation used in these approaches is not formally defined; hence we rely here on the reader's intuition to understand the informal semantics.

The nodes of an object's state transition diagram are arbitrarily chosen by the specifier. As in TLA, we must distinguish between a state (a node) of a state transition diagram and a state of an object. The state of an object is given by the list of values for the object's variables. A node label is a meaningful name representing a *set of object states*. For instance, in the stack example of Figure 6, the node labels are Init, Empty, Loaded and Full.

A perfectly valid state transition diagram for the stack could contain only one node, but it would not be very meaningful for a reader. Node Init is the initial state of the stack, where the values of the object's variables are undefined. Node Loaded represents the case where some elements have been added to the stack; hence, there are several possible values for the object's variables (i.e., several possible object states) when the object is in this node. An extended state transition diagram differs from a Mealy state transition diagram in that the former implicitly contains state variables whereas the latter does not. Variables, which will explicitly appear in the class definition, allow a node in an extended state transition diagram to represent several nodes of a Mealy state transition diagram. For instance, the node Loaded in Figure 6 represents nodes a, b in Figure 1. The node Full in Figure 6 represents nodes aa, ab, ba, bb in Figure 1. The number of nodes in Figure 6 is constant with respect to the number of elements that a stack may contain. In a Mealy stack state transition diagram, the number of nodes grows exponentially with the stack capacity.

An arrow in the graph is labeled with a method name. Optionally, an

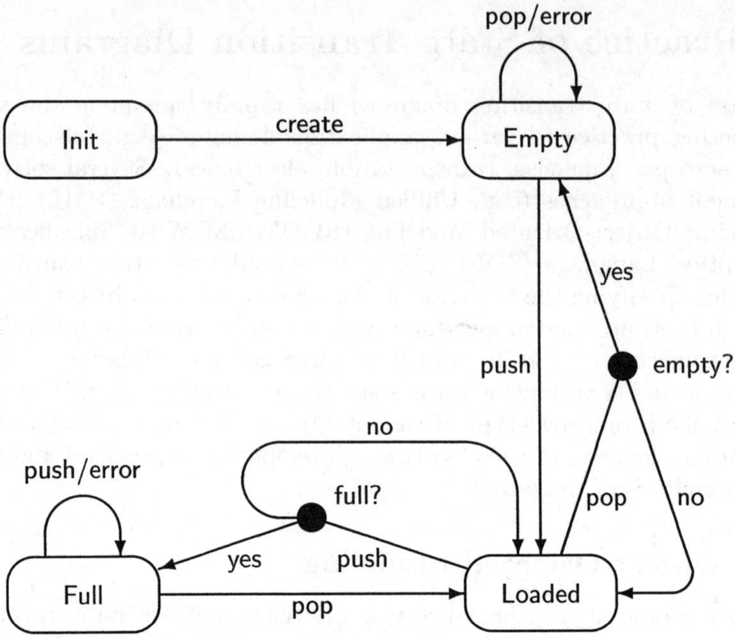

Figure 6: An extended state transition diagram for a stack object

output may be specified on the arrow, separated from the method name by a slash, as in the Mealy notation. The object moves from one node to another when a method of an outgoing arrow is invoked on the object. The end point of an arrow may be a condition with two outgoing arrows. The evaluation of the condition determines which outgoing arrow is selected. The condition usually refers to the object's variables and to the method invocation parameters. The behavior of a method (i.e., the modification to the object's variables and communication with the environment) is usually defined in a separate document (either a class description, a use-case diagram or an interaction diagram [UML97]). The notation used in [JCJÖ92] allows a (partial) definition of the behavior directly on the state transition diagram. In any case, these notations being informal, the designer may write what seems most appropriate to be understood as precisely as possible within the limits of an informal notation. Finally, an object extended state transition diagram may be hierarchically structured if the behavior is too difficult to represent on a single diagram. Figure 7 provides a possible implementation of the stack extended state transition diagram of Figure 6.

```
class Stack
  {   const MaxStack = 1;
      const EmptyStack = -1;
      char  items[MaxStack];
      int   index;

    public:
      Stack();
      void    create();
      status  push(char);
      status  pop();
      boolean empty();
      boolean full();
      char    top();
  };
```

Figure 7: A C++ class for the stack state transition diagram

4.2 Real-Time System Modeling

Several approaches for real-time system modeling have adopted variants of Harel's statecharts for describing the behavior of communicating processes [UML97, SGW94, EHS97]. We may take ROOM [SGW94] as an example, since it restricts Harel's notation to a simple subset and it adopts a more explicit communication mechanism between concurrent states. The notation used in ROOM is object-oriented, in the sense that it allows inheritance for various syntactic categories.

The main syntactic categories of the ROOM notation are actor, port, protocol, state machine and data class. A system is modeled using communicating processes called *actors*. Actors communicate through ports using synchronous and asynchronous message exchange. A protocol is the set of messages that may be sent or received through a port.

An actor is illustrated by two diagrams: a ROOM structure diagram, to define communication links between actors, and a ROOMchart, to define the actor's state transitions. In Figure 8, we present a ROOM structure diagram for the actor AirplanePlant, whose behavior is the same as that of the statechart in Figure 2. In this figure, the outlined little square labeled by externalCom on the outmost rectangle is a port which allows the airplane plant to communicate with its environment. The AirplanePlant actor contains three (component) actors: assembly, counter1 and counter2. These actors also have ports. An arc connecting two actor ports allows these actors to exchange messages. The assembly actor receives the environment messages. When an airplane unit is built, it sends a message to actor counter1 through port oneUnit. When two units are built, actor counter1 sends a message to

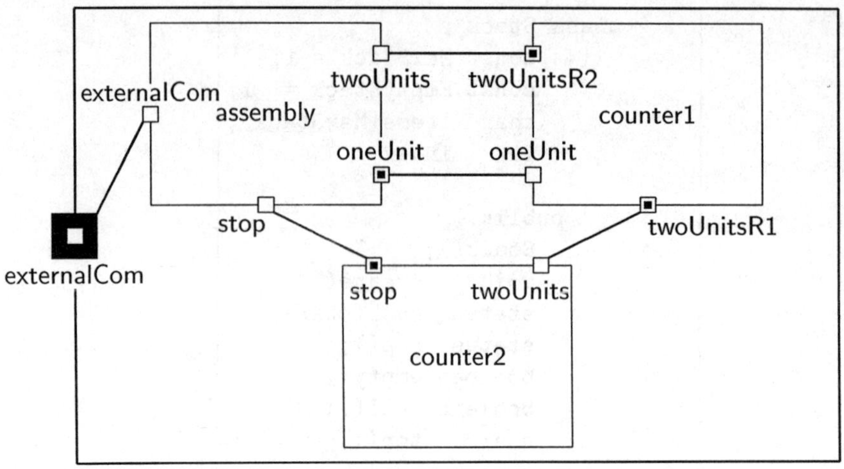

Figure 8: A ROOM actor structure diagram

actors counter2 and assembly through ports twoUnitsR1 and twoUnitsR2, respectively. When four units are built, counter2 sends a message to assembly through port stop. Note that we have represented the AND-state components (the three OR-states) of Figure 2 by three actors, because AND-state components of a statechart execute in parallel.

Figure 9 illustrates the behavior of the assembly actor. It is very similar to the OR-state assembly of Figure 2, except that we have inserted the state idle in order to make the ROOM model simpler. The label of a ROOMchart transition is not the input signal; it is simply a meaningful annotation. The input and output signals are given in the transition definition which is not represented in the diagram. An actor may have variables. They are defined using data classes: a data class is very similar to a class in an object-oriented programming language like SmallTalk. When an actor receives a message in a given node, the transition labeled with this message is triggered. The transition code is then executed: its effect may be to modify the actor's variables or to send messages to other actors through ports. The arrow labeled initialize contains the initialization code that is executed when the actor is started. The ROOMcharts for actors counter1 and counter2 are the same as the OR-states $\mathsf{counter}_1$ and $\mathsf{counter}_2$ of Figure 2.

The main distinguishing characteristics between a ROOMchart and a statechart are the representation of concurrency and the communication mechanism. AND-states are not allowed in ROOMcharts; concurrency is expressed using actors. Events in ROOMcharts are not broadcasted but sent and received between actors through ports. An actor may only modify its own variables.

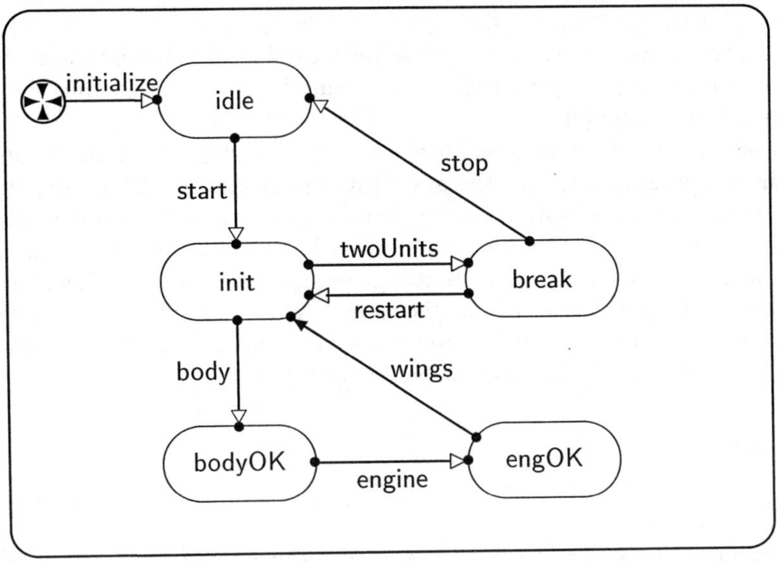

Figure 9: A ROOM actor behavior diagram (ROOMchart)

4.3 Tools

There exist several *verification tools* for state transition systems, such as MEC [Arn89, Arn92], ALDÉBARAN [Fer89] and SPIN [Hol91]. These tools allow one to construct state machines, to apply operations on them and to verify properties (e.g., safety, liveness, reachability, deadlock). When modeling concurrent systems with state diagrams, the number of states grows extremely rapidly; these tools become an absolute necessity.

Several other tools support variants of statecharts (e.g., ObjectGEODE [Verilog], ObjecTime [ObjTim], SDT [Telelog], Statemate [i-Logix]). They provide graphical diagram editors, syntax checkers and simulators for animating state transition diagrams and verifying properties about them.

5 Conclusion

State transition diagrams are now well-established notations in the specification and design of software systems. Software developers used them in various application domains and various system types. The seminal ideas of Moore and Mealy have evolved to mature techniques capable of modeling complex system behaviors in an understandable way. A key strength of state transition diagrams is their evocative graphical representation. Harel contributed to the power of this graphical notation by defining hierarchical state machines and by adding concurrency and communication. Several other contributors have adapted these ideas in different contexts (e.g., hardware design, interface specification, distributed systems, real-time systems, object-oriented modeling).

Paradoxically, the main weakness of state transition diagrams is related to their salient characteristic, the graphical representation. Diagrams require more resources to maintain and adapt than just a plain textual description. It is almost mandatory to use a graphical tool to maintain them. In addition, diagrams are not as compact as textual descriptions. Complex diagrams are decomposed into a hierarchy of diagrams. Thus, the navigation between several levels of diagrams may sometimes be cumbersome. Obviously, it is difficult to achieve a balance between cost, concision and clarity.

Acknowledgments: The authors acknowledge the support of NSERC (Natural Sciences and Engineering Research Council of Canada) and FCAR (Fonds pour la Formation de Chercheurs et l'Aide à la Recherche, Québec).

References

[Arn89] Arnold, A., MEC: a system for constructing and analyzing transition systems, in: J. Sifakis (ed.), Automatic Verification of Finite State Systems, Lecture Notes in Computer Science, Vol. 407, Springer, 1989, 117–132

[Arn92] Arnold, A., Systèmes de Transitions Finis et Sémantique des Processus Communicants, Masson, 1992

[Bee94] Von der Beeck, M., A comparison of statecharts variants. in: H. Langmaack, W.-P. De Roever, J. Vytopil (eds.), Formal Techniques in Real-Time and Fault-Tolerant Systems, Lecture Notes in Computer Science, Vol. 863, Springer, 1994, 128–148

[Boo94] Booch, G., Object-Oriented Analysis and Design with Applications, 2nd edition, Benjamin-Cummings, 1994

[DDQ78] Denning, P. J., Dennis, J. B., Qualitz, J. E., Machines, Languages and Computation, Prentice Hall, 1978

[DKFM97] Desharnais, J., Frappier, M., Khédri, R., Mili, A., Integration of sequential scenarios, in: M. Jazayeri, H. Schauer (eds.), 6th European Software Engineering Conference / 5th ACM SIGSOFT Symposium on the Foundations of Software Engineering, Lect. Notes in Comp. Sci., Vol. 1301, Springer, 1997, 310–326

[Dij68] Dijkstra, E. W., Cooperating sequential processes, in: F. Genuys (ed.), Programming Languages: NATO Advanced Study Institute, Academic Press, 1968, 43–112

[EHS97] Ellsberger, J., Hogrefe, D., Sarma, A., SDL - Formal Object-Oriented Language for Communicating Systems, Prentice Hall, 1997

[Fer89] Fernandez, J., An implementation of an efficient algorithm for bisimulation equivalence, Science of Computer Programming, 13, 1989, 219–236

[Har87] Harel, D., Statecharts: A visual formalism for complex systems, Science of Computer Programming 8, 1987, 231–274

[Har87a] Harel, D., On the formal semantics of statecharts, Proc. 2nd IEEE Symposium on Logic in Computer Science, Ithaca, NY, 1987, 54–64

[Har88] Harel, D., On visual formalisms, Communications of the ACM 31(5), May 1988, 514–530

[Hol91] Holzmann, G. J., Design and Validation of Computer Protocols, Prentice Hall, 1991

[HRR92] Hooman, J. J. M., Ramesh, S., De Roever, W.-P., A compositional axiomatization of statecharts, Theoretical Computer Science 101, 1992, 289–335

[i-Logix] i-Logix Inc. Andover, MA 01810, USA http://www.ilogix.com/

[JCJÖ92] Jacobson, I., Christerson, M., Jonsson, P., Övergaard, G., Object-Oriented Software Engineering: A Use Case Driven Approach, Addison-Wesley, 1992

[Lam94] Lamport, L., The temporal logic of actions, ACM Transactions on Programming Languages and Systems 16, May 1994, 872–923

[Lam95] Lamport, L., TLA in pictures, IEEE Transactions on Software Engineering 21 (9), September 1995, 768–775

[Mea55] Mealy, G. H., A method for synthesising sequential circuits, Bell System Tech. J. 34(5), September 1955, 1045–1079

[MLH86] Mills, H. D., Linger, R. C., Hevner, A. R., Principles of Information Systems Analysis and Design, Academic Press, 1986

[Moo56] Moore, E. F., Gedanken-experiments on sequential machines, Annals of Mathematics Studies, Vol. 34, Automata Studies, Princeton University Press, Princeton, NJ, 1956, 129–153

[ObjTim] ObjecTime Corporation Limited, Kanata, Ontario, Canada, http://www.objectime.on.ca/

[Rum91] Rumbaugh, J., Object-Oriented Modeling and Design, Prentice Hall, 1991

[SGW94] Selic, B., Gullekson, G., Ward, P. T., Real-Time Object-Oriented Modeling, John Wiley & Sons, 1994

[UML97] Rational Software Corporation, Unified Modeling Language for real-time systems design, Santa Clara, CA, USA, 1997, http://www.rational.com/

[Telelog] Telelogic, Malmö, Sweden, http://www.telelogic.se/

[Verilog] VERILOG, Toulouse CEDEX, France, http://www.verilogusa.com/

CHAPTER 8

PIF
The Process Interchange Format

J. Lee, M. Gruninger, Y. Jin, T. Malone, A. Tate, G. Yost

This document describes the rationales and the specification of the Process Interchange Format (PIF). PIF is an interchange format designed to help automatically exchange process descriptions among a wide variety of process tools such as process modelers, workflow software, flow charting tools, planners, process simulation systems, and process repositories. These tools interoperate by translating between their native format and PIF. Then any system will be able to automatically exchange process descriptions with any other system without having to write translators for each pair of such systems. This document specifies the PIF-CORE 1.2, i.e. the core set of object types (such as activities, agents, and prerequisite relations) that can be used to describe the basic elements of any process. The document also describes a framework for extending the core set of object types to include additional information needed in specific applications. These extended descriptions are exchanged in such a way that the common elements are interpretable by any PIF translator and the additional elements are interpretable by any translator that knows about the extensions.

1 Introduction

The needs for sharing process descriptions across heterogeneous representations abound. One may need to build a process model, the pieces of which have to or can come from existing models in multiple representations. One may want to submit that process model to a variety of tools, such as process analyzer or simulator, that uses their own representations. One may then want to reengineer a process model by looking up and plugging in various alternatives for some of its components from a process library that may use yet another representation.

The goal of the Process Interchange Format project is to support sharing process descriptions through a description format called PIF (Process Interchange Format) that provides a bridge across different process representations. Tools interoperate by translating between their native format and PIF.

There are several process representation languages, such as IDEF 0-3 [NIST93a, NIST93b, MME94] and LOTOS [ISO89], which could be potentially used for the purpose of sharing process descriptions. However, most of these languages are originally designed to satisfy a specific set of domain and task needs. PIF differs from them for being a translation language or an interlingua by design. As discussed in Section 3, this difference yields a different set of design tradeoffs. Generality is preferred over efficiency. Extensibility is critical as any process representation language is unlikely to ever completely suit the needs of all applications that make use of business process descriptions. Therefore, in addition to the PIF format, we have defined a framework around PIF that accommodates extensions to the standard PIF description classes. The framework includes a translation scheme called Partially Shared Views that attempts to maximize information sharing among groups that have extended PIF in different ways.

The PIF framework aims to support process translation such that:

- Process descriptions can be automatically translated back and forth between PIF and other process representations with as little loss of meaning as possible. If translation cannot be done fully automatically, the human efforts needed to assist the translation should be minimized.
- If a translator cannot translate part of a PIF process description to its target format, it should:
  - Translate as much of the description as possible (and not, for example, simply issue an error message and give up)
  - Represent any untranslatable parts as such and present them in a way that lets a person understand the problem and complete the translation manually if desired
  - Preserve any uninterpretable parts so that the translator can add them back to the process description when it is translated back into PIF.

These requirements on the translators are very important. We believe that a completely standardized process description format is premature and unrealistic at this point. Therefore, as mentioned earlier, we have provided ways for groups to extend PIF to better meet their individual needs. As a result, we expect that PIF translators will often encounter process descriptions written in PIF variants that they can only partially interpret. Translators must adopt conventions that ensure that items they cannot interpret are available for human inspection and are preserved for later use by other tools that are able to interpret them. Section 6 describes PIF's Partially Shared Views translation scheme, which we believe will greatly increase the degree to which PIF process descriptions can be shared.

In the next section, we provide a brief history behind the PIF project to illustrate our motivation. Section 3 provides the overview of the PIF language itself. Section 4 discusses the rationales underlying the major PIF-CORE constructs. The detail specification of the PIF-CORE 1.2 constructs follow in Section 5. Section 6 discusses the mechanism for extending the PIF-CORE. Section 7 concludes this document with the discussion of the directions in which the project is moving.

2 History and Current Status

The PIF project began in October 1993 as an outgrowth of the Process Handbook project [MCLB93] at MIT and the desire to share process descriptions among a few groups at MIT, Stanford, the University of Toronto, and Digital Equipment Corporation. The Process Handbook project at the MIT Center for Coordination Science aims to create an electronic handbook of process models, their relations, and their tradeoffs. This handbook is designed to help process designers analyze a given process and discover innovative alternatives. The Spark project at Digital Equipment Corporation aims to create a tool for creating, browsing, and searching libraries of business process models. The Virtual Design Team (VDT) project at Stanford University aims to model, simulate, and evaluate process and organization alternatives. The Enterprise Modeling project at the University of Toronto aims to articulate well-defined representations for processes, time, resources, products, quality, and organization. These representations support software tools for modeling various aspects of enterprises in business process reengineering and enterprise integration.

In one way or another, these groups were all concerned with process modeling and design. Furthermore, they stood to benefit from sharing process descriptions across the different representations they used. For example, the Enterprise Modeling group might model an existing enterprise, use the Process Handbook to analyze its tradeoffs and explore its alternatives, evaluate the different alternatives via VDT simulation, and then finally translate the chosen alternative back into its own representation for implementation.

Over the past years, through a number of face-to-face, email, and telephone meetings, the PIF Working Group members have:

- Articulated the requirements for PIF
- Specified the core PIF process description classes
- Specified the PIF syntax
- Elaborated the Partially Shared View mechanism for supporting multiple, partially overlapping class hierarchies
- Created and maintained a database of the issues that arose concerning PIF's design and the rationales for their resolutions

- Implemented several translators, each of which translated example process descriptions (such as a portion of the ISPW-6 Software Change Process) between PIF and a group's own process representation
- Used the translators to port process descriptions across heterogeneous representations (between Kappa PC representation and Lotus Notes representation of process handbook data)

Based on this work, the PIF Document 1.0 was released on December, 1994. Since then, we have received a number of questions and comments on topics that range from individual PIF constructs to how certain process descriptions can be represented in PIF. We have been also assessing the adequacy of the PIF 1.0 by testing it against more complex process descriptions than before. AIAI at the University of Edinburgh also joined the PIF Working Group at this time bringing along their interests in planning, workflow and enterprise process modeling. The Edinburgh group is also providing a valuable service as a liaison between the PIF group and the Workflow Management Coalition as well as the AI planning community (in particular the DARPA/Rome Laboratory Planning Initiative) which has been concerned with the activity representation issues for a while. The Ontology Group at the Stanford University has also joined the PIF Working Group and is sharing the lessons from its experiences in providing the ontology library and the editor.

The revised structure of PIF reflects the lessons extracted from these external and internal input. In particular, two points emerged clearly. One is that the PIF-CORE has to be reduced to the bare minimum to enable translation among those who cannot agree on anything else. The other point is the importance of structuring PIF as a set of modules that build on one another. This way, groups with different expressive needs can share a subset of the modules, rather than the whole monolithic set of constructs. As a result, the PIF-CORE has been reduced to the minimum that is necessary to translate the simplest process descriptions and yet has built-in constructs for "hanging off" modules that extend the core in various ways.

Recently we have been working with other groups whose aim is also to share process descriptions though in their own domains. The goal of the Process Specification Language (PSL) project at NIST is to facilitate process sharing in the domain of manufacturing. It has finished compiling the list of requirements that a process specification language should satisfy and is evaluating the existing process representations with respect to these requirements. We are working with the PSL group in assessing these requirements and comparing the different process representations in the hope that the PSL will be compatible with PIF. The goal of the Workflow Process Description Language (WPDL) is to be an interlingua for sharing workflow descriptions. We have compared the WPDL with PIF, identified similarities and differences, and are communicating with them to make both PIF and WPDL interoperable.

3 PIF Overview

The PIF ontology has grown out of the efforts of the PIF Working Group to share process descriptions among the group members' various tools. We have used the following guidelines in developing this hierarchy:

- Generality is preferred over computational efficiency when there is a tradeoff, for the reason that PIF is an interchange language, not a programming language designed for efficient execution. Therefore, the organization of the entity classes is not necessarily well-suited to performing any particular task such as workflow management or process simulation. Instead, our goal has been to define classes that can express a wide variety of processes, and that can be readily translated into other formats that may be more suitable for a particular application.

- The PIF constructs should be able to express the constructs of some existing common process representations such as IDEF (SADT) or Petri Nets.

- PIF should start with the minimal set of classes and then expand only as it needs to. The minimal set was decided at the first PIF Workshop (October 1993) by examining those constructs common to some major existing process representations and to the process representations used by members of the PIF Working Group.

- Additions to the standard PIF classes could be proposed by anybody, but the proposal had to be accompanied by concrete examples illustrating the need for the additions. The Working Group decided, through discussions and votes if necessary, whether to accept the proposal. PIF allows groups to define local extensions at will (see Section 6), so new classes or attributes should be added to the standard PIF classes only if they seem to be of sufficiently general usefulness.

A PIF process description consists of a set of frame definitions, which are typically contained in a file. Each frame definition refers to an entity instance and is typed (e.g. ACTIVITY, OBJECT, TIMEPOINT) and they form a class hierarchy (see Figure 1). A frame definition has a particular set of attributes defined for it. Each of the attributes describes some aspect of the entity. For example, a PERFORMS definition has an Actor and an Activity attribute that specifies who is performing which activity. The instance of a frame definition has all the attributes of all of its superclasses, in addition to its own attributes. For example, all the instances of ACTIVITY have the Name attribute, since ENTITY, which is a superclass of ACTIVITY, has the Name attribute.

When an attribute of one frame has a value that refers to another frame, the attribute represents a relationship between the two instances that the

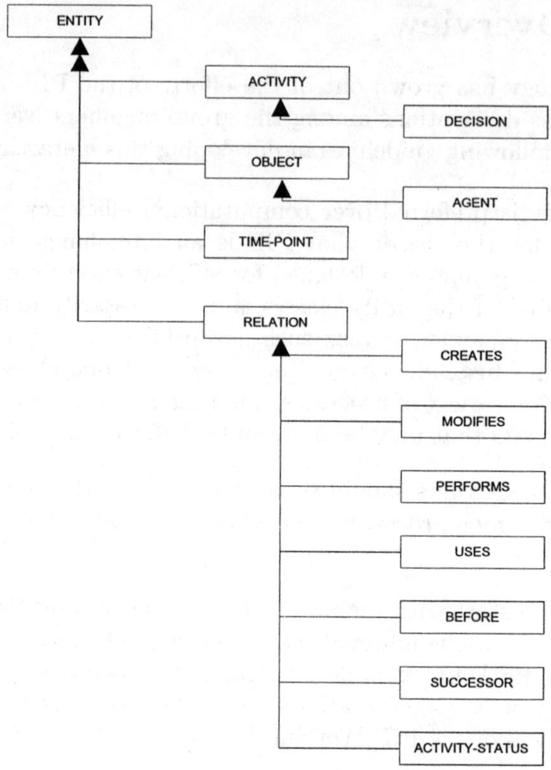

Figure 1: The PIF class hierarchy

two frames refer to. For example, if the Begin attribute of ACTIVITY-1 takes TIMEPOINT-32 as its value, then the Begin attribute represents a relationship between the ACTIVITY-1 and TIMEPOINT- 32 instances. The value of a given attribute in a PIF file holds independent of time. Figure 2 depicts the relationships among the PIF classes. Section 5 describes all of the current PIF classes.

An attribute in a PIF entity can be filled with the following and only the following PIF expressions: a literal value of a PIF primitive value type or an expression of a composite value type.

The PIF primitive value types consist of: NUMBER, STRING, and SYMBOL

- NUMBER: A numeric value. The NUMBER type is subdivided into INTEGER and FLOAT types.
- STRING: A sequence of characters.
- SYMBOL: Symbols are denoted by character sequences, but have somewhat different properties than strings.

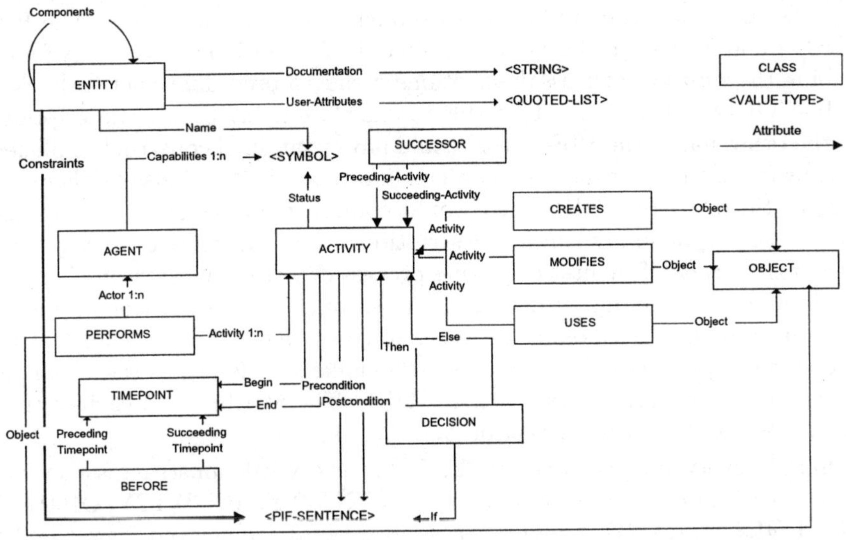

Figure 2: Relationships among PIF classes

The PIF composite value types consist of: LIST and PIF-SENTENCE.

- LIST: A list.
- PIF-SENTENCE: A logical expression that evaluates to TRUE or FALSE.

An object variable is of the form, object-name[.slot-name]*, which refers to either the object named or the object which is the value of the named slot (or, if there are more than one slot-names specified, the object which is the value of the named slot of the object which is the value of the next named slot, and so on.)

4 Rationales

The goal of PIF is to support maximal sharing of process descriptions across heterogeneous process representations. To better serve this goal, PIF consists of not a monolithic set of constructs, but a partially ordered set of modules. A module can build on other modules in that the constructs in a module are specializations of the constructs in the other modules. One can adopt some modules but not others depending on one's expressive needs. Hence, a module typically contains a set of constructs that are useful for a particular domain or a type of task. More details of this module structure are discussed in Section 6.

The PIF-CORE, on the other hand, consists of the minimal set of constructs necessary to translate simple but non-trivial process descriptions.

There is the usual tradeoff between simplicity and expressiveness. The PIF-CORE could have been chosen to contain only the constructs necessary for describing the simplest process descriptions such as a precedence network. Such a PIF-CORE then would not be able to translate many process descriptions. On the other hand, the PIF-CORE could have contained constructs sufficient for expressing the information contained in process descriptions of richer complexity. Such a PIF-CORE then would contain many constructs that may not be needed for many simpler descriptions. The PIF-CORE strikes a balance in this tradeoff by first collecting process descriptions, starting from the simplest and continuing with more complex until we have reasonably many of them, and then by looking for a set of constructs that can translate the process descriptions in this collection. The following describes the rationales for each of the constructs in the PIF-CORE. The attributes of each of these constructs are described in Section 5.

In PIF, everything is an ENTITY; that is, every PIF construct is a specialization of ENTITY. There are four types of ENTITY: ACTIVITY, OBJECT, TIMEPOINT, and RELATION. These four types are derived from the definition of process in PIF: a process is a set of ACTIVITIES that stand in certain RELATIONS to one another and to OBJECTS over TIMEPOINTS.

The following provides intuitive rationales for each of these four constructs. Their precise semantics, however, are defined by the relations they have with other constructs (cf. Section 5).

ACTIVITY represents anything that happens over time. DECISION, which represent conditional activities, is the only special type of ACTIVITY that the PIF-CORE recognizes. In particular, the PIF-CORE does not make any distinction among process, procedure, or event. A TIMEPOINT represents a particular point in time, for example "Oct. 2, 2.32 p.m. 1995" or "the time at which the notice is received." An OBJECT is intended to represent all the types of entities involved in a process description beyond the other three primitive ones of ACTIVITY, TIMEPOINT, and RELATION. AGENT is a special type of OBJECT.

RELATION represents relations among the other constructs. The PIF-CORE offers the following relations: BEFORE, SUCCESSOR, CREATES, USES, MODIFIES, and PERFORMS.

BEFORE represents a temporal relation between TIMEPOINTS. SUCCESSOR (Activity-1, Activity-2) is defined to be the relation between ACTIVITIES where BEFORE (Activity-1.End, Activity-2.Begin) holds. It is provided as a shorthand for simple activity precedence relations.

CREATES, USES, and MODIFIES represent relations between ACTIVITY and OBJECT. In these relations, the object is assumed to be created, used, modified at some non-determinate timepoint(s) in the duration of the activity (i.e. between its Begin and its End timepoint inclusively). Hence the object would have been created, used, or modified by the End timepoint, but no commitment is made as to when the object is actually created, used, or modified. PERFORMS represents a relation between OBJECT (normally an AGENT specialization) and ACTIVITY. In the PERFORMS relation, the actor is assumed to perform the activity at some non-determinant timepoint(s) in the duration of the activity (possibly for the whole duration, but not necessarily). We understand that there are other possible interpretations of these relations. For example, we might want to specify that a given actor is the only one who performs the activity during the whole activity interval. Such a specification, however, will require a PSV extension of the PIF-CORE (for example, by introducing a relation such as PERFORMS-EXCLUSIVELY, cf. Section 6). SUCCESSOR in PIF may not correspond exactly to the notions of successor as used in some workflow or enactment systems because it is common in these systems to bundle into a single relationship a mixture of temporal, causal, and decomposition relationships among activities. PIF provides precise, separate relationships for all three of these activities-to-activity specifications. For example, the temporal relationship is specified with the BEFORE relation, the causal relation with the Precondition and Postcondition attributes of ACTIVITY, and the decomposition relation with the Component attribute. Its intention is to allow the exact meaning to be communicated. Hence, one might have to combine some of these constructs to capture exactly the meaning of SUCCESSOR as used in ones own system.

The attribute value of a PIF-CORE object holds independent of time (i.e. no temporal scope is associated with an attribute value in the PIF-CORE). Any property of an object which can change over time, should be represented by a RELATION that links the property to a timepoint. An example of one such RELATION in the PIF-CORE is ACTIVITY-STATUS which is used to represent the status (e.g. DELAYED, PENDING) of an ACTIVITY at different times. The ACTIVITY-STATUS is provided in the PIF-CORE because it is the one example of a dynamic property of those objects commonly used in process modeling and workflow systems and modeled in the PIF-CORE. Other properties of those objects included in the PIF-CORE are, for the most part, true for all time. As mentioned before, it is possible to extend the PIF-CORE to express additional temporally scoped properties by introducing additional RELATIONS. It is also possible to add temporally scoped version of the static attributes already in the PIF-CORE. In this case, any such static attributes actually specified in a PIF file holds true for all time.

The attribute value of a PIF object can be one of the PIF value types specified above. The PIF primitive value types consist of NUMBER, STRING, and SYMBOL. The PIF composite value types are LIST and PIF-SENTENCE. LIST is used for conveying structured information that is not to be evaluated by a PIF interpreter, but simply passed along (e.g. as in the User-Attribute attribute of ENTITY). PIF-SENTENCE is used to specify a condition that is either true or false, as required, for example, for the Precondition and the Postcondition attributes of ACTIVITY.

PIF-SENTENCE is a logical expression that may include variables, quantifiers, and the Boolean operators for expressing conditions or constraints. A PIF-SENTENCE is used in the Constraint slot of ENTITY, the Precondition and the Postcondition slots of ACTIVITY, and the If slot of DECISION. A variable in a PIF-SENTENCE takes the following positions in the three dimensions that define the possible usage. (1) The scope of the variable is the frame. That is, variables of the same name within a frame definition are bound to the same object, whereas they are not necessarily so if they occur in different frames. (2) A variable is assumed to be bound by an implicit existential quantifier. (3) The constraints on variables in a frame definition are expressed in the Constraints slot of that frame. These constraints are local to the frame.

These positions are expected to be extended by some PSV Modules. Some PSV modules will extend the scope of a variable beyond a single object. Some will introduce explicit existential and universal quantifiers. Yet others will allow global constraints to be stated, possibly by providing an object where such global constraints that hold across all the objects in a PIF file (e.g. All purchase order must be approved by the finance supervisor before sent out.).

Notable Absence:

We have decided not to include ROLE because a role may be defined wherever an attribute is defined. For example, the concept of RESOURCE is a role defined by the Resource attribute of the USE relation. Any object, we view, is a resource if it can be USEd by an ACTIVITY. As a consequence, we have decided not to include ROLE or any construct that represents a role, such as RESOURCE. ACTOR is not included in PIF because it is another role-concept, one defined by the Actor attribute of the PERFORMS relation. Any object, as long as it can fill the Actor attribute, can be viewed as an ACTOR. Hence we resolved that explicit introduction of the constructs such as ACTOR or RESOURCE is redundant and may lead to potential confusions. We should note, however, that the PIF-CORE provides the construct AGENT, which is not defined by a role an entity plays but by its inherent characteristic, namely its capability (for example, of making intelligent decisions in various domains).

5 Alphabetic Class Reference

Activity

Parent Classes: Entity

Attribute	Value Type	Multiple Values Allowed
Component	Activity	Yes
Precondition	PIF-SENTENCE	No
Postcondition	PIF-SENTENCE	No
Begin	TIMEPOINT	No
End	TIMEPOINT	No

Attribute Descriptions:

- **Component:** The subactivities of the activity. For example, if the activity is "Develop Software", its Component may include: "Design Software", "Write Code", "Debug Software", and so on. The field is inherited from ENTITY, but here it is restricted so that its values must all be ACTIVITY entities.
- **Precondition:** The conditions that have to be satisfied at the Begin timepoint of the activity before it can get executed. For example, a precondition of the activity "Run Software" might state that the executable code must be available. Such conditions are expressed using PIF-SENTENCES.
- **Postcondition:** The conditions that are true at the End timepoint of the activity. For example, a postcondition of the activity "Run Software" might be that a log file has been updated. Such conditions are expressed using PIF-SENTENCES.
- **Begin:** The TIMEPOINT at which the activity begins.
- **End:** The TIMEPOINT at which the activity ends.

In the PIF-CORE, the condition in the Precondition is to be true before the Begin timepoint of the ACTIVITY. Similarly, the condition in the Postcondition is to be true after the End timepoint of the ACTIVITY. This requirement may be relaxed later in PSV modules (cf. Section 6) to allow the precondition and the postcondition to be stated relative to other time points.

Many preconditions and postconditions can be expressed in PIF without using the Precondition and Postcondition attributes of ACTIVITY. For example, the USE relation between an activity A and an object O implies that one of A's preconditions is that R is available. In general, the Precondition and Postcondition attributes of ACTIVITY should only be used to express conditions that cannot be expressed any other way in PIF. Doing so will maximize the degree to which a process description can be shared with others.

ACTIVITY-STATUS

Parent Classes: RELATION

Attribute	Value Type	Multiple Values Allowed
Activity	ACTIVITY	Yes
Status	SYMBOL	Yes
When	TIMEPOINT	No

Attribute Descriptions:

- **Activity:** The activity whose status is being specified.
- **Status:** The status being specified such as DELAYED and PENDING.
- **When:** The timepoint at which the status of the activity is being specified.

AGENT

Parent Classes: OBJECT → ENTITY

Attribute	Value Type	Multiple Values Allowed
Capability	SYMBOL	Yes
Component	AGENT	Yes

Attribute Descriptions:

- **Capability:** Its possible values are SYMBOLS that represent the kinds of skills the agent is capable of providing. The symbols are supplied by the source language and simply preserved across translations by PIF. A PSV Module may introduce a restricted set of symbol values.

An AGENT represents a person, group, or other entity (such as a computer program) that participates in a process. An AGENT is distinguished from other ENTITIES by what it is capable of doing or its skills.

BEFORE

Parent Classes: RELATION → ENTITY

Attribute	Value Type	Multiple Values Allowed
Preceding-Timepoint	TIMEPOINT	No
Succeeding-Timepoint	TIMEPOINT	No

Attribute Descriptions:

- **Preceding Timepoint:** The time point that is before the Succeeding Timepoint.
- **Succeeding Timepoint:** The time point that is after the Preceding Timepoint.

BEFORE is a relation between TIMEPOINTS not between ACTIVITIES. A shorthand for a common example of the BEFORE relation is available via the SUCCESSOR relation.

CREATES

Parent Classes: RELATION → ENTITY

Attribute	Value Type	Multiple Values Allowed
Activity	ACTIVITY	No
Object	OBJECT	Yes

Attribute Descriptions:

- **Activity:** The activity that creates the object. The object is assumed to be created at some non-determinate timepoint(s) between its Begin and its End timepoint inclusive.
- **Object:** The object that the activity creates.

DECISION

Parent Classes: ACTIVITY → ENTITY

Attribute	Value Type	Multiple Values Allowed
If	PIF-SENTENCE	No
Them	ACTIVITY	Yes
Else	ACTIVITY	Yes

Attribute Descriptions:

- **If:** The condition being tested to decide which successor relations to follow. Such conditions are expressed using PIF-SENTENCES.
- **Then:** The activity to follow if the condition in the If field holds (that is, if the PIF- SENTENCE in the If field evaluates TRUE).
- **Else:** The activity to follow if the condition in the If field does not hold (that is, if the PIF-SENTENCE in the If field evaluates to FALSE).

A DECISION is a special kind of activity that represents conditional branching. If the PIF Sentence in its If attribute is TRUE, the activity specified in its Then attribute follows. If not, the activity in its Else attribute follows. If the Else attribute is empty, it means no activity follows the DECISION activity in the case where the decision condition is false. If more than one activity in a process is dependent on a decision, then they may be included in the multiple value then or else attributes. To ease description of a complex sub-process which is dependent on the decision, it is possible to describe a set of sub-activities (and any ordering or other constraints on them) in a separate process and to include that process itself within the "then" or "else" attributes.

ENTITY

Parent Classes: None. ENTITY is the roof of the PIF class hierarchy

Attribute	Value Type	Multiple Values Allowed
Name	STRING	No
Documentation	STRING	No
Component	ENTITY	Yes
Constraint	PIF-SENTENCE	No
User-Attribute	LIST	No

Attribute Descriptions:

- **Name:** The entity's name.
- **Documentation:** A description of the entity.
- **Component:** This attribute is used to specify an homogeneous aggregate of the type itself. For example, in an AGENT object, this attribute can be used to specify that the agent is in fact a group of sub-agents. In an ACTIVITY object, this attribute is used to specify its subactivities that make up the activity. If one needs to specify a group of objects of different types, then one can do so by going up to an object of their common ancestor type and specify them in the Component attribute of this object. When interpreted as a relation, this relation holds between the entity and each value, not between the entity and the set of all the values.
- **Constraint:** This attribute is used to specify any constraint that should be true of the other attribute values in the current entity, e.g. constraints on the variables.

User-Attribute: This attribute is used to store additional ad-hoc attributes of an entity that are not part of its class definition. For example, a process modeling application might allow users to specify additional attributes for AGENT entities that are not included in AGENT's PIF definition – the user might want to add an attribute recording the AGENT's age, for example. Such additional attributes can be stored in the User- Attribute attribute, which all PIF entities inherit from ENTITY. Another common use is in the Partially Shared Views translation scheme that we propose for interchanging PIF files (see Section 6). Each value of User-Attribute is a list containing an attribute name and its value(s). For example, an OBJECT entity might have (User-Attribute (Color RED GREEN) (Weight 120))

MODIFIES

Parent Classes: RELATION → ENTITY

Attribute	Value Type	Multiple Values Allowed
Activity	ACTIVITY	No
Object	OBJECT	Yes

Attribute Descriptions:

- **Activity:** The activity that modifies the object. The object is assumed to be modified at some non-determinate timepoint(s) between its Begin and its End timepoint inclusive.
- **Object:** The object that the activity modifies.

OBJECT

Parent Classes: ENTITY

Attribute Descriptions: No Attributes.

An OBJECT is an entity that can be used, created, modified, or used in other relationships to an activity. This includes people (represented by the AGENT subclass in PIF), physical materials, time, and so forth. The PIF Working Group has discussed adding OBJECT attributes such as Consumable, Sharable and so forth, but so far no decision has been made on what attributes are appropriate.

PERFORMS

Parent Classes: RELATION → ENTITY

Attribute	Value Type	Multiple Values Allowed
Actor	OBJECT	Yes
Activity	ACTIVITY	Yes

Attribute Descriptions:

- **Actor:** The object that performs the activity.
- **Activity:** The activity that is performed. The actor is assumed to perform the activity at some non-determinate timepoint(s) between its Begin and its End timepoint inclusive.

RELATION

Parent Classes: ENTITY

Attribute Descriptions: No Attributes.

RELATION entities have no attributes of their own. PIF uses it as an abstract parent class for more specific relation classes such as USES and PERFORMS.

SUCCESSOR

Parent Classes: RELATION → ENTITY

Attribute	Value Type	Multiple Values Allowed
Preceding-Activity	ACTIVITY	No
Succeeding-Activity	ACTIVITY	Yes

Attribute Descriptions:

- **Preceding-Activity:** The preceding activity.
- **Succeeding-Activity:** The succeeding activity.

SUCCESSOR with the Preceding-Activity ACTIVITY-1 and the Succeeding-Activity ACTIVITY-2 is exactly the same as BEFORE with Preceding-Timepoint TP-1 and Succeeding-Timepoint TP-2, where TP-1 is the Begin timepoint of ACTIVITY-2 and TP- 2 is the End timepoint of ACTIVITY-1. That is, the SUCCESSOR relation is true if the ACTIVITY-1 ends before the ACTIVITY-2 begins.

TIMEPOINT

Parent Classes: ENTITY

Attribute Descriptions: No Attributes.

TIMEPOINT represents a point in time. In PIF-CORE, it is used, for example, to specify the Begin and End times of an Activity or the Preceding and Succeeding time points of the BEFORE relation.

USES

Parent Classes: RELATION → ENTITY

Attribute	Value Type	Multiple Values Allowed
Activity	ACTIVITY	No
Object	OBJECT	Yes

Attribute Descriptions:

- **Activity:** The activity that uses the object from its Begin timepoint to its End timepoint. The USES relation is true from the Begin to the End timepoint of the activity. The object is assumed to be used at some non-determinate timepoint(s) between its Begin and its End timepoint inclusive.
- **Object:** The object that the activity uses.

6 Extending PIF

PIF provides a common language through which different process representations can be translated. Between two process representations that support translations into PIF, one can be translated into a PIF description, which can then be translated into the other representation, thus reducing the number of required translators from n*(n-1) to n. However, because there will always be representational needs local to individual groups, there must also be a way to allow local extensions to the description classes while supporting as much sharing as possible among local extensions. The Partially Shared Views (PSV) scheme has been developed for the purpose [LM90]. PSV integrates different ways of translating between groups using different class hierarchies (e.g. pairwise mapping, translation via external common language, translation via internal common language) so as to exploit the benefits of each when most appropriate.

A PSV Module is a declaration of PIF entities which specialize other entities in the PIF- CORE or other PSV modules on which it builds. The class definitions in a PSV Module cannot delete or alter the existing definitions but can only add to them. Examples of PSV Modules are given at the end of this section. A group of users may adopt one or more PSV Modules as necessary for its task.

A group using a PSV module translates a PIF object X into their native format as follows:

1. If X's class (call it C) is known to the group and the group has developed a method that translates objects of class C into their native format, then apply that translation method. C is known to the group if either C is defined in one of the PSV Modules that the group has adopted or the group has set up beforehand a translation rule between C and a type defined in one of the PSV Modules adopted.

2. Otherwise, translate X as if it were an object of the nearest parent class of C for which (1) applies (its parent class in the most specific PSV Module that the group and the sender group both share, i.e. have adopted).

This translation scheme allows groups to share information to some degree even if they do not support identical class hierarchies. For examples, suppose that Group A supports only the standard PIF AGENT class, and that Group B in addition supports an EMPLOYEE subclass. When Group A receives a process description in Group B's variation on PIF, they can still translate any EMPLOYEE objects in the description as if they were AGENT objects. What happens to any information that is in an EMPLOYEE object that is not in a generic AGENT object? That will vary according to the sophistication of the translator and the expressive power of the target process representation.

However, the translator will preserve the additional information so that it can be viewed by users and reproduced if it is later translated back into PIF.

For example, suppose EMPLOYEE has a "Medical-plan" attribute, which is not part of the AGENT object in the PIF-CORE. Then Group A's translator would

- Translate any Medical-plan attributes into a form that the user could view in the target system (even if it only as a textual comment) AND
- When the information is re-translated into PIF in the future (from Group A's native format), it is emitted as an EMPLOYEE object with the same value for the Medical-plan attribute (and not simply as an AGENT object with no Medical-plan attribute). MIT researchers are currently investigating this general problem of preserving as much information as possible through "round trips" from one representation to another and back [Cha95].

Translators that can follow these conventions will minimize information loss when processes are translated back and forth between different tools. The details of PSV can be found in [LM90]. In the current version of PIF, each PIF file begins with a declaration of the class hierarchy for the objects described in the file. PSV uses this class hierarchy to translate objects of types that are unknown to a translator. To eliminate the need for PIF translators to do any other inheritance operations, however, all PIF objects should contain all of their attributes and values. For instance, even if the value of a given attribute is inherited without change from a parent, the attribute and value are repeated in the child.

As the number of PSV modules grows large, we need a mechanism for registering and coordinating them so as to prevent any potential conflict such as naming conflict. Although the exact mechanism is yet to be worked out, we are envisioning a scenario like the following. The user who needs to use PIF would first consult the indexed library of PSV modules, which documents briefly the contents of each of the modules and the information about the other modules it presupposes. If an existing set of modules does not serve the users purpose in hand and a new PSV module has to be created, then the information about the new module and its relation to other modules is sent to a PSV registration server, which then assigns to it a globally unique identifier and updates the indexed library. We foresee many other issues to arise such as whether any proposed PSV module should be accepted, if not who decides, whether to distinguish an ad-hoc module designed for temporary quick translation between two local parties from a well- designed module intended for global use, and so on. However, rather than addressing these issues in this document, we will address them in a separate document as we gain more experience with PSV modules.

To date, two PSV Modules have been specified: Temporal-Relation-1 and IDEF-0 Modules. The Temporal-Relation-1 Module extends the core PIF by adding all possible temporal relations that can hold between two activities (cf. Figure 3). The IDEF-0 Module adds the constructs necessary for translating between IDEF-0 descriptions and PIF. IDEF-0 is a functional decomposition model, which however has been historically used widely as a process model description language. IDEF-0 has been used in various ways with no single well-defined semantics. Hence, the IDEF-0 PSV Module supports translation between PIF and one particular version of IDEF-0. It introduces two additional relations, USES-AS-RESOURCE and USES-AS- CONTROL, as specializations of the USES relation. They are meant to capture the Control and Mechanism input of IDEF-0. The Input and Output relations of IDEF-0 may be translated into PIF by using the Precondition and Postcondition attribute of ACTIVITY. The mapping between IDEF and PIF is shown in Figure 4. These modules have not been officially registered. They are presented here only to provide examples of PSV modules. We are soliciting further inputs before we register them.

Figure 3: Possible Temporal Relations between Two Activities

7 Future Directions

Following the release of PIF version 1.2, PIF developments are expected to follow the following directions.

- We plan to coordinate further development of PIF with other knowledge sharing projects so as to produce compatibility, if not convergence, among the meta-models produced. We will continue working closely with the NIST PSL Group in order to make PSL and PIF compatible. We also plan to work with the International Workflow Management

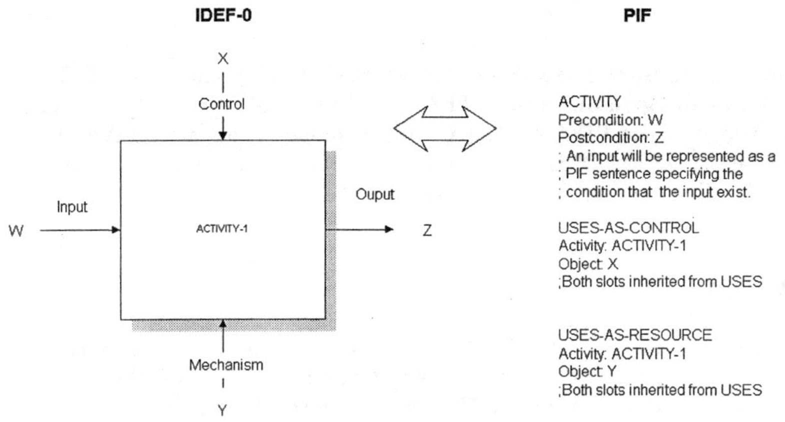

Figure 4: Mapping between IDEF-0 and PIF Constructs

Coalition (http://www.aiai.ed.ac.uk/WfMC), whose goal is to produce interoperability among workflow applications. We have been also talking to the people in the Knowledge Sharing Initiatives [NFFGPSS91], which has produced KIF (Knowledge Interchange Format) described earlier, tools and protocols for sharing knowledge bases, and Web-based ontology libraries among other things. We plan to intensify these coordination efforts through more structured and active forms such as workshops and regular meetings.

- We plan to elaborate on the PIF extension mechanism. We need to discuss and work out the details on such issues as Who can propose and accept PSV modules in which domain and How the modules should be named, registered, organized, and accessed. We also need to carefully lay out the space of PSV modules by identifying an initial set of generally useful ones extending the PIF-CORE. Again, this work will require close interactions with the other knowledge sharing groups as well as the experts in various domains. We hope to pursue this objective as a part of pursuing the first objective of coordination with other groups.

- In order to use PIF to share process descriptions automatically, we need a PIF- translator for each of the local process representations involved. For example, each of the groups represented in the PIF Working Group built a translator for translating between PIF 1.0 and its own representation. Building PIF-translators are ultimately the responsibility of individual groups who want to use PIF. However, we would like to provide a toolkit that will help future groups build PIF-translators.

Acknowledgments: The PIF Working Group's activities are supported by DARPA, NSF, Corporate Sponsors of the MIT Center for Coordination Science, sponsors and organizations of the PIF Working Group members. This article is a revised version of Lee, J. *et al* (1998) "The Process Interchange Format and Framework" in Knowledge Engineering Review 13 (1), pp. 91-122.

References

[Cha95] Chan, F. Y., The Round Trip Problem: A Solution for the Process Handbook, unpublished Master's Thesis, MIT Dept. of Electrical Engineering and Computer Science, May 1995

[GF92] Genesereth, M., Fikes, F., Knowledge Interchange Format v. 3 Reference Manual, available as a postscript file via anonymous ftp from www-ksl.stanford.edu:/pub/knowledge-sharing/papers/kif.ps, 1992

[Gru93] Gruber, T., Ontolingua: A Translation Approach to Portable Ontology Specifications, Knowledge Acquisition 5(2), 1993, 199-200, available via anonymous ftp from www-ksl.stanford.edu:/pub/knowledge-sharing/papers/ongolingua-intro.ps

[ISO89] International Standard Organization Information processing systems – Open Systems Interconnection – LOTOS – A formal description technique based on the temporal ordering of observational behaviour, ISO-8807, 1989

[LM90] Lee, J., Malone, T., Partially Shared Views: A Scheme for Communicating between Groups Using Different Type Hierarchies, ACM Transactions on Information Systems 8(1), 1990, 1-26

[MCLB93] Malone, T., Crowston, K., Lee, J., Pentland, B., Tools for Inventing Organizations: Toward a Handbook of Organizational Processes, Proceedings of the 2nd IEEE Workshop on Enabling Technologies Infrastructure for Collaborative, IEEE Computer Society Press, 1993

[MME94] Menzel, C., Mayer, R., Edwards, D., IDEF3 Process Descriptions and Their Semantics, in: A. Kusiak, C. Dagli (eds.), Intelligent Systems in Design and Manufacturing, New York, ASME Press, 1994

[NIST93a] National Institute of Standards and Technology Integration Definition for Function Modeling (IDEF0), Federal Information Processing Standards Publication 183, Computer Systems Laboratory, 1993

[NIST93b] National Institute of Standards and Technology Integration Definition for Function Modeling (IDEF1X), Federal Information Processing Standards Publication 184, Computer Systems Laboratory, 1993

[NFFGPSS91] Neches, R., Fikes, R., Finin, T., Gruber, T., Patil, R., Senator, T., Swartout, W. R., Enabling Technology for Knowledge Sharing, AI Magazine 12(3), 1991, 36-56

[Ste90] Steele, G., Common Lisp: The Language, Second edition, Digital Press, 1990

[Tat95] Tate, A., Characterizing Plans as a Set of Constraints - the <I-N-OVA> Model - a Framework for Comparative Analysis, ACM SIGART Bulletin, Special Issue on: Evaluation of Plans, Planners, and Planning Agents, Vol. 6 No. 1, January 1995, available as a postscript file via ftp://ftp.aiai.ed.ac.uk/pub/documents/1995/95-sigart-inova.ps

CHAPTER 9

GPN Generalised Process Networks

Günter Schmidt

Business process management is the task to accomplish work in organisations such that processes are carried out in some form of "optimal" way. Two important tasks of business process management are planning and scheduling. Planning is concerned with structuring the processes i.e. determining what needs to be carried out and in what sequence to achieve the objective of the process. Scheduling is concerned with assigning limited resources over time to competing activities of business processes. A modelling language is presented for the purposes of planning and scheduling in support of business process management.

1 Introduction

Modelling languages are required for building models in various application areas. We shall focus on the management of business processes which require the modelling of time-based activities for planning and scheduling purposes. A business process is a stepwise procedure for transforming some input into a desired output while consuming or otherwise utilising resources. Some generic examples are: "Product Development", "Procurement", or "Customer Order Fulfilment"; some more special examples would be "Claims Processing" in insurance companies or "Loan Processing" in banks. The output of a business process should always be some kind of achievement (good or service) which is required by some customer. The customer might be either inside or outside the organisation where the process is carried out [Sch97].

Two major tasks of business process management are planning and scheduling. Planning is concerned with determining the structures of processes before they are carried out the first time. Scheduling in turn is concerned with assigning resources over time to competing processes. Both planning and scheduling focus on dependencies among transformations within one process or between different processes. Malone and Crowston [MC94] formulated the need to merge the paradigms of business process planning and business process scheduling concerning the management of dependencies among transformations. The reason is not only to increase the potential of applying results from planning and scheduling theory to the management of business processes but also to consider the relevance of problems arising from business process management for a theoretical analysis within this area.

Planning and scheduling require a specialised model of the business process. To build the required process model we propose Generalised Process Networks (GPN) [Sch96], a graphical language related to CPM type of networks [SW89]. We will show that GPN are expressive enough to formulate problems related to planning and scheduling of business processes within the same model. Doing this we use a semi-formal kind of presentation of the syntax and the semantics of GPN.

We start with a short discussion of business processes. Then we introduce a framework for systems modelling to define requirements for business process models. Based on this we describe the GPN language and discuss its application to business process planning and scheduling. Finally, we use an example to demonstrate the modelling capabilities of the approach.

2 What is a Business Process?

A business process is a stepwise procedure for transforming some given input into some desired output. The transformation is consuming or using resources. A business process has some form of outcome, i.e. goods or services produced for a customer or customers either outside or inside the enterprise. There are two usual meanings attached to the term "business process"; a business process may mean a process type or a process instance.

The process type can be described by defining the general structure of a process; the process instance is a real process following the rules and structure of a given process type. A process type can be interpreted as a pattern; the behaviour of a corresponding instance matches with the pattern. A process type might be a pattern called "Product Development", and the corresponding instance could be "Development of Product X" carried out according to the pattern of "Product Development". In the sequel a process instance will also be referred to as a job.

The process type is defined by its input and output, functions to be performed, and rules of synchronisation. The process input and output are related to tangible and intangible achievements. For example the major shop floor functions in production have as input different kinds of raw materials which are transformed into various types of output called processed material; office functions are mainly transforming data or information into new data or new information. In general input and output will consist of material and information simultaneously.

A function represents the transformation of some input into some output. Functions are related through precedence relations which constrain the possible ways a process can be executed. E.g. a precedence relation requires synchronisation if the output of a predecessor function is part of the input of the successor function. Before a function can be executed certain pre-conditions have to be fulfilled and after a function has been executed certain post-conditions are fulfilled.

Starting and ending a function is caused by events. In general an event represents a point in time when certain conditions come about, i.e. the conditions hold from that time on until the next event occurs. Conditions related to events are described by values of attributes characterising the situation related to the occurrence of an event.

These event values are compared to pre-conditions and post-conditions of functions. Before carrying out some function its pre-conditions must match with the conditions related to its beginning event and after carrying out a function the conditions related to its ending event must match with the post-conditions of the function. Synchronisation means that there must be some order in which functions might occur over time; in its simplest form a predecessor-successor relationship has to be defined.

To fully determine a process type a number of variables related to the input and output of functions need to be fixed. The input defines the producer who is responsible for carrying out a function, the required resources, and the required data; the output defines the product generated by a function, the customer of the product, and the data available after a function is carried out. Once a process type is defined its instances can be created. A process instance is performed according to the definition of the corresponding process type. The input, output, functions, and synchronisation of a process instance relate to some real job which has to be carried out. The input must be available, the output must be required. Functions that make up a process type have to be instantiated. A function instance is called task. It is created at a point in time as a result of some event and is executed during a finite time interval. To ensure task execution scheduling decisions need to be taken considering the synchronisation and the resource allocation constraints as defined by the process type and resource availability.

Scheduling process instances means to allocate all actual or predicted instances of different process types to resources over time. The process type represents constraints for the scheduling decision [BEPSW96]. In terms of scheduling theory an instance of a business process is a job which consists of a set of precedence constrained tasks. Additional attributes to tasks and jobs can be assigned [Sch96b]. Questions to be answered for process scheduling are: which task of which job should be executed by which resource and at what time. Typically, performance measures for business process instances are time-based and relate to flow time or completion time of jobs; scheduling constraints are related to due dates or deadlines.

3 Views to be Modelled

Modelling is a major component in planning and scheduling of business processes. A framework for system modelling is given by an architecture. An architecture shows the requirements for building models and defines the necessary views on a system. Many proposals of architectures have been developed and evaluated with the objective to find a generic enterprise reference architecture [BN96]. An architecture which fits in such a framework is LISA [Sch96a]. LISA differs between four views on models:

1. the granularity of the model,
2. the elements of the model and their relationships,
3. the life cycle phase of the model, and
4. the purpose of modelling.

According to granularity models for process types and for process instances have to be considered. Concerning the elements and their relationships models of business processes should represent the inputs (data, resources), the outputs (data, products), the organisational environment (producer, customer), the functions, and the synchronisation (events, conditions, dependencies). According to life cycle phase models are needed for analysis, design, and implementation. Finally, concerning the purpose of modelling we need models for the problem description and for the problem solution. The problem description states the objectives and constraints and the problem solution is a proposal how to meet them. Figure 1 shows the different views to be represented by business process models in the framework of LISA.

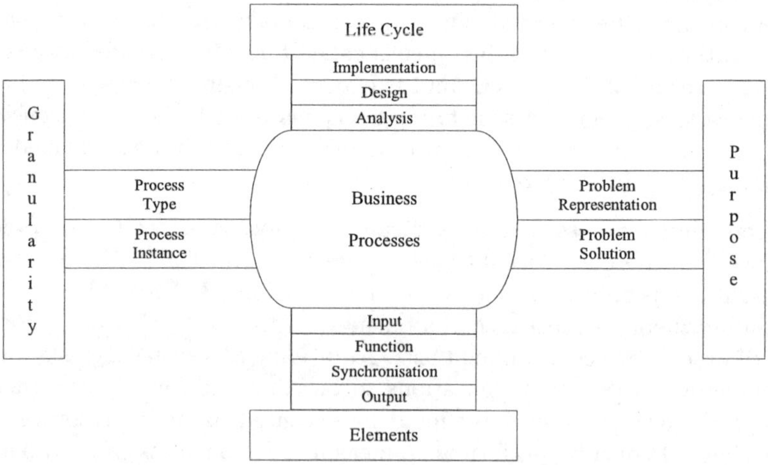

Figure 1: Views on business processes defined by LISA

The views thus identified need to be represented by an appropriate modelling language. First we concentrate on the views concerning the purpose of modelling. We will show that GPN supports the formulation of planning and scheduling models suited both for the problem description and for the problem solution.

4 Generalised Process Networks

There exist many modelling languages to describe business processes. Prominent examples can be found in this volume. Most of these languages have been developed for planning purposes with a focus on the problem description. Models suited for scheduling purposes in particular for optimisation require a representation which is suited for combinatorial problem solving. Existing modelling languages do not support process description which would be suitable for the modelling of the combinatorial structure of the problem, and therefore they are not well suited for the task of scheduling business processes [CKO92]. For this reason GPN was developed.

The modelling language has to fulfil two basic requirements:

- **Completeness and consistency.** All relevant views of a system must be covered and the various view definitions must be defined in a semantically consistent way,
- **Understandability.** The syntax and semantics must be easy to understand and easy to use by the target audience.

The relevant system views for business processes are defined in LISA:

- **Life Cycle.** It is not useful to have only one monolithic modelling language covering all phases of the life cycle. Every phase requires different details to be represented, and different expertise which is best reflected by the selected syntax and associated semantics of the language. GPN is designed for the analysis phase.
- **Granularity.** There are two levels of granularity, i.e. the type of a process and its instances. As these two levels are very much interrelated the modelling language should cover both. GPN models both process types and process instances.
- **Elements.** The inputs, outputs, functions, and synchronisation needs of business processes are modelled. GPN considers all business process elements which are required for planning and scheduling.
- **Purpose.** Most business process models are of descriptive nature and there is no link from these to building constructive models for problem solving. Descriptive models help to answer questions like "what

happens if ...?". In contrast, the purpose of constructive models is to answer the question "what has to happen so that ...?". Descriptive models are mainly used to get an understanding of a problem; the domain of constructive models is more related to (analytical) problem solving. While using GPN a common model for process planning and process scheduling can be formulated which is accessible by descriptive and constructive techniques [Sch96a].

We shall differentiate between a model for a process type (used for planning) and a model for a process instance (used for scheduling), i.e. descriptive modelling is used to represent process types and constructive modelling is used to represent process instances. However, both models are described using one language. The basic syntactical elements of GPN are nodes, arcs, and labels assigned to nodes and arcs (see Figure 2).

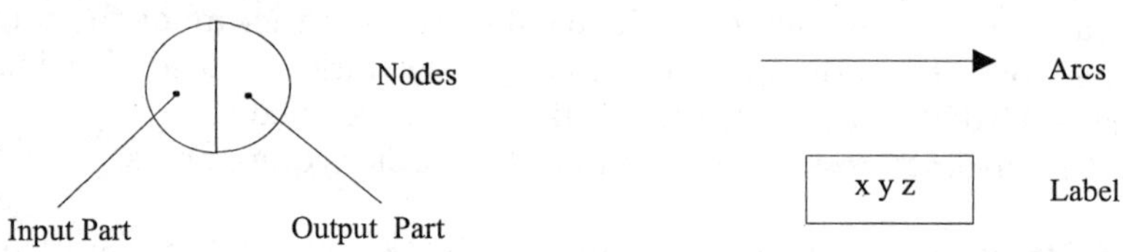

Figure 2: Basic elements of GPN

The semantics of GPN are defined in six layers. The first layer defines the meaning of the basic elements, the second layer is dedicated to the functional specifications, the third to synchronisation aspects representing relationships between functions, the fourth to input and output data, the fifth to required resources and generated products, and the sixth layer describes the customer-producer relationship as related to a function. These semantic layers are shown in Figure 3.

Arcs represent functions. Connected to each function is a number of pre-conditions and a number of post-conditions. The pre-conditions must be satisfied for the function to be carried out; post-conditions are satisfied as a result of performing the function.

Nodes represent events defining constraints for synchronisation of functions. An event separating two functions represents the constraint that the two functions cannot be carried out in parallel but only in a certain sequence. Functions which have no separating event can be performed in parallel. The occurrence of an event is a necessary condition to perform a function. Each event is described by a value list defining the environmental conditions represented by the event. The occurrence of an event is also a sufficient condition for performing a function if its value list meets the pre-conditions of the function adjacent to this event. There are two events connected to each function; one represents its start and the other one its end. Figure 4 is a graphical representation of a function (i,j) with its beginning and ending events i and

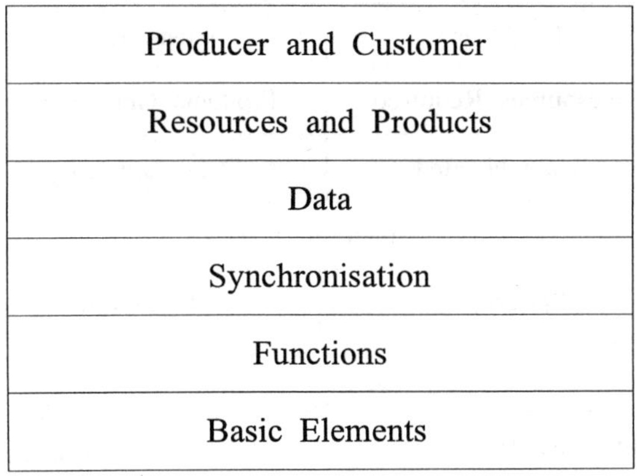

Figure 3: Semantic layers of GPN

j, pre- and post-conditions and the value lists of the input and output parts of the associated events.

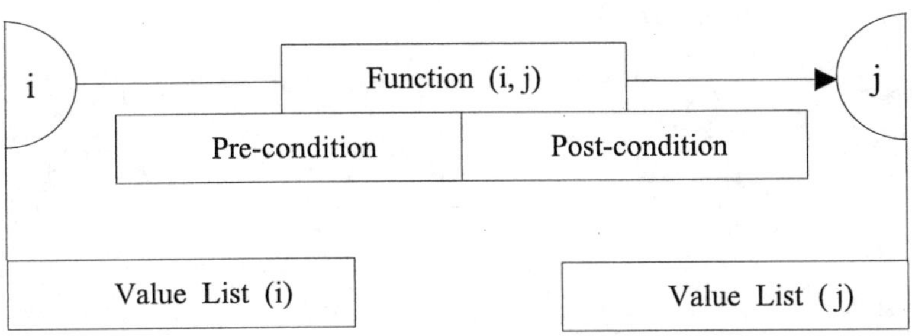

Figure 4: First three layers of GPN

Additional labels may be assigned to the arcs as shown in Figure 5.

- **Producer-Customer label:** The producer is responsible for carrying out some function and the customer needs the results from this function. The inputs of the function are transformed under the responsibility of the producers, and the output of the function is consumed by the customers.

- **Resource-Product label:** Resources are the physical inputs of the function, products are its physical outputs (resources required, products generated).

- **Data-Data label:** Input data represent the information required for performing a function and output data represent the information available after performing it (data needed, data generated).

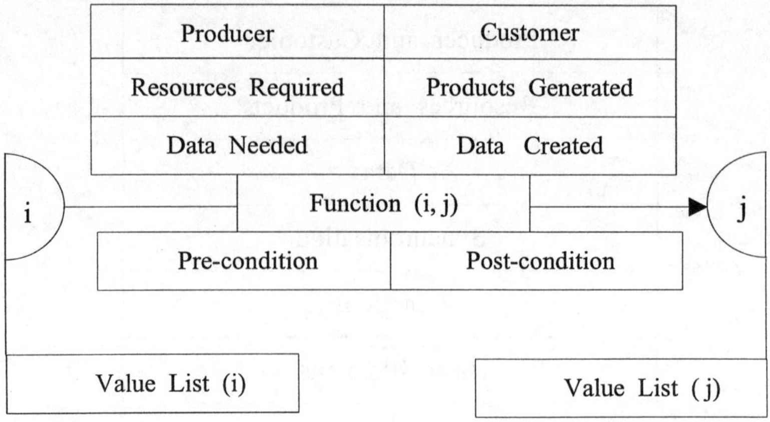

Figure 5: Labelling nodes and arcs of GPN

Nodes represent the dependencies in processing functions. We differentiate between six possible dependencies: three for beginning events and three for ending events (see Figure 6).

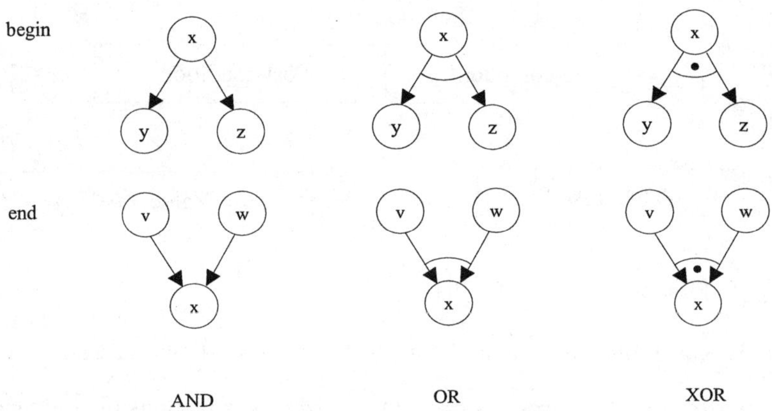

Figure 6: Beginning and ending events

- **begin-AND**: all functions triggered by this event have to be processed (all pre-conditions of all functions must be fulfilled by the value list of the triggering event),
- **begin-OR**: at least one function triggered by this event has to be processed (at least the pre-conditions of one function must be fulfilled by the value list of the triggering event),
- **begin-XOR**: one and only one function triggered by this event has to

be processed (the pre-conditions of one and only one function must be fulfilled by the value list of the triggering event),

- **end-AND**: this event occurs only if all functions ending with this event have been processed (all post-conditions of all functions must be fulfilled by the value list of the ending event),
- **end-OR**: this event occurs if at least one function ending with this event has been processed (at least the post-condition of one function must be fulfilled by the value list of the ending event),
- **end-XOR**: this event occurs if one and only one function ending with this event has been processed (the post-condition of one and only one function must be fulfilled by the value list of the ending event).

We shall now discuss how GPN can be used to model process types and process instances for planning and scheduling purposes.

4.1 Process Types

When building a model for describing process types we represent the process structure on a level where all attributes are defined but their values are not given. To represent a specific process type in some application domain all nodes, arcs and all labels will refer to objects or object types of this application, e.g.

- a producer and a customer might be two distinct organisational units of an enterprise,
- resources might be specific machines or employees with certain qualifications as well as material or incoming products to be processed,
- products might be types of goods or services,
- business functions represent specific activities for the transformations of material and information,
- the value lists of the events, all pre- and post-conditions of the functions, and all input and output data are specific to the application domain.

An example of a process type represented as a GPN schema is shown in Figure 7. The function "Generate Purchase Order" can be interpreted as an activity of a procurement process. Pre-conditions represent the assumption that there must be some "Budget Available" for purchasing. The post-condition "Ready for Ordering" which should be fulfilled after the function "Generate Purchase Order" is processed. The meaning is that the purchase order is ready for sending out. Both conditions match with some values of the list of the beginning and the ending events. Data needed for preparing a purchase order are the "Vendor" (address of vendor) and the "Items" (list of items) to be purchased; data created are all purchase order related: "Total Sum" or "Tax" (to be paid). Required resources might be a "Secretary" and a "Computer"; the product generated is a "Purchase Order Document". The manufacturing department "MD" (the customer) asks the purchasing department "PD" (the producer) to process the function "Generate Purchase Order".

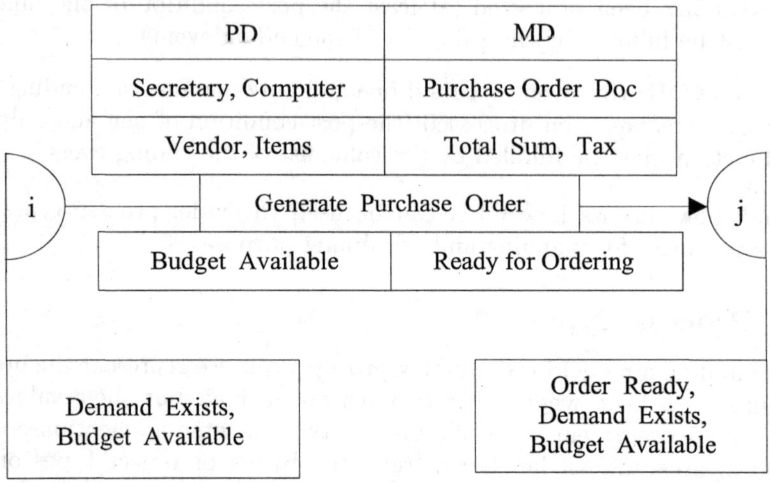

Figure 7: An example for process planning

4.2 Process Instances

In the planning phase the required attributes are defined; their values are determined once an instance of a business process is known. For example the data for "Vendor" or "Items" might be "Vendor ABC" and "Item 123". The emphasis of models for process instances is to find answers to scheduling questions, such as timing and resource allocation, taking into account competing process instances (jobs).

On an instance level a GPN will have detailed labels describing individual jobs, and there will be as many arcs (tasks) and nodes (events) as there are instances of the process. Events will be labelled by the value list describing the actual environmental situation which the event is representing for a particular process instance.

Correspondingly, the labels for the tasks refer to operational aspects essential for scheduling the process instances, such as processing times and actual required resources. Due to the competition for resources between jobs not all events can occur simultaneously. If two tasks require the same resource which cannot be shared only one of those tasks can proceed, i.e. the two tasks cannot be processed in parallel, i.e. neither the two beginning events nor the two ending events can occur at the same time. In case two or more tasks cannot be processed simultaneously, a hyperedge is introduced between the beginning events of the corresponding tasks. A hyperedge is an arc connecting events which cannot occur simultaneously but have to occur in some sequence (e.g., to be determined by the scheduler). In Figure 8 there are four events which are connected by a set of five edges showing five pairs of events which may not happen simultaneously and the corresponding hyperedge consists of nodes 1, 2, 3, and 4 connected by the five edges (1,2), (1,3), (1,4), (2,3) and (2,4).

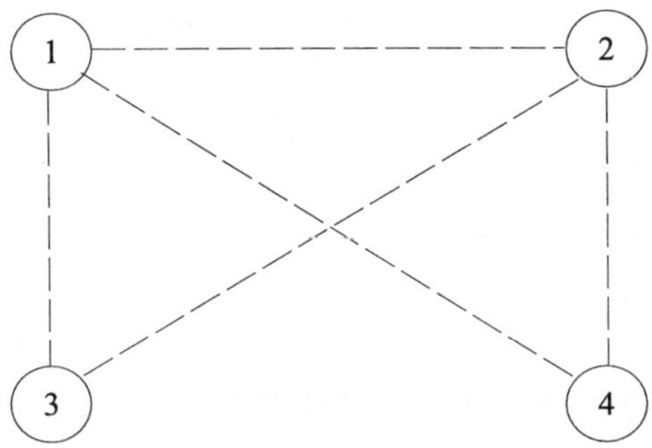

Figure 8: Nodes and edges forming hyperedges

In case of two events the hyperedge consists of one edge and two nodes only; if there are more than two events which are not allowed to occur simultaneously the hyperedge consists of all events and all edges connecting all pairs. Tasks associated with events representing nodes of a hyperedge create conflicts concerning the usage of resources. The scheduling decision has to resolve these conflicts such that a resource-feasible schedule can be generated (compare [Sch89] and [EGS97]).

A GPN schema representing the instance level is shown in Figure 9. There are two instances of the process type "Generate Purchase Order" which are "Generate Purchase Order 1" and "Generate Purchase Order 2"; both tasks have to be performed by the same resource, the employee "Smith". The producer and the customer are the same for both jobs. In order to resolve resource competition for the employee we have to introduce a hyperedge consisting of a single edge between the two beginning events triggering "Generate Purchase Order 1" and "Generate Purchase Order 2". The edges between the events represent the situation that there exists a resource conflict between the two tasks and this has to be resolved by a scheduling decision.

The introduced edges represent the combinatorial structure of the scheduling problem on the instance level. To solve the problem all conflicting events have to be put in some sequence such that a resource-feasible schedule can be constructed. Algorithms to solve this kind of problem are given in [ES93].

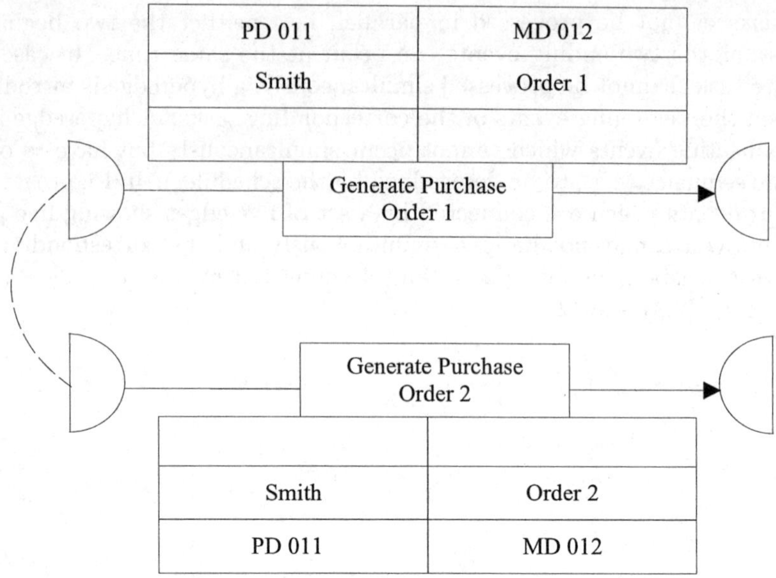

Figure 9: Edges representing a scheduling problem

5 Case Study

We shall now demonstrate how GPN can be used for integrated modelling of a business process on the planning and the scheduling levels. The example problem is related to procurement. This process deals with purchasing goods and paying corresponding bills. Let us start to explain how to build a model on the planning level considering the following setting.

If the manufacturing department (MD) of a company is running out of safety stock for some material it is asking the purchasing department (PD) to order an appropriate amount of items. PD fills in a purchase order and transmits it by mail or fax to the vendor; a copy of the purchase order is passed to the accounts payable department (APD). The vendor is sending the goods together with the receiving document to the ordering company; with separate mail the invoice is also sent.

Once the invoice arrives PD compares it with the purchase order and the goods sent via the receiving document. The documents are checked for completeness and for correctness. If the delivery is approved APD will pay the bill; if not PD complains to the vendor. Invoices for purchased goods come in regularly and have to be processed appropriately.

This process is shown in Figure 10. To be precise there are two processes shown which belong to two different companies. Arcs leading from left to right represent the functions of the purchaser's process and arcs leading from the top to the bottom represent functions of the vendor's process. Each function mentioned above is represented by an arc. The purchasing order can be sent either by fax or by mail. This is represented by the two functions "Fax Order" and "Mail Order". Once the order is confirmed by the vendor a copy of the order is also sent to APD represented by the function "Send Copy". If the ordered goods and the corresponding invoice have arrived the function "Check Invoice" can be carried out. Depending on the outcome of the checking procedure the functions "Pay" or "Complain" are performed. In case there are complains only about part of the delivery both functions are carried out.

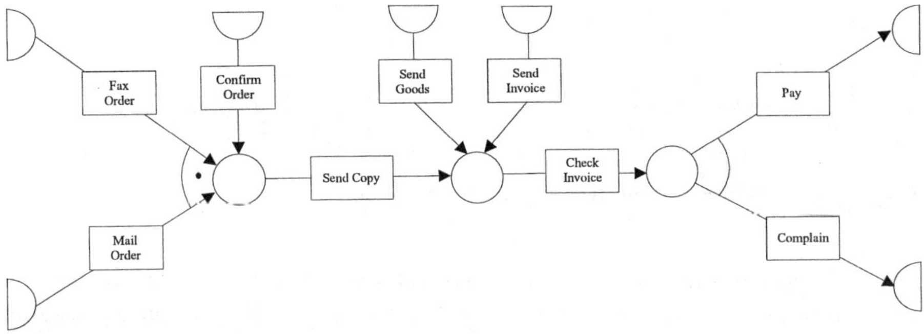

Figure 10: Procurement process

In Figure 10 the labels for most of the layers were omitted. In order to give a small example how labelling is done we concentrate on the function "Check Invoice" using all six GPN layers. The result is shown in Figure 11. We assume that PD has the responsibility for this function and MD and APD need the results. The resource needed is an auditor who is generating a report. Data needed for the "Check Invoice" function are the order and the invoice data; the function creates "Annotated Invoice" data. Before the function can be carried out the ordered goods and the invoice should have arrived; after carrying out the function the condition holds that the invoice has been checked. The remaining parts of the process have to be labelled in an analogous way.

Let us assume that the process structure which is defined on the planning level is agreed on. We now investigate the scheduling decisions considering various instances of the procurement process. We want to assume that with each individual invoice discount chances and penalty risks arise. A discount applies if the invoice is paid early enough and a penalty is due if the payment is overdue.

Now we show how GPN can be used to model this business process for scheduling purposes. Let us focus again on the function "Check Invoice". The corresponding tasks require some processing time related to the work required for checking a current invoice. Moreover, for each instance two dates are important. One relates to the time when the invoice has to be paid in

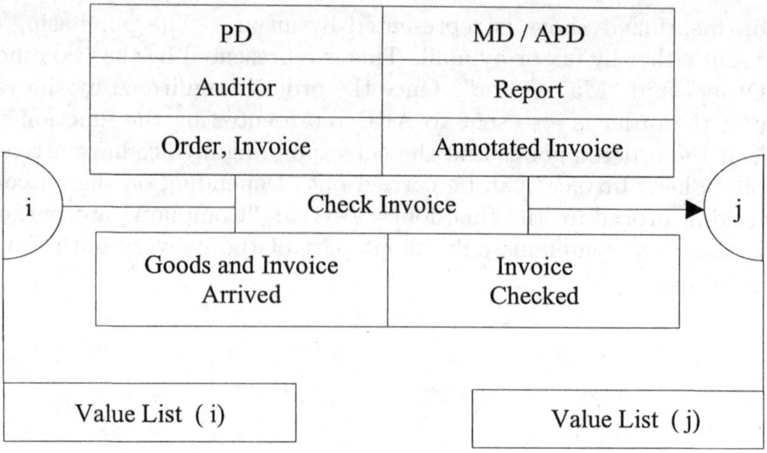

Figure 11: GPN representation of a selected function

order to receive some discount, the other relates to the time after which some additional penalty has to be paid. For the ease of the discussion we assume that discount and penalty rates are the same. Let us furthermore assume that there is only one auditor available to perform these tasks and that there are three invoices waiting to be processed. It is obvious that the sequence of processing is of major influence on the time of payment considering discount and penalty possibilities. Table 1 summarises the scheduling parameters showing invoice number (J_j), total sum of the invoice (w_j), time required to check an invoice (p_j), discount date (dd_j), penalty date (pd_j), and the rate for discount and penalty (r_j), respectively.

J_j	w_j	p_j	dd_j	pd_j	r_j
J_1	200	5	10	20	0.05
J_2	400	6	10	20	0.05
J_3	400	5	10	15	0.05

Table 1: Scheduling parameters for the example problem

In general there are n invoices with n! possibilities to process them using a single resource. The range of the results for the example is from net savings of 30 units of cash discount up to paying additional 10 units of penalty depending on the sequence of processing.

A GPN scheduling model is shown in Figure 12. All labels except resources, input data, and function are omitted. Events 1, 2, and 3 cannot occur simultaneously because there is only one "Auditor X" available for checking the invoices. To show the conflicts between the events a hyperedge is introduced which consists of the nodes 1, 2, and 3 and of the edges (1,2),

(2,3), and (1,3). The data required for scheduling relate to the processing times p_j, the amount of the invoice w_j, the discount and penalty rates r_j, the discount dates dd_j, and penalty dates pd_j; the scheduling objective is assumed to be to maximise the sum of cash discount minus the penalty to be paid.

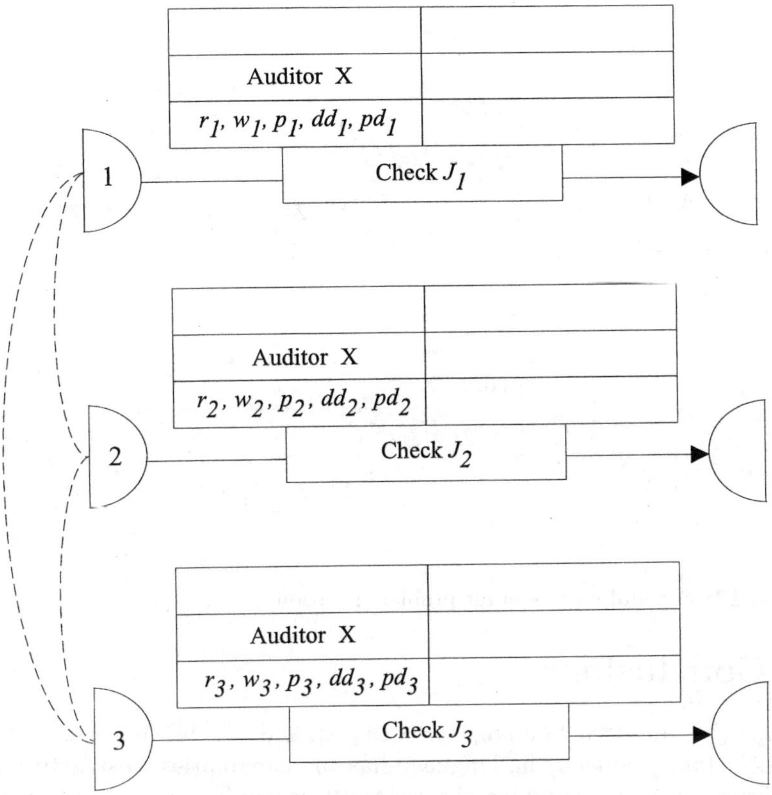

Figure 12: Scheduling model for problem representation

The scheduling decision has to determine the sequence of occurrences of the three events, i.e. the three edges have to be converted into arcs representing a predecessor-successor relationship of the events. The GPN representation is suited to apply directly a scheduling procedure which tries to find an optimal sequence by converting edges into arcs. This is a standard formalism for representing and solving scheduling problems [Pin95]. If the direction of the arcs is determined a complete schedule for the three instances can be generated. The optimal schedule is shown in Figure 13.

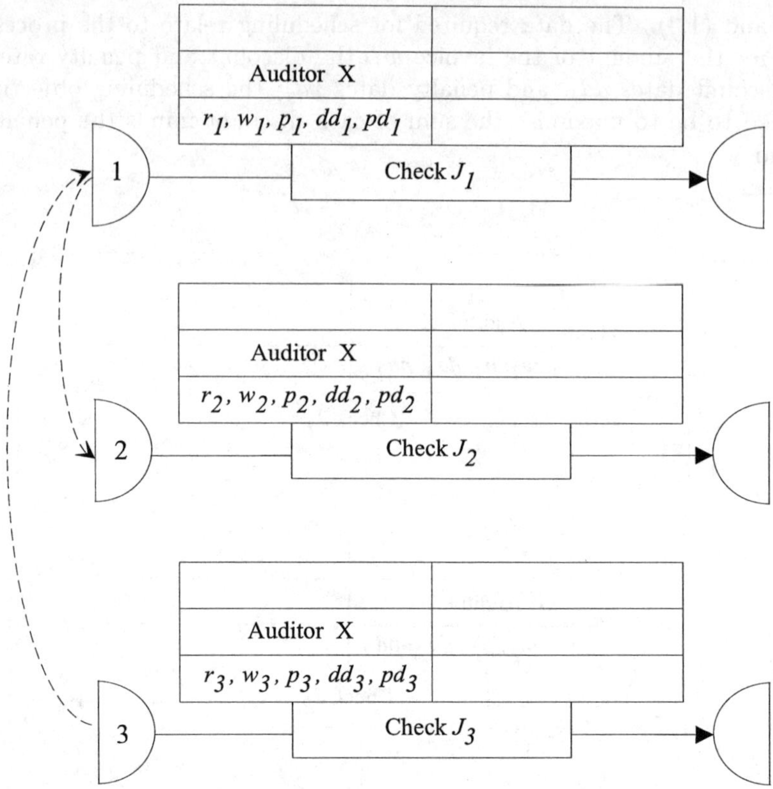

Figure 13: Scheduling model for problem solution

6 Conclusions

We have presented the language GPN to plan and schedule business processes within a single model. The language has the capabilities to structure problems from a descriptive point of view and to show how to optimise business processes when they have to be carried out. The language is easy to understand and easy to use and it is especially suited for modelling time-based assignment problems with a combinatorial structure.

We have not discussed how to evaluate process plans and have not presented algorithms to solve the arising scheduling problems. The scope of this contribution is to demonstrate that planning and scheduling problems can be modelled using a common and easy to use notational framework. We have illustrated this by an example case study. There are many business processes which can be analysed and optimised using the notational framework of GPN.

References

[BEPSW96] Blazewicz, J., Ecker, K., Pesch, E., Schmidt, G., Weglarz, J., Scheduling Computer and Manufacturing Processes, Springer, Berlin, 1996

[BN96] Bernus, P., Nemes, L., Modelling and Methodologies for Enterprise Integration, Chapman and Hall, London, 1996

[CKO92] Curtis, B., Kellner, M. I., Over, J., Process modeling, Communications of the ACM 35(9), 1992, 75-90

[EGS97] Ecker, K., Gupta, J., Schmidt, G., A framework for decision support systems for scheduling problems, European Journal of Operational Research, 101, 1997, 452-462

[ES93] Ecker, K., Schmidt, G., Conflict resolution algorithms for scheduling problems, in: K. Ecker, R. Hirschberg (eds.), Lessach Workshop on Parallel Processing, Report No. 93/5, TU Clausthal, 1993, 81-90

[SW89] Slowinski, R., Weglarz, J., (eds.), Recent Advances in Project Scheduling, Elsevier, Amsterdam, 1989

[MC94] Malone, T. W., Crowston, K., The interdisciplinary study of coordination, ACM Computing Surveys 26(1), 1994, 87-119

[Pin95] Pinedo, M., Scheduling: Theory, Algorithms, and Systems, Prentice Hall, Englewood Cliffs, 1995

[Sch89] Schmidt, G., Constraint-satisfaction problems in project scheduling, in: [SW89], 135-150

[Sch96] Schmidt, G., Scheduling models for workflow management, in: B. Scholz-Reiter, E. Stickel (eds.), Business Process Modelling, Springer, 1996, 67-80

[Sch96a] Schmidt, G., Informationsmanagement - Modelle, Methoden, Techniken, Springer, Berlin, 1996

[Sch96b] Schmidt, G., Modelling production scheduling systems, Int. J. Production Economics 46-47, 1996, 109-118

[Sch97] Schmidt, G., Prozeßmanagement - Modelle und Methoden, Springer, Berlin, 1997

CHAPTER 10

The IDEF Family of Languages

Christopher Menzel, Richard J. Mayer

The purpose of this contribution is to serve as a clear introduction to the modeling languages of the three most widely used IDEF methods: IDEF0, IDEF1X, and IDEF3. Each language is presented in turn, beginning with a discussion of the underlying "ontology" the language purports to describe, followed by presentations of the syntax of the language — particularly the notion of a model for the language — and the semantical rules that determine how models are to be interpreted. The level of detail should be sufficient to enable the reader both to understand the intended areas of application of the languages and to read and construct simple models of each of the three types.

1 Introduction

A modeling method comprises a specialized modeling *language* for representing a certain class of information, and a modeling *methodology* for collecting, maintaining, and using the information so represented. The focus of this paper will be on the languages of the three most widely used IDEF methods: The IDEF0 business function modeling method, the IDEF1X data modeling method, and the IDEF3 process modeling method.

Any usable modeling language has both a syntax and a semantics: a set of rules (often implicit) that determines the legitimate syntactic constructs of the language, and a set of rules (often implicit) the determines the meanings of those constructs. It is not the purpose of this paper is to serve as an exhaustive reference manual for the three IDEF languages at issue. Nor will it discuss the methodologies that underlie the applications of the languages. There are other sources that discuss these issues ([NIST93a, NIST93b, MMP93]). Rather, the purpose of this paper is simply to serve as a clear introduction to the IDEF languages proper, that is, to their basic syntax and semantics. It is thus hoped that the paper will quickly enable the reader both to understand the intended areas of application of the languages and, more specifically, to read and construct simple models of each of the three types.

2 Background to the IDEF Languages

The IDEF suite of modeling languages arose in the 1970s out of the U.S. Air Force Integrated Computer Aided Manufacturing (ICAM) program. The goal of ICAM was to leverage computer technology to increase manufacturing productivity. A fundamental assumption of the program was the need for powerful but usable modeling methods to support system design and analysis. Consequently, the program undertook the development of a suite of "ICAM DEFinition," or IDEF, methods. These included an activity, or "function," modeling method (IDEF0), a conceptual modeling method (IDEF1), and a simulation model specification method (IDEF2). IDEF0 was based loosely upon the Structured Analysis and Design Technique (SADT) pioneered by Douglas Ross [Ros77] and IDEF1 upon the Entity, Link, Key Attribute (ELKA) method developed chiefly at Hughes Aircraft by Timothy Ramey and Robert Brown [RB87]. Since the ICAM program there have been several important developments. First, in 1983, the Air Force Integrated Information Support System (I^2S^2) program added several constructs to the IDEF1 method that were felt to make it more suitable as a database schema modeling method. The result was IDEF1X, which is now more widely used than IDEF1. Beginning in the late 1980s, work began on a process modeling method known as IDEF3, and was completed under the Air Force Information Integration for Concurrent Engineering (IICE) program. IDEF3 subsumes much of the original role of IDEF2, as it can be used for the specification of effective first-cut simulation models. Additionally, the IDEF3 language has an object-state component that can be used for modeling how objects undergo change in a process. The early 1990s saw the emergence of IDEF4 and IDEF5. IDEF4 is an object-oriented software design method that integrates requirements specified in other methods through a process of iterative refinement. It also supports the capture and management of design rationale. IDEF5 is a knowledge acquisition and engineering method designed to support the construction of enterprise *ontologies* [Gru93]. Because of space limitations, these newer methods will not be discussed further in this paper. Interested readers are referred to [MKB95] and [MBM94].

Recent developments have focused on refinement and *integration* of the IDEF languages. That is, the focus has been on the development of both theory and techniques to support the easy exchange of information between different IDEF (and non-IDEF) models, and, ultimately, on the automated exchange and propagation of information between IDEF (and non-IDEF) modeling software applications. To reflect these developments, "IDEF" is now usually taken to be an acronym for *Integration DEFinition.*

The IDEF0, IDEF1X, and, increasingly, IDEF3 methods are widely used in both government and the commercial business sectors. The focus of this paper will be on the languages of these methods. In many presentations of one or another IDEF language, syntax and semantics are intermingled so as to make them difficult to distinguish. A goal of this paper is to keep this distinction sharp. Thus, each major section begins with a discussion of the basic semantic, or *ontological*, categories of the method at hand, independent of any syntactic considerations. Only then is the syntax of the language introduced, first its *lexicon* (i.e., its more primitive elements), then its *grammar* (i.e., the rules determine how complex expressions are ultimately built up from the elements of the lexicon).

3 The IDEF0 Function Modeling Language

We begin with the IDEF0 function modeling language, the method for building models of enterprise activities.

3.1 The IDEF0 Ontology: Functions and ICOMs

In general, an activity is a *thing that happens*, whether (in effect) instantaneously or over some (possibly fragmented, discontinuous) period of time. Simple examples of activities include the death of Caesar, Jessie Owens' running of the 100 yard dash in the finals of the 1936 Olympics, and the writing of this paper. In IDEF0 modeling, however, attention is often focused not just on actual "as-is" activities, but *possible* activities as well — the activities of a merely envisioned company, for example, or those of a proposed virtual enterprise. Thus, one might say, the primary focus of IDEF0's ontology — the things that exist according to IDEF0 — is the class of all possible activities, whether actual or not. However, it is not concerned with just any sort of activity, but with a certain kind, known in IDEF0 as a *function*. Thus, IDEF0 is often referred to as a "function modeling method." An IDEF0 function is a special kind of activity, namely, one that, typically, takes certain inputs and, by means of some mechanism, and subject to certain controls, transforms the inputs into outputs — note the parallel with the notion of a mathematical function wherein a given set of *arguments* (inputs) is "transformed" into a unique *value* (output). (That noted, we shall follow common practice and usually use the generic term 'activity'.) The notions of input and output should be intuitively clear. Controls are things like laws, policies, standards, unchangeable facts of the environment, and the like that can guide or constrain an activity, and mechanisms are resources that are used in bringing about the intended goals of the activity. Thus, for example, in an Implement Software Prototype activity, relevant controls might be such things as a high-level software design, software documentation standards, and the operating systems of the development environment. And the most salient mechanisms would likely be the programmers on the project (together with their computers). Intuitively, there are no salient inputs to this activity, as nothing is actually transformed or destroyed as the activity is actually carried out, and the output is, of course, the completed prototype.

Inputs, controls, outputs, and mechanisms are referred to generally in

IDEF0 as *concepts*, or *ICOMs* (an acronym for the four types of concept). The former term is a bit of a misnomer, for, unlike the ordinary meaning of the term, an IDEF0 concept needn't be an abstract or mental entity. Hence, because it has no connotations from ordinary language, the latter term will be used here. An ICOM, then, can be any entity — mental or physical, abstract or concrete — that plays a certain role in an activity. Note, however, that the same entity might play different roles in different activities. Thus, a particular NC machine might both be the output of a Make-NC-machine activity, and the main mechanism for transforming material input into output in a Make-widget activity. Note also that an ICOM can be a complex object (a car body, for example) that is composed of many other objects.[1]

3.2 IDEF0 Syntax: Boxes and Arrow Segments

The world according to IDEF0, then, consists of activities (functions) and ICOMs. Accordingly, the graphical language of IDEF0 contains two basic constructs: *boxes*, representing activities, and *arrow segments*, representing ICOMs. Arrow segments have a *head* — indicated explicitly by an arrowhead when necessary — and a *tail*. Arrow segments combine to form *arrows*, which will be discussed below. The basic constructs of IDEF0 are built up by connecting boxes and arrow segments together in certain allowable ways. Specifically, the head of an arrow segment can only connect to the bottom, left side, or top of a box, or to the tail of another arrow segment. The tail of an arrow segment can only connect to the right side of a box, or to the head of another arrow segment. The most basic construct of IDEF0 is depicted in a general fashion in Figure 1, along with indications of the type of entity in the IDEF0 ontology each component of the construct signifies.

Notice that the box side to which an arrow segment attaches indicates the type of ICOM that it represents *relative to the activity represented by that box.* Arrow segments representing inputs, controls, and mechanisms for the function in question attach at the head to the left side, top, and bottom of a box, respectively, and are said to be the *incoming* segments of that box. Arrow segments indicating outputs attach at the tail end to the right side of a box, and are said to be the *outgoing* segments of that box. Every box in a model must have at least one incoming control arrow segment and one outgoing output arrow segment. A control segment is required because there must be something that guides, determines, or constrains a well defined enterprise function; random, unstructured, unrepeatable activities are beyond the scope of the IDEF0 method. An output segment is required because oth-

[1] It should be noted that, when talking in general about a certain *kind* of activity, as they are wont, by an ICOM a modeler often means a corresponding *class* of particular ICOMs, e.g., the class of NC machine outputs from all Make-NC-machine activities of a certain sort. Context typically determines whether one is speaking about classes or instances, and, accordingly, we shall not be overly zealous in specifying which "level" we ourselves intend at every point in this article.

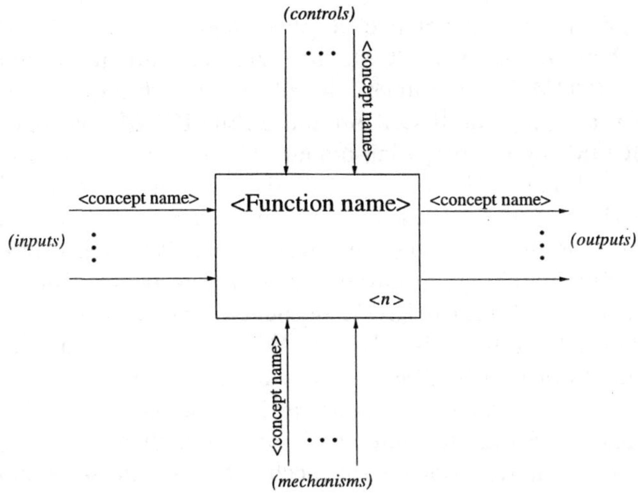

Figure 1: The Basic IDEF0 Construct

erwise there would be no purpose served by the activity, and hence it would add no value to the enterprise. Inputs, though typical, are not required, as not every function involves the consumption or transformation of some object, e.g., writing an email message. Similarly, some activities, e.g., high-level planning, may require no separate, identifiable mechanism.

3.3 IDEF0 Diagrams

Boxes and arrow segments are combined in various ways to form *diagrams*. The boxes in a diagram are connected by sequences of arrow segments, which can fork and join within a diagram as depicted in Figure 2.

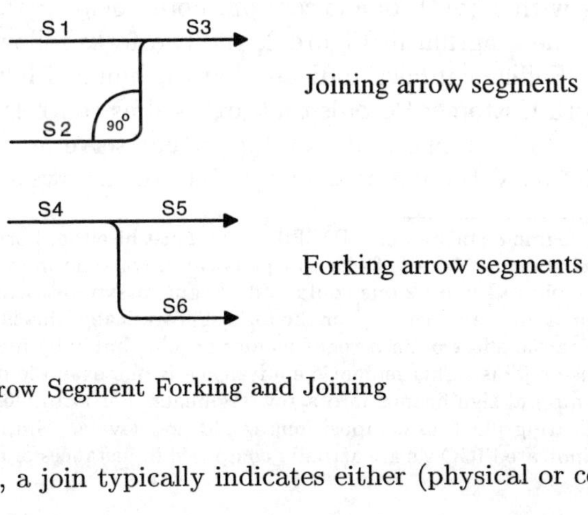

Figure 2: Arrow Segment Forking and Joining

In IDEF0, a join typically indicates either (physical or conceptual) composition or generalization. Hence, a (three-segment[2]) join is often said to indicate the *bundling* of two ICOMs into another, and the more complex or more general ICOM is sometimes referred to as a "bundle." Thus, in Figure 2, S1 might signify the ICOM Ad and S2 the ICOM Envelope and S3 the composite ICOM, or bundle, Mail-promo, whose instances consist of sealed envelopes containing copies of the advertisement in question. (In cases of composition there is often an underlying enterprise activity, but one which is not considered significant enough to warrant explicit representation.) Again, S1 might signify the ICOM Inventory Entry, S2 the ICOM Billing Entry, and S3 the more general, bundled ICOM Account Entries. As the term indicates, it is usually best to think of bundled ICOMs like fiber bundles in fiber-optic cables: instances of two ICOMs that are bundled together into a third are not mingled indistinguishably together, as in a confluence of two rivers; they are simply packaged together and, without losing their original characters, both delivered as inputs, controls, or mechanisms to the same functions.

A join can also simply indicate recognition of a single ICOM whose instances stem from different sources. In this case, all three segments involved in a join indicate exactly the same ICOM. Such cases are usually signified by attaching a label only to the "merged" segment (S3 in Figure 2).

A fork, naturally, is the "dual" of a join. That is, a fork indicates either (physical or conceptual) *de*composition or specialization. Forks are therefore also commonly said to indicate an *un*bundling of one ICOM into two others (one of which might be identical with the initial ICOM). As with joins, a fork can also simply indicate the recognition of a single ICOM whose instances are used as inputs, controls, or mechanism for different functions.

To illustrate, consider the diagram in Figure 3 which represents, from an accounting perspective, the activities initiated by the receipt of a customer order. As illustrated, the connected boxes in an IDEF0 diagram are represented in a "stair step" fashion (on a page or computer screen) from top left to lower right. Each box from top left to lower right is numbered sequentially beginning with 1 (with one exception, noted below); this is the box's *box number*. In the diagram in Figure 3, the two forks following the arrow segment labeled 'Fulfillment Files' indicate that the bundled ICOM Fulfillment Files includes both Customer Records that are used as controls on the Deliver function and the Price Tables and Tax Tables that serve as controls on the Bill function. Similarly, the join that merges into the arrows segment labeled

[2]Because arrow segments in standard IDEF0 syntax must be either horizontal or vertical except perhaps for 90 degree bends, forks and joins can involve no more than four arrow segments — to the join in Figure 2 one could add a segment symmetrical to S2 that joins the other three from above; analogously for the fork. Theoretically, this is no limitation, as one can get the semantic effect of an n-segment fork or join simply by means of a series of three-segment forks or joins. This semantic equivalence is one example of why one ought not to read any temporal significance into arrow segments. For example, a series of joins in a model all indicating physical compositions would not have any implications for how (instances of) the indicated ICOMs are actually composed in instances of the activity being modeled.

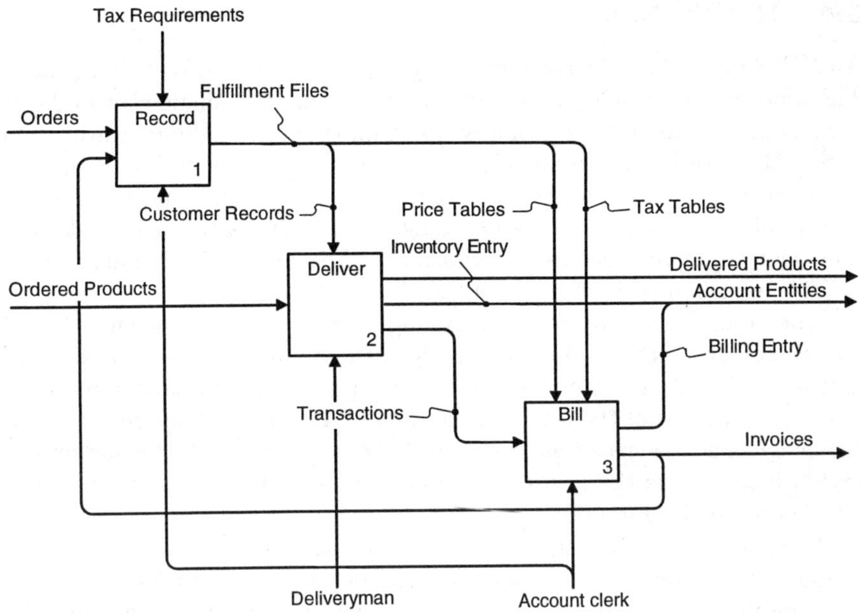

Figure 3: An IDEF0 diagram

'Account Entries' indicates that the Account Entries bundle includes both Inventory Entries and Billing Entries. The fact that the segments forking from the segment labeled 'Account Clerk' are unlabeled indicates that an Account Clerk is used as a mechanism in both the Bill and Record functions.

An *arrow* is a certain kind of sequence of arrow segments within a diagram. An arrow originating at one box and ending at another indicates a resource connection between the indicated functions — though one of those functions may be only implicit if one end of the arrow's initial or final segment is not attached to anything in the diagram. Thus, syntactically, an IDEF0 *arrow* within a diagram D is defined to be a connected sequence of arrow segments in D such that at least one end (i.e., the tail of its initial segment or the head of its final segment) is attached to a box and the other is either attached to a box or unattached to anything in the diagram. Thus, for example, in Figure 3, the Orders arrow segment is itself an arrow, as is the sequence consisting of the Fulfillment Files segment, the unlabeled segment it is attached to it (which, by convention, also signifies the Fulfillment Files bundle), and the segment labeled 'Tax Tables'. Arrows (arrow segments) that are unattached at one end are known as *boundary arrows* (*boundary arrow segments*).

3.4 IDEF0 Models

An IDEF0 *model* is a hierarchically arranged collection of IDEF0 diagrams.[3] The hierarchy is actually an (inverted) tree: there is a single root node, and each node of the tree has some finite number of "daughters"; every node except the root has only one "mother". The root node of an IDEF0 model is known as the *top-level*, or *context*, diagram of the model.[4] Unlike every other diagram in the model, the top-level diagram contains only one box. This box represents — at the coarsest granularity — the single high-level activity that is being represented by the entire IDEF0 model.

The mother-daughter relation holding between two diagrams in an IDEF0 model signifies that the daughter node is the *decomposition* of a box in the mother node. A decomposition of a box B is a diagram that represents a finer-grained view of the function signified by B. Such a diagram D is known variously as a *decomposition diagram*, *detail diagram*, or *child diagram* for B, and B is known as the *parent box* of D. Only one detail diagram per box is allowed in an IDEF0 model.

By convention, a detail diagram contains three to six boxes. The traditional justification for this is that a diagram with fewer than three boxes does not contain sufficient detail to constitute a useful decomposition; similarly, a diagram with more than six boxes contains detail that should be suppressed within that diagram and unpacked in a decomposition. Many users have found this "3-6 box rule" too constraining and have proposed replacing it with a "2-9 box rule," and in fact the latter rule has been incorporated into a proposed IEEE IDEF0 standard [IEEE97].[5]

A simple IDEF0 model for a computer assembly activity can be found in Figure 4. Each diagram within a model has a *diagram number*, and each box within a diagram a unique *node number*. The top level diagram of a model has the diagram number A-0 ("A-minus-zero") and its single box has the node number A0. The number of every other diagram is simply the node number of its parent box (as every diagram but the top-level diagram is the child diagram of some box). The node number of a box in the A0 diagram (i.e., the child diagram of the A0 box) is An, where n is box's box number within the diagram. The node number of a box within every other child diagram is simply the result of concatenating the diagram's diagram number with the box's box number. Thus, the node number of Assemble CPU is A1, while that of Install Storage Devices is A13.

Let B be a box and D a diagram within a model M. B is an *ancestor* of D (within M) just in case B is either the parent box of D (in M), or the

[3] This is not strictly correct, as an IDEF0 model is typically taken also to include textual annotations and glossary, but as the focus of this article is the graphical language proper, we have chosen to ignore these more pragmatic elements of a model.

[4] In fact the top-level diagram for a model can itself be embedded within other, "environmental" context diagrams, but this subtlety will not be discussed in this paper.

[5] At the time of this writing, this document had successfully gone to ballot, and was under revision.

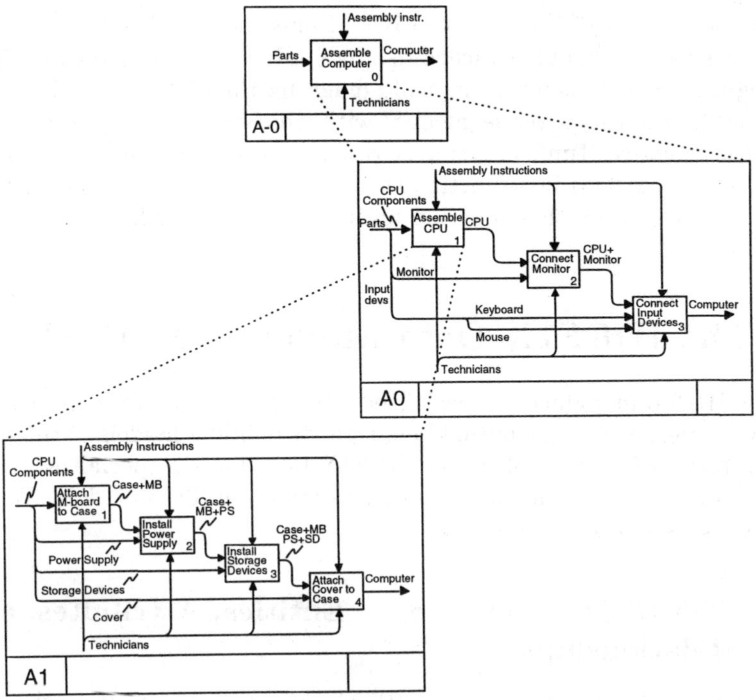

Figure 4: A Simple IDEF0 model

parent box of a diagram containing some ancestor of D (that is, just in case B is either the parent box of D, or the parent box of the diagram containing the parent box of D, or the parent box of the diagram containing the parent box of the diagram containing the parent box of D, and so on). Conversely, D is a *descendent* of B in M just in case B is an ancestor of D in M. Given this, we note that boundary arrow segments in a non-context diagram D within a model indicate ICOMs that are present in the activity indicated by some ancestor B of D — for D is simply a decomposition of B or of an activity indicated by a box in one of the descendents of B. Consequently, a boundary arrow segment that is unattached at its tail (respectively, head) can be correlated with an incoming (respectively, outgoing) arrow segment for some ancestor of D. Such a correlation is typically accomplished by labeling both arrows with the same name.[6] Conversely, and more strongly, every incoming or outgoing segment of a box with descendents *should* be correlated with an appropriate boundary arrow segment in one of its descendents (else

[6]Traditionally, IDEF0 has used a somewhat awkward system of "ICOM codes" to achieve such correlations. However, ICOM codes are both unnecessary, as the same effect can be achieved by the consistent use of names, and are also largely rendered otiose by modern modeling support software which can track such correlations with ease.

the exact function of the indicated ICOM must not be clear).

If an arrow segment S attached to a parent box is correlated with a boundary segment S′ that is not in its child diagram, then S is said to be *tunneled downwards*, and the arrow segment S′ with which it is correlated is said to be *tunneled upwards*. Tunneling simply provides a mechanism for "hiding" the role of a given ICOM in a function through the successive decompositions of the box representing that function until the appropriate level of granularity is reached.

4 The IDEF1X Data Modeling Method

Just as IDEF0 introduces a specialized ontology tailored for capturing business activities, and a specialized language for building models of those activities in terms of that ontology, so IDEF1X introduces a specialized ontology and a corresponding language tailored to build database models. We begin with a discussion of its ontology.

4.1 The IDEF1X Ontology: Entities, Attributes, and Relationships

Not surprisingly, the ontology of IDEF1X corresponds closely to the ontologies other database modeling languages such as the Entity-Relationship (ER) and NIAM modeling languages. The basic ontological categories of IDEF1X are *entities*, *attributes*, and *relationships*. We discuss each category in turn.[7]

4.1.1 Entities

Entities are simply classes of actual or — when "to be" situations are being modeled — possible things in the world. Entities can comprise concrete objects, such as employees and NC machines; more idealized objects such as companies and countries; and even abstract objects like laws and spacetime coordinates. The things comprised by a given entity are known as the *members* or *instances* of the entity. IDEF1X entities thus correspond to ERA entity sets and NIAM entity classes.[8]

[7] It should be noted that we will only be discussing so-called "key-based" views. Officially, IDEF1X models can contain numerous "views", where a view, like the notion of a model here, is a structured collection of entity boxes and relationship links. Views differ in the constraints they satisfy. Specifically, the ER view does not require the identification of keys, and allows "nonspecific", many-to-many relationships (see below for definition of these notions). For the sake of brevity, in this paper we are identifying models with what are known as "fully-attributed" views in IDEF1X, in which keys must be identified and all many-to-many relationships must be resolved into functional relationships.

[8] The term 'entity' is rather unfortunate, since in ordinary language it is a rough synonym for 'thing' or 'object', i.e., for individual *instances* of classes rather than classes themselves. IDEF1 uses the more appropriate term 'entity class'.

4.1.2 Attributes

Every entity has an associated set of attributes. Attributes are simply functions, or mappings, in the mathematical sense: an attribute associates each instance of a given entity with a unique value. An attribute α is *for* a given entity E if it is defined on all and only the instances of E.[9] In IDEF1X, the set of values that an attribute can return is known as the attribute's *domain*.[10] The domain of every attribute referred to in an IDEF1X model is always one of several familiar data types; specifically, it is either the type *string*, a numerical type of some ilk, the type *boolean*, or else a subtype of one of these basic types. So, for example, common attributes for an EMPLOYEE entity might be Name (of type *string*), Citizenship (subtype of *string*, viz., names of countries), Yearly-salary (*positive integer*), Marital-status (*boolean*), and so on.

A central notion in IDEF1X is that of a *candidate key*, or simply, *key*. A key for an entity E is a set of attributes for E that jointly distinguish every instance of the entity from every other. More exactly, where α is an attribute, let $\alpha(e)$ be the value of α applied to e. Let A be a set of attributes for an entity E. Then A is a key for E just in case, for any distinct instances e, e' of E, there is an attribute $\alpha \in A$ such that $\alpha(e) \neq \alpha(e')$. Ideally, a key should be a *smallest* set of this sort, in the sense that no proper subset of a key is also a key. If an attribute α is a member of a key, it is said to be a *key attribute*.

4.1.3 Relationships

Relationships are classes of associations between instances of two (possibly identical) entities. In the context of IDEF1X, one of the two entities is identified as the *parent* entity and the other as the *child* entity. Let R be a relationship, and let E^R_P be its parent entity and E^R_C its child. Then the one general requirement on relationships is that for each instance e of E^R_C there is at most one instance e' of E^R_P such that e is associated (by R) with e'.[11] Also, typically, in an IDEF1X model, no instance of a relationship's child entity fails to be associated with an instance of its parent, though this is not always required. (See the notion of an "optional" non-identifying relationship below.) If E is the child of a relationship R and E' the parent, then R will be said to *link E to E'*. (This is not standard IDEF1X terminology, but it proves very useful for exposition.)

---

[9] Partial attributes — i.e., attributes that are not defined on all the instances of an entity — are allowed in ER views.

[10] This is another unfortunate choice of terminology, as the term 'domain' in mathematics is the usual name for the set of *arguments* for a function, and the term 'range' denotes the set of its possible values, i.e., the attribute's "domain" in the sense of IDEF1X.

[11] In ER views, "non-specific" relationships are allowed that don't satisfy this requirement; specifically, in a non-specific relationship an instance of the child might be associated with more than one instance of the parent.

It is convenient to think of a relationship R as a class of ordered pairs $\langle a, b\rangle$ such that the first element a of each such pair is an instance of R's child entity and the second element b is an instance of its parent entity. The general requirement on relationships, then, can be expressed simply as the requirement that a relationship R be *functional*, in the sense that, for $a \in E_C^R$ and $b \in E_P^R$, if Rab (i.e., if $\langle a, b\rangle \in R$) and Rac, then $b = c$. Given this, to say that a given instance e of R's child entity E_C^R is *associated (by R) with* an instance e' of R's parent entity E_P^R is simply to say that eRe'; likewise, to say that a given instance e of E_P^R is associated with an instance e' of E_C^R is to say that $Re'e$. We say that R is *total* if for each instance e of E_C^R there is an instance e' of E_P^R such that Ree'. Otherwise R is said to be *partial*. Since relationships R are functional, we will sometimes write '$R(a)$' to indicate the unique object b such that Rab (when it is known that there is such an object b).

4.1.3.1 Cardinality The *cardinality* of a relationship R signifies how many instances of the child entity a given instance of the parent is associated with. Often a relationship has no specific cardinality; one instance of the parent might be associated by R with two instances of the child, another with seventeen. The most that can be said in such cases is that the relationship has a cardinality of *zero, one, or more*, which is true under any circumstances. But often enough this is not the case. IDEF1X marks out in particular the following cardinalities for R: *one or more* (signifying that R, viewed as a function from E_C^R to E_P^R, is onto, or surjective); *zero or one* (indicating that R, viewed as a function, is one-to-one, or injective); *exactly n*; and *from n to m*.

4.1.3.2 Attribute Migration The functionality of relationships leads to the important notion of key attribute *migration*. Suppose R links E to E' and let α be a key attribute for the parent entity E'. Because R maps each instance e of E to a unique instance e' of E', a new (migrated) attribute for E can be defined as the *composition* $R \circ \alpha$ of α and R.[12] Thus, more procedurally, to discover the value $R \circ \alpha(e)$ of the migrated attribute $R \circ \alpha$ on a given instance e of E, one first finds the instance e' of E' associated with e by R, and then applies α to e'; i.e., $R \circ \alpha(e) = \alpha(R(e))$. This is the value of the migrated attribute on e. (An example is given below.)

The notion of migration is often documented misleadingly so as to suggest that a migrated attribute in the child entity of a relationship is the very same attribute as the migrating attribute in the parent entity. Since they are attributes for different entities, however, the two must be distinct. It is more correct to characterize migration as a *relation* involving two attributes and a relationship. More exactly, let R be a relationship and α and α' attributes, and let E be the child entity of R and E' the parent entity. Then we say that

[12] Where, as usual, $f \circ g(x) = g(f(x))$.

α' *migrates from* E' *to* E *as* α *via* R if and only if (i) α and α' are attributes for E and E', respectively, (ii) R links E to E' and (iii) for all instances e of E, $\alpha(e) = \alpha'(R(e))$. We will call α' the *migrating* attribute and α the *migrated* attribute (relative to R). Note that a migrated attribute relative to one relationship can itself be a migrating attribute relative another.

4.1.3.3 Categorization Relationships A particularly important type of relationship in IDEF1X is a *categorization relationship.* Basically, a categorization relationship is just the identity relation restricted to a certain subclass of a given entity; that is, a categorization relation maps a member of a subclass of a given entity to itself in that entity. The importance of these relationships is that they are used to form *categorization clusters*, which divide a given entity — known as the *generic* entity in the cluster — into several disjoint subclasses or *category* entities. Thus, the generic entity in a cluster might be the entity EMPLOYEE, and SALARIED_EMPLOYEE and HOURLY_EMPLOYEE the category entities in the cluster. A category cluster is *complete* if the category entities jointly constitute a *partition* of the generic entity, i.e., if every instance of the category entity is an instance of a (unique) category entity.

It is often useful to identify a *discriminator attribute* for a category cluster that returns, for each instance of the generic entity, a standard name for its category. Thus, the discriminator attribute for the EMPLOYEE cluster above would return either the string 'SALARIED_EMPLOYEE' or 'HOURLY_EMPLOYEE' on each generic entity instance. (For incomplete clusters, a discriminator attribute would have to be either undefined on generic instances that are in no category, or else would have to return a string indicating this, e.g., 'NIL'.)

4.2 The IDEF1X Language and its Semantics

Entities, attributes, and relationships constitute the basic ontology of IDEF1X, the basic categories of things that one talks about in the IDEF1X language. In this section we describe the language itself and its semantical connections to these objects.

The basic syntactic elements of the IDEF1X language are *entity boxes*, *attribute names*, and various kinds of *relationship links*. These elements, of course, signify entities, attributes, and relationships, respectively. An IDEF1X *model* is a collection of entity boxes, attribute names, and relationship links that satisfy certain conditions, which we will state in the course of our exposition. As with our account of IDEF0, then, we will continue to use the term 'model' to indicate a certain kind of complex syntactic entity. However, an entity, attribute, or relationship can be said to be "in" a model insofar as that entity, attribute, or relationship is indicated by a corresponding entity box, attribute name, or relationship link in the model.

Entity boxes come in two varieties, ones with square corners and ones with rounded corners, as indicated in Figure 5.

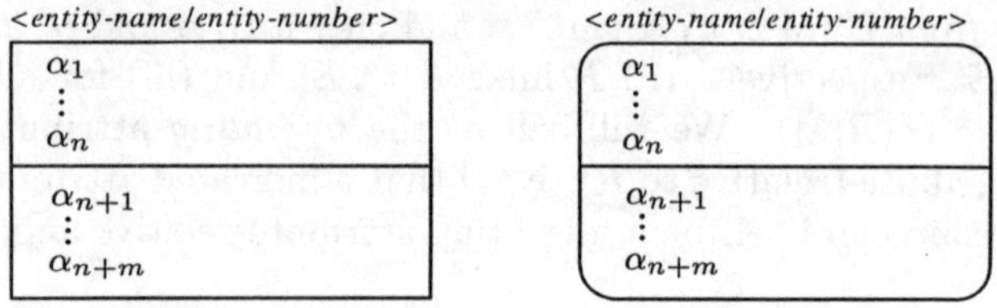

Figure 5: Entity Boxes

The α_i are attribute names. The names $\alpha_1, ..., \alpha_n$, written above the line, indicate the members of a distinguished key for the indicated entity, known (in the context of a model containing the given entity box) as the *primary key* for the entity. n here must be at least 1; that is, it is required that a primary key be identified for every entity indicated in a model. The same entity, of course, could have a different primary key in a different model, although, of course, it would have to be denoted by a correspondingly different entity box in that model. $\alpha_{n+1}, ..., \alpha_{n+m}$ indicate other, non-key attributes for the entity.

Which of the two kinds of box to use for an entity in a model depends on the kinds of relationships that link that entity to other entities indicated in the model. Perhaps the most common type of relationship between entities in a model is an *identifying* relationship, the IDEF1X syntax for which is given in Figure 6. To define this notion, note first that it is a requirement on IDEF1X models that, for any relationship R, all and only the attributes in the primary key of R's parent entity migrate to its child entity via R.[13] R is an *identifying* relationship if all of the attributes in the parent's primary key migrate via R as attributes in the child's primary key; otherwise R is a *nonidentifying* relationship. The idea here is that, procedurally, an instance e of the child entity in a relationship can be identified — i.e., its key attribute values determined — only by first identifying e's associated instance e' in the parent entity, i.e., by first determining all of *its* (e''s) key attribute values. If an entity E is the child entity in an identifying relationship R in a model, then a box with rounded corners is used to indicate E in that model. Otherwise, a box with square corners is used.

A simple example is given in Figure 7. In this example, the primary key attribute Dept_number migrates as the attribute Works_in.Dept_number, which appears as a primary key attribute of EMPLOYEE. The relationship is therefore, by definition, an identifying one. In the example, Emp_numbers alone are not in general sufficient to distinguish one EMPLOYEE from an-

[13]Migrated attributes are sometimes referred to as "foreign keys", or, a bit less problematically, "foreign key attributes", and are often marked with the expression '(FK)'. This marking is otiose if the full name of the migrated attribute is given (i.e., if a role name is used in naming the attribute; see below) but can be heuristically useful if role names are suppressed.

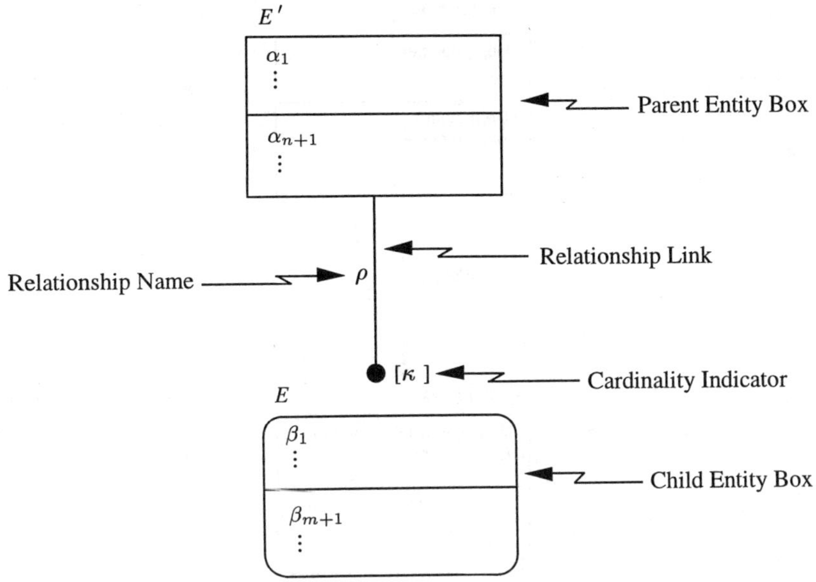

Figure 6: Syntax for Identifying Relationships

other; Emp_numbers are unique only within DEPARTMENTs. Hence, one must also know the Dept_number of the DEPARTMENT in which an EMPLOYEE works to distinguish him or her from every other EMPLOYEE. Hence, the primary key for EMPLOYEE also contains the migrated attribute Works_in.Dept_number. Note that the relationship name 'Works_in', or some related identifier (known in the context as a "role name"), becomes part of the name of the migrated attribute. This is to indicate the relationship relative to which the migration has occurred. By convention, if there is no possibility of confusion, the very same name is used for the migrated attribute. Thus, because there is no such possibility in the example (since there is only one relationship linking EMPLOYEE to DEPARTMENT), 'Dept_number' could have been used in both entity boxes. An attribute like Dept_number or SSN that is not migrated relative to any relationship in the model is said (relative to that model) to be *owned* by the entity it is defined on.

One further construct in Figure 6 requires comment, viz., the cardinality indicator κ. This marker, of course, indicates the cardinality of the relation. The brackets around κ signify that cardinality indicators are optional. If no indicator is present, then the relationship in question can have any cardinality. 'P', by contrast, indicates the relationship is many-to-one; 'Z' that it is one to zero or one; a specific numeral ν indicates that the cardinality is exactly n, where ν denotes n; and ν-μ indicates a cardinality of n to m, where ν and μ denote n and m, respectively.

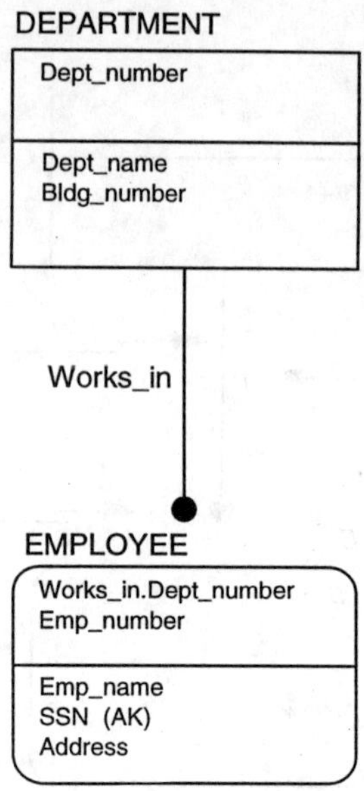

Figure 7: Example of an Identifying Relationship

As noted above, if R is not an identifying relationship (and no identifying relationship links E^R_C to any other entity in the model), then a square-cornered box is used to indicate the child entity. A dashed line rather than a solid line is used to indicate non-identifying relationships. A non-identifying relationship R is said to be *mandatory* if R is a total function from E^R_C to E^R_P, i.e., if every instance of R's child entity is associated with an instance of R's parent entity; otherwise R is said to be *optional*. For example, let E' be a class of offices in a business and let E be the class of computers that exist in the business, and let R be the Located-in relationship. Most, but perhaps not all, computers will be located in offices, but some might, e.g., have been sent out for repair, and hence are not located in any office. If this can be the case, then Located-in is an optional relationship.[14]

An optional relationship is indicated by a dashed line with a small diamond at the parent end of the link, as shown in Figure 8.

[14]Strictly speaking, the difference between mandatory and optional relationships really applies more accurately to the labeled relationship *links* in a model. Entities, attributes and relationships form what in mathematical logic are known as *interpretation* of the basic syntactic elements of IDEF1X. An interpretation can be said to *validate* an IDEF1X model if its entities, attributes, and relationships comport with the constraints expressed in the model (e.g., if the relationship associated with a one-to-n link really is one-n). To call a relationship link mandatory, then, is to say that it can only be associated semantically in any interpretation with a relationship that is a total function. The interested reader is referred to [End72].

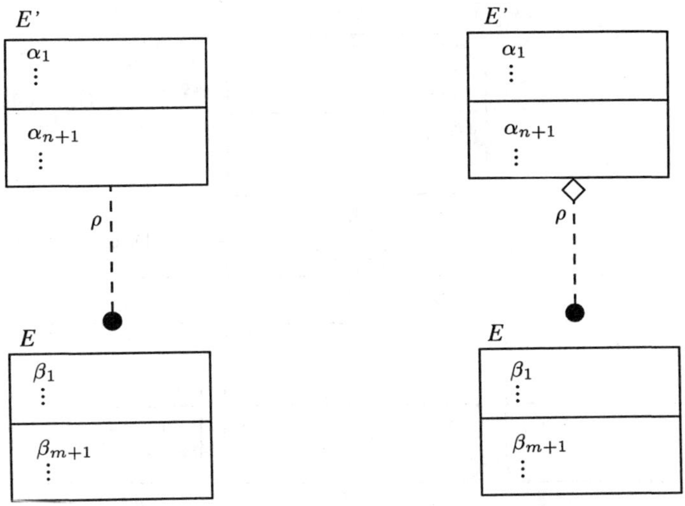

Figure 8: Syntax for Non-identifying Relationships

Any subset of an entity's attributes in a model that constitute a further key is known as an *alternate* key for the entity (relative to that model). The names of members of an alternate key are marked with the string '(AK)', as illustrated by the attribute SSN in Figure 7. Should there be more than one alternate key, then the keys are ordered (arbitrarily) and the names of the attributes in the first key are marked with the string '(AK1)', those in the second with '(AK2)', and so on. (It is possible, but uncommon, that the same attribute be in different alternate keys, and hence for an attribute name to be marked by more than one of the terms '(AKn)').

Finally, the syntax for a complete categorization cluster with three category entities is exhibited in Figure 9. A name for the discriminator attribute is written alongside the circle beneath the generic entity box. In general, clusters with n category entities are represented with n relationship links running from the lower of the two horizontal lines beneath the circle to n entity boxes. Note that the names of the primary key attributes for every category entity are identical with their counterparts in the generic entity. This reflects the fact, noted previously, that the relationship linking a category entity to its generic entity is the identity relation. Hence, each key attribute in the generic entity migrates to each category entity as a restricted version of itself that is defined only on those instances of the generic entity that are instances of the category entity. This "near identity" of the migrating and migrated attributes warrants using the same attribute name in the boxes for both generic and category entities.

Incomplete categorization relationships are indicated in precisely the same

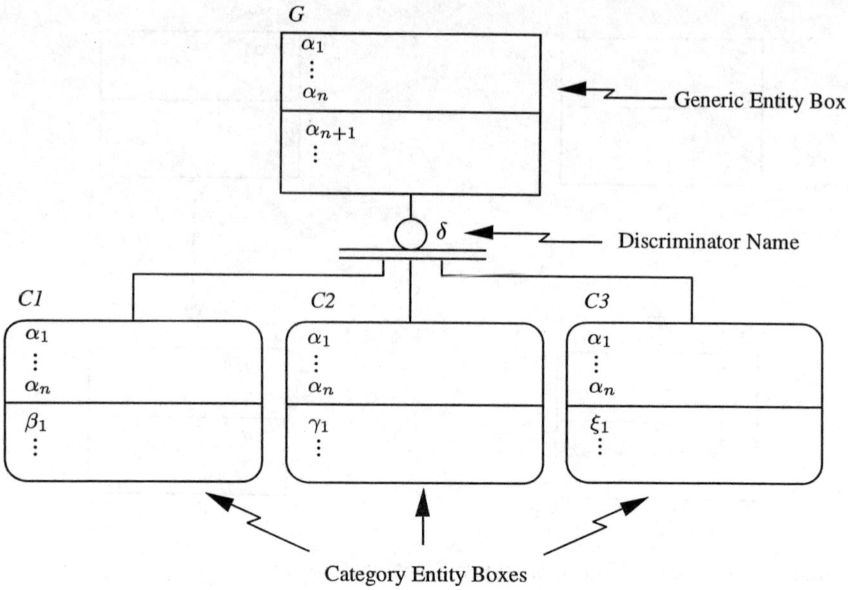

Figure 9: Complete Categorization Cluster Syntax

way, except that a single rather than a double horizontal line is used beneath the circle.

5 The IDEF3 Process Modeling Method

The IDEF3 modeling method is used to construct models of general enterprise processes. Like IDEF0 and IDEF1X, it has a specialized ontology and, of course, a corresponding language, which we detail in the following sections.

5.1 The IDEF3 Ontology: UOBs, Objects, and Intervals

Because the terms 'process' and 'activity' are rough synonyms in ordinary language, one might wonder what distinguishes the subject matter of IDEF0 from that of IDEF3. In one sense, nothing; both are concerned with the modeling of actual and possible situations. The difference is a matter of focus: features of situations that are essential to IDEF0 activities are generally ignored in IDEF3; and, conversely, features essential to IDEF3 processes are ignored in IDEF0. More specifically, because IDEF0 is concerned primarily with the ways in which business activities are defined and connected by their products and resources, IDEF0 activities are characterized first and foremost in terms of their associated inputs, outputs, controls and mechanisms. By contrast, because IDEF3 is intended to be a general process modeling method without, in particular, a specific focus on products and resources, an IDEF3 process — also known as a *unit of behavior*, or *UOB*, to avoid the connotations of more familiar terms — is characterized simply in terms of the *objects* it may contain, the *interval of time* over which it occurs, and the *temporal relations* it may bear to other processes. Thus, IDEF0 (by default) ignores the temporal properties of situations (in particular, it is not assumed that an activity must occur over a continuous interval), and it highlights certain roles that objects play in them. By contrast, IDEF3 (by default) ignores those roles and simply records general information about objects in situations and the temporal properties of, and relations among, situations. IDEF3 is thus particularly well-suited to the construction of models of general enterprise processes in which the timing and sequencing of the events in a process is especially critical. Notably, it is a particularly useful language to use in the design of complex simulation models.

5.2 The IDEF3 Language and its Semantics

The basic elements of the IDEF3 lexicon for building process models are illustrated in Figure 10. UOB boxes, of course, in the context of an IDEF3

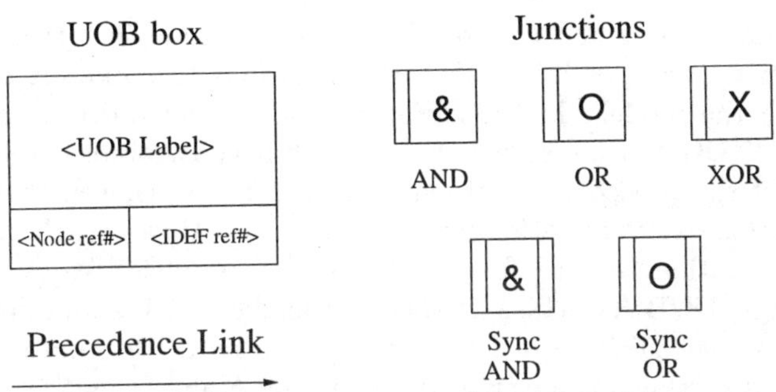

Figure 10: The Basic IDEF3 Process Description Lexicon

model, signify UOBs, and precedence links signify a certain kind of temporal constraint. Every UOB box has an associated *elaboration*, i.e., a set of logical conditions, or constraints, written either in English or, more ideally, in a formal logical language. A UOB box can signify a given UOB A only if the latter satisfies the logical constraints in the elaboration of the former. In such a case we say that A is an *instance* of the UOB box. Junctions, too, can have elaborations.

5.2.1 Syntax for the Basic IDEF3 Construct

The basic construct of IDEF3 is illustrated in Figure 11. Box 1, with the

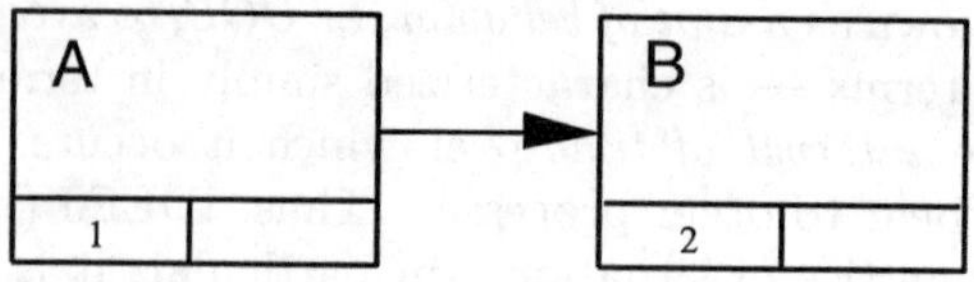

Figure 11: The Basic IDEF3 Construct

label 'A' at the "back" end of the link is known as the *source* of the link and box 2 with label 'B' at the "front" end of the link is known as the *destination* of the link. If Figure 11 is considered as a complete IDEF3 model, box 1 is known as the (immediate) predecessor of box 2 in the model, and box 2 the (immediate) successor of box 1. The '1' in box 1 and the '2' in box 2 are the *node reference numbers* of the boxes, and are assumed to be unique within a model. The corresponding area to the right of the node reference number in a UOB box is optionally filled by an *IDEF reference number*, a broader identifier for the purpose of locating that model element with respect to numerous IDEF models.

5.2.2 Semantics for the Basic Construct

The meaning of an IDEF3 model is best understood in terms of its possible *activations*, the possible real world situations that exhibit the structure specified in the model. In the simplest case, an activation of a model is a collection of UOBs that satisfy the temporal constraints exhibited by the structure of the precedence links in the model. In general, there are many different patterns of activation for a given model. However, there is only one possible activation pattern for simple two box models like Figure 11, viz., when a single UOB A of the sort specified in the box 1 is followed by a UOB B of the sort specified in box 2. More precisely, a legitimate activation of Figure 11 as it stands is any pair of situations A and B that are instances of boxes 1 and 2, respectively, and where B does not start before A finishes.

5.2.3 Junctions

Junctions in IDEF3 provide a mechanism to specify the logic of process branching. Additionally, junctions simplify the capture of timing and sequencing relationships between multiple process paths.

5.2.3.1 Junction Types An IDEF3 model can be thought of as a general description of a class of complex processes, viz., the class of its activations. Such a description is rarely linear, in the sense that the processes it picks out always exhibit the same linear pattern of subprocesses. More typically, they involve any or all of four general sorts of "branch points:"

1. Points at which a process satisfying the description diverges into multiple *parallel* subprocesses;

2. Points at which processes satisfying the description can differ in the way they diverge into multiple (possibly nonexclusive) *alternative* subprocesses;

3. Points at which multiple parallel subprocesses in a process satisfying the description converge into a single "thread;" and

4. Points at which processes satisfying the description that had diverged into alternative subprocesses once again exhibit similar threads.

IDEF3 introduces four general types of junction to express the four general sorts of branch points. The first two sorts are expressed by "fan-out" junctions: Conjunctive fan-out junctions represent points of divergence involving multiple parallel subprocesses, while disjunctive fan-out junctions represent points of divergence involving multiple alternative subprocesses. The last two sorts of branch point are expressed by "fan-in" junctions: conjunctive fan-in junctions represent points of convergence involving multiple parallel subprocesses, while disjunctive fan-in junctions represent points of convergence involving multiple alternative subprocesses. There is one type of conjunctive, or AND, junction, indicated by '&'. There are two types of disjunctive junction: inclusive and exclusive junctions, or OR and XOR junctions, respectively, depending on whether the alternatives in question are mutually exclusive. OR junctions are indicated by an 'O', and XOR junctions by an 'X'.

Junction syntax is illustrated in Figure 12, where γ is either '&', 'O', or 'X'. Although this figure shows only two UOB boxes to the right of a fan-out junction and to the left of a fan-in, arbitrarily many are permitted in an IDEF3 model in general.

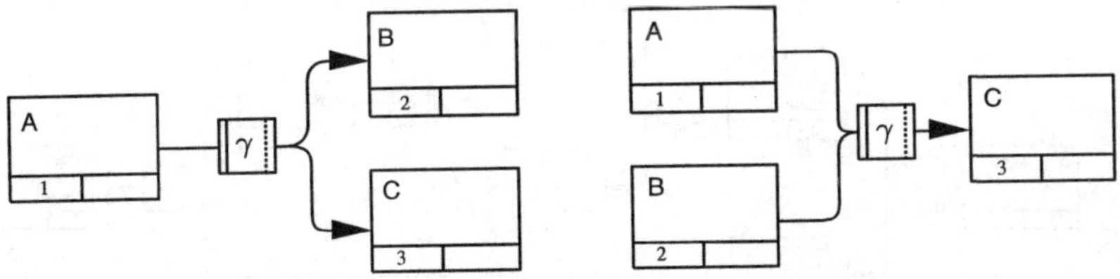

Figure 12: Junction Syntax

5.2.3.2 Junction Semantics The intuitive meaning of junctions is straightforward. It will be enough to use Figure 12. Letting γ be '&' in the figure, an activation of the model on the left will consist of an instance A of box 1 followed by instances B and C of boxes 2 and 3. If the junction is synchronous, then B and C will begin simultaneously. (Note in particular that, for nonsynchronous junctions, there are no constraints whatever on the temporal relation between B and C; all that is required is that both occur after A.) Similarly, an activation of the right model in the figure will consist of instances A and B of boxes 1 and 2 followed by a single instance C of box 3; and if the junction is synchronous, then, A and B will end simultaneously.

For OR (XOR) junctions, if γ is 'O' ('X'), then an activation of the model on the left in the figure will consist of an instance A of box 1 followed by either an instance B of box 2 or an instance C of box 3 (but, for XOR junctions, not both). If the OR junction is synchronous, then, should there be instances of both boxes 2 and 3, they will begin simultaneously. Similarly, an activation of the right model in the figure will consist of an instance of either box 1 or box 2 (but, for XOR junctions, not both) followed by an instance of box 3. If the OR junction is synchronous, then, should there be instances of both boxes 1 and 2, they will end simultaneously.

These semantic rules generalize directly, of course, for junctions involving arbitrarily many UOB boxes. Control conditions on branching and concurrency on a class of processes — e.g., the conditions that determine which of two paths to follow at an XOR junction — are often placed in the elaboration of a junction.

5.3 Models and Schematics

An IDEF3 model is a collection of one or more IDEF3 *process schematics*, which are built from UOB boxes, precedence links, and junctions in natural ways. Intuitively, a schematic is simply a single "page" of a model, a view of (perhaps only a part of) a process from a given perspective at a single uniform granularity.

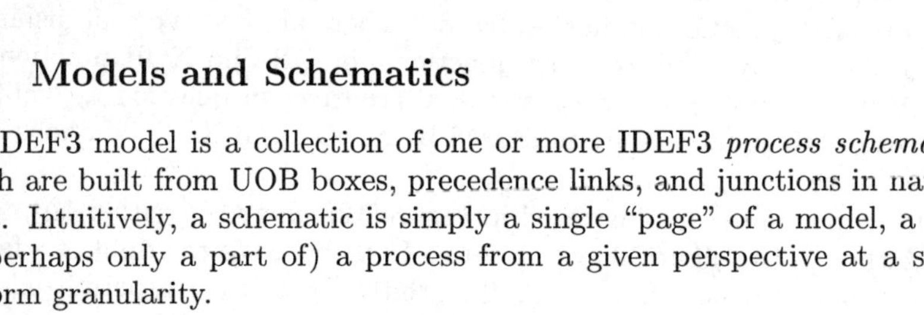

Figure 13: A Small IDEF3 Schematic

A simple example of a schematic is seen in Figure 13. In this schematic, a request for material is followed by either the identification of the current supplier or the identification of potential suppliers. (A condition attached to the junction might indicate that the latter path is taken only if there is no current supplier; but this common sense condition, of course, cannot be derived from the bare semantics of the language alone.) If a current supplier is identified then an order is placed. Otherwise, the identification of potential suppliers is followed by both a report to the manager and a request for bids from the potential suppliers. When both of these tasks are complete, the bids that have arrived are evaluated and an order placed to the winning bidder.[15]

The formal syntax for IDEF3 process schematics is rather laissez-faire; the onus is on the modeler to construct coherent models, i.e., models with possible activations. However, although basically straightforward, the syntax requires more mathematical apparatus than is appropriate here to specify precisely. Informally, though, there are essentially two main rules:

1. A UOB box can be the source or destination of no more than than one precedence link; and

2. A schematic must contain no loops.

The motivation behind the first rule is that precedence links with the same box as source or destination would indicate a point at which there are parallel subprocesses diverging or converging, or a point at which alternative subprocesses can be seen to diverge or converge across different processes satisfying the description. The purpose of fan-out and fan-in junctions is to indicate just such points in a description meant to capture the general structure exhibited by many possible processes.

Regarding the second rule, a *path* through a schematic is a sequence of UOB boxes, junctions, and precedence links such that each element of the sequence (save the last, if there is a last element) is connected to its successor. A loop, or *cycle*, in a schematic is a path in the schematic whose first element is identical to its last. At first blush, the second rule might seem highly undesirable, as loops appear to be very common structural features of many processes. Consider, for example, the process depicted in Figure 14 (in apparent violation of Rule 2).

The problem with loops is that they are inconsistent with the semantics of the precedence link. As noted above, the precedence link indicates temporal precedence. This relation is *transitive*, that is, if UOB A is before B in time, and B before C, then A is before C as well. Given that, suppose box b1 is linked to box b2, and b2 to b3 in a model M, and that A, B, and C are instances of b1, b2, and b3, respectively, in some activation of M. By the basic semantics of the precedence link, A must precede B and B must precede C. But then, by the transitivity of temporal precedence, A must precede C. Now,

[15] Henceforth, junction numbers will be suppressed.

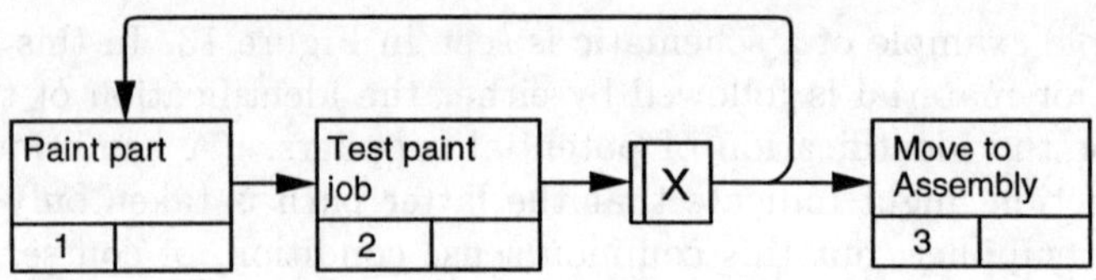

Figure 14: Process with an Apparent Loop

notice that, on this understanding of the precedence link, a loop in a model would mean that one point in an activation of the model — one point in a possible or actual process — could return to an earlier point, and hence that the later point could precede the earlier point. Clearly, though, given the direction of "time's arrow," this is not possible; the past remains ineluctably past and inaccessible; once past, no point in time can be revisited.

Why then is there a temptation to use loops in process models? The answer is clear; in some processes — the one depicted in Figure 14, for instance — a particular *pattern* is instantiated many times. It is therefore convenient and, often, natural simply to indicate this by reusing that part of a model that represents the first occurrence of this pattern, rather than iterating separate instances of it. As noted, though, this is not compatible with the general semantics of the precedence link. Strictly speaking, then, loops must be "unfolded" into noncycling structures. If there is a bound on the number of iterations, the corresponding noncycling model will be finite. Otherwise it will be infinite; the infinite unfolded model corresponding to Figure 14 is exhibited elliptically in Figure 15.

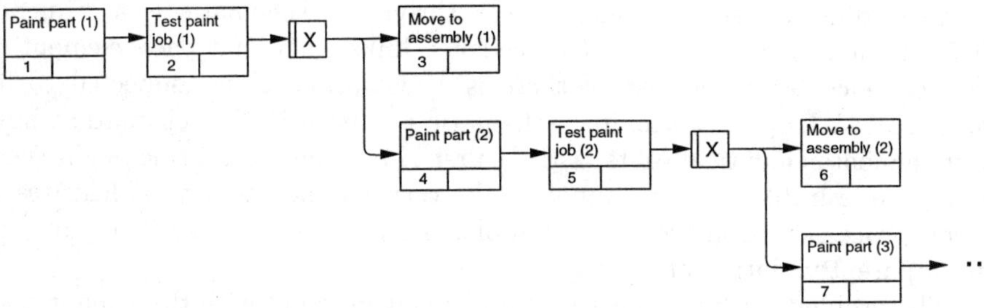

Figure 15: Unfolded Model of the Process Depicted in Figure 14

That noted, it has already been acknowledged that models with loops are often convenient and natural. Indeed, given the ubiquity of processes with iterated patterns, to require modelers explicitly to unfold loops in general would rob IDEF3 of a significant degree of its usability. Consequently, IDEF3 allows models with loops — however, importantly, these are understood syntactically not as primitive constructs but as *macros* for their unfolded counterparts. So understood, loops are semantically innocuous and can be used without qualms.

5.3.1 Referents

Loops are typically indicated in IDEF3 by means of *referents* in process models. Referents are theoretically dispensable, but are useful for reducing clutter. In the context of a process model, referents are used to refer to previously defined UOBs. Referents therefore enhance reuse, as one can simply refer to the indicated schematic or UOB box without explicitly copying it into the referring model.

Referents come in two varieties: *call-and-wait* and *call-and-continue.* Their syntax is seen in Figure 16. The referent type of a referent can be either

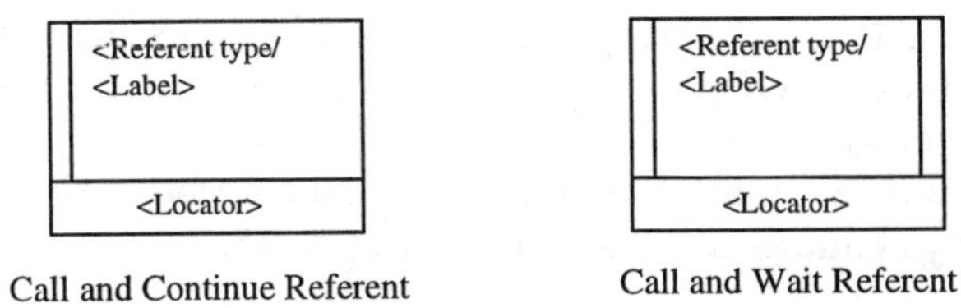

Figure 16: Referent Syntax

'UOB', 'SCENARIO', 'TS', or 'GOTO'. A UOB referent points to a previously defined UOB box, a scenario referent points to a model ('scenario' is the name for the complex UOB described by a model), a TS referent points to an object state transition schematic (see below), and a GOTO points to a UOB box or model. A GOTO referent indicates a change of process control to a UOB or scenario indicated by the referenced UOB box, model, or junction. In each case, the *locator* in a referent specifies the (unique) reference number of the UOB, scenario, or state transition in question. Referents, too, have associated elaborations.

As the names suggest, a call-and-wait referent calls a particular UOB or transition, and execution of the calling model halts until the called UOB or transition completes. By contrast, a call-and-continue referent simply calls a UOB or transition without any halt in the execution of the calling model. Typically, in IDEF3, a GOTO referent, rather than a backward-pointing precedence link, is used to express looping;[16] thus, on this approach, the process intended by Figure 14 would be captured as in Figure 17. Use of precedence links to express looping, however, is permitted.

[16]More than anything, perhaps, this simply reflects the way most IDEF3 support software works.

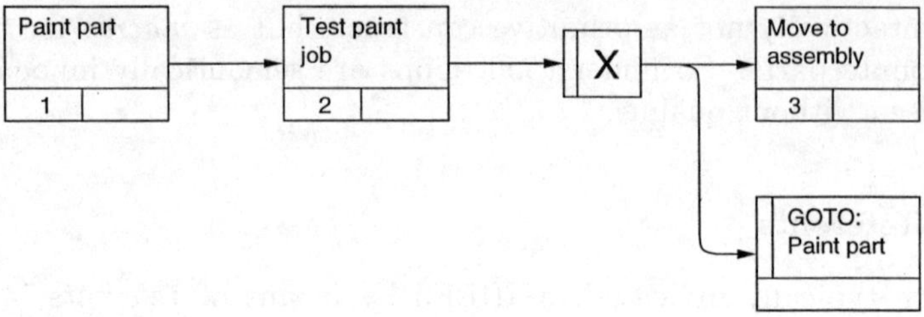

Figure 17: Looping with a GOTO Referent

5.3.2 Decompositions

A *decomposition* of a UOB box in a model is simply another IDEF3 schematic, one that purports to provide a "finer-grained" perspective on the UOB signified by the box. In a fully-fledged IDEF3 model, each schematic is either the decomposition of a UOB box in some other schematic, or else is the unique "top-level" schematic which is not the decomposition of any other schematic. That a given box in a schematic in a model has a decomposition in the model is indicated by shading, as illustrated in Figure 18.

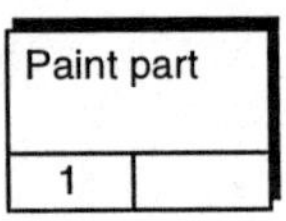

Figure 18: Decomposition Syntax

5.4 Object State Transition Schematics

Initially, process schematics were the only part of the IDEF3 language. However, it soon became apparent that modelers often desired to take "object-centered" views of processes, views that focus not so much on the situations that constitute a process, but on the series of states that certain objects within those processes pass through as the process evolves. This led to the addition of *object state transition schematics*, or simply *transition schematics* to the IDEF3 language.

5.4.1 Syntax for Basic Transition Schematics

The basic lexicon for transition schematics is shown in Figure 19.

As can be seen, the label for a state symbol displays the name of a state and, optionally, the name of the general kind of thing that is in the state. For example, the state of being hot might be labeled simply by means of

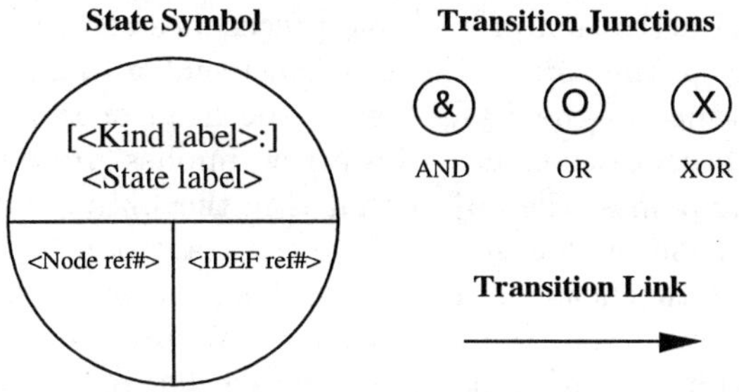

Figure 19: Lexicon for State Transition Schematics

the label HOT. If it is hot *water* in particular, though, and that fact is relevant, then the more complex label WATER:HOT could be used. (Node references and IDEF numbers in state symbols have the same role as in process schematics, and will be suppressed in the examples to follow.) An arrow (indistinguishable from a precedence link), known as a *transition link*, is used to indicate a transition from one state to another, as illustrated in Figure 20. 'K1' and 'K2' indicate optional kind (class) names, and 'S1' and 'S2' names for states.

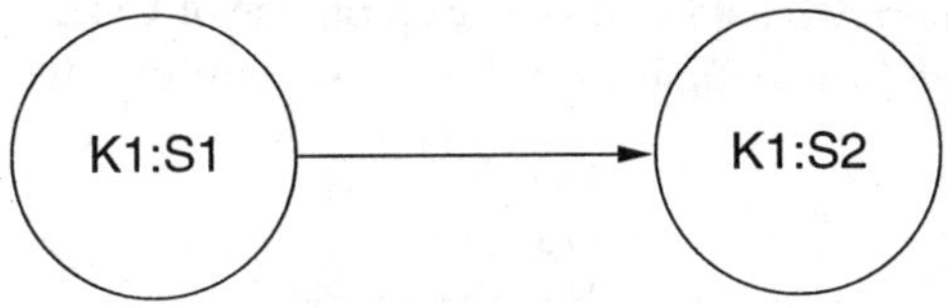

Figure 20: Basic Transition Schematic Syntax

5.4.2 Semantics for Basic Transition Schematics

In general, the semantics of a basic transition schematic is simply that, in an occurrence of the indicated transition, there is first an object x (of kind K1) in state S1, and subsequently an object y (of kind K2) that comes to be in state S2; that is, to have an instance of the transition schematic in question, it is required that x be in state S1 before y comes to be in state S2. It is permitted, though perhaps not typical, that $x \neq y$; and it is permitted, though perhaps not typical, that x remain in state S1 after y comes to be in state S2.

It is important to note that, despite having the same appearance, the semantics of the arrow of transition schematics is somewhat different than the semantics of the precedence link. The precedence link implies full temporal precedence: in an activation of a simple precedence connection, an instance of the UOB box at the tail of the link must end no later than the point at which an instance of the UOB box at the head of the link begins. By contrast, in an object schematic, the arrow implies precedence only with regard to starting points: the object that is in the state indicated at the tail of the arrow must be in that state before the transition to an object in the state indicated at the head of the arrow. The reason for this weaker sort of precedence in state transition schematics is simply the point noted in the previous paragraph: a transition only involves a change from an object in one state to an object (possibly the same object, possibly different) in another; though it may not be typical, the object in the initial state of the transition needn't cease being in that state after the transition. To allow for this type of transition, the weaker semantics is used for the arrow in object transition schematics. There is no potential for confusion, however, as the meaning of the arrow remains constant within each type of schematic.

5.4.3 Using UOB Referents in Transition Schematics

Because (in the context of process modeling) objects are in states within UOBs, and because transitions occur inside UOBs, it is useful and informative to be able to record information about related UOBs in a transition schematic. This is accomplished by attaching UOB referents to various parts of a transition schematic. The most common use of UOB referents is to attach them to the arrow in a transition schematic, as illustrated in Figure 21.

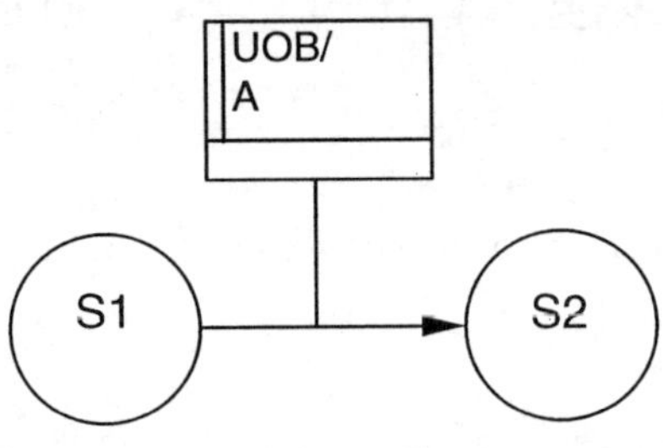

Figure 21: Use of a UOB Referent in a Transition Schematic

The default semantics here is fairly weak. The figure signifies only that in transitions of the indicated sort there will be an object x in state S1 prior to or at the start of a UOB A (satisfying the conditions specified in the referent), and subsequently an object y at some point after the beginning of A. Stronger conditions — e.g., that x=y, that x and y occur in A, that x be in S1 at the start of A and y in S2 at its end, etc. — can be added to the elaborations of appropriate components of the schematic.

Additional referents can be added to a transition link to indicate more information about associated processes. Relative placement on the transition arrow indicates the relative temporal placement of the associated UOBs. For instance, the schematic in Figure 22 indicates a transition involving the occurrence of a pair of UOBs A and B that start simultaneously, and a third UOB C that starts after A and B. Additionally, because the "B" referent is a call-and-wait, in any instance of the transition, UOB B must complete before C can begin. (This will generally be the only sort of context in which call-and-wait referents are used in transition schematics.)

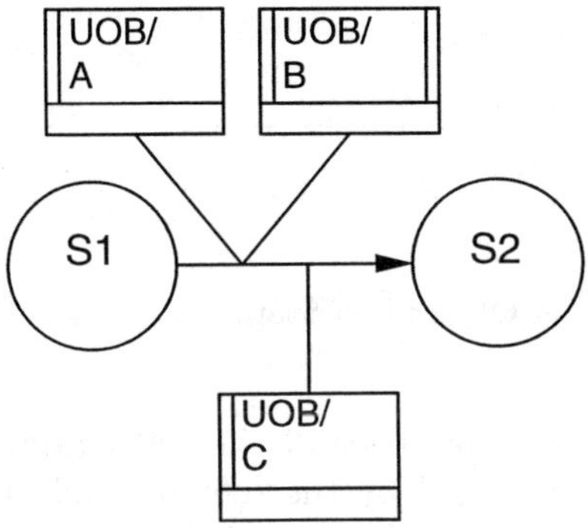

Figure 22: Multiple UOB Referents in a Transition Schematic

The semantics for transitions in schematics with multiple referents is slightly more involved than for simple schematics. In the case of the schematic in Figure 22, for example, the indicated object x in any such transition is in S1 at the start of A and B, and it is in state S2 by the end of C. This semantics generalizes straightforwardly to other cases of multiple referents.

If the relative temporal ordering of the UOBs involved in a transition is unknown or indeterminate from case to case, a small circle is used to "anchor" the referents indicating those UOBs, as illustrated in Figure 23.

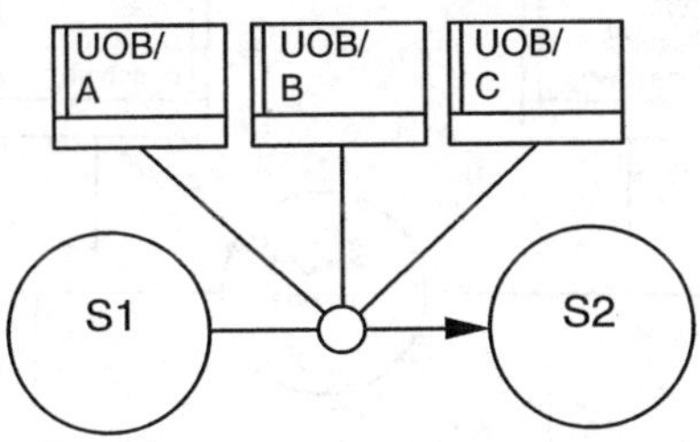

Figure 23: Temporally Indeterminate UOB Referents in a Transition Schematic

It is not uncommon for a given situation to "sustain" an object in a given state; a refrigeration process, for example, might sustain a given substance in a solid state. Situations of this type can be represented by the construct in Figure 24.

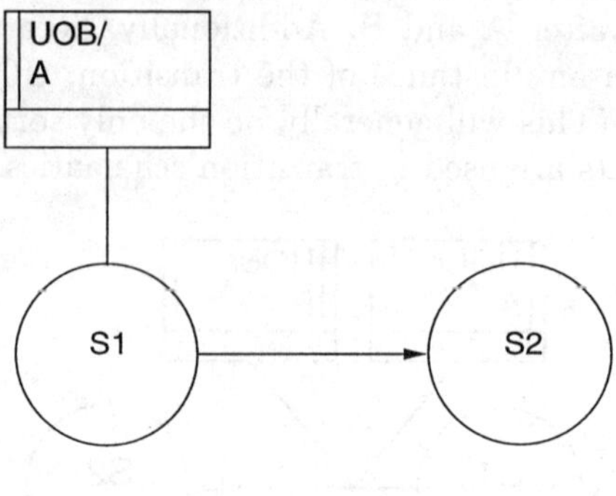

Figure 24: Sustaining an Object in a State

More generally, in any instance of the schematic in Figure 24, there is a UOB A of the sort specified by the referent and an object x in state S1 throughout the duration of A. This requires that such an x must exist when A begins. x could, however, be in state S1 *prior* to the start of A; that is, it could be brought into state S1 by some other process prior to A (the substance noted above might actually become solid through some sort of chemical reaction), and then sustained in that state by A.

5.4.4 Complex Transition Schematics

More complex transition schematics can be constructed by adding further transition arrows and state symbols to existing schematics or by using transition junctions. A complex schematic is illustrated in Figure 25.

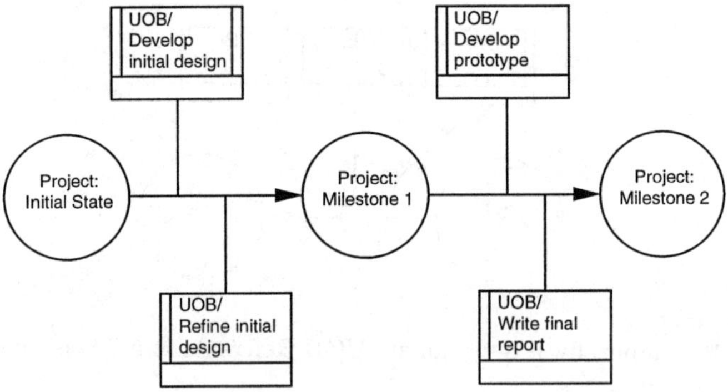

Figure 25: A Complex State Transition Schematic

For the most part, the semantics of complex schematics such as this is a straightforward generalization of simple schematics, only instead of a single transition there are several successive transitions. Thus, the schematic in Figure 25 expresses a transition in which a project evolves from an initial state to a first milestone state and thence to a second milestone state via the UOBs of the sort indicated.

Transition junctions permit the construction of more subtle schematics that express concurrent and alternative paths in a series of transitions. Junctions can take any of the three forms illustrated in Figure 26.

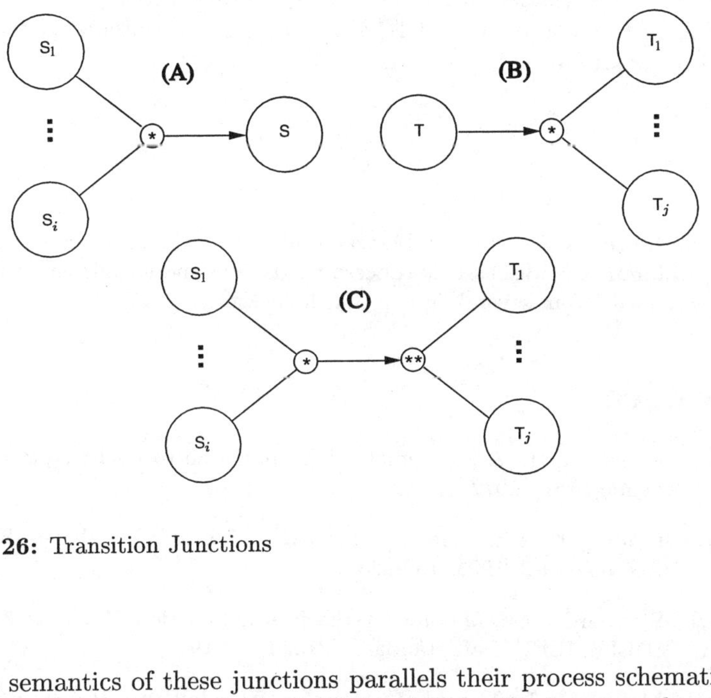

Figure 26: Transition Junctions

The semantics of these junctions parallels their process schematic counterparts. If * is '&' in schematic (A) in Figure 26, for example, then the schematic indicates a transition in which objects $x_1, ..., x_i$ in states $S_1, ..., S_i$, respectively, transition to an object y in state S. If * is 'X' in (B), then the schematic indicates a transition of an object x to an object y in exactly one of the states $T_1, ..., T_j$. Form (C) allows for even more complex transitions. For example, if * is 'O' and ** is '&', then the schematic indicates a transition in which one or more objects $x_1, ..., x_i$ in states $S_1, ..., S_i$ transition to objects $y_1, ..., y_j$ in the states $T_1, ..., T_j$, respectively. Similarly for the remaining possibilities. The syntax and semantics of referents with transition junctions is straightforward but subject to a number of conventions. The reader is referred to [MMP93] for details.

5.5 General Kind Schematics

Early in its development, IDEF3 was focused entirely on the representation of process knowledge, and its language included no transition schematics (see, e.g., [MME94]). The desire of modelers to describe processes from an object-centered perspective led to the introduction of transition schematics. Realization of the importance of general ontologies for understanding, sharing, and reusing process models, however, has led to a deeper integration of the IDEF3 method with the IDEF5 ontology capture method. Indeed, the IDEF5 ontology description language has become incorporated into the IDEF3 transition schematic language. This language permits a modeler to express, not only information about state transitions, but general information about the objects, classes, and relations. Space limitations prevent a detailed discussion of this component of IDEF3. Once again, interested readers are referred to [MMP93].

Acknowledgments: Christopher Menzel would like to thank Alexander Bocast for numerous illuminating discussions concerning IDEF0, and for allowing the authors to borrow heavily from several figures that he designed.

References

[End72] Enderton, H., A Mathematical Introduction to Logic, New York, Academic Press, 1972

[Gru93] Gruber, T., A Translation Approach to Portable Ontologies, Knowledge Acquisition 2, 1993, 199-220

[IEEE97] Standard Users Manual for the ICAM Function Modeling Method — IDEF0, IEEE draft standard, P1320.1.1, 1997

[MMP93] Mayer, R. J., Menzel, C., Painter, M., deWitte, P., Blinn, T., Benjamin, P., IDEF3 Process Description Capture Method Report, Wright-Patterson AFB, Ohio, AL/HRGA, 1993

[MKB95] Mayer, R., Keen, A., Browne, D., Harrington, S., Marshall, C., Painter, M., Schafrik, F., Huang, J., Wells, M., Hisesh, H., IDEF4 Object-oriented Design Method Report, Wright-Patterson AFB, Ohio, AL/HRGA, 1995

[MBM94] Mayer, R., Benjamin, P., Menzel, C., Fillion, F., deWitte, P., Futrell, M., and Lingineni, M., IDEF5 Ontology Capture Method Report, Wright-Patterson AFB, Ohio, AL/HRGA, 1994

[MME94] Menzel, C., Mayer R., Edwards, D., IDEF3 Process Descriptions and

Their Semantics, in: A. Kusiak, C. Dagli (eds.), Intelligent Systems in Design and Manufacturing, New York, ASME Press, 1994

[NIST93a] Integration Definition for Function Modeling (IDEF0), Federal Information Processing Standards Publication 183, Computer Systems Laboratory, National Institute of Standards and Technology, 1993[17]

[NIST93b] Integration Definition for Information Modeling (IDEF1X), Federal Information Processing Standards Publication 184, Computer Systems Laboratory, National Institute of Standards and Technology, 1993

[RB87] Ramey, T., Brown, R., Entity, Link, Key Attribute Semantic Information Modeling: The ELKA Method, ms, Hughes Aircraft, 1987

[Ros77] Ross, D., Structured Analysis (SA): A Language for Communicating Ideas, TSE 3 (1), 1977, 16-34

[Sof81] SofTech, Inc. Integrated computer-aided manufacturing (ICAM) architecture, Pt. II, Vol. V: Information modeling manual (IDEF1), DTIC-B062457, 1981

[17] At the time of this writing, the IDEF0, IDEF1X, IDEF3, IDEF4, and IDEF5 reports listed here are available on the World Wide Web at http://www.idef.com.

CHAPTER 11

The CIMOSA Languages

François Vernadat

CIMOSA is an open system architecture for Enterprise Integration (EI), and especially for integration in manufacturing. The architecture comprises an Enterprise Modelling Framework, an Integrating Infrastructure and a System Life Cycle. This contribution presents the modelling languages used in the Enterprise Modelling Framework. The CIMOSA languages are based on an event-driven process-based model and cover functional, information, resource and organisational aspects of an enterprise (including a workflow language for specifying enterprise behaviour). They can be used at various modelling levels along the system life cycle, including requirements definition, design specification and implementation description. Principles of these languages have influenced standardisation work in the field (CEN and ISO) as well as the development of commercial tools for business process modelling and analysis.

1 Introduction

Enterprise Integration(EI) is a concept emerging from three major Information Technology areas: open distributed processing, co-operative information systems (especially federated databases) and integration in manufacturing, originally named Computer-Integrated Manufacturing (CIM). However, it is now well understood that in addition to these technical aspects, EI also strongly relies on organisation and human resource management principles to include organisational aspects and place people at the heart of the paradigm [BN96, Ver96].

EI is concerned with breaking down organisational barriers and facilitating information exchange and sharing throughout an enterprise to make it more competitive and more reactive in a dynamic and global economy.

Information Technologies, and especially information systems, are of paramount importance in the development of enterprise integration solutions in terms of high speed computer communications networks, distributed databases, distributed computing environments, information exchange (administrative or product data exchange), application interoperability, inter-working or computer supported co-operative work.

Enterprise Modelling(EM) is another fundamental component in the planning and development of EI projects [Ver96]. EM is a generic term which covers the set of activities, methods and tools related to developing models for various aspects of an enterprise.

The aim of EM is threefold: (1) to assist in building an enterprise model or common view of the enterprise which can be shared by the various actors, i.e. building a consensus, (2) to support enterprise analysis and decision making about the parts to be integrated, and (3) to support model-based integration, i.e. using the enterprise model as a federation mechanism to integrate humans, business processes and information systems.

This article presents the CIMOSA languages used for enterprise modelling in the CIMOSA architecture. They cover functional, information, resource and organisation aspects of a manufacturing enterprise at various modelling levels: requirements definition, design specification and implementation description. An application example is provided.

2 CIMOSA

CIMOSA [AMI93] is an Open Systems Architecture for Enterprise Integration. It has originally been developed for Computer-Integrated Manufacturing (CIM) applications as a series of ESPRIT Projects (EP 688, 5288 and 7110) over a period ranging from 1986 until 1994 with the support of the European Commission. More than 30 European companies (including CIM users and IT vendors) as well as academic institutions have contributed to its design and validation.

Its aim is to provide the manufacturing industry with (1) an Enterprise Modelling Framework (EMF), which can accurately represent business operations, support their analysis and design, and lead to executable enterprise models; (2) an Integrating Infrastructure (IIS), used to support application and business integration as well as execution of the implementation model to control and monitor enterprise operations; and (3) a methodology to be used along the System Life Cycle (SLC) to assist users in applying CIMOSA principles [CIM96].

CIMOSA provides a Reference Architecture (known as the CIMOSA cube) from which particular enterprise architectures can be derived. This Reference Architecture and the associated enterprise modelling framework are based on a set of modelling constructs, or generic building blocks, which altogether form the CIMOSA modelling languages. These languages are based on an event-driven process-based model centered on two fundamental and complementary concepts: *business process* to model enterprise behaviour and *enterprise activity* to model enterprise functionality [Ver93]. Other concepts, defined as modelling constructs, are also used to represent various aspects of an enterprise as summarised by Figure 1. For the sake of simplicity, this figure does not show constructs of the organisation view.

The System Life Cycle defines the set of essential and generic phases that an enterprise integration project has to go through, irrespectively of their sequence. It is based on the GERAM (Generalised Enterprise Reference Architecture and Methodology) life cycle [BN96] and comprises the following phases: identification phase, concept phase, requirements definition phase, design specification phase, implementation description phase, operation phase and maintenance and decommissioning phase.

The CIMOSA Integrating Infrastructure is not discussed in this paper. The interested reader is referred to [AMI93] for more details.

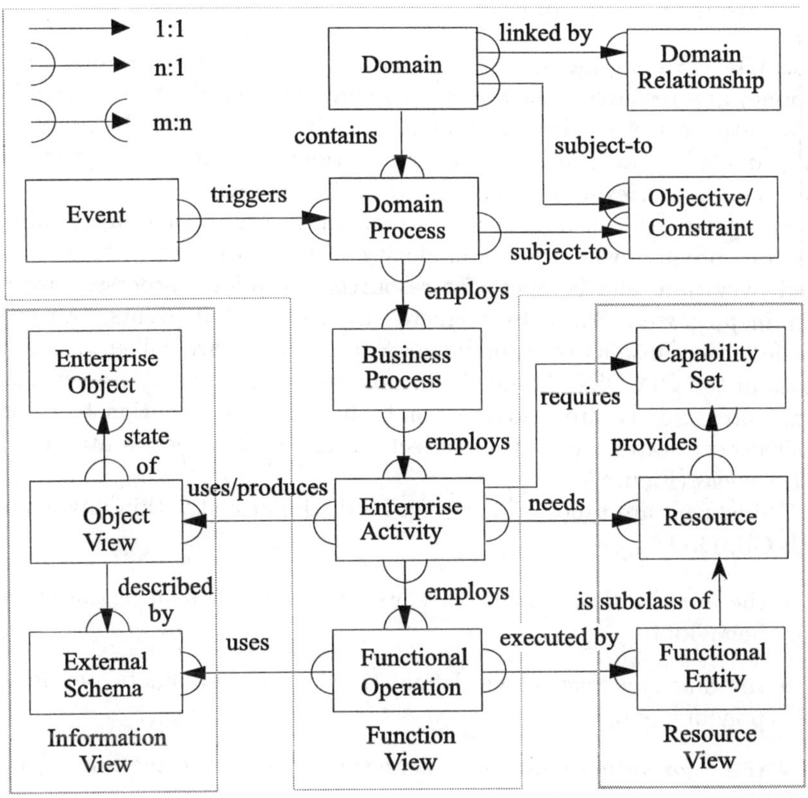

Figure 1: Relationships among essential CIMOSA constructs

3 Business Process Modelling

The earlier methods for enterprise modelling focused very much on the functional aspects, providing an activity constructs and the principle of functional decomposition (such as IDEF0 or GRAI). Later on, new methods have been proposed to focus on causal and precedence relationships among activities and information flows (e.g. ARIS, CIMOSA, IDEF3, IEM). However, in addition to traditional functional and information aspects as found in most business process modelling languages, resource and organisation aspects must also be covered to model industrial business processes [Ver96].

CIMOSA defines an enterprise as a large collection of:

- concurrent processes being executed on request to achieve business goals, and
- interacting agents, or functional entities, executing processes, i.e. processing enterprise objects.

Thus, CIMOSA emphasises a clear separation between processes (what has to be done) and resources (the doers). The link between the two is materialised by primitive actions, called *functional operations* (as required by process steps and provided by *functional entities*). Functional operations are grouped into *enterprise activities* to form elementary process steps.

The processes can be logically organised into functional areas called *domains* to break down system complexity. These processes must be synchronised over time and compete for resources. Top-level processes are called *domain processes.* They are triggered by nothing but events. An event is a solicited or unsolicited happening. Sub-processes are called *business processes* in the CIMOSA jargon. They employ enterprise activities which consume time and require resources for their complete execution to transform input object states into output object states. These object states are called *object views* (Figure 1).

Three separate types of flows can be distinguished within any enterprise with CIMOSA:

- the *control flow* defined as a workflow, which defines the enterprise behaviour,
- the *material flow*, which defines the flow of products or physical components, and
- the *information flow*, which defines the flow of information objects and decisions.

These flows can be modelled separately or altogether. For the sake of clarity, it is recommended to model them separately starting with the control flow, then adding the material flow and finally analysing the information flow. The information flow can be further specialised into a document flow, a data flow or a decision flow, if necessary.

The model must then be enriched with resource constraints indicating for each process step what are the resources required. Conflicts occur in the case of shared resources among several processes and resolution policies must be foreseen.

Finally, according to Bussler [Bus96], business processes can be classified as:

- *well-defined processes* (or deterministic processes), i.e. processes for which the sequence of steps is known and deterministic, and
- *ill-structured (or semi-structured) processes*, i.e. processes for which the complete sequence of steps is partially known.

These are important aspects to be taken into account in business process modelling languages in addition to synchronisation, co-operation, non-determinism and exception handling features of processes. In [Bus96], Bussler presents a workflow modelling language to specify business processes which addresses some of these issues. This language has some similarities with the CIMOSA languages presented in the subsequent sections.

4 The CIMOSA Languages

The CIMOSA modelling paradigm is based on an event-driven process-based modelling approach to cover business requirements definition, system design and implementation description [Ver93]. It places the business process concept at the heart of the approach and it is supported by a set of modelling languages. These languages are made of modelling constructs for each modelling level. A workflow language is also included to describe enterprise behaviour.

Note: A business process is a partially ordered set of activities, as perceived by the business user. It is defined in terms of a flow of control, a flow of materials, a flow of information and resource needs and allocation to process steps. A workflow is a computer representation of the flow of control (or sequence of steps) of a business process.

4.1 Workflow Language

Process behaviour is expressed in terms of a simple declarative workflow language in which all statements are defined as 'HEN (condition) DO action' rules called *behavioural rules*. A complete process behaviour is defined by a Behavioural Rule Set (BRS) as follows in Backus-Naur form:

```
behavioural_rule_set ::= <starting_rules> <behavioural_rules>

<starting_rules> ::= <simple_starting_rule> <event_driven_rules>
<simple_starting_rule> ::= WHEN (START) DO <action>
<event_driven_rules> ::= <event_driven_rule> <event_driven_rule>
                         <next_event_driven_rules>
```

```
<next_event_driven_rules> ::= <event_driven_rules> nil
<event_driven_rule> ::= WHEN ( <event_condition> ) DO <action>
<event_condition> ::= START WITH <event_list>
<event_list> ::= event-id <next_event>
<next_event> ::= AND event-id <next_event> nil

<behavioural_rules> ::= <behavioural_rule> <next_behavioural_rules>
<next_behavioural_rules> ::= <behavioural_rules> nil
<behavioural_rule> ::= WHEN ( <triggering_conditions> ) DO <action>
<triggering_conditions> ::= <triggering_condition>
                            <next_triggering_condition>
<next_triggering_condition> ::= AND <triggering_condition>
                   <next_triggering_condition>
                   AND event-id <next_triggering_condition> nil
<triggering_condition> ::= ES ( process-step-id ) = <ESvalue>
<ESvalue> ::= ending-status-id ANY

<action> ::= process-step-id <asynchronous_spawning>
             <synchronous_spawning> FINISH
<asynchronous_spawning> ::= process-step-id <other_steps>
<other_steps> ::= & process-step-id <other_steps> nil
<synchronous_spawning> ::= SYNC ( <asynchronous_spawning> )
```

where: *event-id* is the identifier of an event, *process-step-id* is the identifier of a process step (process or activity), *ending-status-id* is the name of an ending status of a process step, & is the parallel operator in the action clause.

Using this syntax, it is therefore possible to specify the following situations:

1. *Process triggering rules:* There are two possible cases:

   (a) Starting a domain process by means of one or more events. In the following case, a domain process starts with process step EF1 any time after an occurrence of both event-i and event-j occurred (not necessarily at the same time):

   WHEN (START WITH event-i AND event-j) DO EF1

   (b) Starting a business process called by a parent process using a simple starting rule:

   WHEN (START) DO EF1

2. *Forced sequential rules:* These rules are used when a process step EFx must follow another step EFy whatever the ending status (given by the built-in function ES) of EFx is. The reserved word 'ANY' is used in this case (not an ending status).

   WHEN (ES(EFx) = ANY) DO EFy

3. *Conditional sequential rules:* These rules are used to represent branching conditions in a flow of control. For instance, if EF1 has three exclusive ending statuses, one can write:

   WHEN (ES(EF1) = end_stat_1) DO EF2
   WHEN (ES(EF1) = end_stat_2) DO EF3
   WHEN (ES(EF1) = end_stat_3) DO EF4

4. *Spawning rules:* These rules are used to represent the parallel execution of process steps in a flow of control. Two types of spawning rules can be defined:

   (a) Asynchronous spawning: For instance, when EF1 finishes with status 'value', EF2, EF3 and EF4 will all be requested to start as soon as they are enabled, i.e. when their preconditions are satisfied (& is the parallel operator).

   WHEN (ES(EF1) = value) DO EF2 & EF3 & EF4

   (b) Synchronous spawning: For instance, when EF1 finishes with status 'value', EF2, EF3 and EF4 will all be requested to start exactly at the same time assuming that they are all enabled (SYNC indicates the synchronisation).

   WHEN (ES(EF1) = value) DO SYNC (EF2 & EF3 & EF4)

5. *Rendez-vous rules:* These rules are used to synchronise the end of spawning rules. For instancc, if EF5 must be started after EF2 finishes with status value_2 and EF3 finishes with status value_3 and EF4 finishes with status value_4, we will write:

   WHEN (ES(EF2) = value_2 AND ES(EF3) = value_3
   AND ES(EF4) = value_4) DO EF5

6. *Loop rules:* These rules are used to execute the same process step(s) several times as long as a loop condition is true. For instance, the following statement repeats EF1 as long as EF1 finishes with status loop_value:

   WHEN (ES(EF1) = loop_value) DO EF1

7. *Process completion rules:* These rules are used to indicate the end of a process and only contain the word FINISH in their action part. For instance,

   WHEN (ES(EF1) = end_stat_x AND ES(EF2) = end_stat_y)
   DO FINISH

Using these rules, a process behaviour is said to be consistent if FINISH can be reached from all STARTs and all process steps used in the rules belong to at least one path from START to FINISH (no isolated process steps and no dead-ends are allowed) in the control flow.

Remark: Using this syntax, it is correct to write in CIMOSA:
WHEN (START) DO FINISH
In this case, the process behaviour is limited to one behavioural rule. This is the empty process, i.e. a process which does nothing (neutral element in the set of processes).

Two types of behavioural rules have been added to the previous set to model semi-structured processes: *run-time choice rules* and *unordered set rules.* In these rules, the action part refers to a compound action (variable S), meaning that it is considered as a whole to make possible the definition of its ending status. The extension of the language syntax is as follows (where XOR is the exclusive choice operator):

```
<action> ::= ... <run_time_choice> <unordered_set>
<run_time_choice> ::= compound-action-id = ( process-step-id XOR
                      process-step-id <other_run_time_steps> )
<other_run_time_steps> ::=
                XOR process-step-id <other_run_time_steps> nil
<unordered-set> ::=
        compound-action-id = { process-step-id , process-step-id
        <other_unordered_set_steps> }
<other_unordered_set_steps> ::=
        process-step-id <other_unordered_set_steps> nil
```

1. *Run-time choice rules:* These rules are used when there is an exclusive choice among several alternatives. Exactly one process step in the list will be executed as decided by the resource at run-time, which must be common to all steps in the list.

   WHEN (ES(EF1) = end_stat_1) DO S = (EF2 XOR EF3 XOR EF4)

2. *Unordered set rules:* They are used to indicate that a set of process steps must be executed next but the order of execution is unknown. In this case, all steps must be executed at least once (the semantic is the semantic of the AND logical operator).

   WHEN (ES(EF1) = end_stat_1) DO S = {EF2, EF3, EF4}

4.2 Functional Languages

Within a domain, domain processes are made of enterprise activities and sub-processes, also called business processes, and are triggered by events. Let **P** denote the set of process classes, **A** the set of activity classes, **OV** the set of object view classes, **R** the set of resources and **E** the set of event classes of a business entity. Let also 2^S denote the power set of **S**.

Activities: Enterprise activities are functional units which require the allocation of time and resources for their full execution. By essence, an activity performs something (at least it consumes time), except the activity

NIL which does nothing (neutral element of set **A**). By definition, an activity class A of **A** is a function f which transforms inputs into outputs when some pre-conditions are satisfied. In other words, its occurrences transform an initial state into a final state under the condition C_f (i.e. a logical expression called a *guard*). We can therefore write:

A: final state $= f$(initial state) if C_f (initial state) $=$ true.

Input states and output states are defined in terms of object views of **OV**. The guard can be used to specify special triggering conditions or resource requirements. It is always possible to associate with each activity class A of **A** a finite set ES_A of so-called ending statuses. Ending statuses are defined as 0-argument predicates. They summarise the termination status of the execution of an occurrence of the activity (such as 'successful execution', 'aborted', 'done' or 'less than 100 items produced'). The generic function ES returning the ending status at the end of an activity execution can be defined as follows:

$ES : A \rightarrow \cup A \in \mathbf{A}\ ES_A$ such that $ES(A) \in ES_A$

In CIMOSA, an activity class A is defined as a 10-tuple $A = < A_{id}, FI_A, FO_A, CI_A, CO_A, RI_A, RO_A, \delta_A A, Cap_A, ES_A >$ where A_{id} is the name of the activity class, $FI_A, FO_A, CI_A, CO_A, RI_A, RO_A$ are the function input, function output, control input, control output, resource input and resource output of A, respectively (with $FI_A \cup FO_A \cup CI_A \neq \oslash$; $FI_A \cap CI_A = \oslash$; $FI_A, FO_A, CI_A, RO_A \subseteq 2^{OV}; RI_A \subseteq 2^R; CO_A \subseteq 2^E$), δ_A defines the activity behaviour, i.e. the function f and guard C_f performed by occurrences of A (usually defined as an algorithm for machines and a script for humans) such that $\delta_A(FI_A, CI_A, RI_A) = (FO_A, CO_A, RO_A), Cap_A$ is the set of required capabilities for this activity (defined in the resource view) and ES_A is the finite set of ending statuses. Function input and function output provide the list of object views which are respectively transformed and produced by the activity. Control input indicates object views used by the activity but not modified (control information). Control output provides the list of events which can be generated by the activity. Resource input defines resource requirements. Resource output provides data on resource status after the execution of the activity (optional). If an input (output) receives (sends) a flow of object views, we then use the term *STREAM OF <object-view-class>*

At the design level, time is added in the form of minimum and maximum durations (real numbers *dmin* and *dmax*, $dmin \leq dmax$), defining the time it takes to execute an activity ($dmin = dmax$ for deterministic activities and $dmin \neq dmax$ for stochastic activities). An average duration *davg* with standard deviation could also be specified. Furthermore, the activity behaviour δ_A is defined in terms of elementary actions performed by the activities of class A. These elementary actions are called *functional operations*. These are atomic operations either performed on request by *functional entities*, i.e.

active resources or actors of the system (e.g. drill a hole, move a part, write a letter or fetch data in a data store), or by a CIMOSA model execution service. Each functional operation is formally denoted as (by analogy to a message sent to a method of an agent):

FE.FO (parameter-list)

where *FE* is the name of the functional entity able to execute the functional operation *FO* and parameter-list is the list of formal (input/output) arguments of the operation. Input/output arguments are syntactically differentiated (such as in languages like Ada or CORBA IDL).

A special built-in functional operation, defined as *CreateEvent (e),* can be used in any activity. It will be used within an activity to raise an occurrence of event class e of **E**. Using this function, it is possible to raise an event within an activity of process *P1* which will trigger another process *P2* (within or outside the domain considered). This facility makes it possible to synchronise processes using events.

The activity behaviour δ_A of an activity class A has the following syntax [Ver94]:

```
Activity Behaviour : { <A-behaviour> } [Exception Handling :
                     <exceptions>]
<A-behaviour> ::=    <declarations> <pre-conditions> <statements>
                     <post-conditions>
```

where *<declarations>* is used to declare local variables, *<pre-conditions>* is a set of predicates defining pre-conditions on the execution of the activity (e.g. access to non-empty files, availability of necessary function or resource inputs, variable initialisation, ...), *<statements>* are either functional operation calls or Pascal-like procedural statements (including variable assignments, if-then structures, case structures, loops, etc.) involving functional operation calls, *<post-conditions>* defines a (possibly empty) set of actions to be executed at the end of the activity (e.g. forcing variables to values, closing files or setting ending status values). The *<exceptions>* clause (optional) allows the definition of exception handling mechanisms (such as time-outs or watch-dogs) to face non-deterministic situations (e.g. detection of an infinite loop, conditions never realised or deadlock situations). It has the following structure:

<exception> : <excep_action> ;

where *<exception>* is a Boolean condition (e.g. *elapsed-time = 100* or *Not (C1)* or *Var-A > Threshold-A*) and *<excep_action>* is a set of statements to be applied if the exception condition becomes true or a call to raise an event (using the CreateEvent operation).

An activity can only be executed within a process workflow if its triggering conditions and all its pre-conditions are satisfied, and if its required resources are available. If the pre-conditions are not satisfied, control is either passed to the exception handling mechanism, which can either force the value of the ending status for normal process continuation or call an exception handling procedure if one is defined, or suspend execution and pass control to a supervisor level (i.e. CIMOSA model execution services).

Co-operative Activities: Co-operative activities are activities which involve the exchange of messages (i.e. data, information or object views) and need synchronisation (synchronous or asynchronous mode). Thus, they make use of the following predefined functional operations (where a is an activity identifier, m is the message and c is a communication channel):

- *request (a, m, c)* to ask a for message m via channel c
- *receive (a, m, c)* to receive message m via channel c from a
- *send (a, m, c)* to send message m via channel c to a
- *broadcast (m, c)* to send message m via channel c to anyone interested
- *acknowledge (a)* to let a know that its message has been received

Events: Events are unsolicited happenings (e.g. customer orders, signals, or machine failures) or solicited happenings (e.g. requests, planned orders, or timers) conditioning the execution of the enterprise operations, i.e. execution of business processes and their activities. An event class E of **E** is defined as a 4-tuple:

$$E =< E_{id}, q, OV, t >$$

where E_{id} is the name of the event class, q is a first-order logic predicate, OV is an object view class (optional) defining information carried by events of this class, if any, and t is a time-point indicating when the occurrence of the event happened. q defines a condition describing a real-world situation in the enterprise. When it evaluates to true, an occurrence of the event class is created. For instance, the arrival of a customer order is an event, the customer order itself is an object view. Starting or terminating an enterprise activity can also be considered as events if required.

Processes: Enterprise processes describe the enterprise behaviour, i.e. the order in which activities are chained and executed. Let P be a process class of **P**. P is defined as a 5-tuple:

$$P =< P_{id}, \alpha_P, \beta_P, \delta_P, ES_P >$$

where P_{id} is the name of the process class, α_P is called the alphabet of P and represents the set of steps (i.e. activities) in which occurrences of P can engage, β_P is the set of triggering conditions c (see workflow language) under which a process of P can be started ($\beta_P = (c/(c \rightarrow P))$), δ_P is a set of behavioural rules which defines the process behaviour and ES_P is a finite set of ending statuses of processes of P such that $ES_P = s'_1, s'_2, ..., s'_{mj}, 1 \leq j \leq Card(\mathbf{P}), mj \in \mathbf{N}$ (set of natural numbers). Ending statuses are 0-argument predicates indicating the termination status of the process. They must be ending statuses or logical combinations of ending statuses of enterprise activities employed in the process.

At the design specification modelling level, functional models can be automatically translated into timed Petri nets, and especially generalised stochastic Petri nets. This allows for qualitative analysis (liveness, boundedness, reversibility, p-invariants, etc.) and quantitative analysis (cycle times, bottlenecks, etc.) of business processes using Petri net theory [DHP93, Mur89]. Petri nets are directed graphs made of two types of nodes: places (represented by circles) and transitions (represented by bars). Time is associated to transitions. Translation rules can be provided in graphical form as indicated by Figure 2 (where EF_i denotes a process step, e represents an event, s_j is an ending status, δ denotes an immediate transition represented by a black bar with firing time equal to zero and places with double circles are control places, i.e. their marking is controlled by an external agent to represent external actions on the system).

4.3 Information Languages

At the requirements definition modelling level, CIMOSA uses two constructs in the information view: enterprise objects and object views.

Enterprise objects are actual entities of the enterprise. They are defined by their object class (i.e. structure), their state (i.e. occurrence values) and are characterised by their unique identifier. An enterprise object class O of **O** is defined as a 3-tuple $O =< O_{id}, \{a_k\}_{k=1,2}, \{p_i\}_{i=1,n} >$ where O_{id} is the object class name, a_k is an abstraction mechanism (a_1 is the generalisation mechanism for 'is-a' links associated to property inheritance and a_2 is the aggregation mechanism for 'part-of' links) and each p_i is an object property ($\{p_i\}_{i \neq \emptyset}$) such that:
$p_i : O \rightarrow D_i$ where D_i is a basic domain (i.e. a set of values such as integers, reals, character strings, etc.), if p_i is an atomic property.
$p_i : O \rightarrow O', O' \in \mathbf{O}$, if p_i is defined as an object (for compound objects).
$p_i : O \rightarrow 2^{O'}, O' \in \mathbf{O}$, if p_i is defined as a set of objects of class O'.

Methods, i.e. procedural attachments, can be added to object class definition, but this is not necessary for the scope of this paper. Integrity constraints can also be defined on properties.

Object Views: Material and information objects of the enterprise used as control input, function input and/or function output of at least one enterprise activity are described as object views. An object view, or object state, is a representation or physical manifestation of an object as perceived by users or applications at a given point in time. It is characterised by its embodiment and is described by a set of properties. A class OV of **V** of similar object views can be defined as a 4-tuple (object views are occurrences of the class OV):

$$OV = < OV_{id}, nature, \{p_i\}_{i=1,n}, \{O_j\}_{j=1,m} >$$

where OV_{id} is the name of the object view class, nature = 'physical' if the object view class represents physical objects (e.g. materials, work-pieces or tools) or nature = 'information' if the object views are only made of data (e.g. forms, computer screens, reports, files or messages), $\{p_i\}_i$ is a set of properties of objects of classes $\{O_j\}_j$ of $\mathbf{O}$ on which the object views of the class OV are defined.

At the design specification modelling level, all object views are specified as external schemas of one global conceptual schema derived from enterprise object specification. The conceptual schema defines the structure of the databases to be implemented to support the integrated system. Both the conceptual schema and the external schemas can either be expressed in terms of an extended entity-relationship model or an object-oriented model according to users' requirements. These specifications can then be implemented using the relational model and the SQL language at the implementation description modelling level [JV90].

4.4 Resource Languages

CIMOSA provides two modelling constructs for resource modelling: resource and capability set. Resources can be classified into active resources (functional entities) and passive resources (components) in the sense that one class can execute functional operations and the other cannot. Components and functional entities can be aggregated to form new resources.

Resources: Resources represent any kind of physical enterprise means used to perform tasks (e.g. machines, tools, materials handling systems, devices, computers or database systems) as well as application systems such as CAD systems, CAPP systems or MRP systems and also human beings. Thus, the set of resource classes $\mathbf{R}$ is such that $\mathbf{R} \subset \mathbf{O}$.

Functional entities are active resources offering a finite set of capabilities and able to perform a defined set of so-called functional operations on request or on their own. They represent actors or doers of the system. A class R of functional entities of $\mathbf{R}$ can be defined as a 5-tuple:

$$R = < R_{id}, OV_R, Cap_R, FO_R, f_R >$$

where R_{id} is the name of the functional entity class, OV_R defines the object view providing the set of descriptive properties (variables) describing the state of a resource of class R, Cap_R is the finite set of capabilities offered by resources of class R, FO_R is the set of functional operations (basic commands) that resources of class R can understand and execute and f_R is a table (optional) indicating for a given resource of R when and for how long this resource object is allocated to specific activities (resource scheduling problem). Allocation and assignment modes can also be added.

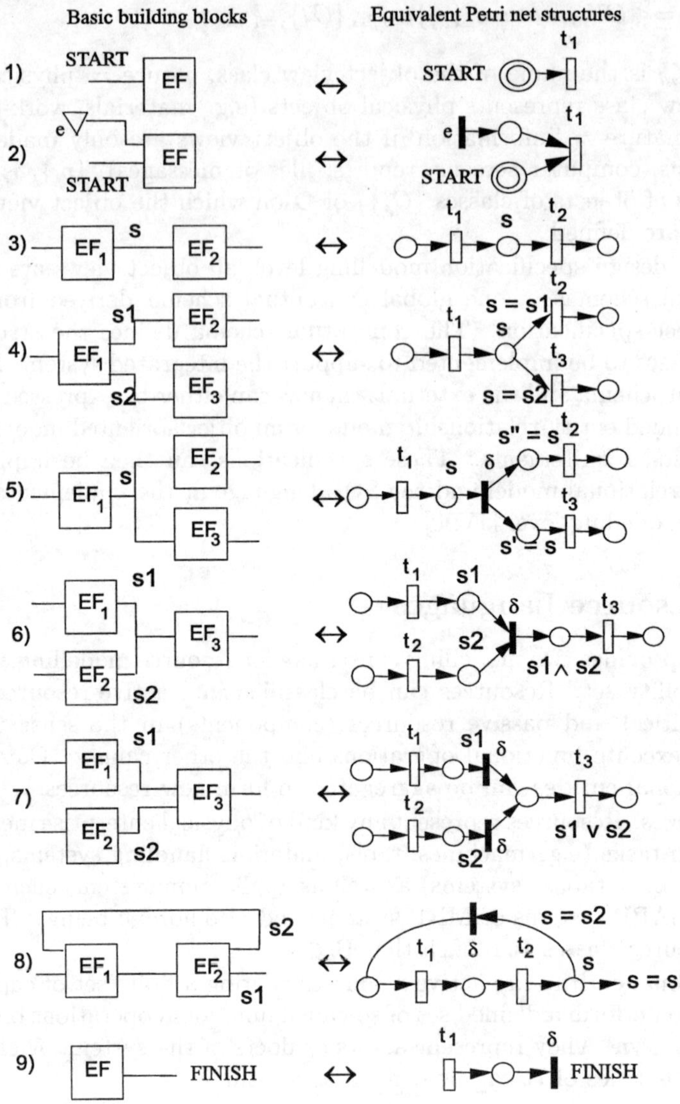

Figure 2: Workflow translation rules into generalised stochastic Petri nets

Functional entities are similar in their definition to the one of agents as used in artificial intelligence. They can receive, send, process or even store information. Active and passive resources can be aggregated into larger functional entities. CIMOSA classifies functional entities into three generic classes: *machines* (for any device having some degree of autonomy or intelligence), *applications* (for computer applications) and *humans* [AMI93]. Each class has characteristics of its own, especially in terms of the set of provided capabilities (i.e. skills, abilities or and competencies) and can in turn be further specialised.

Capability Set: Capability set is a construct used to define capabilities required by an activity and capabilities provided by a resource. When the activity is executed, the resource(s) allocated to the activity must offer the right capabilities.

Capabilities are defined in terms of technical characteristics or constraints for machines and applications (e.g. repeatability or reachability of a robot arm, data access time for a database server or speed and feed range of a machine-tool). They are defined in terms of qualifications, skills and competencies for human beings (for instance, to have a driver's licence for cars and trucks, to speak English, French and German or to be a certified industrial engineer). CIMOSA distinguishes between function, object, performance and operation related capabilities of a resource (for instance, to be able to move 50 Kg heavy parts over a distance of 10 meters, 20 times per hour).

At the requirements definition modelling level, only required capabilities are defined for each activity as resource input. At the design specification modelling level, resources, and especially functional entities, are defined with their complete sets of provided capabilities and functional operations. The same constructs are used at the implementation description level.

4.5 Organisation Languages

CIMOSA defines the organisation view of an enterprise in terms of responsibilities and authorities to be allocated to managerial units being in charge of a particular job or various elements of a particular enterprise architecture (i.e. processes, activities, object views, resources). Two constructs are defined:

Organisation Units: An organisation unit is a decision centre reduced to one functional entity with a specified job profile and well-defined responsibilities and authorities.

Organisation Cells: An organisation cell is an aggregation of organisation units to form a higher level decision centre in the organisation hierarchy. It is placed under the management of one functional entity (must be a human) and it has a set of well-defined responsibilities and authorities on specified elements of the enterprise architecture, i.e. processes, activities, object views, resources or lower level organisation units.

These constructs are used at all modelling levels.

5 Application Example

Let us consider a customer order processing domain. The domain consists of two domain processes: a customer order processing procedure (process-cust-order), occurrences of which are triggered by the arrival of new customer orders (order-A1-arrival events) and a procedure for sending acceptance notification with price and delay (send-notification). The process-cust-order domain process uses four classes of activities: check-customer, check-order, process-order and reject-order. Check-customer and check-order can be done in parallel.

The definitions of the domain, the process-cust-order process and the order-A1-arrival event follow. The domain construct provides a 'table of contents' of this part of the model, stating domain objectives and constraints, listing involved domain processes, events and object views. The domain process template has been provided with entries for process objectives and constraints, which must be sub-objectives and constraints of the domain. It has also an entry for declarative rules which are imperative rules (business rules, administrative rules, regulations, etc.) constraining the design of the process. It has also been provided with input and output entries for traceability of inputs and outputs. However, their use is optional for processes. Finally, the process behaviour is defined by a set of procedural rules. The event template indicates the domain processes to be triggered and the related object view.

```
DOMAIN cust-ord-processing
Domain Description: Concerns receipt, acceptance, processing
                    of customer orders and price and delay
                    notification to customers
CIMOSA Compliant:   Yes
Domain Objectives:  to accept or reject customer orders
                    and notify customers
Domain Constraints: to be able to process at least 100
                    customer orders per day
Domain Processes:   process-cust-order, send-notification
Boundary:           Finance-relationship, MRP-relationship
Object Views:       order-A1, customer-file, customer-data,
                    cust-notification
Events:             order-A1-arrival

EVENT order-A1-arrival
Triggers: process-cust-order
Object View: order-A1
Predicate: arrival (order-A1)

DOMAIN PROCESS process-cust-order
Objectives: to receive customer orders, to check the order, to check
            the customer, and to process or reject the order
Constraints: to be able to process at least 100 customer orders per
             day
Declarative Rules: DC-cust-ord-proc
Function Input: customer-file
Function Output: customer-data
```

```
Control Input: order-A1
Control Output: Nil
Resource Input: Nil
Resource Output: Nil
Events: order-A1-arrival
Process Behaviour: {
WHEN (START WITH order-A1-arrival) DO check-order & check-customer
WHEN (ES(check-order)='OK' AND ES(check-customer) = 'OK')
          DO process-order
WHEN (ES(check-order)='NOT-OK' AND ES(check-customer)=ANY)
          DO reject-order
WHEN (ES(check-order)= ANY AND ES(check-customer)='NOT-OK')
          DO reject-order
WHEN (ES(process-order)='done') DO FINISH
WHEN (ES(reject-order)='done') DO FINISH}
```

Each enterprise activity identified must be defined by description of its inputs and outputs and definition of its full set of possible ending statuses. For instance, the activity check-customer is defined as follows (no activity behaviour is defined at this modelling level and resource requirements are defined in the required capabilities RC-check-customer):

```
ENTERPRISE ACTIVITY check-customer
Objectives: to verify the validity of this customer
Constraints: to be able to process at least 100 customer orders per
             day
Declarative Rules: DC-customer-rejection-rule
Function Input: customer-file
Function Output: customer-data
Control Input: order-A1
Control Output: Nil
Resource Input: Nil
Resource Output: Nil
Required Capabilities: RC-check-customer
Ending Statuses: {'OK' for valid customer, 'NOT-OK' otherwise}
```

where *DC-customer-rejection-rule* is a declarative rule (CIMOSA construct) stating, for instance, that the customer order will be rejected if customer debit is greater than ECU 20.000, customer-file and customer-data are information object views about the customer, *order-A1* is an object view defining the customer order and providing the customer identification, and *RC-check-customer* defines the set of capabilities required for the activity (e.g. process a customer order in less than 5 min).

Finally, all object views identified in the previous constructs must be defined in terms of their properties (information elements with relevant data types or other object views). An object view can be made of other object views (for instance, a technical document structured into sections and including pictures). As an example, the template for the *order-A1* object view is given. The object view defines the leading object and related objects on which this object view is defined and the list of properties describing occurrences of the object view. Among these, *customer-id, status* and *date* are information elements and the others are object views.

```
OBJECT VIEW order-A1
Description: Describes customer orders of type A1 sent
             by customers by EDI
Leading Object: customer
Related Objects: end-products
Properties:
customer-id: string [10]
date: date
customer-address: address
delivery-address: address
itemlist: setof item-quantity
status: (new, in-process, accepted, rejected)
```

At the design specification modelling level, the model is specified in more details. Especially, time is added. Thus, the *order-A1-arrival* event and the *check-customer* activity are further detailed as follows (where *FE-1* and *printer-A* are functional entities, customer is a local variable and SD the system wide information access system of the CIMOSA Integrating Infrastructure):

```
EVENT order-A1-arrival
Source: outside  (* means outside domain *)
Triggers: process-cust-order
Object View: order-A1
Predicate: Arrival (order-A1)
Timestamp: time

ENTERPRISE ACTIVITY check-customer
Objectives: to verify the validity of this customer
Constraints: to be able to process at least 100 customer orders per
             day
Declarative Rules: DC-customer-rejection-rule
Function Input: customer-file
Function Output: customer-data
Control Input: order-A1
Control Output: Nil
Resource Input: FE-1, printer-A
Resource Output: Nil
Required Capabilities: RC-check-customer
Minimum Duration: 100
Maximum Duration: 200
Activity Behaviour: {
Declare cust-id: string [10]; (* declares local variables *)
```

```
Preconditions: not-empty (customer-file);
Begin  (* activity behaviour processing *)
SD.Get (customer-file);
SD.Get (order-A1);
cust-id := order-A1.customer-id;
FE-1.Check (cust-id, customer-file, customer-data, success);
   (* implements the Declarative Rule *)
if success = 0 then begin
printer-A.print (customer-data);
ES (check-customer) := 'OK' end
else ES (check-customer) := 'NOT-OK' end
end;
Postconditions: order-A1.status := 'in-process';
               SD.Put (order-A1);
               SD.Put (customer-data)}
Ending Statuses:
{'OK' for valid customer, 'NOT-OK' otherwise}
```

Pre-conditions and post-conditions can be declared for activities. If the pre-conditions are not verified when the activity is started, control is passed to the entity having responsibility for this construct (organisation unit). This example shows that a type inference mechanism is required to recognise the type of arguments of the functional operations used in the activity behaviour. Formal arguments of functional operations are defined in the specification of functional entities able to execute the functional operations. The example also illustrates how ending status values are initialised during activity behaviour processing. In some cases, ending statuses can be forced by post-conditions.

An example of a resource is given by the functional entity *FE-1* which is a software application installed on a computer workstation to perform functional operations of the check-customer activity. We assume that there is only one copy of this software in the company.

```
RESOURCE FE-1
Description: Software program installed on UNIX station US-1 used to
             check customer data for new customer orders
Class: Functional Entity (* other classes are: Component,
                            Resource Set, Resource Cell *)
Object View: FE-1-desc (* object view containing descriptive data
                          about the resource *)
Cardinality: 1 (* only one occurrence of this resource, called
                  resource unit, exists *)
Location: port-a (* the UNIX station is connected to the CIM
                    architecture by an entry point logically
                    called port-a in the model *)
Capability: C-FE-1 (* set of capabilities provided described in a
                      separate construct *)
Command Set:  (* set of functional operations provided by
```

```
                   the resource *)
Check (IN cid: string  [10], cust-file: customer-file,
              OUT cust-data: customer-data, success: FOstatus)
Allocation Mode: FIFO (* first requesting activity is served first *)
Assignment Mode: FIFO (* first request is processed first *)
```

6 Conclusion

The CIMOSA modelling approach is a business process oriented modelling approach covering functional, information, resource and organisation aspects of an enterprise. It provides a different modelling language for each of the various modelling levels of an enterprise, namely requirements definition, design specification and implementation description. However, consistency among modelling levels is ensured by preserving major concept description from one level to another one.

The languages, although complex because of their richness in terms of number of constructs, can be parsed to check model consistency and be used for model simulation and execution. Especially, transformation rules have been proposed to translate a control flow, expressed in terms of a workflow, into generalised stochastic Petri nets, making its qualitative and quantitative analysis and simulation possible [Ver94]. Finally, CIMOSA ideas and constructs have influenced standardisation work dedicated to enterprise modelling at the European level [CEN90, CEN95] or at ISO (ISO/TC184/SC5) as well as the development of commercial enterprise modelling packages (such as ARIS, FirstSTEP or even IBM's FlowMark).

References

[AMI93] CIMOSA: Open System Architecture for CIM, 2nd extended and revised version, Springer-Verlag, Berlin, 1993

[BN96] P. Bernus, L. Nemes (eds.), Modelling and Methodologies for Enterprise Integration, Chapman & Hall, London, 1996

[Bus96] Bussler, C., Specifying enterprise processes with workflow modelling languages, Concurrent Engineering: Research and Applications 4 (3), 1996, 261-278

[CEN90] CEN/CENELEC, Computer-Integrated Manufacturing, Systems Architecture, Framework for Enterprise Modelling, CEN, Brussels, 1990

[CEN95] CEN/CENELEC, Advanced Manufacturing Technology, Systems Architecture, Constructs for Enterprise Modelling, CEN, Brussels, 1995

[CIM96] CIMOSA Formal Reference Base, Version 3.2. CIMOSA Association e.V., Germany, 1996

[DHP93] Di Cesare, F., Harhalakis, G., Proth, J-M., Silva, M., Vernadat, F., Practice of Petri Nets in Manufacturing, Chapman & Hall, London, 1993

[JV90] Jorysz, H. R., Vernadat, F. B., CIM-OSA Part 2: Information View, Int. J. Computer-Integrated Manufacturing 3 (3), 1990, 157-167

[Mur89] Murata, T., Petri nets: Properties, analysis, and applications, Proceedings of the IEEE 77 (4), 1989, 541-580

[Ver93] Vernadat, F., CIMOSA: Enterprise modelling and enterprise integration using a process-based approach, in: H. Yoshikawa, J. Goossenaerts (eds.), Information Infrastructure Systems for Manufacturing, North-Holland, Amsterdam, 1993, 65-84

[Ver94] Vernadat, F., Manufacturing systems modelling, specification and analysis, in: C. Walter, F. J. Kliemann, J. P. M. de Oliveira (eds.), Production Management Methods (B-19), Elsevier Science, Amsterdam, 1994, 75-83

[Ver96] Vernadat, F. B., Enterprise Modeling and Integration: Principles and Application, Chapman & Hall, London, 1996

CHAPTER 12

ConceptBase
Managing Conceptual Models about Information Systems

M.A. Jeusfeld, M. Jarke, H.W. Nissen, M. Staudt

ConceptBase is a meta data management system intended to support the cooperative development and evolution of information systems with multiple interacting formalisms. It supports a simple logic-based core language, O-Telos, which integrates deductive and object-oriented features in order to support the syntactical, graphical, and semantic customization of modeling languages as well as analysis in multi-language modeling environments.

1 Multi-Language Conceptual Modeling

Conceptual models offer abstract views on certain aspects of the real world (description role) and the information system to be implemented (prescription role) [You89]. They are used for different purposes, such as a communication medium between users and developers, for managing and understanding the complexity within the application domain, and for making experiences reusable. The presence of multiple conceptual modeling languages is common in information systems engineering as well as other engineering disciplines. The reasons are among others:

- the complexity of the system requires a decomposition of the modeling task into subtasks; a frequent strategy is to use orthogonal perspectives (data view, behavioral view, etc.) for this decomposition

- the information system is decomposed into subsystems of different type, e.g. data storage system vs. user interface; experts for those subsystems tend to prefer special-purpose modeling languages

- the modeling process is undertaken by a group of experts with different background and education; the experts may have different preferences on modeling languages
- conceptual modeling has different goals (e.g., system analysis, system specification, documentation, training, decision support); heterogeneous goals lead to heterogeneous representation languages, and to heterogeneous ways-of-working even with given languages.

The pre-dominant approach to solve the integration problem is to "buy" an integrated CASE tool which offers a collection of predefined modeling languages and to apply it in the manner described in the manual. There are good reasons to do so: the method design has already been done and the interdependencies between the multiple modeling languages have already been addressed by the CASE tool designers. Moreover, a CASE tool supports the standardization of information systems development within an enterprise.

Still, there are information systems projects that require more flexibility in terms of modeling language syntax, graphical presentations, and semantics of modeling language interactions. The Telos meta modeling language has been developed to address these concerns. Its implementation in ConceptBase, a meta data management system based on the integration of deductive and object-oriented technologies, supports an Internet-based architecture intended to support flexible and goal-oriented distributed cooperation in modeling projects.

1.1 A Brief History of Meta Modeling

In the mid-1970s, several semiformal notations supporting the development of information systems were developed. The use of some of these became standard practice in the 1980s, especially entity-relationship diagrams for data modeling and dataflow diagrams for function modeling. More recently, object-oriented methods have added notations for behavior modeling, such as Statecharts, giving a broader picture of the specification and an easier mapping to implementations in languages like C++ or Java.

It was recognized early on that managing large specifications in these notations posed serious problems of inconsistency, incompleteness, maintenance, and reuse. Conceptual modeling languages incorporate ideas from knowledge representation, databases, and programming languages to provide the necessary formal foundation for users with limited mathematics background.

In early 1980s, Sol Greenspan was the first to apply these ideas to requirements engineering, when he formalised the SADT notation in the RML language [GMB94]. This was a precursor to numerous attempts worldwide. Initially, these languages embodied a fixed ontology in which requirements engineering could be described. As early as 1984, it was recognized that modeling formalisms must be customizable. Jeff Kotteman and Benn Konsynski

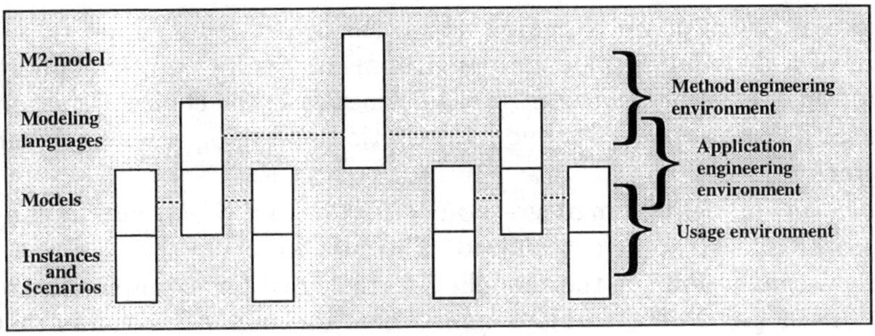

Figure 1: The ISO IRDS architecture applied to conceptual modeling

proposed a basic architecture that included a meta meta model (M2-model for short) as the basis for using different notations within a development environment [KK84]. ISO's Information Resource Dictionary System (IRDS) [ISO90] standard generalized this idea to propose an architecture that combines information systems use and evolution. Figure 1 shows its four-layer architecture applied to the conceptual modeling activity.

The **Instances and Scenarios level** contains objects which cannot have instances. Examples are data, processes, system states, measurements and so on. Objects may have attributes and they may have classes (residing in the model level). During design, when the information system and therefore the instances do not yet exist, this level also contains scenarios of the intended use of the system.

The **Models level** represents the classes of the objects at the instance level. Those classes define the schema (attributes, properties) of the instance level objects as well as rules for manipulating these objects. At the same time the classes are themselves instances of the schema defined at the modeling language level.

At the **Modeling languages level**, meta classes define the structure of the objects (classes) at the model level. In other words, a model is instantiated from the meta classes of the modeling language level. In section 3, the modeling language level will be used to define specific graphical notations *and* their interrelationships.

The **M2-model level** contains meta meta classes (M2-classes). They are classes with instances at the modeling language level. Multiple modeling languages are possible by appropriate instantiations from these M2-classes. Moreover, the dependencies between the multiple languages can be represented as attributes between M2-classes in the M2-model level.

The four IRDS levels can be grouped in pairs that define interlocking environments, as shown on the right side of Figure 1: usage environments, application engineering environments, and the method engineering environment, which manages the interrelationships among modeling languages and the interactions among modeling tools. The interlocking between the models can be read down or up. Reading down, the architecture supports the *generation* of a distributed modeling environment; reading up, it supports the *integration* of existing environments. In either case, the choice of metamodels is crucial for the support the model definition and integration environments can offer.

However, modeling languages do not just have a programming language syntax which needs to be customized. The customization should also address graphical conventions of the modeling formalisms; for example, the mobile phone developer Nokia employs more than 150 method variants in terms of notation, graphics, and ways-of-modeling. Moreover, the correct usage of each formalism and the consistency of models that span across different modeling formalisms should be definable.

Since the late 1980s, more dedicated M2-models have been developed, as discussed in the next subsections. In parallel, the need to have generalized languages dedicated to meta modeling and method engineering was recognized by several people. In several iterations, a number of European projects [JMSV92] jointly with the group of John Mylopoulos at the University of Toronto developed the language Telos [MBJK90] which generalized RML to provide a meta modeling framework which integrates the three perspectives of structured syntax, graphical presentation, and formal semantics.

However, early attempts to implement the full Telos language (as in the first version of ConceptBase [JJ89]) showed that its semantics was still too complicated for efficient repository support based on known technologies. Three parallel directions were pursued by different, but interacting and partially overlapping groups of researchers.

The MetaEdit environment developed at the University of Jyväskylä [KLR96] is a good example of an effort focusing on graphics-based method engineering, i.e. the graphical definition of graphical modeling formalisms.

Starting from early experiences with ConceptBase in the DAIDA project [JR88, JMSV92] the Semantic Index System developed in ESPRIT project ITHACA [CJMV95] focused on an efficient implementation of the structurally object-oriented aspects of the Telos language. It may be worth noting that the recently announced Microsoft Repository [BHSSZ97] has generalized such an approach to full object orientation based on Microsoft's Common Object Model.

Complementing these structural concerns, the first step in the further development of ConceptBase within ESPRIT project Compulog focused on the simplification of the logical semantics. The dissertation [Jeu92] showed that the non-temporal part of Telos, with very minor modifications, can be based on the fixpoint semantics of deductive databases (also known as Datalog) with negation [CGT90], resulting in the O-Telos dialect used in the present version of ConceptBase[1] [JGJSE95]. Thereby, the diagrams denoting the

[1]The current version of the system can be obtained from the address http://www-i5.informatik.rwth-aachen.de/CBdoc for research and evaluation purposes.

structure became explicit facts in the database (of concepts), the syntactical constraints are represented as deductive rules or queries or integrity constraints, and the manipulation services are expressed as restrictions on how to update the database. This simple formalization thus was a prerequisite of the re-integration of syntactical, graphical, and semantic aspects of meta modeling, as discussed in section 2 below.

1.2 Three Basic Modeling Methodologies

As observed in [Poh94], modeling processes proceed along three dimensions: representational transformation, domain knowledge acquisition, and stakeholder agreement. Existing methodologies tend to emphasize one of these dimensions over the others: the modeling *notations*, the available *knowledge* within a specific domain, or the *people* involved in the analysis project. All three methodologies have long histories, with little interaction between them. All of them use multiple modeling perspectives but the purpose of these and therefore the integration strategies are quite different.

Notation-oriented methods manifest their assistance in the set of modeling notations they offer. Their philosophy can be characterized by the slogan *In the language lies the power.* Examples of notation-oriented methods are structured analysis approaches, as, e.g., Modern Structured Analysis (MSA) [You89], and object-oriented techniques, as, e.g., the Unified Modeling Language (UML) [FS97]. A large number of CASE tools in the market offer graphical editors to develop models of the supported notations and check the balancing rules that must hold between models of different notations. The notations as well as the constraints are hard-coded within the tools and are not easily customizable by users.

A completely different strategy is employed by the **domain-oriented analysis methods**. For a specific application domain, e.g., public administration or furniture industry, they offer a predefined set of reference models. Reference models describe typical data, processes and functions, together with a set of consistency tests which evaluate relationships between the models. Reference models represent the knowledge collected in multiple analysis projects within a particular domain: *In the knowledge lies the power.* The reuse of reference models can strongly reduce the analysis effort. However, it can be inflexible since the user can tailor the notations, the constraints or contents only to the degree foreseen by the developers of the reference models, or completely loses the help of the method.

The ARIS Toolset [IDS96] offers a platform for working with reference models. It also offers hard-coded constraint checks within and across the models. These tests are programmed individually and new tests can be added manually, without a coherent theory, even though the concept of event-driven process chain (EPC) provides a semi-formal understanding [Sch94]. Towards a more formal approach, the NATURE project has defined formal problem abstractions [MSTT94] via a M2-model which defines principles for the specification of domain models.

Goal- and team-oriented approaches specifically address the objective to capture requirements from multiple information sources and to make arising conflicts productive. They incorporate stakeholder involvement and prescribe general process steps rather than notations or contents: *In the people lies the power.* Prominent examples include IBM's JAD (Joint Application Design) [Aug91], SSM (Soft Systems Methodology) [Che89], and PFR (Analysis of Presence and Future Requirements) [Abe95]. In these methods highly skilled group facilitators animate the participants, guide the analysis process and keep an eye on the compliance with the specified analysis goals. The general idea is to get as much information as possible from different sources in a short time.

Teamwork remains very informal to enhance creativity. Neither notations nor analysis goals are predefined by the methods but specified by the participants according to the actual problem to be solved. To accommodate the change of goals during project execution, the customization of analysis goals and notations is required even during a running project. Outside ConceptBase few supporting tools are available beyond simple groupware tools. The main reason for this dilemma is the high degree of customizability the tools must offer. They must be extensible towards new notations and flexible enough to support changing analysis goals.

1.3 Goals and Architecture of ConceptBase

The design of ConceptBase addresses the following goals:

1. The system should include a feature to define *and interrelate* specialized conceptual modeling languages in an cost-effective way. The language should reflect the modeler's need of key concepts types and their interpretation of those concepts.

2. The system should be extensible at any time. When the need for a new concept type occurs, it should be possible to include it into the conceptual modeling language definition in terms of language constructs, graphical presentation, and semantic constraints.

3. The system should not only check the syntactic correctness within and between models, but also allow to memorize patterns that indicate semantic errors in the models. The memory of those patterns should be extensible and adaptable to the user's growing experience, thus support organizational knowledge creation [Non94].

ConceptBase is realized in a client-server architecture (Figure 2). The ConceptBase server stores, queries, and updates Telos models. The server offers the method TELL for updating the object base and the method ASK for

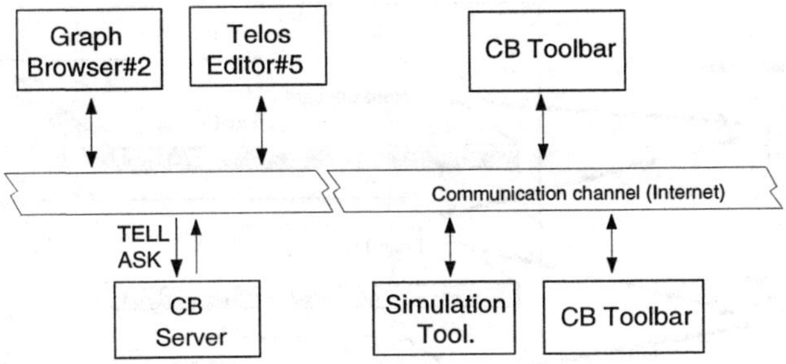

Figure 2: ConceptBase is a client-server meta data manager

querying its contents. Persistent object storage is implemented in C++. Reasoning services for deductive query processing, integrity checking, and code generation are implemented in Prolog.

A ConceptBase client is often a modeling tool, either graphical or textual, but it could be another application, such as a simulation tool. The Internet is the medium for the communication between the server and the clients. Programming interfaces for various toolkits, including Andrew, Tcl/Tk, Ilog Views and Java exist. The distributed version of ConceptBase includes a standard usage interface, along with advice on how to develop your own.

2 The O-Telos Language

Like other conceptual modeling languages, O-Telos offers a textual and a graphical representation. Both are structurally extensible through our meta modeling approach, encoded in the basic language structure. However, the distinguishing feature of O-Telos in comparison with other meta modeling approaches is its simple logical foundation which enables (a) efficient implementation using experiences from deductive database technology, (b) customization of the semantics of modeling formalisms, and most importantly, (c) customization and incremental organizational learning about the analysis of interactions between modeling formalisms. We first discuss the user view of the language (textual and graphical syntax), then the logical foundations and finally its usage in customization and model analysis.

2.1 User View

The four IRDS levels discussed in the introduction define different user classes for O-Telos. Method engineers define a modeling language (here: ER) based on common principles (M2-classes `NodeConcept` and `LinkConcept` in the example). Application engineers learn such a modeling language (symbolized by the meta class `EntityType`) and develop a model (containing for example a class `Employee`). Finally, application users manipulate instance level

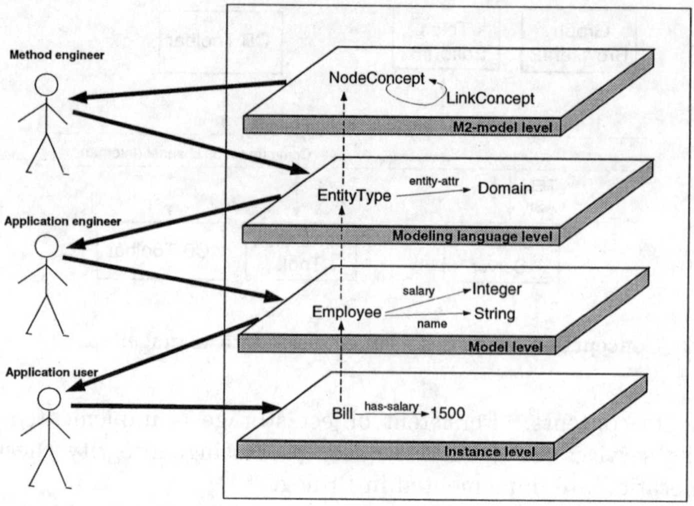

Figure 3: IRDS and O-Telos

objects that conform to the model.

A closer look at Figure 3 reveals that any modeling facility supporting such an interlocked way-of-working requires at least three basic language concepts – one for self-standing labeled objects, a second one for labeled links between them, and the third one to express the instantiation relationship between the IRDS levels. In order to provide formal control over the usage of these base constructs, a fourth concept, that of a logical assertion, is also desirable.

As shown in Figure 4, the kernel of the O-Telos language is just that. All other language facilities (such as generalization hierarchies, cardinality constraints, and so on) can be bootstrapped from this kernel.

In the *textual view* we group together all information for an object (e.g. `Employee`). The class (e.g. `EntityType`) of that object precedes the object name, the attributes of the object (e.g. `salary`) are sorted under *attribute categories* (e.g. `entity_attr`) which refer to the attribute definitions of the object's classes. Note that all objects, i.e. links and nodes, are instances of the builtin object `Object`.

```
Object EntityType with
  attribute
     entity-attr: Domain
end
```

```
EntityType Employee with
  entity-attr
     name  : String;
     salary: Integer
end
```

Besides inserting and modifying O-Telos objects (TELL function), the second main function of the server is the ASK facility. Queries are formu-

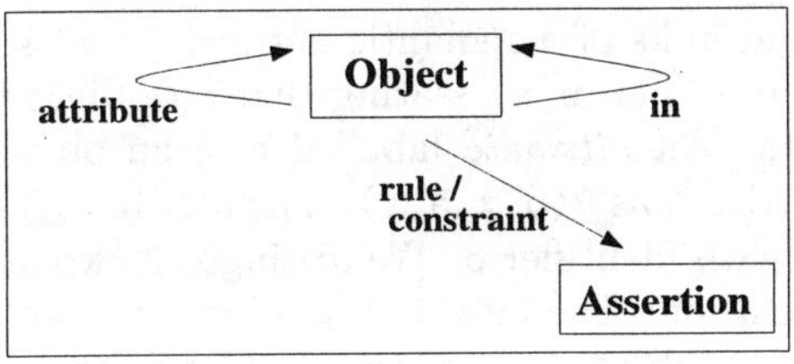

Figure 4: O-Telos' builtin objects

lated like ordinary classes with a (membership) constraint [SNJ94]. They are recognized by the system via the keyword `QueryClass`. The query evaluator computes the answers and establishes an intensional instantiation relationship between the query class and the answers.

The following example presents a query class `RichEmployees` computing all employees with salary greater than 120.000. We restrict the set of answers to the employees by defining the query class as a specialization of `Employee`. The attributes which should be part of the answer are specified as attributes of the query class. In the example we will get the `msalary` attribute for all computed employees. The constraint forms the membership condition, i.e. all only employees that satisfy this constraint become answers to the query class. For the example we require that the value of the `salary` attribute is greater than 120.000.

```
QueryClass RichEmployees isa Employee with
  attribute
     salary : Integer
  constraint
     c : $ salary > 120.000 $
end
```

Note that updates (TELL) and queries (ASK) may refer to any abstraction level. Thus, instance level objects are updated and queried in exactly the same way as the concepts of the modeling language level.

The ConceptBase user interface includes a customizable graph-browser. The base function is to display node objects like `Employee` and link objects like `Employee!salary`. The customization is done by assigning graphical types to nodes and links directly or via deductive rules. It is therefore possible to specify a certain graphical type to all instances of a specific object. An example of graphical customization will be given in section 3.

2.2 Logical Foundations of O-Telos

O-Telos is fully based on the framework of deductive databases, more precisely Datalog with stratified negation [CGT90]. It employs a single relation

P to store nodes and links of a semantic network. *Nodes* are represented by self-referring objects P(x,x,n,x) stating that an object identified by x and labelled by n exists. An *attribute* labelled a of an object x having the attribute value y is written as P(o,x,a,y). The attribute itself is regarded as a full-fledged object with identifier o. We distinguish two attribute labels with predefined interpretation: The fact that an object x is an *instance* of a class c is represented by an object P(o,x,in,c). Moreover, the *specialization* relationship between two objects c and d is stored as an object P(o,c,isa,d) where c is sometimes called a *subclass* of its superclass d.

The P relation allows the representation of arbitrary semantic networks. It serves as the so-called *extensional database* in the deductive interpretation of O-Telos: all explicit information (e.g., a diagram) is stored as objects in the P relation. It should be noted that instances and classes are uniformly represented as objects. Classes may be instances of objects themselves[2]. The ability of O-Telos to represent instances, classes, meta classes, M2-classes etc. uniformly as objects makes it a good framework to store information at different abstraction levels as presented in the subsequent sections.

The extensional database is accompanied by the so-called *intensional database*, i.e. a set of deductive rules and integrity constraints that are stored as attributes of objects. The rules and constraints are logical expressions that are evaluated against the extensional database. The formal interpretation of rules is based on a fixpoint semantics [CGT90] which precisely defines which facts can be derived from the database (extensional plus intensional part). Intuitively, the derivation follows the Modus Pones rule: if the condition A holds and we have a rule "A then B", then the fact B holds. Constraints are special rules of the form "if A does not hold then we have discovered an inconsistency". The object-oriented structure of O-Telos is defined on the simple P-relation via predefined rules and constraints included in any O-Telos database - the so-called O-Telos axioms.

```
forall o,x,c P(o,x,in,c) ==> (x in c)
```

If we explicitly state that x is an instance of c than the fact (x in c) holds.

```
forall o,x,c,d (x in c) and P(o,c,isa,d) ==> (x in d)
```

If x is an instance of a subclass, then it is also an instance of its superclasses.

```
forall p,c,m,d,o,x,l,y P(o,x,l,y) and P(p,c,m,d)
       and (o in p) ==> (x m/l y)
forall x,m,l,y (x m/l y) ==> (x m y)
```

[2]If x is an instance of a class c and c is an instance of a class mc, then we refer to mc as a *metaclass* of x.

The first rule derives an attribute predicate `(x m/l y)` whenever an attribute `o` is declared as an instance of another attribute `p` at the class level. The label `m` is called the *category* of the attribute `p`. The second rule omits the label of the instance level attribute.

Alltogether only 30 such rules were predefined in O-Telos [Jeu92]. The two important things to memorize are

- The single P relation is able to capture semantic networks ("nodes connected by links").
- Rules and constraints are used to fix the interpretation of abstractions like instantiation and specialization. These abstractions are predefined node and link types in the semantic network.

2.3 Conceptual Modeling Languages as Meta Models

The foundation of O-Telos just provides the facilities for representing graphs, plus to constrain and query them via logical conditions. In the following we show that this is enough for not only describing a large collection of conceptual modeling languages but also to relate them in a formal way.

O-Telos treats information at each abstraction level uniformly as objects. The fact that some object is an instance of a class at the upper level is represented as a (derived or stored) fact `(x in c)`. A meta class `mc` of an object `x` is represented by the derived fact `(x [in] mc)`. The corresponding deductive rule in O-Telos is simply[3]:

```
forall x,c,mc (x in c) and (c in mc) ==> (x [in] mc)
```

Attributes are also full-fledged objects: attributes at a class level are the classes of the attributes at the instance level.

Constraints are employed to specify conditions on the instantiation of classes. Rules define information that is derived from explicit information. Note that constraints and rules can be defined at any abstraction level, even crossing several abstraction levels. For example, the instance inheritance rule above is applicable for objects at the model level as well as for objects at the M2-model level. We distinguish the following types of formulae according to the levels involved in the logical condition. As an example, we again use pieces of a formalization of the Entity-Relationship (ER) approach within O-Telos.

- *Model conditions.* Such formulae quantify over instances of classes defined at the model level. For example, there may be a class `Employee` at the model level with an attribute 'salary':

[3]All rules and constraints presented in this paper are part of the intensional database. In principle, any such formula can be inserted into or deleted from the database at any time. This holds for the axioms of O-Telos as well.

```
forall e,s (e in Employee) and (e salary s) ==> (s > 0)
```

- *Modeling language conditions.* Such formulae quantity over instances of meta classes. For example, the meta class EntityType could have a constraint that each instance (like Employee) must have at least one attribute (like salary):

```
forall c (c in EntityType) ==> exists d (d in Domain)
                               and (c entity_attr d)
```

- *M2-model conditions.* Here, the formulae talk about objects at the modeling language level. In our running example, we can think of the two M2-classes NodeConcept and LinkConcept that shall be used to define EntityType and RelationshipType. A M2-model condition could be that links connect nodes but not vice versa:

```
forall x,y (x connects y) ==>
  (x in LinkConcept) and (y in NodeConcept)
```

The reader should have noticed that there is no formal difference between those three kinds of formulae; they are just quantifying over objects at different abstraction levels. The uniform representation of O-Telos objects provides this feature quasi for free. The above examples showed formulae quantifying over objects at the next lower level of abstraction (class to instance). It is also possible to express conditions spanning more than two IRDS levels. Such conditions are needed when the semantics of certain concept types (meta classes) can only be expressed in terms of the instances of the instances of the meta classes. As an example consider "key attributes" of entity types in the ER modeling language.

```
forall x,y,e,k,a,d,v  (x,y in e) and
       (e in EntityType) and P(k,e,a,d) and
       (k in Key) and (x a v) and (y a v)
        ==> (x = y)
```

The formula states that when two entities x,y of the same entity type e have the same value for the key attribute a, then they must be the same.

Such conditions are typical for formal interpretation of conceptual modeling languages. The interesting thing is that those conditions are expressible in the Datalog logic of O-Telos. Thereby, they can be added and evaluated to the (deductive) database at any time. This makes it possible to define specialized modeling languages just by storing appropriate meta classes with their axioms (rules and constraints) in the database. More examples of such formulae crossing multiple IRDS levels can be found in [JJ96].

3 Case Study

The following case study illustrates the management of conceptual models in the context of computer-support for an informal, teamwork-oriented analysis method used by a consulting company. Details and experiences can be found in [NJJZH96].

The consulting firm uses the analysis method PFR (Analysis of Presence and Future Requirements) for rapid, focused requirements capture in settings that alternate between team workshops and individual interviews:

1. In a two-day workshop, stakeholders define an initial *shared vision.* The group makes a rough analysis of the current business processes (mostly in terms of information exchange among organizational units), analyses the goal structure behind the current pattern, identifies goal changes, drafts a redesigned business process, and identify the perspectives of some stakeholders as critical to success.

2. The modeling perspectives identified as critical are then captured in detail by interviews, workflow analyses, and document content studies. This step has the goal of testing the initial vision against the existing and expected organizational context, and to elaborate it, both in terms of deepened understanding and in terms of more formal *representations* (e.g. in the form of activity sequences or data flow models). The acquisition process is accompanied by a *cross-analysis* of the captured conceptual models for consistency, completeness, and local stakeholder agreement.

3. A second workshop is intended to draw the individual perspectives together and to achieve global *stakeholder agreement* on the requirements. The step is accompanied and followed by the development of a comprehensive requirements document of typically several hundred pages.

Even for rather complex projects, the goal is to complete the whole process in a matter of weeks rather than months. A major obstacle in achieving this goal has been the cross-analysis of heterogeneous conceptual models in step 2. Due to time pressure, this analysis often remained incomplete. This led to repeating cycles of steps 2 and 3 due to problems detected only during the second workshop. In a few cases, it even led to problems in the final requirements document which showed up later as errors in the design, coding, or even usage testing phase.

Initially, standard modeling languages like Entity-Relationship diagrams were used both for describing the current procedures and the new (improved) procedures.

Problems with the standard tools emerged with respect to interpretation, extensibility, and analysis functionality. Regarding *interpretation*, customers complained that they wouldn't understand the difference between certain

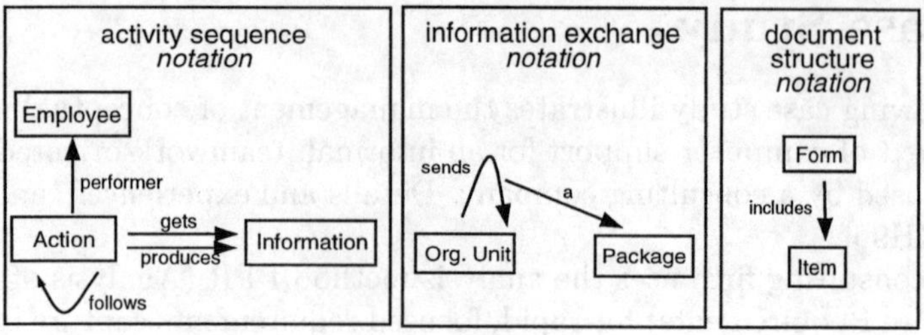

Figure 5: Syntax of the standard PFR notations

concepts of the modeling languages. For example, discussions emerged on whether a certain property of an entity would be a relationship or just an attribute. During these discussions, computer scientists would take the lead and the other participants would loose interest. Customers asked for a graphical method where one has just nodes and links.

Another issue mentioned was *extensibility*. The consulting company has developed its own approach to IT controlling where media was a central concept, i.e. the physical carrier of data like paper and floppy disk. Information on which data would be stored on which medium was important to decide how to improve the current workflow of the customer. Unfortunately, no CASE tool on the market fitted to these needs or could be easily adapted to it.

Finally, the *analysis capabilities* of standard packages were regarded as insufficient. Standard tools concentrate on syntactical correctness of the models and their interdependencies. However, the semantic correctness was seen as much more urgent. The following situation occured in a customer project: A complex data object (tax form) was modeled which contained a smaller data object (tax rate) as a part. A system function was provided to update the tax rate. In this application however, it was required that the numbers in the tax form are updated whenever the tax rate is changed. Since this dependency was detected only after implementation, major error correction costs were induced. As a consequence, the consulting company wanted to memorize this pattern as a possible (not sufficient) cause for a semantic error in the system model.

3.1 Customizing ConceptBase

To tailor O-Telos to the standard PFR modeling languages the consulting firm first defined their syntax in O-Telos, as shown in Figure 5.

The 'activity sequence' notation comprises the concept of an `Employee` who is the `performer` of an `Action`. The `Action` `gets` and `produces` `Information`. The `follows` relation describes dependencies between different `Actions`. The 'information exchange' notation captures `Organisational Units`

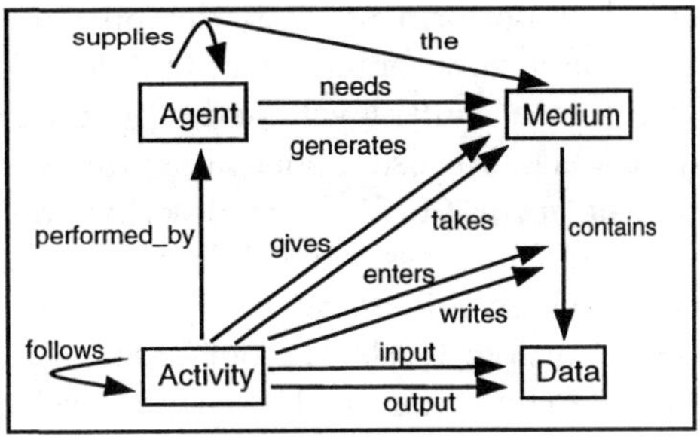

Figure 6: A media-centered meta meta model for PFR

which may `send` a `Package` to another unit. Finally, the 'document structure' notation comprises concepts to define a `Form` and the `Items` it `includes`.

The semantic properties of these notations are specified by integrity constraints and deductive rules. The PFR analysts required, e.g., that every information exchange between `Organisational Units` must be accompanied with the exchanged `Package`. The following integrity constraint expresses this requirement in a formal way:

```
forall s (s in OrgUnit!sends) exists p,a (p in Package) and
         (a in OrgUnit!sends!a) and From(a,s) and To(a,p).
```

Similar constraints specify the semantic properties of the modeling concepts of the other notations.

The semantic analysis of the individual conceptual models exploits the properties of the observed domain and the analysis goals of the specific project. The consulting firm specified the domain structure within a conceptual model on the M2-model level, shown in Figure 6. The modeling language definitions in Figure 5 form partial instances of this model which describes the corresponding perspective. It interrelates all three perspectives mentioned before. An `Agent supplies` another `Agent` with `the Medium`. This `Medium` may contain some `Data`. On this `Data` an `Agent performs` his `Activity`. The `Data` can be used as `input` or `output`. This model defines the extent of the analysis project: exactly the concepts mentioned in this model must be captured and modeled within the acquisition part of the project. It also reflects some of the expected problems. The explicit distinction between the `Medium` and the `Data` it contains allows for the detection of optimizable workflows in the business process. Since the analysis goals may change from project to project, also this domain model may change to cover the actual problems to be investigated.

Beside the domain structure, the meta meta model contains the formalization of the analysis goals. They reflect the problems the analysis project is supposed to discover. Many customers of the consulting firm want to optimize their document flow. Therefore an analysis goal is to detect agents who get a document, but perform no activities on data contained on that document. Thanks to the formal semantics of O-Telos we are able to specify this analysis goal as a formal multi-level condition and to evaluate it on the contents of the object base. We use a special syntax to indicate multi-level literals: A literal of the form `(i [in] c)` describes an instantiation relationship between `i` and `c` that crosses multiple classification levels. A literal of the form `(a [m] b)` where `m` is an arbitrary label describes an attribute predicate that crosses multiple levels. In our case we use a label from the M2-model level to form a condition on the schema level.

```
forall supply,user,medium (supply [in] Agent!supplies) and
    (user [in] Agent) and (supply [to] user) and
    (medium [in] Medium) and (supply [the] medium)
     ==> exists info,action (info [in] Data) and
       (medium [contains] info) and (action [in] Activity)
       and (action [performed_by] user) and
       ((action [input] info) or (action [output] info))
```

In the example environment more than 80 standard analysis goals make semantic statements about single models, inter-relationships between multiple models and properties of the modeled business process. These analysis goals cannot be hard-coded because they may change from one project to another. Further experiences in applying the PFR method lead to the detection of further patterns of potential errors in business processes. These patterns are then formulated as analysis goals to be available in following analysis projects. An example of such a pattern is the situation where an agent gets a document that contains only data that is already supplied to him by other media. This pattern does not always describe an error of the business process, but it is a hint for further investigation. It may indicate an unnecessary media supply which is subject for optimization. But it may also be an intended situation where the agent performs a comparison check of the same data located on different media.

The syntactic and semantic extension of ConceptBase is complemented by a graphical extension. A graphical type can either be specified for a specific object or for all the instances of an object.

Figure 7 presents a screendump of the ConceptBase graph browser. It shows a part of the three repository levels using the graphical types defined by the consulting firm. The part of the meta meta model defining the information exchange is shown on the top. The shape of a human is the graphical presentation of the object `Agent` and the shape of a set of papers of `Medium`. They used the shapes to indicate the abstract nature of these concepts. Below these objects the notation of the corresponding conceptual models is shown. The `Organisational Unit` is presented as a rectangle and the `Package` as a diamond. On the bottom a small excerpt of the 'information exchange' model is given. For the modeled agents and documents they used the filled graphical types of the concepts of the meta meta model to indicate that these objects are more concrete.

4 Summary and Outlook

Conceptual modeling requires the use of multiple interdependent languages. Selecting the right collection of languages and focusing the analysis of their interactions is a not trivial task. For example, the mobile phone company Nokia claims to employ more than 150 different notations and/or methods in their software development processes. In such new application domains, standard languages may very well miss the modeling goal by distracting the modelers to details of notation instead to details of the domain to be modeled.

In O-Telos, as supported by the ConceptBase system, experts can define an adapted collection of languages via meta classes. The customized languages are interrelated via a meta meta model which encodes the overall modeling goals independently from details of the notation of the modeling languages.

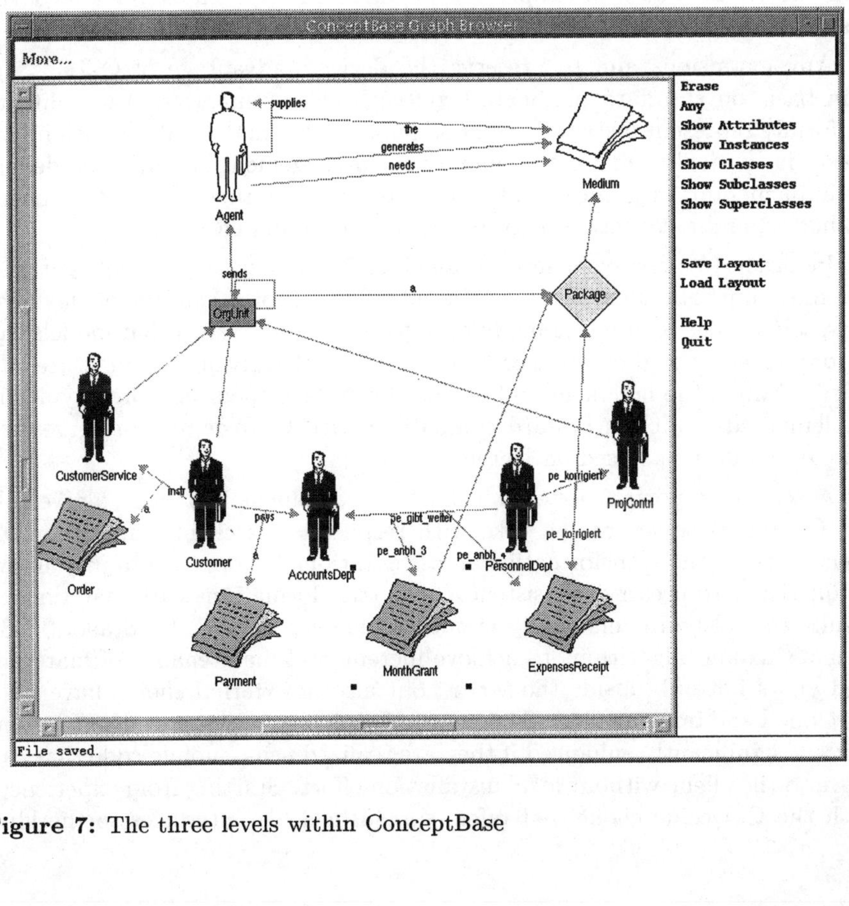

Figure 7: The three levels within ConceptBase

Versions of ConceptBase have been distributed for use in research, teaching, and industrial development since the early 1990s. Currently, a few hundred groups worldwide use the system, a number of such efforts have resulted in spin-off products derived from the ConceptBase prototypes. The main applications have been in cooperation-intensive projects which we have here placed in contrast to notation-oriented standards such as UML or domain-oriented reference models as in the ARIS framework. Especially for the reference models, there is good reason to believe that this competitive situation should be turned into a cooperative one – a cooperative, customized, and goal-oriented modeling process should still be enabled to take advantage of external experiences as encoded in reference models. This attempt to bring goals, teamwork, and formal analysis into the customization process of component software strategies such as SAP or Baan is a major methodological goal of our ongoing research.

In order to support such methodological advances, some advances in the technical support by ConceptBase are also being investigated. The description in this paper corresponds roughly to version 4.1 of the system which has been distributed since 1996. In the following, we sketch some extensions which have been developed for integration into the next versions of the system.

Any extensions aim to preserve the decisive advantage of O-Telos, its firm basis on standard predicate logic with clear semantics. Its ability to uniformly represent instances, classes, meta classes, and attributes as objects makes it an ideal framework for meta data management and meta modeling. Its implementation, ConceptBase, adds persistent storage of objects, a query evaluator, and a collection of graphical and frame-based tools.

In order to offer even more scalability in cooperative modeling tasks, the most important extension is the introduction of a concept of *modeling perspectives*, i.e. interacting modules, into the language such that models can be organized according to accepted principles of software architecture. In [Nis97, NJ97], the language M-Telos has been developed (and prototypically implemented) which is upward compatible with O-Telos and preserves the simple foundations based on Datalog.

A second important extension under development is a more active role the ConceptBase server can take with respect to its clients; an important special case is the transformation across notations (as opposed to just analysis queries). To preserve consistency, such transformations with materialized results should be incrementally maintainable over change. In [Sta96, SJ96], formalisms and algorithms to achieve incremental maintenance of materialized views not only inside the server, but also in external clients have been developed and implemented. The power of such algorithms and the user comfort are significantly enhanced if they are realized using mobile code that can move to the client without local installation effort. Starting from experiences with the CoDecide client that offers spreadsheet-like interfaces to the kind of data cubes used in data warehousing [GJJ97], a complete Java-based user environment is being developed.

Last not least, many cooperative modeling processes require inconsistency management not just for static logical interactions, but along possibly complex process chains. The current deductive approach only allows the analysis of process chains consisting of very few steps. Recently developed process reasoning techniques [BMR93] in a logical framework that is comparably simple to ours appear as a promising candidate for an integration into ConceptBase, without sacrificing its uniform framework and conceptual simplicity.

References

[Abe95] Abel, P., Description of the USU-PFR analysis method, Technical report, USU GmbH, Möglingen, 1995

[Aug91] August, J. H., Joint Application Design: The Group Session Approach to System Design, Yourdon Press, Englewood Cliffs, 1991

[BHSSZ97] Bernstein, P. A., Harry, K., Sanders, P., Shutt, D., Zander, J., The microsoft repository, in: Proc. of the 23rd Intl. Conf. on Very Large Data Bases (VLDB), Athens, Greece, August 1997, 3–12

[BMR93] Borgida, A., Mylopoulos, J., Reiter, R., "... and nothing else changes": The frame problem in procedure specifications, in: Proc. of the Fifteenth Intl. Conf. on Software Engineering (ICSE-15), May 1993

[CGT90] Ceri, S., Gottlob, G., Tanca, L., Logic Programming and Databases, Springer Verlag, 1990

[Che89] Checkland, P. B., Soft systems methodology, in: J. Rosenhead (ed.), Rational Analysis for a Problematic World, John Wiley & Sons, Chichester, 1989, 71–100

[CJMV95] Constantopoulos, P., Jarke, M., Mylopoulos, J., Vassiliou, Y., The software information base: A server for reuse, VLDB Journal 4 (1), 1995, 1–43

[FS97] Fowler, M., Scott, K., UML Destilled: Applying the Standard Object Modeling Language, Addison-Wesley, 1997

[GJJ97] Gebhardt, M., Jarke, M., Jacobs, S., A toolkit for negotiation support interfaces to multi-dimensional data, in: Proc. of the ACM SIGMOD Intl. Conf. on Management of Data, May 1997, 348–356

[GMB94] Greenspan, S., Mylopoulos, J., Borgida, A., On formal requirements modeling languages: RML revisited, in: Proc. of 16th Intl. Conf. on Software Engineering (ICSE), Sorrento, Italy, May 16-21 1994

[IDS96] IDS Prof. Scheer GmbH, Saarbrücken, ARIS-Toolset Manual V3.1, 1996

[ISO90] ISO/IEC International Standard, Information Resource Dictionary System (IRDS) - Framework ISO/IEC 10027, 1990

[Jeu92] Jeusfeld, M. A., Update Control in Deductive Object Bases, PhD thesis, University of Passau, (in German), 1992

[JGJSE95] Jarke, M., Gallersdörfer, R., Jeusfeld, M. A., Staudt, M., Eherer, S., ConceptBase - a deductive object base for meta data management, Journal of Intelligent Information Systems, Special Issue on Deductive and Object-Oriented Databases 4 (2), 1995, 167–192

[JJ89] Jarke, M., Jeusfeld, M. A., Rule Representation and Management in ConceptBase, SIGMOD Record 18 (3), 1989, 46-51

[JJ96] Jeusfeld, M. A., Jarke, M., Enterprise integration by market-driven schema evolution, Intl. Journal Concurrent Engineering Research and Applications (CERA) 4 (3), 1996

[JMSV92] Jarke, M., Mylopoulos, J., Schmidt, J. W., Vassiliou, Y., DAIDA: An environment for evolving information systems, ACM Transactions on Information Systems 10 (1), 1992, 1–50

[JR88] Jarke, M., Rose, T., Managing knowledge about information system evolution, in: Proc. of the SIGMOD Intl. Conf. on Management of Data, Chicago, Illinois, USA, June 1988, 303–311

[KK84] Kottemann, J. E., Konsynski, B. R., Dynamic metasystems for information systems development, in: Proc. of the 5th Intl. Conf. on Information Systems, Tucson, Arizona, November 1984, 187–204

[KLR96] Kelly, S., Lyytinen, K., Ross, M., MetaEdit+: A fully configurable multi-user and multi-tool CASE and CAME environment, in: P. Constantopoulos, J. Mylopoulos, Y. Vassiliou (eds.), Proc of the 8th Intl. Conf. an Advanced Information Systems Engineering (CAiSE'96), Heraklion, Creta, Griechenland, May 1996, Springer-Verlag, LNCS 1080, 1–21

[MBJK90] Mylopoulos, J., Borgida, A., Jarke, M., Koubarakis, M., Telos: Representing knowledge about information systems, ACM Transactions on Information Systems 8 (4), 1990, 325–362

[MSTT94] Maiden, N., Sutcliffe, A., Taylor, C., Till, D., A set of formal problem abstractions for reuse during requirements engineering, Engineering of Information Systems 2 (6), 1994, 679–698

[Nis97] Nissen, H. W., Separation and Resolution of Multiple Perspectives in Conceptual Modeling, PhD thesis, RWTH Aachen, Germany, (in German), 1997

[NJ97] Nissen, H. W., Jarke, M., Goal-oriented inconsistency management in customizable modeling environments, Technical Report 97-12, RWTH Aachen, Aachener Informatik-Berichte, 1997

[NJJZH96] Nissen, H. W., Jeusfeld, M. A., Jarke, M., Zemanek, G. V., Huber, H., Managing multiple requirements perspectives with metamodels, IEEE Software, 1996, 37–47

[Non94] Nonaka, I., A dynamic theory of organizational knowledge creation, Organization Science (1), 1994, 14–37

[Poh94] Pohl, K., The three dimensions of requirements engineering: A framework and its application, Information Systems 19 (3), 1994

[Sch94] Scheer, A.-W., Business Process Engineering, Springer-Verlag, 1994

[SJ96] Staudt, M., Jarke, M., Incremental maintenance of externally materialized views, in: Proc. of the 22nd Intl. Conf. on Very Large Data Bases (VLDB'96), Bombay, India, September 1996, 75–86

[SNJ94] Staudt, M., Nissen, H. W., Jeusfeld, M. A., Query by class, rule and concept, Journal of Applied Intelligence 4 (2), 1994, 133–156

[Sta96] Staudt, M., View Management in Client-Server Systems, PhD thesis, RWTH Aachen, (in German), 1996

[You89] Yourdon, E., Modern Structured Analysis, Prentice Hall, Englewood Cliffs, New Jersey, 1989

CHAPTER 13

Conceptual Graphs

John F. Sowa

Conceptual graphs (CGs) are a system of logic based on the existential graphs of Charles Sanders Peirce and the semantic networks of artificial intelligence. Their purpose is to express meaning in a form that is logically precise, humanly readable, and computationally tractable. With their direct mapping to language, conceptual graphs can serve as an intermediate language for translating computer-oriented formalisms to and from natural languages. With their graphic representation, they can serve as a readable, but formal design and specification language. CGs have been implemented in a variety of projects for information retrieval, database design, expert systems, and natural language processing. A draft ANSI standard for CGs has been developed by the NCITS T2 committee, the liaison to the ISO Conceptual Schema Modelling Facility (CSMF) project under ISO/IEC JTC1/SC21/WG3.

1 Assertions and Constraints

As a system of logic, conceptual graphs can be used to describe or define anything that can be implemented on a digital computer. But their graphic structure resembles the informal diagrams and charts that are commonly used in systems documentation. They have been used as a bridge between the informal diagrams used by computer practitioners and the formalized notations of computer scientists. As an example, Figure 1 shows a CG for an assertion that might be added to a university database: *Student Tom Jones majors in the Biology Department, he enrolls in Section M1B, and Course Calculus I has Section M1B.*

The boxes in a conceptual graph are called *concepts*. Each box has two parts: on the left of the colon is a *type label*, which represents the type of entity; on the right is a *referent*, which can name a specific instance of the type, such as Tom Jones or M1B. The circles or ovals are called *conceptual relations*; they represent instances of relationships as expressed in the *tuples* of a relational database. The labels inside the concept and relation nodes may be copied directly from the relations of a relational database, or they may be taken from a more primitive set of relations, which are used to express

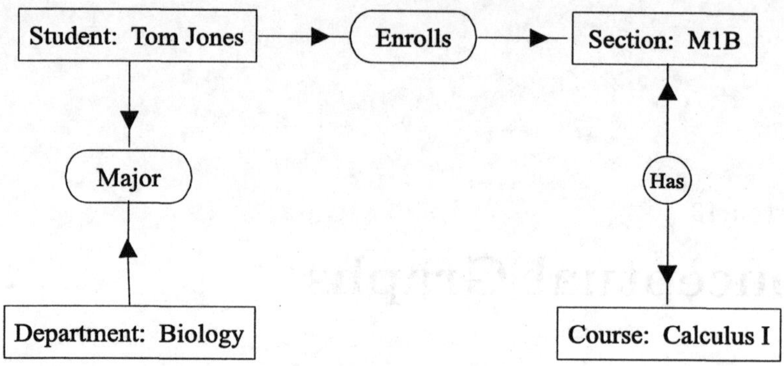

Figure 1: An assertion stated as a conceptual graph

the *thematic roles* or *case relations* of linguistics. The arrows on the arcs distinguish the different arguments of a relation: the arrow pointing towards the relation is the first argument, and the arrow pointing away is the second argument; if a relation has more than two arguments, the arcs are numbered.

The box and circle notation for conceptual graphs, which is called the *display form*, is highly readable, but it takes up a lot of space on the printed page. To save space, there is an equivalent *linear form*, which can be typed at a keyboard. Following is the linear form of Figure 1:

[Department: Biology]←(Major)←[Student: Tom Jones]-
(Enrolls)→[Section: M1B]←(Has)←[Course: Calculus I].

In the linear form, the boxes are represented by square brackets and the ovals are represented by rounded parentheses. If a CG is too long to fit on one line, a hyphen is used to show that it is continued on the next line.

Although Figure 1 looks like an informal diagram, it is a formal representation that can be translated automatically to other formalisms. A companion notation for logic, which is also being standardized by the NCITS T2 committee, is the Knowledge Representation Format (KIF) [KIF95]. When Figure 1 is translated to KIF, a concept like [Student: Tom Jones] becomes the parenthesized pair (student Tom_Jones). Each relation with *n* arguments becomes a list of *n+1* elements, starting with the name of the relation. The dyadic relation between Tom Jones and Section M1B would become the list (enrolls Tom_Jones M1B). The order of the arguments corresponds to the direction of the arrows: Tom_Jones is first, and M1B is second. Following is the complete KIF representation for Figure 1:

(and (student Tom_Jones) (department Biology) (section M1B)
(course Calculus_I) (major Tom_Jones Biology)
(enrolls Tom_Jones M1B) (has Calculus_I M1B))

In KIF, the operator "and" is used to combine all the information from the concepts and relations in a single expression; its arguments may be listed in any order.

In Figure 1, each concept box has a name of a specific instance in its referent field. Besides names, conceptual graphs also permit quantifiers in the referent field. In predicate calculus, the two basic quantifiers are the *existential quantifier* represented by the symbol ∃, and the *universal quantifier* represented by the symbol ∀. In conceptual graphs, the quantifier ∃ is the default, represented by a blank referent field; and the quantifier ∀ is represented by the symbol ∀ or @every in the referent field. The following table compares the quantifiers in English, predicate calculus, conceptual graphs, and KIF:

English	**PC**	**CG**	**KIF**
some student	$\exists x : student$	[Student]	(exists ((?x student)) ...)
every student	$\forall x : student$	[Student: ∀]	(forall ((?x student)) ...)

Figure 2 shows a conceptual graph with four concepts, each of which is existentially quantified (blank referent). Surrounding the graph is another concept box marked with a negation symbol ¬. The complete graph may be read, *It is false that there exists a student who is enrolled in two different sections of the same course.*

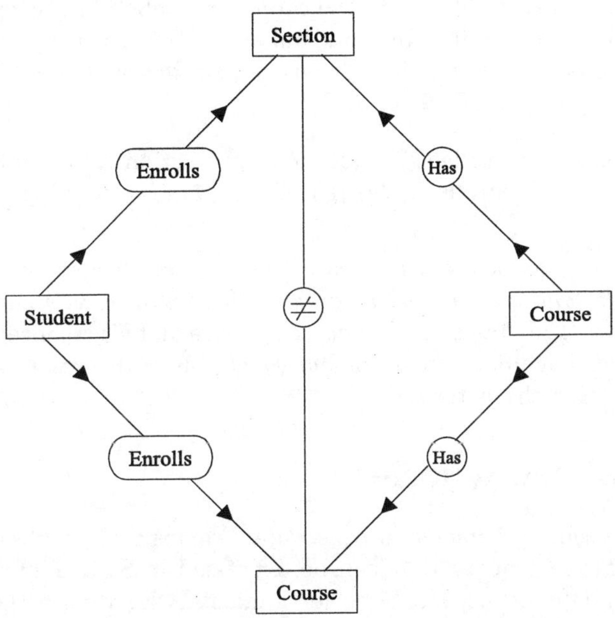

Figure 2: A constraint stated as a conceptual graph

Figure 2 has branches that cannot be drawn on a straight line. In the linear form, it would be represented on several lines; continuations are shown by hyphens, and cross references are shown by *coreference labels*, such as *z and ?z: The first occurrence or *defining label* is marked with an asterisk, such as *z; the subsequent occurrences or *bound labels* are marked with a question mark, such as ?z.

$$\begin{array}{l} \neg[[Student]- \\ \quad (Enrolls) \to [Section]- \\ \qquad (\neq) \to [Section : *z] \\ \qquad (Has) \leftarrow [Course : *w], \\ \quad (Enrolls) \to [?z] \leftarrow (Has) \leftarrow [?w]]. \end{array}$$

In the linear form, hyphens show that relations are continued on subsequent lines, and commas terminate the most recent hyphens. When the linear form is translated back to the display form, the concepts [?z] and [?w] are overlaid on the corresponding concepts [Section: *z] and [Course: *w]. As this example illustrates, complex graphs are usually more readable in the display form than in the linear form, but both forms are semantically equivalent. Their formal syntax is presented in Section 4.

When Figure 2 is translated to KIF, a variable is associated with each of the four concept boxes: ?x for the student, ?y for one section, ?z for another section, and ?w for the course. The question mark distinguishes a variable like ?x from a constant like M1B; the coreference labels in conceptual graphs correspond to variables in KIF, and similar symbols are used for both. The operator "exists" is used for the existential quantifier and "not" for the negation. Following is the KIF form of Figure 2:

```
(not (exists  ((student ?x) (section ?y) (section ?z) (course ?w)) (and
              (enrolls ?x ?y) (enrolls ?x ?z) (/= ?y ?z) (has ?w ?y) (has
              ?w ?z)) ))
```

This statement may be read, *It is false that there exists a student x, a section y, a section z, and a course w, where x is enrolled in y, x is enrolled in z, y is not equal to z, w has y, and w has z*. For readability, conceptual graphs may use special symbols like ≠ for *not equal*; but KIF uses /=, since it has a more restricted character set.

2 Database Queries

Besides representing tuples and constraints, conceptual graphs can also express any database query that can be expressed in SQL. Figure 3 shows a query that might be used to look for students who violate the constraint in Figure 2: *Which student is enrolled in two different sections of the same course?*

The question mark in the concept [Student: ?] of Figure 3 characterizes the graph as a query. When used by itself, the question mark asks the

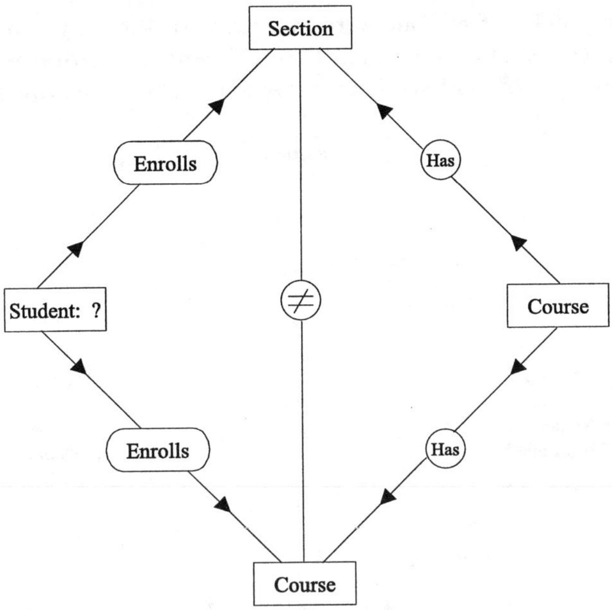

Figure 3: A query stated as a conceptual graph

question *Which student?* When used with a variable, as in ?x, the question mark indicates a variable that corresponds to KIF variables like ?x or ?y. These two uses of the ? symbol correspond to the two uses of the word *which* in English: ? by itself corresponds to the interrogative *which* for asking questions; and ?x corresponds to the relative pronoun *which* used to make a reference to something else in the sentence. In the query language SQL, the question mark maps to the SELECT verb that designates which field in the database contains the answer. Figure 3 would be translated to the following query in SQL:

```
SELECT A.STUDENT
   FROM ENROLLS A, ENROLLS B, HAS C, HAS D
      WHERE A.STUDENT = B.STUDENT
         AND A.SECTION ¬= B.SECTION
         AND A.SECTION = C.SECTION
         AND B.SECTION = D.SECTION
         AND C.COURSE = D.COURSE
```

The SELECT clause in SQL lists the concepts that were marked with the ? symbol; the FROM clause lists the relations; and the WHERE clause is a translation of the conditions stated in the CG.

Any or all of the four concepts in Figure 3 could contain a question mark in the referent field. If all four were marked with the ? symbol, the answer would be the constraint violation in Figure 4, which says *Student Tom Jones is enrolled in two different sections, M1A and M1B, of the course Calculus I*

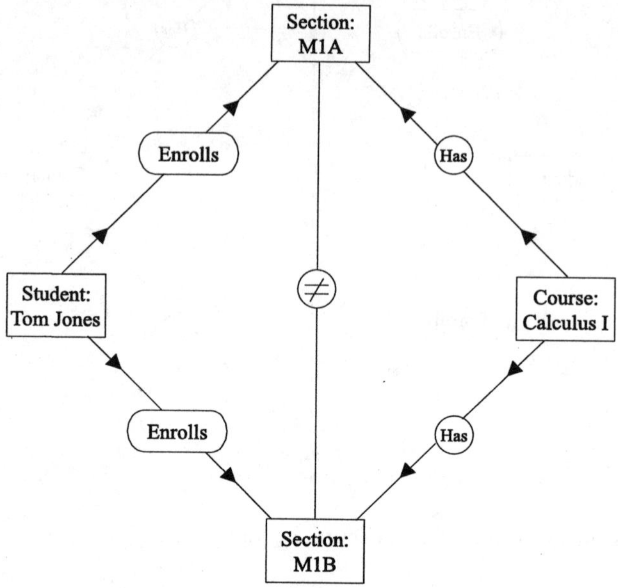

Figure 4: A constraint violation as an answer to a query

3 Relational and Object-Oriented Databases

Besides relating natural language to expert systems, conceptual graphs can be used to relate different kinds of databases and knowledge bases to one another. Relational databases present the data in tables, and object-oriented databases group data by objects. The two kinds of databases have different advantages and disadvantages, but either kind could be translated to the other by means of definitions written in conceptual graphs. To illustrate the differences, consider Figure 5, which shows two structures of blocks and their representation in a relational database.

At the left of Figure 5, the two structures are composed of objects that support other objects. On the right, the Objects relation lists each object's ID (identifier), its Shape, and its Color; the Supports relation lists the Supporter and Supportee for each instance of one object supporting another. In Figure 5, the separation between the two structures is not shown directly in the database: the tuples that represent each structure occur in both tables, and each table mixes tuples from both objects.

Figure 6 shows a conceptual graph that represents the top structure of

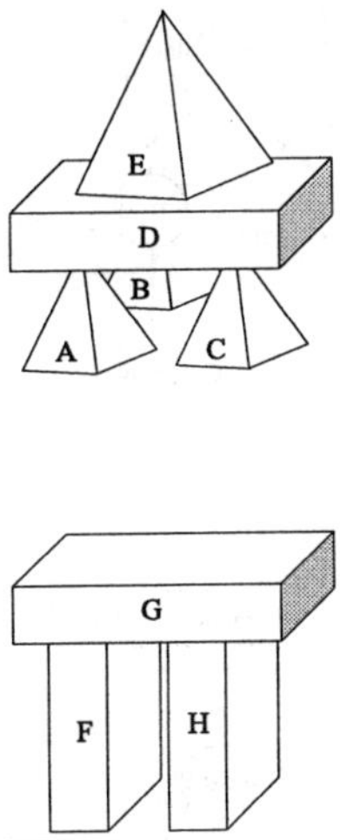

OBJECTS

ID	SHAPE	COLOR
A	pyramid	red
B	pyramid	green
C	pyramid	yellow
D	block	blue
E	pyramid	orange
F	block	blue
G	block	orange
H	block	blue

SUPPORTS

SUPPORTER	SUPPORTEE
A	D
B	D
C	D
D	E
F	G
H	G

Figure 5: Two structures represented in a relational database

Figure 5 in an object-oriented style. Each object in the structure is represented by a concept of type Block or Pyramid. The conceptual relations that link them are derived from the more primitive linguistic relations, such as Characteristic (Chrc), Theme (THME), and Instrument (Inst). Starting from the upper left-hand corner, Figure 6 could be read *Pyramid E has a color orange, it is being supported by block D, which has a color blue; D is being supported by pyramid A, which has a color red, pyramid B, which has color red, and pyramid C, which has a color yellow.* However, the physical placement of the nodes of a CG has no semantic meaning, and the same graph could be translated to different sentences that all express the same proposition. Another way of reading Figure 6 would be *A red pyramid A, a green pyramid B, and a yellow pyramid C support a blue block D, which supports an orange pyramid E.*

The concept and relation types in Figure 6, which map directly to the semantic relationships in natural languages, do not correspond to the names of the tables and fields of the relational database in Figure 5. As an alternate representation, Figure 7 shows another conceptual graph that uses the same names as the relational database.

The graphs in Figures 6 and 7 could be related to one another by selecting a basic set of types and relations as primitives: the types Object, Color, Shape, and Support; and the linguistic relations Chrc, THME, and Inst. Then all of the types and relations in both graphs could be defined in terms of the basic set. For example, following is a definition of the concept type Block:

type Block(*x) **is** [Object: ?x]→(Chrc)→[Shape: block].

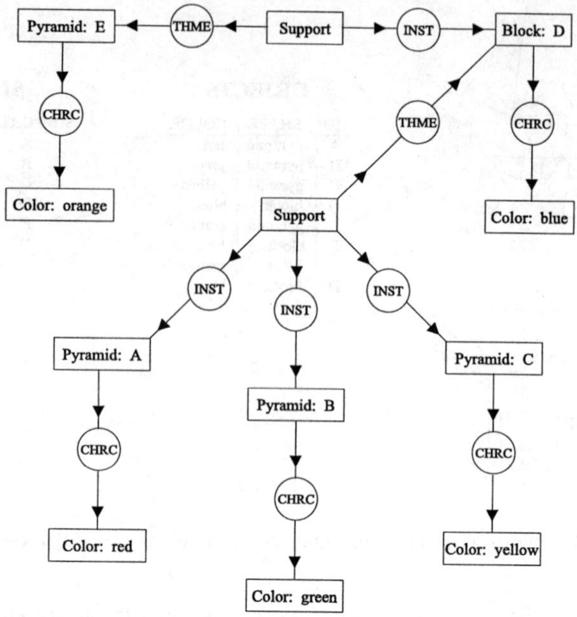

Figure 6: A conceptual graph that represents the top structure in Figure 5

This definition says that a block x is an object x with a characteristic (Chrc) shape of block. Next is a similar definition for the type Pyramid:

type Pyramid(*x) **is** [Object: ?x]→(Chrc)→[Shape: pyramid].

Following is a definition of the dyadic relation Supports:

relation Supports(*x,*y) **is** [Object: ?x]←(THME)←[Support]→
(Inst)→[Object: ?y].

This definition says that the Supports relation links an object x, which is the theme (THME) of the concept [Support], to another object y, which is the instrument (Inst) of the same concept. The Objects relation has three formal parameters:

relation Objects(*x,*y,*z) **is**
[Object: ?x]-
(Chrc)→[Shape: ?y]
(Chrc)→[Color: ?z].

This definition says that the first parameter x is of type Object; the second y is a Shape that is characteristic of the Object; and the third z is a Color that is characteristic of the Object.

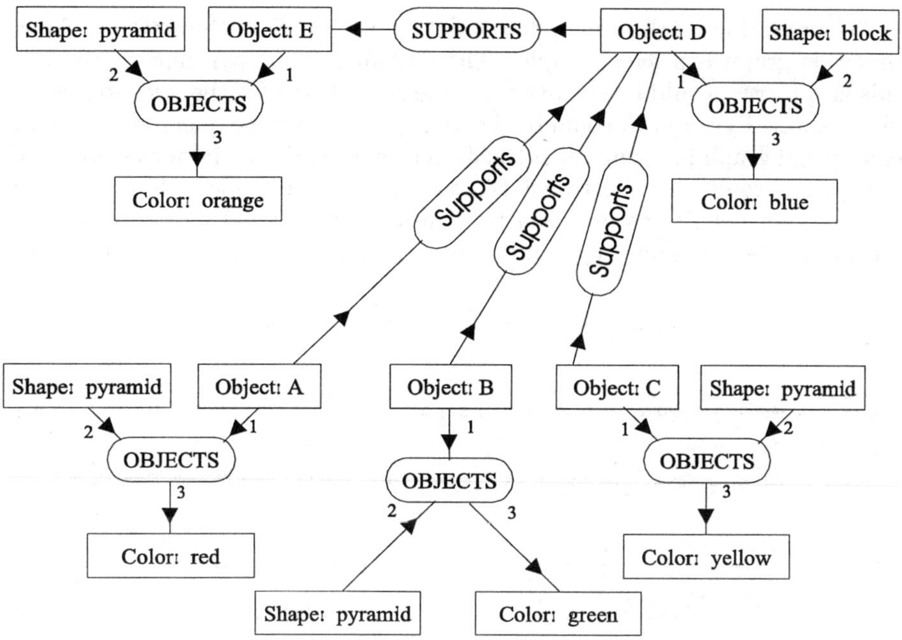

Figure 7: A conceptual graph generated directly from the relational database

For the relational database in Figure 5, the Supports relation has domains named Supporter and Supportee. Those two domain names could also be related to the conceptual graphs by type definitions:

type Supporter(*x) **is** [Object: ?x]←(Inst)←[Support].
type Supportee(*x) **is** [Object: ?x]←(THME)←[Support].

The first line says that Supporter is defined as a type of Object that is the instrument (Inst) of the concept [Support]; the second says that Supportee is a type of Object that is the theme (THME) of [Support]. By expanding or contracting these definitions, Figure 6 could be converted to Figure 7 or vice versa. The definitional mechanisms provide a systematic way of restructuring a database or knowledge base from one format to another.

Restructuring a large database is a lengthy process that may sometimes be necessary. But to answer a single question, it is usually more efficient to restructure the query graph than to restructure the entire database. To access a relational database such as Figure 5, the definitions can be used to translate the concept types in the query graph to concept types that match the domains of the database. As an example, the English question *Which pyramid is supported by a block?* would be translated to the following conceptual graph:

[Pyramid: ?]←(THME)←[Support]→(Inst)→[Block].

The question mark in the referent field of the concept [Pyramid: ?] shows that this graph is a *query graph* . The identifier of the pyramid that makes this graph true would be the answer to be substituted for the question mark. The answer, Pyramid E, could be derived by matching the query graph to the conceptual graph in Figure 6. If the data is in a relational database, however, the query graph must be translated to SQL. Figure 8 shows how the type and relation definitions are used to translate the original query graph to a form that uses the same types and relations as the corresponding SQL query.

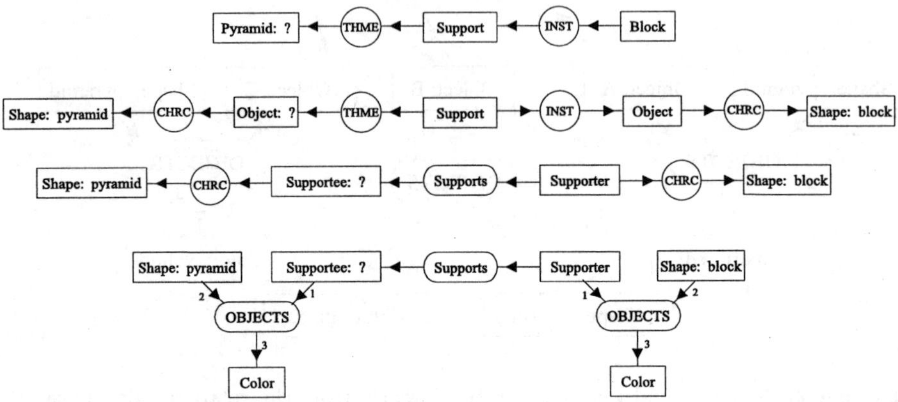

Figure 8: Translating a query graph to a form that maps directly to SQL

The graph at the top of Figure 8 is the original query graph generated directly from English. The second graph replaces the concepts [Pyramid] and [Block] by the definitions Object with Shape pyramid or Object with Shape block. The third graph replaces the concept [Support] and the relations THME and Inst with the relation Supports, which links the supporting object [Supporter] to the supported object [Supportee]. Finally, the bottom graph replaces the two occurrences of the Chrc relation with the Objects relation. Since the Objects relation has three arcs, two concepts of type Color are also introduced; but they are ignored in the mapping to SQL, since colors are irrelevant to this query. By translating the bottom graph of Figure 8 to SQL, the system can generate the following SQL query for the original English question *Which pyramid is supported by a block?*

```
SELECT SUPPORTEE
    FROM SUPPORTS, OBJECTS A, OBJECTS B
        WHERE SUPPORTEE = A.ID
            AND A.SHAPE = 'PYRAMID'
            AND SUPPORTER = B.ID
            AND B.SHAPE = 'BLOCK'
```

The question mark in the concept [Supportee: ?] maps to the SELECT verb in the first line of the SQL query. The three relations in the query graph are listed in the FROM clause on line two. Since the Objects relation appears twice, it is listed twice on line two – once as OBJECTS A and again as OBJECTS B. Then the WHERE clause lists the conditions: the supportee must be equal to the identifier of object A; the shape of object A must be pyramid; the supporter must be equal to the identifier of object B; and the shape of object B must be block. Every feature of the SQL query is derived from some feature of the transformed query graph at the bottom of Fig. 8.

4 Dataflow Graphs and Recursive Functions

Functional programs, which do not have side effects, are the easiest to represent in conceptual graphs, KIF, or any other system of logic. By definition, a *function* is a relation that has one argument called the *output*, which has a single value for each combination of values of the other arguments, called the *inputs*. In conceptual graphs, the output concept of a function is attached to its last arc, whose arrow points away from the circle. If F is a function from type T1 to type T2, the constraint of a single output for each input can be stated by the following conceptual graph:

[T1: ∀]→(F)→[T2: @1].

This graph says that for every input value of type T1, F has exactly one output value of type T2. Combinations of functions can be linked together to form dataflow diagrams, as in Figure 9.

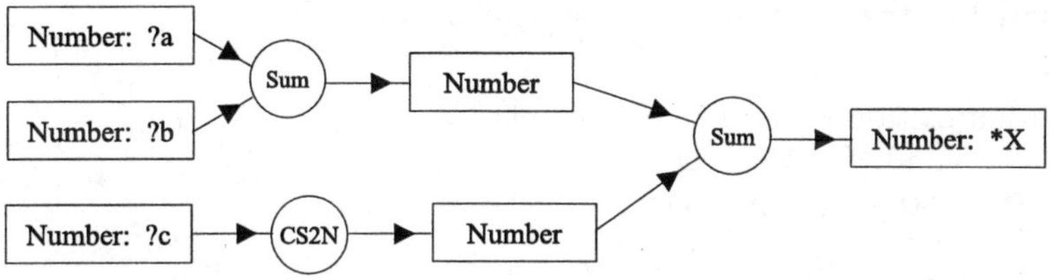

Figure 9: A dataflow diagram written as a conceptual graph

The input labels ?a, ?b, and ?c refer back to defining labels *a, *b, and *c on other concept nodes of other diagrams. The output label *x defines a node that could be referenced in another graph by ?x. The functions (Sum) and (Prod) take two numbers as input and generate their sum or product as output. The function (CS2N) converts a character string input to a number as output. Figure 9 could be mapped to the following statement in KIF:

(= ?x (* (+ ?a ?b) (cs2n ?c)))

In a more conventional programming language, Figure 9 or its KIF equivalent would correspond to an assignment statement

x := (a + b) * cs2n(c);

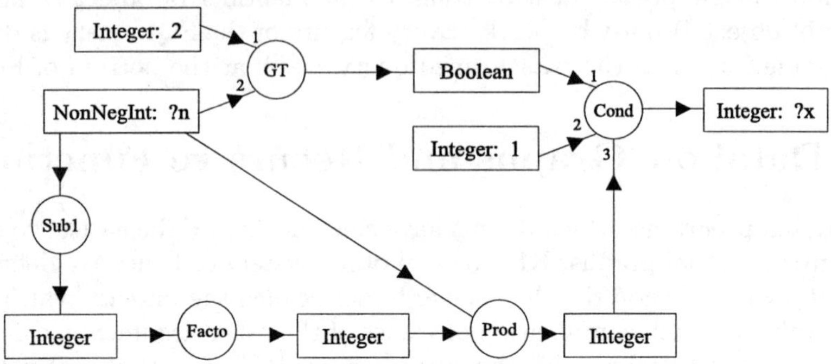

Figure 10: Defining a recursive function with a conceptual graph (relation Facto(*n,*x) is functional)

Dataflow diagrams by themselves are not sufficient for a complete computational system. But when combined with a conditional relation and the ability to define recursive functions, they form the basis for a complete programming language that can compute any function that is computable by a Turing machine. Figure 10 shows a conceptual graph for defining the function Facto, which computes the factorial x of a nonnegative integer n It could be translated to the following function definition in KIF:

```
(deffunction facto ((?n nonnegint)) :=
    (cond ((> 2 ?n) 1)
        (true (* ?n (facto (1- ?n)))) ))
```

In Figure 10, both variables ?n and ?x are marked with ? rather than * because their defining occurrences are already specified in the top line with the keyword "relation". The relation (Sub1) corresponds to the KIF function 1-, which subtracts 1 from its input. The relation (Cond) corresponds to the conditional in KIF or the ternary ?: operator in C. Its first argument is a Boolean value; if true, the output of Cond is equal to the second argument; otherwise, the output of Cond is equal to the third argument. The features illustrated in Figures 9 and 10 represent all the structure needed for a language that can specify any computable function. The inference rules of logic can make such diagrams executable, and a compiler can translate them to more conventional programming languages.

5 Encapsulated Objects

To represent the encapsulated objects of object-oriented systems, logic must support contexts whose structure reflects the nest of encapsulations. In conceptual graphs, contexts are represented by concept boxes with nested graphs that describe the object represented by the concept. In KIF, the nesting is represented by the description relation dscr and a quoted KIF statement that describes the object. As an example, Figure 11 shows a graph for a birthday party that occurred at the point in time (PTIM) of 26 May 1996.

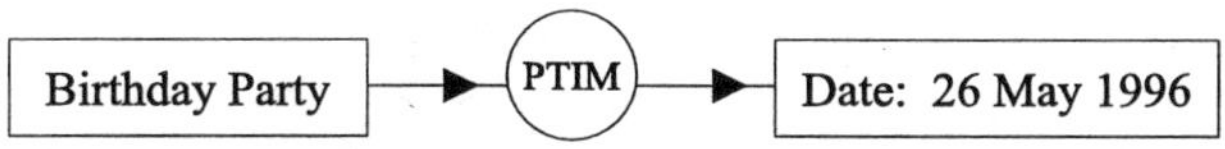

Figure 11: A birthday party on 26 May 1996

The concept with the type BirthdayParty says that there exists a birthday party, but it doesn't specify any details. The PTIM relation for point-in-time indicates that it occurred on the date 26 May 1996. To see the details of what happened during the party, it is necessary to open up the box and look inside. With a graphic display and a mouse for pointing, a person could click on the box, and the system would expand it to the context in Figure 12. In that graph, the large box is the same concept of type BirthdayParty that was shown in Figure 11, but it now contains some nested conceptual graphs that describe the party.

Inside the large box in Figure 12, the first graph says that 40 guests are giving presents to a person named Marvin, and the second one says that 50 candles are on a cake. The relations AGNT, THME, and RCPT are linguistic case relations that indicate the agent (guests who are giving), the theme (presents that are being given), and the recipient (the birthday boy, Marvin). The *generic set symbol* * indicates a set of unspecified things; the types Guest and Candle indicate the types of things; and the qualifiers "@40" and "@50' indicate the count of things in each set.

6 Zooming in and Zooming out

At the bottom of the box in Figure 12 is another concept [Process], which says that there exists some process in the birthday party. By clicking on that box, a viewer could expand it to a context that shows the steps in the process. In Figure 13, the process box contains three other nested contexts: a state with duration 15 seconds, followed by an event that occurs at the point in time 20:23:19 Greenwich Mean Time, followed by a state with duration 5 seconds. The relation Dur represents duration, PTIM represents point in time, and Succ represents successor. Dur links each state to a time interval during which the graphs that describe the state are true; PTIM links the

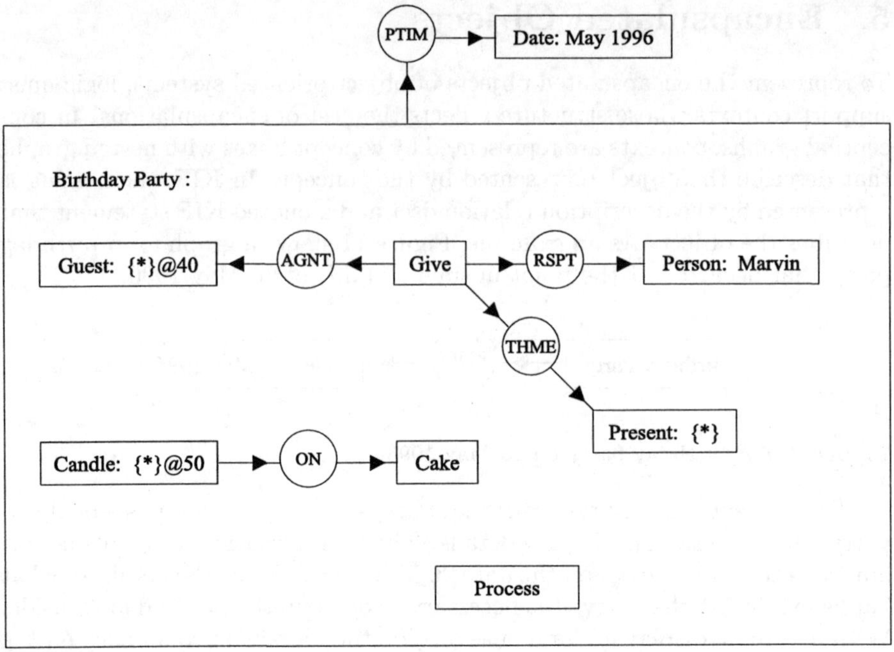

Figure 12: Expanded view of the birthday-party context

event to a time point, which is a short interval whose starting and ending times are not distinguished.

At the top of Figure 13, two new variables *x and *y appear in the concepts of the 40 guests and the 50 candles. Those variables mark the *d*efining nodes, which are referenced by the *b*ound variables ?x and ?y in graphs nested inside the process context. In the pure display form, variables are not needed, since coreference is shown by dotted lines. But when the graphs contain a lot of detail, variables eliminate the need for crossing lines. An interactive display could provide an option of showing coreference links either as variables or as dotted lines.

In Figure 13, the graphs nested inside the concepts of type State and Event are too small to be read. By clicking on the box for the first state, a person could zoom in to see the details in Figure 14. The expanded state shows the candles ?y burning while the guests ?x sing the song "Happy Birthday". Then the event box could be expanded to show Marvin blowing out the candles, and the next state would show the candles smoking for 5 seconds. Context boxes can encapsulate details at any level. At a lower level, the concept [Sing] might be expanded to show one guest singing in the key of G while another is singing in G flat. In this way, the encapsulated description of any object could be contained in a single context box, which could be expanded to show the details or contracted to hide them.

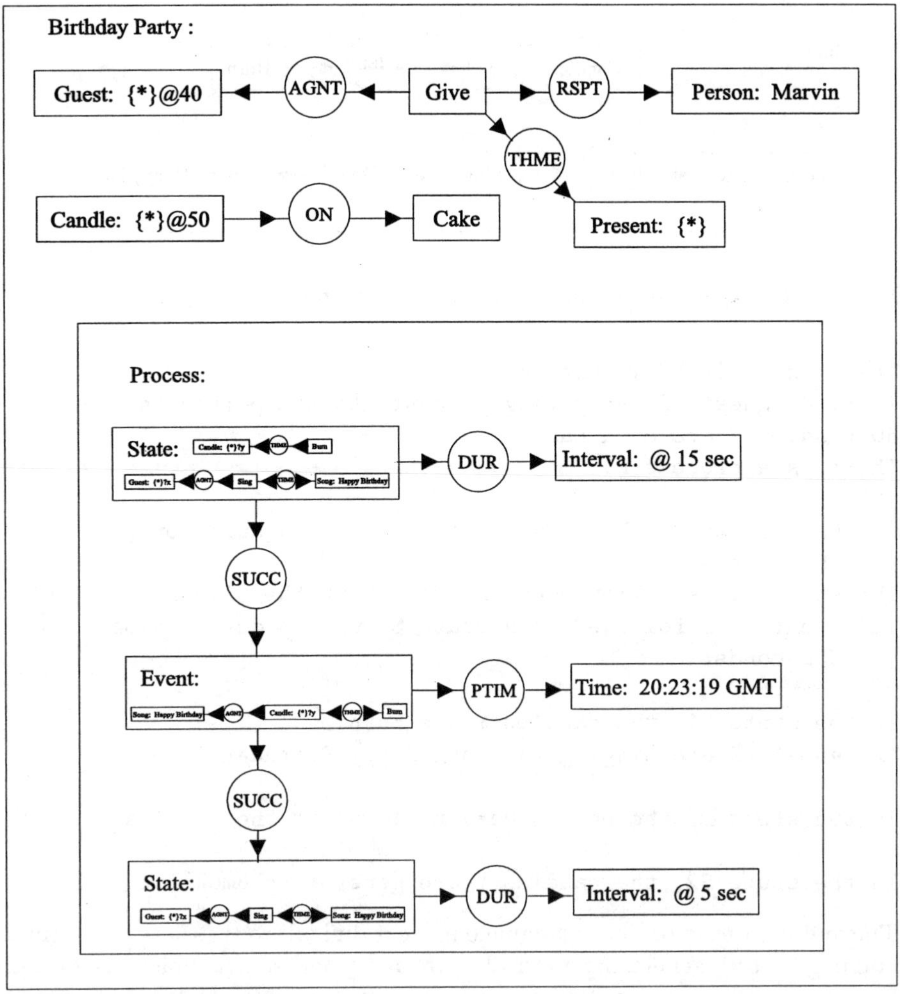

Figure 13: Expanded view of the birthday party to show details of the process

7 Stylized Natural Language

Although conceptual graphs are quite readable, they are a formal language that would be used by programmers and systems analysts. Application users would normally prefer natural languages. But even programmers use natural language for comments, documentation, and help facilities. Conceptual graphs were originally designed as a semantic representation for natural language, and they can help to form a bridge between computer languages and the natural languages that everyone reads, writes, and speaks. Following is a stylized English description that could be generated directly from Figure 13:

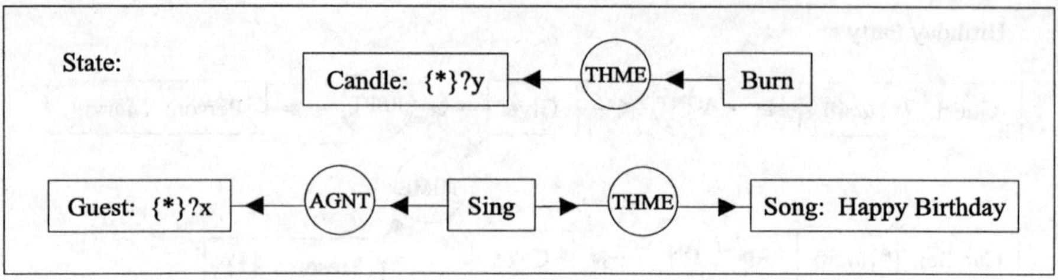

Figure 14: Expanded view of the first state of the process in Figure 13

```
There is a birthday party B.
In B, 40 guests X are giving presents to the person Marvin.
50 candles Y are on a cake.
There is a process P.

In the process P, there is a state S1 with a duration of
    15 seconds.
The state S1 is followed by an event E at the time 20:23:15 GMT.
The event E is followed by a state S2 with a duration of
    5 seconds.

In the state S1, the candles Y are burning.
The guests X are singing the song Happy Birthday.

In the event E, the person Marvin blows out the candles Y.

In the state S2, the candles Y are generating smoke.
```

The ambiguities in ordinary language make it difficult to translate to a formal language. But generating natural language from an unambiguous formal language, such as conceptual graphs, is a much simpler task. For stylized English, the generation process can be simplified further by using variables instead of pronouns and mapping the context structure of the graphs to separate paragraphs. Such stylized language may not be elegant, but it is useful for comments and explanations.

8 First-Order Logic

In conceptual graphs, as in Peirce's existential graphs, there are three logical primitives: conjunction, negation, and the existential quantifier. All the operators of *first-order logic* can be defined by combinations of these three primitives. As an example of the basic logical notation, Figure 15 shows a conceptual graph for the sentence *If a farmer owns a donkey, then he beats it.*

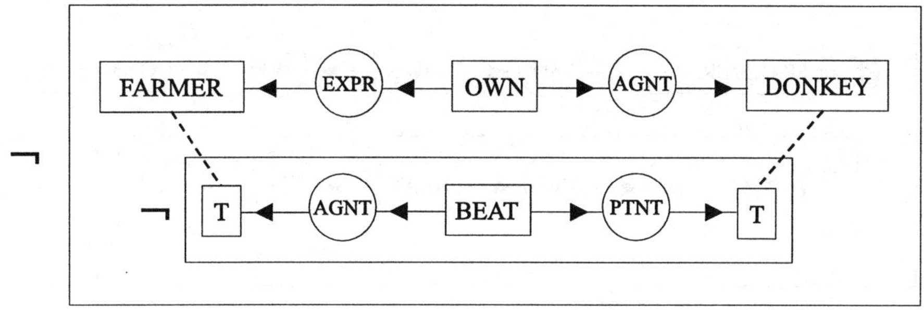

Figure 15: A conceptual graph with nested negations and coreference links

The context boxes, which were used to encapsulate object descriptions in previous examples, are also used to show the scope of the logical operators and quantifiers in Figure 15. The dotted lines are *coreference links*; they show that the concepts of type ⊤, which represent the pronouns *he* and *it* , are coreferent with the concepts [Farmer] and [Donkey]. The dyadic conceptual relations represent the linguistic case roles experiencer (EXPR), theme (THME), agent (AGNT), and patient (PTNT). Literally, Figure 15 may be read *It is false that a farmer owns a donkey and that he does not beat it.*

To make conceptual graphs simpler or more readable, definitional mechanisms can be used to define new concept and relation types. Two nested negations in the form ¬[p ¬[q]] are logically equivalent to *If p, then q.* Therefore, the keywords If and Then may be defined as synonyms for a negation applied to a context of type proposition:

type If(*p) **is** ¬[Proposition: ?p].
type Then(*q) **is** ¬[Proposition: ?q].

By these definitions, If and Then are defined to be type labels for propositions that are enclosed inside a negation. When the context of type Then is enclosed inside a context of type If, the combination is logically equivalent to the two nested negations of Figure 15, but with the more readable syntax of Figure 16.

Figure 16 may now be read as the more natural sentence *If a farmer x owns a donkey y, then x beats y.* The dotted lines, which showed coreference links in Figure 15, have been replaced with pairs of *coreference labels* in Figure 16. The pair *x and ?x represents the farmer, and the pair *y and ?y represents the donkey. The labels marked with asterisks, *x and *y, are called the *defining nodes*; and the corresponding labels marked with question marks, ?x and ?y, are called the bound nodes. Dotted lines are used in the pure graph notation, but the equivalent coreference labels map more directly to KIF variables. Following is the KIF translation of Figure 16:

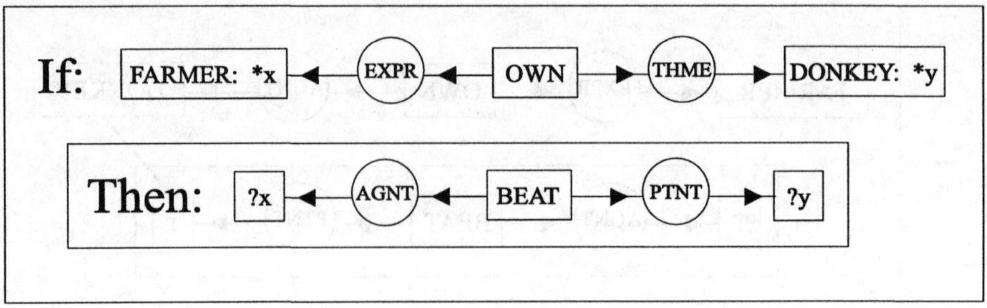

Figure 16: A conceptual graph with an If-Then combination

```
(forall ((?x farmer) (?y donkey) (?z own))
    (=> (and (EXPR ?z ?x) (THME ?z ?y))
        (exists ((?w beat)) (and (AGNT ?w ?x) (PTNT ?w ?y)))
))
```

Other Boolean operators can also be defined by combinations of negations and nested contexts. The *disjunction* or logical *or* of two graphs p and q is represented by the combination

¬[Proposition: ¬[Proposition: p] ¬[Proposition: q]].

For better readability, a dyadic conceptual relation OR may be introduced by the following definition:

relation OR(*p,*q) **is symmetric**
¬[Proposition: ¬[Proposition: ?p] ¬[Proposition: ?q]].

The definition of the OR relation implies that it is symmetric: the order of the formal parameters p and q may be interchanged without affecting the meaning. In the heading of the definition, the keyword **symmetric** affirms the symmetry and indicates that the arrows on the arcs of the OR relation may be omitted.

The universal quantifier ∀ may be defined in terms of an existential quantifier ∃ and two negations: $(\forall x)$ is equivalent to the combination $\sim(\exists x)\sim$. As an example, the following conceptual graph represents the sentence *Every cat is on a mat*:

[Cat: ∀]→(ON)→[Mat].

The concept [Cat: ∀], which has a universal quantifier, may be replaced by two negative contexts and the concept [Cat], which has an implicit existential quantifier. The expansion is performed in the following steps:

1. Draw a double negation around the entire graph:

¬[¬[[Cat: ∀]→(ON)→[Mat]]].

2. Move the concept with the universal quantifier between the inner and outer negations, and replace the symbol ∀ with a coreference label, such as *x, which represents a defining node:

   ¬[[Cat: *x] ¬[→(ON)→[Mat]]].

3. Insert the concept [?x], which represents a bound node corresponding to *x, in the original place where the concept [Cat: ∀] had been:

   ¬[[Cat: *x] ¬[[?x]→(ON)→[Mat]]].

4. With the concept types If and Then, the graph could be written

   [If: [Cat: *x] [Then: [?x]→(ON)→[Mat]]].

   This graph may be read *If there exists a cat x, then x is on a mat.*

With the above definitions, the following English sentences can be translated to conceptual graphs and then to KIF:

- *Every cat is on a mat.*

  [Cat: ∀]→(ON)→[Mat].
  (forall ((?x cat)) (exists ((?y mat)) (on ?x ?y)))

- *It is false that every dog is on a mat.*

  ¬[[Dog: ∀]→(ON)→[Mat]].
  (not (forall ((?x dog)) (exists ((?y mat)) (on ?x ?y))))

- *Some dog is not on a mat.*

  [Dog: *x] ¬[[?x]→(ON)→[Mat]].
  (exists (?x dog) (not (exists ((?y mat)) (on ?x ?y))))

- *Either the cat Yojo is on a mat, or the dog Macula is running.*

  [Either:
  　　[Or: [Cat: Yojo] → (ON) → [Mat]]
  　　[Or: [Dog: Macula] ← (AGNT) ← [Run]]].
  (or (exists ((?x mat)) (and (cat Yojo) (on Yojo ?x)))
  　　(exists ((?y run)) (and (dog Macula) (AGNT ?y Macula))))

- *If a cat is on a mat, then it is happy.*

```
[If: [Cat: *x]→(ON)→[Mat]
     [Then: [?x]→(ATTR)→[Happy] ]].
(forall ((?x cat) (?y mat))
     (=> (on ?x ?y)
          (exists ((?z happy)) (attr ?x ?z))))
```

9 Generalization Hierarchies

The *rules of inference* of logic define a generalization hierarchy over the terms of any logic-based language. Figure 17 shows the hierarchy in conceptual graphs, but an equivalent hierarchy could be represented in KIF or other logical notation. For each dark arrow in Figure 17, the graph above is a generalization, and the graph below is a specialization. The top graph says that an animate being is the agent (AGNT) of some act that has an entity as the theme (THME) of the act. Below it are two specializations: a graph for a robot washing a truck, and a graph for an animal chasing an entity. Both of these graphs were derived from the top graph by repeated applications of the rule for restricting type labels to subtypes. The graph for an animal chasing an entity has three subgraphs: a human chasing a human, a cat chasing a mouse, and the dog Macula chasing a Chevrolet. These three graphs were also derived by repeated application of the rule of restriction. The derivation from [Animal] to [Dog: Macula] required both a restriction by type from Animal to Dog and a restriction by referent from the blank to the name Macula.

Besides restriction, a join was used to specialize the graph for a human chasing a human to the graph for a senator chasing a secretary around a desk. The join was performed by merging the concept [Chase] in the upper graph with the concept [Chase] in the following graph:

```
[Chase]→(ARND)→[Desk].
```

Since the resulting graph has three relations attached to the concept [Chase], it is not possible to represent the graph on a straight line in the linear notation. Instead, a hyphen may be placed after the concept [Chase] to show that the attached relations are continued on subsequent lines:

```
[Chase]-
     (AGNT)→[Senator]
     (THME)→[Secretary]
     (ARND)→[Desk].
```

For the continued relations, it is not necessary to show both arcs, since the direction of one arrow implies the direction of the other one.

The two graphs at the bottom of Figure 17 were derived by both restriction and join. The graph on the left says that the cat Yojo is vigorously

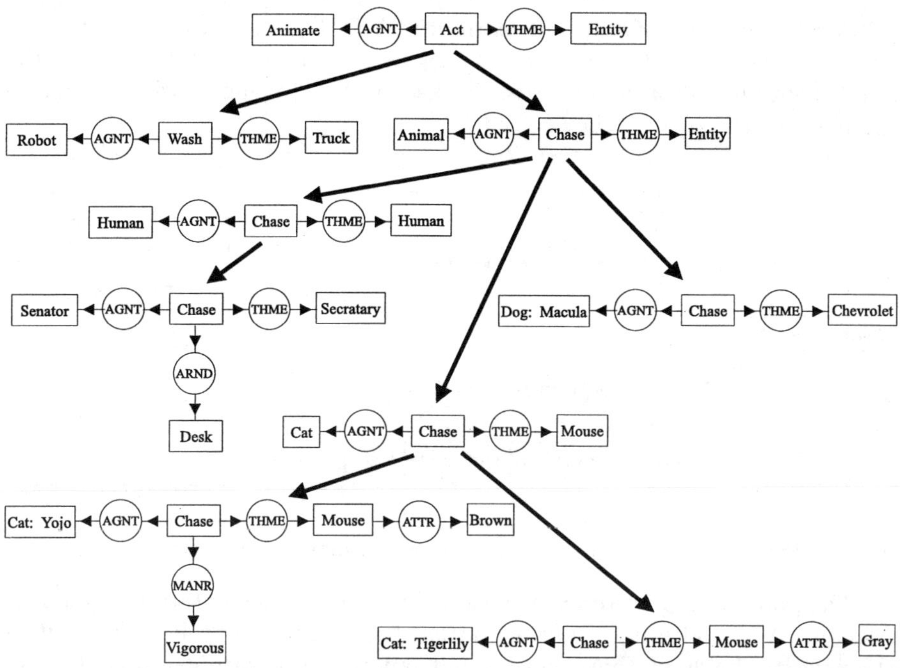

Figure 17: A generalization hierarchy

chasing a brown mouse. It was derived by restricting [Cat] to [Cat: Yojo] and by joining the following two graphs:

> [Mouse]→(ATTR)→[Brown].
> [Chase]→(MANR)→[Vigorous].

The relation (MANR) represents manner, and the relation (ATTR) represents attribute. The bottom right graph of Figure 17 says that the cat Tigerlily is chasing a gray mouse. It was derived from the graph above it by one restriction and one join. All the derivations in Figure 17 can be reversed by applying the generalization rules from the bottom up instead of the specialization rules from the top down: every restriction can be reversed by unrestriction, and every join can be reversed by detach.

10 Multimedia Systems

The boxes of a conceptual graph can be used as frames to enclose images of any kind: pictures, diagrams, text, or full-motion video. Figure 18 shows a conceptual graph that describes a picture; it may be read *A plumber is carrying a pipe in the left hand and is carrying a tool box in the right hand.* The conceptual relations indicate the linguistic roles: agent (AGNT), theme

(THME), location (LOC), and attribute (ATTR). The picture itself is enclosed in the referent field of a concept of type Picture. Concepts in the graph contain *indexical referents*, marked by the ♯ symbol, which point to the parts of the picture they refer to.

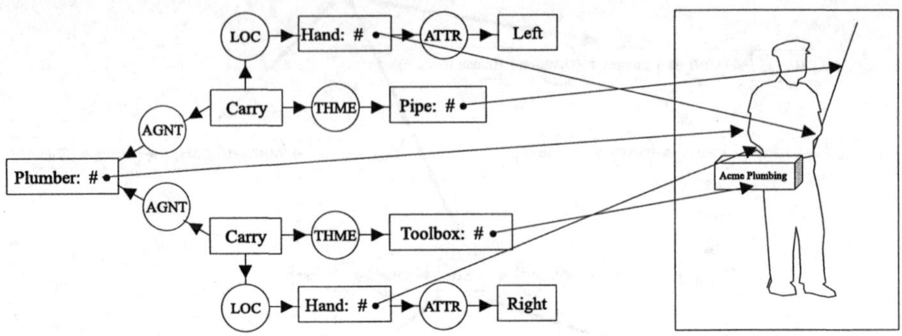

Figure 18: Referring to parts of a picture with indexical referents

The pointers in Figure 18 are encoded in some implementation-dependent fashion. As an alternate representation, the pointers may be taken out of the referent fields of the concepts and put in a separate catalog. In Figure 19, the picture of Figure 18 has a catalog indexed by serial numbers. Then the concepts may contain the serial numbers like ♯14261 instead of the implementation-dependent pointers.

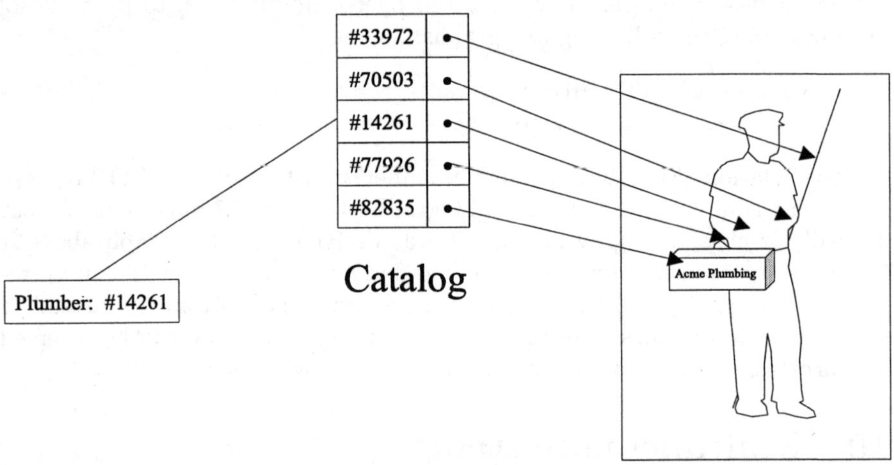

Figure 19: Mapping via a catalog of objects

When a picture is enclosed in a concept box, conceptual relations may be attached to it. Figure 20 shows the image relation (IMAG), which links a concept of type Situation to two different kinds of images of that situation:

a picture and the associated sound. The situation is linked by the description relation (DSCR) to a proposition that describes the situation, which is linked by the statement relation (STMT) to three different statements of the proposition in three different languages: an English sentence, a conceptual graph, and a KIF formula.

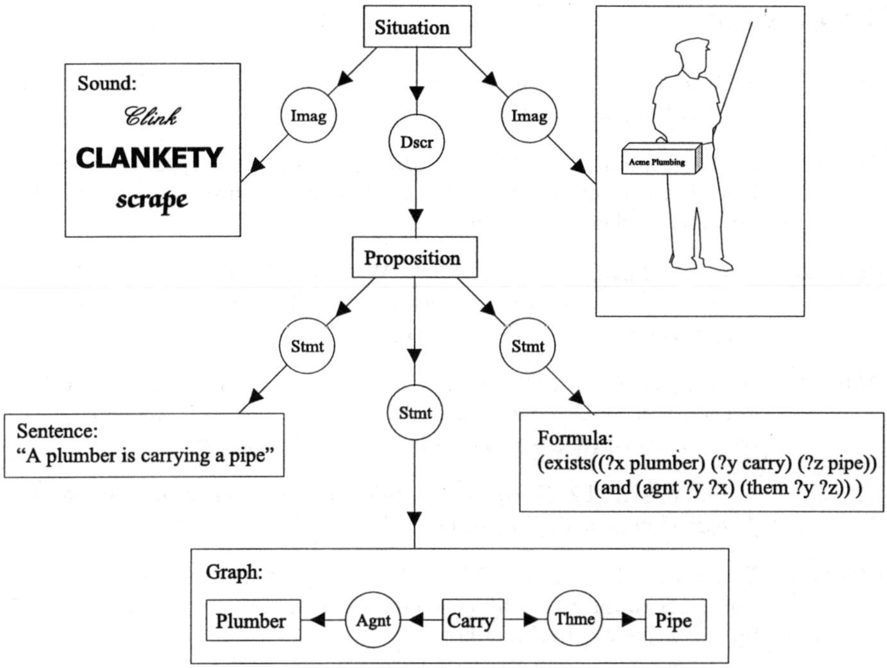

Figure 20: A conceptual graph with embedded graphics and sound

Figure 20 shows how the nested contexts in conceptual graphs can be used to encapsulate information either in conceptual graphs themselves or in any other medium – including graphics, sound, natural language, or KIF. A conceptual graph like Figure 20 resembles a hypertext network where each concept box corresponds to a hypertext card that can encode information in any arbitrary form. But unlike hypertext, a conceptual graph is a formally defined version of logic that can be processed by rules of inference, be translated to English or KIF, and be used to pass parameters to and from application programs.

In multimedia systems, conceptual graphs have been used in conjunction with the Standard Generalized Markup Language (SGML) and the HyperText Markup Language (HTML). The markup languages specify the syntactic organization of a document in chapters, paragraphs, tables, and images; but they don't represent the semantics of the text and pictures. Conceptual graphs provide a bridge between syntax and semantics: they can be translated to the syntactic tags of SGML or HTML; they are a semantic representation, which can be translated to database and knowledge-base languages, such as SQL and KIF; and they can be translated to natural language text and speech.

References

[Che96] M. Chein, (ed.), Revue d'Intelligence artificielle, Special Issue on Conceptual Graphs, vol. 10, no. 1, 1996

[EEM66] P.-W. Eklund, G. Ellis, G. Mann, (eds.), Conceptual Structures: Knowledge Representation as Interlingua, Lecture Notes in AI 1115, Springer-Verlag, Berlin, 1966

[ELRS95] Ellis, G., Levinson, R. A., Rich, W., Sowa, J. F., Conceptual Structures: Applications, Implementation, and Theory, Lecture Notes in AI 954, Springer-Verlag, Berlin, 1995

[HMN92] Hansen, H. R., Mühlbacher, R., Neumann, G., Begriffsbasierte Integration von Systemanalysemethoden, Physica-Verlag, Heidelberg, Distributed by Springer-Verlag, 1992

[KIF95] ANSI ASC X3T2, Knowledge Interchange Format, available via http://logic.stanford.edu/kif/kif.html, March 1995

[LDKSS97] D. Lukose, H. Delugach, M. Keeler, L. Searle, J. F. Sowa, (eds.), Conceptual Structures: Fulfilling Peirce's Dream, Lecture Notes in AI 1257, Springer-Verlag, Berlin, 1997

[NNGE92] T. E. Nagle, J. A. Nagle, L. L. Gerholz, P. W. Eklund, (eds.), Conceptual Structures: Current Research and Practice, Ellis Horwood, New York, 1992

[MMS93] G. W. Mineau, B. Moulin, J. F. Sowa, (eds.), Conceptual Graphs for Knowledge Representation, Lecture Notes in AI 699, Springer-Verlag, Berlin, 1993

[PN93] H. D. Pfeiffer, T. E. Nagle, (eds.), Conceptual Structures: Theory and Implementation, Lecture Notes in AI 754, Springer-Verlag, Berlin, 1993

[Sow84] Sowa, J. F., Conceptual Structures: Information Processing in Mind and Machine, Addison-Wesley, Reading, MA, 1984

[Sow92] Sowa, J. F., Knowledge-Based Systems, Special Issue on Conceptual Graphs, vol. 5, no. 3, 1992

[Sow99] Sowa, J. F., Knowledge Representation: Logical, Philosophical, and Computational Foundations, PWS Publishing Co., Boston, MA, 1999

[TDS94] W. M. Tepfenhart, J. P. Dick, J. F. Sowa, (eds.), Conceptual Structures: Current Practice, Lecture Notes in AI 835, Springer-Verlag, New York, 1994

[Way92] E. C. Way, (ed.), Journal of Experimental and Theoretical Artificial Intelligence (JETAI), Special Issue on Conceptual Graphs, vol. 4, no. 2, 1992

CHAPTER 14

GRAI Grid Decisional Modelling

Guy Doumeingts, Bruno Vallespir, David Chen

Among formalisms used to model complex systems and organisations, the GRAI Grid has a special status because it focuses on the decisional aspects of the management of systems. The GRAI grid defines the points where decisions are made (decision centres) and the information relationships among these. Models built using the grid allow the analysis and design of how decisions are co-ordinated and synchronised in the enterprise.

1 Introduction

Among formalisms used to model complex systems and organisations, the GRAI Grid has a special status because it focuses on the decisional aspects of the management of systems and it enables to build models at a high level of globality, higher than most of other formalisms.

The GRAI Grid is a management-oriented representation of the enterprise. The GRAI Grid does not aim at the *detailed* modelling of information processes, but puts into a prominent position the identification of those *points* where decisions are made in order to manage a system. These points are called *decision centres.* Decision centres are the locations where decisions are made about the various objectives and goals that the system must reach and about the means available to operate consistently with these objectives and goals.

To manage a system, many decision centres operate concurrently, each with its own dynamics reflecting the various time-scales and dynamic requirements that management decisions need to address. The links existing between decision centres are influenced by several concepts of control (situation in a hierarchy, temporal aspects, information handled, etc.). That is why models built up by the way of the GRAI Grid are in fact *architectures* of decision centres. These architectures remain at a high level of globality because the elementary building block of the GRAI Grid is the decision centre. Other formalisms may be used for modelling the internal behaviour of decision centres, i.e. to describe how decisions are made; e.g. GRAI nets were specifically designed for that purpose, however, other functional modelling languages may also be suitable.

The GRAI Grid is a modelling tool with several concepts to model a decisional system. These concepts are proposed within and are presented consistently by the GRAI Model. The GRAI Model is a generic (reference model) and the GRAI Grid enables its user to instantiate these concepts on real individual cases (Figure 1).

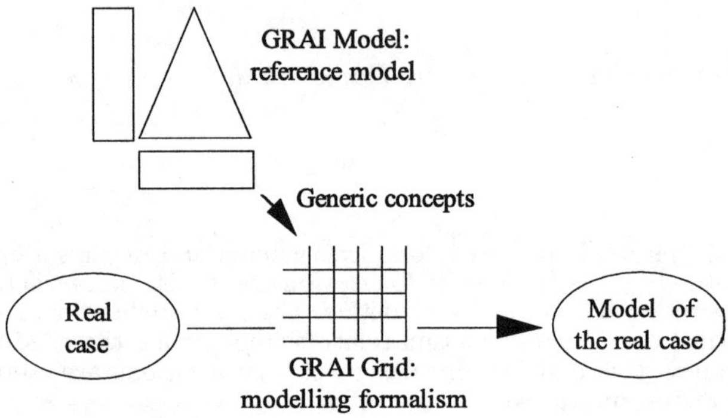

Figure 1: GRAI Model and GRAI Grid

The first part of this contribution will present the GRAI Model and the associated concepts. The second part will focus on the GRAI Grid.

2 The GRAI Model

The two main domains contributing to the GRAI model are control theory and the systems theory. We will show now what these contributions are.

2.1 From Control and Systems Theories Towards Management Systems

Control theory describes an artificial system as a couple: the *physical system* and the *control system.*

The physical system aims at the transformation of inputs into outputs. E.g. in manufacturing raw materials are transformed into products. Requirements about the physical system are directly linked to what the system is expected to do. Thus the physical system is the key part of the whole because it is the physical system that supports the implementation of the systems main aim. If the system is an enterprise then it is the physical system that creates the products and services which are the reason for the existence of the enterprise.

However, the physical system must be controlled to process consistently with the objectives of the system. The control system ensures that this aim, or objective is achieved by sending "orders" to the physical system. Moreover the control system communicates with the environment relating to the systems aims, accepting orders, making commitments, and exchanging any other information with the environment that is necessary to make decisions about how to control the physical system to successfully achieve overall system aims and objectives[1]. The control system acts (makes its decisions) by using *models* of the physical system. However, for these models to reflect reality to a sufficient degree the control system must receive information, or *feed-back*, from the physical system (Figure 2).

Systems theory enables us to enrich this understanding of systems, taking concepts into account, particularly relevant for our interest, such as those below:

Information processing. The simplest systems are assumed to process only physical flows, i.e. material and energy. However, when a system goes higher in complexity, part of its activity is dedicated to the *processing of information* necessary to control its own behaviour. Information processing assumes the existence of a *model* based on which stimuli from the environment or signals from the physical part of the system can be interpreted, and thus become information.

Decision-making. Some systems appear to be able to choose their own behaviour; in other words, given a situation to be in the position to carry out any one of a set of activities and to choose one of them as the next course of action, i.e. to *decide* on the system's behaviour. Such systems appear to follow an internal logic and can be characterised as "goal seeking." The system's goal is usually not a simple objective function, but can be described as a system of *objectives*[2].

Memory. A system may be able to store and restore information for control purposes. The structure and form of information to be stored is related to what information will need to be re-used: since information is used

[1]Note that the distinction between decision system and physical system is less evident when the system aims at the transformation of information (production of services generally speaking) than when it aims at the transformation of products (manufacturing). In fact, when the service of the physical system involves information transformation, this dichotomy remains valid: the physical system inputs and produces information (e.g. a design office receiving customer requirements and produces designs) and adds a value to this flow of information while decision system processes information only in order to control the physical system.

[2]Operating under a system of objectives instead of a simple objective function normally means that there is no one single optimal behaviour, but there are several possible behaviours which can satisfy to some degree the system of objectives.

for decision making memory can be defined in relation to decision-making[3].

Co-ordination. When a system is too complex, it must structure its activities. Structuring of the system's overall activity results in an activity decomposition and accordingly the overall system objective may be decomposed into a system of objectives. The system can be considered as a multi-objective, or multi-goal system. Individual constituent activities can not be *independently* controlled so as to achieve their respective individual objectives without regard to one another; they must be *co-ordinated* in order for the entire system to meet overall system objectives.

Based on the above discussion the GRAI model describes the control system as consisting of two parts: the information system and the decision system (Figure 2). Note that the term information system is used here in a more restrictive sense than it is generally understood in the IS discipline (see also Section 2.4).

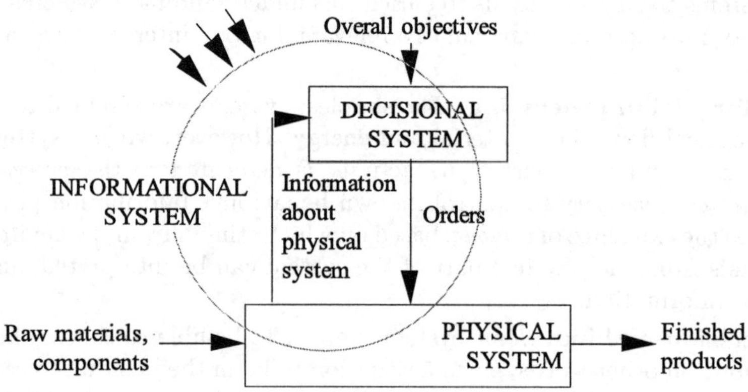

Figure 2: The three sub-systems

2.2 Hierarchy, Co-ordination and Decomposition

Any complex system can be assumed to be hierarchycally controlled (see co-ordination above). To support this assumption we must define more precisely what is meant by a hierarchy. Two types of hierarchies are relevant for our discussion: layers and echelons [MMT70] and are separately defined below.

2.2.1 Layers

Layers are related to the decision complexity. In this case, the hierarchy supports a sequence of transformations and decisions. A layer is therefore a

[3]We consider the information needed for the control of the system; information that is transformed by the physical system as part of its production activity is not considered here.

step in a sequence of decision-making[4] and the position of a layer related to the other layers is the result of the logical form of the sequence. Figure 3 shows an example from the domain of production management.

In this example, we can see that a layer is characterized by the contents of the decision made and the nature of the result. E.g. the task of calculating a material requirements plan is different from the task of calculating a schedule. The hierarchy is defined by a sequence: material requirements planning is higher in the hierarchy than load planning because a material requirements plan is needed as an input to load planning.

In Section 2.4, we shall come back to how the GRAI model takes layers into account.

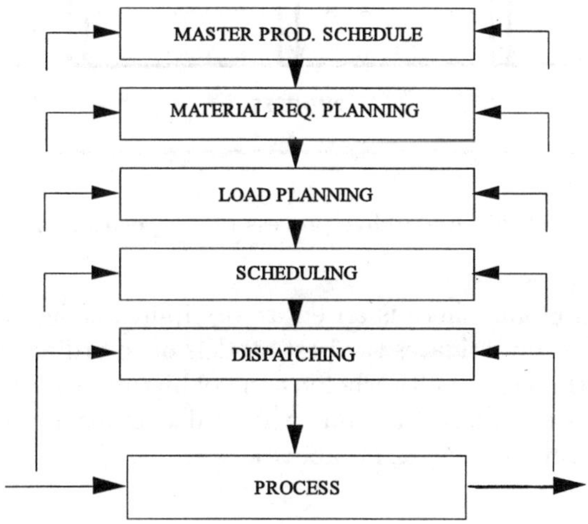

Figure 3: Layers in production management

A multi-echelon (or multi-tier) hierarchy corresponds to a decomposition of the process and its dynamics. A system with any appreciable degree of complexity has multiple functions or objectives which need to be controlled. To ensure a harmonious process of the whole system, i.e. of the set of individual controls, upper levels of control are needed. These levels are echelons. Thus the multi-echelon hierarchy is the hierarchy of co-ordination (Figure 4).

A multi-echelon hierarchy is always based on the co-ordination principle of control: if a process P that is to be controlled is decomposed into $P_1, P_2, ..., P_n$ and each such part is *separately* controlled by decision functions $D_1, D_2, ..., D_n$ respectively from echelon level k, then there must be a decision function D on level k+1 (or higher) which co-ordinates the decisions taken by $D_1, D_2, ..., D_n$. There are several different techniques to implement

[4]We are speaking about the "main stream" of decision-making, then the decomposition in layers does not exclude possible iterations.

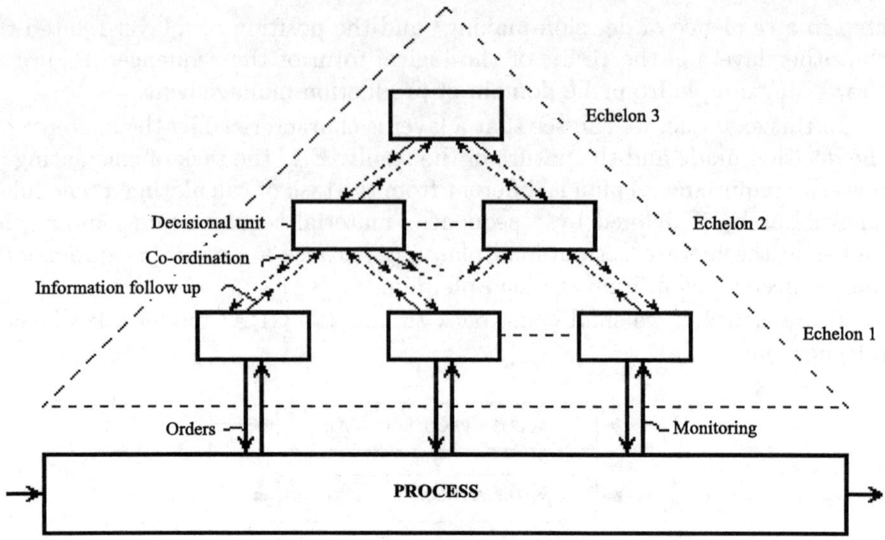

Figure 4: Multi-echelon hierarchy: process decomposition and co-ordination

such co-ordination and there is an entire discipline, called co-ordination science [MC94], that investigates the best models of co-ordination. It is possible to design more than one multi-echelon control hierarchy for any given system, e.g., because there is more than one way of decomposing processes (such as decomposing P into $P_1, P_2, ..., P_n$ above).

2.2.2 Echelons

A process can be decomposed based on various possible criteria such as

- resource structure (organizational decomposition), or
- steps[5] of transformation (functional decomposition).

Figure 5 shows an example of decomposition of a production[6] system based on resource structure. In this example, the criteria of decomposition is the organization of manufacturing resources: a factory is decomposed into shops, which are decomposed into sections, which are further decomposed into work-centres.

[5]Previously, we have presented layers as steps of transformation of information inside the decision system. The steps we are speaking about here are related to the transformation of products (physical system).

[6]Production systems are systems which have an aim to produce products and, or services for the external environment.

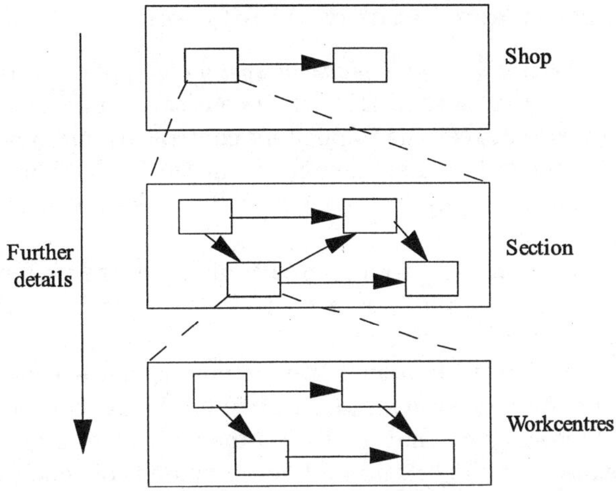

Figure 5: Organizational decomposition of a production system

The decomposition by steps of transformation (functional decomposition) is based on the process of production (for instance, procurement, machine-tooling, painting, etc.) without taking the organization into account (who does what).

Within this framework, the time to process a task is a major characteristic from a control point of view. Thus the functional decomposition of the process supporting the definition of a multi-echelon hierarchy can be based on the criteria of time to process each task. Figure 6 illustrates this. In this figure the tasks processed by the physical system are decomposed into three levels. The first level ($n-1$) corresponds to a set of elementary tasks which are assumed to have a time to process of value D_{n-1}. Based on the decomposition presented in the figure, the tasks of the intermediary level (n) have a time to process $D_n = 3 * D_{n-1}$. Finally, the upper level of decomposition is composed of one task, the time to process of which is $D_{n+1} = 6 * D_{n-1}$.

The right part of the figure presents the multi-echelon hierarchy of control related to this decomposition. There are three echelons, each of them being characterised by a temporal concept: the horizon (part of the future taken into account to make the decision). Then, echelon $n-1$ is characterised by a horizon equal to H_{n-1} and so on. To ensure the complete controlability of the whole system, an important rule says that the horizons must have a value equal or more to the time to process of the task controlled by the echelon ($_{Hn-1} \geq D_{n-1}$, and so on).

This concept is of paramount importance in the GRAI model and the GRAI grid. We shall come back to this notion of horizon Section 3.1.

2.2.3 Recursivity and Cognitive Limitation

The dichotomy *control system / physical system* is applicable to any level of the decomposition. E.g., a shop (Figure 5) consists of a physical system (described as a network of sections implicitely controlled) and a control system (which can be described as a shop control function). Sections must in turn also be understood as a physical system (a network of Workcentres) and a control system (section control).

These considerations lead to a recursive model of the system where each element of the decomposition has a control system and a physical system which latter is a network of elements.

Cognitive limitation is another reason for using multi-echelon hierarchies in the control of complex systems. Cognitive limitation can be expressed as the quantity of information that a decision-maker is able to process in a unit of time. Decisions must be taken in a limited amount of time (in accordance with the dynamics of the system) therefore the amount of information that can be considered to make the decision must also be limited. Above this limitation, the decision-maker is overwhelmed by information.

The quantity of information handled by the decision-maker grows with the level of detail and the size of the space, or scope of decision-making which is the extent of the system meant to be influenced by the decision. E.g., in the manufacturing domain this extent is defined in the space of resources, products and time.

Roughly speaking, this limitation may be illustrated by assuming that it is impossible to think in globality and in detail at the same time.

However, the complexity of manufacturing systems makes it necessary to understand them at several levels from details to globality (from machine control to factory management). Thus, a decision-maker in charge of a detailed level (e.g., control of a machine) uses information which is very detailed, and the space of decision-making is very small (one machine, products operated

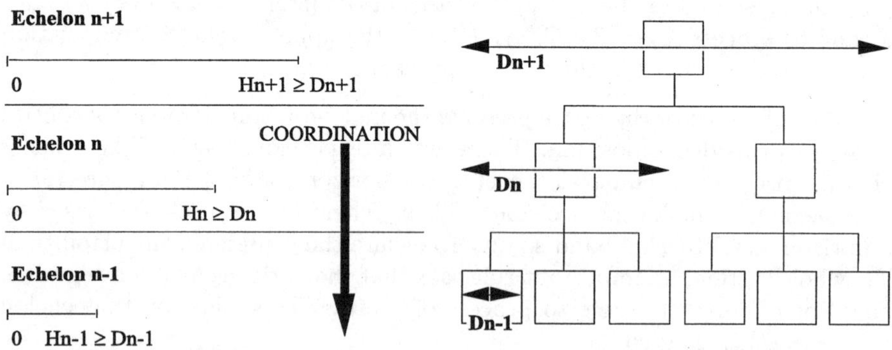

Figure 6: Multi-echelon hierarchy based on time to process (H = horizon)

on by this machine, and with a time span of one day or less). At the opposite side, a decision-maker in charge of a global level (of the management of a factory) uses global information with a space of decision-making very broad (the factory, all products with a time span of one year or more). Intermediate levels exist as well.

2.3 Functional Decomposition and Synchronization

Any concrete activity[7] is defined by a product (or a set of products[8]) and a resource (or a set of resources[9]) (Figure 7). This is the definition of an activity from a static point of view.

From a dynamic point of view, this definition is expanded in order to take time into account; the triplet [Product, Resource, Time] must now be considered. The dynamic definition of an activity is necessary to be able to synchronise its execution with other activities.

Figure 7: Definition of an activity from a static point of view: Activity = Product x Resource

Figure 8 presents all the combinations of the above three dimensions. Every area can be interpreted as describing some information about the activity of the system. Let us consider the seven combinations in Figure 8a. T is related only to time [Time]; in itself a list of time points (events) does not provide any useful information on the system, therefore this area is concealed (see Figure 8b).

The six remaining combinations are split into two parts as in Figure 8c.

- combinations where time is involved and
- combinations where time is not involved.

The three combinations within the first case are related to the domains of production management. We find:

---

[7] A concrete activity is an occurence of an activity type, thus needs a resource to perform it. An activity type of which the concrete activity is an occurence could be defined by defining what input is transformed into what output.

[8] Input-output definitions.

[9] It may be that a set of resources is only able to carry out the activity if the set of resources is in a given *state*, e.g. if it is configured in a certain manner. For this discussion resource means a physical machinery or human in a state necessary to be able to perform the activity.

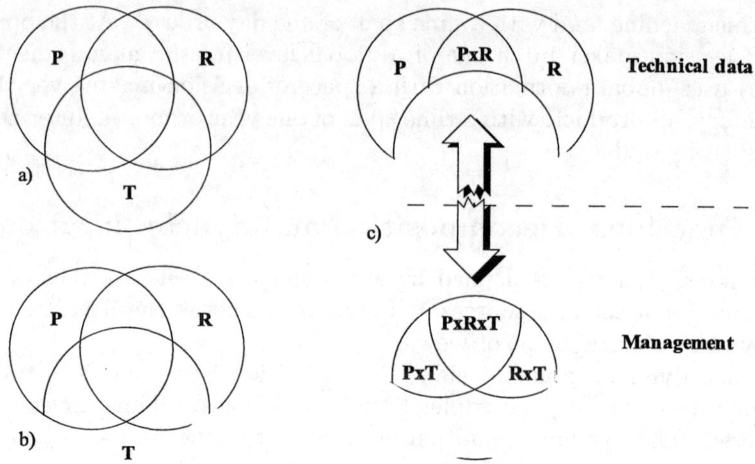

Figure 8: From the triplet Product, Resource, Time to the definition of domains of production management

[Product, Time]: **To Manage Products** which is related to decisions about products (flows management, inventory control, purchasing, etc.),

[Resource, Time]: **To Manage Resources** which is related to decisions about resources (means, manpower, assignment, etc.) and

[Product, Resource, Time]: **To Plan** which is related to decisions dealing with the transformation of products by resources. Its main purpose is to manage the activity by synchronizing **To Manage Products** and **To Manage Resources.**

The three combinations within the second case are related to the domains of definition of products and resources. Thus they are related to technical data. We find:

[Product]: Definition of products, bill-of-materials,

[Resource]: Definition of resources and

[Product, Resource]: Definition of Routes.

It is obvious that time is also involved in the three last domains because technical data evolve. However, the assumption here is that technical data evolve more slowly than physical products do. Thus technical data are considered constant related to the operational time base.

Figure 9 completes Figure 6 by taking these new concepts into account.

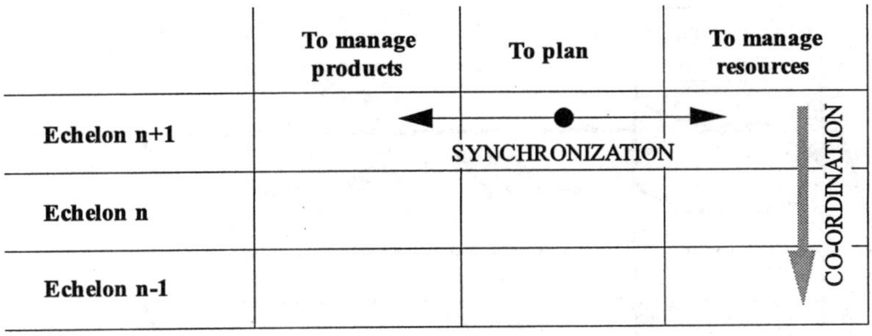

Figure 9: Time hierarchy and domains of decision-making

2.4 Synthesis: The GRAI Model

All the notions presented in this paper are taken into account within the *GRAI modcl* which is shown Figure 10.

2.4.1 Physical System

The physical system is presented as a set of organized resources the aim of which is the addition of value to the flow of products by the transformation of raw materials and information into final products.

2.4.2 Decision System

The decision system is composed of a set of decision centres which are the locations of decision-making for the management of the physical system. Mapping the domains of decision-making (Figure 8) to a hierarchical description of the system allows us to define *decision centres* more precisely as sets of decisions made on one hierarchical level and one domain of decision-making (see below).

The hierarchical structure of the decision system is put in prominent position. This hierarchy is defined consistently with the organization of the physical system. The hierarchy is multi-echelon based and has a main purpose of co-ordination. However, because the GRAI model aims at being a frame for decisional models, it neither prescribes nor proposes anything about the nature of decision made in the frame. Thus the GRAI model is fully open to multi-layer approach which is generally relevant in production management (as seen for instance Figure 3).

Production management system is assumed to mainly run periodically. However, the lowest part runs in real-time. That it is why the GRAI model set it apart by calling it *operating system* (but the GRAI Grid does not aim at the modelling of the operating system).

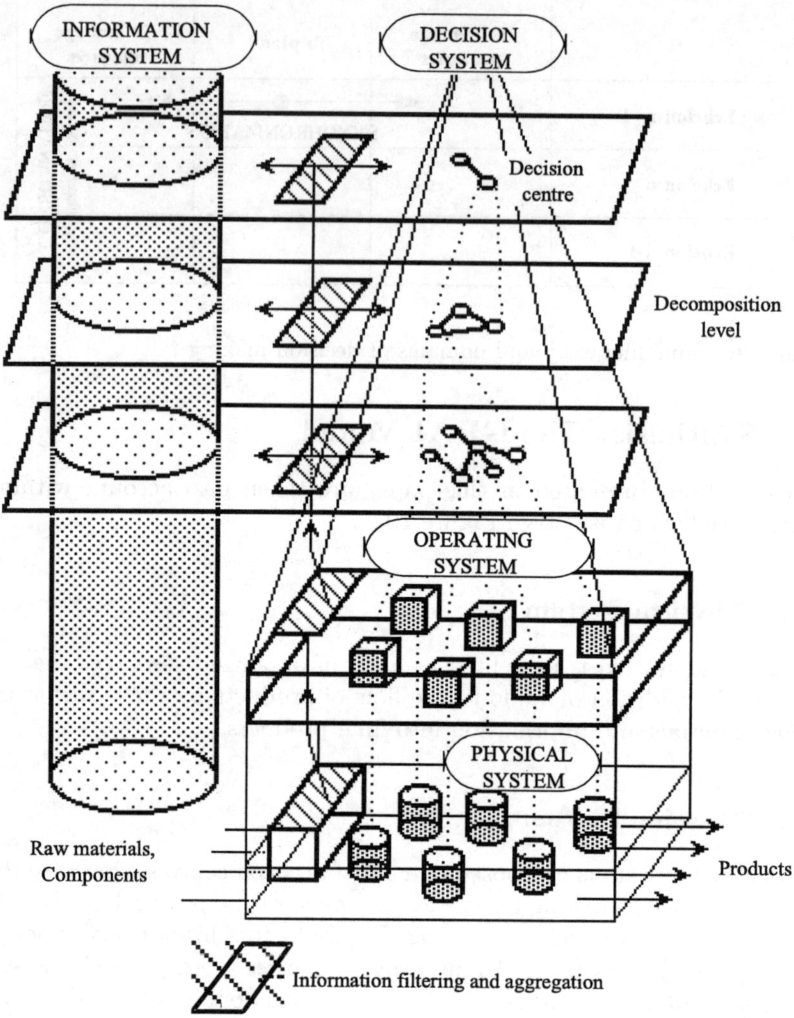

Figure 10: GRAI model

2.4.3 Information System

The information system is in charge of communication within the system and between the system and the environment, it also serves as the memory of the system and prepares information for the decision system.

Similarly to the decision system, the GRAI model does not propose any *particular* structure for the information system. However, it puts emphasis on the fact that the global structure of the information system is constrained by the structure of the decision system. However, invariably two categories of important functions: filtering and aggregation are emphasised in the GRAI model, filtering functions are related to domains of decisions (what information is to be selectively presented for individual decision centres) and aggregation functions are those which summarise information flowing from the buttom to the top of the information system.

More precisely, the information system must enable each level of the hierarchy to maintain a relevant model of the physical system. Information must be aggregated at every level based on a trade-off between detail and size which is exploitable (constrained by the earlier discussed principle of cognitive limitation).

3 The GRAI Grid

Figure 11 demonstrates the main concepts appearing in a GRAI grid. These concepts are now detailed.

3.1 Levels

Levels of the GRAI grid correspond to the echelons presented in the previous section. Each level is defined by a horizon and a period.

3.1.1 Horizon

A horizon is the part of the future taken into account by a decision. E.g., when a plan is made for three months, the horizon is three months. The notion of horizon is closely related to the concept of planning. In this way this notion is also very closed to the notion of terms (long term, short term, ...) but is more precise because a horizon is quantified. In industrial production systems and because of control considerations already discussed in Section 2.2 and Figure 6, horizons are directly valuated in relation with the customer order lead time, the material requirements cycle times, the manufacturing cycle etc.

3.1.2 Period

The notion of period is closely related to the concept of control and adjustment. When, based on an objective, a decision has been made to carry out some activity or activities during a subsequent horizon, the execution of these activities needs to be monitored. The intermediary results obtained need to be measured with respect to the objective before this activity is completely finished and the horizon ran out. If the measurements show that there is a deviation with reference to the objective, adjustments must be made. A period is the time that passes after a decision when this decision must be re-evaluated. E.g., a three months plan may be re-evaluated and decided upon every two weeks, i.e., the horizon is three months and the period is two

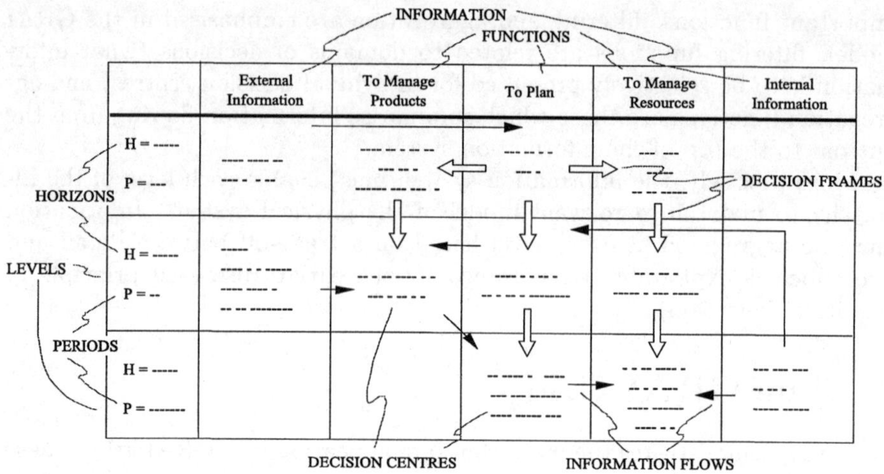

Figure 11: Concepts of the GRAI Grid

weeks. The concept of period allows the manager to take into account the changes in the environment of the decision system. This change comes from the internal behaviour of the system (disturbances, machine breakdowns, ...) and from outside (new customers orders arrive, problems arise related to providers, ...).

The value (length) of a period is determined as the result of trade-off between stability and reactiveness: if the period is too short, the system will not be stable enough; if it is too long, reactiveness is too weak. A period is directly linked to the frequency of the occurence of events relevant to the level considered. Although it is not optimal to react with changed decisions to every single relevant event, the shorter the time between these events the more frequently will it be necessary to re-evaluate the decisions which are influenced by these events. This rule can be used as guide for designers of the decision system.

An echelon-hierarchy is represented as rows of the grid, using these temporal criteria. Further consistency criteria are a) an echelon with a longer period must be considered to be higher in the hierarchy, and b) if two levels have the same period, the level with the longer horizon is higher.

3.2 Functions

Decision-making tasks are classified into *functions* depending on the basic items they handle (Products, Resources and Time). The three domains of decision (called functions within the GRAI Grid) were previously described (Figure 8c) and are fundamental for the management of any kind of system.

When describing the management functions of an enterprise these functions are broken down into separate functional areas either by functional decomposition or by organizational partitioning as described in Section 2.2.

Here is a sample list of typical functions which would appear as separate columns in the grid. Note that each of the functions below may or may not have individual product and resource management components.

- Decisions about engineering: Function to manage engineering

  To manage the engineering task means to manage the product of the engineering department and to manage engineering resources. Depending on whether the enterprise engages in repetitive or one of a kind production the relative importance of the engineering management (both a product and resource) is different – with one of a kind production being in the need of more sophisticated engineering management functions.

- Decisions about maintenance: Function to manage maintenance

  Maintenance is carried out, e.g. by a maintenance workshop, which is a kind of service enterprise that gets its orders from the factory rather than from the outside environment. Clearly, from the point of view of the maintenance workshop the machines to be maintained are products. Managing maintenance from the maintenance workshop point of view is a product management task. The human resource that does the maintenance task and the necessary equipment needs to be managed as well, which is a resource management task of the maintenance workshop.

  From the point of view of the factory the management of machine maintenance is a separate resource management task, e.g. it needs to be planned when and which machine will be available (or not available because it is scheduled for maintenance).

- Decisions about quality control: Function to manage quality control

  Quality management is a kind of product management, deciding on the quality control tasks needed at any stage of the product transformation. It may or may not need separate resource management for quality control.

- Decisions about delivery: Function to manage delivery

  Delivery is one function out of the many in the product transformation process. Delivery can be separately managed and therefore delivery management can be decomposed into product management (which product to deliver and when), resource management (which delivery resource, such as trucks, people should be available, and when) as well as delivery planning and scheduling (which delivery is to be done by which delivery resource at what time).

  Delivery management may also be considered as part of the overall management of a factory, whereupon the product and resource management and planning and scheduling tasks of management include delivery as well as all other transformation functions. The only difference between manufacturing and delivering a part is that manufacturing changes the shape while delivery changes the physical co-ordinates (space) of the part.

3.3 Decision Centres

A decision centre is defined as the set of decisions made in one level and belonging to one decision function.

3.4 Information

The decision system (often called the production management system) receives information internally, mainly from the physical system and from outside the system.

3.4.1 Internal Information

The column on the right side of the grid is used to describe the information[10] generally coming from the physical system. This column identifies the feedback information needed for control (see upward pointing arrows in Figure 3). Based on this information the recipient decision centres can keep up to date their respective models of the physical system.

3.4.2 External Information

The column on the left is related to information coming from outside the system. This information corresponds to the fact that a production system is open to its environment. Most of the time, the main part of external information arc of commercial nature (orders, forecasts, etc.).

On the level of the GRAI grid the identification of internal and external information is qualitative in nature; commonly used data modelling languages are readily available to develop the corresponding data descriptions in form of database schemata[11].

3.4.3 Information Flows

Decision centres receive information through *information flows.* These flows may be emitted by another decision centre, by an entity outside the production system (external information) or by the physical system (internal information). Because the GRAI Grid does not aim at a detailed model of

[10] Or the source of information.

[11] In case the information is not received through a database system, the precise description may be in any other form that pragmatically specifies the meaning of the information identified.

the production management system, only major information flows are presented (those needed to understand the overall operation of the system). Information flows are represented in the GRAI Grid by single arrows.

3.5 Decision Frames

The concept of *decision frame* is of paramount importance in a management-oriented representation of the enterprises control. The global structure of management is represented by decision centres and the decision frames linking them.

A decision frame is a complex information entity which can be one of two types: structural decision frame and operational decision frame. Structural decision frames are qualitative in nature, while operational decision frames are quantitative.

3.5.1 Structural Decision Frame

A structural decision frame describes for a decision centre the frame within which it can make decision. This frame is structural because it cannot be modified by a decision made within the model. To avoid conflicts, a decision centre is under the influence of only one structural decision frame. Structural decision frames are represented in the GRAI Grid by double arrows.

A structural decision frame is composed of:

- one or more *objectives,*
- one or more *decision variables,*
- zero or more *criteria* and
- zero or more *structural constraints.*

Objectives indicate which types of performances are targeted. These performances may be the production costs, the delivery lead time, the level of quality, etc. Objectives are needed everywhere a decision is made. Global objectives refer to the entire production system and, according to the principle of co-ordination are consistently detailed to give local objectives to all decision centres[12].

Decision variables are the items which the decision centre can act on to make its decisions in order to allow the decision centre to reach its objectives. E.g., for scheduling of workers working hours a decision variable can be the number of extra work hours, i.e. the decision frame of scheduling declares that scheduling decisions may decide upon the value of extra working hours

[12] Whether the local objectives were actually *derived* from global objectives or the global objective was derived from local objectives by way of some form of aggregation or generalisation is immaterial; as long as the global objective is valid, the local objectives are feasible, and the two sets are consistent.

in order to reach the objective of scheduling. A decision centre may act upon one or more decision variables through determining their respective values. In other words decisions are made in a *decision space* the dimension of which is the number of decision variables.

If several solutions can be found to reach the objectives in the space of decision-making then criteria must be used to discriminate these solutions.

Constraints are the limitations on possible values of decision variables. Structural constraints describe limitations which are not decided by the production management system itself: they come as given and can not be transgressed unless the production system itself or its environment is changed, e.g. resource limits in terms of capabilities and capacities, regulations, etc.

3.5.2 Operational Decision Frame

The use of a structural decision frame is not sufficient from an operational point of view. A decision centre receives an operational decision frame through its structural decision frame. The operational decision frame is quantitative and changes each time the decision centre that determines this frame makes a decision. A decision centre receives only one operational decision frame at a time.

An operational decision frame consists of:

- the valuation of the objectives and
- one or several operational constraints.

In a structural decision frame objectives were only qualitative, not valuated. An operational decision frame provides actual values for the qualitatively defined parts of a structural decision frame.

Operational constraints aim at a limitation of the space of decision-making for the decision centre receiving the frame. This limitation applies to the decision variables in the structural decision frame of the same decision centre. Operational constraints are defined in the same form as structural constraints.

3.5.3 Decision Variables and Constraints

Decision constraints limit the freedom of a decision centre to select any arbitrary value for its decision variables (Figure 12).

Because structural constraints represent limitations that must not be transgressed by decisions, the space of freedom defined by operational constraints must be contained in the space of freedom defined by structural constraints[13].

[13]To avoid Figure 12 to be too complex, structural constraints are not represented. However, as noted above, the space defined by structural constraints must contain at least the space defined by operational constraints.

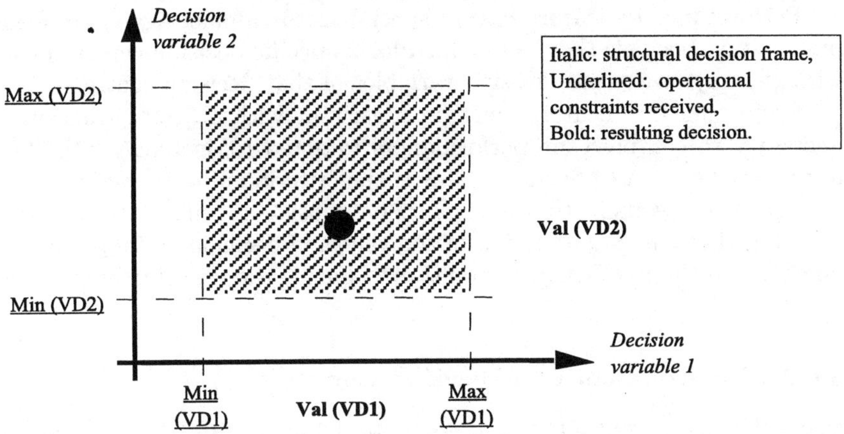

Figure 12: Space with two decision variables and two operational constraints

3.6 A Complete Environment of a Decision Centre

Two more concepts are needed to define a complete environment of decision-making for a decision centre.

3.6.1 Commands

The decision frame contains all the elements indicating to a decision centre *in which frame* (partially *how*) it can decide. Commands represent *what* must be processed. A decision centre interprets commands in the context given by the decision frames.

A decision centre may receive one or more commands and may emit one or several ones as well. In the GRAI Grid, a command is represented as a information flow or is implicit within a decision frame.

A command may come from another decision centre or from outside the system, e.g. an order (sent by a customer) is a command.

In the same way, a command may be sent to a resource. Sending a command to a resource is the way for the management system to control its physical system.

3.6.2 Performance Indicators, Observability and Controllability

A performance indicator is an aggregated piece of information allowing the comparison of the performance of the system to the systems objectives. A performance indicator may be defined by its name, a value domain or dimension, and a procedure that describes how its value can be calculated.

Performance indicators have a special status among aggregate feedback information because they are defined for a specific decision centre consistent with the objectives and decision variables of that decision centre.

Performance indicators must be consistent with objectives because it is necessary to compare the performances targeted (objectives) with the performances reached (indicator). This is the criterion of observability.

Performance indicators must also be consistent with decision variables meaning that the manipulation of the values of decision variables must have an effect on the performance monitored. This is the criterion of controllability.

3.6.3 Environment of a Decision Centre

Using the above concepts it is possible to define a complete decision-making environment (i.e. the set of all inputs) for each decision centre of the decision system. Table 1 summarizes these concepts. Note that on the output side the centres decision variables are valuated and are received as parts of the operational frames (valuated objectives and constraints) and commands of lower level decision centres.

STRUCTURAL	OPERATIONAL
Objective (type)	Objective (value)
Decision variable (type)	/
Structural constraint (value)	Operational constraint (value)
Criteria (type)	/
Command (type)	Command (value)
Performance indicator (type)	Performance indicator (value)

Table 1: Environment (or input) of a decision centre (Legend: type means qualitatively defined, value means quantitatively defined, / means not applicable)

Figure 13 shows a simple example of a GRAI grid[14]. The grid is the result of an as-is analysis and could be used to uncover various problems with the present production management system.

3.7 Example

This section presents the use of the GRAI Grid in an industrial case study. The company studied manufactures industrial butterfly floodgates. The subject of the study was an assembly shop and warehouse (for more detail concerning this study, see [DVM95a]). The study aimed at re-engineering the shop in order to meet the following objectives:

[14]Note that the function which was called to deliver by the analysis team is in fact a delivery *planning* function (of the To plan type).

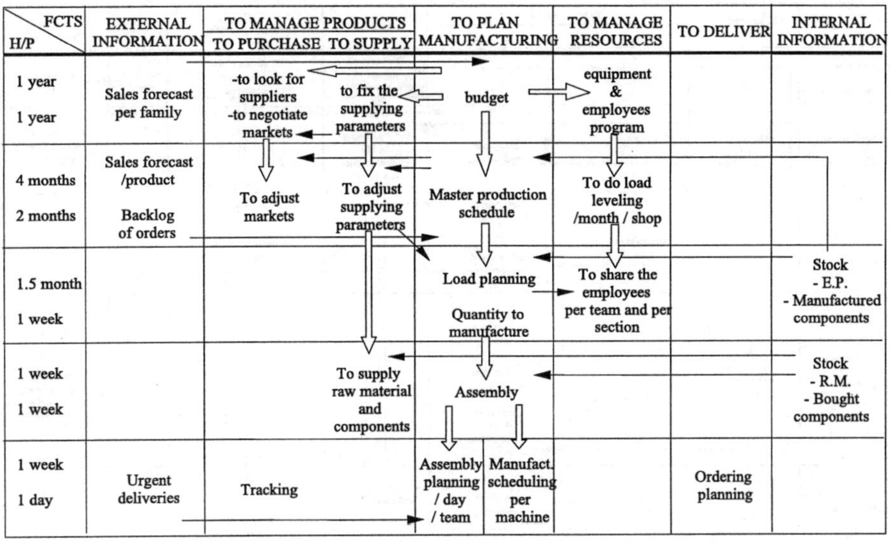

Figure 13: Example of a GRAI Grid (as-is analysis)

Regarding the customers:

- meet the strategic requirements in terms of manufacturing volume,
- respect delivery due dates,
- increase reliability of delivery lead times,
- improve load and product flexibility, and
- monitor and improve quality.

Regarding the factory organization:

- decrease inventories,
- decrease production costs, and
- enrich operating and management tasks, for employee motivation.

The objective of the use of the GRAI Grid was to identify the elements and organization of the production system, and to present a model understandable by various users. This task had to allow existing inconsistencies to be brought to the fore and their origin to be identified. Finally, the aim was to allow the participants in the study to understand the system and to know its specific features.

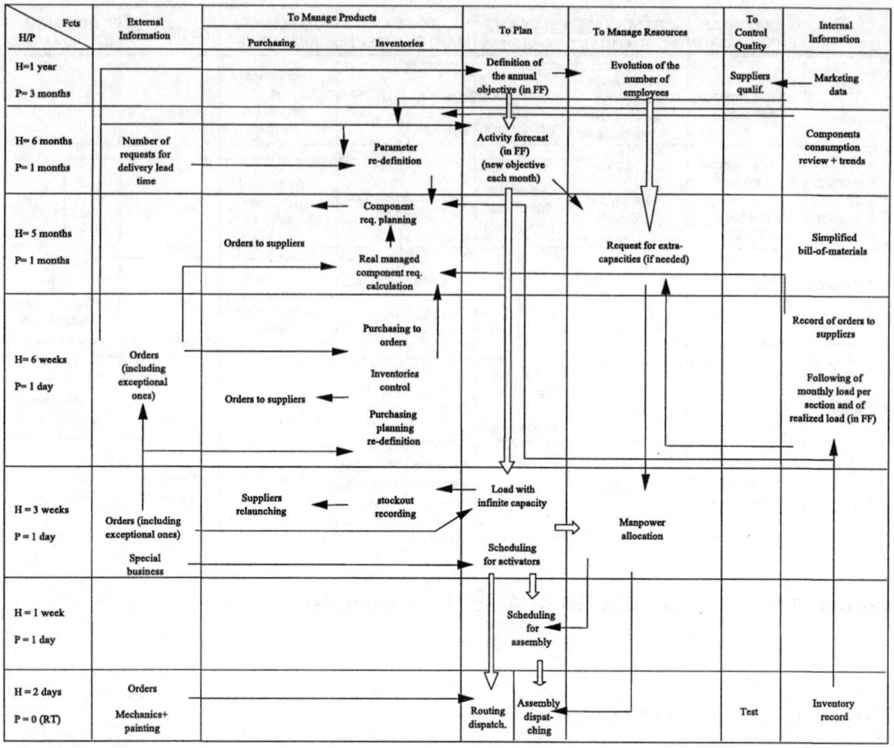

Figure 14: The assembly management system (GRAI grid) - as-is situation

A grid representing the current assembly management system was built (Figure 14). From this grid, the most important inconsistencies were identified, as well as the consequences of these for the production. What follows is a sample analysis of the inconsistencies which were discovered in the three main types of management functions "To plan," "To manage products" and "To manage resources."[15] Such analysis can be carried out by a production management expert who can compare known production management with the explicit model of present production management as brought to light by the model.

Long-term / To plan. Planning is only expressed in terms of money (French Francs [FF]) and is based on orders. There is therefore no Master Production Schedule taking manufacturing and procurement lead times into account. Thus, it is not possible to define manufacturing parameters and procurement rules over the long term. There is no criterion for processing exceptional orders or project-like orders which may run over several months.

[15] Note that for the reader of this handbook it is harder to interpret this grid than for those involved in the study, since the grid utilises the terminology commonly shared in the studied shop and is interpreted in that context.

Long-term / To manage products. Incoming goods or products should normally be procured on the basis of requirements planning, component consumption review, or inventory control rules. Planning expressed in terms of money is not suitable for the calculation of a procurement plan (see Long-term / Plan). Thus, production objectives and procurement management are not consistent, leading to both stockouts and inventory inflation.

Long-term / To manage resources. Because of the long-term plan being expressed in terms of money there is no real long-term resource management. Especially, the relationship between load and capacity cannot be taken into account by resource management.

Middle-term / To plan. There is no load planning. The acceptance of an order with a lead time less than the standard lead time is based only on the availability of components. Thus the main aspect of dispatching is based on a rigid sequencing rule, and resources shared by several routes do not know their future loads.

Middle-term / To manage products. Because of the lack of load planning it is impossible to adjust the procurement plan. Thus the inventory is sizeable but inappropriate for the needs of the assembly unit.

Middle-term / To manage resources. Because of the lack of load planning it is impossible to adjust capacities, mainly the allocation of operators.

Short-term / To plan. Scheduling is not really planned because it is based only on a so-called infinite capacity calculation. The only real planning is carried out by dispatching. Thus there is no synchronization. This leads to stockouts and inventory inflation. The scheduling decision centre receives an objective expressed in terms of money and as a monthly forecast. This is inappropriate for the short-term level and the objective cannot be achieved.

Short-term / To manage products. Because of the inappropriateness of the long- and middle-term product management, routing is triggered two weeks before real requirements. This leads to increased Work-In-Process, information flows and processing.

Short-term / To manage resources. Because of the status of the middle-term resource management the optimization of the use of resources is not possible.

4 Conclusion

The GRAI Grid was used in many studies, in SMEs and large companies as well, in several business domains. Generally, the GRAI Grid is not used alone but as one of the modelling formalisms brought into play within GIM (GRAI Integrated Methodology) [DVZC92].

The success of the GRAI Grid may be explained through two main points. First, the GRAI Grid is operationaly very practical because it gives a comprehensive, one-page model generally sufficient to explain the structure of the management system to the executives of a company. Second, the GRAI Grid is management-oriented and enables the understanding of the production system in terms of *performances* (related to the notion of objectives) and *integration* (related to the notion of co-ordination and synchronisation).

It is considered particularly that the decomposition and transmitting of objectives is a key point for integration. Integration is not only related to the physical connection of machines and computers, but also to the coherence of objectives of the various decision-making activities. Without coherence of objectives, the physical connection of machines and communication network cannot improve the performance of a manufacturing system.

The main items that make up the frames of decision making (objectives, decision variables, constraints) are primarily determined by the hierarchy of the decision system. These items are decomposed in a consistent way by descending the hierarchy of the system. E.g., *suppose* that the global objectives of a manufacturing system can be described by a triplet $< Costs, Quality, Leadtimes >$, i.e. cost objectives, quality objectives and lead time objectives. These objectives are the objectives of the highest level of the hierarchy. The objectives of lower levels are different but must be consistent with these three objectives. Conversely the performance of a lower level decision centre contributes to the global performance of the system.

The GRAI Grid enables its user to analyse the consistency of the decision system and helps in designing improved systems of management. Note that a number of analysis rules exist which can be applied to GRAI grids to uncover common problems of co-ordination and synchronisation thus improving the level of integration in the enterprise.

References

[CVD96] Chen, D., Vallespir, B., Doumeingts, G., GIM: GRAI Integrated Methodology, a methodology to design and specify integrated manufacturing systems, in: Proceedings of ASI'96, Annual Conference of ICIMS-NOE, Life Cycle Approaches to Production Systems, Toulouse, France, 1996, 265-272

[Dou84] Doumeingts, G., Méthode GRAI: méthode de conception des systèmes en productique, Automatic Control, Université de Bordeaux I, 1984

[DVZC92] Doumeingts, G., Vallespir, B., Zanettin, M., Chen, D., GIM: GRAI Integrated Methododology, a methodology for designing CIM systems, A technical report of the IFAC/IFIP Task Force on Architectures For Integrating Manufacturing Activities And Enterprises, GRAI/LAP, Version 1.0, 1992

[DVM95a] Doumeingts, G., Vallespir, B., Marcotte, F., A Proposal for an Integrated Model of Manufacturing System: Application to the reengineering of an Assembly Shop, Control Engineering Practice, Special Section on Models for Management and Control 3(1), 1995, 59-67

[DVC95b] Doumeingts, G., Vallespir, B., Chen, D., Methologies for Designing CIM systems – A survey, Computers in Industry, Special Issue on CIM in the Extended Enterprise, Amsterdam, 25 (3) 1995, 263-280

[DV95c] Doumeingts, G., Vallespir, B., A Methodology Supporting Design and Implementation of CIM Systems including Economic Evaluation, in: P. Brandimarte, A. Villa (eds.), Optimization Models and Concepts in Production Management, 1995, 307-331

[MC94] Malone, T. W., Crowston, K., The interdisciplinary study of coordination, ACM Computing Surveys 26 (1), 1994, 87-119

[Mar95] Marcotte, F., Contribution à la modélisation des systèmes de production: extension du modèle GRAI, PhD Thesis, CIM, Université Bordeaux I, 1995

[MMT70] Mesarovic, M. D., Macko, D., Takahara, Y., Theory of hierarchical, multilevel, systems, Academic Press, New York and London, 1970

[Moi84] Le Moigne, J.-L., La théorie du système général, Presses Universitaires de France, collection Systèmes-Décisions, Paris, 1984

[Vall90] Vallespir, B., Hierarchical aspect of production management systems, associated modelling tools and architecture, in: Proceedings of the 1st International Conference on Automation Technology, Taipei, Taiwan, 1990

[VMD93] Vallespir, B., Merle, C., Doumeingts, G., GIM: a technico-economic methodology to design manufacturing systems, Control Engineering Practice, Oxford 1 (6), 1993, 1031-1038

CHAPTER 15

SOM
Modeling of Business Systems

Otto K. Ferstl, Elmar J. Sinz

SOM is an object-oriented methodology for comprehensive and integrated modeling of business systems. It is based on a framework consisting of the layers business plan, business process model, and business application system as well as views on these layers focusing on specific aspects. This contribution presents the SOM language for business process modeling and shows how business application systems can be linked to business process models. The language uses concepts of systems theory and is based on the notions of business object, business transaction, task, event, and service. Business objects are coordinated by feedback control or by negotiation. Decomposition rules allow a stepwise refinement of a business process model. The contribution includes a detailed example to illustrate the methodology.

1 Introduction

SOM is a methodology for modeling business systems [FS90, FS91, FS95]. The abbreviation means 'Semantic Object Model', expressing that the SOM methodology is fully object-oriented and designed to capture business semantics explicitly. General basis of the SOM methodology are concepts of systems theory.

SOM supports the core phases of business engineering, such as analysis, design, and redesign of a business system. A business system is an open, goaloriented, sociotechnical system. Thus the analysis of a business system focuses on the interaction with its environment, goal pursuing business processes, and resources. Moreover, the dynamic behavior of a business system requires investigation of properties such as stability, flexibility, and complexity [Bah92].

The backbone of the SOM methodology is an enterprise architecture which uses different perspectives on a business system via a set of models. These models are grouped into three model layers referring to a business plan, business process models and resource models. Each layer describes the business system as a whole, but with respect to the specific perspective on the model. In order to reduce complexity, each model layer is subdivided into several views, each focusing on specific aspects of a model layer. On the meta level, the modeling language of each layer is defined by a meta model and derivated view definitions. Thus the enterprise architecture provides a modeling framework which helps to define specific semantics and to manage complexity of the model [Sin97]. In this contribution we outline the methodological framework of SOM as well as its modeling language.

2 Characteristics of Business Systems

In terms of systems theory a business system is an open, goaloriented, sociotechnical system [FS98]. It is open because it interacts with customers, suppliers, and other business partners transferring goods and services. The business system and its goods/services are part of a value chain which in general comprises several consecutive business systems. A corresponding flow of finance runs opposite the flow of goods and services.

The behavior of a business system is aimed at business goals and objectives. Goals specify the goods and services to be provided by the system. Objectives (e.g. profit and turnover) are defined measurable levels against which business performance can be measured.

Actors of a business system are humans and machines. Human actors are persons in different roles. Machine actors in general are plants, production machines, vehicles, computer systems etc. SOM pays specific attention to application systems which are the machine actors of the information processing subsystem of a business system (information system). An application system consists of computer and communication systems running application software. The degree of automation of an information system is the ratio of tasks carried out by application systems to all tasks of the information system.

The notion of a business system as open and goal-oriented reflects a perspective from outside the system. An inside perspective shows a distributed system of autonomous, loosely coupled components which cooperate in pursuing the systems goals and objectives. The autonomous components are business processes [FS93, FS95] which produce goods and services and deliver them to other business processes.

The cooperation of business processes is coordinated primarily through process specific objectives which are derived from the overall objectives of a business system. This is done by the business systems management. Within the degrees of freedom defined by the process specific objectives a secondary coordination is done by negotiation between the business processes.

Inside a business process there are components which also cooperate and have to be coordinated. This coordination is done by an intra-process management which controls the activities of the process components by sending instructions to them and supervising their behavior. In contrast to the coordination between business processes, the components inside a business process are guided closely by the process management.

The components of a business process as well as the business processes as a whole take care of functions which are essential to every business system. The following classification of these functions helps to identify business processes and their components: (1) input-output-function to implement the characteristic of openness, e.g. a production system, (2) supply function to provide material resources and energy, (3) maintenance function to keep the system running, (4) sensory function to register disturbances or defects inside or outside the system, (5) managing function to coordinate the subsystems [Bee81].

3 Architecture of Business Systems

The SOM methodology utilizes an enterprise architecture which consists of three layers (Figure 1) [FS95]:

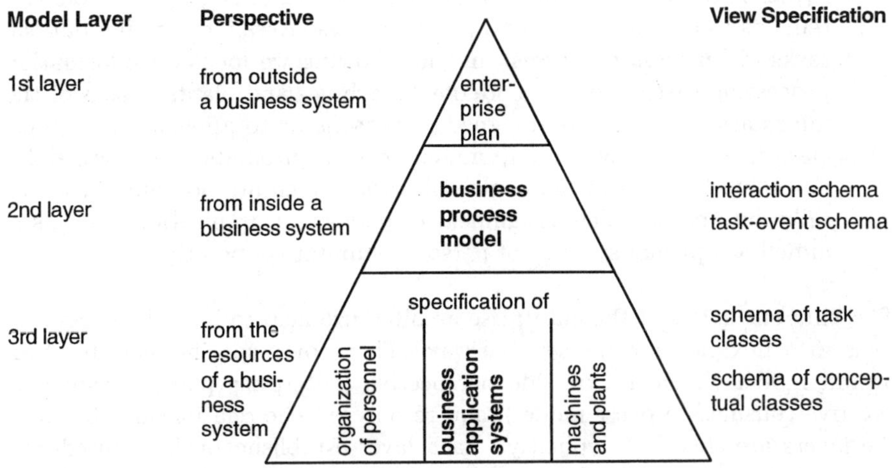

Figure 1: Enterprise architecture [FS95]

- **Enterprise plan:** The enterprise plan constitutes a perspective from outside a business system. It focuses on the global task and the resources of the business system. The specification of the global task includes the universe of discourse, the goals and objectives to be pursued, as well as the goods and services to be delivered. Requirements on resources are derived from the global task and have to be cross-checked to the capabilities of available resources. So both global task and resources determine themselves mutually.

A first evaluation of an enterprise plan is done by an analysis of chances and risks from a perspective outside the business system, and an additional analysis of the strengths and weaknesses of the business system from an inside perspective. Strategies on products and markets, strategic actions, constraints, and rules serve as guidelines to realize an enterprise plan.

- **Business process model:** The business process model constitutes a perspective from inside a business system. It specifies main processes and service processes. Main processes contribute directly to the goals of the business system, service processes provide their outcome to main processes or other service processes. The relationships between business processes follow the client/server concept. A client process engages other processes for delivering the required service. Business processes establish a distributed system of autonomous components. They cooperate in pursuing joint objectives which are derived from the overall objectives of a business system.

- **Specification of resources:** In general, personnel, application systems as well as machines and plants are resources for carrying out the tasks of business processes. In the following we focus on information processing tasks and therefore omit machines and plants. Tasks of the information system are assigned to persons or to application systems classifying a task as non-automated or fully-automated. A task partly-automated has to be split into sub-tasks which are non-automated or fully-automated. The assignment of persons or application systems is aimed at optimal synergy of person-computer cooperation.

The different layers of the enterprise architecture help to build business systems in a flexible and manageable way. They cover specific aspects of an overall model which are outside perspective (enterprise plan), inside perspective (business process model), and resources. The relationships between the layers are specified explicitly. Each layer establishes a distributed system of autonomous, loosely coupled components. In contrast to a single-layered monolithic model, the multi-layered system of three models allows local changes without affecting the overall architecture. For example, it is possible to improve a business process model (inside perspective) yet retaining goals and objectives (outside perspective), or to replace actors of one type by other ones.

Following an outside-in approach it is advisable to build the three model layers top down the enterprise architecture. But the architecture does not force this direction. There may be good reasons to depart from this guideline e.g. when analyzing existing business systems. Here it is sometimes difficult to find an elaborated enterprise plan, so modeling starts at the business process layer focusing on the inside perspective. The enterprise plan may be completed when the other layers are fully understood. In each case effects on other layers have to be balanced and approved.

The enterprise architecture implies that functionality and architecture of the business application systems are derived from the business process model. The relationships between both layers are formalized to a high degree. Design decisions and results at the business process layer are translated automatically into the layer of application systems. The architecture of the layer of application systems uses the concept of object-integration to combine conceptual and task classes [Fer92]. Alternatively it is possible to link a business process model to an existing, traditional application system which follows the traditional concepts of function integration or data integration. In this case tasks to be automated are linked to functional units of the application system.

4 Language for Business Process Modeling

In this section we define the language for business process models. The language is specified by a meta model (Section 4.1) and a set of decomposition rules (Section 4.2). The section is completed by an example, introducing the business process *distribution* of a trading company (Section 4.3).

4.1 Meta Model for Business Process Models

The meta model for business process modeling shows notions and relationships between notions (Figure 2). It is specified as a binary entity-relationship schema. Relationships between notions are associated with a role name as well as two cardinalities to denote how many instances of the one notion can be connected to one instance of the other notion at least and at most. Within the meta model the notions are represented by entities. Each entity also contains the symbols used for representation within a business process model.

As introduced in Section 3, a business process model specifies a set of business processes with client/server relationships among each other. A business process pursues its own goals and objectives which are prescribed and tuned by the management of a business system. Cooperation between processes is a matter of negotiation. The term 'business process' denotes a compound building block within a business process model and therefore it is not a basic notion of the language. A business process consists of at least one business object and one or more business transactions.

At the initial level of a business process model, a business object (object in short) produces goods and services and delivers them to customer business processes. Each business object belongs exclusively to a business process of the universe of discourse or to the environment of a business system. A business transaction (transaction in short) transmits a good or service to a

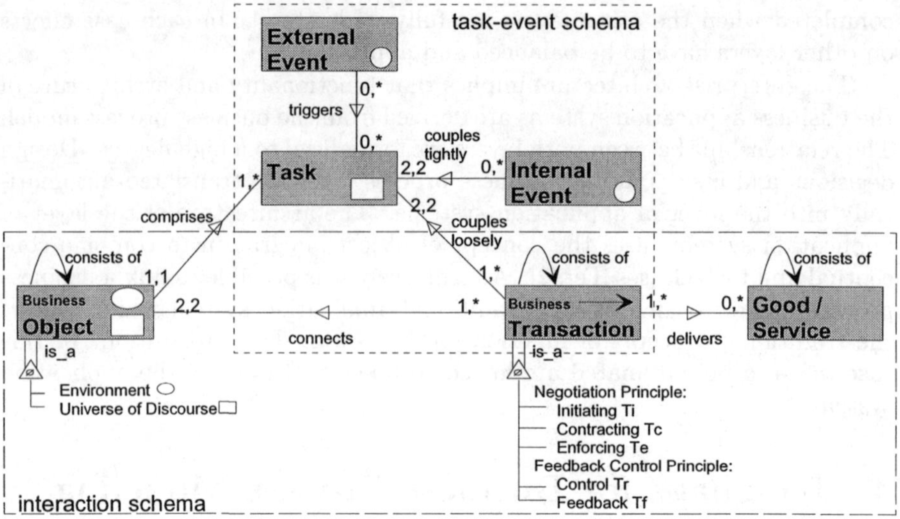

Figure 2: Meta Model for Business Process Models [FS95]

customer business process or receives a good or service from a supplier business process. A transaction connecting different business processes belongs to both processes.

A business process may be refined using the decomposition rules given below. At a more detailed level of a business process model, each business object appears in one of two different roles: an operational object contributes directly to producing and delivering of a good/service while a management object contributes to managing one or more operational objects using messages. A business transaction transmits a good/service or a message between two operational objects or a message between two management objects or between a management object and an operational object.

A business transaction connects two business objects. Conversely, a business object is connected with one to many (*) in-going or out-going business transactions. From a structural viewpoint a transaction denotes an interaction channel forwarding goods, services, or messages. From a behavioral viewpoint a transaction means an event which is associated with the transmission of a specific good, a service package, or a message.

A business object comprises one to many tasks, each of them driving one to many transactions. A transaction is driven by exactly two tasks belonging to different business objects. The tasks of an object share common states and are encapsulated by the object. These tasks pursue joint goals and objectives which are attributes of the tasks.

The SOM methodology uses two different concepts of coupling tasks (Figure 3, top): Loosely coupled tasks belong to different objects and therefore operate on different states. The tasks are connected by a transaction which

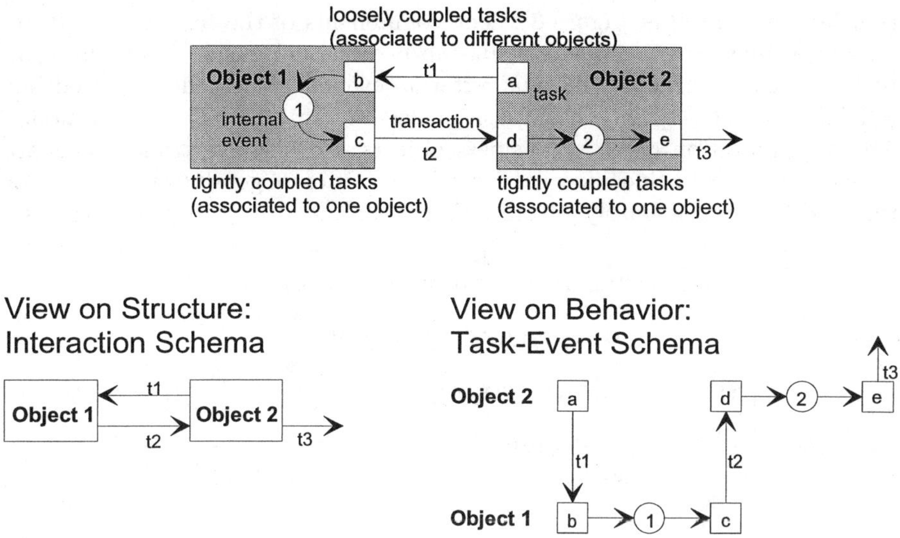

Figure 3: Representation of structure and behavior in a business process model

serves as an interaction channel for passing states from one task to the other. A task triggers the execution of another task by an event (good, service package, or message) riding on the interaction channel. Tightly coupled tasks belong to the same object and operate on the same states. The tasks are connected by an internal event which is sent from one task to trigger the execution of the other. The concept of encapsulating tightly coupled tasks by an object and loosely coupling the tasks of different objects via transactions is a key feature of the object-oriented characteristic of the SOM methodology.

A third type of event is the external event. An external event denotes the occurrence of an event like 'the first day of a month' which is not bound to a transaction.

Due to its complexity, a business process model is represented in two different diagrams (Figure 3 bottom and Figure 2): The Interaction Schema is the view on structure. It shows business objects which are connected by business transactions. The Task-Event Schema is the view on behavior. It shows tasks which are connected by events (transactions, internal events, or external events).

4.2 Decomposition Rules

The SOM methodology allows a business process model to be decomposed by stepwise refinement. Decomposition takes place with the components of the interaction schema specifying the structure of a business process model, i.e. business objects, business transactions, and goods/services (see the relationship *consists of* in Figure 2). The components of the task-event schema which specify the behavior of a business process model (tasks, events riding on transactions, internal events, and external events) are not decomposed but redefined on subsequent decomposition levels of a business process model. The decomposition rules for business objects and business transactions are shown in Figure 4 . Specific rules for decomposition of goods/services are not required because of simply decomposing them into sub-goods/sub-services.

Decomposition rules for business objects:

O	::={O',O",T_r(O',O"),[T_f(O",O')]}	(1)
O	::={O',O",[T(O',O")]}	(2)
O	::={spec O'}$^+$	(3)
O'|O"	::=O	(4)

Decompostition rules for business transactions:

T(O,O'	::=[[T_i(O,O') seq] T_c(O',O)] seq T_e(O,O')	(5)
T_x	::=T'_x{seq T''_x}$^+$ | T'_x{par T''_x}$^+$ (x=i,c,e,r,f)	(6)
T_x	::={spec T'_x}$^+$ (x=i,c,e,r,f)	(7)
T_i|T_c|T_e	::=T	(8)
T_r|T_f	::=T	(9)

Figure 4: Decomposition rules for business objects and business transactions (::=replacement,{} set, {}$^+$ list of repeated elements, [] option, | alterantiv, seq sequential order, par parallel order, spec specialization)

The decomposition of a business process model helps to manage its complexity, allows to separate the management system of a business process from its operational system, and uncovers the coordination of a business process.

The SOM methodology uses two basic coordination principles within decomposition [FS95]:

- Applying the **feedback control principle** (rule 1) a business object is decomposed into two sub-objects and two transactions: a management object O' and an operational object O" as well as a control transaction T_r from O' to O" and a feedback transaction T_f in opposite direction. These components establish a feedback control loop. The management object prescribes objectives or sends control messages to the operational object via the control transaction. Conversely the operational object

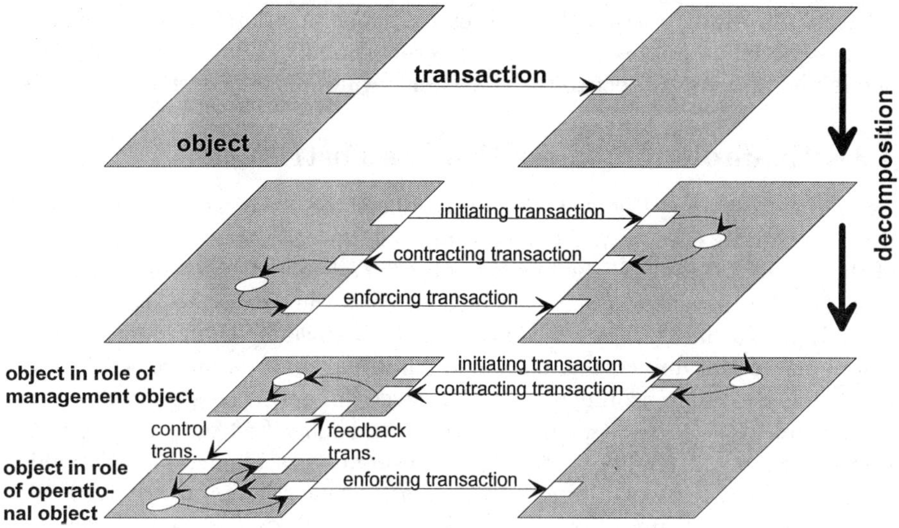

Figure 5: Decomposition of business process models

reports to the management object via the feedback transaction.

- Applying the **negotiation principle** (rule 5) a transaction is decomposed into three successive transactions: (1) an initiating transaction T_i where a server object and its client learn to know each other and exchange information on deliverable goods/services, (2) a contracting transaction T_c, where both objects agree to a contract on the delivery of goods/services, and (3) an enforcing transaction T_e, where the objects transfer the goods/services.

The types of transactions resulting from the decomposition are shown in the meta model (Figure 2) as specialized transactions.

Figure 5 illustrates the application of the coordination principles for the decomposition of business process models. The decomposition of the first level into the second level is done by applying the negotiation principle. Applying the feedback control principle leads to the third level.

In addition to the coordination principles given above, a transaction may be decomposed into sub-transactions of the same type which are executed in sequence or in parallel (rule 6). Correspondingly, a business object may be decomposed into sub-objects of the same type (management object or operational object) which may be connected by transactions (rule 2). Objects as well as transactions may be specialized within the same type (rules 3 and 7). The other rules (4, 8, and 9) are used for replacement within successive decompositions.

It is important to state that successive decomposition levels of a business process model do not establish new, different models. They belong to exactly one model and are subject to the consistency rules defined in the meta model.

4.3 Example: Business Process Distribution

To give an example, Figure 6 (left) introduces the business process *distribution* of a trading company. At the initial level, the interaction schema consists of three components, (1) the business object *distributor* which provides a service, (2) the transaction *service* which delivers the service to the customer, and (3) the business object *customer* itself. *Distributor* is an internal object belonging to the universe of discourse while *customer* is an external object belonging to the environment. At this level the entire cooperation and coordination between the two business objects is specified by the transaction *service*. Figure 6 (right) shows the corresponding sequence of tasks which is very simple. The task names in the task-event schema are derived from the name of the transaction. Here, the task *service>* (say send service) of *distributor* produces and delivers the service, the task *>service* (say receive service) of *customer* receives it. The arrow *service* here defines the sequence of the two tasks belonging to the transaction *service* which is represented in the interaction schema by an arrow, too.

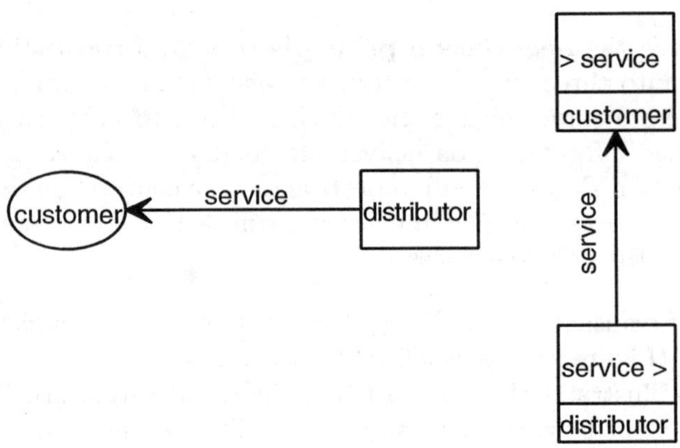

Figure 6: Interaction schema (left) and task-event schema (right) of business process distribution (1st level)

Transactions like *service* connect business objects inside the universe of discourse and link business objects to the environment. When modeling a value chain the business process model of a trading company includes a second business process *procurement*, which receives services from a business object *supplier*, belonging to the environment, and delivers services to *distributor*.

The example (Figure 6) will be continued now. As *customer* and *distributor* negotiate about the delivery of a service, the *service* transaction is

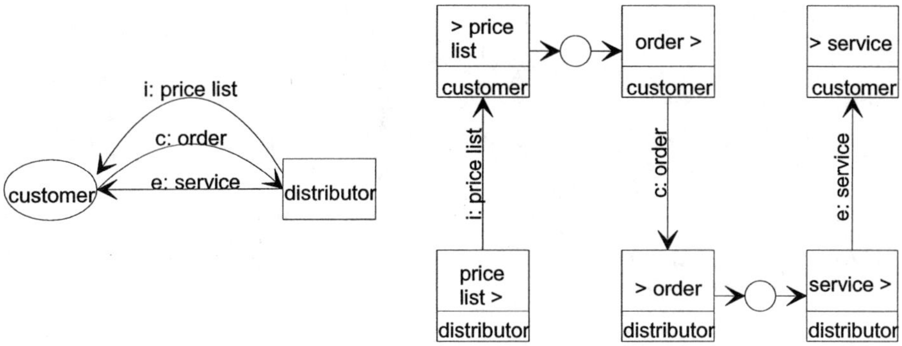

Figure 7: Interaction schema (left) and task-event schema (right) of business process distribution (2nd level)

decomposed according to the negotiation principle into the sub-transactions *i: price list* (initiating), *c: order* (contracting), and *e: service* (enforcing transaction). The corresponding task-event schema is determined implicitly because the sub-transactions are executed in sequence (Figure 7). The tasks of each business object are connected by object-internal events. In the next step, the feedback control principle is applied to *distributor* to uncover the internal management of the business object. This leads to the sub-objects *sales* (management object) and *servicing system* (operational object) as well as the transactions *r: service order* (controlling transaction) and *f: service report* (feedback transaction). At the same time the transactions assigned to the parent object *distributor* are re-assigned to the new sub-objects. The *sales* sub-object deals with *price* list and *order*, the *servicing system* operates the *service transaction* (Figure 8).

Continuing the example, the final decomposition of the business process *distribution* uses the additional rules given above (Figure 9 and 10). Here, the *servicing system* and the *service* transaction are decomposed to find business objects and transactions which operate homogeneous goods or services. First, the *e: service* transaction is decomposed into the sequence *e: delivery* and *e: cash up*. The *cash up* transaction is decomposed again according to the negotiation principle into the sequence *c: invoice* and *e: payment*. The initiating transaction is omitted because the business objects already know each other. The contract of the *invoice* transaction refers to amount and date of payment, not to the obligation to pay in principle which is part of the transaction *c: order*.

As a result of this refinement, some other decomposition are necessary. The business object *servicing system* is decomposed into *store* and *finances*, responsible for goods and payments respectively. The transaction *r: service order* is decomposed into the parallel transactions *r: delivery order* and *r: debit*. And likewise the transaction *f: service report* is decomposed into *f:*

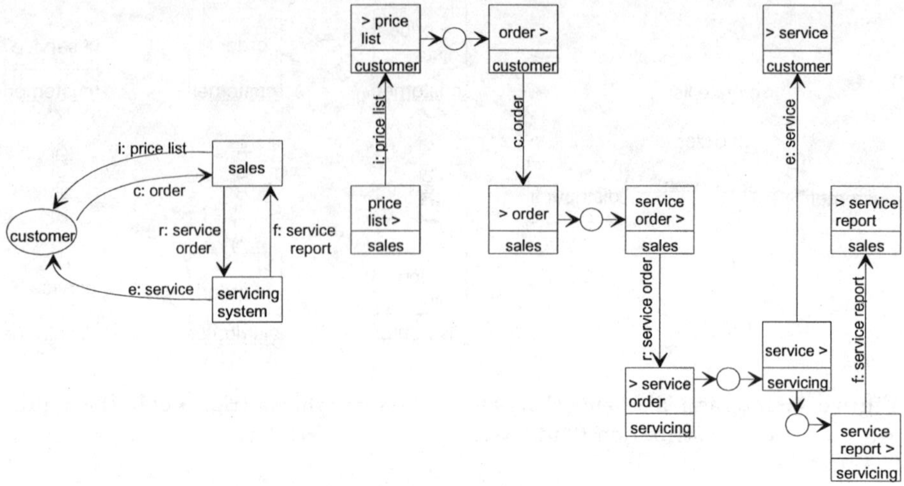

Figure 8: Interaction schema (left) and task-event schema (right) of business process distribution (3rd level)

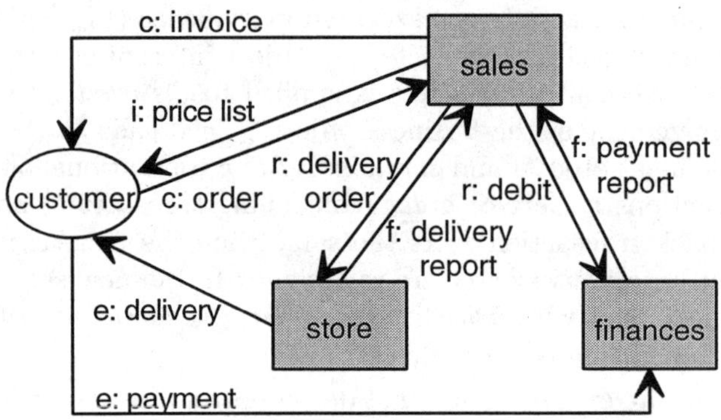

Figure 9: Interaction schema of business process distribution (4th level)

delivery report and *f: payment report.*

5 Linking Business Application Systems to Business Process Models

As outlined in Section 3, personnel and business application systems are resources to carry out business processes. In addition to the language for business process modeling, the SOM methodology provides a concept for explicitly linking business application systems to business process models. To introduce this concept, we investigate the automation of business processes

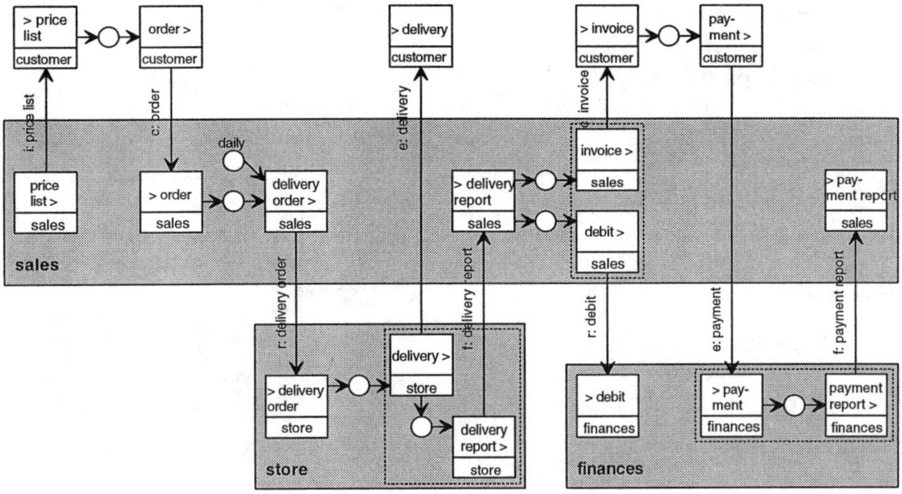

Figure 10: Task-event schema of business process distribution (4th level)

using business application systems, define a meta model for the domain-specific specification of business application systems and discuss the impact of this concept on the architecture of business application systems.

5.1 Automation of Business Processes

The automation of a business process is determined by the automation of tasks and transactions. An information processing task is fully-automated, if it is carried out completely by an application system, it is non-automated if it is carried out by a person, and it is partly-automated if it is carried out by both a person and an application system cooperating [FS98].

Similar considerations hold for the automation of transactions within information systems. A transaction is automated if it is performed by an electronic communication system and it is non-automated if it is performed e.g. paper-based or orally.

Prior to defining the degree of automation, a task or a transaction have to be investigated if they are suitable for automation. A task is suitable for automation if its states and operations can be handled by a computer system. A transaction is suitable for automation if message passing and protocol handling can be done by an electronic communication system.

The relationship between business process model and business application systems is based exactly on the concept of automation of tasks and transactions. The interaction schema of a business process model is convenient to record the extent of both the achievable and the achieved degree of automation. Figure 11 (left) shows degrees of automation of tasks and transactions (see also [Kru97]) and applies them to the business object *sales* of the business

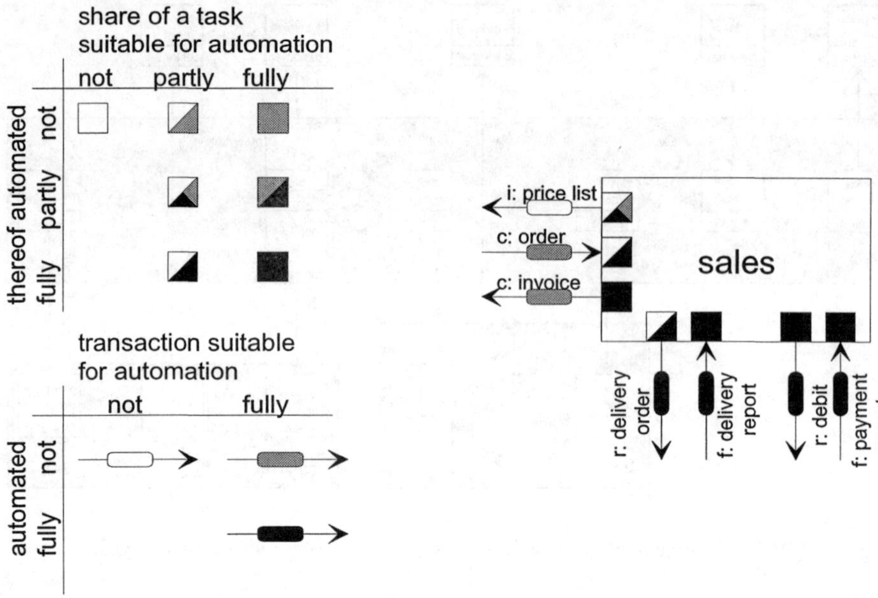

Figure 11: Automation of tasks and transactions of the sales business object

process *distribution* (Figure 11 right).

5.2 Meta Model for Specifications of Business Application Systems

The SOM methodology uses an object-oriented approach for the domain-specific specification of business application systems. The corresponding meta model is shown in Figure 12. The notion of *class* follows the general understanding of object-orientation. Classes have *attributes* and *operators* and they are connected by binary *relationships*. Relationships are either *is_a*, *interacts_with*, or *is_part_of* relationships. *Interacts_with* relationships denote channels for message passing between two classes, *is_a* relationships are used to model the specialization of a class using inheritance, and *is_part_of* relationships allow the specification of the component classes of a complex class.

To specify the linkage of business application systems to business process models the meta model in Figure 12 is related to the meta model in Figure 2. The relationships represented as dashed lines connect notions of a business process model to notions of a specification of an application system. A business object is connected to an *object-specific* class. A *good/service*, *business transaction*, or *task* is connected to a *service-specific*, *transaction-specific*, or *task- specific* class respectively as well as some *interacts_with* relationships. *Object-specific*, *service-specific*, and *transaction-specific* classes together with

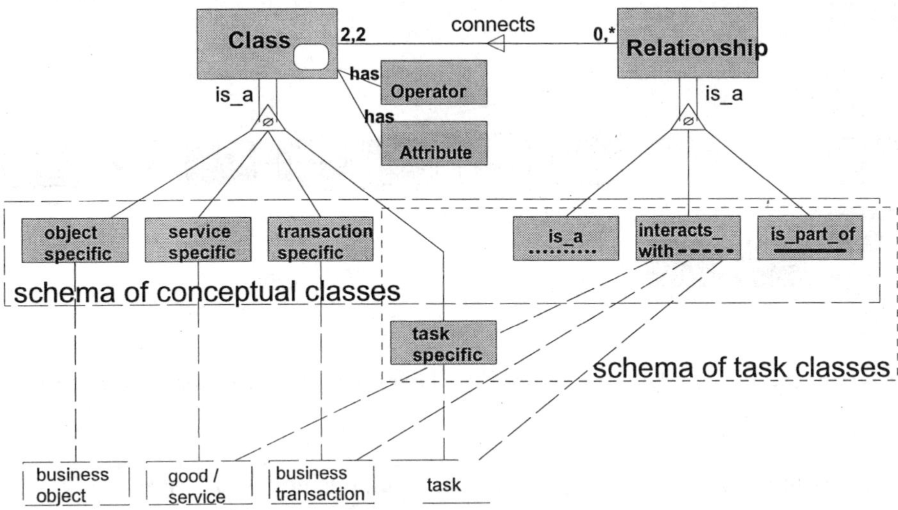

Figure 12: Meta Model of Business Application Systems

their relationships are arranged to the schema of conceptual classes. *Task-specific* (*task class* in short) together with their relationships belong to the schema of task classes. *Is_a* relationships and *is_part_of* relationships cannot be linked directly to a business process model. They have to be included during the further specification of the schema of conceptual classes or the schema of task classes.

5.3 Architecture of Business Application Systems

The way of linking a business application system to a business process model following the SOM methodology has impact on the architecture of business application systems. Again we concentrate on domain-specific aspects and omit details of design and implementation.

The SOM methodology leads to (1) strictly object-oriented, (2) distributed, (3) object-integrated, and (4) evolutionary adaptable specifications of business application systems [FS96]:

1. The domain-specific specifications of the schema of conceptual classes and of the schema of task classes are strictly object-oriented. Conceptual classes encapsulate (a) the states of the (automated) tasks of a business object as well as the states of the corresponding transactions and goods/services, and (b) the operations defined directly and exclusively on these states. Using the linkage of business process models and specifications of business application systems in Figure 12, the initial structure of the schema of conceptual classes can be derived from the most detailed level of the interaction schema in conjunction with the

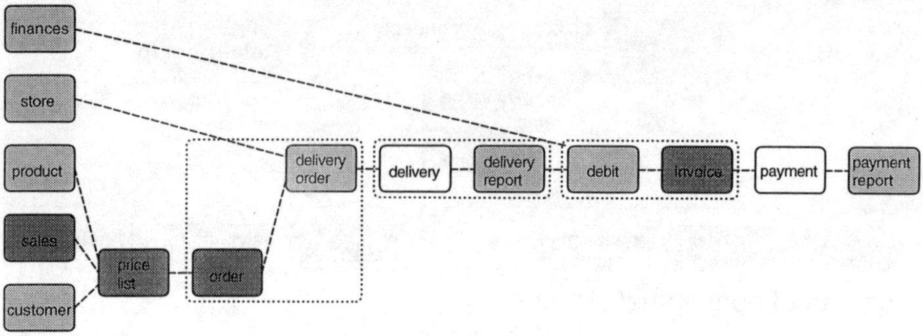

Figure 13: Initial schema of conceptual classes of the business application system sales

task-event schema of the corresponding business process model.

Figure 13 shows the initial schema of conceptual classes derived from the business process model in Figures 9 and 10. The classes at the left side correspond to the business objects and the *product.* The class *price list* is derived from the corresponding transaction, connecting *sales* and *customer* with reference to *product.* The same way the other classes are derived from transactions. Figure 13 refers to the complete *distribution* process. The shaded classes belong to the *sales* application system. Dark shaded classes belong exclusively to the *sales* application system, light shaded classes are shared with other application systems.

Task classes coordinate the cooperation of conceptual classes and/or other task classes when executing a task automated fully or partly. In other words, task classes specify the work-flow within a business application system. The initial structure of the schema of task classes is almost identical to the most detailed level of the task-event schema of the corresponding business process model. Tasks lead to task classes, internal events and transactions lead to *interacts_with* relationships. Therefore Figure 10 illustrates the schema of task classes too. The shaded areas delimit the schema of task classes for the *sales* business application system as well as for *store* and *finances.*

2. A distributed system is an integrated system which pursues a set of joint goals. It consists of multiple autonomous components which cooperate in pursuing the goals. There is no need for a component which has global control of the system [Ens78]. Starting with a business process model with business objects loosely coupled by business transactions, the SOM methodology leads to a specification of distributed business application systems in a very natural way. Initially, each conceptual class and each task class derived from a business process model is an autonomous component. During the further specification process

classes may be merged due to domain-specific reasons. For instance in Figure 13 *debit* and *invoice* are merged to reduce redundancy of attributes, in Figure 12 *invoice>* and *debit>* are merged to avoid sources of functional inconsistency.

3. The most common way to integrate application systems is data integration. Several application systems share a common database, the functions of the application systems operate on this database via external views. Although this kind of integration preserves consistency and avoids redundancy of data, it is not sufficient to support flexibility and evolution of application systems. The SOM methodology completes the concept of data integration by the concept of object integration [Fer92, FS98]. This concept supports distributed application systems consisting of autonomous and loosely coupled sub-systems which themselves may be internally data integrated. To achieve consistency of the application system as a whole, the sub-systems exchange messages according to detailed communication protocols. These protocols are derived from the transaction-oriented coordination of business objects as specified in the business process models.

4. The SOM methodology uses similar structures of distributed systems at the business process model layer and the business application systems layer [FS96]. A balanced and synchronized development of business process models and business application systems allows a simultaneous evolution of both layers during their life cycle [FS97]. There is a strong need that local changes in the business process model should only effect local changes in the business application systems. Both features, distributed systems at the two layers and the synchronized evolution, show that the business process model of a business system proves to be the backbone of a widespread architecture of business application systems.

6 Related Work

In literature and practice, there are several approaches to business process modeling. The approaches take different perspectives on a business system and specify models based on different views. The differences will be illustrated exemplary at the modeling languages IDEF and CIMOSA.

IDEF (Integration Definition) is a family of languages which evolved since the 1970's adapting to different modeling methods [MM98]. Applied to business systems, it basically covers the universe of discourse which is supported by an application system. Personal actors of a business system are not subject of these languages. With respect to the SOM enterprise architecture the IDEF languages refer to the model layers of business process model and specification of business application systems. They use traditional views on functions, data, and processes to specify structure and behavior of a system. The first language IDEF0 is based on the method Structured Analysis and Design Technique (SADT). It helps to specify the functions of the universe of discourse hierarchically. IDEF1X is suitable for modeling database schemes and IDEF3 is aimed at processes. IDEF4 refers to software design. IDEF5 as the end of the chain supports the construction of enterprise ontologies. It comes closest to the requests taken up for business process modeling within the SOM methodology. The IDEF languages viewing functions, data, and processes fail to integrate the three views within a single object-oriented concept.

Another approach for modeling of business processes and business application systems corresponding to the model layers 2 and 3 of the SOM enterprise architecture are the CIMOSA languages [Ver98]. CIMOSA is an open system architecture for enterprise integration in manufacturing. Like the IDEF family the CIMOSA modeling languages also use views on functions, data, and processes to specify structure and behavior of a system. They supplement views on resources and organizational aspects. There are different types of flows within a system of business processes i.e. control flows defined as workflows, material flows and information flows. This approach also fails to integrate the views within an object oriented concept.

IDEF and CIMOSA views a business process as a sequence of activities (also called steps, process elements, functions), which are tied together by joint marks and which have to be equipped with resources [FS93, VB96]. From the viewpoint of the SOM methodology, IDEF and CIMOSA describe the behavior of a business system. In contrast, the SOM methodology specifies structure and behavior of a business system. The specification of structure consists of business objects and transactions and refers to the handling of goods and services. The coordination of the business objects involved in the handling of goods and services is specified explicitly.

7 Summary and Outlook

The previous sections give a brief introduction to the SOM methodology for business systems modeling. A comprehensive enterprise model consists of sub-models for each layer of the enterprise architecture (Figure 1). The sub-models are balanced carefully within the architectural framework. It is not necessary to start top down with the enterprise plan, followed by the business process model and ending with the specification of business application systems. The starting point depends on the goals pursued in the specific project.

More and more, enterprise models prove to be indispensable for business engineering, information management, and organization. Enterprise models following the SOM methodology show several characteristics which support the management of large enterprise models: (a) several model layers, each focusing on specific characteristics of a business system, (b) definition of views on each model layer, outside and inside perspectives, (c) different levels of abstraction and decomposition within a single model, and (d) notions with precise semantics which are arranged to meta models. Compared to other approaches of enterprise-wide modeling, e.g. enterprise-wide data modeling, a comprehensive model of a business system offers advantages and is more likely to be handled successfully.

There is a lot of research around the kernel of the SOM methodology which cannot be shown in this contribution due to limitation of space. These features include management of complexity (i.e. decomposition of large business process models into models of main and service processes), reuse of model components (using patterns, reference models, application objects), tool support (for modeling, reporting, business process management, information management, work-flow management) [FS+94], an in depth consideration of distributed business processes and distributed business application systems [FS96] as well as first findings on virtual business processes [FS97].

References

[Bah92] Bahrami, H., The Emerging Flexible Organization: Perspectives from Silicon Valley, in: California Management Review, Summer 1992, 33-52

[Bee81] Beer, S., The Brain of the Firm, 2nd Edition, Wiley, Chichester, 1981

[Ens78] Enslow, P. H., What is a 'Distributed' Data Processing System? in: IEEE Computer, Vol. 11, No. 1, January 1978, 13-21

[Fer92] Ferstl, O. K., Integrationskonzepte betrieblicher Anwendungssysteme, Fachbericht Informatik 1/92, Universität Koblenz-Landau, 1992

[FS90] Ferstl, O. K., Sinz, E. J., Objektmodellierung betrieblicher Informationssysteme im Semantischen Objektmodell (SOM), in: Wirtschaftsinformatik 32 (6), 1990, 566-581

[FS91] Ferstl, O. K., Sinz, E. J., Ein Vorgehensmodell zur Objektmodellierung betrieblicher Informationssysteme im Semantischen Objektmodell (SOM), in: Wirtschaftsinformatik 33 (6), 1991, 477-491

[FS93] Ferstl, O. K., Sinz, E. J., Geschäftsprozeßmodellierung, in: Wirtschaftsinformatik 35 (6), 1993, 589-592

[FS98] Ferstl, O. K., Sinz, E. J., Grundlagen der Wirtschaftsinformatik, Band 1, 3. Auflage, Oldenbourg, München 1998

[FS95] Ferstl, O. K., Sinz, E. J., Der Ansatz des Semantischen Objektmodells (SOM) zur Modellierung von Geschäftsprozessen, in: Wirtschaftsinformatik 37 (3), 1995, 209-220

[FS+94] Ferstl, O. K., Sinz, E. J., Amberg, M., Hagemann, U., Malischewski,

C., Tool-Based Business Process Modeling Using the SOM Approach, in: B. Wolfinger (ed.), Innovationen bei Rechen- und Kommunikationssystemen, 24. GI-Jahrestagung im Rahmen des 13th World Computer Congress, IFIP Congress '94, Hamburg, Springer, Berlin, 1994

[FS96] Ferstl, O. K., Sinz, E. J., Multi-Layered Development of Business Process Models and Distributed Business Application Systems - An Object-Oriented Approach, in: W. König, K. Kurbel, P. Mertens, D. Premar (eds.), Distributed Information Systems in Business, Springer, Berlin 1996, 159-179

[FS97] Ferstl, O. K., Sinz, E. J., Flexible Organizations Through Object-Oriented and Transaction-oriented Information Systems, in: H. Krallmann (ed.), Wirtschaftsinformatik '97, Internationale Geschäftstätigkeit auf der Basis flexibler Organisationsstrukturen und leistungsfähiger Informationssysteme, Physica-Verlag, Heidelberg 1997, 393-411

[Kru97] Krumbiegel, J., Integrale Gestaltung von Geschäftsprozessen und Anwendungssystemen in Dienstleistungsbetrieben, Deutscher Universitätsverlag, Wiesbaden 1997

[MM98] Menzel, Ch., Mayer, R. J., The IDEF Family of Languages, in: P. Bernus, K. Mertins, G. Schmidt (eds.), Handbook on Architectures of Information Systems, this volume, 1998

[Sin97] Sinz, E. J., Architektur betrieblicher Informationssysteme, in: P. Rechenberg, G. Pomberger (eds.), Informatik-Handbuch, Hanser-Verlag, München, 1997, 875-887

[Ver98] Vernadat, F. B., The CIMOSA Languages, in: P. Bernus, K. Mertins, G. Schmidt (eds.), Handbook on Architectures of Information Systems, this volume, 1998

[VB96] G. Vossen, J. Becker (eds.), Geschäftsprozeßmodellierung und Workflow-Management, International Thomson Publishing, Bonn, 1996

CHAPTER 16

Workflow Languages

Mathias Weske, Gottfried Vossen

We survey the requirements, concepts, and usage patterns of workflow languages which are used in today's commercial or prototypical workflow management systems. After briefly reviewing workflow application development processes, basic notions of workflow modeling and execution and their relevant properties are introduced. A coarse classification of workflow languages is presented, and the main features of common workflow languages are described in the context of a sample application process.

1 Introduction

Workflow management aims at modeling and controlling the execution of processes in business, scientific, or even engineering applications. It has gained increasing attention in recent years, since it allows to combine a *data-oriented* view on applications, which is the traditional one for an information system, with a *process-oriented* one in which activities and their occurrence over time are modeled and supported properly [VB96, GHS95]. Workflow management combines influences from a variety of disciplines, including cooperative information systems, computer-supported cooperative work, groupware systems, or active databases. Its major application area has so far been in the business field; as the *modeling* of business processes has become a strategic goal in many enterprises, a further step is to *optimize* or to *reengineer* them, with the goal of automation in mind. Once the modeling and specification of business processes has been completed, they can be verified, optimized, and finally brought onto a workflow management system. It is here where *languages* for describing or specifying workflows, or *workflow languages* for short, enter the picture. These languages will be discussed in what follows.

Generally, workflow languages aim at capturing workflow-relevant information of application processes with the aim of their controlled execution by a workflow management system [RS95, GHS95, She96]. The information involved in workflow management is heterogeneous and covers multiple aspects, ranging from the specification of process structures to organizational modeling and the specification of application programs and their respective execution environments. We here survey the requirements, concepts, and usage patterns of workflow languages which are used in today's commercial or prototypical workflow management systems. To embed workflow languages in the context of their purpose and usage, workflow application development processes are reviewed, and a simple application process is described which serves as our running example.

Workflow languages are yet another species of languages for human-computer interaction. In contrast to general-purpose programming languages, workflow languages are highly domain specific, i.e., they are tailored towards the specific needs of workflow applications. Moreover, computational completeness is not an issue in a workflow language, since they are not used to describe computations. While control structures play an important role in both programming languages and in workflow languages, low-level constructs are missing in workflow languages. On the other hand, workflow languages support constructs to integrate external applications, and to describe and organize their interaction, cooperation, and communication relationships. They are hence similar in nature to software specification languages, which also have to be able to describe control flow as well as data flow between modules or components. Since workflow models are used as an information basis for the modeling and optimization of application processes, it should be obvious that graphical languages play an important role.

There are numerous approaches to model related and potentially concurrent activities, which stem from different domains. A set of rigorous mathematically founded approaches have been developed in the area of distributed computing, among which process algebras play a key role, namely to formally define concurrently executing processes and their communication behavior. Important approaches are Milner's CCS [Mil80] and Hoare's CSP [Hoa85]. These approaches focus mainly on formal properties of distributed computations; since technical and organizational aspects, which are important for workflow languages, cannot be represented in these calculi, they are not discussed in further detail here.

The organization of the remainder is as follows: In Section 2 basic concepts and notions of workflow modeling are presented, and an example is provided which will serve as our running example. Since process modeling languages have been discussed elsewhere in this book, we focus on the specific aspects workflow languages have to cover. Section 3 focuses on categories of workflow languages. For each category we choose a typical language, and we show how it can be used to model the sample application process as a workflow. A summary and concluding remarks complete our survey.

Information Gathering
↓
Business Process Modeling
↓
Workflow Modeling
↓
Implementation, Verification, Execution

Figure 1: Workflow Application Development Process

2 Workflow Modeling

Workflow management aims at modeling and controlling the execution of complex application processes in a variety of domains, including the traditional business domain [LA94, GHS95, JB96] and the natural sciences [Ioa93, VW97]. Workflow models are representations of application processes to be used by workflow management systems for controlling the execution of workflows. Workflow languages are used to specify workflow models. Since workflow modeling aims at mapping relevant information about application processes into workflow models, workflow languages need to have constructs for a variety of aspects, as explained below in Section 2.3.

2.1 Workflow Development Process

In general, workflow models capture the information of application processes which is relevant for the purpose of workflow management. Before workflow languages will be discussed, the general development process of workflow applications is described. While the workflow application development process differs from one project to the next, the following phases typically are involved.

The first phase of the workflow application development process, which generally shares a number of aspects and steps with a database design process or an information system development process, deals with gathering information, relevant for the application process under investigation (Figure 1). In this phase, empirical studies like interview techniques and available documentation is used. The techniques used in this phase are mostly informal. The activities of this phase are centered around the application, and technical issues are not considered.

The next phase involves *business process modeling*, in which the information previously gathered is used to specify business process models. In this phase semi-formal techniques are used, typically some simple form of Petri net formalism, often without exploiting their formal semantics. The main purpose of business process modeling is to provide a general and easy-to-read notation, which enables information system experts and domain experts to validate and optimize business process models, an activity called business process reengineering. The result of this phase is a business process model, which is used as a basis for the next phase.

The purpose of the subsequent *workflow modeling phase* is to enhance the business process model with information needed for the controlled execution of workflows by a workflow management system. In this phase workflow languages are used. Typically, different languages are used for business modeling and workflow modeling. Hence, business process models have to be translated into the constructs of a workflow language. Notice that there are languages that cover both phases, as discussed below. Besides the translation, information which is relevant for the controlled execution of workflows by a workflow management system is added to the model. On the other hand, information which is irrelevant for workflow executions is omitted from the business process model. Hence, workflow modeling abstracts from irrelevant information and adds relevant information, mainly of technical nature. For instance, in workflow models application programs used to perform workflow activities are specified, including their execution environment. The result of the workflow modeling phase is a workflow model, which is used by a workflow management system for controlling the execution of the workflow. We point out that the workflow development process can be iterated so that workflow execution data is used to improve business process models; it may also depend on the methods and tools used.

2.2 Sample Application Process

In order to keep the presentation of workflow languages concise and to provide a common basis to study and to compare different workflow languages, we now present an example of a business process from the area of credit processing in a banking environment. This example originates from the documentation of FlowMark, IBM's workflow management system [FM96]; when using the example with other workflow languages, it is modified according to the needs of the workflow language used.

Informally, the application process starts when a customer requests a credit from the bank. The customer does so by filing a credit request form and by sending it to the appropriate department in the bank. The information in the credit request form is transferred into the bank's computer system. After the validity of the data is checked, the next step involves an assessment of the risks involved in granting the credit request. Depending on the amount requested, checking activities of different complexity may be involved. We assume that the checking activity is performed by a financial expert, subject to the credit amount requested and the financial situation of the applicant. If the expert grants the credit, administrational activities to allocate the requested amount to the customer's account are launched. If it is not granted in this activity then a second, more advanced expert re-evaluates the case, possibly after getting hold of new information on the financial situation of the customer. Depending on his or her judgment, the credit is rejected or granted. In any case, the customer is informed of the decision.

While this description of a credit processing application simplifies real-world applications considerably, it provides a basis for a presentation of workflow aspects and of typical workflow languages. Notice a typical aspect of such informal descriptions, namely that errors and failures which may be encountered while the process is executed are not included. Indeed, a vastly open problem today is to specify exceptions as well as repair or compensating actions for possible errors and failures, or to build corresponding features into languages that allow the specification of normal activities in workflows.

2.3 Workflow Aspects

As discussed above and as indicated in the example, workflow modeling aims at specifying different aspects of the application process and of the technical and organizational environment in which the workflow will be executed. To provide modularity in workflow modeling and to refer to the different dimensions of workflow modeling explicitly, workflow aspects are described [JB96]. The description of the workflow aspects includes basic notions of workflow modeling and execution.

2.3.1 Functional Aspect

The functional aspect covers the functional decomposition of activities as present in application processes, i.e., it specifies which activities have to be executed within a workflow. To deal with the high complexity of application processes, the concept of nesting is used to describe the functional aspect of workflows. In particular, workflows are partitioned into complex and atomic workflows, where complex workflows are composed of a number of (complex or atomic) workflows. Due to their relative position, the components of a complex workflow are known as subworkflows. Hence, workflows typically have a tree structure, such that the root node of the tree represents the top-level (complex) workflow, the inner nodes represent other complex workflows, and the leaf nodes represent atomic activities. While different approaches to workflow modeling denote the entities of the functional aspect differently, we adopt the approach that activities generally are represented by workflows, which can be complex or atomic. Synonyms for complex workflow include process, complex activity, block; atomic workflows are also called (atomic) activities or steps.

In the sample application process, the functional aspect covers the functions performed during the process. When the credit is requested, a credit form is received by the bank. One function is entering the data from the credit request form into the system followed by searching for invalid or missing data. The functional aspect describes what has to be done during a workflow execution. It does not specify how it is done. In the sample workflow, the functional aspect does not define how the data entering and checking is done – this is covered by the operational aspect, discussed below. Constraints on the functions performed in a workflow are also not described in this aspect – these properties are defined in the behavioral aspect, discussed now.

2.3.2 Behavioral Aspect

In general, workflows consist of a set of interrelated activities. Hence, the controlled execution of a complex workflow by a workflow management system has to take into account interrelationships of the complex workflow's subworkflows. While the functional aspect does not cover the relative ordering of subworkflows, these issues are covered in the behavioral aspect. This aspect specifies under which conditions the subworkflows of a given complex workflow are executed during workflow executions. Important components of this aspect are control flow constraints, which represent the control structure of activities of the application process. When in the application process subworkflow j can only be started after subworkflow i has terminated then a control flow constraint can be used to model this relationship. When the workflow is started, the workflow management system makes sure that activity j is started only after i has terminated. There are other forms of interrelationships between subworkflows, covered by other concepts in the behavioral aspect, for instance start conditions and termination conditions. For each subworkflow, a start condition specifies the precondition of its execution. Hence, an activity is started during a particular workflow instance only if the start condition of that activity is evaluated to 'true'. The information specified in the behavioral aspect of workflow models is important for a workflow management system to control the execution of workflows. This aspect is covered by all workflow languages, and workflow management systems support mechanisms to guarantee that the interrelationships between workflows as defined in the behavioral aspect of workflow models are satisfied by all workflow instances.

In the sample workflow, the behavioral aspect specifies relationships between workflow activities. For instance, it specifies that entering credit form data is done before the checking for incorrect values, which in turn is performed before the risk is assessed and the decision on granting or rejecting the credit is taken. Another example of this aspect in our example is the branching of control flow depending on the amount requested. If the amount is smaller than a predefined value x then a quite simple checking procedure is applied. If the requested amount exceeds x then a more complex procedure is performed to either grant or reject the credit request. In general, the semantics of branches can be parallel, alternative, or it can be controlled by predicates which are evaluated at execution time of the workflow. An example of the latter form is discussed above, which can be specified by $amount <= x$ and $amount > x$, respectively.

2.3.3 Informational Aspect

An important aspect of workflow languages is the modeling of workflow relevant application data. Modeling data is required to permit workflow management systems to control the transfer of workflow relevant data as generated or processed by workflow activities during workflow executions. In graph-based approaches, the informational aspect includes data flow between workflow activities. In particular, each activity is assigned a set of input and a set of output parameters. On its start, an activity reads its input parameters, and on its termination it writes values it generated into its output parameters. These values can be used by follow-up activities in the workflow as input data. This transfer of data between workflow activities is known as data flow. By providing graphic language constructs to represent data flow between activities, the informational aspect can be visualized and used to validate and optimize application processes. While the basic principle of the informational aspect is straightforward, there are many technical issues to solvc, for instance different data formats of a given data flow, which may require the use of filters to allow seamless integration of different tools using different data formats. To this end, it is desirable that data as specified in a data flow is strongly typed. Clearly, this would require a typing scheme for data which occurs as parameters of workflow activities. In doing so, potential typing incompatibilities can be detected in the workflow modeling phase.

The informational aspect in the sample workflow describes the data types involved, for instance data types for customer data, credit forms and risk assessments. Besides the specification of the data types, data flow constraints between activities of a workflow are also described in the informational aspect. Data flow constraints in the sample workflow occur between the activity in which the credit form is entered into the system and follow-up activities, which use this information to decide on granting or rejecting the credit request. In addition, there is a data flow from the decision taking activity to the activity in which the customer is informed of the result of his or her credit request.

2.3.4 Organizational Aspect

Workflows are executed in complex organizational and technical environments, and a major goal of workflow management is enhancing the efficiency of application processes by assigning work to persons or software systems as specified by workflow models. To reach this goal, a workflow management system has to be provided with information on the organization and on the technical environment in which the workflows will be executed. In general, atomic workflows can be either automatic or manual. Manual atomic workflows are executed by persons who may use application programs to do so; automatic atomic workflows are executed by software systems without human involvement. Since a strict assignment of workflow activities to persons is not feasible in most cases, the role concept is used. A role is a predicate on the structure of an organization in which the workflow is executed. When an activity is about to start, the system uses predefined role information to select one or more persons which are permitted, competent and available to perform the requested activity. The process of selecting one or more persons to perform a workflow activity is known as role resolution. Depending on the scope of workflow management systems, the role concept has different complexity. While some systems support a simple role concept others provide additional features for substitution of persons or they take into account the overall structure of the organization to select persons to perform activities during workflow executions.

People involved in the execution of the sample workflow are part of the bank's credit department. Activities of the sample workflow are scheduled to persons in the department according to their positions, which are specified by roles. Clerk, financial expert, and credit expert are sample roles. While the data entering is done by clerks, the decision on granting requested credits is done by financial experts, capable of assessing the risks and of deciding on the credit, provided the requested amount is below a predefined margin. The assignment of workflow activities to persons is done by role resolution, for example the data entering is done by a clerk while the assess credit activity is performed by a financial expert. The role concept can be enhanced to allow context sensitive features, e.g., a person is selected to perform an activity of a credit workflow which the person previously has decided on. In this case, workflow execution data is used to allow more complex role resolution.

2.3.5 Operational Aspect

The integration of existing tools and application programs into workflow applications is an important feature of workflow management systems. The information required is specified in the operational aspect. The operational aspect covers mainly technical issues, like the invocation environment of application programs (including host and directory information of the executable program), the definition of the input and output parameters of the application program and their mapping to input and output parameters of workflow activities. As described above, persons are selected by role resolution to perform workflow activities. When a person chooses to perform an activity then the defined application program is started, and the input data as specified in the workflow model is transferred to that application program. When the person completes that activity, the output data generated by that activity is collected in the output parameters of the activity to be transferred by the workflow management system to the next workflow activity, as specified in the respective workflow model. Notice that during business modeling, no information on the operational part is (and needs to be) present. Business process modeling aims at mapping high level and domain specific features of the application process; the technical details – the main components of the operational aspect – are taken into account in the workflow modeling phase.

In the banking example, different information systems are used to perform different tasks. Entering customer and credit request data by clerks is typically done by forms-based software systems as front-ends of an integrated data repository. The activities of assessing the risk of a credit may involve other information systems, some of which may reside remotely. In this case, the execution environment includes detailed information which allows the workflow management system to invoke the desired applications in the respective sites, using different kinds of middleware technology.

2.3.6 Flexibility Aspect

Recently, the need to enhance the flexibility of workflow applications arose in different application areas [EKR95, VW97, RD98]. Starting from applications in non-traditional domains like the natural sciences or hospital environments, flexibility also became an issue in business applications. Providing flexibility to workflow applications is based on the understanding that during workflow modeling not all aspects of the application process can be specified completely. There may be unforeseen situations during workflow executions, which require flexible reactions by the user or administrator of the system. Hence, additional features to model workflows and additional functionality to support the functionality is required by workflow management systems to deal with flexibility issues. We believe that the future success of workflow management systems to a large extent depends on the way workflow model changes or changes to the organizational or technical environment are supported in a user-friendly way. There are different forms of flexibility, ranging from the change of role information and application program information to the change in the functional and behavioral aspects of workflows. Adding an activity to a complex workflow while the workflow executes corresponds to a dynamic change in the functional aspect; changing the control structure of subworkflows of a given workflow (e.g., parallel execution of workflow activities, originally defined to be executed sequentially) corresponds to the change in the behavioral aspect. Providing user intervention operations to allow uses to skip, stop or repeat subworkflows is another form of flexibility in the behavioral aspect. A change of role information and of application program information changes the organizational and operational aspects, respectively. We remark that supporting flexibility has to be supported by the workflow language and also by the workflow management system, supporting the respective functionality. For instance, workflow languages should allow to specify which activities can be skipped or repeated, and how data issues due to deleting workflow activities which would generate required data are solved.

Although the general structure of the sample credit request workflow is static, numerous unforeseen events may occur during workflow executions, which require flexible reactions. For instance, assume while a credit request is processed, the applicant comes into an inheritance. This changes the financial situation of the applicant considerably, which may require a re-evaluation of the credit request. On the side of the customer, the inheritance may lead to canceling the credit request. In this case, the workflow has to be canceled, and steps already executed on its behalf have to be undone, for instance the allocation of funds to the customer. Simpler forms of flexibility occur when it comes to changes in role information or in application programs used to process workflow activities.

3 Workflow Languages

In general, workflow languages can be classified according to their underlying methodologies and underlying meta models. A meta model describes the constructs and their relationships of workflow models of particular workflow languages. An important class of workflow languages are graph-based languages, which allow the specification of workflows using different forms of directed graphs. While the functional and behavioral aspects can be specified using graph notation, the informational and operational aspects require additional specifications, like data types of transferred data objects or information on the execution environment of application programs. This information can be provided textually, often supported by workflow management systems using forms interfaces. Hence, the categories discussed below do not indicate that all workflow aspects are specified using the respective notation. The second category of workflow languages use the Petri nets approach to specify workflow models. Petri nets have widely been used to specify the behavior of a dynamic system with a fixed structure.

Besides these classes of workflow languages, script languages are widely used. Often, these languages are closely related to workflow management system development. Workflow languages can also have multiple representations. For instance, there may be a graphical language for the specification of workflow models, which is translated into a script language, to be processed by a workflow management system. An example of this strategy is provided in the remainder of this section. State and activity charts, originally developed to model reactive systems, are used to model workflows. We discuss this approach briefly.

Due to space limitations, we restrict ourselves to workflow languages which are currently used in workflow management systems, commercially available or prototypical. In particular, graph-based languages, net-based languages and script language approaches are considered in some depth; the state and activity chart approach is discussed briefly. Further approaches to workflow languages, like speech act theory are not widely used in workflow management systems and are therefore not discussed here.

3.1 Graph-Based Languages

Graph-based languages allow to specify workflow activities, their hierarchical relationships and their data flow and control flow constraints using directed graphs. These graphs are enhanced to cover the workflow aspects presented above. Workflow graphs are nested, such that each node can be refined into a subgraph, known as a subworkflow. In addition, there are two forms of directed edges, i.e., control flow edges and data flow edges. Control flow edges belong to the behavioral aspect, while data flow edges belong to the informational aspect. In particular, a control flow edge $i \rightarrow j$ specifies that activity j can start only after activity i has terminated. Data flow edges specify data dependencies between workflow activities; if activity i generates data which is required as input to activity j then there is a data flow edge connecting these activities. Explicit modeling of data flow between workflow activities is an important means to describe interrelationships between workflow activities due to the generation and use of data.

3.1.1 Workflow Process Definition Language

The Workflow Management Coalition (WfMC) is a consortium of workflow vendors, users and researchers, aiming at promoting the use of workflow technology in business organizations [WMC96a]. By specifying a set of interfaces of workflow management systems, the WfMC builds a framework to enhance the interoperability of workflow systems of different vendors. In their effort, the WfMC loosely specifies a workflow language which is based on graphs. Since the language has to be supported by the systems the WfMC members develop and use, the language is described in an abstract way using graph notation. Activities are represented by nodes; control flow is defined by explicit control flow constructs, for instance (AND, OR, XOR) split and the respective join nodes [WMC96b]. However, the WfMC is focused primarily on technical issues of workflow system interoperability. Instead of defining a complete workflow language which is mandatory for all workflow system vendors which are members in the coalition, it adopts the strategy that different workflow products are free to use different workflow languages.

3.1.2 FlowMark Workflow Language

One of the first workflow management systems that reached the market is IBM's FlowMark. This paragraph discusses the graphical workflow language used in FlowMark, while its textual representation (FlowMark Definition Language, FDL) is sketched below. To describe its workflow language, the main components of the FlowMark workflow meta model have to be described [LA94, FM96]. The main entity of the FlowMark workflow meta model is the activity, which can either be complex or atomic. Complex activities are called processes, while atomic activities are called program activities, typically implemented by application programs. Processes are composed of a number of activities with accompanying control flow and data flow constraints. A set of activities can be grouped using the block construct. The activities in a block are executed repeatedly until an end condition of the block signals its termination. With regard to the informational aspect, each activity has an input container and an output container, consisting of a set of input parameters and output parameters, respectively. In FlowMark, data flow is specified by connecting an output parameter of an activity i to an input parameter of an activity j. This data flow is permitted only if there is a path of control flow edges from i to j. Control flow is defined by control flow edges. Each control flow edge is assigned a transition condition, which is a predicate to be evaluated at runtime. When an activity terminates, the transition conditions of all outgoing control flow edges of that activity are evaluated. Depending on the value, the control flow edge is fired with either 'true' or 'false'. The start of activities is governed by start conditions. In general, start conditions of an activity can be evaluated if and only if all incoming control flow edges have been fired. When a start condition evaluates to 'true', the respective activity can be launched. To guarantee that control flow edges fired with 'false' do not hamper the start of workflow activities, a technique called *dead-path-elimination* is performed [LA94]. Workflow models in FlowMark are generally acyclic; loops can be modeled using the block construct, as discussed above.

The sample workflow can be specified graphically in the FlowMark system as shown in Figure 2. Activities are represented by nodes; data flow is represented by dotted lines, and solid lines are control flow edges. Control flow edges are labeled with transition conditions, which are evaluated on termination of the source node of the respective control flow edge. For instance, to model that a credit request can be granted if less than 100 K$ is requested and if the risk factor determined by the AssessRisk activity is low, the transition condition from the AssessRisk to the AcceptCredit activity in Figure 2 is labeled "CreditAmount < 100000 AND RiskFactor="L"". Notice that the AssessRisk activity has CreditAmount and RiskFactor as output parameters. In an alternative form of data flow, a complex workflow can transfer data to its subworkflows. Analogously, data can be transferred from subworkflows to their respective superworkflows. In these cases, the data flow is vertical rather than horizontal (data flow between subworkflows of a common superworkflow is called horizontal data flow). A fragment of a textual representation of the sample workflow using FDL is discussed shortly.

3.1.3 WASA

The workflow language in the WASA project [VW97] on flexible workflow management is based on the FlowMark workflow language. Since the WASA project aims at enhancing the flexibility of workflow management systems, the language supports the flexibility aspect, discussed above [VW97, Wes98]. For instance, for each workflow model the user may specify if it can be skipped, stopped or repeated during particular workflow executions. Skipping workflow activities may lead to missing data. Hence, the workflow language specifies how these data issues are solved by providing the appropriate language constructs. In addition to enhancing the workflow language w.r.t. flexibility, the workflow management system has to support flexibility operations, e.g., dynamic modeling operations and user intervention operations. With dynamic modeling operations, workflow models of running workflow instances can be changed to reflect changes in the environment of the process. Changes can apply to the changing workflow instance only, or changes may apply to all workflow instances of the changed workflow model. User intervention operations allow the user to perform changes to the control flow structure of the workflow for a particular workflow instance.

3.1.4 ADEPT

In the ADEPT framework, workflow models are specified as symmetric graphs with special workflow relevant nodes [RD97, RD98]. Branching nodes are explicitly marked as AND split, OR split, XOR split; these nodes are followed by the respective join nodes. Based on this framework, a complete and minimal set of change operations are specified to define the ADEPT$_{flex}$ framework. In this framework, change operations to the structure of running workflows can be performed by users in a controlled manner. For instance, enhancing a workflow model with an activity involves the embedding of the added activity into the workflow model. This is specified by defining a set of activities which have to be completed before the added activity can start and a set of

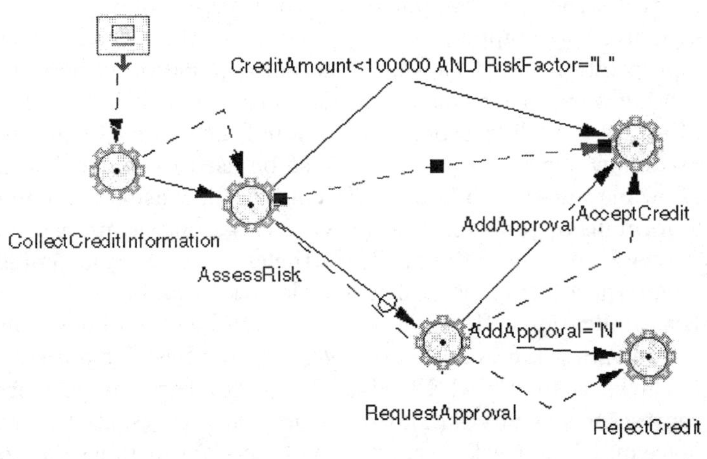

Figure 2: FlowMark: Sample Workflow Model

activities which can only be started after the added activity as terminated. The monitoring of data flow constraints between activities is also supported by the ADEPT$_{flex}$ framework.

3.2 Net-Based Languages

We now elaborate on Petri nets, which are specifically tailored towards the requirements of workflow modeling and execution.

3.2.1 FUNSOFT Nets

FUNSOFT nets are based on higher Petri nets and enhances them to incorporate different workflow aspects [Gru91]; FUNSOFT nets are structured as follows: The node set is partitioned into places and transitions. Each place may include one or more typed data objects. Workflow activities are represented by transitions. Controlling workflow instances is done by passing documents and information between activities. The traditional Petri net formalism is enhanced with special constructs, e.g., there is a special form of transitions to represent alternative execution paths, represented by a 'switch' transition.

The basic idea of this approach is the integration of different workflow aspects into a single formalism, namely FUNSOFT nets. This concept has implications on its usability. In particular, it allows to use a single formalism in different phases of the workflow application development process, i.e., FUNSOFT nets can be used in business process modeling, in workflow modeling and in workflow execution. These nets provide a graphical notation to model the control structure of application processes; organizational modeling is also supported by mapping role information to the net formalism. By providing appropriate means to specify external application programs to be used in the workflow executions, the operational aspect is also covered by this formalism. Besides modeling aspects, FUNSOFT nets can also be used as input for a workflow engine, i.e., they can also be used to control the execution of workflow instances. While the different workflow aspects are mapped into a single formalism, tools exist to provide views on certain aspects, for instance behavioral and operational. Nevertheless, the internal representation can become quite complex, which may lead to scalability problems in large workflow applications. However, the FUNSOFT net workflow language covers many interesting issues and is therefore chosen here for presentation.

Figure 3 shows a simplified FUNSOFT net for the sample workflow. Places are represented by circles, and transitions are represented by rectangles. Each place may hold a set of typed data objects, for instance data object *Credit Form*. 'Switch' transitions allow to model alternative executions. *Assess Risk* and *Request Approval* transitions have alternative outgoing edges to allow the explicit modeling of alternative branches, which are evaluated at runtime. The workflow starts with collecting the Collect Credit Info ac-

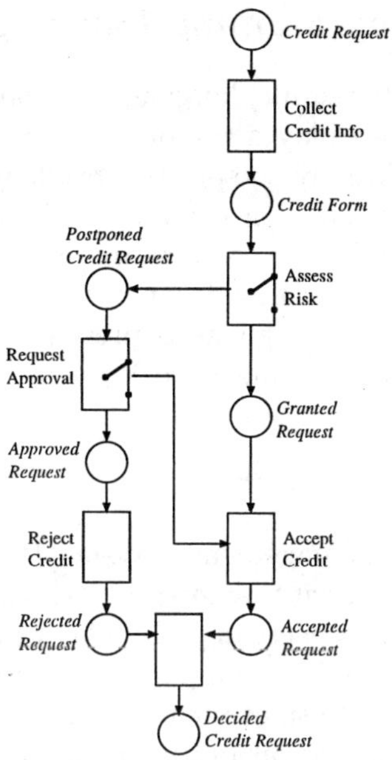

Figure 3: FUNSOFT Nets: Sample Workflow Model

tivity, which takes a Credit Request as an input document and generates a Credit Form as an output document. The Assess Risk activity can either grant the credit request, in which case the Granted Request is transferred to the Accept Credit activity or it can postpone the decision, in which case a Postponed Credit Request is transferred to the Request Approval activity. The workflow continues as specified in Figure 3.

3.2.2 Flow Nets

Ellis *et al* present the Flow Net formalism [EKR95]. Based on higher level Petri nets, their focus is on providing flexibility, namely by allowing the change of Flow Nets at runtime. Flow Nets do not provide formalisms for the operational aspect or organizational aspects like tool integration or role management, respectively. The focus of this approach is on the specification of the control flow structure of workflows as Flow Nets and their use to control the execution of workflows in the presence of dynamic modification operations. In particular, dynamic modification in Flow Nets is done by substituting subnets with other subnets, governed by rules for the correct substitution and embedding of subnets into the Flow Net, representing a workflow model.

3.3 Workflow Programming Languages

Workflow programming (or script) languages are often used in projects where system development issues play a major role. Workflow programming languages are either used directly to specify workflow models or they are used as an internal representation with the aim of the controlled execution by a workflow management system or to allow the import and export of workflow models. One approach of the first form is the Mobile approach – the second form of workflow script language is present in the FlowMark workflow management system, whose graphical workflow language was sketched above.

3.3.1 Mobile

In the Mobile workflow management system [JB96], workflow models are specified using the Mobile script language. The Mobile project aims at supporting different workflow aspects in a modular way. This goal is reflected in the Mobile workflow language by supporting constructs for the definition of different workflow aspects. Besides the focus on workflow aspects, the Mobile workflow language provides extensibility. In particular, based on a set of predefined control flow operators, the user can define new control flow constructs to support the specific requirements of particular workflow applications. For instance, constructs to execute a set of activities in any sequential order can be specified. From a system development point of view, each workflow aspect is covered by a server devoted to keeping track of workflows w.r.t. its particular aspect. The aim of this conceptual design and system architecture is to provide the system administrator with facilities and tools to use the aspects which are important for the particular workflow applications and to be able to extend the system with additional aspects as they are required.

An incomplete specification of the sample workflow using the Mobile workflow language is given in Table 1. Each workflow aspect is represented by language keywords and accompanying language constructs. Workflow models are specified in sections, delimited by `WORKFLOW_TYPE` and `END_WORKFLOW_TYPE` keywords. Analogously, the behavioral aspect is described in a section delimited by `CONTROL_FLOW` and `END_CONTROL_FLOW`. The set of constructs in this section includes sequential execution and branching, represented by the `sequence` and `ifthen` constructs, respectively. A complete workflow specification of the sample workflow can be found in [JBS97].

3.3.2 FlowMark Definition Language (FDL)

While the FlowMark system presents a graphical interface to the user, there is an internal workflow language which is used as an interface to import or export workflow models. Fragments of the FDL specification of the sample workflow are shown in Table 2.

```
WORKFLOW_TYPE CreditRequest (IN PersonInfo: CreditRequestor)
  /* definition of subworkflows */
  WORKFLOW_DATA CreditInfo: c
  END_WORKFLOW_DATA

  CONTROL_FLOW
    sequence (CollectCreditInfo,
      sequence(AssessRisk,
      ifthen(c.CreditAmount<100000 AND c.RiskFactor == ``L",
        AcceptCredit,
        sequence(RequestApproval, ifthen(c.AddApproval == ``Y",
          AcceptCredit, RejectCredit)))))
  END_CONTROL_FLOW

  DATA_FLOW
    CreditRequest.CreditRequestor -> ci.CreditRequestor;
    AssessRisk.out_ci -> AcceptCredit.in_ci;
  END_DATA_FLOW
  /* definition of organizational aspect */
END_WORKFLOW_TYPE
```

Table 1: Mobile workflow language

3.3.3 State and Activity Charts

The statechart formalism is an extension of finite state machines; it was developed by Harel [Har88] to specify the behavior of reactive technical systems. To describe such systems, statecharts specify potentially nested states and state transitions, while accompanying activity charts describe events that may trigger state transitions. Provided with a formal semantics and with a commercially available tool (Statemate [HP96]), statecharts are widely used in designing technical systems, like remote control systems or car radio systems; they are also popular in software engineering environments for system specification. One of the first workflow management systems to exploit the formalism is the Mentor project, where state and activity charts have been used to model workflows [WWWK96]. In terms of workflow aspects, statecharts describe the informational aspects while activity charts describe when state transitions are performed and which activities are launched when a particular state transition occurs. Hence, activity charts define the behavioral aspect. The separation of control flow and data flow in state and activity charts can lead to control structures which are not easily understandable by application domain experts. On the other hand, the statechart formalism provides techniques and tools to formally prove properties of statecharts. These properties are used in the Mentor project to formally prove that the execution of workflows in centralized and distributed environments are equivalent [Wod96].

```
STRUCTURE 'CreditInfo'
    'CreditRequestor':   'PersonInfo';
    'Address':           STRING;
    'RiskFactor':        STRING;
    'AddApproval':       STRING;
    'CreditAmount':      LONG;
END 'CreditInfo'

PROCESS 'CreditRequest' ('PersonInfo')
    PROGRAM_ACTIVITY 'AcceptCredit' ('CreditInfo')
        PROGRAM 'NAcceptCredit'
        DONE_BY STARTER_OF_ACTIVITY 'CollectCreditInformation'
    END 'AcceptCredit'

    PROGRAM_ACTIVITY 'AssessRisk' ('CreditInfo', 'CreditInfo')
        PROGRAM 'NAssessCreditRisk'
        DONE_BY STARTER_OF_ACTIVITY 'CollectCreditInformation'
    END 'AssessRisk'
    PROGRAM_ACTIVITY 'CollectCreditInformation'
        ('PersonInfo', 'CreditInfo')
    PROGRAM_ACTIVITY 'RejectCredit' ('CreditInfo')
    PROGRAM_ACTIVITY 'RequestApproval'
        ('CreditInfo', 'CreditInfo')

    CONTROL FROM 'CollectCreditInformation' TO 'AssessRisk'
    CONTROL FROM 'AssessRisk' TO 'AcceptCredit'
        WHEN 'CreditAmount<100000'
    CONTROL FROM 'RequestApproval' TO 'RejectCredit'
        WHEN 'AddApproval=''N"'
    CONTROL FROM 'RequestApproval' TO 'AcceptCredit'
        WHEN 'AddApproval=''Y"'
    CONTROL FROM 'AssessRisk' TO 'RequestApproval'
        OTHERWISE
END 'CreditRequest'
```

Table 2: FDL specification

4 Conclusions and Summary

We have discussed general design principles of workflow languages. Starting from general workflow notions, we have described a variety of aspects relevant to workflow management. A sample application process has been provided, and a set of workflow languages was described by presenting their underlying methodology; they have been used to model the sample application process as a workflow.

Due to space limitations, our selection of workflow languages is by no means exhaustive. We have tried to present the major categories of workflow management which are used in today's workflow management systems. For each category, a specific language has been presented in some detail using the sample workflow.

Current research issues in workflow languages focus on usability studies, on flexibility issues, and on correctness properties of workflow models. The latter may require workflow languages to represent additional properties which are not yet found in current languages. Today's workflow languages require a high degree of specialization on the user's side; in other words, workflow modeling has be done by experts who are well familiar with the respective workflow language used. This situation is similar as it was with early database design tools 20 years ago; with database systems becoming a mass product, their design tools have been simplified such that nowadays even non-experts can get a grasp on them. We expect a corresponding development for workflow languages, in particular since the details of an operational workflow are often in the heads of the end-users, so that it is crucial to have them participate more heavily in the description and specification phase of a workflow they are about to become involved in.

Regarding executions of workflows, current workflow languages are still rudimentary with respect to a distinction between transactional and non-transactional tasks, and with respect to recovery issues. One reason for this may be seen in the fact that the proper exploitation of transactional concepts in the context of workflows and their executions is still under heavy discussion [WS97]. On the other hand, there has been positive experience with using a transaction specification framework for describing execution aspects of workflow instances [SK97, Dog97]; it may therefore be expected that future workflow languages will also provide transactional capabilities. In addition, enhancing the flexibility in workflow management systems is a current research topic. It is expected that this topic will lead to new developments in workflow languages and in methods and tools to prove correctness properties of workflow models and workflow executions.

References

[Dog97] Dogac, A. *et al*, Design and Implementation of a Distributed Workflow Management Systems, METUFlow, in: Springer ASI NATO Series, NATO ASI Workshop, Istanbul, August 12–21, 1997

[EKR95] Ellis, C., Keddara, K., Rozenberg, G., Dynamic Change Within Workflow Systems, in: Proc. Conference on Organizational Computing Systems (COOCS), Milpitas, CA 1995, 10–22

[GHS95] Georgakopoulos, D., Hornick, M., Sheth, A., An Overview of Workflow Mangement: From Process Modeling to Workflow Automation Infrastructure, Distributed and Parallel Databases 3, 1995, 119–153

[Gru91] Gruhn, V., Validation and Verification of Software Process Models, Ph. D. Thesis, University of Dortmund, 1991, Available as Technical Report No. 394/1991, University of Dortmund, Germany

[Har88] Harel, D., On Visual Formalisms, Communications of the ACM 31, 1988, 514–530

[HP96] Harel, D., Politi, M., Modeling Reactive Systems with Statecharts, The Statemate Approach, Part No. D-1100-43, i-Logix Inc., Andover, MA 01810, 1996

[Hoa85] Hoare, C.A.R., Communicating Sequential Processes, Prentice-Hall, 1985

[FM96] IBM, IBM FlowMark: Modeling Workflow, Version 2 Release 2, Publ. No SH-19-8241-01, 1996

[Ioa93] Ioannidis, Y., (ed.), Special Issue on Scientific Databases, Data Engineering Bulletin 16 (1) 1993

[JBS97] Jablonski, S., Böhm, M., Schulze, W., (eds), Workflow Management: Development of Applications and Systems (in German), dpunkt-Verlag, 1997

[JB96] Jablonski, S., Bußler, C., Workflow-Management: Modeling Concepts, Architecture and Implementation, International Thomson Computer Press, 1996

[LA94] Leymann, F., Altenhuber, W., Managing Business Processes as an Information Resource, IBM Systems Journal 33, 1994, 326–347

[Mil80] Milner, R., A Calculus of Communicating Systems, Springer LNCS 92, 1980

[RD97] Reichert, M., Dadam, P., A Framework for Dynamic Changes in Workflow Management Systems, Proc. 8th International Workshop on Database and Expert Systems Applications 1997, Toulouse, IEEE Computer Society Press, 1997, 42–48

[RD98] Reichert, M., Dadam, P., ADEPT_{flex} – Supporting Dynamic Changes of Workflows Without Loosing Control, in: Journal of Intelligent Information Systems, Special Issue on Workflow and Process Management, Vol. 10, No. 2, 1998

[RS95] Rusinkiewicz, M., Sheth, A., Specification and Execution of Transactional Workflows, in: K. Won (ed.), Modern Database Systems: The Object Model, Interoperability, and Beyond, ACM Press, 1995, 592–620

[She96] Sheth, A., Georgakopoulos, D., Joosten, S.M.M., Rusinkiewicz, M., Scacchi, W., Wileden, J., Wolf, A., Report from the NSF Workshop on Workflow and Process Automation, in: Information Systems, Technical Report UGA-CS-TR-96-003, University of Georgia, Athens, GA, 1996

[SK97] Sheth, A., Kochut, K. J., Workflow Applications to Research Agenda: Scalable and Dynamic Work Coordination and Collaboration Systems, in: Springer ASI NATO Series, NATO ASI Workshop, Istanbul, August 12–21, 1997

[VB96] Vossen, G., Becker, J., (eds.), Business Process Modeling and Workflow Management: Models, Methods, Tools, (in German), International Thomson Publishing, Bonn, Germany, 1996

[VW97] Vossen, G., Weske, M., The WASA Approach to Workflow Management for Scientific Applications, in: Springer ASI NATO Series, NATO ASI Workshop, Istanbul, August 12–21, 1997

[Wes98] Weske, M., Modeling and Execution of Flexible Workflow Activities, in: Proc. 31st Hawaii International Conference on System Sciences, Software Technology Track (Vol. VII), IEEE Computer Society Press, 1998, 713-722

[WWWK96] Wodtke, D., Weissenfels, J., Weikum, G., Kotz Dittrich, A., The Mentor Project: Steps Towards Enterprise-Wide Workflow Management, in: Proc. 12th IEEE International Conference on Data Engineering, 1996, 556–565

[Wod96] Wodtke, D., Modeling and Architecture of Distributed Workflow Management Systems (in German), Ph.D. Thesis, University of Saarbrücken, 1996

[WS97] Worah, D., Sheth, A., Transactions in Transactional Workflows, in: S. Jajodia, L. Kerschberg (eds.), Advanced Transaction Models and Architectures, Kluwer Academic Publishers, 1997, 3–33

[WMC96a] Workflow Management Coalition, Workflow Handbook 1997, John Wiley in association with Workflow Management Coalition (WfMC), 1996

[WMC96b] Workflow Management Coalition, Terminology & Glossary, Document Number WFMC-TC-1011, 1996 (Available from http://www.aiai.ed.ac.uk:80/project/wfmc)

Part Two

Software Engineering Methods for Information System Construction

As described in Chapter 1, methodologies for Information Systems development are not independent from Enterprise Engineering Methodologies but form a hard to separate part of enterprise engineering. This is especially true for the identification and concept phases of the system life-cycle, and to a lesser extent is true for the requirements definition phase. Consequently the reader should expect that the presented methodologies would to some extent address the issues of business strategy making and business planning. This is indeed true, especially for the second contribution on Information Engineering. However, the focus in this part of the handbook is on the eventual construction of an Information System, and the methodologies presented here are more detailed on questions related to this particular aim.

Wojtek Kozaczynski gives an overview of software engineering methods for the construction of Information Systems, especially its software component. Two simple Information Systems Reference Models are presented and through that the author identifies the domains for which methodologies are needed. The important concept to watch for is the design and building of large-scale systems on the basis of *components.* In terms of Information Systems Architecture, these components are characterised as *partial models*, i.e. reusable models of the whole or part of the system. The components themselves are *modules*, which are implementations of these models. The result of the component based approach to software design and construction is, that requirements level models are a) constrained by available modules thus ensuring feasibility and b) component based design ensures rapid development and high quality.

Clive Finkelstein's contribution presents a version of Information Engineering, a methodology based on the recognition that data in the enterprise are more stable than processes, and therefore data / information modelling can be used to create a longer lasting model for the business than models which are solely based on process models. To correctly interpret the message of Information Engineering needs of course the realisation that eventually there will be process models constructed, but the volatility and changability of the two are different. This allows the methodology to be employed in various situations, including deployment of green field information systems, re-design or integration of legacy systems, re-engineering of the processes and supporting applications, or a combination of these.

Brian Henderson-Sellers presents a detailed overview and comparison of object-oriented methods for the design and construction of Information Systems. Each of these methods aims at a complete life-cycle support, and promote the construction of object-oriented models corresponding to the supported phases. At any moment in time during the life history of a system potentially multiple life-cycle activities are carried out – either simultaneously or quasi simultaneously, therefore the transition between models must be almost seamless.

Alfred Helmerich presents Euromethod, which is a method developed in the European Union for contract management. This is a useful addition to the methods presented in the preceding contributions, describing how software development and acquisition is managed between suppliers and customers through a tendering process.

The reader who wishes to adopt an in-house methodology will notice that the above contributions are not in competition; using Chapter 18 one could identify the system in question and its development direction, using Chapter 17 one could determine the necessary direction for implementation (in-house development, component based development or off-the-shelf system); Chapter 20 offers methods for the customer to procure a system through a tendering process, and Chapter 19 describes processes to use object-oriented models (and their supporting tools) to actually carry out the development.

The reader may also ask whether and how the languages presented in Part 1 of the handbook relate to this part on methodology. Clearly, some methodologies favour one given modelling language or another; however, by separating the system development methodology from the *modelling methodology* often embedded in it, the reader has a wide choice of languages and associated tools. Although it is beyond the scope of this handbook, we must mention the trend which aims at the establishment of interoperability of models by semantic translation between various modelling languages. In this way one could use e.g. an underlying object-oriented design database, which may provide a number of useful abstractions, or views to the designer, including Entity Relationship views, IDEF0 and IDEF3 views, the CIMOSA views etc. (see for a more complete list in Part 1). This of course hinges on the ability of developers to formally define the semantics of their languages.

Finally, the reader is reminded that the design and implementation of the Information System includes the design of those components which are implemented by humans (individuals and groups of individuals). For this reason the methodology utilised for Information System design must also include organisational analysis and design methods. These questions will be dealt with in detail in the forthcoming Handbook on Enterprise Integration.

Peter Bernus

CHAPTER 17

Software Engineering Methods

Wojtek Kozaczynski

This contribution attempts to take a systematic look at the methods and tools for the design and construction of Software/Information System (ISs) of today and the future. Development of an ISs is a set of many complex and inter-related activities. These activities are shaped not only by the information technology, but also by the business need and trends. The paper provides a (conceptual) framework that the author found very useful while thinking about different aspects and activities of IS development, methods prescribing these activities and tools that support them. The paper also tries to "predict the future" of the methods and tools by taking into account the new developments in the areas of distributed computing and the Internet.

1 Introduction

Webster's Third New International Dictionary defines methodologies and methods as follows:

a methodology:

1. a body of methods, procedures, working concepts, rules, and postulates employed by a science, art, or discipline
2. the process, techniques, or approaches employed in the solution of a problem or in doing something

a method:

1. a procedure or process of attaining an object
2. a way, technique, or process of or for doing something
3. a body of skills or techniques

Software Engineering Methods and Methodologies capture best practices for designing, constructing (or developing), deploying, and maintaining Software/Information Systems (ISs). The key words are "best practices", that is, proven techniques, processes, concepts and models, and rules for assuring quality of produced systems and productivity of S/W Engineering Processes.

Information Systems are complex software artifacts that have only one purpose; enable and support business processes of the companies and organisations that use them. Although this definition may suggest a subservient role of ISs and Information Technology (IT), this is not exactly the case. The information technology has had increasingly more impact on the way companies conduct their business - it shapes how businesses are organised and ran.

To best answer what is the state-of-the-art of the S/W Engineering Methods and more importantly what is their future, we have to take a look at the forces shaping the IT/IS domain.

2 Major Forces Shaping the IS/IT Domain

There are two types of forces (or drivers) that shape the IS/IT domain: the business drivers, and the technology drivers.

2.1 Business Drivers

Globalization and Streamlining of Business Processes. On one hand, Information Systems of a global company must support operations at multiple locations, different countries, different time zones, etc. On the other hand, business processes of and between companies are intricately interrelated. Streamlining them becomes a competitive necessity and potential for savings. The impact of these two trends on ISs is rather obvious:

- complexity - support for multiple locations, distributed processes, different cultures, languages, legal systems, etc.
- size and distribution - support for remote locations, support for global organisations, etc.
- openness and interoperability - ability to support processes spanning multiple systems.

Concentration on Core Business Competencies. Companies recognize, that in majority of cases building and maintaining complex ISs in-house is expensive, not strategically necessary, and should not be one of their core competencies. There are two important consequences of this:

- Definitive move towards using vertical software products (or packages). In late 1996 The Gartner Group forecast, that by the year 2000 companies will invest most in Packaged Business Applications, and

- Outsourcing of IT operations or IS development (many companies will also retain process improvement and customization groups to provide customer responsive systems and service differentiators).

2.2 Technology Drivers

Probably the most important technology driver is **Maturation of Distributed Computing.** On one hand, the tele-communication technology has already delivered both local and global networks with virtually unlimited connectivity and access from anywhere.

On the other hand, Client/Server has matured and is a well understood and broadly used architecture for corporate computing. This architecture is now evolving into Object Oriented distributed computing architecture. The leading force in OO computing has been the Object Management Group (OMG)[1] with its de-facto CORBA Object Management Architecture standard[2]. OMG brought to its fold almost everybody but Microsoft, which is offering an alternative direction with its DCOM[3]. Despite differences at the detailed level, both OMG's and Microsoft's solutions are conceptually equivalent and are based on principles first introduced by DEC's DCE[4].

The other dominant driver has been the **Internet**. From a purely technological point of view, the Internet technology has brought a universal GUI standard (the Web Browser) and "wire shippable" software (Java applets and ActiveX components). But it also has had a tremendous impact on millions of IS users. It reformulated their expectations on how new ISs should look and feel, how simple to use they should be, and how available they should be.

3 Impact on S/W Engineering Methods

What impact do the above forces have on Software Engineering Methods for IS Construction? Interestingly, the most profound impact is usually not well recognized. Exploding complexity and globalization of ISs, growing use of packages, and multiplicity and complexity of distributed systems technologies created ideal market climate for growth of large vertical software product companies (also referred to as Independent Software Vendors or ISVs) and IT consultants and integrators. Best examples are Andersen Consulting with its 45K-plus employees world-wide, and the short list of Enterprise Resource Planing (ERP) systems providers including SAP, Baan, SSA, and J.D Edwards.

What does it have to do with methods? Surprisingly, a lot. Leading ISVs (SAP, PeopleSoft, Oracle, SSA, Baan, ...) and Large Consultants and IT

[1] http://www.omg.org/
[2] http://www.omg.org/library/omaa.htm
[3] http://www.microsoft.com/work\-shop/prog/com/dcom-f.htm
[4] http://www.opengroup.org/tech/dce/

Integrators invest significant sums of money in development and adoption of IS construction methods, because they have become strategically important to them. This is a significant change from what was happening until recently where most of the methods work was sponsored by governments. In the US it has been DARPA (Software Engineering Institute[5], the STARS or DSSA programs, and the ill-conceived I-CASE initiative) and NIST (the Advanced Technology Program)[6]. In Europe it is still EC's Esprit funding, and the UK's government sponsored SSADM (System Software Analysis and Design Method)[7].

Today, true market forces make large Consultancies and ISVs put significant resources into developing new IS design and construction methods. Methods, that will support building large business software solutions (both customized and packages) providing new levels of services:

- effective support for current business processes
- ability to evolve these processes without being constrained by the ISs supporting them
- configurability
- interoperability, and
- scalablility.

Majority of these new methods are based on three general principles:

1. Component-based S/W Engineering - an approach to system construction in which a system is assembled from well-defined parts, and
2. S/W Reuse - an approach to developing components in such a way, that they can be used in many different situations, and
3. Process driven - to optimise development time scales and response to changing business needs.

4 Framework for IS Construction Methods and Tools

A methodology for constructing a distributed, component-based system comprises of a large body of guidelines for team organisation, development processes, concepts and tools, and reusable designs and components. In order to address its (the methodology's) most important aspects in an organised fashion, we need a reference model. A layered architecture of component-based IS provides a convenient model.

[5]http://www.sei.cmu.edu/
[6]http://www.atp.nist.gov/atp/atphome.htm
[7]http://www.ipsys.com/ssadmeth.htm

4.1 Layered Architecture of a Component-Based System

A high-level layered architecture of component-based systems is shown in Figure 1. The layers are described from the bottom up.

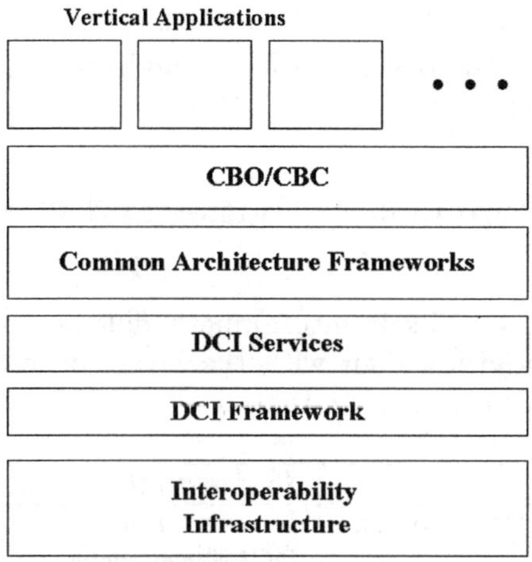

Figure 1: IS Layered Architecture Reference Model

Interoperability Infrastructure. This is a commodity layer such as a CORBA ORB, DCOM, or IBM's MQ Series Queue Manager [OHE96a] that provides communication between distributed system components

Distributed Computing Infrastructure (DCI) Framework. A plain interoperability infrastructure is not a convenient level at which one builds large distributed systems - it provides a relatively low level of building-block abstractions. Therefore, there is an emergence of higher level abstraction frameworks like those submitted to the OMG in response to the Business Object Framework Request for Proposal (BOF RFP)[8].

DCI Services. This layer provides a set of services such as Component Persistency, Component Life-cycle, Event Handling, etc., that are commonly used by all ISs.

Common Architecture Frameworks. This is the next-up level of commonly used funcitonality that is more than just individual services. These are frameworks such a Error Handling Framework, Transaction Management Framework, User-Unit-Of-Work Framework, GUI Framework, Failure Recovery Framework, Mega-data Management Framework, etc.

Common Business Objects/Components (CBO/CBC). This is the first layer of business software and it can be multi-tier itself. ISs share objects and components that are common to them in general or are common to

---

[8]http://www.omg.org/members/doclist-97.html

a particular business domain. Address, Currency, Employee, and Time are examples of very generic objects and components, while Invoice or Vendor exemplify more domain specific components.
Vertical Business Applications. This is finally the application-specific part of the system that uses and/or embeds all lower layers. In particular, it includes run-time representation of business processes and unifies business process patterns and workflow that is rule oriented and structured.

Note, that this model does not explicitly address legacy migration, wrapping, interoperability, etc.

4.2 Key Development Activities and Computational Domains

In most current (and very likely future) methodologies, major system design and construction activities align with the layers of system decomposition presented above. This is shown in Table 1.

Activity	*IS Architecture Layer*
Infrastructure Development	Interoperability Infrastructure DCI Framework DCI Services
Architecture Development	Common Application Frameworks
Application Development modelling and design application construction	 CBO/CBC Vertical Applications

Table 1: Activities and IS Architecture Layers

A brief discussion of these activities, from the perspective of methods supporting them, is presented in the subsequent paragraphs. Before we continue, however, we introduce another very useful reference model that will help the discussion of IS construction methods. It is a model of so-called computational domains [Sim94] and it is depicted in Figure 2.

The model indicates, that IS system design and construction takes place in three "spaces" that satisfy different purposes and have different characteristics.

1. **Shared Resources Domain (SRD)** - is responsible for providing a set of services to one or more clients, in most cases executing concurrently, and for ensuring the integrity of shared resources required to implement those services. The principal shared resource is one or more data bases. Resources in this domain generally tend to be static in nature. That is, they are used by clients or agents, in the course of

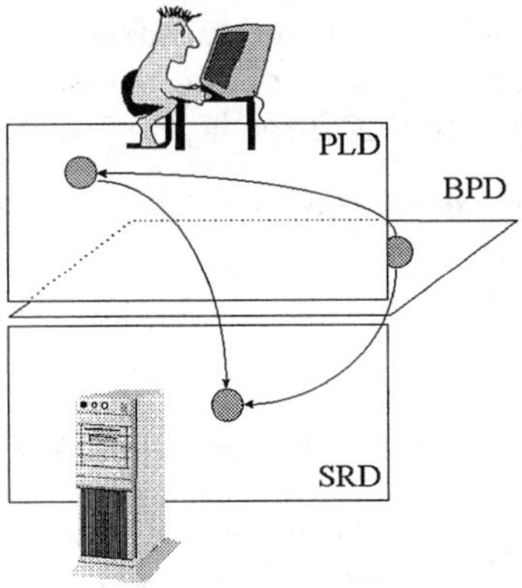

Figure 2: Computational Domains Reference Model

performing some function, activity, or process. The SRD is an implementation of what is often called the "corporate object model" or the "entity" model [Boo94]. The scope of an SRD is coterminous with the scope of ACID transactions against resources. Often a resource manager, such as a Database Management System (DBMS) or a Transaction (Processing) Monitor (TPM) [OHE96b], is the provider of ACIDity. In a more general case, the SRD stretches across two or more resource managers which may not know anything about one another.

2. **Presentation Logic Domain (PLD)** - is a domain responsible for ensuring maximum productivity and ease-of-use for system users, who accesses the system through some form of an human-compute interface (HCI). The scope of a PLD is that function required to support a single person. Often the PLD functionality can be provided in identical form to all users. In this case, the developer sees a single PLD, but at run-time there will be as many PLDs as there are users.

3. **Business Process Domain (BPD)** - is responsible for the execution of configurable business processes of various kinds - workflows, activities, and business transactions. The BPD acts on components in all other domains including itself. An example is a "Place Order" business process which may act on Inventory, Customer, Order and CreditChecker components. Different techniques and methods are used for designing and constructing components in the three domains. These are briefly described in the next three paragraphs.

5 Infrastructure Development

In the future, Distributed Computing Infrastructures (DCIs) will become commodities, but this is not going to happen for a while. Therefore, infrastructure development, or more correctly infrastructure assembly, has been and will remain an important part of the overall system construction processes. A complete DCI contains three layers introduced above:

- Interoperability Infrastructure
- DCI Framework, and
- DCI Services.

A DCI cuts across all three computational domains.

- In the PDL, the infrastructure may integrate a GUI technology framework such as Java-based Bongo[9] or MFC[10].
- In the SRD the infrastructure may include:
  - a transaction monitor (TPM) such as Tuxedo or CICS
  - one or more DBMSs
  - real time input/output devices, like card readers an ORB or a Message Oriented Midleware[11], etc.
- Finally in the BPD, the infrastructure may integrate a document management system, a group-ware environment like Lotus Notes[12], electronic mail, a Web-like[13] enviroment, a work-flow engine, etc.

The methods for developing, or more correctly assembling, DCIs are characterized by highly technical work packages and large-grain component reuse and integration. The emphasis of these methods will be on:

- providing a convenient set of abstractions to framework and application developers
- providing most general-purpose functionality (not business-domain specific), and
- performance and reliability of the services.

Standard Object-oriented (OO) S/W methods will dominate this area from the software construction viewpoint. Also important will be different component Application Programming Interface (API) standards such as the Workflow Coalition's APIs[14] to Workflow engines. For good examples of a complete DCIs the reader is referred to SSA's submission[15] to the OMG's BOF RFP.

[9] http://www.marimba.org/
[10] http://www.microsoft.com/msdn/
[11] http://www.hursley.ibm.com/mqseries/
[12] http://www2.lotus.com/domino.nsf
[13] http://developer.netscape.com/library/one/index.html
[14] http://www.aiai.ed.ac.uk/project/wfmc/
[15] http://www.omg.org/members/doclist-97.html

6 Architecture Development

The architecture development activities provide solution patterns and frameworks in all three computational domains. These frameworks and patterns, in turn, provide proven approaches to structuring applications. Examples include:

- Transaction Management Framework
- Mega-Data Framework
- User-Unit-Of-Work (or Activity) Pattern
- Security Framework
- System-Level Error Management Framework, and
- Batch Transaction Processing Framework.

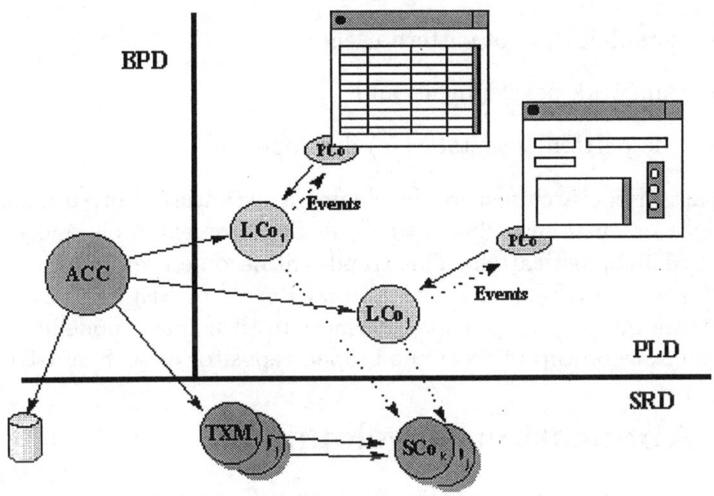

Figure 3: A common pattern of User-Unit-Of-Work Coordination

Figure 3 illustrates a common pattern for handling User-Units-Of-Work - a group of activities that the user considers to be a complete business activity. Central to this pattern is an Activity Coordination Component (ACC), that orchestrated the work of other components:

- LCos (Local Components), which are local representations (or copies) of persistent business objects
- PCos (Presentation Components), which are responsible for handling user interfaces (the GUI)
- TXMs (Transaction Managers), that coordinate ACID DB transactions, and
- SCos (Shared resource Components), that provide access to persistent object storage.

This pattern uses lower-level patterns and frameworks. LCos and PCos communicate using a Model-View-Controller pattern [GHJV94] and PCos internally use a GUI framework such as Bongo. SCos use a Persistency Framework to store and retrieve object state in/from a data store.

Architecture Development Methodologies focus on:

- component models
- capturing and describing patterns
- using some form of a (semi)formal notation
- exemplification of pattern usage
- framework development, and
- code pattern (skeletal code) development.

As part of the architecture development activities many organisations also produce or customise their own S/W development tools and environments of varying sophistication. This trend will become even more common. S/W development toolsets such as Rational Rose[16] or SELECT Enterprise[17] are becoming more open, provide interfaces to their meta-modelling capabilities, and migrate on top of a common, open repositories such as UREP[18].

7 Application Development

Application development is the focal set of IS construction activities. Emerging component oriented methodologies further divide these activities into:

- development of Common Business Objects (CBO) and Components (CBC), and
- development of vertical applications.

[16] http://www.rational.com/products/rose/
[17] http://www.selectst.com/Component/SCF/SCFFrames.htm
[18] http://www.unisys.com/marketplace/products/\-urep/

7.1 CBO/CBC Development

A Common Business Object is at the level of an OO-language object. A Common Business Component is larger than an object, that is, it may contain multiple objects. A business component is usually a unit of system distribution, while a business object it not. Specifically, a business component instance is a network-addressable system unit. A business object may be sent between components by value (in a message) and internalised within the receiving component, but it does not have a system-wide identity.

Both Common Business Objects and Components are the building blocks used in many vertical applications. Example may include: Address and Address Book, Currency, Voucher, Order, Customer, etc.

From the methodology view point, development of common business objects and components starts from Enterprise Business Entity Modelling. A good Enterprise Business Entity Model should identify many of business objects in a system (both common and specific) and the aggregation and use relationships between them. Further process-driven analysis should reveal business objets that are collection managers, such as Address Book.

Common business objects and components form layered structures. At the bottom are simple objects (sometimes simple abstract data types) such as Postal Code. Progressing up the layers, objects become more complex and semantically rich. An example is shown in Figure 4.

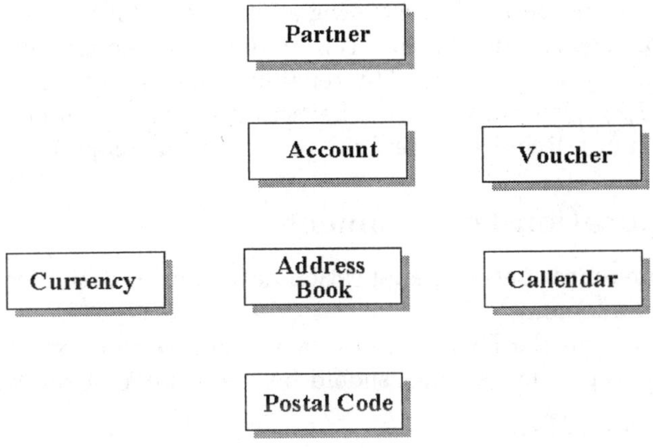

Figure 4: An example Common Business Component/Object Hierarchy

It is not always obvious what should be a CBO and what should be a CBC. The rule-of-thumb criteria include network visibility, independent context, and user access. Most of CBC span across PLD and SRD, that is, they have both the persistent side as well as a GUI side. For example, a Vendor Component should support all maintenance operations of a vendor including requests like changing its address. This particular operation would be, of course, delegated to the Address component or object.

The methodology of building CBOs and CBCs is that of building common purpose reusable OO software [JGJ97]. It focuses on detailed interfaces specification, implementation hiding, and testing. A well defined component/object interface specification should include:

- Provided Interfaces - the operations the component provides to its clients
- Required Interfaces - the operations the components will request from other components/servers
- Operation Semantics
- Pre- and Post-Conditions
- Invariants
- One-Sided Protocols - temporal dependencies between Provided Interfaces.

Probably still the best example of a good support for interface specification is the Eiffel language [Mey88]. Also, there are extensions of the CORBA IDL to provide for better component interface specifications [BBKLNO77].

Another focus of CBO and CBC development is testing. This means both reliability and performance testing as well as usability testing. Usability testing is particularly difficult and can be done only empirically, that is, by repeated use of a component. The reliability and performance testing can be simplified by generation of test harnesses - sets of dummy components delivering dummy Required Interfaces to the tested components.

7.2 Application Development

There are differences between application development activities in the three computational domains.

Development in the **PLD** is concerned with how to make a system most usable to its users, that is, what should be the System's User Model:

- Visualization - the look
- Interaction - the feel, and
- User's Conceptual Model - concepts that the user operates on when using the system via the user interfaces.

Only a small part of developing a good system presentation layer is related to building a GUI itself, that is, the screens (the visualization). Most of the work is related to developing user interactions, navigation, interactions with SRD and BPD, and choosing proper system metaphors. However, except for

GUI frameworks, there are no good methods for overall system-user interface design and development for ISs. Most of the existing implementations borrow metaphors from desktop computing. This is an area where methods have ample room for improvement and will be definitely driven by the developments in the area of Internet computing.

Development in the **SRD** is dominated by the system's storage design and implementation. It starts from traditional Enterprise Business Object (or Entity) Modelling and follows with:

- Mapping of Business Objects into physical DBs - currently, most of the large, enterprise-wide ISs utilise Relational DBMSs. This trend will continue due to the maturity and scaleability of the technology. Therefore, most of current and future systems will have to use a mapping between Business Objects and Components and DB tables. The mapping process is well understood, but often error prone, and there are approaches and tools to support it[19].
- Determining clustering of objects into components - objects are not used individually, but in clusters determined by the static and dynamic relationships between them. Determining how to group objects into stable, usable components is one of the most difficult and poorly understood tasks in SRD development. In most cases, developers rely on their domain experience, static object dependencies, and less on analysis of how objects are used together in business and system processes and use cases [JCJO93]. Object clustering into components is always a trade-off between
  - component size, that is, number of objects brought into a component at execution time, and
  - number of relationships that have to be managed between components. In an ideal situation, a component has a few relationships with other components and high cohesion between the objects implementing its internal behavior.
- Coordinating transactions and data consistency management - since components are interrelated, changes in one component may cause changes in other components. This usually requires designing support for nested transactions and/or transactions on multiple DBs. That in turn leads to development of TXMs (transaction management components) that are capable of coordinating ACID DB transactions.

BPD development starts form a different place, which is, business process modelling. The objective is to produce a collection of business ACC (Activity Coordinator Components) that best represent business activities supported by the system.

[19] http://www.persistence.com/

An ACC may be best described as a work-flow-like entity. It represents a well-defined User Unit of Work (cf. CIMOSA functional operation [Ver96]) (sometimes referred to as a Logical Unit of Work) which is a part of a business process. ACC is invoked from the top-most layer of the system interface and coordinates a multi-step business transaction such that each step:

- will request one or more business components to be brought to the PLD
- may involve interactions with the user via one or more presentation components
- may request to commit, in an ACIDized way, changes to the business components that were brought to the PLD; invoke an ACID transaction in the SRD.

A user unit of work is a long lasting business transaction, that may take an unspecified time and in a degenerate case can be interrupted for an unpredictable time or fail entirely. At the end of each step, however, changes must be committed to the system's SRD (DB in particular). For these reasons, construction of ACC is complex (see Figure 3 again):

- they must log their state change history
- they must log the requested and committed SRD changes
- they must be able to recover their state after they were suspended or interrupted, and
- they must be able to undo the SRD changes by issuing compensating transactions (since the changes have been already committed).

In even more complicated cases, an ACC may have to involve different users in different steps, but this is not common unless the ACC is implemented as a true work flow activity.

There are no well-defined methods for developing business process components (the ACCs). Methodologists seem to agree, that the design starts at Process Modelling, Scenarios and Use Case Analysis, and Enterprise Business Object Modelling [JCJO93, JEJ94]. However, there are no good methods for mapping these analysis models into distributed component models.

8 Component-Based IS Development Process

Figure 5 below puts all of the described IS development activities together.

The "squares" in the Vertical System Components Development block represent design, construction, assembly and testing of System Components. A System Component is a basic system fabrication unit and a unit of packaging. A system component should have strong business semantics, but may

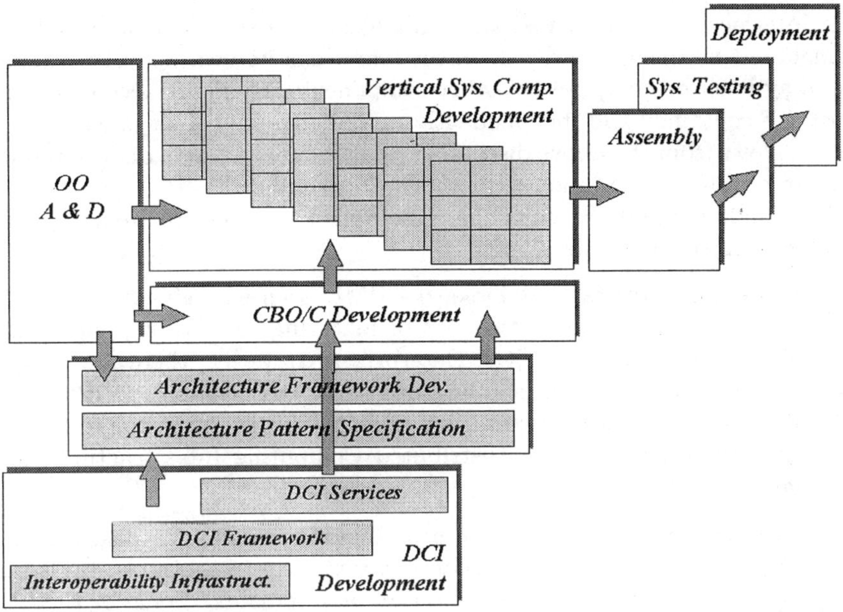

Figure 5: IS Development Activities

not be exactly equal to a business component. For example, a system may contain an Inventory Management System Component that manages Inventory Items that are first-order business components. The structure of the "squares" is shown in Figure 6.

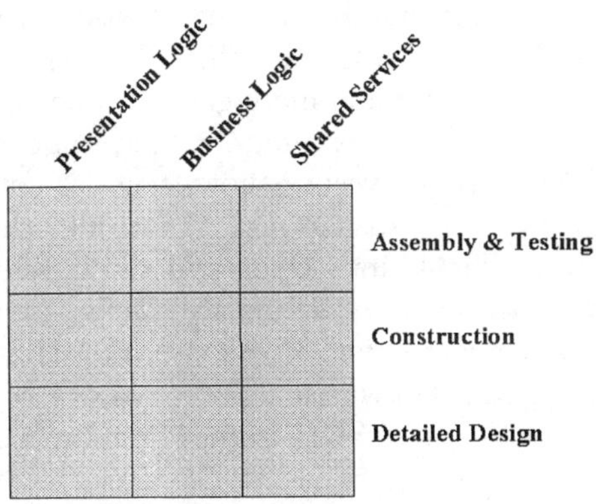

Figure 6: System Component Development Activity areas

The figure suggests that a system component is a so-called wall-to-wall unit. Such a unit contains a services/persistency layer, business logic, and user interfaces. It is designed and built like an independent, large software element. It is assigned a development team, has its own delivery schedule, and may itself be composed of other components. By many accounts, it is a most self-contained and independently marketable unit of a system.

It follows from the above discussion, that to build a large, distributed IS a number of different techniques, methods, tools and skills are required - there isn't a single method. Some of these methods and tools are already mature and some must still be developed.

1. **Object Analysis and Design** - UML is an emerging de-facto standard in this domain with a set of maturing tools to support it (like Rational Rose or SELECT Enterprise). However, there are no good methods to guide the mapping from a UML[20] system specification to its component model (execution model). This is partly due to the fact, that there isn't a singe Distributed Computing Infrastructure Model yet.

2. **Vertical System Components Development** - as discussed (see Figure 6), this is an area that requires a set of methods, skills, and tools that cover all three computational domains. Some of them are better understood than others, but they are not really integrated into one comprehensive component development approach:

   - **PLD** - there exist good GUI development tools (like Ilog Views[21] or Bongo) at the so-called windows-&-controls level. However, there still exists little support for the development of complex, usable user dialogs. In most cases designers are free to do what they feel right.
   - **SRD** - this has been a relatively well understood domain until the OO impedance mismatch occurred. A standard approach to managing the SRD was to use a TPM. However, TPMs usually play two roles: (1) transaction management, and (2) resource management. Components, unfortunately, tend to be very independent in terms of where they execute (how they use computing resources) and how they join transactions. As a result, there still is no clean integration of TPMs into DCIs and the development of SRD for distributed component systems still lacks a mature methodology. What is expected to change the situation is a new generation of TPMs (e.g. MS Transaction Server and associated tools), or a general purpose set of SRD frameworks (and a set of supporting tools).
   - **BLD** - this domain is conceptually simple, yet there are many details that must be taken into account. In particular, coordination of multiple alternative steps and activity roll-back. Today

[20] http://www.rational.com/uml/index.html

[21] http://www.ilog.com/html/product_visualization_suite.html

almost every big project develops its own User Unit of Work Management Pattern or/and Framework. In the future, we should see emergence of scripting languages designed to write component coordination logic. Some of these languages and tools will be probably derived form rule languages of inference engines.

3. **System Assembly, Testing, and Deployment** - these activities are well understood and the component-based system development should make them only easier. This is because components naturally follow the rules of loose coupling and strong cohesion and provide very well articulated demarcation lines between system parts. These properties have always been the key to efficient system assembly and configuration management, testing, and deployment.

4. **Distributed Computing Infrastructure Development** - from the software construction methodology and tools point of view, this is a well understood area.

5. **Common Business Component Development** - depending on granularity, this activity can be either similar to developing an object class or developing a system component. Development of individual object classes is well supported by design tools such as Rational Rose and code development tools such as MS Developer Studio. The development of system components has been discussed above.

6. **Architecture Pattern and Framework Specification and Development** - this is an important, yet one of the least understood and appreciated development areas, and a corner stone of large-grain reuse. There is an extensive literature on software patterns[22] and a lively Internet[23] discussion on the subject. However attempts to formalise pattern specification have been refuted by the fathers of the pattern movement who belive that the "software patterns are not supposed to be formalised". This hinders development of tools. There is also little in the way of support for development of frameworks, which are the next level up of encoding commonly used approaches to handling a specific computing requirement. We hope to see some improvements in this area.

7. **Finally, the DCI Development** - from the methods and tools point of view, this is a well understood domain. The questions are usually about what distributed computing and programming model to use and what services to expose, but not how to develop them. Usually standard OO methods and techniques are used.

[22] http://st-www.cs.uiuc.edu/users/patterns/books/
[23] http://st-www.cs.uiuc.edu/users/patterns/

9 Summary

Sometimes it is not that important to predict the future, as much as to understand where it is coming from and what shapes it. In this paper, we described a framework that we found quite convenient when thinking about IS construction methods, tools, and skills.

It is clear, that the next paradigm shift, after Client/Server (C/S) Computing, will be Distributed, Component-Based Computing that to some degree is a natural evolution of the C/S computing. The indications are very clear and can be found in many places[24]. There is much that we can reuse or leverage from the existing methods and tools. There are also areas, like development of wall-to-wall system components, that we still have to master. So who will master them and when? When will an average S/W shop be able to buy a new toolset in an Internet store?

Unfortunately, the answer to the second question is that some of these new tools may remain proprietary (at least partially) for a while. The reason is in the answer to the first question. The new tools and methods will come from different coalitions of S/W tool companies, big S/W product companies, and information integrators and consultants. This is all due to the business drivers described at the beginning of the paper. A few current examples include:

- IBM teaming up with Rational to provide a toolset for its Java set of general-purpose business objects developed by the San Francisco project[25],
- Prise Waterhouse teaming up with IntelliCorp to provide a set of tools for business modelling to support customization of the SAP family of packages, and
- PeopleSoft teaming up with SELECT and Rational to provide a customized set of tools to their software packages.

Another alternative, although less likely, is integration of Open Repositories like UREP with MetaCASE Tools like ToolBuilder[26] or open or extensible tools like Rational Rose. Meta-CASE tools are almost extinct species, victims to their original immaturity and unfulfilled promises. However, with emergence of open repositories that provide support for meta-modelling, their premise becomes attractive again. Many of their proprietary functions such as their own scripting languages can be now provided in a much more open fashion. For example, Visual Basic can be used as a scripting language to access and manipulate the content of the repository.

Both areas will be very interesting to watch, but we do not expect a very fast progress. Developing a complex Distributed Computing Architecture

[24] http://splash.javasoft.com/beans/WhitePaper.html
[25] http//www.ibm.com/Java/Sanfrancisco/
[26] http//www.ipsys.com/tb.htm

and Frameworks is a task for several years. Adding to that the development of common components, vertical components, and then proving that all this works and scales will take time. Despite all enthusiastic claims, large scale distributed, component-based computing is not with us yet and will be slow in delivery. Andersen Consulting, the most progressive of all technology integrators have learned this first hand on its publicly touted Eagle project[27]. The project has lasted for over four years, consumed undisclosed millions of dollars and yet failed to deliver a commonly accepted set of tools and methods.

References

[Boo94] Booch, G., Object-Oriented Analysis and Design with Applications, Benjamin/Cummins Publishing Company, 1994

[BBKLNO77] Bronsard, F., Bryan, D., Kozaczynski, W., Liongosari, E., Ning, J., lafsson, A., Proceedings of the Symposium on Software Reusability, Boston, May 1997

[GHJV94] Gamma, E., Helm, R., Johnson, R., Vlissides, J., Design Patterns - Elements of Reusable Object-Oriented Software, Addison-Wesley, 1994

[JGJ97] Jacobson, I., Griss, M., Jonsson, P., Software Reuse: Architecture, Process and Organization for Business Success, Addison-Wesley, 1997

[JEJ94] Jacobson, I., Ericsson, M., Jacobson, A., The Object Adventage - Business Process Reengineering with Object Technology, Addison-Wesley, 1994

[JCJO93] Jacobson, I., Christerson, M., Jonsson, P., Overgaard G., Object-Oriented Software Engineering: A Use CaseDriven Approach, Addison-Weslay, 1993

[Mey88] Meyer, B., Object-Oriented Software Construction, Prentice-Hall, 1988

[OHE96a] Orfali, R., Harkey, D., Edwards, J., The Essential Client/Server Survival Guide, John Wiley & Sons, 1996

[OHE96b] Orfali, R., Harkey, D., Edwards, J., The Essential Distributed Objects Survivor Guide, John Wiley & Sons, 1996

[Sim94] Sims, O., Business Objects: Delivering Cooperative Objects For Client-Server, McGRAW-HILL Book Company, 1994

[Ver96] Vernadat, F. B., Enterprise Modeling and Integration: Principles and Application, Chapman & Hall, London, 1996

[27] http//www.ac.com/eagle/spec/

CHAPTER 18

Information Engineering Methodology

Clive Finkelstein

This chapter discusses the history and evolution of Information Engineering, with emphasis on the business-driven IE variant. It describes the methods used at each phase in the systems development life cycle: strategic business planning; strategic, tactical and operational data modelling; process modelling; systems design; and systems implementation. It describes the application and use of IE for Forward Engineering, Reverse Engineering and Business Re-Engineering, and illustrates business-driven IE principles with a Business Re-Engineering example. The chapter concludes with a summary of Internet and Intranet technologies; discussing development of Client/Server systems and Data Warehouses, and their deployment via the Internet and corporate Intranets.

1 Introduction

The need to design and build systems that fully support the information requirements of users of those systems has long been recognised since the first computers were introduced. But the complexity of systems development has demanded a detailed knowledge of analysis and design techniques and an understanding of computer technology. Methodologies such as Software Engineering helped. First introduced in the early 1970s, Software Engineering focused first on Structured Programming, then on Structured Design with Structure Charts, and on Structured Analysis with Data Flow Diagrams (DFDs) [Jac75, Orr77, YC78, DeM82].

But business processes change, often more frequently than the data they use. And business changes invariably require that the programs used to automate those processes must also be changed. In contrast, data has been found to change less often than processes and so is more stable. Systems designed first from the perspective of the data needed by the business, and then from the processes that operated on that data, were found to be more flexible - able to accommodate change more readily. These are fundamental principles that are used by the object-oriented analysis and design methods of today, but these principles had already been recognised in the mid-1970s as important concepts for analysis and design generally.

Relational theory, developed by Edgar Codd at IBM, provided some important insights into the analysis and design of systems based on data [Cod70, Cod79, Dat82]. Three independent developments emerged in the mid 1970s; in Europe, in the UK, and in Australia. It was the Australian initiative that lead to the development of Information Engineering (IE).

2 History of Information Engineering

From 1976 in Australia, at Information Engineering Services Pty Ltd (IES) we felt that by focusing on data we could identify the information that business users needed to carry out their job responsibilities. The business processes that operated on that data we felt could then be identified and analysed. But how could we determine data and information that was required? And how could we identify the relevant business processes?

Normalisation theory, developed by Edgar Codd as part of relational theory, provided some insight. We found that systems analysts and Data Base Administrators (DBAs) could use the rules of normalisation to interview business users at operational levels, and they could then identify the data and information that was needed. DBAs used this knowledge to design databases that were stable and able to accommodate business change more readily. We called these first two analysis and design methods, developed from 1976-1977: *Data Analysis* and *Data Base Design.*

From 1978-1980 we developed three additional methods. *Information Analysis* was based on Drucker's principles of management [Dru74] and was used to identify information needed by managers. *Procedure Formation* was used to derive processes from data. This was an early representation of today's object-oriented methods that operate against classes ie. data. *Distributed Analysis* was used to analyse and design for remote distribution of data and processing.

Together with the first two methods above, we found that we had developed a rigorous, repeatable discipline like *Engineering* for the identification of *Information* and the development of information systems. At IES we coined the word *Information Engineering* (IE) to describe the overall methodology. A more detailed history of Information Engineering is provided in [Fin81] and [Fin89].

Information Engineering was first published as six InDepth articles in May-June, 1981 by Computerworld USA [Fin81]. But it was the publication in November 1981 of the Savant Institute Technical Report on Information Engineering [FM81], co-authored by Clive Finkelstein and James Martin, that lead to its wide-spread adoption - as IE was popularized world-wide by

James Martin. From 1982-1986 IE began to evolve into two distinct variants.

2.1 DP-driven IE Variant

The first variant was developed in the USA by Database Design Inc (later to be renamed KnowledgeWare, Inc) and Texas Instruments (TI). They changed the data-driven emphasis of IE from 1976-1980 instead to a process-driven focus for use by DBAs, systems analysts and Data Administrators (DAs). These are Data Processing (DP) staff roles; people in these roles generally take a DP-driven focus. Four systems development phases were defined:

1. Information Systems Planning,
2. Analysis,
3. Design,
4. Construction.

This was very effective for analysis and design of information systems using third generation and fourth generation languages in the early 1980s. IE evolved during this period into what is now called the *DP-driven variant of IE* [Mar87]. Many Computer-Aided Software Engineering (CASE) tools today still only support this DP-driven IE variant.

2.2 Business-driven IE Variant

The second variant was developed by IES in Australia. We found that the use of third and fourth generation languages to develop systems and databases with the DP-driven variant of IE resulted in long development times. But in many cases, the business changed before those systems could be completed. We found that by designing systems based on the processes and information needs of operational users, the resulting systems were too volatile. Business changes could not easily be anticipated, as these changes often occur without warning at the operational levels of organisations. As there was no knowledge of possible changes, systems could not be designed proactively to accommodate them.

We realized that there had to be greater awareness of the directions that were set by management for the future. These directions were not unknown; they are defined in the Strategic Business Plans for the organization. We recognised then that IE had to draw more effectively on business expertise: not by interview in the DP-driven variant, but by the active participation of business experts in the analysis and design process. Business-driven methods that draw upon business expertise, rather than computer expertise, were needed to encourage a design partnership between business experts and computer experts. Business experts know the business; while computer experts know computers. We realized that this required business-driven Joint Application Development (JAD) methods. This recognition resulted in our development of the *Business-driven variant of IE* by 1986.

Business-driven Information Engineering uses methods that are understandable and applied by business managers and their staff (the business experts) as well as by IT staff. It uses a number of phases to capture the business knowledge and understanding vital for success, summarized below and illustrated in Figure 1:

- *Strategic Planning* uses the strategic directions set by management to identify their information needs.
- *Data Modelling* documents in data models the information and data needed to achieve those directions.
- *Process Modelling* defines the business processes based on information usage, to implement the plans.

These three phases focus on the business and so are *technology-independent*; they use the knowledge of the business experts. The end-result is the development of a Business Model based on strategic, tactical and operational business plans, and on information, data and business processes that are needed to implement those plans.

The next two phases utilize the Business Model as input. From a computer perspective they determine the systems requirements and decide the available technology to achieve the performance requirements. They depend on computer knowledge and are *technology-dependent.*

- *Systems Design* defines the application design and database design needed to build the required information systems and databases.
- *Systems Implementation* deploys the systems and databases using the available technologies.

Systems and databases developed using business-driven IE were found to be capable of being built rapidly with priority systems delivered early and changed easily to respond readily to rapid business change in the 1990s. Business-driven IE resulted in the development of object-oriented systems that were directly aligned with corporate goals and strategic plans. Business changes could be easily accommodated without the massive redevelopment often required with systems that had been built with the process-oriented, DP-driven variant. Furthermore, these systems were often able to take advantage of new technologies without causing massive business disruption. Some modern CASE tools support the business-driven IE variant for modelling; a few support both IE variants [1].

We shall now examine the phases of business-driven Information Engineering in more detail.

[1] Visible Advantage (previously called IE: Advantage) fully supports and automates

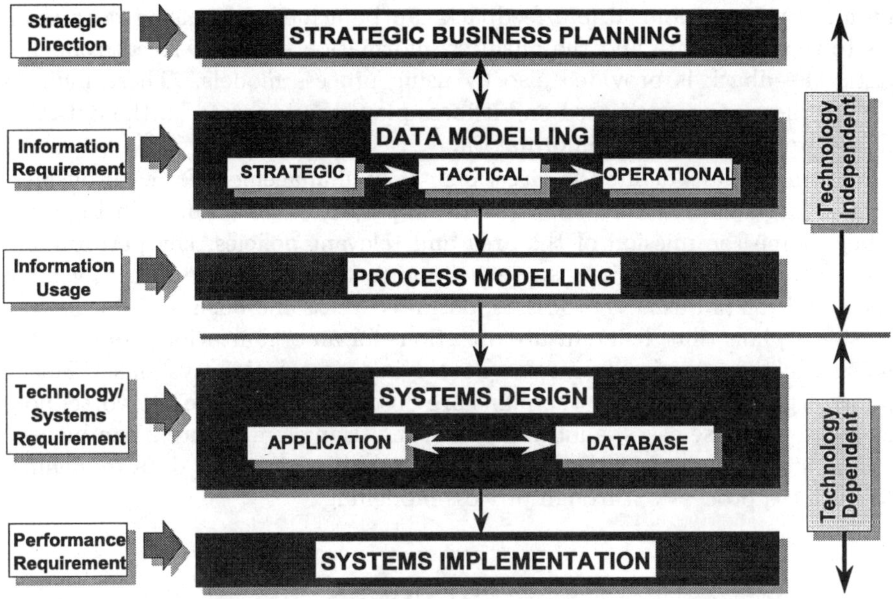

Figure 1: The Phases of Business-driven Information Engineering

3 The Phases of Information Engineering

3.1 Strategic Business Planning

The business directions that senior managers set for the future are defined in strategic business plans, with their greater definition in tactical business plans and implementation in operational business plans. Most organizations acknowledge today a vital need to develop such business plans. But it has often been difficult for these plans, expressed in terms that are relevant to senior management, to provide clear direction also at the tactical and operational levels of organizations. Feedback is needed, so that any problems that occur due to miscommunication and misinterpretation of business plans can be corrected early. This is illustrated in Figure 2.

Business plans indicate the business information that is needed to measure achievement of goals and objectives within defined policy boundaries. These plans also indicate the business processes that implement the strategies and tactics to implement those plans, operate on data and deliver the

all phases of Business driven IE. It supports Forward Engineering, Reverse Engineering and Business Re-Engineering. Visible Analyst and EasyER/EasyOBJECT support the DP-driven variant of IE, as well as many Structured and Object-Oriented development methods. These Modelling tools are all developed and supported by Visible Systems Corporation. See Web Sites http://www.visible.com/ and http://www.ies.aust.com/~ieinfo/ for further details.

required information. Rapid feedback can be achieved by using data models to represent data and the business information that is derived from that data. Feedback is provided also by using process models. These indicate the business processes based on business plans that operate on the data and deliver required business information.

Business plans define the directions set by management for each business area or organization unit, shown as the top apex of the triangle in Figure 2. They define the mission of the area and relevant policies, key performance indicators, goals, objectives, strategies and tactics. These are all catalysts for the definition of business processes, business events and business information. Business plans that define future directions for an organization represent the most effective starting point for developing information systems. But in many organizations today the plans are obsolete, incomplete, or worse, nonexistent. In these cases, another apex of the triangle in Figure 2 can be used as the starting point: either business information, through data modelling; or business processes, through process modelling.

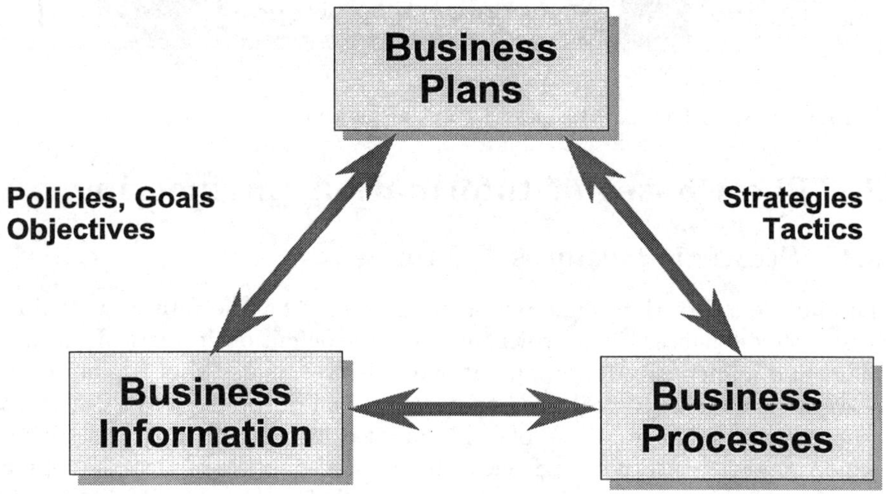

Figure 2: Business Processes and Business Information must support Business Plans

3.2 Data Modelling

Data models should ideally be based on directions set by management for the future. As discussed, these are defined in business plans. Where business plans are not available or are out-of-date, or the reasons why business processes exist are lost in the dark recesses of history, data models of business information provide clear insight into future needs.

Data models can be developed from any statement, whether it is a narrative description of a process, or a statement of a policy, goal, objective or strategy. Redundant data versions that typically have evolved over time in different areas of an organization (each defining its own version of the same data) can be consolidated into integrated data models so that common data can be shared by all areas that need access to it. Regardless of whichever area updates the common data, that updated data is then available to all other areas that are authorized to use it.

Consider the following example, based on the analysis of a data model developed for business processes involved in Sales and Distribution, stated as follows:

- Order Processing *"A customer may have many orders. Each order must comprise at least one ordered product. A product may be requested by many orders."*
- Purchase Order Processing *"Every product has at least one supplier. A supplier will provide us with many products."*
- Product Development *"We only develop products that address at least one need that we are in business to satisfy."*
- Marketing: *"We must know at least one or many needs of each of our customers."*

Figure 3 is an integrated data model that consolidates these functions of Order Entry, Purchasing, Product Development and Marketing. It illustrates an important principle of business-driven Information Engineering, used to develop and rapidly deliver priority business systems as sub-projects from subsets of data models. This principle is stated as:

> *Intersecting entities in a data model represent functions, processes and/or systems.*

We will later see (in *Business Re-Engineering*) that this leads to identification of business re-engineering opportunities from a data model, from examination of cross-functional processes that arise from data model integration of the Order Entry, Purchasing, Product Development and Marketing functions.

Referring to Figure 3, ORDER PRODUCT is an intersecting (or "associative") entity formed by decomposing the many to many association between ORDER and PRODUCT (an order comprises many products; a product may be requested in many orders). It represents the *Order Entry Process* used in the Order Entry business area. When it is implemented, it will become the Order Entry System; but we will focus on identifying processes from the data model at this stage. Similarly, PRODUCT SUPPLIER is an intersecting entity that represents the *Product Supply Process* in Purchasing. PRODUCT

NEED is the *Product Development Process* used in the Product Development area. Finally, CUSTOMER NEED represents the *Customer Needs Analysis Process* used in Marketing. These are summarized in Figure 3.

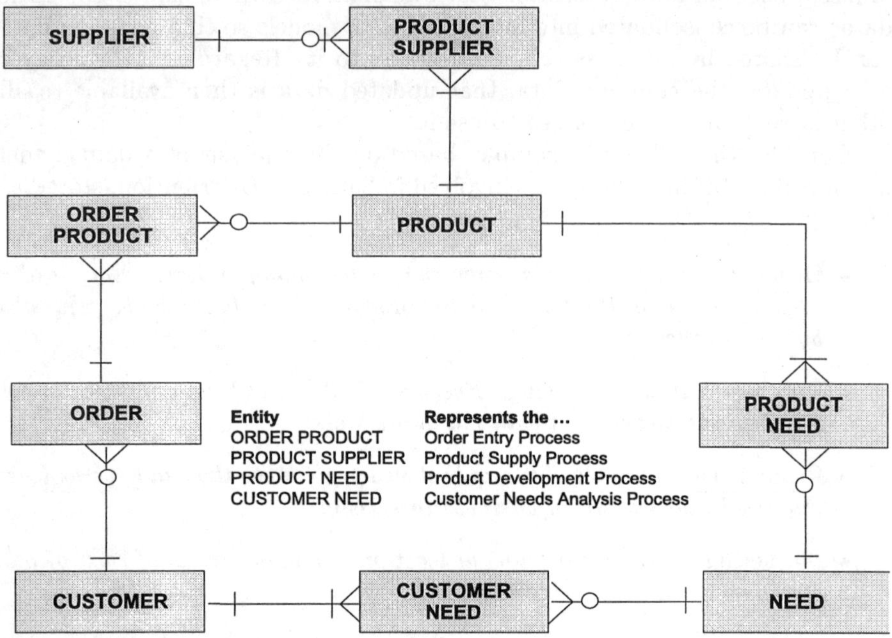

Figure 3: Integrated data model

3.3 Process Modelling

A business event is the essential link between a business plan and a business process. It initiates strategies and tactics (see Figure 2). In the plan, an event is defined as a narrative statement. Physically, it may be a transaction that invokes a business process. Or it may represent a change of state. The process invoked by each event should be clearly indicated.

Without a link to the plan, the business reason(s) why the process exists may not be clear. It may be carried out only because *we have always done it that way*. If the process cannot be seen to support or implement relevant plans at a strategic, tactical or operational level of the business, or provide information needed for decision-making, then it has no reason to remain. To implement these processes without first determining whether they are needed also for the future is an exercise in futility.

If the process is essential, then the strategies or tactics implemented by the process must be clearly defined. Associated goals or objectives must be quantified for those strategies and tactics. Relevant policies that define the boundaries of responsibility for the process and its planning statements must be clarified. Missing components of the plan can thus be completed, with clear management direction for the process and hence the business.

Process modelling documents processes using a variety of diagrams. These include data flow diagrams, state transition diagrams and object-oriented process and class hierarchy diagrams. These documented processes are used to provide input to systems design and systems implementation.

3.4 Systems Design and Implementation

The Business Model, comprising data models and process models that are developed from business plans, indicate the business needs to be addressed by relevant information systems and data bases. They define the systems requirements from a business perspective, which is one part of systems design. The other part considers available technologies to be used for design and implementation.

These technologies may be used for the design of client/server systems using relational data base management systems and object-oriented development tools. Or technologies may be used for design of Data Warehouses, accessed using Executive Information Systems (EIS), Decision Support Systems (DSS), OnLine Analytical Processing (OLAP), Relational OnLine Analytical Processing (ROLAP) and Decision Early Warning Systems (DEWS) based on the information and processing needs indicated by the Business Model.

Client/Server systems and Data Warehouses, designed and developed using technologies as described above, may be deployed using LANs or WANs across the corporate Intranet, or via Extranets with customers, suppliers and business partners, or may be deployed directly to the Internet. The Systems Implementation phase ensures that the performance requirements, identified in the Systems Design phase, are achieved using the available technologies.

4 Application Categories

CASE tools developed to support the DP-driven variant of IE typically focused on one of three application categories: *Forward Engineering, Reverse Engineering* or *Business Re-Engineering.* If an organization's requirements addressed more than one category, different CASE tools therefore had to be used. But most business applications cannot be so conveniently pigeon-holed. There may be new or enhanced databases and systems to be developed (using Forward Engineering techniques). There may also be existing databases and systems that need to be captured (using Reverse Engineering techniques) and integrated with the new systems. And there may be business processes that have to be reengineered (using Business Re-Engineering techniques).

Recognizing this, Business-driven Information Engineering and the Modelling tools that support it were designed so that Forward Engineering, Reverse Engineering and Business Re-Engineering application categories can be supported for any project, and in any combination. Typical applications in each of these categories are discussed below.

4.1 Forward Engineering Applications

Forward Engineering is based on business plans set for the future, and applies the IE phases in the sequence described above. The business plans provide the input for data modelling and process modelling to develop Business Models that support those plans. Four types of Forward Engineering applications are:

- *Strategic Systems Development:* Develops information systems from corporate-wide strategic business plans.
- *Business Systems Development:* Uses IE for rapid development and delivery of high priority systems.
- *Data Warehouse Development:* Develops corporate Data Warehouses or smaller Data Marts (such as for Customer, Product or Market) with EIS, DSS, DEWS, OLAP and ROLAP access for decision-makers.
- *Commercial Application Software Package Evaluation:* Uses a variation of Strategic Systems Development or Business Systems Development to evaluate and acquire externally developed software package solutions.

Forward Engineering addresses top-down, business-driven systems development. Its goal is to build, or buy, complete systems and implement them in the organization with all of the infrastructure components that ensure its success. It may be used for any type of system in business, science, engineering or government. The system and its components are linked rigorously to business plans, models and designs created in a systems development project using Information Engineering.

4.2 Reverse Engineering Applications

Reverse Engineering uses existing systems and databases to provide input for the redevelopment of systems often using different software and hardware platforms from those presently utilized. This may be necessary to save the investment in legacy systems and databases, or to conserve resources by not replacing systems that still meet enterprise needs. The three types of Reverse Engineering applications are:

- *Current Systems Analysis:* Documents and cross-references components of an existing system to the business plans and business model developed using another application type or category.

- *System Reengineering:* Migrates an existing system from its current implementation environment to a new one, while cross-referencing it to a business model as an interim result.
- *Systems Integration:* Combines the functionality of two or more existing systems into one new system cross-referenced to the business model.

Applications developed using Reverse Engineering integrate legacy systems with each other and with new systems, or update existing systems to support new business requirements. Reverse Engineering starts at the Systems Design phase to capture existing application and database designs, developing data models and process models of those existing systems. These are integrated with data and process models addressing the new business requirements. The resulting integrated data models and process models are then implemented on new hardware and/or software platforms.

4.3 Business Re-Engineering Applications

Business Re-Engineering applications have the purpose of facilitating change in the enterprise to enable it to become more effective. Three types of Business Re-Engineering applications are:

- *Reorganization Planning:* Uses a logical analysis of the business model representing the enterprise as the basis for planning infrastructure evolution.
- *Business Process Reengineering:* Streamlines the enterprise through innovative, often radical, changes to its infrastructure, business rules, processes and activities to improve its productivity, quality and effectiveness.
- *Strategic Business Planning:* Uses a sophisticated series of internal and external analysis techniques to determine new directions, and identify the opportunities that are necessary for success.

These Business Re-Engineering applications represent an opportunity to facilitate change in the enterprise; to improve effectiveness by identifying necessary infrastructure changes, allocating resources and improving procedures.

With the consolidation of redundant data versions using integrated data models as discussed in relation to Figure 3, redundant business processes earlier needed so those redundant data versions could be maintained up-to-date are no longer required. Instead, new cross-functional processes are needed. The following example illustrates how these cross-functional processes can be identified from integrated data models by using *Re-engineering Opportunity Analysis*, an IE technique used in Business Re-Engineering. Elements of Forward Engineering and Reverse Engineering are also included indirectly in the example.

5 Business Re-Engineering Example

As common data is integrated across parts of the business, data that previously flowed to keep redundant data versions up-to-date no longer flows. With integrated data models, implemented as integrated databases, data still flows to and from the outside world but little data flows inside the organization. Processes that earlier assumed that data existed redundantly may no longer work in an integrated database environment. New, integrated, cross-functional processes are required. But how can cross-functional processes be identified? Process models using Data Flow Diagrams provide little guidance in this situation.

Cross-functional business processes can be identified from an analysis of data models using an objective technique called *Entity Dependency* as described in [Fin92]. Its importance was acknowledged in [McC93]. Entity dependency is rigorous and repeatable: it can be applied manually, or can be fully automated. When used to analyze a specific data model, the same result will always be obtained - regardless of whether the analysis is done by man or machine. Entity dependency automatically identifies all data entities that a specific process is dependent upon; this is important for referential integrity or data integrity reasons. It automatically identifies inter-dependent and pre-requisite processes, and indicates cross-functional processes. It uncovers and provides insight into re-engineering opportunities.

The data model in Figure 3 is common to many organizations and industries. We can use it to illustrate the principles of reengineering opportunity analysis. For example, we can assess re-engineering opportunities to integrate the functions shown in that data model based on our understanding of the business. But what of mandatory rules we are not aware of, that have been defined in other business areas? How can we ensure that these mandatory rules are correctly applied in our area of interest? The complexity of re-engineering based on business knowledge is difficult; it can be greatly assisted by automated entity dependency analysis from this simple data model.

5.1 Entity Dependency Analysis

A Business-driven IE Modelling tool, *Visible Advantage* (see footnote in section 2.2) that fully automates entity dependency analysis using *Reengineering Opportunity Analysis*, was used to analyze the data model in Figure 3. The results are shown in Table 1, an extract from the Cluster Report produced by entity dependency analysis of the data model.

Each potential function, process or system represented by an intersecting entity (as discussed above) is called a *Cluster*. Each cluster is numbered and named, and contains all data and processes required for its correct operation. It can be implemented as a sub-project for early delivery of priority systems. A cluster is thus self-contained: it requires no other mandatory reference to data or processes outside it. Common, shared data and processes are automatically included within it to ensure its correct operation.

Business Re-Engineering and the Internet	**Cluster Report**
Thu Oct 8 10:00:00 1998	**Page 1**
1.CUSTOMER NEEDS ANALYSIS PROCESS (derived)	
1) CUSTOMER	
1)NEED	
2)CUSTOMER NEED	
(CUSTOMER NEEDS ANALYSIS PROCESS)	
2. ORDER ENTRY PROCESS (derived)	
1)SUPPLIER	
2)PRODUCT SUPPLIER	
(PRODUCT SUPPLY PROCESS)	
1)NEED	
2)PRODUCT NEED	
(PRODUCT DEVELOPMENT PROCESS)	
1)PRODUCT	
2)CUSTOMER NEED	
(CUSTOMER NEEDS ANALYSIS PROCESS)	
1)CUSTOMER	
2)ORDER	
3)ORDER PRODUCT	
(ORDER ENTRY PROCESS)	

Table 1: Entity dependency analysis

Table 1 shows Clusters 1 and 2, representing the *Customer Needs Analysis Process* and the *Order Entry Process.* These have been automatically derived from the data model in Figure 3. Each of these clusters addresses a business process, structured as a potential sub-project; common data and processes appear in all clusters that depend on the data or process. The intersecting entity that is the focus of a cluster appears on the last line of that cluster.

Notice that a right-bracketed number precedes each entity in Table 1: this is the project phase number of the relevant entity in the process. Shown in outline form above for each cluster, it represents a conceptual Gantt Chart as the Project Plan for implementation of the process. Modelling tools that use entity dependency can automatically derive Project Plans from data models.

An intersecting entity indicates a process; the name of the process in Table 1 is shown in brackets after the name of the entity. The intersecting entity on the last line of the cluster is called the "cluster end-point". It is directly dependent on all entities listed above it that are in **bold:** it is also dependent on those entities above it that are not bold (ie. plain text). These entities indicate common data and processes that may also be shared by many other clusters.

Cluster 2, the *Order Entry Process* (based on ORDER PRODUCT in Table 1) depends on three processes: *Product Supply Process, Product Development Process* and *Customer Needs Analysis Process.* We can see that these are all prerequisite processes as their end-point entities are shown in plain text. Analysis of the data model has determined that they must all be carried out prior to the *Order Entry Process.* Furthermore, we see that the *Customer Needs Analysis Process* (Cluster 1, based on CUSTOMER NEED) has only bold entities within it, indicating that it is not dependent on any other processes and therefore is an independent, prerequisite process.

Table 2 next shows that the first two of these processes are fully interdependent: a product supplier cannot be selected without knowing the needs addressed by the product (as each supplier names its products differently to other suppliers).

Business Re-Engineering and the Internet **Cluster Report**
Thu Oct 8 10:00:00 1998 **Page 1**

---

3. PRODUCT DEVELOPMENT PROCESS (derived)
    1)SUPPLIER
    2)PRODUCT SUPPLIER
    (PRODUCT SUPPLY PROCESS)
  1)PRODUCT
  1)NEED
    2)PRODUCT NEED
    (PRODUCT DEVELOPMENT PROCESS)

---

4. PRODUCT SUPPLY PROCESS (derived)
  1)NEED
    2)PRODUCT NEED
    (PRODUCT DEVELOPMENT PROCESS)
  1)PRODUCT
  1)SUPPLIER
    2)PRODUCT SUPPLIER
    (PRODUCT SUPPLY PROCESS)

Table 2: Further entity dependency analysis

5.2 Automatic Data Map Generation

A cluster in outline form can be used to display a data map automatically. For example, vertically aligning each entity by phase, from left to right, shows the data map in Pert Chart format as illustrated in Figure 4. Or instead the data map can be rotated 90 degrees clockwise so that the entities are horizontally displayed by phase, from top to bottom, in an Organization Chart format. An entity name is displayed in an entity box; the attribute names may also be displayed in the entity box. And because the data map is generated automatically, it can be easily displayed using different data modeling conventions: for example by using the IE data modeling notation in Figure 4 or instead by using the IDEF1X notation.

This ability to automatically generate data maps in different formats is a characteristic of many of the Modelling tools that support the business-driven IE variant: data maps can be automatically displayed after entity dependency analysis; the entities within specific clusters can also be displayed. These data maps are not manually drawn; they are generated automatically. When new entities are added, or associations changed, data maps do not have to be changed manually: they can be automatically regenerated. This eliminates much of the delay and potential for error of manually-updated data maps. Furthermore, project plans for related clusters that represent other sub-projects are automatically updated. The impact of the changes on these related project plans can then be readily assessed.

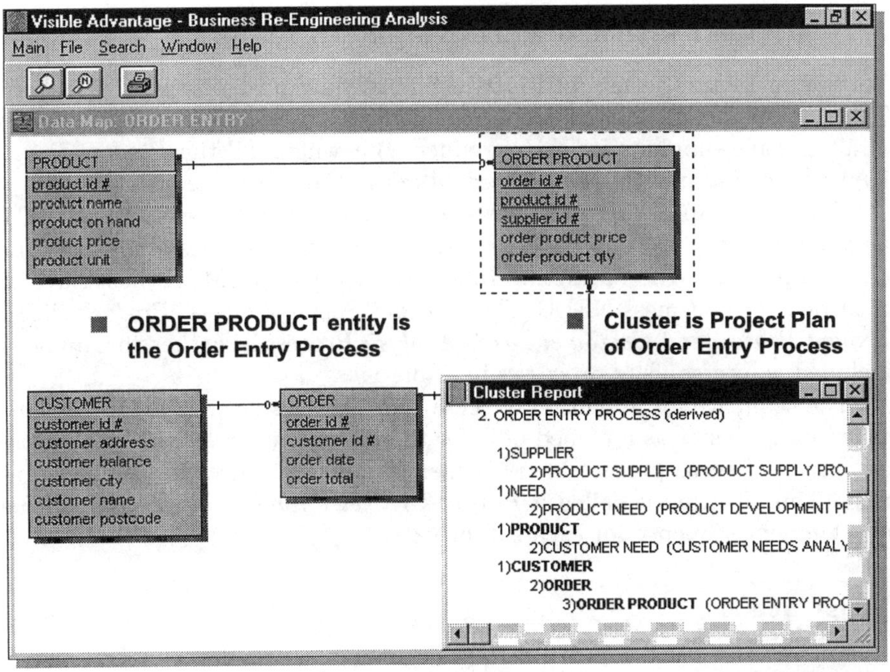

Figure 4: Data Map in Pert Chart format

5.3 Building Business Objects from Data Models

Similarly, process maps can be generated from data models. For example, data maintenance and data access processes (Create, Read, Update, Delete) can be automatically generated from entities in data models. These processes operate against the relevant entities as reusable object-oriented methods. They can be used to build reusable business processes that are documented as object-oriented process maps for business objects such as *Customer* or *Product*.

For example, the *Customer* business object represents all data relating to a Customer. It includes methods to *Create a Customer, Read a Customer, Update a Customer* and *Delete a Customer.* It also includes standard Customer screen formats and standard report formats for different security levels. Thus any changes made to the *Customer* object are automatically reflected in all processes that use the Customer business object; they automatically apply those Customer changes. Similarly methods derived from Product, with Product screen and report formats, exist for the Product object. Any Product changes can be made to this Product object, so automatically changing all processes that refer to Products.

5.4 Project Critical Path Maps

We saw in Figure 3 that a PRODUCT must have at least one SUPPLIER. Table 1 thus includes the *Product Supply Process* to ensure that we are aware of alternative suppliers for each product. But where did the *Product Development Process* and *Customer Needs Analysis Process* come from?

The data map in Figure 3 shows the business rule that each PRODUCT must address at least one NEED relating to our core business. Similarly the data map follows the Marketing rule that each CUSTOMER must have at least one core business NEED. The *Product Supply Process, Product Development Process* and *Customer Needs Analysis* Process have therefore all been included as prerequisite processes in Table 1.

The sequence for execution of these processes is shown in Figure 5. This shows each cluster as a named box, for the process represented by that cluster. Each of these process boxes is therefore a sub-project for implementation. This diagram is called a *Project Critical Path Map* as it suggests the development sequence for each sub-project.

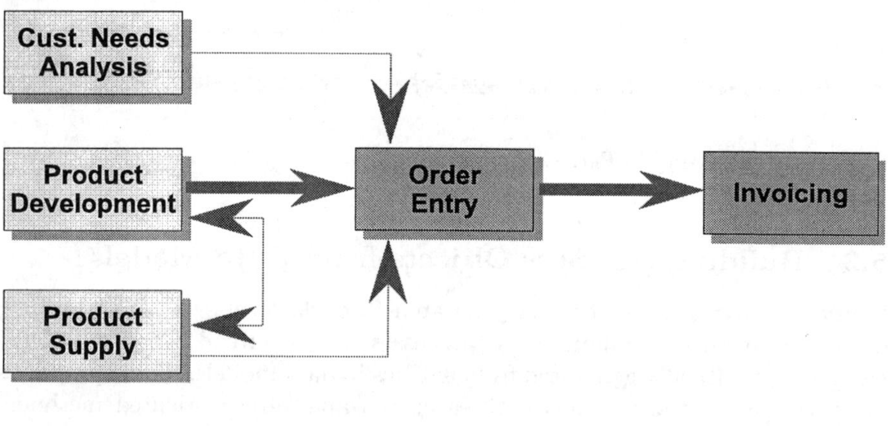

Figure 5: A Project Critical Path Map

We can now see some of the power of entity dependency analysis: it automatically applies business rules across the entire enterprise. As business rules are defined in the data model, the case tool becomes a business expert: aware of all relevant business facts. It determines if other business areas should be notified of relevant business rules, data and processes. It derives a Project Critical Path Map for project management of each sub-project process that is needed to implement those processes as potential computer systems.

So why have these prerequisite processes been included in the cluster in Table 1 for the *Order Entry Process*, and in the Project Critical Path Map in Figure 5? What do these processes suggest? Do they help us to identify re-engineering opportunities? Entity dependency uses Reengineering Opportunity Analysis to provide direct assistance for Business Re-Engineering.

5.5 Reengineering Opportunity Analysis

Figure 5 shows that the prerequisite processes for Order Processing are cross-functional; these separate processes can be integrated. Consider the following scenario for Order Processing - *before Business Re-Engineering:*

Customer:	*"Customer 165 here. I would like to order 36 units of Product X."*
Order Clerk:	*"Yes, certainly. ... Oh, I see we are out of Product X at the moment. I'll check with the Warehouse. I will call you back within the hour to let you know when we can expect more of Product X into stock."*
Customer:	*"No don't bother, I need to know now. Please cancel the order."*

Clearly, this example shows that the Order Clerk has no access to the Inventory Control System in the Warehouse. There is no way to determine when outstanding purchase orders for out-of-stock products will be delivered. It requires a phone call to the Warehouse staff to get that information. A call-back in an hour is no longer responsive for today's customers. The sale was therefore lost. Now consider the same scenario - *after Business Re-Engineering:*

Customer:	*"Customer 165 here. I would like to order 36 units of Product X."*
Order Clerk:	*"Yes, certainly. ... Oh, I see we are out of Product X at the moment. One moment while I check with our suppliers. ... Yes, we can deliver 36 units of Product X to you on Wednesday."*

What has happened in this scenario? Product X was out of stock so the *Product Supply Process* then automatically displayed all suppliers of Product X. The Purchasing function had been re-engineered so the Order Clerk can now link directly into each supplier's inventory system to check the availability and cost of Product X for each alternative source of supply. For the selected supplier, the Clerk placed a purchase order for immediate shipment and so could confirm the Wednesday delivery date with the customer.

But there are problems with this approach, due to incompatibilities between the supplier's Inventory Control System and the Order Entry System. There may be incompatibilities between the Operating Systems, Data Base Management Systems, LANs, WANs and EDI data formats used by both organizations. We will discuss these problems and their resolution, shortly.

The re-engineered *Product Supply Process* discussed above seems revolutionary, but other industries that also take orders online consider this inter-enterprise approach to Order Entry the normal mode of operation. For example, consider the Travel Industry. We phone a travel agent to book a flight to Los Angeles (say) because we have business there. We need to arrive on Wednesday evening for business on Thursday and Friday. But we also decide to take the family and we plan to stay for the weekend, returning Sunday evening. The travel agent uses an Airline Reservation terminal to book seats on suitable flights. These are ordered from an inventory of available seats offered by relevant suppliers: the Airlines. Let us now return to the customer on the phone - still talking to the Order Clerk, who says:

Order Clerk:	*"By the way, do you know about Product Y. It allows you to use Product X in half the time. I can send you 36 units of Y as well for only 20%. Also users of Product X enjoy Product Z. Have you used this? It has the characteristics of ... ... and costs only ... ... Can I include 36 units of Product Z as well in our Wednesday delivery?"*
Customer:	*"Yes and thanks for those suggestions. I confirm that my order is now for 36 units each of Products X, Y and Z - all to be delivered on Wednesday."*

The *Product Development Process* displayed related products that met the same needs as Product X. This suggested that Product Y may be of interest. An order for Y, based on the current order for X, was automatically prepared and priced ... and Y was in stock. This extension to the order only needed the customer's approval for its inclusion in the delivery. Once again, this is commonplace in the Travel Industry. The travel agent knows the customer will be in Los Angeles over several nights and so asks whether any hotel accommodation is needed. If so, a booking is made at a suitable hotel using another supplier's system: Hotel Reservations.

The *Customer Needs Analysis Process* then indicated that customers in the same market as Customer 165, who also used Products X and Y, had other needs that were addressed by Product Z. A further extension to include

Z in the order was automatically prepared and priced. Z was also in stock and was able to be included in the delivery, if agreed. This is analogous to the Travel Agent asking if a rental car and tour bookings are also needed: quite likely if a family is in Los Angeles for a weekend, and thus near the theme parks and tourist resorts.

Instead of waiting for stock availability from the Warehouse in the first scenario based on separate, non-integrated processes for each function, the re-engineered scenario let the Clerk place a purchase order directly with a selected supplier so that the customer's order could be satisfied. And the Product Development and Customer Needs Analysis processes then suggested cross-selling opportunities based first on related products, and then on related needs in the customer's market.

Cross-functional processes identified with reengineering opportunity analysis can suggest reorganization opportunities. For example, inter-dependent processes may all be brought together in a new organization unit. Or they may remain in their present organization structure, but be integrated automatically by the computer only when needed - as in the re-engineered scenario discussed above.

But what about the incompatibilities we discussed earlier with inter-enterprise access to suppliers' Inventory Systems? This is achieved by linking customers, suppliers and business partners together by Extranets, using the Internet. This use of Internet technologies offers us dramatic new ways to deploy applications and address otherwise insurmountable incompatibilities.

6 Deployment of Information Engineering Applications

Databases and information systems are today implemented using many technologies. These include Data Warehouses with Executive Information Systems, Decision Support Systems, Online Analytical Processing and Decision Early Warning. They also include Client/Server systems developed using object-oriented languages. These are implemented today via Intranets or Extranets, or are deployed directly to the Internet. Reviewing the status of Internet and Intranet technologies today we find that:

- Web browsers are available for all platforms and operating systems, based on an open architecture interface using HyperText Markup Language (HTML). A key factor influencing future computing technologies will be this open architecture environment.
- The Web browser market is largely shared between Microsoft and Netscape. But the strategy adopted by Microsoft has seen it rapidly gain market share at the expense of Netscape: it is using its desktop ownership to embed its browser technology (Internet Explorer) as an integral and free component of Windows NT and the successors to Windows 95.

- The Internet is based on TCP/IP communications protocol and Domain Naming System (DNS). Microsoft, Novell and other network vendors recognize that TCP/IP and DNS are the network standards for the Internet and Intranets. This open architecture network environment benefits all end-users.

- The battle to become THE Internet language - between Java (from Sun) and ActiveX (from Microsoft) will likely be won by neither. Browsers support both languages and automatically download code as needed from Web servers in a relevant language (as "applets") for execution. Instead, the winners of this battle will again be the end-users, who will benefit from the open architecture execution environment.

- Data Base Management System (DBMS) vendors (those that plan to survive) support dynamic generation of HTML for browsers, with transparent access to the Internet and Intranets by applications using these tools. They accept HTML input direct from Web forms, process the relevant queries and generate dynamic HTML Web pages to present the requested output. DBMS products with this capability include: Microsoft SQL Server, IBM DB2, Oracle, Sybase, CA-OpenIngres and Informix. Extensible Markup Language (XML) promises even more powerful dynamic capabilities.

- Client/Server vendors (again those that plan to survive) also provide dynamic generation of HTML for browsers that are used as clients, with transparent access to the Internet and Intranets for applications built with those tools. Client code - written in either ActiveX or Java - is downloaded as needed for execution and for generation of dynamic HTML or XML output to display transaction results. Products include: Microsoft Visual Basic, Visual J++, Access; Powersoft Optima++ and Powerbuilder; Centura and SQLWindows; Borland Latte, Delphi & C++.

- Data Warehouse and Data Mining products provide a similar capability: accepting HTML input and generating HTML output if they are to be used effectively via the Intranet and Internet. Screen Scraper tools with GUI interfaces for Legacy Systems have also become internet-aware: accepting 3270 data streams and dynamically translating them to (or from) HTML to display on the screen. Thus they provide a transparent HTML interface for easy migration of 3270 Legacy Systems to the Internet and Intranets.

6.1 Internet and Intranet Deployment

The Internet has emerged since 1994 as a movement that will see all businesses inter-connected in the near future, with electronic commerce as the norm. It indicates that most DBMS and Client/Server tools will interface directly and transparently with the Internet and Intranet. Web browsers, Java, HTML, XML, the Internet and Intranet all provide an open-architecture interface for most operating system platforms. Previous incompatibilities between operating systems, DBMS products, Client/Server products, LANs, WANs and EDI disappear - replaced by an open architecture environment based on HTML, XML and Java.

6.2 Client/Server Systems

The client software for Client/Server systems becomes the web browser, operating as a "fat" client by automatically downloading Java or ActiveX code when needed. Client/Server tools typically offer two options, each able to be executed by any terminal which can run browsers or HTML-aware code:

1. Transaction processing using client input via web forms, with dynamically-generated HTML or XML web pages presenting output results in a standard web browser format, *OR*

2. Transaction processing using client input via Client/Server screens, with designed application-specific output screens built by client/server development tools. This client environment recognizes HTML and XML, dynamically translating and presenting that output using the designed application-specific screens.

6.3 Data Warehouses

Client/Server development tools provide transparent access to data base servers using HTML-access requests, whether accessing operational data or Data Warehouses. In turn data base servers process these requests - transparently using object-oriented logic developed with O-O languages such as Java, or with ActiveX, to access new or legacy data bases as relevant. These may be on separate servers, or instead may be on mainframes executing legacy systems.

Web servers then operate as application servers, executing Java, ActiveX or conventional code as part of the middle-tier of three-tier Client/Server logic distribution for operational databases, with data base servers also executing Java, ActiveX or conventional code as the third logic tier. Data Warehouses then take periodical extracts from operational databases for multi-dimensional, time-dependent analysis using EIS, DSS, OLAP and DEW software products.

7 Conclusion: What does the Future hold?

Managers of organizations in all industries and environments whether Public Sector, Private Sector or Defense now recognize that the design and development of successful information systems depends on business knowledge as well as expertise in Information Technology. Business-driven Information Engineering provides a very productive design partnership between business experts and IT experts. Together they are able to utilize their respective knowledge to design databases and systems that are more flexible and so are able to accommodate business change more readily. This rapid change capability will be essential for survival and prosperity in the competitive years ahead.

Development is also becoming easier: many of the incompatibilities we previously had to deal with will soon be a thing of the past. Open architecture development using the technologies of the Internet enables deployment on any PC with any hardware, operating system, DBMS, network, client/server tool or Data Warehouse. This will be the direction that the IT industry will take for the foreseeable future.

The open-architecture environment enjoyed by the audio industry - where any CD or tape will run on any player, which can be connected to any amplifier and speakers - has long been the holy grail of the IT industry. Once the industry has made the transition over the next few years to the open-architecture environment brought about by Internet and Intranet technologies, we will be close to achieving that holy grail!

References

[Cod70] Codd, E., A Relational Model for Large Shared Data Banks, CACM 13 (6), 1970, 377-87

[Cod79] Codd, E., Extending the Database Relational Model to Capture More Meaning, ACM Trans. on Database Systems 4 (4), 1979, 397-434

[Dat82] Date, C., Introduction to Data Base, Volumes 1 and 2, Addison-Wesley, Reading, 1982

[DeM82] De Marco, T., Software Systems Development, Yourdon Press, New York, 1982

[Dru74] Drucker, P., Management: Tasks, Responsibilities, Practice, Harper & Row, New York, 1974

[Fin81] Finkelstein, C., Information Engineering, six InDepth articles in: Computerworld, Framingham, 1981

[Fin89] Finkelstein, C., An Introduction to Information Engineering, Addison-Wesley, Sydney, 1989

[Fin92] Finkelstein, C., Information Engineering: Strategic Systems Development, Addison-Wesley, Sydney, 1992

[FM81] Finkelstein, C., Martin, J., Information Engineering, Volumes 1 and 2, Savant Institute, Carnforth, Lancs, 1981

[Jac75] Jackson, M., Principles of Program Design, Academic Press, New York, 1975

[Mar87] Martin, J., Information Engineering, Volumes 1, 2 and 3, Prentice-Hall, Englewood Cliffs, 1987

[McC93] McClure, S., Information Engineering for Client/Server Architectures, Data Base Newsletter, Boston, 1993

[Orr77] Orr, K., Structured Systems Development, Yourdon Press, New York, 1977

[YC78] Yourdon, E., Constantine, L., Structured Design: Fundamentals of a Discipline of Computer Program Systems Design, Prentice-Hall, Englewood Cliffs, 1978

CHAPTER 19

Object-Oriented Software Engineering Methods

Brian Henderson-Sellers

Object-oriented software engineering is coming of age. The focus in the first two generations of object-oriented (OO) methods (around 1990 and 1994 respectively) was on techniques and modelling. In the current third generation approaches, exemplified here by OPEN, a software engineering process is the key element which supplies the necessary underpinning to link together the second generation techniques into a viable approach to software development in a commercial/business environment.

1 Introduction

Object-oriented software engineering methods are relatively new. Whilst object-oriented (OO) ideas have been developing since the late 1960s when the language Simula was first developed, the real interest in OO methods, from an information systems perspective, only commenced around 1990; and even in the subsequent few years, the subject was dominated by technical arguments rather than the the considerations of the full lifecycle implementation for employment in commercial IS projects (Section 2).

Consequently, most OO "methods" are in fact highly technically focussed and are no more than a set of (usually coherent) techniques (see Section 3). As research and practice both progressed, a large number of OO methods were developed (Section 4) so that by around 1995/6 there was a strong impetus to try to "slim down the choice" and standardize, at least on a common metamodel (Section 5). Full OO software engineering methods are now beginning to "come of age" with new, third-generation, full-lifecycle development approaches such as OPEN (Section 6). The need is not only for a technical lifecycle focussed on the creation of the software product almost considered independently of the people who build it and the environment in which this manufacture occurs, but also on the project management, business focus, customer focus and usability/quality issues (including GUIs) that are vital for modern software developments.

Whilst many OO approaches are traditionally referred to as either an OO method or methodology (the terms will be taken as synonomous for the purposes of this discussion) or as OO analysis and design, it is important in this contribution to focus not only on OOAD (object-oriented analysis and design – some OOAD techniques are discussed in Section 7) but also on the broader issues. Indeed, this contribution attempts to integrate both the technical and the broader management issues in its evaluation of the state-of-the-art of OO software development.

2 The Software Process and Lifecycle Seamlessness

2.1 Process

The overall *process* of software development can be considered to possess three dimensions:

a) Methodology: which can be viewed as the manifestation of attempts to introduce rigour into software development, at least by capturing and standardizing recognised good practice as well as by seeking good underpinning theory.

b) People and organizational influences — directly related to the management of the human activities that lead to the development of software systems; and

c) Technology.

It is the balance of elements from these three dimensions that defines a specific software process and allows an approximation and subsequent comparison of the level of the capability, in process assessment terminology (e.g. Capability Maturity Model: CMM), of an instance of such a process. Indeed, it is a well-defined software process that is the central requirement for attaining a CMM or ISO-SPICE (Software Process Improvement and Capability Determination) [EDM97] level 3 maturity.

We can therefore consider a software process as being defined in terms of a mix of an instance of a methodology, being conducted within a particular organizational context and utilizing a specific set of technologies [YH97]. A high quality software process, however, not only has to cover the three areas above, but also has to be understandable, enactable, repeatable, and improvable. To achieve these attributes, a software process has to be formal, granular, precise and measurement-based.

2.2 Lifecycle Seamlessness

In many OO methodologies, the words analysis and design are retained. However, in doing so, it is sometimes not clear whether traditional definitions (analysis = breaking down, sometimes called discovery; design = building up or synthesis, sometimes called invention) are being used or not. Often it is the case that a distinction similar to the second one in Figure 1 is being used: the word analysis covers all activities through to the beginning of language-specific design details. This is generally the flavour, for instance, in two second-generation OO methods: BON (Business Object Notation) [WN95] and MOSES (Methodology for Object-Oriented Software Engineering of Systems) [HE94a] — where, in the latter, the word analysis was replaced by the word Specification to avoid confusion. There is also a recent trend to talk about requirements engineering and how to incorporate that into methodologies (see e.g. discussion on FOOM (Formal Object-Oriented Method) by Swatman [Swa96] and on BIO by Moser [MCF96]).

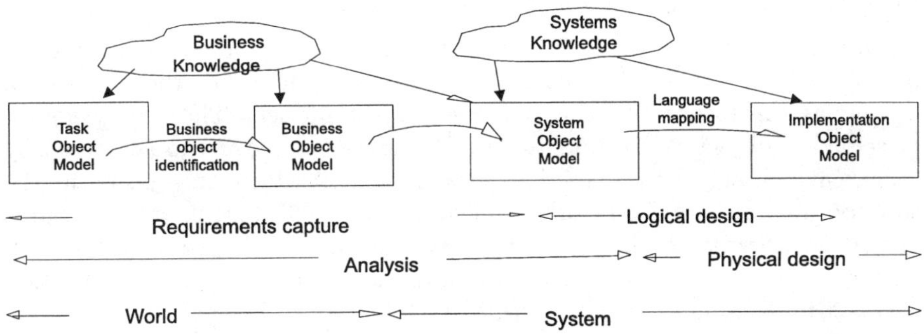

Figure 1: Seamlessness and the various object models [GHY97b]

Whatever the words that are used, we can consider that

(i) there is indeed a highly seamless transition across the lifecycle. The gaps between the four boxes of Figure 1 are minimal.

(ii) there is a need to address the transitions between the task object model to the business object model (business focus) to the system object model (software focus) and also from the system object model to the implementation[1] model (the code).

The last (third) transition is most discussed. It is essentially the transition from logical design (OOPL-independent) to physical design, in which the nuances and capability of the chosen OOPL are utilized to their full. The

[1]Note that sometimes, confusingly, not only is the coding stage referred to as implementation but so too is the act of installing the software with the end user.

boundary between systems design and implementation in object-oriented systems is a blurred one, although perhaps more identifiable than the OOA/D boundary in that design documentation is of a very different nature to implementation documentation (viz. code). Although it could be argued that implementation is merely a continuation of design, just at a very detailed level, it is more realistic to differentiate design and implementation as two different activities, design being at a level of abstraction above implementation. A good design (as represented by the System Object Model) is one that represents the problem and also has a number of good software engineering traits. Design thus combines knowledge gained in analysis (of the problem domain) with more detailed *solution* techniques — the focus is on semantics. Coding in a chosen programming language finalizes the solution using techniques available in that language, and is syntactically-focussed. Indeed, it is argued that, for some OOPLs, such as Eiffel supported by a methodology such as BON or OPEN, this transition is so smooth as to be almost unnoticeable. For C++ the transition is not so smooth, but is well catered for by the detailed discussions of a methodology like Booch.

We should remember that the (physical) design model is not a model of the UoD (universe of discourse) but rather a model of the conceptual model, as represented by the Business Object Model. The purely logical or semantic object classes identified in "analysis" are now supplemented by "physical" object classes, used to model entities which only occur in the solution domain and not in the problem domain. This also involves resource allocation, security checks, efficiency considerations etc. Reuse should be even better supported than in design, both in terms of process (e.g. generalization and testing techniques) and in terms of quality control.

As part of quality control, a significant post-development activity (at all granularities) must include defect management procedures such as testing as well as verification and validation. In current methods, neither are well described; in fact, generally being omitted totally in methodologies other than OPEN. However, testing procedures for object hierarchies are currently under development and verification and validation (V&V) techniques increasingly stressed. These techniques must address both technical (software) competency as well as user satisfaction; the latter, especially, being relevant throughout the lifecycle. Methodologies should therefore support peer, expert and customer review, as well as consistency and completeness checking plus a mechanism to support auditability. Indeed, in OPEN (Section 6), we go even further and mandate testing as part of the post-condition on *all* lifecycle Activities.

Good, reusable classes require additional effort. The methodological metamodel supports reuse through generalization and class refinement specifically (as well as a higher level class reuse mindset throughout the lifecycle). Such class reuse strategies should be seen both as part of the normal object-oriented lifecycle as well as activities needed for modification, extension and maintenance.

The first two transitions, however, provides more challenge. Translating from the task object model which represents the business knowledge to the business object model, still capturing business knowledge but now described in object-oriented terms, followed by the transition into the software domain to create the System Object Model, described by an OOAD modelling language such as OML (OPEN Modelling Language) or UML (Unified Modeling Language), requires significant skill. The OPEN approach is to ensure that this transition is as smooth as possible.

Figure 2 shows how this seamlessness is accomplished in both SOMA (Semantic Object Modelling Approach) and OPEN. From the Mission, a set of objectives is derived. By analyzing the business objectives using hierarchical task analysis (roughly a higher-level, business-focussed type of use case), which gives a set of task scripts, the objectives can thus be represented by Task Object Models which can then be decomposed down to atomic tasks. Each of these atomic tasks corresponds to a single business object in the software domain. The trick is to notice that these task trees constitute "plans" for interaction during task performance and, thus, for system execution. Then each root task corresponds to EXACTLY ONE system operation: in the class that initiates the plan. By making this link, we can generate event traces which correspond to aspects of the system functionality (what the user requires to be delivered). This now gives us a seamless link from mission down to the code — AND BACK! [Gra96].

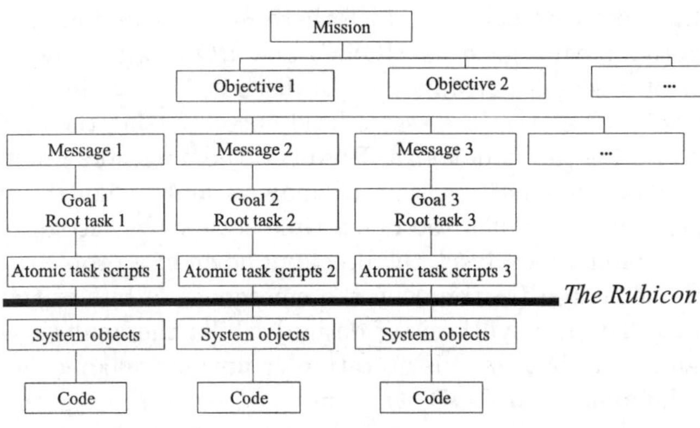

Figure 2: A seamless process from Mission to Atomic Task Script and on into code [Gra96]

2.3 "Analysis" and "Design"

It is often argued that the reason for separating analysis from design is related to the target of the modelling at each level. At the analysis or conceptual modelling phase, we are trying to represent a part of the real world, whereas at the design stage we are representing an information systems design. Thus "information systems *analysis* is the process of creating a *model* of (the human perceptions of) the real system to be represented in the information system," [WW89] while "design is the process of creating a model of the information system (artifact) to be constructed based upon the model of the real system".

An analysis-level model is then primarily concerned with providing an accurate picture of the real-world situation, and an object-oriented requirements engineering (OORE) and object-oriented analysis (OOA) must have this as their primary objective. The object-oriented design (OOD) model's major objective is to support "good" software engineering design in terms of correctness, modularity, reusability, and abstraction. The goal of a "seamless" transition between phases should be subsumed by the primary goals of each level of modelling identified above.

This separation of analysis and design, and the explicit recognition of language constructs and analysis constructs, are reflected in, and supported by, many of the current analysis and design methodologies. This leads some authors to offer a notation that is slightly different between OOA and OOD. However, the graphics of the two stages should be as compatible as possible to provide as seamless a transition as possible from analysis to design, yet support powerful enough concepts to be useful modelling tools at each stage.

The problem of moving from analysis to design is obviated in a different way in other methodologies in which there is no distinct analysis/design boundary. Methodologies such as MOSES and BON, which focus strongly on the notion of a seamless transition (as discussed above in Section 2.2), have a single "phase" at the large scale level encompassing the analysis and design phases of other methodologies. However, these authors point out that they are not suggesting that the acts of analysis and design do not occur; rather that they do so at much too fine a time scale to be recognized within any full lifecycle model. Analysis, the breaking down of a problem, is almost inevitably complemented (in time) by the emergence of bits of the solution being stuck together (the synthesis of design) whilst the analysis continues. Another advantage is that there is no rationale now for making the notation in OOA any different from OOD. Of course, at some time in the process, OOPL-specific notation will be needed. However, this is seen as part of the implementation decision (after all, it can only take place after an implementation language choice has been made); the modelling process of creating the final models being totally independent of the technology. This, for instance, then allows object modelling also to be applied to modelling large scale enterprises and elevates the technique beyond a simple computing aid.

In a fully object-oriented (i.e. pure OO) lifecycle systems development, the object-oriented paradigm is utilized during analysis, design, and coding, thus providing a single model valid *throughout* the lifecycle stages. The use of this "seamless transition" permits a continuity across phase "boundaries" (Figure 1) and also allows highly similar terminologies and graphical notation to be used at each successive stage. At the same time, it blurs the analysis/design boundary so much that it often becomes difficult to distinguish between these two traditional phases. Indeed, in methodologies like MOSES, SOMA, OPEN and BON, discussed below, the analysis/design dichotomy is not recognized; rather the emphasis is on a smooth, full lifecycle transition.

In general, a methodology should be programming-language independent; although in some, particularly in OOD, there may be a (partial) influence from one specific language. This occurs because some methodologies have clearly grown "backwards" from OOP — for instance, RDD from Smalltalk, Booch91 from Ada, BON from Eiffel. Others have evolved from an information systems environment and thus show no programming language bias (e.g. OMT – Object Modeling Technique, Martin/Odell, MOSES, OPEN).

2.4 An Alternative to Sequential Analysis and Design

In the alternative process view, as recommended here, OOA and OOD are not segregated at the macroscale. Instead, it is argued that software developers, whilst undertaking analysis and design in the sense described above, do so in a way in which they alternate between the two over a timescale of minutes or seconds. Analyzing the problem often leads rapidly to thoughts of likely solution (design); discovery (analysis) immediately leads on the human brain to building a model of the discovered artefact which by its very nature is the design process. In other words, in methodologies such as MOSES, SOMA and OPEN which use this approach of merging OOA and OOD at the macro- or activity-level, the arguments discussed above remain valid but the timescale of their applicability is very much shortened (possibly by several orders of magnitude).

In the OPEN process lifecycle (Section 6.1) the object model is constructed during the Evolutionary Development Activity which is a programming-independent language process of gradual refinement, elaboration, discovery of business objects and then computer-specific objects but *not* in a constrictive way. Towards the end of each iteration, it is likely that the classes being discovered and refined will have more "computer-specificity" — they may be newly demanded classes or themselves derived from concerns already present from the earlier requirements analysis. Flexibility is thus supported and the methodology acts as a roadmap [UM95] rather than a straightjacket for construction.

Thus, in this approach, Modelling is an iterative development which is a refinement and elaboration, augmented by the discovery of new object classes as appropriate. The "end point" is a detailed design deliverable ready for coding. Analysis and design activities occur concurrently, often on very short timescales; whilst the deliverables (on the timescale of weeks or months) are clearly delineated and refer to the detailed design documentation not intermediate "analysis diagrams".

It is this notion of "Specification" (a term also used by [CD94]) for the same SDLC structuring) or "Modelling" (as preferred in OPEN) which corresponds to the optimal support for a seamless transition and a discrimination between language-independent system object model construction and the detailed design and coding towards the implementation model (the code itself).

3 The Evolution of Object-Oriented Software Development Approaches

Let us trace the history of object-oriented "methods". In the late 1960s, object orientation was in its infancy; yet this decade was when many of the object-oriented concepts were laid down. Object orientation had little real-world application and object-oriented tools were generally confined to university and industry research laboratories. At this stage, it was understood that, with regards to object orientation;

"Methodology" = set of programming level standards, tips and hints

Concepts are important but do not intrinsically contain information on how, when and where these should be used. In the 1970s and 1980s, techniques such as CRC cards, scenario analysis, the use of interaction diagrams and how to object model became well-developed. This laid the foundation for the development of object-oriented design methods. At this stage, our understanding was extended to encompass these new considerations, such that the popular view of object orientation in this era was

"Methodology"
=
set of design level techniques guidelines supporting documentation

As object technology matured, a veritable explosion of published OOAD methodologies occurred. Dependent on your definition of a "methodology" (a.k.a. method), there are between 20 and 80 of these for industrial software developers to choose from. This is an unenviable task for the project manager. Not only are there technical considerations (lifecycle coverage, metrics support, implicit object (meta)model) but there are also pragmatic concerns regarding ongoing support, industry norms, perceived methodology "market share" as well as the degree of support from CASE tool vendors. Some were purer OO than others, some fuller lifecycle, some more influenced (or you may say biased) towards one particular programming language, supporting the adoption of OT in mainstream markets such as finance, insurance, banking, health, airlines.

It also takes time for any software development approach to become established. Consequently, the most well-known methods are those published some years ago. Thus the choice often focusses on the older methods such as RDD, OMT, Booch, Coad/Yourdon, Shlaer/Mellor, OOSE/Objectory. A second crop of methods was published in the 1994/1995 period. These have, in general, a broader scope, plugging some of the gaps of the pioneering OOAD methodologies, particularly the non-technical, reuse, quality and process omissions. Whilst they are newer and have a lower user base (because of their shorter time in the marketplace), they should not be disregarded simply on market share arguments. Some examples here are Fusion, SOMA, MOSES, BON and OOram.

Around 1993, there was concern raised among the methodologists themselves that this plethora of methods might be in fact retarding, rather than encouraging, industry adoption of OT, and particularly of an appropriate OOAD methodology. Whilst not wishing to slow down progress, as evident in more recently published books and articles, it was clearly time to try to consolidate our knowledge of OT in its "analysis and design" guise.

Towards the end of 1994 it began to be realized that text books describing methods were inadequate for many organizational needs [Jac94]. Textbook-based methods are fine for learning the techniques and for pilot projects and small industries. However, even the best are somewhat deficient with respect to real process support — in other words, they have no or little method! Published methods were often limited to particular foci e.g. a modelling focus in OMT [RBPEL91], a telecommunications influence on OOSE [JCJO92] etc. No single method (of those published up to 1995) is complete, mostly because they don't fully deal with the difficult issues of project management, quality assurance and project practicalities. Granted there is some embryonic evidence of some of these in these books — for instance OOSE [JCJO92] includes some discussion on testing, SOMA [Gra95a] on requirement analysis and user interaction, MOSES [HE94a] on metrics, quality and project management. Neither do any of these pre-1995 methods integrate well in hybrid environments in which interfacing to traditional code is vital. Graham [Gra93a, Gra93b] in some of his Object Magazine articles, discusses the ideas of interfaces in terms of wrapper technology.

Overall, this led to disenchantment with Booch [Boo94], OMT [RBPEL91], OOSE [JCJO92] and the like by many organizations who, instead, chose to "roll their own" by merging together bits of all these familiar methods. There are, however, dangers in this [HKM94]. This leads us to presume that what is now meant by methodology is:

"Methodology"

=

client-specific methods that cover
the lifecycle requirements of the particular project

By the end of 1994, it was clear that there were potentially three types of methodology. Henderson-Sellers and Edwards [HE94b] proposed a three level discrimination

1. Teaching methodologies — smaller than those published to date, not commercially complete but useful for learning.

2. Public domain methodologies — the backbone of the "methodology industry". These are almost all the ones we have talked about here — they are published in a book, they have CASE tool support, etc.

3. Sophisticated yet proprietary methodologies, such as Objectory, Syntropy and Mentor. Such level 3 methodologies are often strongly linked, like Mentor, to a Level 2 methodology (in this case, OPEN).

Most of the work is focussed on Level 2 methodologies; although there is likely to be significant action at Level 3 as large consulting firms develop their proprietary versions of an OO methodology. I would also like to think that we shall soon see some smaller methodologies for teaching purposes, as suggested by Susan Lilly [Lil94].

Over the period 1991–6, OMT, Booch, RDD, Coad and Yourdon and OOSE became the most widely known of the "OO methods". *However,* as we began to suggest above, these well-known "OO methods" are not really methods at all but rather a somewhat coherent set of useful techniques. What is needed is full process support, but a process that is not frozen as a particular model (e.g. waterfall), but is flexible and tailorable and may be applied to many project domains. We need to consider the larger scale issues of organizational structures, corporate as well as departmental reuse strategies, component-based development and costing models.

A good method or process, be it OO or not, has several rôles: it can provide a set of standards for what is to be done, when these actions are to be undertaken and in what order, what the elements are that are involved in the process as well as what will be delivered. It can give guidance and support through its techniques and guidelines; it can provide a framework for monitoring and control. At the higher (Software Process) level this monitoring and control may be achieved through advice on project management and quality procedures and by the use of appropriate technologies. In an object-oriented domain, these must be selected in such a way that are sympathetic with an OO development approach [Hen95]. Consequently, as many have pointed out, an object-oriented process is not simply a recipe book by which a series of steps is followed slavishly to produce the perfect "meal". Access to business knowledge is mandatory as is creativity and skill in design. Rather than a "cookbook", a process or method may be better regarded as a good guidebook or roadmap [UM95]. Such a book provides the traveller with the basic layout of the streets, complete with hints, procedures and rules that apply, thus providing for a successful navigation. However, no-one expects it to predict occasional disturbances such as burst water mains or closed paths for renovation.

A well-defined process or method thus provides a standard, yet flexible, framework for developing systems that blend engineering rigour with engineering creativity thus permitting success to be repeated and repetition of failures to be avoided. Adoption of such an approach will be instrumental in permitting the organization to improve their process capability as measured by capability maturity assessment models such as the CMM or ISO-SPICE.

The above brief outline of the history of OO methodologies and a short description of some of the key players in the methodology field does not attempt to give any real detail; more just a flavour. Over the last few years, there has been a flurry of publication of books on methodologies augmented by books on comparisons of methodologies. The interested reader is recommended to study the books by the methodologists themselves.

4 First and Second Generation Methodologies

There is, as yet, no obvious clear winner in the "methodology stakes". Indeed, any such consensus would be immediately visible in the computing press worldwide. Whilst many papers e.g. [ABCGH91, CF92, MP92] focus on the differences between these various published (and therefore public domain i.e. Level 2) methodologies, overall, these methodologies are more similar than they are different. The newer methodologies clearly use (and credit) ideas abstracted from the methodologies published in the previous three or four years intermingled with brand new ideas. For example, Booch [Boo94] uses OMT and OOSE; Fusion uses OMT and Booch [Boo91]; MOSES uses RDD, OMT, Booch and OOSE; SOMA uses OOSE and MOSES. The list could go on.

On the other hand there are some differences. Some are differences of focus. For instance, Booch [Boo91, Boo94] and Firesmith [Fir93] have more focus on real-time and large systems; Coad and Yourdon [CY91a, CY91b] on data-driven systems; MOSES, SOMA and OPEN on MIS/business applications and on a quality approach to software development; and OOSE on telecommunications. Others focus on particular lifecycle phases — RDD [WWW90] and [Boo91] have a design focus; [CY90, CY91a] on analysis; Fusion uses a different approach in analysis cf. design; MOSES, SOMA, BON and OPEN encapsulate the OO ideas of a seamless transition across *all* lifecycle phases and also incorporate business issues which other methodologies do not; UML has a modelling focus[2].

Some slight technical differences would also appear to exist: for instance, OMT has a two-way association as its default whilst MOSES has a one-way

[2]Whilst UML is not a methodology, being simply a notation plus metamodel, it is still of significance in the broader "methods" discussion.

association; Booch [Boo94] differentiates explicitly between association and using relationships by use of different symbols, whereas OMT and MOSES do not do so explicitly; rather they discuss one-way and two-way associations. Complexity management is less evident in RDD and OMT than in MOSES and OPEN. Concurrency and timing issues are only well addressed in, e.g., ROOM (Realtime Object-Oriented Method), Booch and ADM3/4.

One categorization which is often used is the difference between, on the one hand (one extreme), the evolutionary OO methodologies which tend to treat objects as if they were predominantly (or indeed totally) data, to consider objects to be static with a relatively weak form of information hiding and closely allied to traditional (relational) data stores and to use graphical techniques which are weak extensions of structured analysis and design techniques. Both Eckert and Golder [EG94] and Berard [Ber95] gives examples of these as including OMT, Shlaer/Mellor, Embley *et al*, Fusion and Martin/Odell. Revolutionary OOAD approaches are obviously at the "other extreme". In these, Berard notes, concepts such as inheritance and polymorphism are paramount, there is a strong emphasis on information hiding, information is localized around objects (as opposed to data), and concepts such as abstract, parameterization and/or metaclasses are used. An OO mindset prevails; objects can be active and classes and instances are clearly differentiated. Typical examples are given as Berard, Booch and RDD (the newer methodologies in this category such as BON, SOMA, MOSES, OOram and OPEN were, of course, not included in this evaluation). Of course there are many other methodologies which try to capitalize on a range of techniques without going to either extreme. More detailed comparisons of methodologies have also been previously made ([vGBH92, Gra94, HE94a]).

A significant, and more revolutionary, approach in many ways is that of responsibilities and contracting. Responsibilities were introduced in the design approach of Rebecca Wirfs-Brock and colleagues in 1990 and their approach is now commonly known as RDD standing for Responsibility-Driven Design; although other methodologies, notably BON and OPEN, also place emphasis on this way of OO thinking and modelling.

5 Standardized Methodologies?

Over the period 1994–1997 there has been growing interest in the possible "standardization" and/or "convergence" of object-oriented analysis and design methodologies. Discussion on the internet bulletin boards in late May/early June of 1994 underlined this. Over a similar period, at least three "standards" organizations, OMG (Object Management Group), ASC X3H7 and CDIF, have been working towards a commonality of understanding within object technology and particular between OO methodologies.

Some authors have used a "check box" type of approach ([ABCGH91, CF92]) to compare methodologies which has a tendency to focus on differences between models and breadth of support in an individual model. Underlying such an approach might be an implicit assumption that "more is better". It is all too easy to assume, upon reading such a work, that because Methodology A does not possess many of the features of Methodology B, then Methodology B must be unquestionably better. Of course, the missing elements may be because of a lack of quality; but more likely are to do with a different focus and/or level of granularity. It is obvious, once pointed out, that if your methodology is focussing on, say, transaction processing, then support for embedded real time applications may well be irrelevant. Thus we would not expect to find many of the elements of, for example, the real-time method ROOM [SGW95] present within a data-processing-oriented method such as Coad/Yourdon [CY91a, CY91b]. This does not degrade either; but merely suggests we should provide (and use) methodological "horses for courses". Indeed, it is even arguable that a methodology satisfying every conceivable project type would be so unwieldy as to be incomprehensible and hence unmanageable and unuseable.

Whilst comparisons such as these are undoubtedly useful in helping the developer choose the most appropriate set of techniques, they also, unfortunately, give the impression of disarray between methods. The published descriptions often seem hard to reconcile. Object models, terminology and notation all tend to obfuscate the reality of the *similarities* between approaches. The perception was that differences are all important (for marketing presumably) and that the methodologists themselves were all waging internecine war.

In fact, the reverse has been true for some time. Studying any recently published (say 1994 onwards) book on OOAD, the reader will see significant citations to other work. Thus Booch [Boo94] acknowledges influences of OMT and OOSE; SOMA [Gra95a] acknowledges the work embodied in MOSES [HE94a] which in turn acknowledges Booch [Boo91, Boo94], OMT [RBPEL91], UON (Unified Object Notation) [PCW90] etc[3]. Rather than competition, many of the methodologists have already opted for collaboration. This new spirit of "togetherness" is best evinced in three ways — the building of metamodels, convergence of terminology and the convergence of methods themselves.

Proponents for standardization note that for the more rapid acceptance of OOAD methodologies by industry, something that is solid and ready for adoption, something that is widely accepted and widely supported is vital. It is felt that this is likely to give them some confidence in the long term survival of OO [Gra94, Jac93].

Arguments against standardization/agreement include the possible stultification of the field before it's sufficiently mature; huge investments of time and money by each individual methodologist to create a coherent whole – viz.

[3]And in many unpublished documents from a wide variety of reputable sources

an amalgamation might be the "camel" designed by the committee, which no-one finds acceptable. Even if agreement were feasible and/or desirable, then with a single agreed methodology it is arguably inevitable that someone else will come along with a better "OO mousetrap".

5.1 Standardization or Interoperability?

Obviously, since OOAD methodologies are still rapidly maturing, it is inappropriate to simply adopt any one at present as being "the industry standard". Interoperability is perhaps the most fruitful way forward. With this approach, a common core is identified and agreed and each extant methodology elaborates (and sells) OT in its own guise — yet, the underlying core is agreed so that in practice an industry can move relatively freely between the various "brand methodologies" as they mature further.

One way of building a "common" methodology is to try to identify *all* the features in the various published methodologies and construct some superset methodology. Such a methodology rapidly becomes overly complex and provides a barrier to entry to the OO market rather than the support that a good methodology should provide.

Another approach is to try to identify a critical "core". This has dangers, as outlined in [MSBRSBAW93]. If, say, aggregation was identified as a core concept, then any analysis or design method not using aggregation would be seen as being penalized. Secondly, the delineation of such a subset might restrict growth of new ideas. Forcing everyone to use only the minimal set of concepts *cannot* provide support for more than the standard, run-of-the-mill application; which in any case are probably going to be undertaken by experienced analysts rather than a neophyte software engineer following "the book" page by page.

Identification of this core (which may itself mature of course) requires, in the opinion of many, the use of metamodelling techniques [Car94a, Car94b, Hen94, Jac93]. On the other hand, it is critical to retain flexibility so that

(i) individual methodologies can retain their own identity, and continue to be marketed as such, addressing their own markets and growing in time,

(ii) methodologies can be made available for specific domains, such as MIS, realtime, process control, and

(iii) methodologies can be applied for specific contexts such as greenfield development, enhancements, maintenance and conversions.

The time is ripe for the identification of such a common core. Despite fears that such identification will stultify the field [MSBRSBAW93], current efforts of the OMG [Jou97], in particular, are creating an atmosphere in which the methodologists can share experiences directly or indirectly. The consequences of this are highlighted in Section 4 below. One important component of this identification is the use of metamodelling techniques, which we shall now explain briefly.

5.2 Metamodels

A metamodel of a methodology effectively describe the rules underlying the methodology itself. It provides a model of the methodology. Metamodelling at the same time abstracts the real "guts" of the method, yet, as with any metamodelling, loses detail. Generality is gained at the loss of granularity.

In terms of methodologies, the corresponding metamodel will describe things such as how class, type and instance are related; when certain relationships are valid and when invalid — essentially the semantics as well as the syntax of the methodology. In doing so, a formal language is needed. Terms need to be tightly defined and the metamodel itself "strips away" all but the essential detail. Using a set of metamodelling rules and notation then permits the construction of a definitive core metamodel for any published methodology. This is the focus of the COMMA (Common Object Methodology Metamodel Architecture) project [HB96, HB97]. Then with this metamethodology, each particular methodology can inherit from this core (Figure 3), specializing it in whatever way seems desirable. In parallel, some groups of methodologists are also taking the initiative of rationalizing methodologies by actively merging their approaches. Notable examples here are Booch + OMT + OOSE (the "Unified Method", later the Unified Modeling Language) and SOMA + MOSES + Firesmith together with strong influences from RDD, BON, OOram, OBA (Object Behavioral Analysis) (the "OPEN" method).

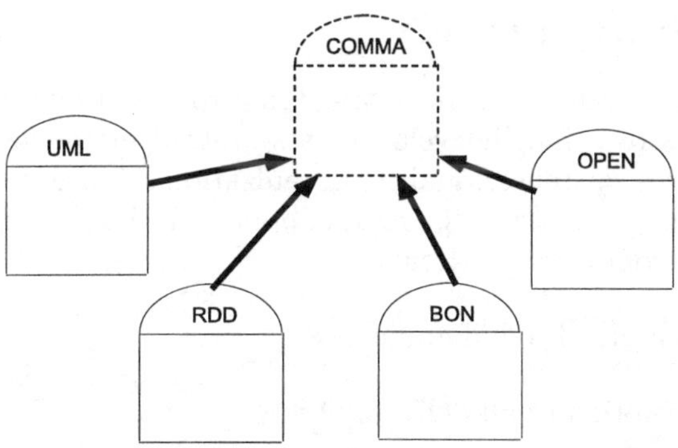

Figure 3: COMMA and its subsets [HB97]

6 Emerging Third Generation Approaches

So what is available? A high quality process-supported method requires many aspects: procedures, QA, metrics, techniques, tools, guidelines, lifecycle, rôles, deliverables, representation (notation), project management, coding standards and models. A match between a commercial process tool such as MeNtOR or Objectory (a Level 3 method: [HE94b]) and a public domain method (Level 2) provides both full commercial-strength support and, at the same time, international validity and entry level documentation through the corresponding public-domain version.

The new, third generation, full lifecycle methodology OPEN fits this bill; together with a commercial process embodiment in the MeNtOR process. OPEN is an example of a fully object-oriented, responsibility- and contract-driven approach. OPEN's metamodel is derived strongly [HFG97c] from the core COMMA metamodel of Henderson-Sellers and Firesmith [HF97] (Figure 4). OPEN also has a preferred notation known as COMN = Common Object Modelling Notation (Figure 5). Collectively, these are known as OML or the OPEN Modelling Language [FHG97]. OML is at the same level of detail as Rational's UML; whilst OPEN, the method (see discussion below), comprises *much* more than UML.

UML, on the other hand, consists of a notation and an underlying metamodel. It makes no contribution to analysis and design techniques nor to software engineering process or methodology. UML's focus is on use cases and modelling (particular its graphical representation). It is an example of a more data-driven approach in which responsibilities play a minor rôle.

Since UML does not address any process issues (including OOAD) which are the focus of this contribution, only providing the representational component of a method, it will not be discussed further here. Instead, we concentrate on the full lifecycle, software engineering characteristics of OPEN.

6.1 The Heart of OPEN

OPEN (OPEN stands for Object-oriented Process, Environment and Notation), consists of a full lifecycle process-centred methodology with wide-ranging emphases on reuse, quality, organizational issues including people, and project management and so on. It supports all the elements of a methodology that one would expect [Hen95]:

- a collection of rules and guidelines
- a full description of all deliverables
- a set of techniques and tools
- a set of appropriate metrics, standards and test strategies

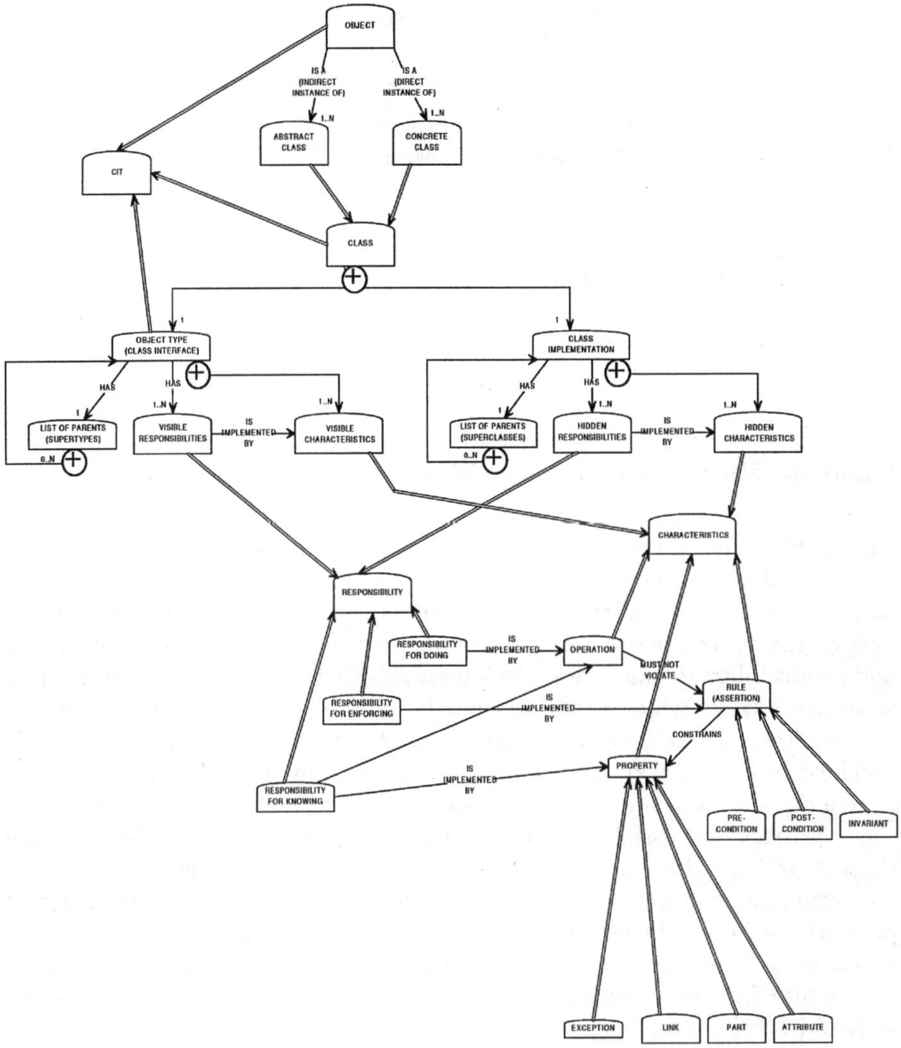

Figure 4: The proposed COMMA core metamodel [HF97]

- a description of the underlying models for product and lifecycle i.e. process
- identification of organizational rôles e.g. business analyst, programmer
- guidelines for project management and quality assurance
- advice on library management and reuse

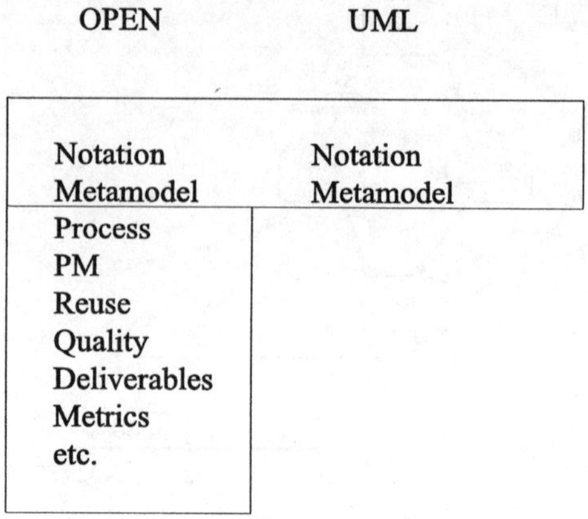

Figure 5: Elements in UML and OPEN

The architecture of OPEN, at the metalevel, is of a set of lifecycle Activities represented as objects [Gra95b]. These objects have contracts with each other so that the flow of control can pass between these objects in any order so long as the contracts are met (Figure 6). This gives the necessary flexibility and tailorability to the overall architecture. Each Activity has a number of associated Tasks which describe what is to be done. These Tasks are the services/responsibilities/operations of the Activity objects. How the goals specified in these Tasks are achieved is described by a set of Techniques.

On the left hand side of Figure 6 are Activities which are associated with a single project (discussed here); on the right hand side, in the shaded box, are those Activities which transcend a single project and are associated more with strategic planning and implementation concerns e.g. resources across several projects; reuse strategies; delivery and maintenance aspects (not discussed here). OPEN includes both projects and organizational software strategies.

Detail of these Activities is outside the scope of this article but are described in [HGSWR97a].

Each Activity has a number of associated Tasks which describe what is to be done. They are the smallest unit of work [GR95]. OPEN Tasks can be loosely grouped. Some occur typically earlier in the lifecycle; others group around a particular domain such as distribution or database management. OPEN Tasks are grouped under seven loose headings:

1. Tasks which focus on modelling or system construction* include:
    - *Analyze user requirements*
    - *Construct the object model*
    - *Design user interfaces*
    - *Identify CIRTs* (= class or instance or rôle or type)

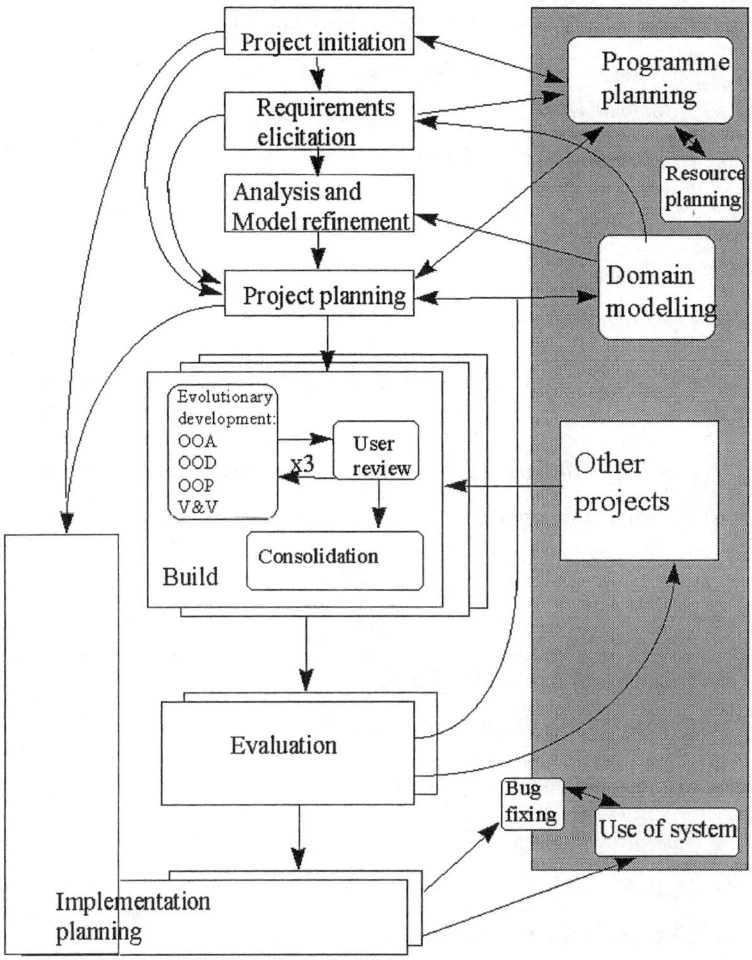

Figure 6: Contract-driven process lifecycle model [GHY97b]

- *Map rôles on to classes*
- *Optimize the design*
- *Undertake usability design*
- *Write manuals and other documentation*

2. Database focussed tasks are:
   - *Design and implement physical database*
   - *Map logical database schema*
3. Tasks which focus on user interactions and business issues include:

- *Problem definition and user requirements*
- *Business process engineering*
- *Approval to proceed*
- *Business object modelling*

4. Tasks which focus on large scale architectural issues include:
   - *Architecture*
   - *Optimization*
5. Tasks which focus on project management issues, which are described in detail in [HD97], include:
   - *Develop software development context plans and strategies*
   - *Develop and implement resource allocation plan*
   - *Undertake feasibility study*
6. Tasks which focus on reuse issues include:
   - *Optimize reuse* (with reuse)
   - *Create new reusable components*
7. Tasks focussing on quality issues are:
   - *Evaluate quality*
   - *Test*
   - *Undertake in-process review*
   - *Undertake post-implementation review*

Notes: These tasks deal specifically with the 'technology' of object technology and utilize those tips and techniques which are often all there is to an OO "methodology". In OPEN, these Tasks are only a small portion of the overall approach. For further details, consult standard texts or the forthcoming OPEN manuals and user guides.

Detail of these Tasks is outside the scope of this article but are described in [HGFRSW96b, GHY97b].

How the goals specified in these Tasks are achieved is described by a set of Techniques. Techniques are ways of doing things. They include the ways that have been tried and tested over the last decade; but also may include new techniques that are more experimental. Some indication on the level of maturity of the individual technique is thus given as part of its full specification.

The key is how to choose the appropriate Technique or Techniques[4] to fulfil the Tasks. This is accomplished by the use of a "probabilistic" matrix (Figure 7) which gives couplings between them. In fact we specify the links with a probability selected from one of five levels: M (=mandatory), R (recommended) O (=optional), D (=discouraged) and F (=forbidden). The values in this matrix can either be determined as "industry averages" or they can be calculated at lower levels such as industry sectors (e.g. banking) or for your own particular organization or department or, indeed, at the individual project level; although preferably the values, once determined, should be retained from project to project, assuming the project characteristics are not vastly different.

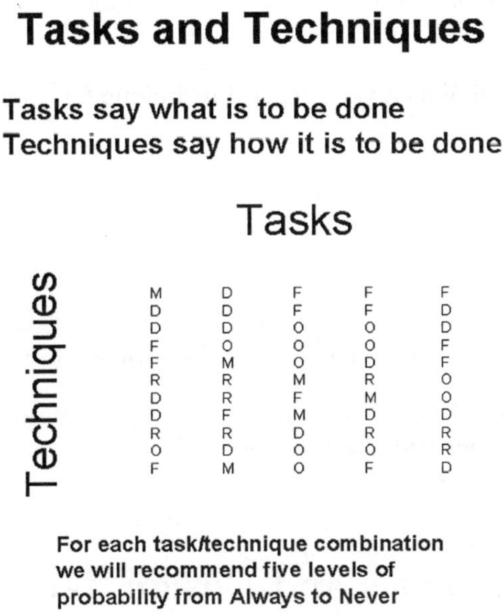

Figure 7: The two-dimensional relationship between Tasks and Techniques Activities

Techniques are intrinsically orthogonal to the notion of Tasks. They cannot readily be grouped in any unique way. They are akin to the tools of the tradesperson — a carpenter's toolbox contains many tools, some of which have superficial resemblances but may have operational affinity to tools of different outward appearance. Since a full description of the OPEN toolbox of Techniques (currently over 150 techniques have been catalogued) is a book in itself (which is currently being prepared), we only give a brief review here (in Section 7).

[4]Often choices are available. For example, in order to find objects, the choice may be between, say, using use cases, using noun analysis, identifying concepts and their responsibilities, using CRC cards, etc. In reality, many tasks are best accomplished by a mixture of techniques rather than just one.

6.2 OPEN Principles

Finally, OPEN embodies a set of (object-oriented) principles. It permits enhanced semantics for object models based on the contributions of methods such as SOMA, BON, Syntropy, Firesmith etc. Furthermore, OPEN is fully object-oriented in that encapsulation is a basic principle. To this end, bi-directional associations are not first-order members of the metamodel, but are instead modelled as a pair of uni-directional associations that are semi-strong inverses of each other. It is a logical consequence of this that class invariants are not an optional extra in the modelling semantics [GBH97]. Rulesets (which generalize class invariants) can be used to model intelligent agents as objects.

In OPEN, OO principles are basic and should be adhered to. These include:

- object modelling as a very general technique for knowledge representation
- encapsulation
- polymorphism

together with

- clear, jargon-free and well-founded definitions of all terms
- extensive use of abstraction techniques, a foundation for semantically cohesive and encapsulated "objects"

7 Some Analysis and Design Techniques

Object-oriented systems at compile time consist of classes whose structure and relationships represent the static aspects of the system. At run-time, the system state consists of objects, that is, instances of classes, and references. In analysis and design, the system is described in terms of types and rôles which represent *concepts*. Sometimes it is hard to be crystal clear whether we are talking about Classes, Instances, Rôles or Types; so we often use a generic term, CIRT, made up from their four initials.

In order to show the dynamics of the system graphically, CIRTs must be displayed as a network of methods and the messages passing between them. A relationship between any two CIRTs, whether expressed by aggregation and association or represented by client–server, provides a connection channel that allows messages (or events) to be sent. These messages trigger methods (or processes) that lead to changes of state in the CIRT to which the messages were sent. By recognizing that a static relationship exists between two CIRTs, providing a link for many different events, processes, and state changes to occur in a server CIRT, we explicitly recognize the dynamic and static aspects of the system. One static architecture, therefore, does not imply a one-to-one mapping with any single dynamic arrangement of calls to the supplier class. The static link allows the client to call any exported feature of the supplier in whatever way its implementation sees fit. Thus the sequence of calls to the supplier may be changed, altering the dynamic arrangement, while the static structure remains unchanged.

7.1 Static Object Modelling

Object modelling focusses on two issues: (i) descriptions of the CIRTs or "objects", and (ii) description of interactions between CIRTs.

A core concept is that of type or interface (the external view) versus the internal view of the full implementation of an "object". It is this dichotomy between the external view or specification, much used in analysis and design, and the internal or implementation view (the inside of the class) that is, at the same time, a major strength of OT and an often-neglected description. The external view is taken by the modeller and designer; the internal view by the coder. Focussing your attention, at appropriate times in the development lifecycle, on external and internal views, assists in managing what would otherwise be a confusing situation. This confusion has perhaps been exacerbated by many OO programming language texts where this twin view is ignored. Examples of code often make it difficult for the novice reader to discriminate between external considerations and internal implementation details.

The external view provides a name, services or responsibilities offered, and rules and constraints (e.g. valid ranges, necessary preconditions on services). This is the specification or interface. It describes the type which represents a well-understood concept [MO92]. A concept is an idea that is sufficiently well-developed to have an identical, shared meaning. An idea held by an individual person which means nothing to anyone else does not count. So for instance, common words such as dog, student, person, tree all denote shared concepts and thus qualify as potentially useful concepts. However, it must be stressed that an object type is *not* simply a *set* of objects. A set is a mere collection of extant individuals; for instance, just the people that are in your view at present. Wrongly equating the *set* with the *concept* will preclude later additions of perfectly valid instances from becoming part of the concept. Concept (the intension) first; instances which belong to the concept thus forming the set (or extension of the type) come later. That means that certain concepts can exist (e.g. unicorn, Father Christmas, tooth fairy) which define the intension but for which the extension is a null or empty set [MO92, MO95].

Since OT is about modelling business problems with objects and/or classes, an initial search for CIRTs should be in the problem domain itself. Obvious candidate CIRTs (and we should start with the notion of candidates which may later be cast aside in favour of better concepts) are real-world objects. These can be found by looking for nouns in the user requirements specification [Abo83]; although it should be noted that rigorously taking the user requirements specification and underlining every single noun can waste a *lot* of time for a large user requirements specification (apparently this has been done on real projects). During system development those "first pass" objects (substantive and abstract) will be significantly augmented by objects created as artifacts of constructing the conceptual model. A better approach may thus be to identify objects in terms of their services offered or their responsibilities — this avoids the danger of OOA becoming simply data modelling (see earlier discussion). Task scripts or use cases are also useful here (Section 7.3) as are rôles (Section 7.2).

A service or responsibility is the ability of a CIRT to respond to some request for action. A responsibility may be a "responsibility for knowing" (also called a property or query); a "responsibility for doing" (also called an operation or command); or a "responsibility for enforcing" (rulesets). A property always returns an object (indicated by the type statement after the property name whilst an operation does not — it just does something. It is also important that each service does only one thing. For instance, a request to withdraw an amount from a *BANK_ACCOUNT* class should not also give you the balance. This requires two services: a `withdraw` service and a `tell_me_my_balance` service. Normally, you do not depict services for `create`, `read`, `update` and `delete` (or CRUD services – create, read, update and delete services).

Properties often relate to adjectives in the user requirements specification. They are services that return (tell you) information (usually by accessing hidden data). The information received back is an object. This object may be a simple value such as an *INTEGER* or a more complex object such as an *ENGINE* or a *WING*. The use of properties in the interface *does not* imply that the information requested by the property is stored as data. It may or it may not be. For instance, consider the property of a person's age. This is a number. It may be stored as a number within the instance; or, equally, it may be calculated from other stored information such as birthdate and today's date. It is, however, not good style to put attributes in the service list; rather, any data should only be accessed by methods which implement the services. Properties can be regarded as a shorthand for services offering read and write methods to the hidden attributes.

Operations are roughly equivalent to verbs in the user requirements specification. They represent functionality or commands (procedures). A good identification rule is found from taking an anthropomorphic perspective and asking "can I suffer this operation?". One useful and simple technique for following up this anthropic principle is that of CRC cards [BC89, Wil95]. Here each person takes a single index card to represent a type and asks what is my name? (we saw above how important a good name is); (ii) what are my responsibilities i.e. what services can I offer to other object types?; and (iii) in providing these services with whom do I have to collaborate first?

Modeling is the key focus to build the object model. In OOA/D, the issues of implementation are of no concern and the notation should therefore reflect semantically important concepts rather than be concerned with later design issues that may or may not be object-oriented. In other words, the concepts of uniform reference and information hiding are paramount. The distinction between properties and operations often becoming unnecessary. With a true responsibility-driven design these are dealt with together as "services".

In detailed design, it may be necessary to graphically depict internal (hidden) services (Figure 8). For example, it may be clear that certain services really will be stored as attributes (data) because they already exist in the database. For services which do not relate directly to stored data, the operation is likely to be coded within the class as a method (a procedure or a function). In languages such as C++ and Eiffel these methods resemble miniature procedural programs.

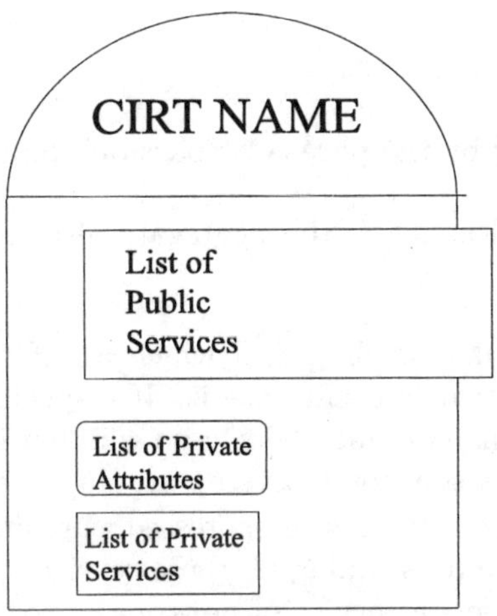

Figure 8: Internal and external information may be depicted visually as internal or external (actually cross-boundary) on the icon (MOSES notation) [Hen97]

7.2 Relationships between CIRTs

It is generally agreed that there are three (maybe four) main relationships between CIRTs: inheritance (including generalization/specialization and implementation inheritance); association (which may include the using relationship or this may be a separate, fourth relationship); and aggregation (which is alternatively regarded by some as a special form of association). However, it should be noted that for detailed design/coding typically only two relationships (inheritance and client–server) are supported.

An association is a named "uses-a" relationship; for example, a *CUSTOMER* uses a *CAR* and also the financial services of a *BANK*. It is generally pictured by a line joining icons representing each of the two participating classes. In OPEN, the default is unidirectional (a mapping); whereas in UML it is bidirectional.

Aggregations depict a tighter, more permanent affiliation: the "is-composed-of" relationship. For example, a room is composed of door(s), walls, a ceiling, a floor and often windows. It is fairly permanent. A room is not an aggregate of the people or the furniture inside it since these are patently temporary and (re)movable. Equating aggregation with the containing relationship is a mistake frequently made — the containing relationship is valid but different. Aggregations

- reflect an inherent asymmetry (whereas associations are often symmetrical),
- describes a parts hierarchy,
- can be described by the phrase "is-part-of", and
- in many cases destroying the aggregate also destroys its component parts.

Aggregation is a useful modelling tool which assists in rationalizing many levels of abstraction. If it is useful, use it. If a specific relationship creates argument between your team members as to whether it really is an aggregation, then the optimum solution is to stop arguing and use association.

Often properties are equally well expressed as relationships (often association). For example (and assuming all these services are externally visible), a *CUSTOMER* may have a service of `personal_profile`. But it is equally useful, especially as you elaborate the detail of the design, to make this an explicit relationship to a class *PERSONAL_PROFILE*; which itself then may have services, such as `name`, `address` and `credit_rating`. These services may, in turn, also be replaced, at an appropriate time, with explicit relationships to other CIRTs.

Inheritance covers many sins. The most discussed is the difference between specialization inheritance (or generalization) and implementation inheritance. The distinction relates to knowledge representation and the merging and equating of the notions of abstract data type and module in OT. Generalization is to be encouraged; implementation inheritance to be strongly discouraged. Generalization represents the "is-kind-of" relationship in which the subclass is a kind of its superclass. This makes the relationship between class and subclass also a type/subtype relationship. In implementation inheritance, only the class/subclass relationship holds and the knowledge represented by the relationships between types is destroyed. Typically, a subclass inherits all the "knowledge" of its parent. This makes it a very open relationship insofar as the subclass is concerned.

One sin which inheritance should not cover directly is that of rôles (the R of CIRT) — a focus of OOram [RWL96]. For example, an example commonly seen to illustrate an inheritance relationship might be that of a class *MANAGER* inheriting from class *PERSON*. From a knowledge representation viewpoint, applying the rule of **is-a-kind-of** sounds OK at first. However, that manager later in the day may return home, becoming first an object of type *COMMUTER* and then an object of type *HOUSEOWNER* and possibly *PARENT*. It may be that two rôles are played concurrently. Perhaps the *COMMUTER* takes his daughter to a hockey match by train and is thus also a *PARENT*. Drawing separate inheritance relationships for the many rôles an individual can play in a single day even can lead to a veritable explosion. In the worst case, a subclass can often by created for each valid combination of rôle and state. In other words, be careful in using the inheritance relationship when really a rôle relationship is needed. Rôles can be very useful in modelling and ways to implement them in an OOPL have recently been proposed, both in extensions to MOSES [RH95] and in the rôle-focussed approach of OOram [RWL96].

7.3 Dynamic Modelling

The behaviour of objects rather than the collaboration of sets of objects can be shown using some form of state-transition diagrams, often based on the statechart of Harel [Har87].

At a system level, sequencing of messages may also be necessary. These are often shown in two flavours: some form of a collaboration diagram or a sequence diagram. In a collaboration diagram, icons representing objects are shown with message paths. The ordering of message passing along those paths is then enumerated so that it is clear in what order these should occur. The sequence diagram, as used in OOSE for example, lays out similar information in a two dimensional fashion. The objects are named across the top and time flows vertically. A good visual impression is thus given of the dynamic nature of the specific part of the system being scrutinized. Of course, in large systems both representations become unwieldy. However, this sort of fine granularity of objects and their messages only usually occurs over a small portion of the system. These diagramming notations should therefore be used in that smaller spatial framework.

Another way of showing particular uses of a system and the control flow patterns, yet again at a fairly abstract level are the task script, the scenario and the use case. In books a few years old, these last two terms tended to be used interchangeably to describe a prototypical user's involvement with the system and their sequence of actions. Now it is generally agreed that a use case is at a more abstract level than a scenario and can be regarded as a "set of scenarios" [Gra97].

The purpose of use cases and task scripts is to describe in natural language a small number of typical interaction sequences of a user with the system. The notion of the user playing a rôle is also important since it is not people that are important here as users but rather their rôle which determines the type of interaction they wish to have with the system. The word actor is thus often used to typify the user.

Use cases and task scripts are good for identifying user requirements; they identify the dynamic aspects of the system; they can help to identify the operations (services) offered by particular classes; and they can be used for testing and evaluation against user requirements. Use cases and task scripts show a trace of events and the response by the supplier. These traces should show the interactions involved in fulfilling the responsibilities of the subsystem leading to a detailed examination of how the system behaves.

Task scripts or use cases should be developed for different situations that the system is to handle, concentrating on those "typical" for the system. Such task scripts are useful in identifying external events and how they are handled by the system. Each use case and task script should be significantly different; minor differences may be recorded within the same use case or task script. Differences between use cases and task scripts become more obvious when more amplification is made.

7.4 Business Rules and Contracting

As well as using a graphical representation for object–object interactions, a second concept should be applied to each and every client–server relationship: the notion of a service contract. The terms of these contractual obligations/benefits are spelled out in a 2×2 matrix (Figure 9), which can be clarified in a contract diagram as a table of features and requirements [Mey92]. This states the obligations and the benefits to each of the two participating parties (see below regarding relationships between pairs of CIRTs). The obligation imposed by any CIRT and a particular service is, in effect, a precondition which any other CIRT wishing to avail itself of this particular service must meet.

The idea of contracts is related to that of "responsibilities" by defining a contract as a cohesive set of responsibilities that a client can depend on (the interface contract) [WWW90]. Many authors stress this need to use a responsibility-driven conceptual approach since a data-driven approach "inherently violates encapsulation." Furthermore, a contract diagram is necessary not only for association relationships but also for aggregation responsibilities, as both are represented by client–server relationship at the design level.

Contracting is an excellent way of moving software towards fuller support

	Obligations	Supplier
Client	Details of obligation on client	Details of benefit to client
Supplier	Details of obligation on supplier	Details of benefit to supplier

But benefits to both client and supplier contingent upon client meeting obligation

e.g. buying your lunch

Figure 9: Contracting matrix [Hen97]

of the business. Business rules, which are essentially statements of policies and conditions, are essentially captured in this way. In a more general sense, we can think of modelling business rules at the class level by supplementing the notion of a class as having "name", "properties" and "operations" by a fourth classification: "a ruleset". Rules are non-procedural and include representation of control constraints, business rules, exception handling and triggers. They may be written in IF THEN ELSE structures or in natural language. Rules need to be at the same time rigorous and understandable by the end users in the business domain.

8 Summary and Conclusions

The use of object-oriented techniques for developing commercial software is rapidly increasing and the methods by which this development takes place are themselves maturing. From first and second generation methodologies are now emerging collaboratively so-called "third generation" OO development approaches. OPEN is one such example which is typified by its full lifecycle process support for building object-oriented information systems. At the same time, the Object Management Group are aiming to standardize on an underpinning metamodel for the modelling component of such advanced methodologies. From a focus on technical modelling aspects, more concern is currently being shown on an integration of these into the information systems culture involving project management, organizational culture and people. These emerging third-generation OO methodologies should thus fulfil most, if not all, of the requirements for facilitating the adoption of object technology as a key technology by commercial IS software development organizations.

Acknowledgments: I wish to thank Houman Younessi and Simon Moser for constructive comments on an earlier draft of this manuscript. This is Contribution no 97/9 of the Centre for Object Technology Applications and Research (COTAR). Figures 1 and 6 were reprinted by permission of Addison-Wesley Longman Ltd.

References

[ABCGH91] Arnold, P., Bodoff, S., Coleman, D., Gilchrist, H., Hayes, F., An evaluation of five object-oriented development methods, JOOP Focus on Analysis and Design, 1991, 107-121

[Abo83] Abbott, R. J., Program design by informal English descriptions, Communications of the ACM 26 (11), 1983, 882-894

[BC89] Beck, K., Cunningham, W., A laboratory for teaching object-oriented thinking, SIGPLAN Notices 24 (10), 1989, 1-6

[Ber95] Berard, E. V., What is a "methodology?", comp.object newsnet, 1995

[Boo91] Booch, G., Object Oriented Design with Applications, Benjamin/Cummings, Menlo Park, CA, 1991

[Boo94] Booch, G., Object-Oriented Analysis and Design with Applications (2nd edition), The Benjamin/Cummings Publishing Company, Inc., Redwood City, CA, 1994

[Car94a] Carmichael, A., Towards a common object-oriented meta-model for object development, Chapter 19, in: A. Carmichael (ed.), Object Development Methods, SIGS Books, New York, 1994, 321-333

[Car94b] Carmichael, A., Methods war, methods truce, methods trade, in: ObjectExpo Europe Conference Proceedings, 1994, 26-30, London, England, SIGS Conferences, Inc., 1994, 41-50

[CD94] Cook, S., Daniels, J., Designing Object Systems, Prentice Hall, UK, 1994

[CF92] de Champeaux, D., Faure, P., A comparative study of object-oriented analysis methods, J. Object-Oriented Programming 5 (1), 1992, 21-33

[CY90] Coad, P., Yourdon, E., Object-Oriented Analysis, 1st edition, Prentice-Hall, 1990

[CY91a] Coad, P., Yourdon, E., Object-Oriented Analysis, 2nd edition, Prentice-Hall, 1991

[CY91b] Coad, P., Yourdon, E., Object-Oriented Design, Prentice-Hall, 1991

[EDM97] Emam, K., Drouin, J.-N., Melo, W., SPICE, The Theory and Practice of Software Process Improvement and Capability Determination, IEEE Computer Society Press, Los Alamitos, CA, USA, 1997

[EG94] Eckert, G., Golder, P., Improving object-oriented analysis, Inf. Software Technol. 36 (2), 1994, 67-86

[FHG97] Firesmith, D., Henderson-Sellers, B., Graham, I., OPEN Modeling Language (OML) Reference Manual, SIGS Books, NY, 1997

[Fir93] Firesmith, D. G., Object-Oriented Requirements Analysis and Logical Design: A Software Engineering Approach, J. Wiley and Sons, New York, 1993

[GBH97] Graham, I. M., Bischof, J., Henderson-Sellers, B., Associations considered a bad thing, J. Obj.-Oriented Programming 9 (9), 1997, 41-48

[GHY97b] Graham, I., Henderson-Sellers, B., Younessi, H., The OPEN Process Specification, Addison-Wesley, 1997

[GR95] Goldberg, A., Rubin, K. S., Succeeding with Objects, Decision Frameworks for Project Management, Addison-Wesley, Reading, MA, 1995

[Gra93a] Graham, I., Migrating to object technology, Object Magazine 2 (5), 1993, 22-24

[Gra93b] Graham, I., Interoperation: reusing existing software components and packages, Object Magazine 2 (6), 1993, 25-26

[Gra94] Graham, I. M., Object-Oriented Methods (2nd edition), Addison-Wesley, Wokingham, UK, 1994

[Gra95a] Graham, I. M., Migrating to Object Technology, Addison-Wesley, Wokingham, UK, 1995

[Gra95b] Graham, I. M., A non-procedural process model for object-oriented software development, Report on Object Analysis and Design 1 (5), 1995, 10-11

[Gra96] Graham, I., Linking a system and its requirements, Object Expert 1 (3), 1996, 62-64

[Gra97] Graham, I., Some problems with use cases ... and how to avoid them, OOIS'96, D. Patel, Y. Sun, S. Patel (eds.), Springer, London, 1997, 18-27

[Har87] Harel, D., Statecharts: a visual formalism for complex systems, Sci. Computer Program. 8, 1987, 231-274

[HB96] Henderson-Sellers, B., Bulthuis, A., The COMMA project, Object Magazine 6 (4), 1996, 24-26

[HB97] Henderson-Sellers, B., Bulthuis, A., Object-Oriented Metamethods, Springer, New York, 1997

[HD97] Henderson-Sellers, B., Dué, R. T., OPEN project management, Object Expert 2 (2), 1997, 30-35

[HE94a] Henderson-Sellers, B., Edwards, J. M., BOOKTWO of Object-Oriented Knowledge: The Working Object, Prentice Hall, Sydney, 1994

[HE94b] Henderson-Sellers, B., Edwards, J. M., Identifying three levels of OO methodologies, Report on Object Analysis and Design 1 (2), 1994, 17-20

[Hen94] Henderson-Sellers, B., COMMA: an architecture for method interoperability, Report on Object Analysis and Design 1 (3), 1994, 25-28

[Hen95] Henderson-Sellers, B., Who needs an object-oriented methodology anyway?, J. Obj.-Oriented Programming 8 (6), 1995, 6-8

[Hen97] Henderson-Sellers, B., A BOOK of Object-Oriented Knowledge (2nd edition), Prentice Hall, NJ, 1997

[HF97] Henderson-Sellers, B., Firesmith, D., COMMA: Proposed core model, J. Obj.-Oriented Programming (ROAD) 9 (8), 1997, 48-53

[HFG97c] Henderson-Sellers, B., Firesmith, D., Graham, I., OML metamodel: relationship and state modeling, J. Obj.-Oriented Prog. (ROAD) 10 (1), 1997, 47-51

[HG96a] Henderson-Sellers, B., Graham, I. M., with additional input from C. Atkinson, J. Bézivin, L.L. Constantine, R. Dué, R. Duke, D. Firesmith, G. Low, J. McKim, D. Mehandjiska-Stavrova, B. Meyer, J.J. Odell, M. Page-Jones, T. Reenskaug, B. Selic, A.J.H. Simons, P. Swatman and R. Winder, OPEN: toward method convergence?, IEEE Computer 29 (4), 1996, 86–89

[HGFRSW96b] Henderson-Sellers, B., Graham, I. M., Firesmith, D., Reenskaug, T., Swatman, P., Winder, R., The OPEN heart, TOOLS 21, C. Mingins, R. Duke, B. Meyer (eds.), TOOLS/ISE, 1996, 187-196

[HGSWR97a] Henderson-Sellers, B., Graham, I. M., Swatman, P., Winder, R., Reenskaug, T., Using object-oriented techniques to model the lifecycle for OO software development, Procs. OOIS '96, D. Patel, Y. Sun, S. Patel (eds.), Springer-Verlag, London, 1997, 211-220

[HKM94] Henderson-Sellers, B., Kreindler, R. J., Mickel, S., Methodology choices — adapt or adopt?, Report on Object Analysis and Design 1 (4), 1994, 26-29

[Jac93] Jacobson, I., Time for a cease-fire in the methods war, J. Obj.-Oriented Programming 6 (4), 1993, 6 - 84

[Jac94] Jacobson, I., public communication on OOPSLA 94 panel: Methodology standards: help or hindrance?, 1994

[JCJO92] Jacobson, I., Christerson, M., Jonsson, P., Övergaard, G., Object-Oriented Software Engineering: A Use Case Driven Approach, Addison Wesley, 1992

[Jou97] Joukhadar, K., OMG committee meets on object analysis & design proposals, Object Magazine 7 (1), 1997, 12-13

[Lil94] Lilly, S., Planned obsolescence, Object Magazine 3 (5), 1994, 79-80

[MCF96] Moser, S., Cherix, R., Flueckiger, J., BI-CASE/OBJECT (BIO) V3, Bedag Informatik, Berne, Switzerland, 1996

[Mey92] Meyer, B., Applying "design by contract", IEEE Computer 25 (10), 1992, 40-51

[MO92] Martin, J., Odell, J. J., Object-Oriented Analysis & Design, Prentice Hall, Englewood Cliffs, NJ, 1992

[MO95] Martin, J., Odell, J. J., Object-Oriented Methods. A Foundation, PTR Prentice Hall, New Jersey, 1995

[MP92] Monarchi, D. E., Puhr, G. I., A research typology for object-oriented analysis and design, Comms. ACM 35 (9), 1992, 35-47

[MSBRSBAW93] Mellor, S. J., Shlaer, S., Booch, G., Rumbaugh, J., Salmons, J., Babitsky, T., Adams, S., Wirfs-Brock, R. J., Premature methods standardization considered harmful, J. Obj.-Oriented Programming 6 (4), 1993, 8-85

[PCW90] Page-Jones, M., Constantine, L. L., Weiss, S., Modeling object-oriented systems: the Uniform Object Notation, Computer Language 7 (10), 1990, 69-87

[RH95] Renouf, D. W., Henderson-Sellers, B., Incorporating rôles into MOSES, in: C. Mingins, B. Meyer (eds.), TOOLS15, Prentice Hall, 1995, 71-82

[RBPEL91] Rumbaugh, J., Blaha, M., Premerlani, W., Eddy, F., Lorensen, W., Object-oriented Modelling and Design, Prentice Hall, New Jersey, 1991

[RWL96] Reenskaug, T., Wold, P., Lehne, O. A., Working with Objects. The OOram Software Engineering Manual, Manning, Greenwich, CT, USA, 1996

[SGW95] Selic, B., Gullekson, G., Ward, P. T., Real-Time Object-Oriented Modelling, John Wiley & Sons, Inc., New York, 1995

[Swa96] Swatman P. A., Formal Object-Oriented Method — FOOM, in: H. Kilow, W. Harvey (eds.), Specification of Behavioural Semantics in Object-Oriented Information Systems, Kluwer Academic Publishers, Norwell, Massachusetts, 1996

[UM95] Unhelkar, B., Mamdapur, G., Practical aspects of using a methodology: a road map approach, Report on Object Analysis and Design 2 (2), 1995, 34-36, 54

[vGBH92] van den Goor, G. P., Brinkkemper, S., Hong, S., A comparison of six object-oriented analysis and design methods, Method Engineering Institute, University of Twente, 1992

[Wil95] Wilkinson, N., Using CRC Cards: An Informal Approach to O-O Software Development, SIGS Books, NY, 1995

[WN95] Waldén, K., Nerson, J.-M., Seamless Object-Oriented Architecture, Prentice Hall, 1995, 301

[WW89] Wand, Y., Weber, R., An ontological evaluation of systems analysis and design methods, in: E. D. Falkenberg, P. Lindgren (eds.), Information Systems Concepts: An In-depth Analysis, Elsevier Science Publishers (North Holland), Amsterdam, The Netherlands, 1989, 79-107

[WWW90] Wirfs-Brock, R. J., Wilkerson, B., Wiener, L., Designing Object-Oriented Software, Prentice Hall, 1990, 368

[YH97] Younessi, H., Henderson-Sellers, B., Cooking up improved software quality, Object Magazine, 7(8), 1997, 38-42

CHAPTER 20

Eurometh od Contract Management

Alfred Helmerich

Acquiring an information system to meet new business needs is not a trivial task. It includes deriving the acquisition goal, developing a strategy for its implementation, contracting for parts of the acquisition goal, integrating the parts into the complete information system and into the business processes of the acquiring organisation. Properly addressing these issues during acquisition significantly increases the likelihood of a successful outcome. Effective acquisition of an information system and related services requires clear descriptions of the desired final state and the current situation. It is important that the customer and supplier have the same understanding of the current situation and the information system and related services to be achieved. Eurometh od has been designed to help organisations with the acquisition of effective information systems and related services in a variety of situations. It encourages customers and suppliers to control costs and timescales, to manage risks, to improve mutual understanding and to reach a fair contract. Through the achievement of these objectives, the European Commission aims to encourage the opening of the information system (IS) market, to improve the mobility of people internationally, to ease the organisation of international projects by a flexible contract management.

1 Introduction

One of the principles of the European Union is the completion of a single market. Therefore the EC requires for their administrations that the call for tenders be open throughout Europe to allow competition to take place and refer to product descriptions based on standards rather than on brand names [EGKS94]. In the private sector various disciplines have defined procurement guidance and standards for procurement, e.g. the telecommunication initiative SPIRIT (Service Providers Integrated Requirements for Information Technology) or SOTIP (The Swedish Government Open Telecommunications Systems Interconnection Profil). Other procurement guidelines issued by various countries, like TAP [TAP91] (Total Acquisition Process of CCTA), UfAB

(Unterlagen für Ausschreibung und Bewertung von DV-Leistungen, BMI, 1985) or EPHOS [Ephos94] (European Procurement Handbook for Open Systems of the EC) have already been or will be harmonised with Euromethod [SPRITE97].

1.1 Why should the Tenders be open?

There are good reasons for any customer to favour open tenders, even though they might require more work in the beginning and result in starting dates of projects to be shifted in time:

- competition will generally lead to more cost-effective solutions,
- competition increases the variety of solutions and generally will lead to better solutions,
- standards will prevent a lock-in to one supplier and secure the investment for future updates,
- better planning of the acquisition leads to better control and results.

However, not only the customers but also the suppliers profit from an increased market. Indeed many standards are rooted in initiatives by suppliers to make their products interchangeable and secure their investment in research.

1.2 Why are the Council Directives not enough?

The EC has regulated the public procurements of various types, e.g. the procurement of:

- construction work (Works Dirctive),
- IS-products (Supplies Directive [EEC93a]),
- IS-services, e.g. for processes that represent an economic value not related to the production of material goods (Service Directive [EEC92]),
- for IS-services in special branches, e.g. telecommunications (Utility Directive [EEC93b]).

As can be seen by the number of directives, the various types of procurements require special treatments. Whereas in the procurement of products standards can be defined and off-the-shelf products therefore exist, it is impossible to do likewise with defining services that entail creative work and problem solutions. Moreover, information has become a cornerstone of modern organisations. And the procurement of an information system (IS), whether in the private or the public sector, be it paper-based, partially or fully computerised, often is a key to the success and often the survival of an organisation. Also the complexity of a computerised system may range from a single PC to a distributed heterogeneous system containing many complex and interacting applications. Uncertainty will depend on the type of application, organisational aspects, technology to be used, etc. Applications that are common across organisations and are well understood present little risk. Novel and/or specific applications have the potential to provide competitive advantage but may be more risky. However, neither standards nor the Council Directives alone can guarantee a good quality of the solution. A method - Euromethod [EM96] - is needed to install the directives in practice.

1.3 Why should Euromethod be applied?

1.3.1 The Method Euromethod

Euromethod was designed to support the definition, planning, and execution of the effective acquisition of information systems and related services. With Information system (IS) Euromethod understands the aspect of the organisation that provides, uses and distributes that information, together with the associated organisational and technical resources. It is used to assess and determine:

- the problem situation and the associated risks [FA94],
- the goal of the acquisition,
- the strategy for the acquisition, for the IS-adaptation and service provision,
- the delivery plan showing the customer-supplier relationships at contractual level including the exchange of deliverables [Fra94].

Euromethod does not address legal aspects. Neither is it an IS-development method.

1.3.2 The Framework Euromethod

Euromethod provides a framework i.e. a set of concepts and a terminology:

- to improve the customer-supplier relationship,
- to harmonise methods,
- to standardise the procedure,
- to provide standardised templates.

One of the main obstacles in achieving mutual understanding is the variety of methods using different concepts and terminology. These methods often use a vocabulary that stems from software engineering and may be difficult to understand by IS users, procurers and contract managers. Euromethod addresses this problem by considering adaptations and service provisions from an acquisition point of view rather than an engineering point of view. A bridging dictionary enables people to understand the types of deliverables proposed by a method without having been trained in that method. Bridging dictionaries already exist between some methods (like SSADM [SSADM96], SPICE [ME98], Merise [QCKI91], MEiN, Dafne) and Euromethod [EM96]. A standardised procedure and templates reduce the efforts for the next tender and generally lead to more transparent and fairer contracts.

1.3.3 The Project Euromethod

In a first phase in early 1989 the European Union Member states agreed on the needs and requirements for a Euromethod [Fra94]. In a second phase from May 1990 - Feb. 1991 the CEC DG XIII/PPG funded a Feasibility Study performed by an pan-European consortium (Eurogroup). From May 1992 - April 1994 Version 0 of Euromethod [EM94] was developed and put to trial in the next phase. From July 1994 - July 1996 Euromethod was applied within seven projects throughout Europe, including a PHARE project in Hungary. The results were used to develop the current version 1 of Euromethod [EM96].

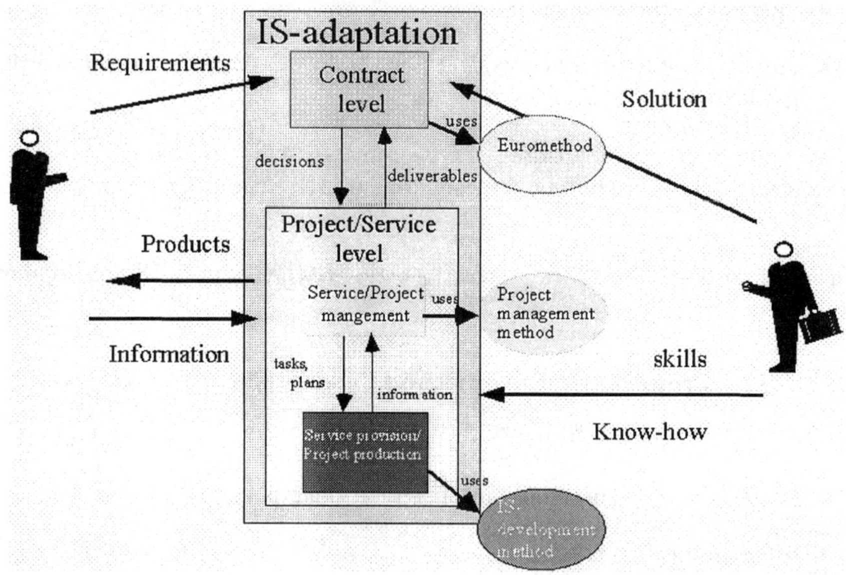

Figure 1: Structure of an acquisition organisation

The customer/supplier relationship takes place on three distinct levels (Figure 1):

- the contract,
- management and
- production/provision level.

1.4 How is the Contract Relationship defined?

Euromethod addresses the first level, whereas most IS-development methods address the second and/or third level.

1. Contract level
The acquisition management function controls the acquisition and its various contracts. It is responsible for the service and system requirements that are documented in the request for proposals, tender responses and contracts. It controls whether requirements are met by the services and system and takes the appropriate measures when they are not.

2. Management level
The service or project management function plans and monitors the service or the production. It organises the team, allocates resources to the tasks, and makes sure that the required quality is achieved within timescales and budget.

3. Production/provision level
The service provision or project production function provides the required service or systems for the customer, e.g. business process engineering, computer system operation, network maintenance, software development. For this purpose it uses resources (skills, knowledge, products, etc.) from the supplier and sometimes from the customer.

In complex acquisitions, this level may be split into acquisition management and contract management and the various contracts may involve different people in their management.

2 Making a Contract

Due to the complexity of information systems acquisitions are usually split into several procurements regulated by contracts allowing for smaller lots and increased competition. Acquisitions may involve more than one supplier, each one being responsible for a subset of systems and services. Suppliers in their turn may have sub-contractors providing them with some services and systems. The offside is an increase in preparation and administration especially at the beginning. A very common example of a stepwise acquisition is a pre-study performed internally or externally, before the actual procurement with a call for tender is launched.

2.1 The Initiation of the Acquisition

The acquisition process (or acquisition for short) is the process of obtaining a system or a service, or any combination thereof. Its necessity usually arises from some business needs. The acquisition goal is used to drive the acquisition process, which starts with the formulation of an acquisition strategy determining the number and the kinds of adaptations, service provisions, and contracts, that are needed to reach the acquisition goal. The planning of the acquisition process on the other hand usually results in a further refinement of the acquisition goal, in terms of

- target domain affected,
- systems and services requirements,
- cost/benefit analysis,
- stakes and stake holders.

The acquisition planning will start by determining the overall adaptations and service provisions scenarios, then analysing the risks and designing an acquisition strategy within a risk management framework; setting up the acquisition organisation; and finally planning the main decision points of the acquisition:

- decide to change some situational factors,
- decide to change or refine requirements prior to tendering,
- decide to use external assistance in the acquisition management,
- decide the types of suppliers: internal or external,
- determine the types of tendering (open, restricted, negotiated),
- determine the interaction with suppliers (single-phase, multi-phase tendering),
- determine the flexibility of contracts (capability to modify or refine),
- decide the strategy regarding standards,
- identify contracts and sequencing constraints (one or several contracts),
- decide to buy or develop,
- determine requirements to adaptation strategy,
- determine the type of service arrangement,
- determine requirements to service provision strategy.

An acquisition strategy may be to perform the acquisition in more than one step, e.g. split the hardware procurement from the software procurement, or the feasibility study from the implementation. Each step is called a procurement and is defined within a separate contract. A procurement usually consists of a sequence of three processes:

- tendering process,
- contract monitoring and
- contract completion process.

2.2 Mode of Tendering

The EC directives [EGKS94] ask that all call for tenders with a value above a certain limit (GATT-limit) are officially and openly announced in the European Journal or electronically in Tenders Electronically Daily (TED; telnet: echo.lu). The directives regulate the structure and scope of the announcements; Euromethod prescribes the structure and supports the preparation of the accompanying detailed technical information. A standardised structure of the tender information and tender response already reduces the work load of both suppliers and customers. It is only natural that in Euromethod the tender information as well as the tender response are already in the same format as the technical annex of the final contract. According to the EC directives there are four modes of tendering described:

- Open call for tender:

  The default for any procurement allowing unlimited participation of suppliers.

- Restricted call for tender:

  In special cases the call for tender can be given to a short list of suppliers only. Generally this is admissible when the short listed suppliers effectively are all possible suppliers for the specific procurement. The above condition can be verified by a market study, a previous open call for tender or by a previous open call for application.

- Negotiated call for tender:

  Allows the customer to make a contract with one supplier, if an open competition is proofed to be without success, not possible or not justified by the procurement. Mostly it is used to contract some additional work (less than 20% of the original contract) or if there is only one supplier.

- Open call for application:

Describes a two phase tender process, where the customer first calls openly for suppliers to claim their interest. In a second step the call for tender is given to those suppliers only that have applied in the first step.

In UK customers use the open call for application mode to generate a short list of possible suppliers. That is, they first call for mini-proposals, select admissible suppliers and then call the short listed suppliers for their full proposals. It is conceivable that the customer uses the mini-proposals to generate options for solutions that are then discussed with all short listed suppliers on a round table prior to the call for a full proposal for one selected option.

3 What contains a Contract?

A contract is a binding agreement between two parties especially enforceable by law or a similar internal agreement wholly within an organisation, for the supply of services or systems. Several contracts may be required for the acquisition of the systems and services needed by an organisation. It is the main goal of any contract to describe clearly the deliverables that are to be exchanged between customer and supplier. Deliverables can be products or services and are described

- by their goals, constraints and quality characteristics (e.g. deliver a certain product to a customer within a certain time and cost and to the customers satisfaction),
- by their results (e.g. delivered product),
- by their activities (or sub-process) (e.g. the delivery process will consist in getting the product out of stock, checking its characteristics, selecting the transportation means).

3.1 Description of Goals

The goals of an acquisition are described in terms of a business strategy with market survey and estimates for costs and benefits. The acquisition goal is needed to co-ordinate all subsequent procurements and to guarantee the overall success. Ideally the acquisition goals should well fit into the objectives of the enterprise. However, the complex of strategic planning, where objectives are analysed, mission statements formulated and business strategy planned, is outside the scope of Euromethod. The point of view Euromethod takes on the acquisition goal is that of the final state of the IS-adaptation or the service level that has to be achieved by the acquisition. Both are part of the delivery model of Euromethod and supported by templates and concepts that can be used. In other words the final state captures the results or deliverables of the acquisition.

3.2 Description of Results

The description of results is easiest if the products are already standardised as described in the European Procurement Handbook of Open Systems [Ephos94]. If the results are information systems, they can be described in Euromethod by the concepts of initial and final states.

3.2.1 The Levels of Abstraction

In analogy of the different levels of customer/supplier relationship, products of different level of abstraction are passed on between the levels. As Euromethod supports the contractual relationship, it only provides templates or profiles to characterise descriptive items. These profiles do not contain a summary of the content of the descriptive items, they rather classify the scope, the quality and functional properties of the descriptive item. For that reason the profiles are very flexible and can be

- used to describe information at the contract abstraction level for decision making,
- used as acceptance criteria for controlling the contract,
- adapted to the situation by defining the granularity of the grid to suit its objective.

The latter can be used to describe the necessary deliverables for decision points. The common decisions are the selection of suppliers in the tendering phase, decisions about system design, future investments, and system acceptance in the contract monitoring and completion phases.

3.2.2 The Types of Deliverables

When characterising descriptive items by profiles, Euromethod recognises three main types of deliverables, for which different default profiles are provided (Figure 2).

3.2.3 Initial and Final States

The profiles of all deliverables available at the starting point of the IS- adaptation are called the initial state profile. Likewise is the set of profiles at the expected end point called the final state profile. The two are used to illustrate the transition the information system is meant to undergo during the IS-adaptation.

An IS-adaptation is defined by its initial and final state. System development methods help create documents that describe the IS (IS-descriptions). Euromethod in addition helps to create profiles that characterise and describe the IS-descriptions

3.3 Description of Tasks

Task descriptions are used to steady state processes outsourced to some supplier supporting the day-to-day functioning of the organisation. They are usually continuous and they contain activities that are repeated regularly during the life of the organisation. They remain in the same steady state, or incur only slight changes, for long periods. Task descriptions are also used to manage contracts and allow for the flexibility of contracts needed during the adaptation of an organisation to its changing environment. Each adaptation is a specific process that has a beginning and an end and that executes a state transition in the organisation, i.e. it moves the organisation from an initial state to a final state in a certain elapsed time. The adaptation process can be adjusted to the problem situation and monitored to guarantee success by the following activities:

- Risk Analysis,
- Strategy Selection,
- Decision Point Planning.

3.3.1 Risk Analysis

Euromethod provides a list of situational factors that need to be analysed as to their potential to cause risks, e.g. their likelihood of happening and the severity of consequences.For each situational factor, Euromethod proposes heuristics to diminish the inherent risk. Some actions are rather local and

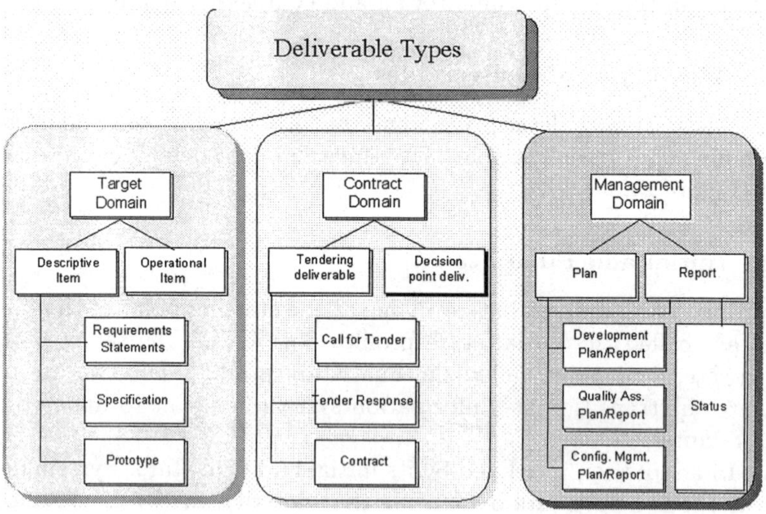

Figure 2: Deliverable types in Euromethod

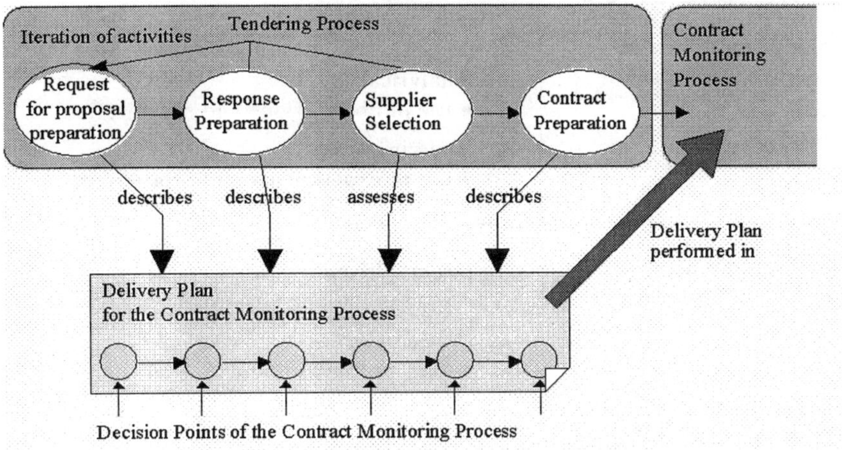

Figure 3: The connection of delivery planning and contract monitoring

address one situational factor only, others are more global and affect the strategy selected for the IS-adaptation, like the splitting of the project into various steps or the evolutionary development.

3.3.2 Strategy Selection

Table (1) lists the strategy options among which one can choose in Euromethod. The choice is determined by the situational factors as explained in the previous section. Risks that are not covered by the chosen strategy have to be specially treated and monitored by the project control.

3.3.3 Decision Point Planing

A key element of flexible contracts are decision points (Figure 3). They allow the customer in co-operation with the supplier to make intelligent decisions based on the deliverables produced.

Although the outcome of a decision can not be planned, it is possible to plan the decision and to specify the necessary deliverables. Actually, during the tendering process a refinement of that planning takes place and finally leads to the formulation of a delivery plan as a basis of the contract.

4 Conclusion

In Euromethod, a contract is not used as a legal means to pull the wool over the partner but as an instrument to come to a fair and clearly understood agreement that can be tailored to the problem situation and is flexible enough to adopt if needed.

Adaptation approach	Strategy options
Description approach – cognitive approach	1. Analytical: • use of abstractions and specification 2. Experimental: • use of experiments and prototypes
Description approach – social approach	1. Expert-driven: • production and assessment separated 2. Participatory: • joint production and assessment
Construction approach	1. One shot construction: • a single version constructed and tested in one step 2. Incremental construction: • parts constructed and tested in a sequence of steps • no change of descriptions after first construction 3. Evolutionary construction: • versions constructed and tested in a sequence of steps • changes of descriptions are possible after learning from test
Installation approach – system coverage	1. One shot installation: • a single version installed in one step 2. Incremental installation: • parts installed in a sequence of steps • no change of descriptions after first installation 3. Evolutionary installation: • versions installed in a sequence of steps • changes of descriptions are possible after learning from usage
Installation approach – geographical coverage	1. Global installation: • installation in all locations in one step 2. Regional installation: • stepwise with more and more locations

Table 1: Strategy options

Benefits to customers

- Clearer expression of requirements
- Improvement of risk management
- Guidance in choosing the appropriate acquisition approach for a specific problem situation
- Better understanding of suppliers' proposals
- Easier evaluation of suppliers' proposals
- Easier system and service acceptance, through better requirements definitions and planning
- Improved decision process relating to deliverables and services
- Avoidance of lock-in to a supplier
- Avoidance of lock-in to a specific method
- Better information to control costs
- Easier control of ambitions

Benefits to suppliers

- Better information to control ambitions and costs
- Enhanced management of risks involved in a project and/or a service provision
- easier system and services acceptance, through better requirements definitions and planning
- Selection of the appropriate methods, techniques and tools
- Determination of the appropriate approach for a project or service provision
- Easier to obtain a clear endorsement from customers of the key design decisions
- A clearer view of the customer's IS
- Better understanding of customer's needs

References

[EEC92] 92/50/EEC: Service Directive, 1992

[EEC93a] 93/36/EEC: Supplies Directive, 1993

[EEC93b] 93/38/EEC: Utilities Directive, 1993

[EGKS94] EGKS, Öffentliche Auftragswesen in Europa, Brüssel-Luxemburg, 1994

[EM94] Euromethod V0: Eurogroup, Euromethod Version 0, 1994

[EM96] Euromethod V1: Eurogroup, Euromethod Version 1, 1996

[Ephos94] European Procurement Handbook for Open Systems, Conference Proceedings, Na, DIANE Publishing Co, 1995

[FA94] Franckson, M., Anderson, N. E., The Euromethod Situational Approach, (unpublished presentation), 1994

[Fra94] Franckson, M., The Euromethod Deliverable Model and its contribution to the objectives of Euromethod, in: A. A. Veriihn-Stuart,T. W. Olle (eds.), Methods and Associated Tools for the Inormaitno System Life Cycle, A-55, Elsevier Science B.V., North-Holland, 1994

[ME98] Melo, W., Emamn, K., The Theory and Practice of Software Process Improvement and Capability Determination, in: K. Emamn, J. N. Drouin (eds.), IEEE Computer Society, 1998

[QCKI91] Quang, P. T., Chartier-Kastler, C., Intl, S., Merise in Practice, MacMillan Computer Science, 1991

[SPRITE97] SPRITE-S2 Initiative, http://www.ispo.cec.be/sprites2/spriobje.htm, 1997

[SSADM96] SSADM, Version 4.3, CCTA Library, 1996

[TAP91] TAP, A Guide to Procurement within the Total Acquisition Process, CCTA M Treasury, 1991

PART THREE

Tools for Analysis and Design

This part is about those tools which can support information systems modelling helping management and technical personnel to collect, organise, store, and analyse information about the system, and to produce system descriptions on various levels of formality. Originally, CASE tools were developed with the aim of supporting the hard aspects of information systems design, i.e. the detailed design, implementation, validation, and testing of *software* ("Lower CASE" tools).

With time it has become clear that this approach was limited, on two accounts:

- Designers need tools which support the requirements of management and technical personnel throughout the entire life-cycle of the system. A number of CASE tools have been built in support of the softer aspects of design, to help the task of requirements specification and analysis (collectively called "Upper CASE" tools).
- It is clear that the information system life-cycle does not end at the design or implementation phase; a continuity between the design and implementation tools, and execution environments is highly desirable. This includes the management of executable models of the information system i.e. the management of the *release to operation* of implementations (of human and computer implemented processes), and the management of the execution of these processes, commonly referred to as *workflow management*.

The above realisation resulted in a) the need for modelling entire business processes, including human and computer implemented activities, with the requisite need for analysis, as well as b) following the models after their implementation to operation through the implementation of some form of *model based control.*

Naturally, the relevant analysis questions and synthesis rules of human implemented processes is markedly different from the analysis questions and synthesis rules of computer software, and today we are just at the beginning of being able to develop tools which support both. A complete treatment of the CASE tool area would have required a very extensive volume in itself. There are many fine CASE tools which for one reason or another are not represented in this volume and the editors had to decide to contend with a sample of typical tools – this is enough for the reader to appreciate the various types of functionality that an end user may wish to expect from such tools, and equip the reader with a shopping list of features when selecting a CASE tool for in-house use. However the handbook can not be used as a recommendation of preferred tools, only a very extensive survey of the area could find answers to such questions.

One should read the part on information systems design tools in conjunction with the part on modelling languages (Part 1), because the tools support the design process using these modelling languages. Nevertheless the separation of tools from languages is useful because all too often the blurring of the difference results the end user being *locked in* in the use of a tool if the selected tool is not based on well defined and published languages: as a result the produced models may only be usable in conjunction with the given tool. An end user committing to a tool of which the underlying modelling language is not public and is not exposed to outside scrutiny is playing a dangerous game, or at least is exposed to the tool vendor to an undesirable level.

Given (a set of) languages supported by a tool the user (or more likely a group of users) will be able to produce models with the tool's help. These models are then used for a variety of tasks, limited by the *language's expressive power* and afforded by the *capabilities of the tool.* Provided the underlying modelling language allows the representation of the requisite information, the tool may support static or dynamic analysis of the system, the derivation of various system characteristics (such as expected performance indicators e.g. processing times and cost), sensitivity analysis, what-if analysis, etc. These can be achicved either by analytic or statistical evaluation of the design models, or through using simulation and statistical experimentation.

This part presents examples of tools for analysis and design, as well as one example tool for detailed design and implementation which are available in the marketplace. There are seven contributions dedicated to such products or families of products.

Florence Tissot and Wes Crump describe an integrated enterprise modeling environment based on the IDEF family of languages. They provide an overview of this approach, explaining the primary motivations for developing the software and describing its main features and characteristics.

Walter Rupietta presents WorkParty, a family of tools for business process and workflow management. The contribution describes the concepts and the members of the family.

Günther Schuh, Thomas Siepmann, and Volker Levering present Proplan, a tool for the representation, analysis and documentation of business processes.

August-Wilhelm Scheer presents the Architecture of Integrated Information Systems (ARIS). ARIS aims at addressing the entire information system life-cycle: from business process design to information technology deployment.

Gay Wood and Herrmann Krallmann present Bonapart. It is a general-use modeling, simulation and dynamic analysis tool designed to support both experts and non-experts in organizational decision making and planning.

Kai Mertins and Roland Jochem present MO^2GO, a tool for object-oriented modelling and analysis of business processes.

Finally, Alois Hofinger presents VisualAge, a comprehensive development environment, which is a tool supporting the detailed design and implementation life-cycle phase of the software component in the information system, including its Human-computer Interface.

Peter Bernus

CHAPTER 21

An Integrated Enterprise Modeling Environment

Florence Tissot, Wes Crump

Increasingly complex systems have stimulated the development of sophisticated methods and tools for enterprise design and analysis. Advances in information technology as well as significant progress in analytical and computational techniques have facilitated the use of such methods in industry. However, enterprise modeling and analysis methods are yet to make a significant impact in the decision-making process of most companies and organizations. In this contribution, we provide a detailed analysis of some of the major roadblocks to a broader use of enterprise modeling methods in industry. We then describe an approach that addresses each of those roadblocks. Finally, we provide an overview of a commercial software environment that implements the approach, explaining the primary motivations for developing the software and describing its main features and characteristics.

1 Enterprise Design and Analysis

To survive in today's extraordinarily competitive and ever expanding worldwide economy requires a skillful management capable of monitoring and controlling highly complex situations and systems involving a growing number of interdependent parameters and variables. This phenomenon can be witnessed in a variety of organizations, institutions, and industries ranging from traditional manufacturing industries, to software development, medical facilities, government agencies, and universities.

Increasingly complex systems have stimulated the development of sophisticated methods and tools for enterprise design and analysis. Fueled by tangible benefits in many domains and by the synergy between academia and industry, many industries have increasingly accepted enterprise analysis methods such as optimization, simulation, cost analysis, and stochastic analysis. Two key factors have accelerated the use of such methods: (1) advances in information technology (increased efficiency in the collection, storage, and control of information) and (2) significant progress in analytical and computational techniques. Nevertheless, enterprise analysis methods remain largely unharnessed, and advances in enterprise analysis theories have yet to filter into the mainstream of managerial decision-making.

The reason for the limited success of enterprise analysis methods on a large industrial base is that these methods are generally very elaborate and require acute expertise to be used effectively. They operate on very intricate models of the enterprise being analyzed. Such models require specific formats and use technical jargon hardly comprehensible to the non-initiated. In this regard, an interesting parallel can be drawn between enterprise analysis and modern physics [Gig91]. A common approach to analyzing complex systems or phenomena consists of providing abstractions of the system being analyzed. These abstractions isolate certain system characteristics from others. In the study of physical phenomena, physicists have repeated the process of abstracting to the point that it has become impossible to visualize the resulting abstractions. Zukav [Zuk79] writes:

> We have come a long way from Galileo's experiments with falling bodies. Each step along the path has taken us to a higher level of abstraction; first to the creation of things that no one has ever seen (like electrons), and then to the abandonment of all attempts even to picture our abstractions.

In the process of modeling the world around us while trying to account for all of its complexity, physicists have created powerful and sophisticated models. These models enable us to predict events, understand their impact, and manage and react more efficiently to the changes they generate. However, most people find it difficult to relate these complicated models to their own perception of the world. A similar situation has developed in the area of enterprise analysis. This field of science and engineering has made tremendous progress in its ability to answer questions, determine optimums, and weigh alternatives. However, it has done so by providing abstractions that are far removed from the systems they model and hence that are inaccessible to the average decision-maker. While in physics the path from our perception of the real world to intricate mathematical models is paved with intermediate abstractions, in enterprise analysis there still exists a significant breach between a decision-maker's perception of an enterprise and an executable model of that enterprise.

This dichotomy between the executable models created for analysis and the actual enterprises they model has promoted the impression that enterprise analysis is complex, time consuming, and prohibitively expensive. This perception is reinforced by the following characteristics of today's analysis efforts.

1. *Enterprise analysis efforts are analyst-dependent.* To produce executable models, most enterprise analysis methods rely heavily on an

expert. Applying a particular analysis technique requires the abstraction and classification of enterprise concepts and elements into non-intuitive categories. In addition, enterprise analysis methods make use of specialized languages that demand a substantial amount of training to learn. For example, the building of an optimization model necessitates the expression of business rules and constraints with mathematical equations and the classification of elements and concepts of the enterprise into parameters and variables. Hence, most domain experts do not have the training necessary to generate and execute analysis models and instead must rely on experts in the various analysis fields.

2. *Enterprise analysis involves time- and communication-intensive activities.* The domain experts' dependence on experienced analysts to generate an executable model of a complex enterprise has made effective communication imperative. Domain experts possess in-depth knowledge of the enterprise to be analyzed. They understand the concepts underlying its functioning, the rules that constrain and govern its operations, and the interfaces and relationships among its components. Analysts, on the other hand, are experts in their particular analysis methods but typically have no understanding of the intricacies of an enterprise. Hence, the success of enterprise analysis depends on how well the domain expert can transfer his knowledge of the enterprise to the analyst and on how well the analyst can understand that enterprise, extract needed information, and design a valid executable model from that information.

3. *A significant amount of the effort spent is not reusable.* The knowledge transfer between a domain expert and an analyst is mostly an ad-hoc one. The analyst directs the activity to extract the information and data needed to create a specific type of executable model of the enterprise. The analyst abstracts the domain expert's enterprise knowledge and directly encodes the resulting abstractions into mathematical formalisms and highly technical languages. It is seldom possible to reuse that knowledge later in other analysis efforts of a different nature. Because knowledge transfer is one of the most critical and most time-consuming activities of an enterprise analysis effort, this situation is one that can greatly influence its cost.

4. *Decision-makers are not in control of the enterprise analysis effort.* The analysis models used to respond to a particular problem or to improve a certain aspect of an enterprise depend on the nature of the problem or on the desired improvement. The prevailing approach is to develop piecemeal custom models tailored to each specific decision-making situation. Hence, given a series of questions about a particular enterprise, an analyst may develop as many as 5 different models encoded in 5 different formalisms. This customization is often necessary because each

analysis method is better suited to answer a particular type of question. Nevertheless, since there is no underlying representation of the knowledge from which the various models are obtained, there is no mechanism to help the domain expert interpret the results of the various analyses as a whole and ascertain their impact on the overall enterprise. Hence, each question or goal is answered in isolation from the rest of the analysis process, and the burden falls on the decision-maker to relate and integrate these independently obtained results.

These four characteristics are often viewed by decision-makers as significant, if not insurmountable, obstacles that are far too costly to overcome. Therefore, a major challenge to increasing the use of enterprise analysis methods in businesses and organizations is to provide the tools and methods that will address those obstacles and render analysis activities more attractive to all participants.

2 Enterprise Models as Intermediate Representations

To overcome these obstacles, practitioners and researchers have followed an approach that consists in providing intermediate representations between a practitioner's perception of an enterprise and a typical executable model of that enterprise. Computer programming is a field in which this approach has been used successfully. In the early 1950's, first generation computers required programs written in machine language. Using machine language, a programmer encodes a set of instructions as strings of zeros and ones that specify the desired states of a computer's internal circuits and memory banks. Programming in machine language was (and still is) extremely tedious and time consuming. In addition, only a limited number of experts actually understood the language. The next generation of computer language was the assembly language. This language is a direct symbolic representation of the strings of zero and ones from the machine language. Although it still requires programmers to understand fully the computational model of the computer they are programming, it simplifies the programming tasks by providing a syntax that is more intelligible to humans. Over the years, to further the development of software and render programming accessible to more researchers and engineers, high level languages (such as LISP) were developed and refined. By providing an additional level of abstraction, these languages enable programmers to follow a simplified model of computation that is more natural because it is closer to the human way of individuating the world. Each step in the evolution of programming languages has resulted in programs that are closer to the human mental model of computational activities and, hence, that are easier to create, manipulate, and maintain.

In enterprise analysis, representations that lie between a decision-maker's perception and an analyst's model of the same enterprise are often called conceptual models in recognition of their basic conceptual nature [BMS84]. These special-purpose representations describe the various aspects of an enterprise with the goal of supporting a business (usually decision-making) activity. Conceptual models are formal or informal abstractions of a system that are expressed using special-purpose modeling constructs. Typically part of a modeling language's syntax, these constructs include simple graphical elements such as circle, boxes and arrows. These graphical elements are combined into easy-to-understand diagrams that can generally be augmented using annotations (Figure 1 gives an example of such type of diagrams).

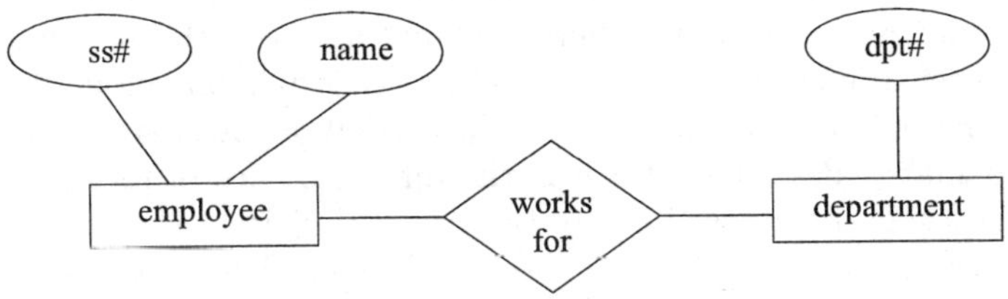

Figure 1: A Sample Entity-Relationship Diagram

The rationale for using relatively simple diagrams to represent a particular aspect of an enterprise derives from the original objective for building these models, best summarized by van Gigh [Gig91]:

> The first objective of modeling is to attempt a simplification of the real world situation through abstraction. [...] A good model must display the same characteristics or properties as the slice of the world from which it has been extracted. However, because a model is much simpler, it can more easily be studied and manipulated to yield a solution.

Note that the use of diagrams or graphical means to represent an enterprise does not imply a lack of formality. Some of the IDEF modeling methods, for example, have precise syntax and semantics.

2.1 Enterprise Models and their Characteristics

The term *enterprise model set* is used to refer to a group of conceptual models built to obtain a coherent and comprehensive picture of an enterprise. This set includes models of various types, and each type of model defines "a perspective or viewpoint from which the system is considered for a given purpose, concentrating on some aspects and hiding irrelevant ones to reduce complexity" [Ver96]. An enterprise model set can include various activity, process, organization, information, and behavioral models. This diversity of model types is based on an important insight. A typical enterprise contains many different information types arising from different aspects of that enterprise: the relatively static information that might be stored in an employee database, the dynamic information involved in planning or processing, the complex array of information found in a detailed product design, etc. Consequently, a particular model type is tailored to a given kind of information, and models tailored to one type of information may be quite unsuitable with regard to another.

Enterprise model sets have three critical characteristics. First, as stated above, each type of model in a set is different in nature from any other model type. This fact is worth emphasizing. A model of a given type does not simply provide a view on the information known about an enterprise, but also captures information that is different in nature from the information captured in other model types. The central way in which one model type differs from another is not in the amount of information or the characteristics of the enterprise that it describes. Rather, the difference lies in its semantic categories, the kinds of things that are taken as primitive (processes, activities, classes, attributes, etc.) and the logical relations those categories can bear to one another. Zachman writes [Zac86]:

> A significant observation regarding these architectural representations is that each is of a different nature than the others. They are not merely a set of representations, each of which is an increasing level of detail than the previous one. Level of detail is an independent variable, varying within each architectural representation.

The second critical characteristic of these models is that all model types are equally important in describing an enterprise. Each model type is necessary to capture different aspects of the enterprise and, ideally, all types of models should be developed to provide a comprehensive and coherent description of the enterprise. Again, Zachman writes [Zac86]:

> [...] there is not an architecture, but a set of architectural representations. One is not right and the others wrong. The architectures are different. They are additive, complementary. There are reasons for electing to expend the resources for developing each architectural representation. And, there are risks associated with not developing any one of the architectural representations.

Finally, the third major characteristic of an enterprise model set is that the models constituting the set are not independent from one another. Each model describes some aspect of the enterprise that depends upon and is constrained by aspects of the enterprise described in other models. For example, the information captured in a data model may limit the execution of tasks described in a process model. The dependencies and relationships across models ultimately enable the projection of a comprehensive, consistent, and coherent enterprise view.

2.2 Today's Enterprise Modeling Methods and Tools

The potential of conceptual models to describe, design, and analyze complex systems was recognized in the late 1970's, and enterprise modeling technology has made steady progress since then. Today enterprise modeling methods and software tools exist for a variety of model types including data, function, process, object, and organization models (IDEF, SADT, GRAI/GIM, CIMOSA, etc.). Because these modeling methods typically provide intuitive, easy-to-understand graphical languages to represent concepts and their relationships, domain experts are able to directly and explicitly capture and represent some of their domain knowledge with limited training in the corresponding methods and tools.

The use of these methods and tools benefits enterprises and organizations in several important ways. First, conceptual models can be used to transfer knowledge between domain experts and system analysts in three steps. In the first step, domain experts record their knowledge of the enterprise in an enterprise model set. The system analyst then studies this set to gain a good understanding of the enterprise and its characteristics. Finally, the two parties meet to discuss missing pieces of information and ambiguities in the models. Thus, the time and associated cost of knowledge transfer activities is significantly reduced in two ways. First, the interview process, formerly an activity in which success depended largely on the analyst's interviewing and the domain expert's description skills, is now replaced by the structured best-practice guidelines and procedures provided by the modeling methods. Second, the amount of time required for meetings between the two parties is dramatically reduced.

Another way in which enterprise modeling positively impacts analysis efforts is reuse. Because enterprise models are not committed to a low-level representation language (such as a particular simulation language), they provide the foundation from which a variety of analysis models can be built to satisfy various goals. Enterprise models created by a domain expert can be reused by a number of analysis method specialists to build a variety of analysis models. Even as the enterprise changes over time, the enterprise models can evolve to reflect these changes and, hence, be reused in future analysis efforts. Finally, because analysis models are built from an explicitly represented set of conceptual models, decision-makers and domain experts can more easily relate the results of analysis efforts to the enterprise being analyzed. These conceptual models enable them to exercise better control over these efforts and to participate more fully in the design and evaluation of alternatives. The benefits of using conceptual models therefore increase domain expert's acceptance and motivations to using analysis methods.

Not surprisingly, these important advantages have prompted great interest and expectations in enterprise modeling. Kosanke writes [Kos92]:

> Enterprise modeling has to fulfill a number of requirements to meet the needs of day-to-day operation. Modeling has to result

> in better understanding and handling of complexity in enterprise operation. Modeling has to enable simulation of alternatives and identification of optimum solutions. The ultimate use of a model will be its direct execution to control and monitor enterprise operations.

Similarly, Grosof and Morgensten [GM92] expect enterprise models to enable rigorous reasoning about an enterprise and to generate executable specifications that can then be used for experimentation and simulation. These expectations, however, have yet to be fulfilled. Although enterprise models are gaining popularity in industries and organizations and are at the center of a number of success stories, particularly in business process reengineering, enterprise technology has yet to realize its full potential in a commercial setting. Four major challenges stand in the way.

The first challenge originates in the critical characteristics of enterprise model sets, namely the differential and complementary nature of the models that comprise the set. Recall that the various conceptual enterprise models (data, activity, process, organizational models, etc.) each focus on a specific type of information that differs in nature from that dealt with by any other model types. Each is necessary to describe a particular aspect of an enterprise, and only a set that includes all of the models can provide a comprehensive representation of an enterprise's operations. Consequently, the use of enterprise models for controlling and monitoring an enterprise requires the generation of a number of different model types. Today, this model generation can typically be accomplished only by developing each model separately, using independent software applications with proprietary storage mechanisms and formats. Hence, it is at best cumbersome and at worst impossible for a domain expert to reuse, in some automated fashion, the information captured in a model of one type in a model of another type. This situation has made the development of a complete enterprise model set a time consuming and effort-intensive endeavor that requires the use of a number of disjointed software applications. Call this the challenge of heterogeneous modeling methods and tools.

The second challenge facing enterprise modeling technology stems from the third major characteristic of enterprise modeling sets, namely the interdependency of the conceptual models that constitute the set. Because all models of an enterprise capture some aspect of the same enterprise, there will be a number of relationships and dependencies among the concepts represented in the various models. Consequently, to develop a comprehensive and coherent picture of the enterprise, the various models must be correlated to permit understanding of the relationships and constraints between the elements represented in the various models. Only such correlation can make it possible for decision-makers to detect conflicts and inconsistencies between models, identify missing information, and calculate the impact of changes in one aspect of the enterprise on other aspects. However, in today's modeling development environments, each type of model is generally captured, represented, and stored using a stand-alone application. Hence, it is impossible, for all intents and purposes, to explicitly correlate enterprise models and use the correlations effectively to (1) obtain a coherent view on the enterprise and (2) evolve the models over time while maintaining consistency between them. Call this the model correlation challenge.

As discussed earlier, each modeling method focuses on a particular aspect of an enterprise. For example, a process modeling method focuses on the processes or tasks that are performed, on the partial ordering of these tasks with respect to time, and on the objects involved in each task. A data model, on the other hand, captures information about the types of data stored and managed in the enterprise, the characteristics of the data, and the relationships and constraints between them. While soundly motivated, this restriction on the types of information managed by each modeling method leads to the third challenge facing enterprise technology. When representing their knowledge using a modeling tool, decision-makers and domain experts will often feel the need to record some information elements whose type is not supported by that particular modeling method and tool. These information types can be critical for providing a good understanding of the enterprise's operations and/or for generating analysis models of the enterprise. Usually, these types of information elements are not supported by the modeling methods because they are too specific to a particular domain or enterprise and fall outside the scope of each particular method. To capture and store such information elements, practitioners are therefore reduced to using ad-hoc notes and annotations (when the modeling tool supports them). Consequently, the effectiveness with which this additional information can be used (and reused) is dependent on the communication skills of the domain expert, in effect going against one of the primary reasons for using modeling methods in the first place. Call this the challenge of representation extensibility.

Finally, the last challenge to effective use of enterprise model technology concerns the automatic generation of executable analysis models (such as simulation or optimization models) from conceptual models. The goal of compiling an enterprise model into an executable model is not to reduce the role of analysis experts in the analytical process. Given the complexity and the expertise needed to apply analysis methods effectively and to interpret the results of analysis effort, this exclusion would not be a realizable goal. Rather, the goal is to minimize the non-value-added activities that are involved in transferring knowledge from domain experts to system analysts. Once automatically generated, an initial executable model can be completed, fine tuned, validated, and finally run by an expert in the corresponding analysis method. Call this the challenge of enterprise modeling compiling.

Today only a handful of commercially available software applications exist that are capable of compiling enterprise models into executable models. The reason is that automatic generation of executable models is a difficult problem that requires expertise from both fields of enterprise analysis and enterprise modeling. Building even a draft executable analysis model requires extensive expertise in the chosen analysis method. Creating one based on the information contained in a conceptual model is not simply a matter of translating knowledge from one language to another. Not only does it require a deep understanding of both the modeling method and the targeted analysis method, but it also demands the development of generic, and often complex, mappings from one method to the other. The development of such a compiler is made even more difficult because analysis models require types of information that are generally not accounted for in high-level conceptual models. Consequently, this type of information must either be added after the executable models have been generated, in which case that information is never explicitly linked to the original model elements, or it must be captured as part of the conceptual models, which requires ad-hoc additions and modifications to the original modeling methods and tools.

Another issue about enterprise model compilers is the quality of the executable models generated. Today, most commercially available compilers generate executable models from one type of model (e.g., simulation models are generated from process or activity models, but not both). This restriction limits the quality of the executable models being generated as they can only rely on the description of one focused aspect of the enterprise. More effective and better initial models generated by an integrated set of enterprise models would together capture various but interdependent aspects of the enterprise.

In summary, then, enterprise modeling faces four significant challenges: (1) heterogeneous modeling methods and tools; (2) model correlation; (3) representation extensibility; and (4) enterprise model compiling. In 1980, Brodie, Mylopoulos, and Schmidt wrote [BMS84]:

> We believe that further advances in conceptual modeling require the integration of the concepts, tools, and techniques that were developed for system description.

Although some advances have been made in conceptual model integration since then, the four challenges described above remain major roadblocks to the use of enterprise modeling technology on a large industrial base. For a description of some research efforts in this field, the reader is referred to [Ver91, Fox91, HJKSMC91, Kos92, MSJ91, Que91, FMM95]).

In the next two sections, we will describe a truly integrated enterprise modeling environment that addresses the challenges described above. Section 3 focuses on the underlying conceptual approach to addressing those challenges while section 4 provides a detailed description of the resulting commercial software. The development of the approach and of the commercial software that implements it is the result of over six years of research and development in the area of enterprise integration, enterprise model integration, and enterprise model compiler technology.

3 A Truly Integrated Approach to Enterprise Modeling and Analysis

Our approach to overcoming the four challenges described in the previous section is the development of an integrated modeling environment that supports the following elements: capture of the entire enterprise model set within a single application, model integration, and extensions to the information types managed by the various model types. In the following subsections, we describe how our approach provides a solution to each of the identified challenges.

3.1 Overcoming the Challenge of Heterogeneous Modeling Methods and Tools

Our approach to overcoming the challenge of heterogeneous modeling methods and tools involves two goals. The first is to provide an environment that supports the capture, representation, and storage of a variety of model types within one application. This application is composed of a variety of modules, each providing the necessary functionality for capturing and manipulating the information types relevant to a particular model type and each responsible for enforcing the rules and procedures of the associated modeling method. All models in the enterprise model set can then be concurrently viewed and manipulated within the application's uniform user interface. The information captured in the various models that constitute the enterprise model set is stored in a single integrated information base.

Our second goal is to provide a mechanism for reusing information captured in one model type to create different model types. This is done by identifying relationships and dependencies among the concepts (i.e., information types) supported by the various modeling methods. The identified relationships are used to define rules for automatically generating a given perspective of an enterprise (i.e., a given model type) from one or more existing enterprise models of different types. In this manner, the creation of a variety of model types to describe an enterprise is partly automated, and the potential for model and model element reuse is increased dramatically.

3.2 Overcoming the Challenge of Model Correlation

Recall that the model correlation challenge concerns the capture, representation, and storage of inter-model relationships and the use of these relationships to maintain consistency across the enterprise model set. Our approach to solving this problem is to provide users with the means to identify and record relationships between model elements across model types. Because the integrated modeling environment enables users to view multiple models concurrently, the identification of relationships is simply of matter of selecting the model elements to be related and the relationship that relates them.

Once identified, the relation instance is stored in the integrated information base and used to maintain consistency between the related elements.

Our approach to using relation instances for maintaining inter-model consistency is based on a simple but powerful observation. Inconsistencies across models in an enterprise model set can be of three types. The first type occurs when one or more properties of an element in a model (or of the model itself) conflicts with properties of one or more elements in another model. An example is the duration of a process in a process model differing from the duration of an activity representing the same real-world event in an activity model. The second type occurs when an association between two elements in one model conflicts with associations between elements in another model. As an example, consider a process in a process model being associated to a particular type of resource through the 'use-as-input' relation. Suppose that the real-world event represented by the process is recorded as an activity A and the type of resource as a concept C in an activity model of the same enterprise. Then, an inconsistency between the two models occurs if C and A are not related through the 'input' relation (or some similar relation) in the activity model. Finally, the third type of inconsistency that can occur between two models of the same enterprise happens when one of the models lacks information the other contains. The detection of this type of inconsistency is harder to automate as it may simply be the result of a conscious decision on the part of the domain expert to describe an aspect of the enterprise with more details than those used in another model.

Given the nature of inter-model inconsistencies, it is possible to automate conflict detection and consistency maintenance in the following manner. The relationships between elements across models are characterized by the way they constrain (1) the properties of the elements they relate and (2) the relationships that these elements have to other elements in their respective models. The impact of a change on an information element in an enterprise model can then be automatically assessed based on the characterization of the relationships it bears to elements in others models. This assessment is then used by the environment to detect conflicts and propagate changes automatically.

3.3 Overcoming the Challenge of Representation Extensibility

An important characteristic of enterprise models is that each type of model focuses on a very specific aspect of an enterprise and therefore is limited with regard to the types of information that it can represent. As described in previous sections, although soundly motivated, this feature of enterprise models hinders the ability of domain experts to capture information that is highly domain-specific and hence may not fall within the types of information supported by the environment. Our approach to overcoming this challenge is to enable seamlessly integrated extensions to the information types supported by the environment. Such extensions are made possible by the flexible underlying structure of the integrated information base.

The integrated information base's underlying structure is rooted in a flexible knowledge representation system developed at Knowledge Based Systems, Inc. (KBSI) called the Container Object System (COS) [SBMM91]. Briefly stated, the COS representation scheme is based on the separation of existential knowledge from descriptive knowledge. A container object has a non-qualitative, unique property that distinguishes it from any other object. The existence and identity of the object is therefore determined by that property. The set of descriptive information elements for that object, including the object's qualitative properties and the relationships that it bears to other objects, forms a 'container' that is simply attached to the object and can be easily modified over time.

The integrated information base is thus structured to represent the various information types needed by modeling methods as types of containers. In this manner, an object can have multiple sets of descriptive knowledge (or containers) that are used to describe it according to various perspectives. In effect, the containers capture the information known about the model elements that represent, in the various models, the real-world object corresponding to the container object (as illustrated in Figure 2). This approach enables and facilitates extensions to the properties of existing information types (an activity which corresponds to adding a property or relation to a type of container) and the creation of new information types (an activity which corresponds to the construction of new types of containers). Because relationships are explicitly represented in the information base, new information elements and types can easily be related to existing ones, and behaviors can be assigned to those relationships in the manner described in Section 3.2. Extensions made in such a manner are seamlessly integrated with existing information elements in the information base and can be manipulated and reused as if they were an integral part of the enterprise model set.

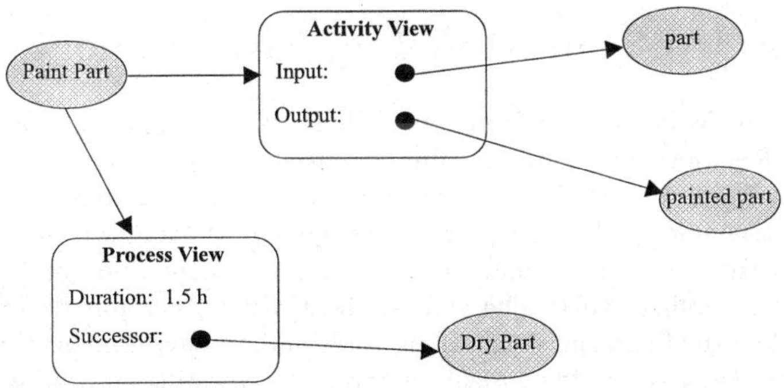

Figure 2: Logical View of the Information Base

3.4 Overcoming the Challenge of Enterprise Model Compiling

Recall from Section 2 that the generation of executable models requires detailed information typically not found in more abstract conceptual models and that, traditionally, executable models have been generated from a single perspective (i.e., a single type of model). There are three ways in which our approach addresses these problems associated with the challenge of enterprise model compiling. The first two ways, which also provide solutions to the other challenges to enterprise modeling technology, come in the form of the integrated information base and its extensibility. The extensible property of the information base allows information specific to analysis methods to be captured, represented, and stored in the information base as well as explicitly linked to the appropriate model elements. In this fashion, information captured for the purpose of generating a particular executable model can be reused for other analysis efforts of a different nature. The integrated information base also enables enterprise model compilers to generate executable models from the total set of enterprise models. In our integrated modeling environment, because the various models that constitute the enterprise model set are tightly coupled through meaningful relationships and constraints, executable models can be generated from a coherent and comprehensive picture of the enterprise.

The third way in which our approach addresses the enterprise model compiling challenge is by providing the means to extend the functionality of the environment and to integrate such extensions through a uniform user interface. This feature allows for the total integration of the various compilers with the original environment. With such extensions, the integrated modeling environment truly supports all phases of analysis efforts, from conceptual modeling to the generation of executable models, while maximizing reuse and minimizing non-value-added activities.

4 The Uniform Modeling Environment

The Uniform Modeling Environment (UME) is a commercial software application developed at KBSI that implements the approach described in the previous section. In addition to addressing the major challenges of enterprise modeling technology, the design and development of the UME has been motivated by the need for the effortless and rapid specialization and extension of current modeling tools. The goal of the UME is therefore to provide an integrated suite of enterprise modeling tools and an environment that can be easily extended to provide an ideal setting for performing enterprise analysis.

The impetus for the system design was to support two fundamental audiences. One is the end users or model builders. They have the task of analyzing a real-world domain, of creating and abstracting out of that domain the various enterprise models that represent different aspects of the enterprise, and of generating initial executable analysis models from these enterprise models. The second audience is the developers of modeling tools and enterprise model compilers. They are responsible for building and supporting modeling activities by maintaining and extending the environment as necessary. The UME's architecture supports the activities of both audiences by (1) supplying a team-based integrated modeling environment and (2) providing developers with the mechanisms to rapidly and easily generate inter-operable extensions to the UME.

Figure 3 illustrates the system architecture that supports these objectives. The heart of the system, the core component, provides three main pieces of functionality, the user interface shell, the database access services, and the mechanisms for model integration. The user interface shell provides the foundation for the common user interface, which includes basic user gestures support, common menus, toolbars, etc. The database access services implement the basic functionality for storing and managing models and other types of information in the integrated database via a common database interface. Finally, the core component encapsulates a powerful inference engine that is responsible for providing model integration through inter-model consistency maintenance and automatic change propagation.

The first echelon of the architecture contains the various modeling modules, called modelers, that operate within the environment. Each modeler supports the creation and management of a single model type. Each modeler is a separate, complete component that interfaces with the core through the common database and common user interface. Each modeler provides the core component with a description of the types of model elements that must be managed in the common database. The core component uses this description to create the necessary database tables and entries as requested by the modeler. This technique allows new modelers to be added to the environment without disturbing the database. The modelers also provide their own user interfaces that extend the core's user interface to enable the creation and management of models and model elements.

At the second echelon, the plug-in applications provide another level of functionality and integration. They extend the environment even further by building on the core component and one or more of the modelers. In particular, this echelon is designed to facilitate and support the development of enterprise model compilers to create bridges between the basic modelers and a variety of analysis tools.

At the third and final tier lie the custom extensions. Custom extensions are only a degree different from applications as they are melded with the environment in a similar way. The goal is to provide an easy point of access for end users to create their own extensions to the modeling environment. This echelon allows virtually unlimited extensibility to the environment while maintaining the integrity and consistency of the formal methodologies supported by the tool.

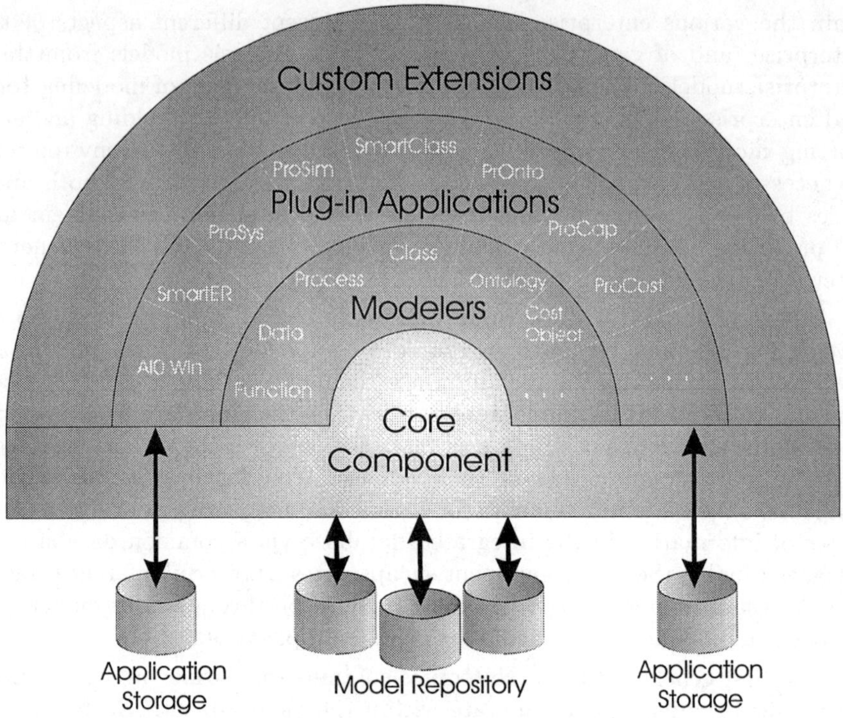

Figure 3: Conceptual Architecture of the UME

4.1 Providing for the Modeling Tool End-Users

In striving to satisfy the needs of two very different groups, end-users of modeling modules and modeling modules developers, programmers invariably face conflicting requirements: enhance the application being developed to provide maximum assistance to the end-user, or program the application to optimize the time, money and effort spend on the development phase. Our focus at KBSI has always been on helping the end-users first and only then assisting the tool developers. After all, software is ultimately built to enhance and assist end users, not to make the developers' jobs easier. While this seems like an obvious objective, in reality, software is frequently written to satisfy given functionality requirements while minimizing effort and cost, a situation that often shortchanges the user.

Enterprise modeling is an extraordinarily complex endeavor requiring many skills and detailed thought processes. Developing software tools that supports domain experts in performing modeling activities requires that tool developers design user interfaces that are as transparent as possible while still providing users with the power to handle complex modeling tasks. An effective user interface should be invisible, allowing the modeler to concentrate on the complex systems being modeled rather than on how to operate the supporting tool. A key focus in the design of the UME was to facilitate enterprise modeling activities by making the user interface as pleasant and transparent as possible.

4.1.1 User Interface Based on Sound Principles

While each application has its own special needs and concerns for the user interface, general guidelines help make the difference between an exceptional user interface and just an average one. Our first objective was to make the user interface fade from the user's mind, to make it invisible to the users. The second objective was to follow, as closely as possible, the users' mental model of the system and of the data being manipulated to make interfacing with the environment intuitive and logically consistent. The third and final aim was to allow as much direct manipulation of the models and model elements by enabling user gestures such as drag-and-drop actions, single and multi-element selection, edit-in-place, etc.

4.1.1.1 Provide an Invisible Interface A simple design technique to improve an application's user interface is to replace most dialog boxes with direct manipulation, edit-in-place, and status bar messages. Dialog boxes interrupt the user's thought process, demanding answers and forcibly extracting acknowledgments. These interruptions distract users from the task at hand and often make using a software application a frustrating experience. In the UME, we have carefully analyzed the process of building enterprise models and used the analysis results to drastically reduce the number of unnecessary interruptions caused by dialog boxes.

The modeling modules of the UME allow users to pace themselves when developing models by allowing them to enter information in a variety of ways and in any order they chose. Normally, when a complex system description is constructed, the process of refining a model includes various stages of incompleteness, inconsistency, and inaccuracy. To support this kind of environment, the system allows incomplete data to be entered and completed later whenever possible. The ability to postpone filling in all information and to delay the validation phase allows the model builders to continue working uninterrupted until the model has reached a stable point.

In the UME, we used a variety of techniques to achieve such user interface, including typical defaults, user input saving and reuse, input validation delays, automatic translation, and automatic information completion. Although these changes are more difficult and time consuming to implement, they do eliminate the peevish tone of an application that continuously forces perfection on the user. One aspect of our approach to designing and building the user interface is to plan for the most common case and allow users to deviate from it without any complaints from the tool. To paraphrase Alan Cooper [Coo95] on user interface design, 'no matter how good your interface is, less of it would be better.' By removing environmental obstacles and distractions, the UME allows model builders to concentrate on their thought process and the task at hand, and to only notice the user interface when necessary or convenient for them.

4.1.1.2 Follow Users' Mental Models Another aspect of our approach to user interface design is to let the user do the thinking but the software do the work. The UME provides the ability to do complex tasks with simple user gestures. In order to provide this capability, we identified common repetitive tasks that occur during the creation and manipulation of enterprise models and implemented sensible manipulation techniques to allow users to easily perform these tasks. For example, a common characteristic of modeling tools is the ability to create and manipulate diagrams and graphs. In the UME, these graphs can be manipulated directly through multiple selection and drag-and-drop actions, (e.g., to create a link between to nodes in a graph). These features facilitate the interaction between the user and the environment, in effect, enabling users to concentrate on the task of creating diagrams rather than on interacting with the tool.

Our tools have traditionally supported auto placement and auto routing capabilities, eliminating the problem of tiresome manual placement of graphical elements. The UME continues this tradition but adds a few enhancements that give the user more control over model element placement. Our guiding principle in providing enterprise modeling tools continues to be to provide end-users with as much automated support as possible but always provide a way for the user to override the default behavior of the tool. In this manner, the tool automatically performs actions grounded on the probable case and then provides the ability for the user to change that default behavior. In the case of diagrams, this principle translates into letting the user place and reposition diagrams elements within a diagram while providing basic auto routing of links between those elements and a feature that can redraw entire diagrams automatically.

An important characteristic of today's end-users is that they never make mistakes (that is, in their minds, at least). Their mental model of how an application should operate does not include the possibility of their making an error. Error messages generated by an application are really just indications that the software is not robust enough to handle input from the user. The way to mitigate this shortcoming is by providing the user with an undo capability. Thus, when the tool users and the tool developers differ in their expectations of how the application should operate, the user does not lose. The UME supports the undo command through the use of special-purpose objects, which allow users to roll back undesired actions until a previous (and desired) state of the information base is reached. This functionality, while usually invoked to correct mistakes made by the user, is also useful for experimentation. Users can try out various actions and features and, if the results aren't the ones desired or expected, can undo the action and recover the previous model state.

4.1.1.3 Allow Direct Manipulation Direct manipulation is an essential component to providing an immersive environment for users. An immersive environment is one that allows users to fully concentrate on the task at hand by never having to interrupt their thought process to ponder on how to make the application behave in some particular fashion. This means that, for every possible action that the user can take to change the models, the tool should provide a way to do it directly. For example, if users can see a model element on the screen, then they should be able to directly edit and manipulate it. Almost everything that can be done to an object in the environment using dialogs and menu commands must also be supported by direct manipulation in the form of edit-in-place; multi-select; drag-and-drop move, copy, etc.

4.1.1.4 Enable a Novice to Perform at an Expert Level Clearly there is an enormous gap in the skills and abilities between novice and expert model builders. While it is not possible to immediately provide novices the years of experience of the expert, novice users can be guided through the modeling processes, helping them to perform at much better than novice levels. The system aids the novice user in several important ways. First, it supports and enforces the rules and the syntax of the modeling methods, thereby guiding the user through the proven benefits of using these formal methods. By doing so, it enables users with a limited knowledge and understanding of the methods to build meaningful and valid models. Second, by providing automatic input completion and allowing users to build their models in a piece-wise manner, it allows novices and beginners to experiment with the tools and work at their own pace. In turn, this characteristic of the UME allows model builders to slowly gain confidence in their ability to build models and use advanced modeling techniques, without being intimated by the environment. Finally, by providing automatic translation and consistency maintenance, it provides tremendous support for users to validate and refine their models.

4.1.2 Integrated Modeling Environment

The UME is an integrated environment at both the data and the user interface levels. As described in previous sections, our approach to solving some of the challenges to enterprise modeling technology and model integration in particular is to automate the reuse of enterprise models and their elements. Traditionally, applications have attempted to support such automation through the ability to import or export files between applications. Although the ability to import or export files between applications is a necessary feature, creating a foundation that will support the integration of the various perspectives is even more imperative. The goal of such capability is to make the user more effective by removing burdensome excise tasks. The UME introduces a radically different paradigm that allows the model builder to work in all perspectives, as needed, without needing to switch between applications via export/import operations. With this paradigm, model builders can manipulate a variety of models concurrently and generate automatically, with a simple user gesture, a model of a given type from one or more models of different types.

4.1.2.1 Make Modelers More Effective The ultimate purpose of any application is to make its users more effective, to remove any obstacle that stand in the way of performing their tasks, and to simplify and automate otherwise tedious and non-value-added activities. The UME is specifically designed for those performing modeling and analysis tasks. Enterprise modeling is a very creative mental activity. It is an activity that requires a high level of concentration on the part of the model builder due to the very complex nature of the systems being modeled. The suite of modeling tools that are seamlessly integrated in the UME allows the model builder to effortless switch among the many perspectives of an enterprise, moving, copying, and linking model elements across method borders. This integration is made possible by special-purpose components called translators. Recall from an earlier section that our approach to solving the challenge of heterogeneous modeling methods and tools is to provide automatic generation of enterprise models from existing enterprise models. This functionality is made possible by the identification and characterization of relationships between the information types supported by the various modeling methods. These relationships, in turn, are used to define translation and mapping rules between model types. The translators that are provided by the UME implements these rules, effectively enabling the automatic translation of model elements from one model type to any other model type supported by the UME.

In accordance to our objectives and guiding principles for the user interface, this translation functionality is made available to user in a transparent and unobtrusive way. Simply selecting and dragging part of a model (e.g., elements in a diagram) and dropping the selected items in another model stirs the translators into action and causes the selected items and their inter-relationships to be translated into appropriate model element types and added to the target model. For example, when a user drops an element from an IDEF0 model into a diagram of an IDEF3, the UME examines the source and target objects, determines the appropriate translation mapping, and invokes the resulting translation procedure. This feature of the UME is critical to providing users with an environment in which the effective manipulation and management of their enterprise through an enterprise modeling set becomes a reality.

4.1.2.2 Visualize the Integrated Information Base The UME allows domain experts to model their enterprise in a number of ways using a variety of perspectives. In addition to supporting a number of modeling methods to enable the representation of various aspects of an enterprise, the UME supports a multitude of techniques to visualize the information stored in the integrated information base. These techniques include an assortment of diagram types, various customizable matrices that depict summaries of fundamental relationships and associations among model elements, and a project node-tree built on the model of the Windows 95^{TM} Explorer. The project node-tree provides both an overview of the entire enterprise model sets and powerful navigation mechanisms to view and manage the information contained in the set.

4.1.3 Knowledge and Rule Base

The system, built upon a modeling knowledge base, uses a powerful production rule system to provide total integration between the different models of an enterprise. There are several advantages to using a rule-based engine as the foundation for model integration. Rules for maintaining consistency between models and model elements do not need to be coded into the program but simply explicitly captured and stored in the knowledge base. Because the rules are not represented in the source code, they can be changed without rebuilding the application. This means that they can be changed without intervention or support from a developer. This flexibility allows the user to customize the behavior of the model integration mechanisms to better fit their specific domain and needs. Currently, only basic rules are used to provide behavior for keeping the various complementary perspectives consistent with each other. The rationale for providing only these basic rules is to provide robust model integration while avoiding users to be overwhelmed with unexpected or unnecessarily complex tool behavior. However, experienced end-users can extend, modify, and enhance the rule base to include additional change propagation and consistency maintenance behavior.

Note that giving the tool the ability to maintain and manipulate meta information (i.e., the information types supported by the various modeling methods) allows users to work at a higher, more generic level of abstraction. At this meta level, users can make connections and define relationships between model and model element types. This unique feature greatly increases the flexibility and the power of integrating models to maintain consistency among the various enterprise perspectives, focuses, and levels of detail.

The use of a rule base engine to maintain consistency and propagate changes across models is made possible by the encoding of all the information contained in the enterprise model set (as well as other types of information) in the integrated information base. The set of model integration rules, together with the integrated information base, form a knowledge base that is used by the UME to provide expert system-like functionality. When changes are made to some part of the information base, the expert system is invoked and the rules are evaluated and applied as appropriate. In this manner, the various aspects of the enterprise are synchronized and remain consistent without any cumbersome effort on the part of the user.

To maintain consistency across the various aspects of an enterprise, the UME expert system requires users to identify relationships between model elements across models. To this end, and through simple drag and drop user gestures, it lets users designate associations between model elements displayed on the screen. Once such associations have been explicitly captured, consistency across models is maintained automatically by the firing of rules in the knowledge base. To simplify the model integration task, the UME provides users with a set of predefined relationships that can be used to relate model elements in a meaningful way.

4.1.4 Representational Flexibility

The primary enabling technology for the UME modeling environment is the enhanced level of integration of information in the information base. The common storage mechanisms facilitate the use of modular modeling tools and plug-in applications, supplying an extensible and flexible foundation. To supplement this capability, the system's common storage mechanism currently uses the ODBC standard and the OLE structured storage specification, providing users with a choice of database formats. The use of OLE structured storage technology permits the UME application to embed OLE objects directly into the modeling database, allowing the user to attach documents, spreadsheets, or other OLE-enabled applications' objects to the models. The use of ODBC technology allows users to share and reuse their integrated information base across various database management systems.

The power of the common storage mechanism, the consistency maintenance and automatic change propagation provided by the inference engine, and the automatic translation of model elements make the UME an unparalleled integrated modeling framework.

4.2 Providing for the Modeling Tool Developers

Although providing for the end user is our primary objective in development of the UME, we also feel it necessary to allow developers and end-users to further extend the capabilities of the environment in a way that allows them to take part in the integrated features of the system. To this end, the UME provides the interfaces necessary to allow customization of existing functionality and the further addition of modelers and plug-in applications.

4.2.1 Extensible Component-Based Architecture

One of the primary requirements for the system was to make it easy for developers to extend without laborious re-design and re-programming cycles. The design of the system had to allow the developers to use and reuse components and, through this reuse, extend the environment without unnecessarily disturbing the existing code base or the structure of the database. To this end, the system is partitioned so that the various modeling methods are encapsulated yet can be completely integrated through the database with both model data and meta information shared among the modules.

At the foundation is the information manager, which all modeling modules use to access relational databases via ODBC and OLE structured storage, and the generic user interface, which provides the core functionality for interacting with the environment. The database schema is designed to accommodate the seamless integration of new model types and new information. The underlying database is relational; however, the design allows the modeling tool developers to treat it as if it were an object-oriented database. This database design gives developers the ability to add new information, relationships, meta information, and meta relationships without restructuring the database or changing the application to adapt to the new information. Another important benefit of this design is that it allows developers to use an object-oriented approach without being chained to the underlying database representation.

4.2.2 Inter-Operability

An extensible component architecture is just the first requirement to support the tool developer. Another is the ability of those components to interoperate with other applications and tools. The UME supports the integration of external applications as well as internal modeler and plug-in applications. The Microsoft^{TM} COM architecture allows the use of OLE servers, OLE clients, and OLE automation. This technology allows the UME to be invoked from within other applications such as Word^{TM} for Windows^{TM} or Excel^{TM}. It allows the use and storage of objects, documents, and spreadsheets from other applications inside the UME database. OLE automation permits access to internal functionality by providing an interface that can be used by external applications, such as analysis and simulation tools. This is a critical innovation that will greatly simplify the design and development of enterprise model compilers and the use of enterprise model to generate executable models that can then be run by specialized analysis tools.

4.2.3 Open Architecture

The UME provides an open architecture that facilitates the addition of new modelers, plug-ins, and customizations by the end user or third party developers. This open architecture is supported by the extensible, centralized storage mechanism based on ODBC and OLE structured storage. The use of OLE automation provides external access to UME functionality as well as support for automatic model translation via translators and translation rules.

4.2.3.1 Extensible Centralized Storage Mechanism The core component provides a simple programming interface used by all other components to store information in the integrated relational database. Each component using the interface must describe the objects that are to be stored in the database. The database manager uses this description to create the necessary tables in the database and to store and retrieve data as needed. As new components are added to the environment, their data can be integrated seamlessly into the existing database. The new component's objects are easily linked to the other model elements through the use of explicitly defined objectified relations that are stored together with the objects in the database. The addition of a new component to the UME thereby expands the environment to include more information and functionality with little extra effort on the part of the developer. New components added to the framework are not required to use their own particular storage mechanism but rather rely on the one provided by UME. When a component needs an object, the component requests the object through the database interface. The database uses its registered description for the object to find it in the relational database. This registration of object descriptions ensures that the information created using one of the UME components is accessible by the other components or plug-in applications.

This feature is critical to support major advances in enterprise modeling technology. In particular, it provides the means to extend and customize the environment to support domain-specific information types. Using this feature, each enterprise can customize the environment to support their particular modeling and analysis needs.

4.2.3.2 OLE Automation Support OLE Automation is a technology that allows the system to reveal features and functionality to other applications. Using OLE Automation, developers can create and manipulate model objects within the UME from another application. With this capability, developers can easily create tools that access and manipulate model elements. These modeling tools can include embedded macro languages, external programming tools, object browsers, analysis tools, simulators, and compilers. Using OLE Automation to expose internal UME objects provides a way for the developer or end user to manipulate the models and model elements programmatically.

This feature is critical to ensure the ultimate use of enterprise models to facilitate and accelerate system analysis efforts. Through the UME's open architecture and the use of OLE Automation, powerful and flexible enterprise model compilers can be built that take full advantage of the UME's integrated information base. Since all compilers rely on the same data to generate executable analysis models, all generated executable models are guaranteed to be consistent and can be traced back to a single source of information. This unique feature provides domain experts with an extremely powerful tool to analyze their enterprise while staying in control of the analysis effort.

4.2.3.3 Translators While the UME provides unprecedented levels of integration for modeling tools, there still exists the need for translation functionality. Translation modules furnish this functionality in the UME for the various model types and by the rules of translation in the knowledge base. These two elements work together to provide the interoperability of the modeling components with one another. For the developer, this makes the burden of creating a modeling tool that will operate in the UME much simpler. To integrate a new modeling tool, the developer can simply map the new tool's model elements to the existing elements. Using the mapping, the translators and translation rules can be built and registered with the environment, completely integrating the new tool into the system.

5 Conclusion

In this contribution, we have provided an analysis of the challenges facing a broader use of enterprise modeling and analysis techniques and presented an approach that addresses these challenges. Some of the most significant of these challenges are:

1. The proliferation of stand-alone enterprise modeling support applications that makes it difficult for domain experts to reuse existing models and to obtain a comprehensive view of the entire enterprise.
2. The lack of automated support to integrate in a meaningful way the various models that constitute an enterprise model set and, consequently, the lack of support for maintaining consistency and propagating changes across these models.
3. The lack of support for capturing information that falls outside the scope of enterprise modeling methods and for linking that information to knowledge captured in the various enterprise models.
4. The relative immaturity of enterprise model compiling technology, which renders using enterprise models to generate executable analysis models a cumbersome and time-consuming endeavor.

Our proposed approach to overcoming these critical challenges is to provide an integrated modeling environment that supports (1) the development of all types of models needed to capture the various aspects of an enterprise, (2) the seamless integration of these models and the use of inter-model relationships to automate consistency maintenance across models, and (3) information and functionality extensions to the environment. This approach has served as the foundation for the development of a the Uniform Modeling Environment (UME), a commercial software application developed at KBSI.

The UME satisfies two main objectives: (1) provide an intuitive, easy-to-use, but powerful environment to domain experts to create and manage enterprise model sets, and (2) facilitate information and functionality extensions to the environment. The first objective is attained by using state-of-the-art user interface techniques, automating the process of building and integrating models, and using an underlying integrated information base that provides a comprehensive and coherent view of the enterprise. The second objective is attained by providing a flexible framework using a component-based system development architecture, which enables developers to extend, enhance, and evolve the environment.

Acknowledgments: We gratefully acknowledge the technical contribution and guidance of the following people. Without them, none of this work would have been possible: Dr. Richard Mayer, Dr. Christopher Menzel, Richard Henderson, Sridevi Subramanian, Thomas Blinn, David Hart, Tom Landrum, Michael Biggerstaff, and Dr. Perakath Benjamin. We also extend our thanks and appreciation to Kathryn Alexander for her help in editing this contribution.

References

[BMS84] Brodie, M. L., Mylopoulos, J., Schmidt, J.W. (eds.), On Conceptual Modeling, Springer Verlag, New York, 1984

[Coo95] Cooper, A., ABOUT FACE, The Essentials of User Interface Design, IDG Books Worldwide, Inc., California, 1995

[FMM95] Fillion, F., Menzel C., Mayer, R. J., Blinn, T., An Ontology-Based Environment for Enterprise Model Integration, Presented at the Workshop on Basic Ontological Issues in Knowledge Sharing at IJ-CAI95, Montreal, Canada, November 1995

[Fox91] Fox, M. S., The TOVE Project: Towards a Common-Sense Model of the Enterprise, published in [PET91], 1991

[Gig91] Gigh, J. P. van, System Design Modeling and Metamodeling, Plenum Press, New York, 1991

[GM92] Grosof, B., Morgenstern, L., Applications of Logicist Knowledge

Representation to Enterprise Modelling, Workshop on Artificial Intelligence in Enterprise Integration, AAAI-92, July 1992

[HJKSMC91] Huhns, M. N., Jacobs, N., Ksiezyk, T., Shen, W.-M., Singh, M. P., Cannata, P. E., Enterprise Information Modeling and Model Integration in Carnot, published in [PET91], 1991

[Kos92] Kosanke, K., CIMOSA - A European Development for Enterprise Integration. Part 1: An Overview, published in [PET91], 1991

[MSJ91] Mertins, K., Süssenguth, W., Jochem, R., An Object-Oriented Method for Integrated Enterprise Modeling as a Basis for Enterprise Coordination, published in [PET91], 1991

[PET91] Petrie, C. J. (ed.), Enterprise Integration Modeling Proceedings of the First International Conference, The MIT Press, Cambridge, 1991

[Que91] Querenet, B., CIMOSA - A European Development for Enterprise Integration, Part 3: Enterprise Integrating Infrastructure, published in [PET91], 1991

[SBMM91] Sanders, L. K., Browne, D., Menzel, C., Mayer, R. J., Container Objects: A Description Based Knowledge Representation Scheme, Proceedings of Autfact'91, 1991

[Ver91] Vernadat, F. B., CIMOSA - A European Development for Enterprise Integration, Part 2: Enterprise Modeling, published in [PET91], 1991

[Ver96] Vernadat, F. B., Enterprise Modeling and Integration, Chapman & Hall, London, 1996

[Zac86] Zachman, J., A Framework for Information Systems Architectures, Report No. G320-2785, IBM Los Angeles Scientific Center, March 1986

[Zuk79] Zukav, G., The Dancing of Wu Li Masters: An overview of the New Physics, William Morrow, New York, 1979

CHAPTER 22

WorkParty

Walter Rupietta

Workflow management is concerned with the execution of business processes, supporting division of labor between participants and partial automation of individual tasks. Currently, workflow management systems are primarily employed in the service business, e.g. banks, insurance companies, and public authorities. However, the objectives of introducing workflow applications - improved productivity, faster and more reliable processing of workflows, immediate availability of information in response to customer inquiries - are equally important in industrial business processes. Workflow management systems can serve as a platform for process design in areas like purchasing, sales, order processing, human resources management, and quality management for industrial processes. Workflows are well-defined work processes that are repeatedly carried out according to predetermined rules. Labor may be divided between multiple participants. Rules determine which work steps are carried out, in which sequence, and who is responsible. Workflow management systems like WorkParty from Siemens Nixdorf comprise tools for the definition of business case templates and workflows and support their execution in the corresponding runtime environment. This contribution describes the concepts and tools of the scaleable workflow product family WorkParty. It concludes by presenting the idea that the architecture of future application systems will rely on a workflow management infrastructure.

1 Introduction

This section presents a framework for workflow management by defining basic terms, standards and procedures for implementing workflow applications. In this section, the term *organization* refers to the result, not to the process of organizing.

1.1 Organization, Processes, and Workflow Management

The aim of organization is to set a suitable structure for work in a company. Organization can be decomposed into static and dynamic aspects. Static aspects are referred to as *structural organization* dynamic aspects as *workflow organization.* Structural organization comprises the entities and persons involved, tasks and authorities, resources, structures and relationships. These are limiting conditions for work processes. The regulation of work processes is termed *workflow organization* and defines work steps, the timing and sequence of the steps, division of labor, participants, work objects and results, and dependencies. The workflow organization defines *how* work is done in an enterprise or public authority. Every enterprise or public authority is organized in one way or another and can thus be called an organization. *Business processes* are well-defined work processes within an organization, characterized by division of labor between multiple participants working at different times and different places. Basically, they come in two different varieties:

- *Organization-directed* business processes are continuously repeated in the same or a similar way. They are carried out according to predetermined, permanently valid rules.

- *User-directed* business processes show only few similarities or repetitions. They are carried out according to permanently changing rules or with no predetermined rules at all.

These define the extreme ends of a continuum of business processes. Real-world examples are neither completely organization controlled nor completely user controlled. An organization-directed business process needs some degree of flexibility to cope with unforeseen situations. User-directed business processes take place within a company or public authority and have to comply with its regulations. They are user-directed only as far as the organization permits. Business processes are characterized by attributes, e.g. customer number, order number, related documents and data, workflows, persons and organizational entities involved. *Workflow management systems* support the definition and developmen of *process types* or templates to make use of the similarity of organization-controlled work processes. Repetition is handled by (partial) automation of the execution of *process instances* in a runtime environment. Rules are transformed into workflow specifications. Each process instance belongs to a corresponding process type or template. Basically, all workflow management systems exhibit this distinction between workflow template development and workflow execution (see for example [Jab95]). However, different workflow management systems use different solutions for workflow definition, different tools and interfaces (see [KRK95], for example).

1.2 Standards and Procedures

The Workflow Management Coalition (WfMC) is an international organization whose aim is to develop specifications for software that will allow different workflow management products to interoperate in various key areas [WfMC94]. For this purpose, the WfMC developed a reference model that

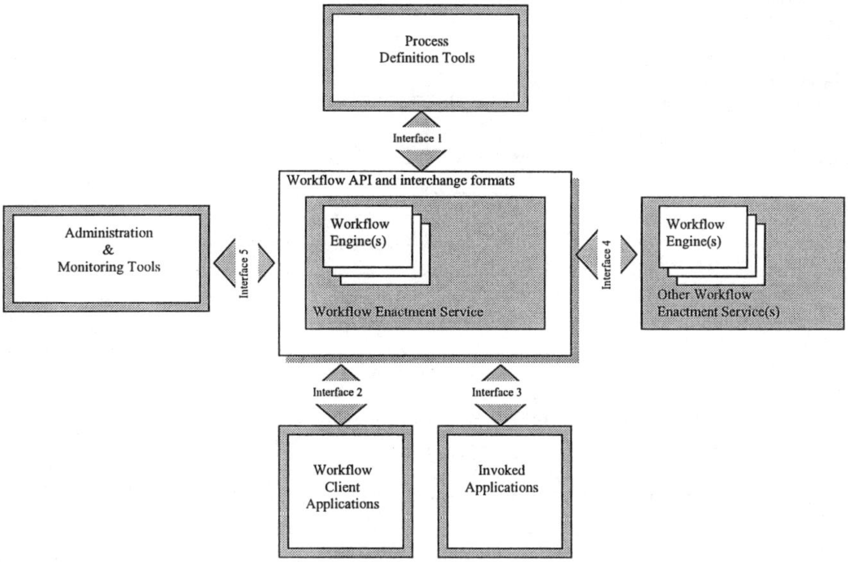

Figure 1: Workflow reference model developed by the WfMC

describes an architecture for workflow management systems and interfaces between the different entities of the model (Figure 1).

In the context of the WfMC model, a workflow enactment service consists of one or more workflow engines and is used to process instances. Workflow templates are developed using process definition tools and then managed with the help of administration & monitoring tools. Users interact with the workflow enactment service using workflow client applications (e.g. a worklist handler). The workflow enactment service invokes other applications while executing workflows and possibly interoperates with other workflow enactment services.

As of today, the interface definitions have not been finally released. Existing products like WorkParty adhere to the reference model and consequently provide comparable interfaces. This implies, of course, that interoperation requires conversions and individual adaptations.

The topic of workflow management applications is frequently introduced in the context of business process reengineering projects. Optimizing business processes implies corresponding organizational changes and appropriate redesign of the information processing infrastructure. This is where workflow management systems are brought into play.

Workflow management is often seen as a means to implement the results of business process reengineering. On the other hand, workflow management should not be introduced without prior consideration of business processes and their optimization. This is why the deployment of workflow applications

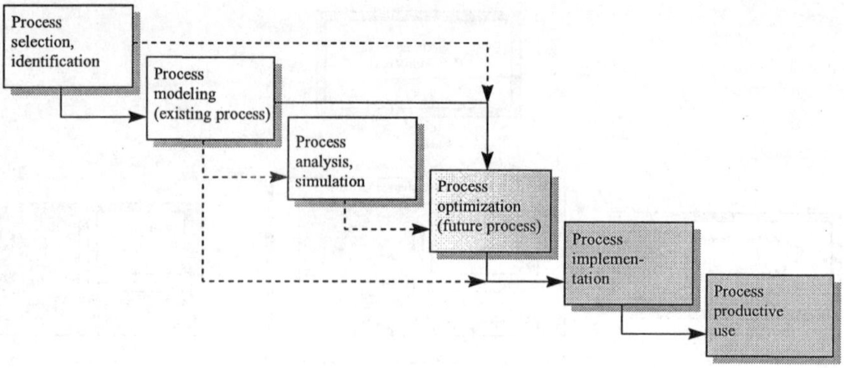

Figure 2: Procedure for introducing workflow applications.

should follow the procedure sketched in Figure 2. The shaded areas represent workflow-related phases, the earlier phases correspond to reengineering tasks. In the process optimization phase both aspects overlap. Dotted lines represent alternatives and shortcuts.

After identifying and selecting a business process, it must be modeled either in its existing form or in its future, optimized form. An existing process will then be analyzed and possibly simulated resulting in an optimized process. The latter is modeled in terms required by the workflow management system and subsequently deployed. The final stage is productive execution of the resulting workflow application. This procedure has been adopted in several WorkParty projects (see for example [Jor94, RH97]).

This arrangement neither prevents the use of a workflow management system like WorkParty for reengineering tasks nor does it imply that the workflow-phases necessarily require the use of a workflow management system. The procedure is independent of any specific technology.

2 WorkParty - The Business Case Manager

The reason for calling WorkParty a business case manager is given in the next paragraph. The business case model is the foundation for WorkParty's architecture and operations. The following paragraph introduces the scaleable workflow product family from Siemens Nixdorf and demonstrates the role of WorkParty in this context. The rest of this section is devoted to a detailed description of the WorkParty architecture, tools, and interfaces.

2.1 The WorkParty Business Case Model

WorkParty considers a business process as a self-contained pattern of organizational behavior devoted to a specific business purpose. Workflow processes

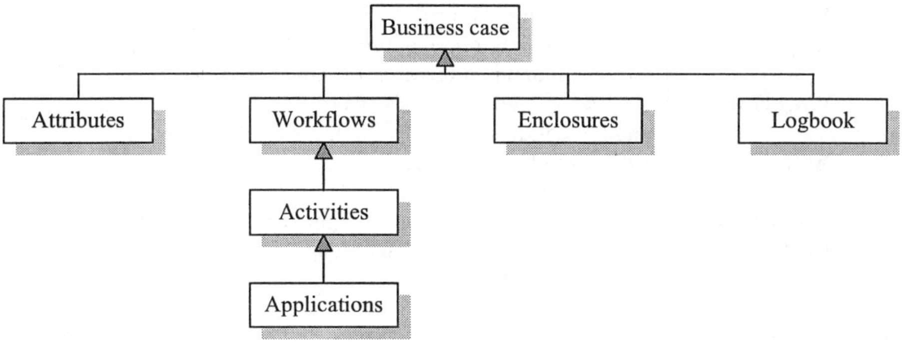

Figure 3: The WorkParty business case model

are concerned with those portions of business processes that are supported by information systems. WorkParty uses the term ***business case*** to refer to computer-represented portions of a corresponding business process (Figure 3). A *workflow* is regarded as a specific work process in the context of a business case.

A business case is represented as a case file collecting all items pertaining to that particular business process. Each business case has a set of attributes (e.g. customer number, account number, order number, interest rate, credit limit, loan amount) that characterize a specific case. It can have one or more workflows which in turn contain several activities. An activity is defined by being an atomic portion of work that is completely carried out by a single employee at his workplace. Each activity may be connected to an application. Enclosures are case-related documents or references to such documents or data. The case logbook collects data concerning the life cycle of a business case (e.g. start and end times of activities, the employee who performed an activity ...). The applications are usually not considered part of the business case, but part of the system infrastructure. This is partly due to technical reasons: most applications are complex software packages that need to be installed and not simply programs that can be moved around and used in any place.

An example of such a business case is the opening of a loan account in Table 1. In this example, the business case exists for several years. After an initial phase of activity (workflows related to the establishment of the credit) it remains inactive as long as regular payments are received. Then conditions for the credit (e.g. the interest rate) change and new work processes (workflows for condition changes) are carried out. Finally, the business case is closed when the credit has been paid back. This may again require a workflow to be executed. This example shows the advantages of distinguishing between workflows and business cases: during the lifetime of a business case several related workflows may be executed at different times. The busi-

Business case	Loan case file "Jones"
Attributes	Start date, customer name & address, phone number, subject matter, interest rate, amount of credit, ...
Workflows	Apply for loan, raise mortgage, change conditions, ...
Activities	Fill in application form, calculate financing, ...
Applications	Spreadsheet application, customer accounts access, ...
Enclosures	Loan application form, mortgage documents, letter of consent, ...

Table 1: Example of a Loan Account

ness case is still alive during phases without active workflows. There is no workflow overhead during phases of inactivity.

2.2 WorkParty - The Workflow Product Family

Business cases are handled at different levels, depending on the size of the organization: at the desk of an individual, within a small team or company, within units of a large enterprise. Workflows for routine tasks at the desk of an individual are certainly user-directed. Workflows at team level tend to be user-directed, but this is not necessarily so. Workflow at the enterprise level is normally organization-directed. These differing requirements led Siemens Nixdorf to the introduction of a scalable family of workflow products for different purposes (Table 2). Scaleability includes the option to upgrade to a more complex workflow product without losing the time and work already invested.

SmartAssist workflows are sequences of actions (simple branching features are available) executed under user control. Activities can be chosen from an extensible set of predefined building blocks. Team Edition extends SmartAssist by integration with the business case manager, worklist handler and limited use of the Organization & Resources management component of WorkParty. Enterprise Edition replaces SmartAssist with the native WorkParty engine and its associated tools, the graphical workflow editor and the activity editor, which allow the definition and execution of more complex workflows. The rest of this section will focus on the Enterprise Edition, its architecture, tools, and interfaces.

2.3 WorkParty Architecture and Tools

WorkParty is designed in accordance with the reference model of the WfMC. The operation of WorkParty is best comprehended by examining the architecture of workflow applications based on WorkParty. Such a *workflow application* is an ensemble of one or more business case templates, one or

	SmartAssist	*WorkParty Team Edition*	*WorkParty Enterprise Edition*
	Personal productivity tool, automation of routine tasks	*User-directed business case management*	*Organization-directed business case management*
Business case manager		WorkParty business case manager	WorkParty business case manager
Workflow and activity definition	SmartAssist definition tools	SmartAssist definition tools	Graphical workflow editor and activity editor
Workflow execution	SmartAssist engine	SmartAssist engine	WorkParty engine
Worklist handler		WorkParty worklist handler	WorkParty worklist handler
Organization management		Organization and Resources Manager (limited use)	Organization and Resources Manager

Table 2: The WorkParty product family

more libraries containing workflows and activities, the application programs and functions invoked by the activities, and an organizational model. WorkParty provides a set of tools that enable a workflow designer to produce these entities (at development time). Application programs may be existing applications that are unaware of the workflow environment or specifically integrated applications with interfaces to the underlying WorkParty environment. The latter can be developed using common programming environments (e.g. C++, Microsoft Visual Basic). The execution of workflow applications (at runtime) is supported by the WorkParty runtime system, which executes and controls workflows designed with the development tools. Activities are processed in the order determined by the workflow, and associated applications are subsequently executed (Figure 4).

WorkParty uses a relational database and a central file store located on a server system for coordination and information exchange between workstations of a workgroup; its software components reside on the users' PC workstations. The file store houses executable workflow specifications (com-

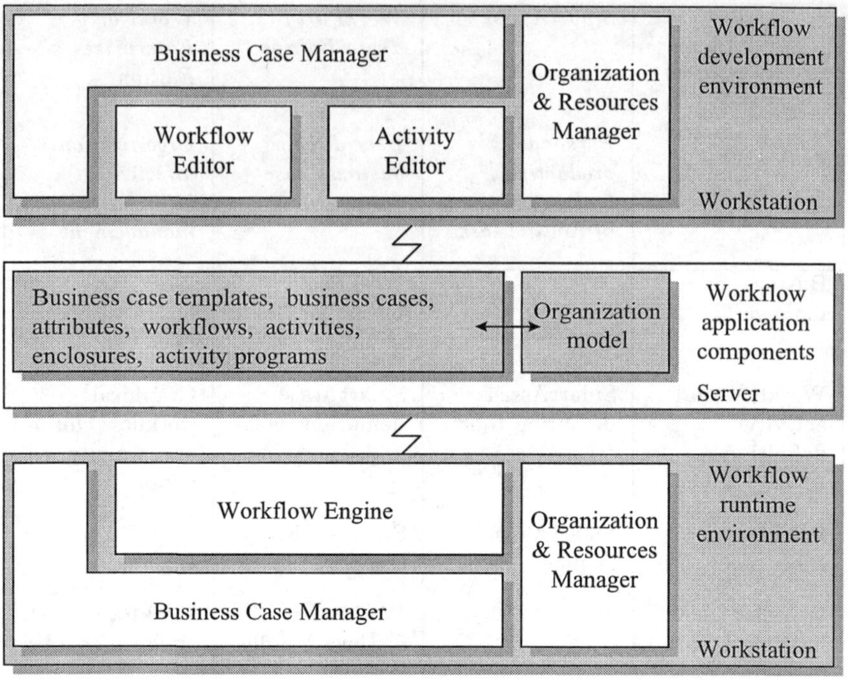

Figure 4: WorkParty development and untime architecture

piled from the graphical representation of the workflow editor), activities, and enclosures. The database contains administration data about these entities and business case attributes. Business case templates and libraries of workflows and activities have to be released before they can be used in the runtime environment. Enclosures can also be references to documents stored in other locations, e.g. in a document management system. Users cooperating across different WorkParty locations can exchange business cases via electronic mail.

2.3.1 Business Case Manager and Worklist Handler

The business case manager is the control center of WorkParty. In terms of the WfMC reference model it is a workflow client application as well as an administration and monitoring tool. At development time the business case manager controls business case templates, libraries of workflows and activities. At runtime, it manages business case instances and worklists. The business case manager is a uniform interface for viewing, editing, and administering different entities of workflow applications. It also controls access to business case entities (Figure 5). Each user has to enter his or her ID and password to log on to the business case manager. This data is passed on

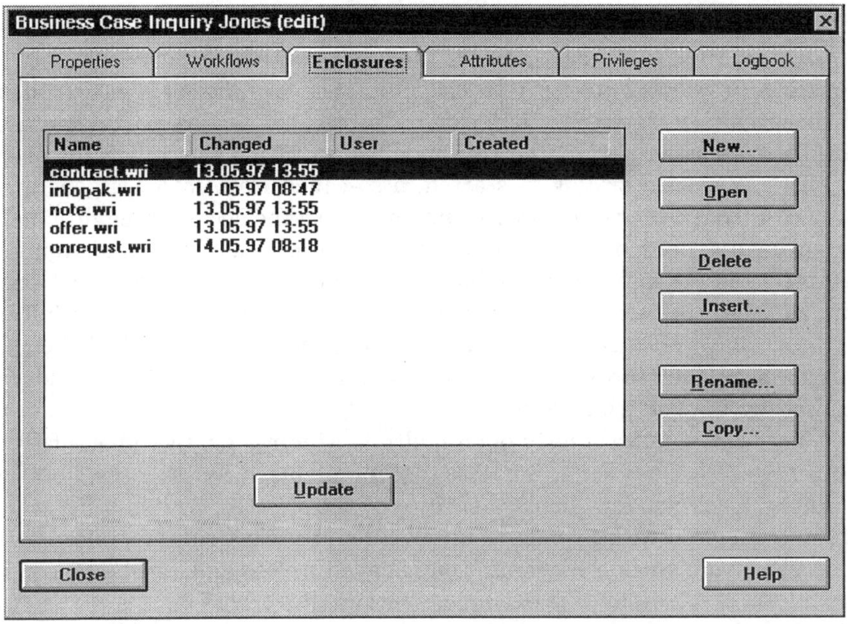

Figure 5: WorkParty business case template editor showing enclosures

and checked by the Organization & Resources Manager. Access is granted if an employee with the ID and password given exists in the organizational model. The business case manager then retrieves the user's profile with respect to positions, roles, organizational units, and authorities. The profile is matched against privilege profiles defined for accessing individual business case entities.

A *business case template* comprises basic properties, workflows, enclosures, attributes, privileges, and the logbook (see WorkParty business case model in section 2.1). A template specifies the initial state of each instance of this business case. Its properties define name, initial case ID, version, and validity period of the template. Workflows reside in libraries also managed by the business case manager and are only referred to from within a case template. Enclosures and attributes may be added or removed at runtime. Privileges specify access rights for the case template. This topic will be discussed later. The logbook refers to the template, each business case (instance) possesses its own logbook. Creating a *business case* involves copying the template to be used and specifying individual properties.

A *library* collects related workflows and activities. Activities are referred to from within workflows. Workflows are referred to from within business case templates. Workflows can be created and edited using the graphical workflow editor. Activities can be created and edited with the activity editor. Activities can be used in multiple workflows. Workflows can be used in multiple business case templates.

At any point in time, several workflows from different business cases can be executed simultaneously. Each of them is positioned at a specific activity executing or waiting its turn to execute. The *worklist* of a user collects all those current activities that can be processed by this particular user. Worklists are assembled at the very moment when the user opens his or her worklist. When a workflow is started, a so-called *work folder* is generated. For each activity, the work folder is prepared with the necessary environment, i.e. enclosures needed for this activity are automatically retrieved from the file store and copied into the folder. On activation of an activity from a worklist, the work folder is moved to the workstation where the activity is executed, and the corresponding application program is invoked. When the activity ends, enclosures in the file store are updated from the work folder as required by the particular activity.

A user can simultaneously open multiple windows for the different types of business case entities, i.e. business case templates, business cases, libraries, worklists. Each window displays entities of the selected type in a list which can be configured with respect to order, filters to select subsets, information to be displayed. Such a configuration is called a *view* and can be stored for later reuse. A view can, for example, contain all worklist entries that newly arrived in the last half hour.

2.3.2 Graphical Workflow Editor and Activity Editor

The *graphical editor* is the main tool for workflow design in WorkParty (Figure 6). Workflows are designed following a metaphor of visual programming. Starting with an empty workflow graph, flows are composed from graphical representations of activities, subworkflows, and control structures. These elements are entered by simply dragging them from a toolbox to the desired anchor point in the workflow graph. The construction process guarantees syntactical correctness of the workflow graphs. The editor docs not allow syntactically illegal flows to be constructed. WorkParty's control structures comprise alternatives, loops, and parallel processing. Workflow graphs are directed graphs with a single start point, at least one end point, and possibly loops. The graphical representation of workflows has been proven to be rather intuitive. It is therefore well suited to communicate workflows and work regulations with users. In addition, workflow graphs are executable workflow specifications.

The subworkflow element allows the modular development of workflows. The nodes of the resulting workflow graph refer to activities or subworkflows. Each workflow can serve as a subworkflow in another workflow definition. Thus, complex workflows can be developed either top-down, by hierarchical decomposition into subworkflows, or bottom-up, by combining existing workflows. At runtime, the graphical editor can be used to view the workflow graph of an active workflow. The current activity is then marked to trace the status of execution.

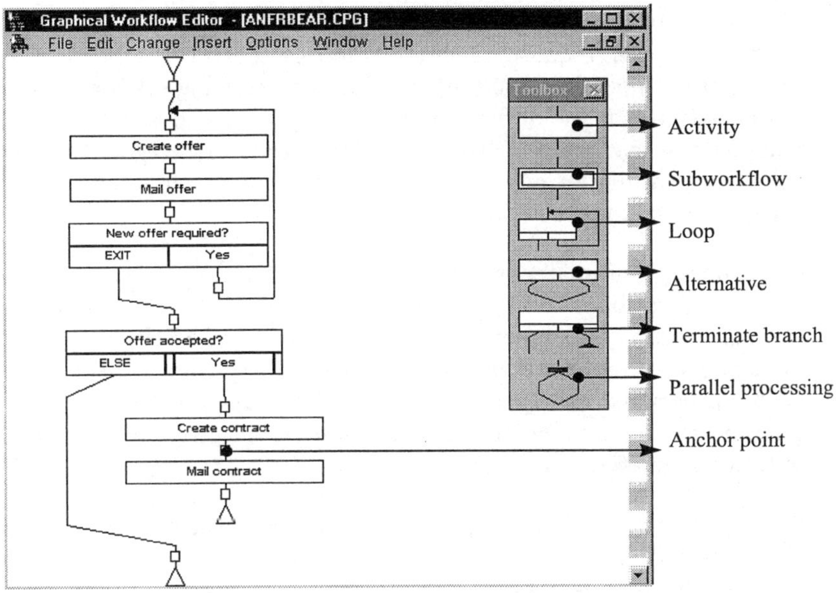

Figure 6: Graphical workflow editor

From a top-down view, the final step in workflow design is the definition of activities and their implementation via activity programs. Activities in WorkParty are rather complex objects that provide for detailed control of invoked applications. The *activity editor* is used for:

- User specification: The user for an activity can be specified in three different ways. First, a reference to the workflow history may specify the user of a previous activity as the user for the actual activity. Second, a profile referencing the underlying organizational model can specify a set of possible users (see below), and third, a program can be specified that determines the user for the current activity.

- Specification of start conditions: Conditions can be specified that determine whether the current activity can be executed. Conditions may require specific attribute values, the existence of documents or events (see [Wor96]). At runtime, execution of the current activity will be deferred until its start conditions are satisfied. A current activity whose execution is deferred - for example waiting for an event to occur - is not displayed in any worklist. As part of this specification, attributes, attribute values, and necessary documents can be defined. At runtime, attributes and necessary documents will be attached to the corresponding work folder.

- Specification of execution conditions: Execution conditions encompass the control of whether the activity is started or ended either automatically or at user request. These conditions control whether the user can skip or repeat the activity at runtime, exchange it for an alternate activity or insert additional activities. It is also possible to specify whether the current activity may be forwarded or delegated to other users. Forwarding or delegation can be restricted to users of the same organizational unit, role, or authority.

- Program and parameter specification: This part of an activity describes which application is to be invoked when executing the activity. Parameters or necessary documents can be specified. Invoked applications can be arbitrary programs unaware of the WorkParty environment or integrated programs that use the WorkParty interface to retrieve workflow-related attributes or documents. For integrated programs, input and output parameters can be specified.

- Specification of end conditions that have to be satisfied in order to conclude the activity: In the same way that start conditions for an activity can be defined, it is possible to define end conditions. An activity will not reach the status "ended" unless it fulfills its end conditions.

A workflow graph together with all its activities provides an executable workflow. If no activity programs are defined, all activities are carried out manually. In this case, WorkParty acts as a check list. The graphical workflow editor and the activity editor are process definition tools in terms of the WfMC reference model.

Flexibility in application development is enabled through re-use of existing processes, activities and activity programs as building blocks for new business case templates. Flexibility in application execution is controlled by the workflow designer through the definition of appropriate execution conditions for activities. If specified, the user can at runtime skip, repeat, or exchange an activity with another one, insert additional activities, and forward or delegate activities to other users. Thus, it is possible to design workflows where some sections are strictly regulated and allow no deviation while in other sections the user is given more control.

2.3.3 Organization and Resources Manager

The Organization & Resources Manager (ORM) serves to manage the structural organization that defines the framework for business cases. Structural organization is modeled in terms of *organizational units* (e.g. departments, groups), *positions* (workplaces of an individual employee), *employees*, *roles* (organizational roles, e.g. department manager), *authorities* (which may be interpreted as authorization, responsibility or capability), *resources* (e.g. a file server, a specific file system resource), and their mutual relationships as

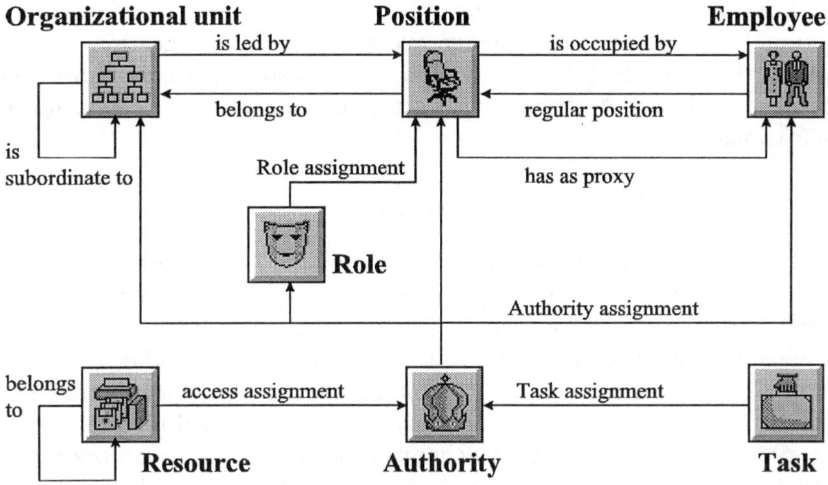

Figure 7: Conceptual model of the ORM

shown in Figure 7. (Icons represent objects, i.e. terms; arrows represent relationships.) All entities of the organizational model are characterized by the values of a set of predefined attributes. Additional attributes can be attached according to the needs of applications.

In ORM a statement like "Sam Spade is the section lead of the Sales section in the Household Appliances division" can be represented as follows: The position *LA* belongs to the organizational unit *Sales* and is occupied by the employee *Sam Spade*. The sales unit is subordinate to the organizational unit *Household Appliances* and led by the position *LA*. LA is assigned the role*Section lead*. The hierarchy level of Sales is *section*; the hierarchy level of Household Appliances is *division*.

ORM was designed to reflect the fact that an employee's work is regulated by his or her placement in the organization and does not depend on the individual person. This is why authorities assigned to abstract organizational entities like organizational units, positions, or roles will be inherited by employees via their assignment to positions according to configurable rules. Thus, if an employee gets moved to a different position, his authorities will be adapted automatically.

Depending on the organization involved in individual application environments, not all of these entities and relationships are needed. This is provided for in the user interface of ORM, which is configurable to hide entities and relationships not needed. ORM provides a generic framework that makes it possible to model different types of organizations.

ORM can be used independently from WorkParty to serve as "electronic organization manual" or extended user management for applications. In contrast to pure analysis and design tools, the information stored in an ORM model can be used at runtime by arbitrary applications to adapt to organizational structures or to manage access rights for application resources. Using authorities instead of individual users to specify access rights results in more flexible and organization-directed management of access control for applications.

2.4 Roles and Authorizations

The connection between the organizational model and a workflow process is established via the concept of a *process-related role* (see [Rup97]). A process-related role is a placeholder whose purpose is to provide an abstraction for the person assigned to a workflow process activity or any other task related to a workflow process. However, combining it with the organizational model, causes it to be associated with organizational entities and relationships and thus makes it a very powerful mechanism for defining generic workflow processes that can automatically adapt to specific organizational structures.

An activity is part of a workflow process. At execution time each workflow process produces a series of logbook entries that constitute its history. At development time, when a process template is developed, the history of its instances does not yet exist. However, references to this history can specify previous entries relative to an activity. In an activity definition, a process-related role is a placeholder for the performer of the workflow activity. This process-related role is called "Workflow participant". At definition time, the workflow participants for all activities of the workflow are defined. The definition refers to either the history of the workflow selecting the user of any previous activity, or specifies a profile that selects, through a combination of user, position, organizational unit, role, and authority, a set of candidates as potential performers who are responsible and authorized to perform the corresponding activity during process execution. Finally, the definition can specify a program that selects a user (possibly from the organizational model according to application-specific criteria). This latter option provides for great flexibility in controlling responsibilities for activity execution and adapting to application-specific policies (Figure 8).

In this way, workflow processes can be tied to entities of the enterprise organizational structure and do not depend on specific users. Workflow participants can be specified referring to employees, positions, organizational units, (organizational) roles or authorities, for example, and not to specific employees. If the assignments of employees to positions or assignments of authorities change, the workflow definition remains unaffected as long as it relies on abstract concepts rather than on concrete users.

The same kind of profile is used to specify access privileges for business case templates, business cases, and libraries. For each of these object types, three classes of privileges have been defined for editing, administration, and information. Each privilege class is associated with a specific set of functions. Its profile describes, through a combination of user, role, position, author-

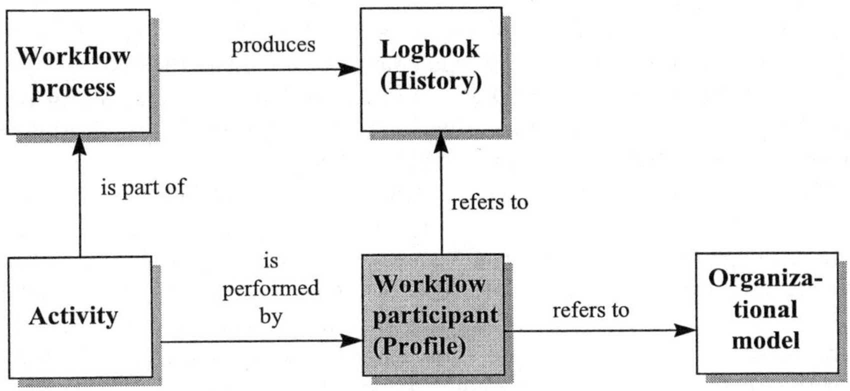

Figure 8: Specification of workflow participants

ity, and organizational unit, a set of users who may execute the functions pertaining to that particular privilege class.

For example, a business case has a profile for each of the three privilege classes editing, administration, and information. Each of these profiles selects a set of users who are allowed to execute the functions pertaining to that particular privilege class for the specific business case. The administration privilege class for business cases, for example, contains functions for deactivating and activating a business process.

2.5 WorkParty Interfaces

Following the WfMC reference model, WorkParty incorporates equivalents of interfaces 2 (workflow client application - workflow enactment service), 3 (invoked applications - workflow enactment service) and 5 (administration & monitoring - workflow enactment service). Interface 3 corresponds to the WorkParty interface for programming activities; interfaces 2 and 5 are combined in the WorkParty API.

When activity programs are called, WorkParty makes a standard set of data available, the so-called *folder instance attributes*. These are in part technical data required for using the WorkParty API (e.g. technical keys for identifying business cases and workflows); to a greater extent it contains information that describes the current environment of the activity (e.g. the case ID, the name of the user), and finally it contains values that can be returned (in modified form) to the WorkParty enactment service (e.g. the results of an activity, data for a logging entry).

Besides the folder instance attributes, WorkParty supplies an additional set of data, the so-called *InPins*, which can be defined individually for each activity with the help of the activity description. These can be the contents of attributes of the business case, the contents of local attributes of the workflow, or simple strings. Programs can return data to WorkParty; this is done with the help of the so-called *OutPins*, the counterparts of the InPins.

The interface for programming activities consists of a collection of functions for connecting and disconnecting to WorkParty, retrieving and returning folder instance attributes, InPins, and OutPins.

The WorkParty API contains a comprehensive set of functions for about every task that is normally handled by the client tools, e.g. administering business case templates, executing workflows, evaluating logbooks, administering worklists, and more. [RSD97] describes an example of an application, that integrates worklist handling and application functions into new workplace interfaces, so that users of this applications never use WorkParty directly. They use their application interface and need not be aware of the fact that it is driven by workflow technology. This appearance is achieved through the WorkParty API which has been used to replace the business case manager with application-specific user interfaces.

3 WorkParty - Case Study

The growing demand for healthcare is placing new pressures on hospitals and the information systems which support them. At the same time, hospitals and other healthcare providers are increasingly being held accountable for both the quality and the cost of the patient care they offer. Meeting the changing needs of hospitals and other healthcare providers requires open healthcare systems which can be customized and adapted for all aspects of administrative and clinical use. Workflow management appears to be well suited for providing such a system. A case study was conducted to evaluate the suitability of workflow systems in a university gynecological hospital. The case study closely followed the procedure described in section 1.2 and focused on clinical and not on administrative aspects (see [RSD97]).

The first step of the study was the identification of the relevant business processes of the hospital. Four main processes and a couple of elementary service processes were identified. The main processes were minimal-invasive surgery, invasive surgery, in-patient chemotherapy, out-patient chemotherapy. Examples of elementary service processes were diagnostics, ordering of drugs, and laboratory analyses.

The four main processes were then analyzed in detail and modeled using BONAPART (see [Ubis97]). Next, the minimal-invasive surgery process was selected for optimization and implementation. Reasons for selecting this process were its limited complexity and duration on the one hand and its clear potential for improvement on the other hand.

The process model was optimized and then manually transformed into a WorkParty business case. The manual transformation was necessary because the previous analysis identified manual activities (e.g. transport of a patient from a ward to an operating room) as well as computer-supported activities.

Furthermore, the levels of detail in the analyzed processes and the resulting WorkParty workflows sometimes differed significantly. In some parts, entire subprocesses collapsed into a single WorkParty activity.

The minimal-invasive surgery process was successively decomposed into smaller subprocesses in the WorkParty environment. The result was a hierarchy of (sub-)processes constituting a patient's complete stay, from her registration, medical examinations and operation to her dismissal from the hospital. The hospital's organizational structure was modeled using ORM. To demonstrate the integrative capabilities of the workflow management approach, legacy applications as well as newly developed applications were integrated in the workflow as activity programs. The newly developed applications used a relational database to store patient records and related data.

Another outcome of the process analysis was the requirement for application- and workplace-specific user interfaces. The normal WorkParty user interface (i.e. business case manager, worklist handler) was designed with typical office work in mind. The majority of hospital personnel is not as familiar with computer use as, for example, bank personnel. Thus, different workplace interfaces were designed and implemented for the out-patient department, the ward nurse, the ward physician, and the operating room staff.

This case study proved that the business case approach is appropriate for clinical environments and that workflow management is a suitable technique for providing flexible, process-oriented healthcare systems. Especially the ability to implement specifically adapted user interfaces for different types of workplaces while maintaining the underlying workflow control mechanism was very useful. The graphical representation of workflows was successfully used to communicate ideas with hospital personnel.

4 Conclusion

WorkParty's graphical editor is well suited to modeling existing workflows (regardless of whether they are carried out manually or supported by application programs) and to re-modeling them in order to optimize the processes. An optimized model can then be implemented to execute in the WorkParty runtime environment. In the same way, ORM can be used to model existing organizational structures and re-model them according to the requirements of optimized business processes. Our experience shows that the hierarchical structure of organizational units, positions, employees, and their relationships are easily identified. On the one hand, the distribution of authorities and roles is usually more difficult to define, on the other hand, it provides great potential for optimization and adaptation to redesigned processes. As organizational structures tend to flatten in the course of optimization, regulations formerly contained implicitly in hierarchical structures must be explicitly expressed using authorities.

WorkParty and the Organization & Resources Manager are specially created to design and implement workflow applications and have limited capabilities for analysis and simulation of business processes. If the requirements for analysis and simulation exceed the limits of WorkParty and ORM, tools designed specifically for this task are used: for example ARIS-Toolset (see [Sch91]), BONAPART (see [Ubis97]), or GRADE (see [Inf97]). Results achieved with these tools are then transformed and, where appropriate, converted to a WorkParty implementation. WorkParty's domain is the efficient implementation and execution of workflow applications.

Workflow management systems like WorkParty provide an *infrastructure* for process-oriented applications (see [Den94, Rup95]). Conventional applications mainly consist of programs and rely on the underlying operating system and, for example, a database management system as infrastructure. Workflow applications replace part of the programs with models, e.g. graphical workflows and an organizational model. Programming is restricted to well-defined components with clearly defined interfaces (activities). Models are easier to comprehend and easier to adapt to changing requirements. Workflow applications require the workflow runtime system as an additional infrastructure component which provides for workflow control, integrity and audit trails. Consequently, these aspects need not be handled within the application.

An initial learning process and the requirement for business process (re-) design as well as the initial overhead for implementing the first workflow application add to the costs of introducing workflow management to application development. The benefits are

- Models used for workflow applications are more transparent for organizers than programs.
- Increased flexibility for organizational structure and process adjustments.
- Well-defined tasks and interfaces for application program modules enable re-use.
- Immediate availability of information in response to customer inquiries.

This is the perspective represented in the ComUnity application architecture from Siemens Nixdorf in which WorkParty figures as the workflow component and ORM as the organization component.

As the improvement of workflow technology continues, monolithic applications will become decomposed into self-contained components that are combined to process-oriented applications with the aid of a workflow management system such as WorkParty. The functional view of conventional programs (a set of functions made available via menus) will shift to a process-oriented view (a process in which individual functions are used in a specific order).

Fixed processes will evolve to flexible processes, and programs will partly be replaced with models (e.g. graphical workflow models, organizational models). Workflow technology will become as natural a part of the infrastructure required for applications as database systems are today.

References

[Den94] Denning, P. J., The Fifteenth Level, Proc. of ACM SIGMETRICS Conference on Measurement & Modeling of Computer Systems, May 1994

[Jab95] Jablonski, S., Workflow-Management-Systeme, Modellierung und Architektur, Thomson, Bonn, 1995

[Inf97] GRADE Graphical Re-engineering Analysis & Design Environment (Product brochure), Infologistik GmbH, München, 1997

[Jor94] Jordan, B., Praxisbericht: Einführung einer ganzheitlichen Kreditbearbeitung, in: U. Hasenkamp (ed.), Einführung von CSCW-Systemen in Organisationen, Vieweg, Braunschweig, 1994, 11-124

[KRK95] Kock, T., Rehäuser, J., Krcmar, H., Ein Vergleich ausgewählter Workflow-Systeme, Information Management 1, 1995, 36-43

[RH97] Reinhold, M., Hachinger, H., Einführung von Workflow: Schnelligkeit wird zum entscheidenden Wettbewerbsfaktor, INFOdoc 3, 1997, 16-24

[RSD97] Reichert, M., Schultheiß, B., Dadam, P., Erfahrungen bei der Entwicklung vorgangsorientierter, klinischer Anwendungssysteme auf Basis prozeßorientierter Workflow-Technologie, Proc. 42. Jahrestagung der GMDS, 1997

[Rup95] Rupietta, W., Flexible Geschäftsprozesse mit Workflow-Anwendungen in: Rundbrief Informationssystem-Architekturen of GI FA 5.2, No 2, December 1995, Proceedings of the conference 'Geschäftsprozesse und Workflow-Systeme in der evolutionären Unternehmung', Bamberg, Oktober 1995, 79-81

[Rup97] Rupietta, W., Organization and Role Models for Workflow Processes, in: P. Lawrence (ed.), Workflow Handbook 1997, Wiley & Sons, Chichester, 1997, 165-172

[Sch91] Scheer, A.-W., Architektur integrierter Informationssysteme, Springer, Berlin, Heidelberg, 1991

[Ubis97] BONAPART home page: http://www.ubis.de/

[WfMC94] Workflow Management Coalition Members, Glossary, Brussels, November 1994

[Wor96] WorkParty Enterprise Edition, Benutzerhandbuch, Siemens Nixdorf Informationssysteme AG, 1996

CHAPTER 23

PROPLAN

Günther Schuh, Thomas Siepmann, Volker Levering

With PROPLAN any business process can be analyzed, depicted, documented and described by a standardized language. Hence it is an instrument to provide a high transparency of business processes and activities. Furthermore it supports strategic management tasks by improving the overall department information flow from sales to delivery. The examined process is depicted as a sequence of symbols following the applied modeling language. Therefore, weak points are revealed for optimizing the process. The implemented middleware concept PRAGMA enables PROPLAN's mobile computing ability used in combined locations. Combined with Inter-/Intranet browsers in WWW formats PROPLAN can easily be integrated in an existing LAN or WAN environment.

1 Introduction

"Everything is in a flow." European industry found some truth in a philosophical statement. Dropping market prices - due to an increasing number of new arriving competitors - forces industrial companies to radical changes. During the last 5 years Europe's industry applied a variety of different methods and concepts for reorganization. Business Process Reengineering (BPR) [HC93] represents one of them as it can lead to significant lead-time improvements in manufacturing processes. Figure 1 shows the results of an empiric study conducted by the Aachen University of Technology's Laboratory for Machine Tools (WZL).

Still the good concept is a source but not a guarantee for successful restruction. Even Mike Hammer and James Champy, the two BPR protagonists admitted frequent problems during implementation. Some 70 % of major Business Process Reengineering projects turned out to be ineffective, about 40 % of the process owners showed dissatisfaction with the results of BPR projects.

In 1995, European Community set up the project MOTION to examine problems during change management like BPR. The project's aim is to

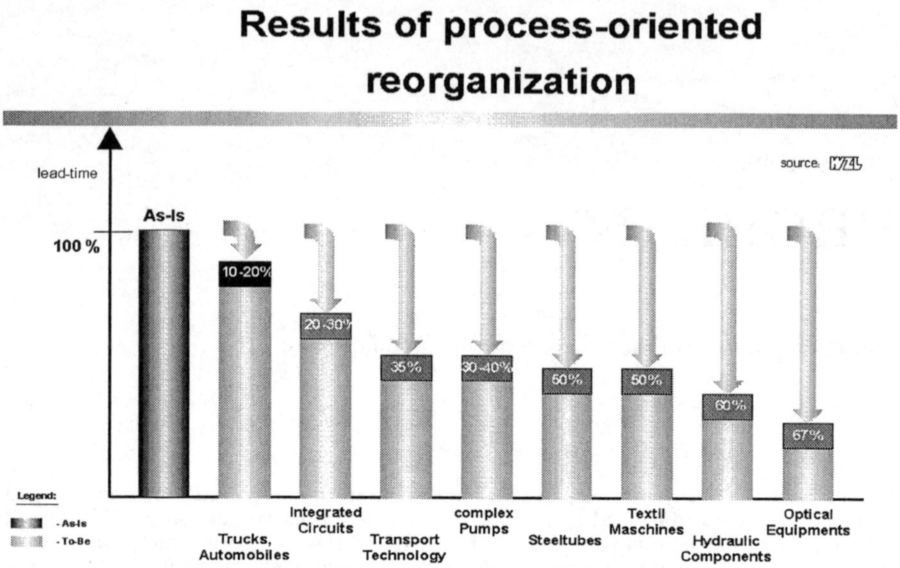

Figure 1: Results of process-oriented reorganization

identify critical success factors for the successful implementation of corporate change management. About 30 important industrial companies, consulting and software firms as well as scientific institutes took part in the project. The MOTION team identified 10 main critical success factors for change management as Figure 2 shows.

As an overall result the examination reveals team orientation to be the precondition for successful implementation. The team approach is valid for all 10 factors. It takes place on two different level: First, external team participation of all employees involved in the process is a prerequisite for successful BPR projects. Second, the team-oriented internal cooperation in project teams is equally important for BPR implementation.

Successful BPR projects lead to process organization within the company. The problem remains that process organization itself is unable to detect weak points in the process. It takes additional efforts to model the entire process for an intense analysis. First, the project team examines entire processes. On the basis of the intense analysis the team member are able to reorganize the process with the aim for efficiency improvements (of the process).

The question remains: "How do I support my BPR project?" The obvious need for continuous improvements of business processes caused serious problems in many companies as the methodical projection as well as an appropriate IT support were absent. The software and consulting firm GPS Prof. Schuh Komplexitätsmanagement GmbH together with the Aachen University

Success Factors in Change Management

1. Top Management Commitment
2. Motivation and Acceptance
3. clearly defined Aims
4. Tight Project Management
5. Customer-oriented Processes
6. Set up of Project Teams
7. Project Marketing
8. Sufficient Resources
9. Conflict Management
10. Motivation for Implementation

Figure 2: Critical Success factors as result of EC-MOTION project

of Technology's Laboratory for Machine Tools (WZL) (both joined the MOTION project) developed a method for process-oriented enterprise modeling and process optimization.

The model's tenet is the consideration of all necessary aspects for a successful reorganization. It includes procedures for implementing customer-oriented organizational structures and process-control. The method forms the basis for the software PROPLAN, developed by GPS. PROPLAN supports an integrated optimization of business objectives like cost and lead-time reduction as well as quality improvements. It is used in BPR projects as well as for ISO 9000 certification.

2 Application of the Model in PROPLAN

The PROPLAN method defines 14 process elements as symbols for an overall process depiction. They are employed by the modeling language and visualize corporate processes as an entire sequence, e.g. from order placement to delivery. They are divided into direct and indirect elements. Indirect elements such as linkage, decide, communication, etc. are characterized by their indirect contribution to the added value of order processing. Direct elements on the other hand symbolize activities directly specified for the examined process, e.g. designing, process planing and manufacturing as Figure

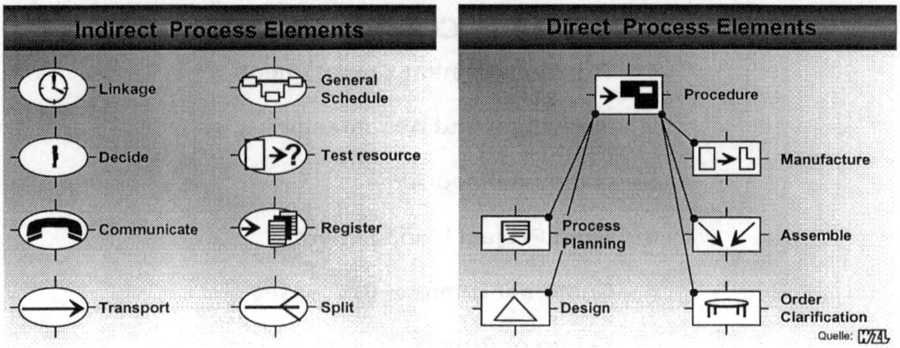

Figure 3: Elements of modeling language

3 shows.

With PROPLAN, process plans can easily be drawn to visualize business processes by applying the elements proposed by the modeling language. The symbols are assembled to a sequence as the depicted process is proceeded. All elements show an entry on their left side and outlets on top, bottom and/or right hand side of the symbol. The outlet on the right hand side represents the normal outcome for a trouble-free executed process. The bottom outlet shows an interrupted process in case of an interrupted process execution. For instance, it could be a design process with all test data available and required essential market information provided by sales department. A process will take the top outlet of an element, if the following process remains undefined. An entire process is visualized in the above mentioned process sequence plan shown in Figure 4.

The method of Business Process Reengineering represents a general approach forming the theoretical basis for the use of PROPLAN symbols in practice. Weak points such as lack of information, critical resources and unnecessary idle time are revealed in discussions between all employees involved in the process. Besides PROPLAN offers the possibility to determine the process' cost and lead-time. Additionally benchmarks allow users to measure and compare different processes in the company. The underlying method for the program system PROPLAN "Method for Process Oriented Reorganization in Technical Order Transaction" follows four steps:

1. Building up the process-oriented model of order processing: The examined business process is depicted as a sequence of process symbols and interconnecting lines. As every element has several outlets for different process' outcomes, failures or ramifications are depicted clearly.

2. Quantification of relevant process parameters: The average lead-time and/or cost for each process element is determined. After the quantification PROPLAN calculates the overall lead-time and cost for the

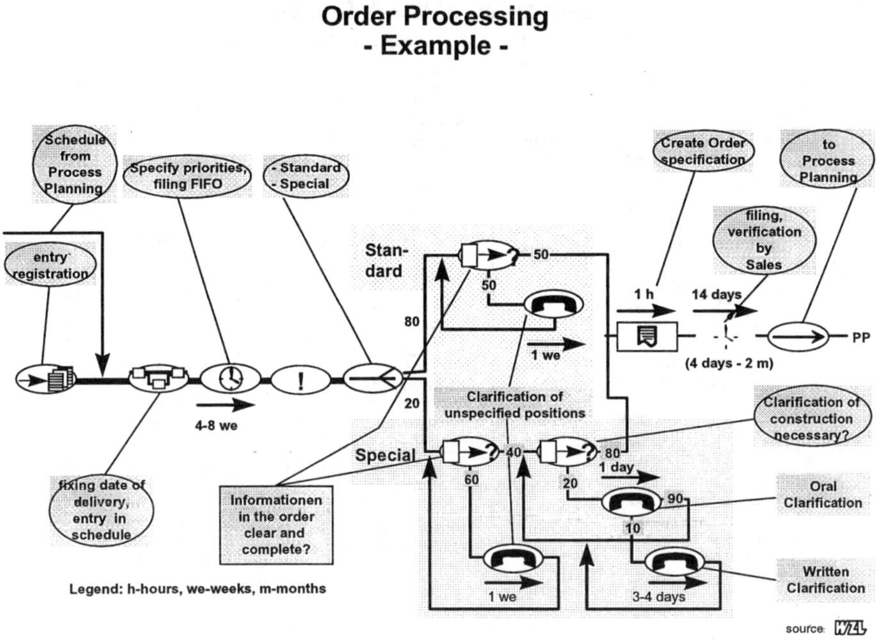

Figure 4: PROPLAN IT-Tool for Business Process Reengineering

entire process or parts of process.

3. Problem identification in the sequence: Problems are detected in corporate areas directly or indirectly involved in the process (Figure 5). Most frequently weak points concern lead time, frequency of failures and lay days.

4. Evaluate measures to be taken: The process team develops plans for improvements on the basis of previous steps. Before implementation the plans are projected in the business process sequence plan in order to evaluate their impact on the process. The results serve as an aim for the examined main business process plans.

The process analysis starts with selecting a team documenting corporate processes on the basis of interviews. Operative worker (process owner) are questioned to give detailed information about particular process chains. The process owners report how the incoming orders are proceeded. According to their descriptions process elements are assembled to a process plan. Then the involved employees have to verify "their" processes by a further questioning. Due to the elements' high transparency the process owners identify themselves rapidly with the depicted process and will indicate potential improvements, which remain unconsidered by the first questioning.

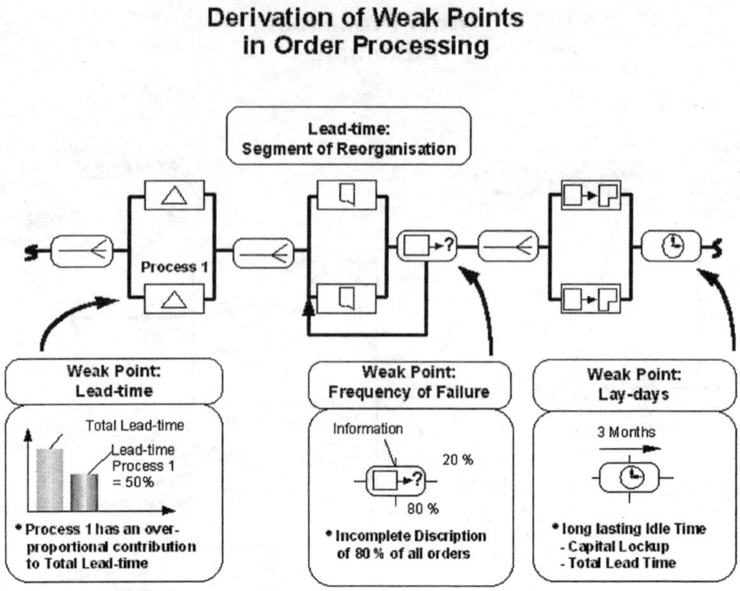

Figure 5: Problem Identification

The software PROPLAN was initially developed to support the above defined approach and make it easy to handle. Even a non-trained user can easily record all important information about the examined process. The software was brought to market maturity by a cooperation formed by GPS and WZL as well as ten industrial companies. PROPLAN was introduced into the market in 1994 and has supported various successful BPR projects in many companies during the last years. The software is operative on IBM compatible PCs under WINDOWS.

Some developments with a long lasting impact on information technology become visible already today. Thanks to Internet and technologies based thereon, a closely knit global network will play an important role in future. Combined locations, cooperation among different companies and branched corporate structures require solutions on the basis of IT-networks. Often mixed teams are working at different sites with shared databases. The following requirements for commonly used databases are essential: Multi-user abilities, guarantee of always up-to-date data and the capability to provide data for mobile users without permanent connection. It requires high standards regarding data consistence, information security and software services.

On the basis of PROPLAN version 2.1, GPS developed version 3.0 to meet rising demand for team-oriented and mobile data sharing. It is built on the GPS software PRAGMA (Professional Application's Generic Middleware

Architecture) for middleware architectures. Version 3.0 extends PROPLAN version 2.1 as it enables several users to share a common database.

The middleware is a software layer on the basis of standardized interfaces and protocols. It provides services for transparent communication and shared applications. It consequently represents an infrastructure to integrate applications in a heterogeneous environment. The middleware might include Internet as well, while using standardized TCP/IP protocols.

Data transmission plays the key role in mobile computing, even if speed of data exchange is normally uncritical in LAN. In WAN, however, slow data transfer may jeopardize the useful employment of the whole software. The middleware minimizes data exchange by transmitting data only if commonly used data is changed. Additionally an optimized timing for data exchange allows mobile users to work independently as long as possible. Even slow 9600 baud connections can then provide a service comparable to LAN.

The concept of data replication helps minimizing time and cost for data exchange. For mobile users the software keeps a copy (or replicate) of original data. The user applications are then allowed to work with copies only. In order to preserve data consistence a comparison is needed between centralized original data and the various copies. Problems may arise by two different users changing identical data fields simultaneously. In this case the comparison between data would provoke an error. Implementing priorities of possible changes could avoid this situation. However a manual test of consistence will be necessary if two different applications with an equal priority change identical data at the same time. A more severe solution is the exclusive use of certain data fields (or areas) by only one user and consequently locked for others. This is favorable for mobile computing, as transmission of changed data is reduced to minimum. PROPLAN 's version 3.0 includes the software module PRAGMA as middleware. So PROPLAN uses the above described advantages of data replication with lockable data. The generic architecture provides a maximum of compatibility to already existing databases via SQL or ODBC. Therefore it simplifies administration and data backup. The concept defines different layers as shown in Figure 6.

The important layers are:

- application layer
- transport layer
- database layer.

The structure offers extensions to alternative database modules. The model's upper layer defines the exchange with the application software. This application uses data description language (DDL) to transmit to the system its data structure. It is registered as new user and has access to other databases as well. Data exchange between different users uses commands like "get data, which is more actual than mine" or "get all information about deleted

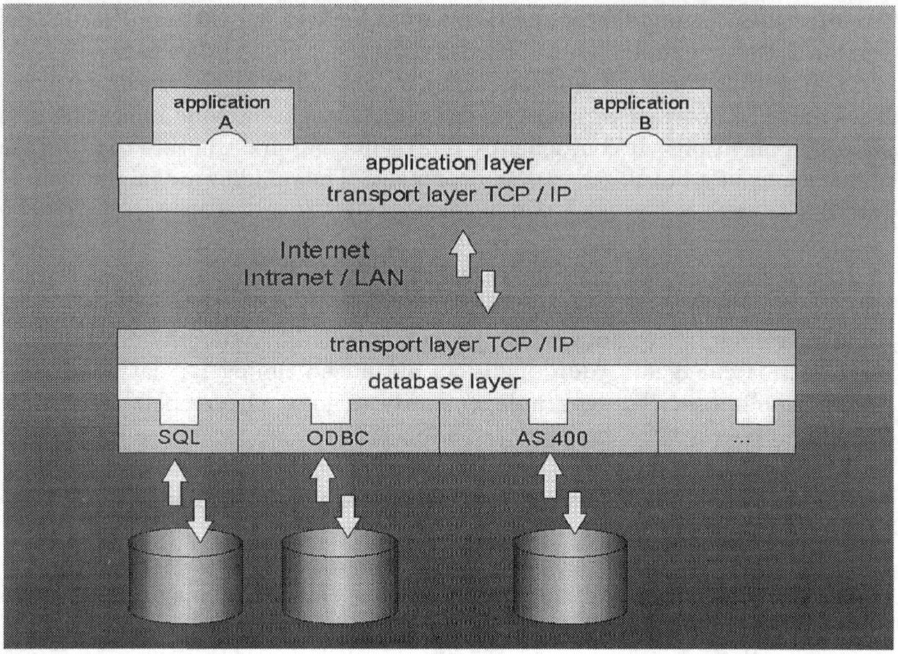

Figure 6: Generic Model with different layers

data". Synchronization between different databases is arranged by timestamps. Changes in databases will be indicated to the user by transport and application layer.

The combination of PROPLAN with PRAGMA adds to a software tool supporting Business Process Reengineering the possibilities of a Middleware architecture with multiple databases. Users have then access to up-to-date information, mobile computing becomes effective.

3 PROPLAN Implementation with Intranet

ISO 9000 certification has internal and external effects on a company. It should not only focus on quality definitions for customers and competitors but increase employees' level of information and acceptance about order processing as well. Documentation of business processes serves as an instrument for staff members to ensure defined quality standards. A GPS customer in Germany (1600 employees, Sales: US$ 270 Mill) intended to introduce a software tool in order to minimize the costly documentary period during the certification. Requirements for the tool were defined as easy handling, a comprehensive modeling language and, as result, an explicit readability of the documentation. The company chose PROPLAN to support ISO 9000 certification as documentation was defined as key factor for business process certification.

The documentation was focused on:

- Optimization of existing processes regarding Quality Management (QM), for instance feedback of quality control test results to R&D.

- Introduction of new business processes to complete company-wide automatic closed control loops, for instance feedback of QM-relevant customer information to the sales department.

- Integration of QM in order processing, for instance in regard of the interface between order control and quality test management.

Flow Charts, as normally employed within the ISO 9000 certification were replaced by PROPLAN documents. Additionally, process descriptions by PROPLAN offer the possibility to detect hidden potential for reorganization. After fixing the specific lead-time and probability for each process result, PROPLAN shows the difference between the actual process and its determined target. In some cases the potential for reorganization can sum up to 90% (Figure 7).

An Intranet service [SWS97] was available at the GPS customer and suited well for the company-wide distribution of the quality manual. The document was defined in HTML description language employed in the WWW. While integrated in company's Intranet, PROPLAN offered:

- the description of PROPLAN documents with all necessary HTML parameters.

- an identical graphic surface maintaining the variable zoom function. With already installed Internet browsers the user can navigate through all different process plans.

- easy handling, even for non IT-experts.

The representation of WWW's formats GIF, JPEG and PNG caused conflicts with process plans documents described by PROPLAN , as the conversion in WWW formats leads to increased data volume, with the result of a slow software application. The solution consists of transforming the document into a vector oriented format, which is linked to selected Intranet pages with usual HTML code. A free, worldwide available extension to the browser displays the converted document. This solution ensures a comfortable handling as a profound knowledge of Internet tools by the user is not required. He simply starts his usual browser, which is able to handle both, Internet and Intranet. His PROPLAN environment on the screen does not change. An example of a possible screen shows the Figure 8.

By using digital media the GPS customer established a state-of-the-art solution for its guideline to business processes. In comparison to former

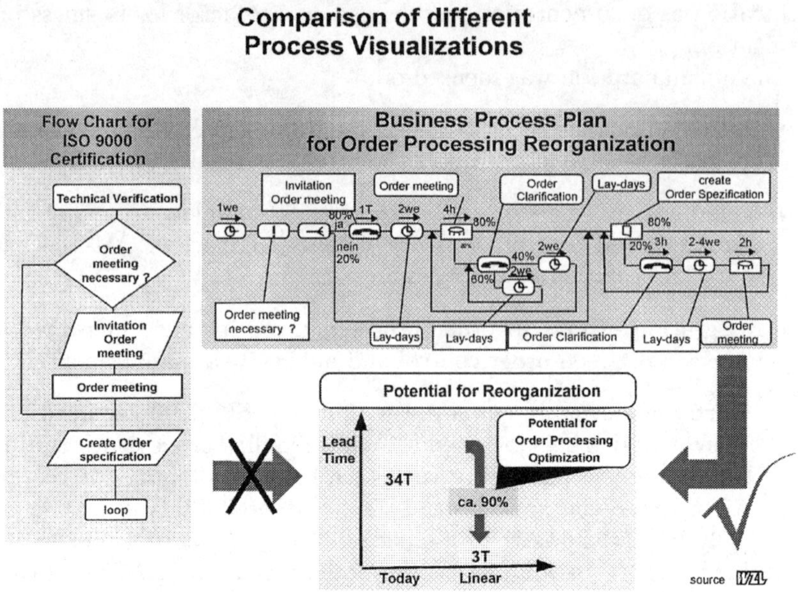

Figure 7: Target orientation of different process presentations

quality manuals printed on paper, the Intranet application can be noticed by many more employees. The higher availability of actual documents together with an easy and comfortable handling led to a significant higher acceptance in the company.

Before certification the provision, copying, distribution and review of paper-printed quality manuals were expensive and inefficient. Other inconveniences were missing indices and a poor availability. Company's former organizational manual contained 150 valid guidelines and instructions, being updated and revised more than 250 times until today. The effort was drastically reduced by employing the Intranet-based organizational manual. Still the main advantage consists in the possibility to get all staff members immediately informed by the actual manual. Quality in information provision within the company was improved significantly, nearly without any financial effort.

The realization and successful ISO 9000 certification of the GPS customer can be summarized as follows:

- Low cost of implementation and minimized time for user training. Also time for PROPLAN -implementation is reduced due to already existing Internet applications.

- According to ISO 9000 certification, documents' provision and distribu-

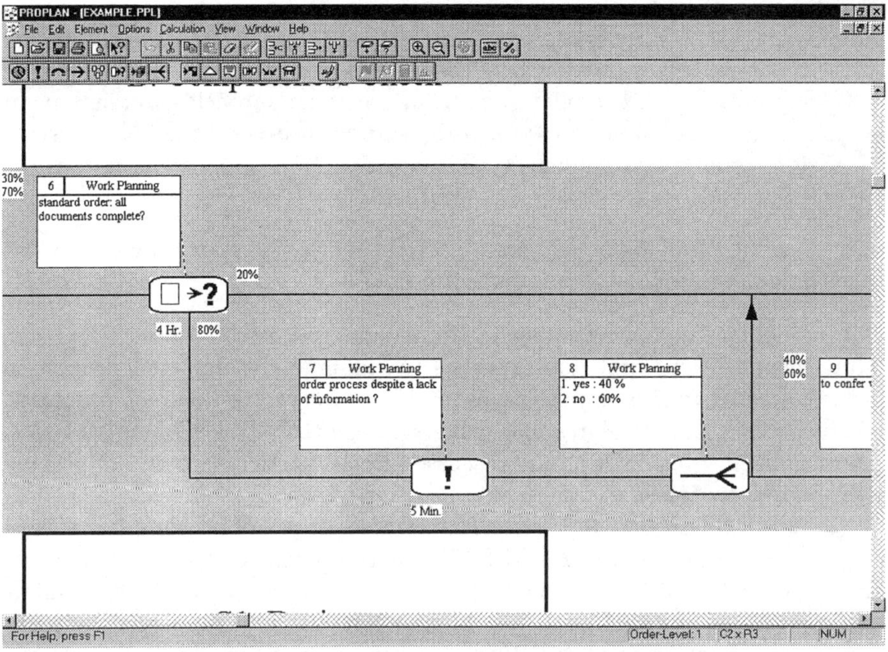

Figure 8: Presentation of PROPLAN documents in Internet or Intranet

tion is now under the responsibility of a certain designated office. It is equally accountable for the manual's update and review. It guarantees a direct access to the actual version of the quality manual by everyone in the company as there is only one actual version of the manual.

- A process depiction in the organizational manual can now be updated and reviewed by minimized cost. After the certification all adjustments in manuals are carried out by a central office and there is only one change needed. These measures decrease IT-cost significantly.

- An up-to-date level of information leads to increased QM-acceptance by staff members. Due to the fact that employees have access to actual descriptions of business processes, frustration and confusion owing to a lack of information can be diminished.

4 Conclusion

The standard software tool PROPLAN developed by GPS allows the visualization and depiction of corporate processes. PROPLAN offers 3 major advantages:

1. First it represents a very efficient tool for enterprise modeling. Efforts just take some 5-10% in comparison to most other modeling tools.

2. Second PROPLAN follows the team-oriented approach. All team members get the chance to work with an easy to understand tool. Discussions among team members concentrate on the process and not on the tool.

3. Finally PROPLAN delivers objective results. It clearly reveals "as-is" defaults and not "should-be" situations.

The modeling language employs a limited number of 14 process elements. After visualization even non-experts can examine the depicted process in order to reveal weak points. The process is compared to different processes, where PROPLAN simulates and calculates respectively lead-time and cost. An optimized solution is finally discussed by all participants and implanted with high acceptance.

To meet rising demand for team-oriented and mobile computing with commonly used database, PROPLAN was combined to the middleware architecture PRAGMA. Now multiple users have access to up-to date information without internal conflicts. Mobile computing is supported by minimized data transmission, as PROPLAN can work effectively on a notebook and a mobile phone without permanent connection to the server. Users will notice PRAGMA only by the system's multi-user ability, as ordinary Internet/Intranet browsers ensure the software's integration in company's Intranet. The system allows several users to work simultaneously on different processes handling a common database.

References

[Eve95] Eversheim, W., Prozeßorientierte Unternehmensorganisation, Springer-Verlag, Berlin Heidelberg New York, 1995

[HC93] Hammer, M., Champy, J., Reengineering the Corporation, Harper Collins Pubisher, New York, 1993

[PEKW94] Pfeifer, T., Eversheim, W., König, W., Weck, M., Manufacturing Excellence, The competitive Edge, Chapman & Hall, London Glasgow New York Madras, 1994, 3-34

[SSJ97] Schuh, G., Siepmann, T., Jansen, T., Durch Middleware Standorte vernetzen, Zeitschrift für wirtschaftlichen Fabrikbetrieb 3/97, 119–121

[SWS97] Schuh, G., Webersberger, P., Siepmann, T., Qualitätshandbuch und Prozeßpläne im INTRANET, Industrie Management 3/97, 47–49

CHAPTER 24

ARIS

August-Wilhelm Scheer

In this article a general business process architecture is presented, which is based on the Architecture of Integrated Information Systems (ARIS) and which is composed of the four levels of process optimization, process management, workflow and application. The ARIS-House of Business Engineering encompasses the whole life-cycle range: from business process design to information technology deployment, leading to a completely new process-oriented software concept. At the same time, the architecture bridges the gap between business process modeling and workflow-driven applications, from Business Process Reengineering to Continuous Process Improvement.

1 Introduction

Despite an abundance of various reengineering concepts in recent years, business processes have emerged as the focal point of business reengineering [Dav93, Gai83, Har91]. Business processes in manufacturing have been governed by clear methods for quite some time [Sch94, Sch92, DCVF93]. This is not the case, however, for processes in the indirect areas within manufacturing, the service industry or public services [Sch96, SNZ96].

In this article, the 'ARIS-House of Business Engineering', a general architecture of business processes consisting of the following four levels: Process Design, Process Management, Process Workflow and Process Application is introduced. This architecture is applicable for every type of business process: in manufacturing, in the service industry and in the public services. Constant feedback between these levels guarantees Continuous Process Improvement (CPI).

2 Business Process Design and Control

At a business breakfast. Two executives are sitting across from each other and are discussing the current situation in their respective departments. The

Plant Manager is complaining to the sales manager that in the previous month the machine load factor in his department had dropped by 3%. Yet the lead time of processed manufacturing orders had risen by 2%, while the gap between planned costs of an important order and actual costs had leaped to over $350,000. On the other hand, the production scheduling system had helped him squeeze in an unexpected high priority order, without having to compromise the delivery dates of other orders. Then he asks the sales manager how things are going over at sales. His peer is only able to make general comments regarding the order book. He is, however, not capable of determining the precise load factor of his employees, the lead times of order processing, their respective costs or obtaining precise information on the dispatch of high priority orders.

This tiny example demonstrates that methods for controlling manufacturing processes are far more perfected than for the control of procedures in other operational areas. It raises the question as to why these methods are not customary beyond the area of manufacturing and whether the basic principles of controlling manufacturing processes can also be applied to other areas. Various operational buzz words, such as CIM (Computer Integrated Manufacturing), lean management and BPR (Business Process Reengineering) have cropped up in the past few years and have been a constant source of discussion in management circles. Today, the business community seems to unanimously agree that designing and controlling business processes is one of the premier organizational tasks in enterprises.

The term "business process" is defined universally. A business process is described as a procedure relevant for adding value to an organization. It is viewed in its entirety, from beginning to end. Figure 2 illustrates the business process of order entry processing. The initial requirements of the customer lead to order acceptance by the manufacturer's sales department. Sales then relays information to purchasing, in order for them to supply bought-in parts. Finally, production plans and executes the work-order.

Figure 2 illustrates this procedure by a series of events triggering functions. The initial event of the process is the customer requirement. The final event is the completion of the product in Manufacturing. Events not only trigger functions, they are themselves the results of functions. Processes can be split into sub-processes. Conversely, sub-processes can be joined together. By introducing logical operators, the control structure with its event-driven process chain (EPC) can be expanded to accommodate variously complex procedures [Sch92, KNS92, Sch94].

Besides describing the procedural structure of events and functions, there must also be a focus on describing the organizational units assigned to the functions. Many reengineering projects are actually directed at re-allocating functions to organizational units.

A business process consists of two function classes. The first function class describes how processing rules transform input data into output data.

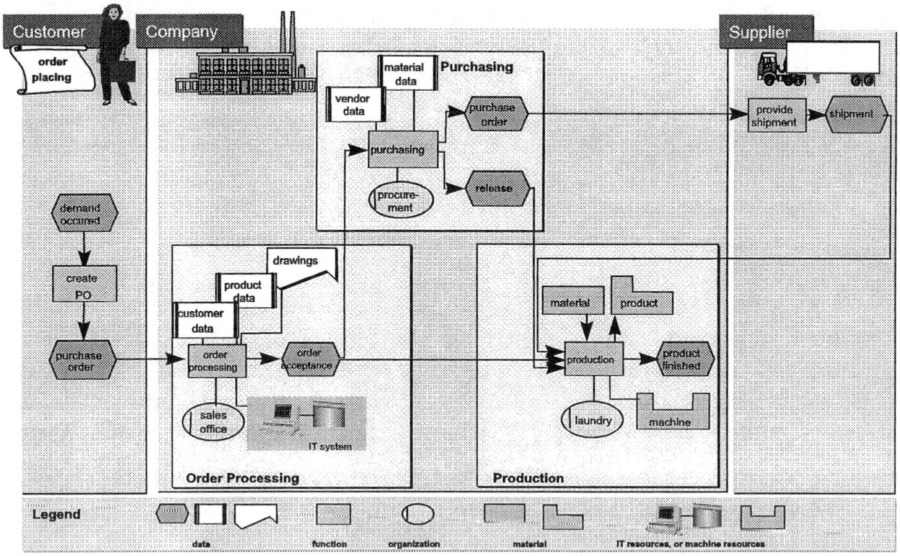

Figure 1: Modeling of a business process, using event-driven process Chains

Functions of this kind are executed in the "office area". For example, customer order data is supplemented by data pertaining to the article (e.g. inventory) or the customer (e.g. credit worthiness), respectively. It is then transformed into result data (accepted order, reserved warehouse stock, increased customer order balance). Thus, input and output data both belong to the description of a business process. In addition to the transformation of data, a second type of transformation can be carried out in a business process: the transformation from input material to output material. This process is called manufacturing. Material transformation comprises physical change, but can also involve a change in location, that is the function of material handling.

For many years now, the process of material transformation in industrial enterprises has been mastered quite well. This process can be described minutely and is usually controlled precisely regarding its scheduling and costs. On the other hand, management's knowledge regarding administrative processes is usually quite scant. Whereas the process of a production order is described minutely by the routing, descriptions regarding the business process in sales, purchasing or accounting are rare. Finally, to make matters even worse, in many industrial enterprises, scheduling and cost shortcomings are more frequently found in administrative rather than in production departments. Therefore it seems appropriate to examine whether and how procedures, which have proven to be most successful in controlling manufacturing processes, might also be applicable in the back office. The back office usually feeds into production. The same concept would then apply to service providers, such as banks, insurance companies and even government agencies.

Considering how many industrial enterprises augment their products with various services such as 'engineering' or 'after sales service', it becomes apparent that industrial enterprises and service providers are reaching out toward each other. By the same token, due to a continuing rise in automation, services providers, software houses for instance, are beginning to assume the shape of industrial structures [Nüt95].

The basic concept of ARIS will now be briefly outlined and then the fundamental architecture of controlling business processes (ARIS-House of Business Engineering) will be introduced. This leads to a new kind of software architecture, supporting these processes. While analyzing the processes, we will stress the analogies between production and services in the various steps.

3 ARIS - The Basic Concept

Aligning the enterprise along its processes offers the possibility to hit several business targets. But a process-oriented business management not only requires a concept for the systematic design and organization of the business processes themselves (by means of so-called Information System Architectures). Process-oriented business management also calls for tools and concepts to design the information systems supporting these processes. The aim is to design and control the organizational structures in a very flexible way so they can rapidly adapt to changing conditions (of the market, competitors etc.) [SNZ95].

The Architecture of Information Systems (ARIS) can be used as a keystone for Business Process Reengineering and Business Process Management [Sch92]. With ARIS the business processes of an enterprise can be described in order to represent the underlying business problems.

The components and their interrelationships to be described in a computer-supported business process include processes, activities, events, conditions and organizational units. Considering all the effects on all the elements of the process when reengineering it would severely complicate the design process.

In order to reduce this complexity, the model is divided into individual views that represent discrete design aspects and can be handled (largely) independently, which simplifies the task. Events such as "order", "order reception" or "production release" are information objects that are represented by data. Reference field conditions such as "customer status" and "article status" are also represented by data. Conditions and events thus form the data view. The functions to be performed and their relationships form a second view, the function view. The structure and relationships between staff members and organizational units constitute the organization view.

Dividing the initial problem into individual views does reduce its complexity, albeit at the expense of the description of the relationships between the views as expressed by the arrows in the process model. For this reason, a "control view" is used to restore the relationships between the components. The control view is an essential ARIS component that distinguishes it from other proposed architectures.

By introducing the control view into the architecture, it is possible to retain the relationships between the views, although previously the views were isolated and could therefore be treated in a more simplified form. The subsequent explicit input of the relationships between the views makes it possible to systematically enter all the relationships. This process results in the four ARIS views shown in Figure 2.

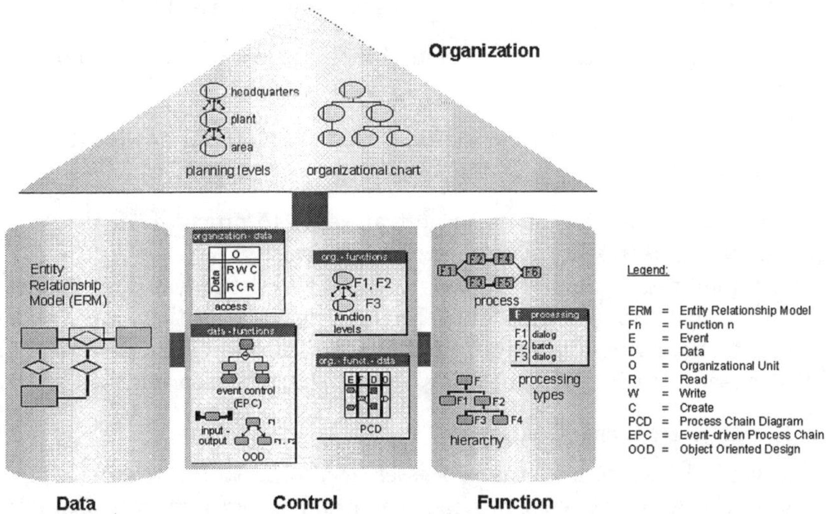

Figure 2: Views and methods used on requirements definition level

The term "tool" is employed here in the sense of computerized aids used to support the use of the methods in the software development process. Their use can apply to the creation of designs within the individual ARIS fields or to the transformation of a design result to superordinate or subordinate levels. In addition to the design support provided by descriptions, tools can also help navigate within and between the design results. Furthermore they should offer support for analyzing, evaluating or simulating the models.

The "ARIS-Toolset", a product of the IDS Prof. Scheer GmbH, provides developers and consultants with a product that meets these requirements. It provides user-friendly tools for the modeling, analysis and navigation of business processes, thus ensuring the productive translation of the methodology [IDS94].

On top of that the evolution of ARIS in research and development leads to new concepts and products for optimized business processes based on the ARIS-Architecture. The latest developments were integrated into a new framework called the "ARIS-House of Business Engineering", which will be described in the next sections.

4 The Architecture of the ARIS-House

When analyzing the methods used for process control in manufacturing, we deduce the following four main tasks:

1. Describing and optimizing the process structure, based on routings.
2. Optimization planning of current business processes with regard to capacity, time and costs (production scheduling control).
3. Controlling the execution of individual processes (material flow control).
4. Supporting the function execution, that is, material or data transformation rules.

On the whole, these tasks can also be translated to processes in the service sector, where data transformation has a high priority.

These four tasks can be allotted to the 4 Level Model. This model is called the 'ARIS-House of Business Engineering' and is the focal point of the subsequent discussion. Figure 3 sums up the individual Levels of the 'ARIS-House of Business Engineering' and depicts their correlation.

- **Level I: Process Design**

  Level I describes business processes according to the routing. Therefore, the ARIS Concept provides a method to cover every aspect of the business process. Methods for optimizing and guaranteeing the quality of processes are also available.

- **Level II: Process Management**

  Level II plans and monitors every current business process from the "business process owner's" point of view. Various methods of scheduling and capacity control and cost analysis are available. By monitoring the process, the process manager is aware of the status of each process instance.

- **Level III: Process Workflow**

  Level III transports the objects to be processed, such as customer orders with the corresponding documents or insurance claims in insurance companies, from one workplace to the next. The documents are then stored in "folders". Workflow systems carry out the material handling in electronically stored documents.

- **Level IV: Process Application**

  Level IV processes the documents transported to the individual workplaces, that is where the functions of the business process are executed. Computer-aided application systems - from simple word processing programs to complex standard software modules and Internet applets - are used at this Level.

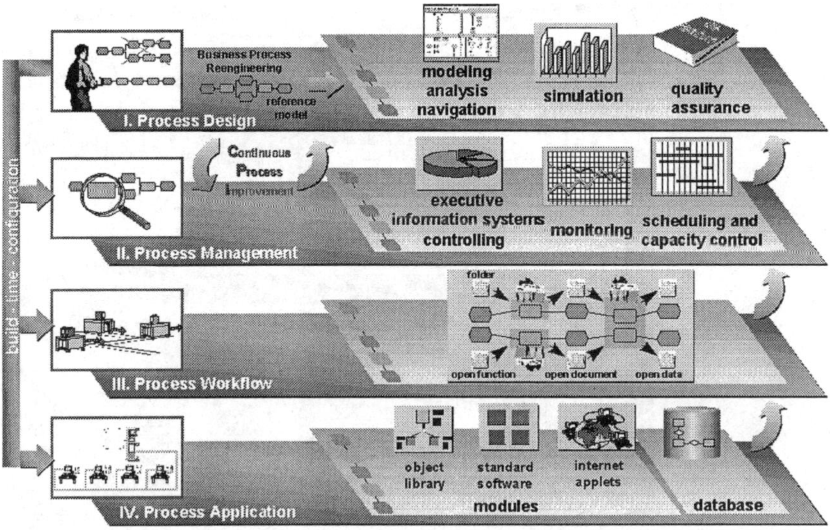

Figure 3: The 'ARIS-House of Business Engineering' Architecture

The four Levels of the 'ARIS-House of Business Engineering' are interdependently connected. Information at Level II regarding the profitability of current processes, is the point of departure for continuous adjustment and improvement of the business processes at Level I. We call this Continuous Process Improvement (CPI). Process Workflow is linked to Level I, because Process Workflow at Level III requires the description of business processes. At the same time, Process Workflow reports actual data regarding the processes to be executed (amounts, times, organizational allocation) back to Level II. Applications at Level IV are executed from the workflow system at Level III and configured according to the business process models at Level I. Up to now, only the 'ARIS-House of Business Engineering' in Figure 3 has been outlined. We will now describe each Level in detail. For illustration purposes, we will present typical screens from systems developed by the IDS Prof. Scheer GmbH. In Section 5, we will focus on future developments and show what is in store for the concept and the software solutions based upon it.

4.1 Process Design - Level I

ARIS consolidates various views into one business process as mentioned above. The Control View records the relationships between the other Views; it also utilizes the event-driven process chain (EPC) method, as illustrated in Figure 2. The ARIS-Toolset is based on the ARIS Concept and supports the user in modeling, analyzing and navigating through its business processes. Figure 4 depicts the user interface of the ARIS-Toolset [IDS94].

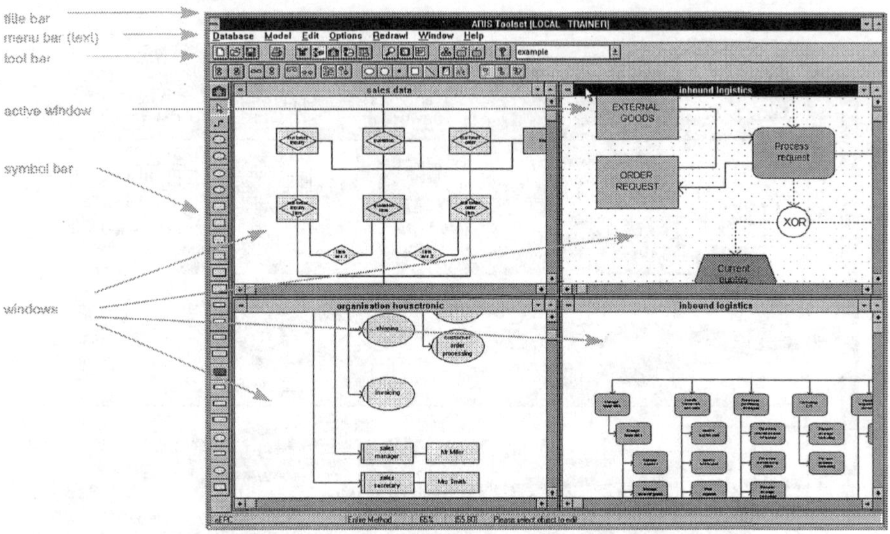

Figure 4: ARIS-Toolset - User's interface

In order to demonstrate that process representation can be utilized universally, in Figure 5 we offer an example of application processing in a governmental agency. Figure 6 shows a work schedule, including the material flow, modeled as an EPC. On the one hand, both figures show that the ARIS-Toolset can be employed as a front end for managing manufacturing routings and material flows. This offers more variations for representing alternate procedures. Obviously, presenting the manufacturing methods in a graphical form is much more user-friendly than listing routings in tables. By including the material flow in the ARIS Concept, relationships between product and business process models can also be addressed. On the other hand, concepts designed to manage different versions of manufacturing routings (even expert systems) are well suited for describing business processes in the service sector.

Thus, Level I corresponds to the description of the master routing in manufacturing. In the service sector, it is not customary to define each and every object that is to be processed. This is done in a more general way, by object groups. For example, in purchasing, this would involve a purchasing process for spare parts, standard purchasing, just in time processing and

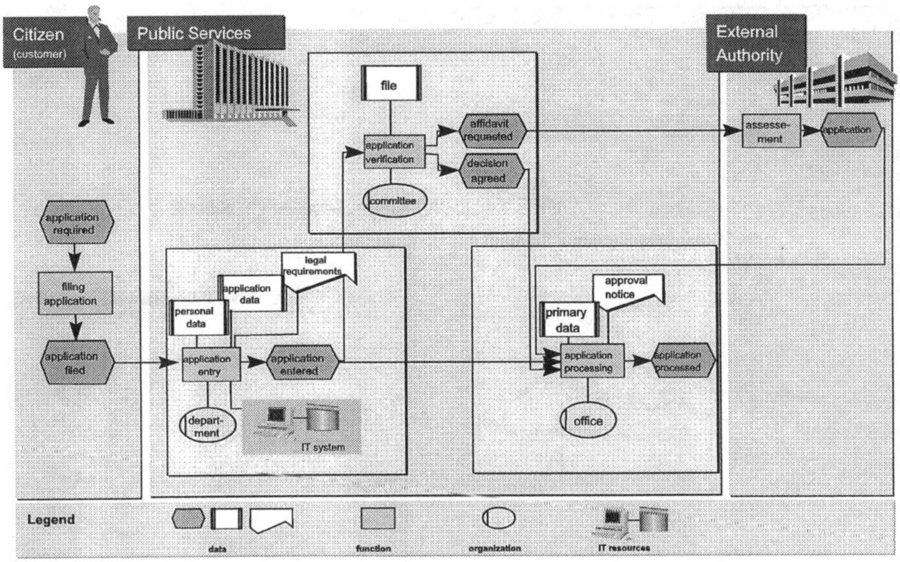

Figure 5: Administration process as an event-driven process chain

other similar groups as a whole, not a process for individual products. In production, however, routings for every single part are maintained.

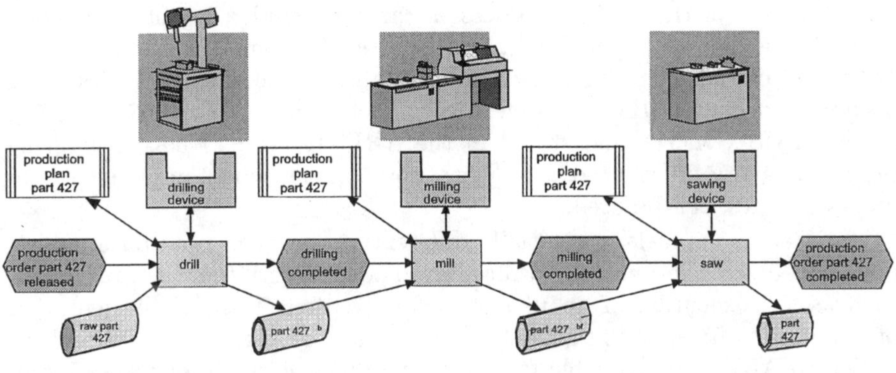

Figure 6: Routing and material flow as event-driven process chain

Using ARIS-Analysis, processes can be evaluated and compared according to their time and costs (see Figure 7). Using ARIS-Simulation, bottlenecks in business processes can be analyzed. They are then removed by restructuring the processes (see Figure 8). ISO 9000 definitions include criteria for the quality definition of business processes. These descriptions and forms can be generated directly from the ARIS business process description (see Figure 9).

This summary shows the comprehensive methods and tools available from

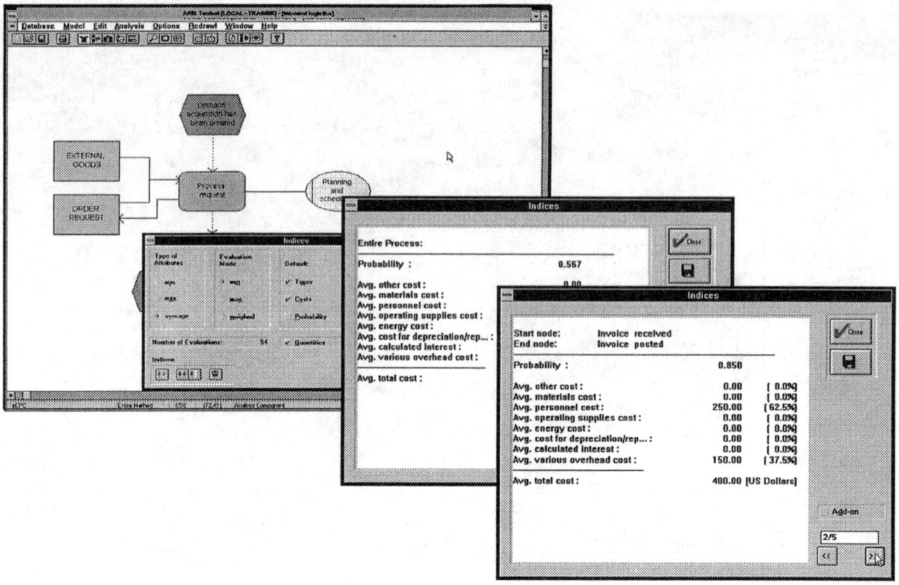

Figure 7: Evaluating business processes: user interface of ARIS-Analysis

ARIS for optimizing business processes.

As an aid to modeling business processes, existing information on useful structures of the business processes can be included in the basic solution. These reference models, derived empirically from Best Practice cases or theoretical considerations, lead to substantial time savings in designing optimal procedures [Har94]. Reference models can be described according to the ARIS Concept and stored in the ARIS-Toolset. When structuring processes, every function, e.g. analysis, comparison, model adjustment and model changes, can be used.

In reference models, we initially differentiate between procedure models and industry-specific models. Procedure models describe project processes, such as the execution of an ISO 9000 certification or the implementation of standard software. Special reference models, developed by IDS and included in ARIS, are available for the above tasks or the implementation of workflow systems. Figure 10 shows the reference model part for SAP R/3 implementation.

Industry-specific models refer to typical operational business processes, such as logistics, product development or finance. In ARIS, they are available, among others, for the following vertical markets: Paper, Chemical, Mechanical Engineering, Plant Engineering as well as Construction and Utilities. They are continually supplemented and enhanced.

Furthermore, models contained in financial standard applications are also documented in ARIS. For users who have not yet decided upon a particular

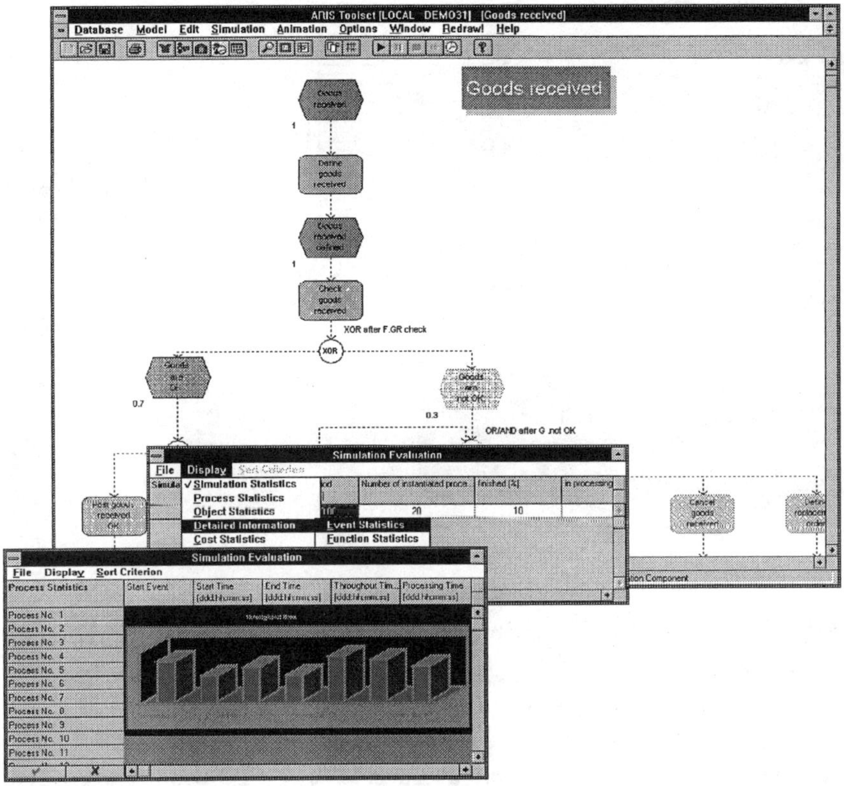

Figure 8: Analyzing bottlenecks and testing alternatives: user interface of ARIS-Simulation

software package, these models can be adopted as an additional information source for designing business processes. When selecting and implementing software, they are also ideal for comparing the requirements or functionality of various packages and for customizing.

4.2 Process Management - Level II

In order to control the scheduling and capacity of business processes, functions are allocated to the individual workplaces or organizational units. Thus, scheduling- and location-related processes as well as the load of the individual capacity units is known. This information also leads to a consolidated view of the capacity situation in the individual work groups. In project procedures, such as the execution of a BPR project or the implementation of standard software, project process chains and resource definitions compatible with MS Project can be generated automatically. They can then be displayed and managed in Gantt charts or networks. Changes in MS Project

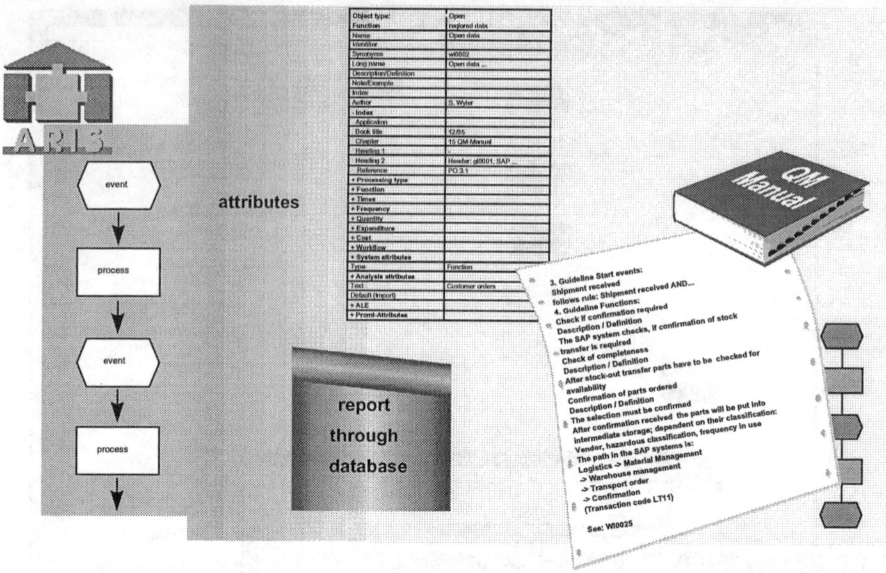

Figure 9: ISO 9000-report generated from ARIS models

are automatically reflected in the ARIS reference model.

In operational processes, it may be necessary to employ more powerful control systems than are available at Level II. The FI-2 production scheduling system [IDS90], initially developed by IDS to control manufacturing processes, is now being used to control software development processes. It is also under review as a tool to control administration processes and even medical operations.

Project and production scheduling systems also provide information on "to-be" and "as-is" deviations from the schedule and costs of the business processes that are to be executed. This, as well as other information, is utilized to continuously improve business processes. This creates a closed loop between Level I (Process Design) and Level II (Process Management), leading to Continuous Process Improvement (CPI).

Every method used in describing Level I, such as process analysis, model comparison, ISO 9000 certification or simulation, can be employed for CPI. BPR and CPI should be regarded in the same vein. When a certain situation arises, causing a company to reflect on its structures, this in turn can lead to a BPR project. However, even after resolving the problem, processes still change. New organizational concepts can arise. New Best Practice cases become available as reference models. New technologies are invented. New knowledge is obtained from processes, which have just been implemented, leading to an adjustment of the process. Hence, Process Design is a continuous process. Frequently, conflicts of interest lead to apparent disparities

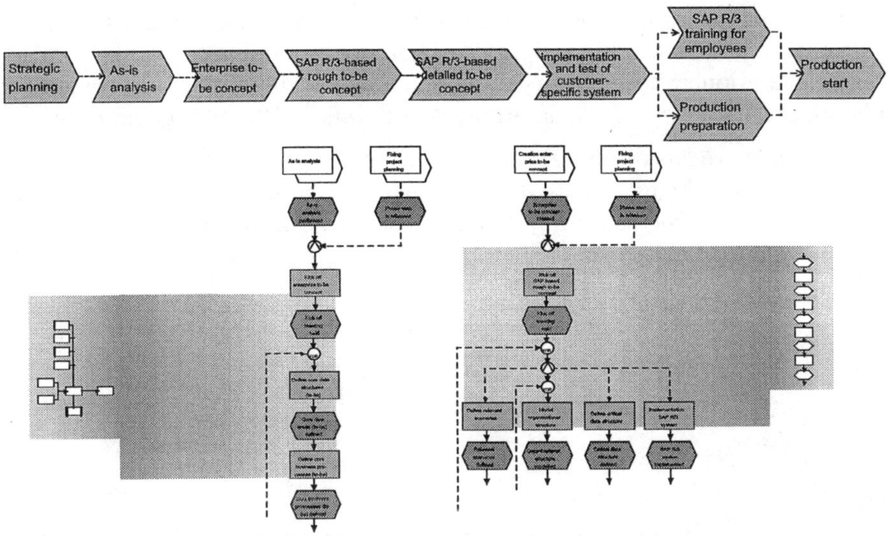

Figure 10: ARIS procedure reference model for the implementation of SAP R/3

between BPR and CPI: applications vendors are sometimes blamed for the lengthy procedure occasionally necessary to implement their software. They are concerned that their product could be held responsible for any additional delay if they are connected with a BPR project. Therefore, they oppose BPR strategies and recommend rapid installation of their software and subsequent CPI. Due to their interest in selling consulting services, consulting companies, on the other hand, recommend the opposite approach: first, develop a new engineering (organizational) concept and then support it with the new software. This prevents unnecessary and awkward procedures from being carried over into the new software concept. The contradictions of these two approaches are resolved in the 'ARIS-House of Business Engineering' because BPR and CPI are so closely intertwined.

The integration of a process costing component within ARIS is important for implementing a permanent Improvement Process. With their focus on cost center accounting, current financial cost accounting systems mainly provide a functional view. For example, the objective of standard product costing is to cost-optimize cost centers according to their functions. Conversely, the costs of business processes are not known. The ARIS-Promt module, developed jointly by Plaut AG and IDS Prof. Scheer, provides the concept and tool for process costing. The cost rates of traditional cost accounting systems are linked with the business processes modeled in ARIS. This determines the cost per process (see Figure 11).

The intense debates in business administration circles in recent years regarding process costing generally dissipate if one adheres to this basic view of business processes [JK87, CK88]. Process costing has always been around, however, only in areas in which process descriptions are available, such as in calculating manufacturing processes. That is why we use terms like concurrent calculation, where as-is costs of a manufacturing order, and thus of a manufacturing process, are determined in parallel with an ongoing process.

Business process owners are also interested in the processing status of processes currently being executed. Using ARIS-Monitoring , they can display each individual process during its execution and can highlight the functions that have already been concluded.

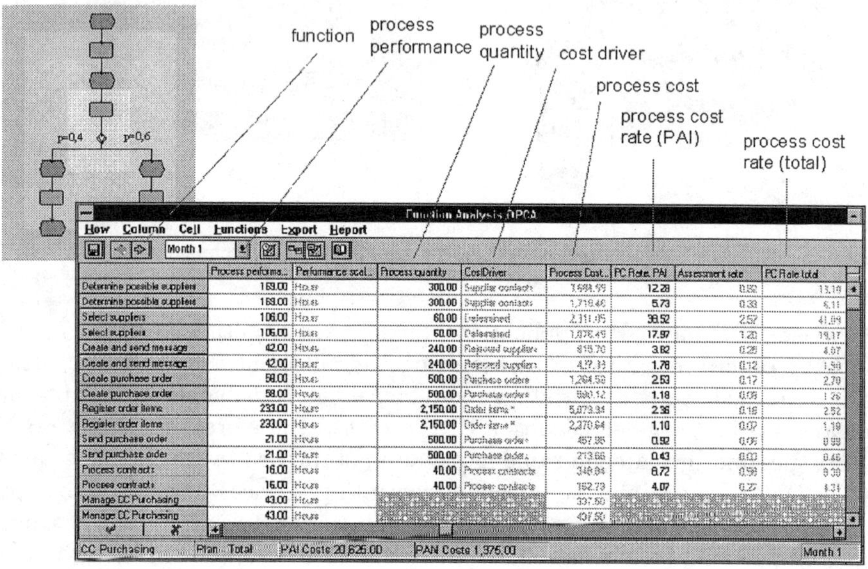

Figure 11: Supporting process costing with ARIS-Promt

In addition to the cost point of view, business process owners are thus kept up to date on the various states of the processes regarding scheduling, capacity and organization. The IDS production scheduling system, initially developed for manufacturing control, can also be used to control business processes in public services. Process data can also be summarized in an executive information system (EIS) or data warehouse, supporting process management. When turning the concept of an enterprise-wide business process control into reality, the following guideline must be kept in mind:

"A process is a process is a process," regardless of whether it is in production, purchasing or in sales. Going back to the example at the very beginning of this article, we can see that this concept will guarantee that the sales manager can actually communicate with his peer in production, having the same reference numbers at his disposal.

4.3 Process Workflow - Level III

Thirty years ago, a software application used to be comprised of a function description (program statements), procedure control (defined by the sequence of statements) and data. Because data does not belong to an individual function, but rather is processed by several functions, it was stripped of the individual function programs and defined as an enterprise-wide organization object.

We can observe a similar development as with data when controlling individual function commands [Don94]. The entire business process procedure (see Figure 2) is generally not handled by a single software application system. Moreover, several function-oriented systems are usually used by sales, purchasing, production or finance. None of these systems is capable of providing information on the entire process, such as the processing state of an order. Therefore, is seems obvious that we should not hand over the responsibility for the whole process control to a single function, but rather to a separate system level. This level is known as workflow.

Workflow systems transport the objects to be processed (documents) from one workplace to the next. Better yet, they send them from the computer system at one workplace to the computer system at the next work step. Therefore, the procedure must be described in detail and must include each individual type of process or business user, respectively [GS95].

In Figure 3 the document flow is illustrated by a “folder”, which is transported from one workplace to the next. This folder contains electronic references regarding the data required for processing and the function elements that need to be called up. Figure 12 illustrates how a specific process in the execution level is derived from the procedure defined in Level I. Instead of the general attributes of the organizational unit, we now find actual business users. Instead of the general term, we find an order that is linked to an actual customer.

After the conclusion of a workstep, the workflow system retrieves the document from the electronic out-bin of the business user and transports it into the electronic in-bin of the next business user. If several business users are involved in processing, the procedure can be placed in several in-bins. As soon as a business user has begun with the process, the procedure is deleted in the other in-bins. The workflow system is informed of the process status, execution time and the appropriate business user of every business process. Thus, the workflow procedure is also the foundation for Process Management in Level II. It reports the data for cost and scheduling evaluations and provides process information for process monitoring. An agreement by the Workflow Management Coalition, a group of workflow vendors, has standardized interfaces. Now, various workflow systems can be linked with one another [Hol95].

The process representation of workflow systems can also be used to guide business users. This increases their knowledge of the interrelationship of

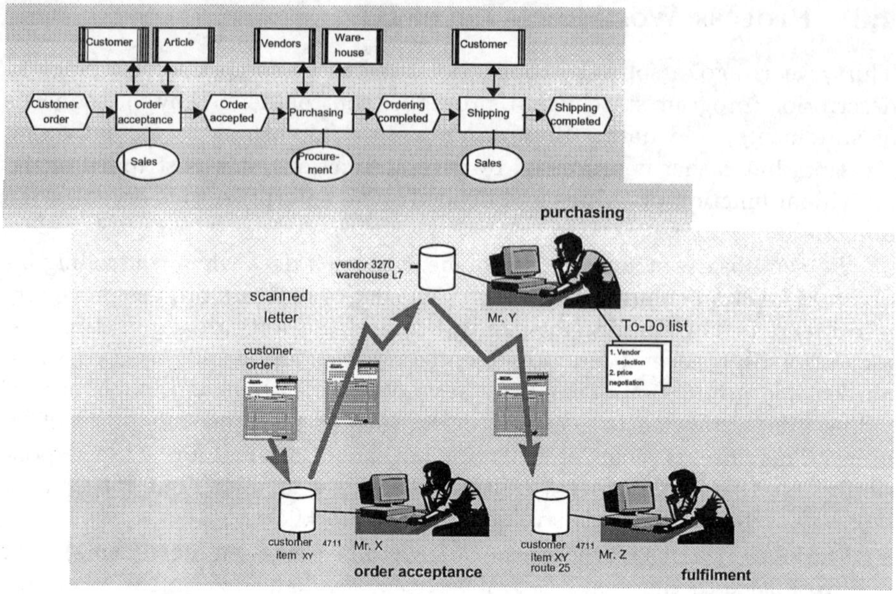

Figure 12: An as-is procedure is derived from a business process model

organizational business processes.

The specific procedure in Figure 13 (right box) follows from the general business process procedure. You create a specific procedure by giving information on particular business users and by selecting a certain path outlined in the general business process description. Thus, business users can always see how their activity is embedded in the process, who will precede and who will succeed them within the process. For example, they can also see that only the left branch of a business process is relevant for them; the control flow of the right branch might be deleted. Since a particular process has not been created for the business user of the succeeding activity, only the department name, "Warehouse", is listed. Depending on the capacity situation at that time, the business user of the next workstep is not determined until the conclusion of the task. During Process Workflow, processes with precisely defined procedural structures can be differentiated from processes with only roughly defined procedural steps.

In many operational or repetitive procedures (such as order or loan processing), functions, their procedural branches and organizational units are determined from the start. Thus, the process is well-structured and can be described with the EPC method. On the other hand, other processes can only be described partially since functions become apparent during the process. This is also the case when the sequence of the process steps is determined ad hoc or the organizational units to be processed become apparent on an ad hoc basis. In these cases, we define the process as being poorly structured. It

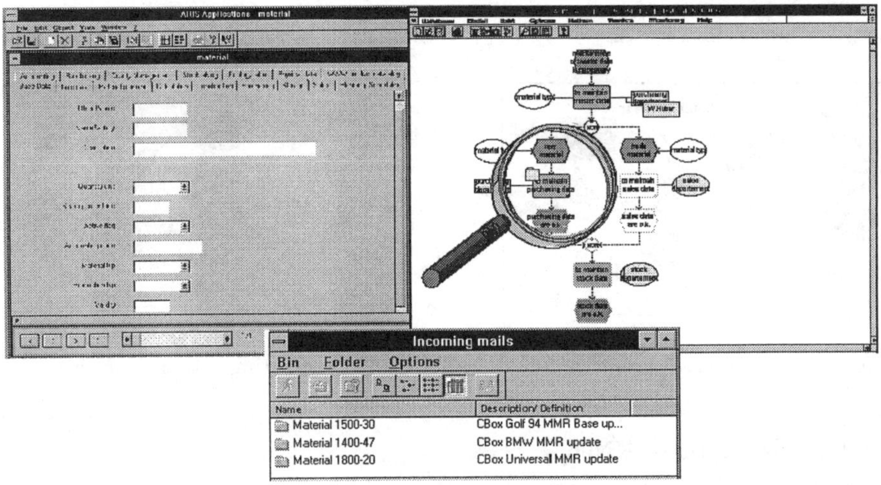

Figure 13: The workflow component guides users according to processes

can only be modeled in an imperfect way. For example, functions can only be presented in a "TO DO" list; the sequence will be determined by the project team during the process. It is at this time that the person to whom the task has been assigned, is also determined.

Workflow systems seem to be more suitable for controlling well-structured processes. Likewise, less structured processes are supported by groupware systems, which only offer tools such as electronic mail, video conferencing, shared conferencing etc., but which do not require logical knowledge of the processes. In real-life situations, we will always find a mix of these two structure forms. Thus, workflow systems are capable of "exception handling", that is, procedure control can be changed ad hoc during processing. This functionality can be linked with groupware tools, complementing workflow and groupware. In the future, these two systems will even grow together. In Figure 14, a process is first depicted as a structured procedure and secondly, after a team organization has been implemented, as a less structured procedure.

4.4 Process Application - Level IV

Current vendors of integrated software systems are splitting their systems into smaller modules. Many of them are now just loosely coupled. This makes it possible to release upgrades for each individual module and not across-the-board for the entire system. On the whole, there is a strong tendency today towards splitting application software into individual components (componentware). These modules are re-assembled into complete solutions according to process models. The operational data in these applications are managed

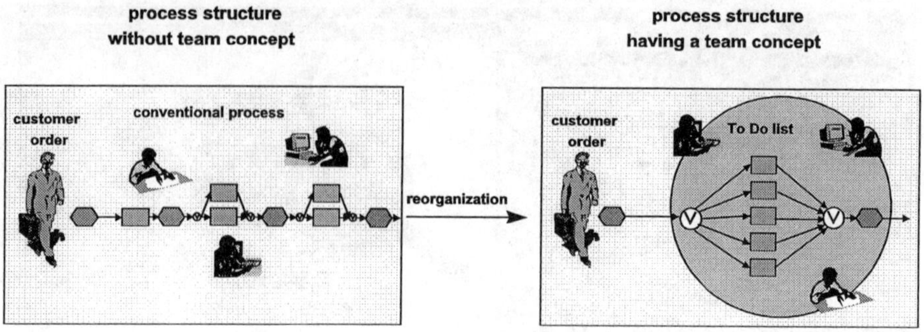

Figure 14: Process structure before and after implementing a team concept

by database systems [KN96].

In the object-oriented approach, data and functions are encapsulated and communicate via a messaging system, which performs material handling for the workflow system. The objects correspond to the "folder" and provide references to data and functions. It is important to note that Level III is responsible for the entire process of the operation. It calls up objects to be processed, such as electronic forms for filing insurance claims, loan application forms for loan processing operations or customer orders for customer order processing. It then passes them on to the appropriate processing station and calls up the program modules.

This separation of the control flow of programs and function execution is bringing about tremendous changes in the software market. Vendors of conventional application software will have to decide whether they want to be brokers' at Level IV and just provide "componentware" with some editing functionality - or if they want to move up to the rapidly growing workflow systems market. Conversely, softwarc manufacturers without much experience in applications are reaching a new point of departure, now that workflow systems are being developed. Particularly in service applications, the processing rules in Level IV can be so simple that they only involve data entry or document editing. Many functions could therefore be executed at this level, such as calling up a spreadsheet or a word processing program. This makes workflow systems that control the coherence of a procedure all the more important.

What this means for users is that a new architecture for application software is on its way (see Figure 15). Service providers, such as banks and insurance companies, do not have a large selection of standard applications at their disposal to support their operational procedures. Now they can document (model) their business procedures in Level I and can control their procedures by implementing a workflow system in Level III. In Level IV, they can still use their existing software to support the processing rules. Nevertheless, today it is necessary to split software in Level IV and make it accessible to workflow control. By separating procedure control from function execution statements, information systems are split into data management, procedure control and function execution.

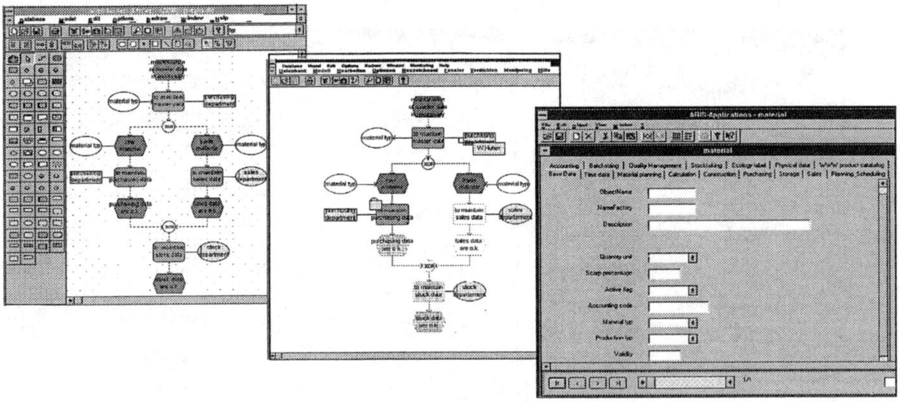

Figure 15: Process-oriented, workflow-supporting application software

4.5 Interaction between the Levels (Customizing)

When supporting business processes in their entirety, it is not sufficient to simply split the whole process into the four parts intellectually or as a physical system, as described above. We must also separate their links with one another. We have already noted that the individual business events in the Process Workflow Level are generated by copying the business process design in Level I. The generating of this business design is thus a link between the business process modeling tool and the workflow system. In the Workflow Management Coalition, experts are working on creating accepted standards for this link [Hol95]. The same goes for delivering workflow results to Level II, for example, by delivering details regarding as-is schedules or as-is amounts to Level II for evaluation purposes.

These two links make it possible to immediately update a business process procedure, even in execution and evaluation levels. This occurs without having to manipulate any computer programs. Thus, organizational Design Level I plays a tremendous role within the whole architecture.

From an organizational point of view, the link between Level I and Level IV is equally important. Thus, the modeling level not only generates procedure control, but also processing rules and data transformation. After starting with a group of processing rules that are only very roughly defined, for example, it is possible to filter and adapt only those that are really important for the business procedures.

ARIS-Applications is consistent in carrying through this concept of model-driven customizing:

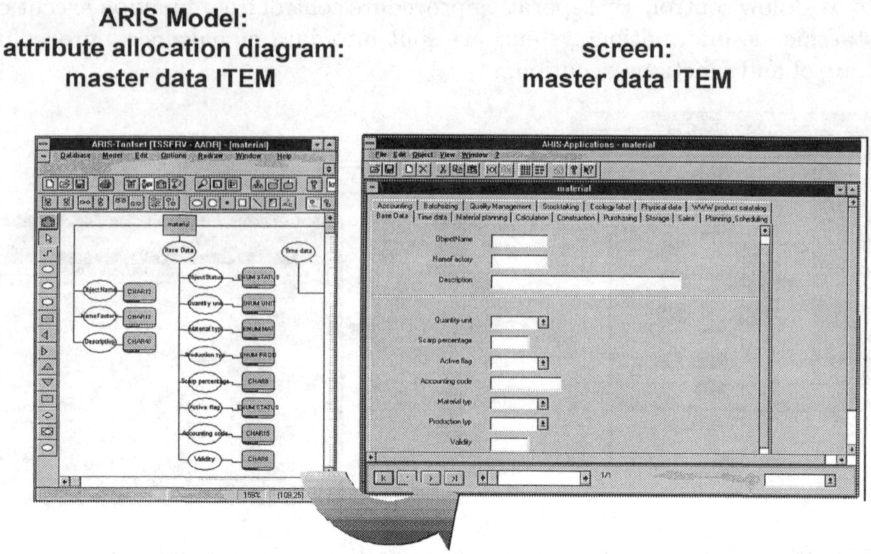

Figure 16: Model-based customizing with ARIS-Applications

Changing the attributes of the data model in Level I alters the data tables in Level IV. Modifying process models, in turn, varies the sequence of function procedures. Changing function models either switches off or activates functions. Finally, employing the organizational model allocates functions to certain organizational units and determines the screen sequence. ARIS-Applications are derived directly from industry-specific market reference models described according to the ARIS Method. Using the ARIS-Toolset, they can then be developed into company-specific "to-be" models.

In order to transfer the model into application software, a build-time-system, class library and configuration model are at your disposal. The build-time-system converts the company-specific ARIS model, based on object-oriented programming, into an operational application system (run-time system). The build-time system utilizes a class library consisting of predefined business administration and data processing classes. The processing rules for this conversion are comprised in the configuration model. Here is an example: Processing rules guarantee the DP-conversion of the ARIS models into database objects. They further govern the description of database objects and links between external and internal identifiers (e.g. for tables and columns). Besides modifying procedure rules, model-based customizing enables the adjustment or expansion of data models, dialogue masks and process organization. Thus, the application is derived directly from the process model of the enterprise and then configured from business-objects.

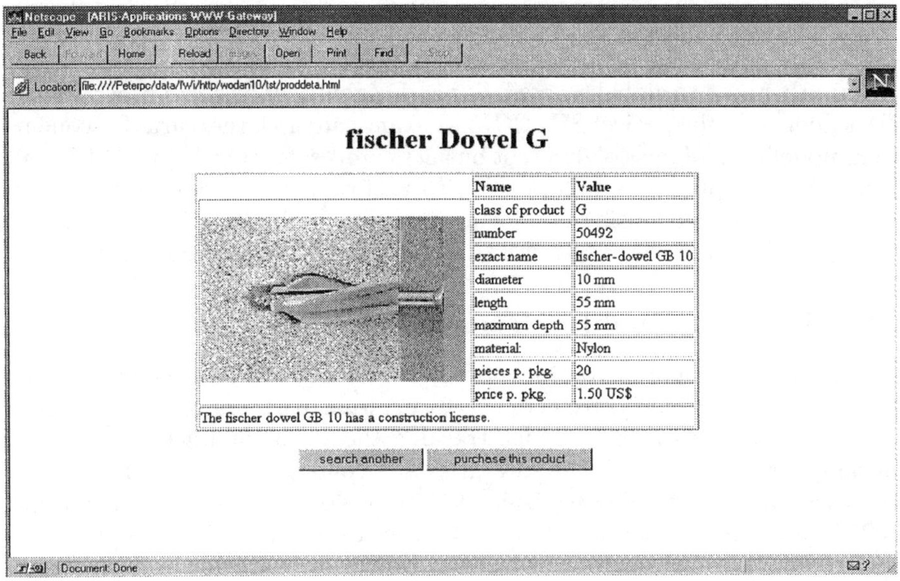

Figure 17: Internet user interface of WODAN

5 Outlook - Further Developments

The 'ARIS-House of Business Engineering' is designed to make it easily adaptable for further development. Currently, work is being done on the following approaches:

- Distributed Modeling and Model-Warehouses,
- Internet-Enabled Business Process Control and
- Business Process Control in Virtual Enterprises (only selected examples !).

Some of these approaches are still in the R&D stage. Others will soon be in production.

5.1 Distributed Modeling and Model-Warehouse

Due to the fact that multiple organization units are involved in business processes, they must also take part in their respective definition (modeling). This can take place in a cooperative way across multiple locations, even across national borders. In a cooperative effort involving IDS and IBM, the IWi at Saarbrücken, Germany, have developed a prototype, ContAct, to control asynchronous modeling projects. This prototype contains groupware techniques for modeling as well as procedures for consistent query and reply processing within the modeling process [GHS95].

Another step to global accessibility and usability of business process models is done with the project SETCOM (Semantically rich thesaurus for concurrent modeling). Models of different business processes, modeled with different tools could be placed in a database with an Internet-Frontend. With an extensive search-engine using ontologies, examples and descriptions a common understanding and easy accessibility to business process models is available.

5.2 Internet-Enabled Business Process Control

As follows from Figure 2, business processes can range from several company locations for sales and production - to external partners of the enterprise (suppliers and customers). Thus, tracking the status and active control of business processes beyond the enterprise is becoming increasingly important. Internet standards are distinguishing themselves as a key networking concept. ARIS-Workflow system and ARIS-Applications are generic by design. This makes them ideal for world-wide business processes conducted in the Internet. Due to the fact that Internet standards are becoming increasingly common in enterprises, these products also support corporate applications (Intranets).

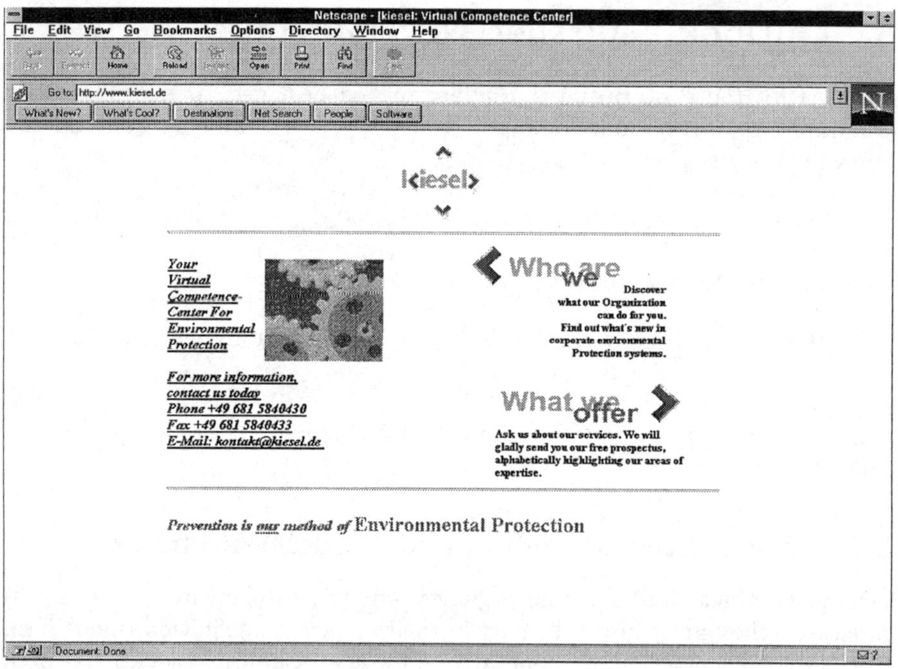

Figure 18: KIESEL: Virtual competence center for Enviromental Issues on WWW

A prototype for logistic applications has been developed, using the WO-

DAN system [LKSS96]. A (private) customer logs into a manufacturer's multimedia catalog (in this example, of a manufacturer of dowels). They select the items they want to purchase, fill out the order and send it to the manufacturer via the Internet. The manufacturer loads the order into an internal logistics system and actually enables the customer to monitor the status of the order during the entire order process. WODAN is a component of ARIS-Applications. That is, the application is generated employing reference models, and is workflow-driven. Figure 17 illustrates the system's interactive form and the multimedia product catalog.

5.3 Business Process Control in Virtual Enterprises

Information technology is especially significant when it leads to new organizational concepts. So-called virtual enterprises are profiting from new networking technology, enabling distributed work on teamworking projects. Virtual enterprises operate like any other traditional company, but without their legal properties. They are common in joint ventures in the construction industry. What makes this topic so special, is the fact that partners can be located through an electronic cooperation network. All their joint activities, from e-mail and video conferencing to shared applications, are supported.

The IWi is targeting its KIESEL project at designing a virtual enterprise for medium- sized firms in the environmental industry. The processes for designing the organization and managing the processes are controlled by ARIS. In all probability, more and more virtual enterprises will appear in the future - culminating in "mini enterprises" that consist of one person offering his or her services via networks from a home office. The more these organizational forms become "softer", the more it is important to assign responsibilities to the individual persons involved in the processes - the more important is process modeling [KMNSS95, SK96].

References

[CK88] Cooper, R., Kaplan, R. F., Measure costs right: Make the right decisions, in: Harvard Business Review, 66 (1988) 5, 96-103

[Dav93] Davenport, T. H., Process Innovation - Reengineering Work through Information Technology, Boston, 1993

[Don94] Donovan, J. J., Business Reengineering with Information Technology, Englewood Cliffs, 1994

[DCVF93] Doumeingts, G., Chen, D., Vallespir, B., Fénié, P., GIM - GRAI Integrated Methodology and its Evolutions - A Methodology to Design and Specify Advanced Manufacturing Systems, in: H. Yoshikawa, J. Goossenaerts (eds.), Proceedings of the JSPE/IFIP TC5/WG5.3,

Workshop on the Design of Information Infrastructure Systems for Manufacturing, Tokyo, Japan, 8. - 10. November 1993, 101-120

[Gai83] Gaitanides, M., Prozeßorganisation: Entwicklung, Ansätze und Programme prozeßorientierter Organisationsgestaltung, München, 1983

[GS95] Galler, J., Scheer, A.-W., Workflow-Projekte: Vom Geschäftsprozessmodell zur unternehmensspezifischen Workflow-Anwendung, Information Management 1/95, 20-27

[GHS95] Galler, J., Hagemeyer, J., Scheer, A.-W., ContAct - Coordination of Cooperative Information Modeling Activities, in: Conference Supplement to the European Conference on Computer Supported Cooperative Work, Stockholm, Sweden, 1995, 25-26

[Har91] Harrington, H. J., Business Process Improvement: The Breakthrough Strategy for Total Quality, Productivity and Competitiveness, New York, 1991

[Har94] Hars, A., Referenzdatenmodelle - Grundlagen effizienter Datenmodellierung, Wiesbaden, 1994

[Hol95] Hollingsworth, D., The Workflow Reference Model, in: Workflow Management Coalition (ed.), Document TC00-1003, Draft 1.1, 1995

[IDS90] IDS Prof. Scheer GmbH (ed.), Dezentrale Fertigungssteuerung: Der Intelligente Leitstand FI-2, Systembeschreibung, Saarbrücken, 1990

[IDS94] IDS Prof. Scheer GmbH (ed.), ARIS-Toolset - Business Reengineering mit dem ARIS-Toolset, Saarbrücken, 1994

[JK87] Johnson, H. P., Kaplan, R. F., Relevance lost: The rise and fall of management accounting, Boston, 1987

[KMNSS95] Kocian, C., Milius, F., Nüttgens, M., Sander, J., Scheer, A.-W., Kooperationsmodelle für vernetzte KMU-Strukturen, in: A.-W. Scheer (ed.), Veröffentlichungen des Instituts für Wirtschaftsinformatik, Nr. 120, Saarbrücken, 1995

[KN96] Kruppke, H., Nelles, Ch., Modellbasierte Standardsoftware: Ein Weg zur Kundenorientierung, in: A.-W. Scheer (ed.), Rechnungswesen und EDV, 17. Saarbrücker Arbeitstagung, Heidelberg, 1996, 439-453

[KNS92] Keller, G., Nüttgens, M., Scheer, A.-W., Semantische Prozeßmodellierung auf der Grundlage "Ereignisgesteuerter Prozeßketten (EPK)", in: A.-W. Scheer (ed.), Veröffentlichungen des Instituts für Wirtschaftsinformatik, Nr. 89, Saarbrücken, 1992

[LS95] Loos, P., Scheer, A.-W., Vom Informationsmodell zum Anwendungssystem - Nutzenpotentiale für den effizienten Einsatz von Informationssystemen, in: W. König (ed.), Wettbewerbsfähigkeit, Innovation, Wirtschaftlichkeit, Wirtschaftsinformatik 95, Heidelberg, 1995, 185-201

[LKSS96] Loos, P., Krier, O., Schimmel, P., Scheer, A.-W., WWW-gestützte überbetriebliche Logistik - Konzeption des Prototypen WODAN zur unternehmensübergreifenden Kopplung von Beschaffungs- und Vetriebssystemen, in: A.-W. Scheer (ed.), Veröffentlichungen des Instituts für Wirtschaftsinformatik Nr. 126, Saarbrücken, 1996

[Nüt95] Nüttgens, M., Koordiniert-dezentrales Informationsmanagement: Rahmenkonzept - Koordinationsmodelle und Werkzeug-Shell, Wiesbaden, 1995

[Sch91] Scheer, A.-W., Principles of Efficient Information Management, Berlin, 1991

[Sch92] Scheer, A.-W., Architecture of Integrated Information Systems: Principles of Enterprise-Modeling, Berlin, 1992

[Sch94] Scheer, A.-W., Business Process Engineering - Reference Models for Industrial Enterprises, Berlin, 1994

[SNZ95] Scheer, A.-W., Nüttgens, M., Zimmermann, V., Rahmenkonzept für ein integriertes Geschäftsprozeßmanagement, in: Wirtschaftsinformatik, 37 (1995) 5, 426-434

[SK96] Scheer, A.-W., Kocian, C., Kiesel - Das Virtuelle Umweltkompetenzzentrum - Theorie und Praxis der virtuellen Unternehmung, m&c Management & Computer 4/96, 221 - 228

[Sch96] Scheer, A.-W., Industrialisierung der Dienstleistung, in: A.-W. Scheer (ed.), Veröffentlichungen des Instituts für Wirtschaftsinformatik, Nr. 122, Saarbrücken, 1996

[SNZ96] Scheer, A.-W., Nüttgens, M., Zimmermann, V., Business Process Reengineering in der Verwaltung, in: A.-W. Scheer, J. Friedrichs (eds.), Innovative Verwaltungen 2000, Schriften zur Unternehmensführung (SzU57), Wiesbaden, 1996, 11-30

CHAPTER 25

Bonapart

Herrmann Krallmann, Gay Wood

Bonapart is a general use modeling, simulation and dynamic analysis tool designed to support both experts and non-experts in organizational decision making and strategic planning. Bonapart's OO (object-oriented) design supports most key organizational and IS (information system) methodologies so it can be effectively used in organizational design, restructuring (e.g. BPR), communication, organizational memory management, IT design and implementation, cost control (e.g. activity-based costing) and documentation (e.g. ISO 9000 standards). Tailored interfaces to other critical work-related and IS applications maximize the usefulness of Bonapart data when implementing workflow, CASE technologies, data warehouse and enterprise-wide (e.g. SAP) applications. Since both process and actor-oriented views are modeled, information processing is considered from both the technological and the organizational perspectives allowing information within an organization to be more visible and controllable.

1 Development History

Bonapart is an outgrowth of expert system research performed at the Technical University in Berlin during the 1980's. Its earliest predecessor, KSA (Kommunikationsstrukturanalyse), was a SQL-based relational database which collected information regarding organizational structures, processes, jobs, individuals, information flows and the implementation of technologies and resources. The goal of this system was to support the definition and analysis of critical success factors as measured by key performance measures and existing or proposed information structures [Kra90].

In 1988, an university spin-off company, UBIS GmbH (Unternehmensberatung für integrierte Systeme), was grounded to continue research, development and consulting in the application of KSA and KSA-based technologies within commercial and public organizations. In 1990, UBIS' first PC non-commercial product, ODESSA (OrganisationsDEsign durch Strukturierte SystemAnalyse), was available for use by UBIS consultants and university researchers. ODESSA expanded the relational database capabilities of KSA and added a dynamic index, import/export capabilities, enhanced graphic presentation features and a user-friendly MS-Windows, pop-up menu GUI (graphical user interface). In spite of attempts to make ODESSA user-friendly, its rigid relational structure limited its use to Expert System experts.

The development of ODESSA corresponded to the gaining popularity of BPR (Business Process Reengineering) [Ham90]. BPR methodologies fit perfectly with the capabilities of ODESSA. Consulting in this area rapidly expanded. In spite of the strong methodological ties to expert system research, it was the multi-organizational consulting experience which determined new system specifications.

In early 1992 UBIS made a strategic decision to develop a marketable product which could be used by non-experts. After considering available expert system shells and C++, it was decided to use new object-oriented technologies. Object-oriented methodologies were expected to insure maximum product flexibility, decrease development and maintenance costs, shorten development cycles and allow direct interfaces to CASE tools. IntelliCorp's KAPPA-PC was chosen as the object-oriented development platform and the KEE (IntelliCorp) expert system shell formed the basis of the simulation. The integration of these two products made Bonapart one of the first available object-oriented products with simulation and analysis capabilities. In addition to object-orientation, built-in dynamic data exchange (DDE) links allowed Bonapart analysis results to be directly available to Microsoft applications (e.g. MS-EXCEL), SQLWindows and other predefined interfaces. The new object-oriented modeling and simulation version of ODESSA was renamed to BONAPART 1.0. To maximize modeling flexibility and ease-of-use without sacrificing the advantages gained from using embedded expert system controls, Bonapart 1.0 controlled for inconsistencies in the following ways:

- only previously defined objects are available for use in process and organizational chart diagrams
- identical class names are not allowed
- a consistency analysis report is generated

Analysis was based on a query language with constructs for accessing object types, objects of an object type, and all subtypes etc. When making associations, queries indirectly associated with objects were also accessible. For example, the analyzer is able to select all employees which report to a particular manager or a particular division. Set operations can be applied to subquery results. In cases where numeric information is generated, usual arithmetic operations are available. Bonapart queries are specified using a graphical language. Therefore the results of queries can be exported to spreadsheet programs for additional calculations or to presentation programs to generate graphic images such as pie charts.

The next generation of Bonapart 2.0 products was developed on a Windows platform with Kappa 3, an object-oriented expert system shell from IntelliCorp Inc. The GUI (graphical user interface) was designed to function with Microsoft Windows. Previous tool limitations, such as simulation and model size constraints, were either eliminated or improved. New multiple refinement capabilities allowed for subprocesses to have more than one parent process.

Bonapart 2.1 added OLE automation and links to Microsoft EXCEL. Interface enhancements allow full integration of user-defined attributes and more sophisticated analysis capabilities. User-defined analysis capabilities can also be defined using tools such as VisualBasic. In addition, a bottom-up modeling feature was included.

The current version Bonapart 2.2 is a 32 bit application with even more seamless plug-in type interfaces. Further developments continue to maximize user-friendliness and applicability in a wide range of modeling environments. Bonapart interfaces to best-of-class applications such as Microsoft Office products and other specialized interfaces such as LiveModel (IntelliCorp) and Rational Rose (Rational).

2 Organizational Modeling

The main problem in successful IS or organizational design is not what analysts and managers know, it is what they do not know. This unknown information is responsible for significant unanticipated costs during all phases of analysis, design, implementation and maintenance. Tools which make unknown information known, especially early in the design cycle, save time, save money and contribute to overall project success. Modeling, simulation and dynamic analysis tools assist managers, information engineers, consultants and other experts in their organizational planning by collecting and organizing data about existing or proposed organizational and process structures so that information flows, workflows and management control structures can be optimized to maximally achieve organizational goals.

2.1 What are Models?

Since cavemen started drawing hunting scenes on cave walls, humans have attempted to model their work in order to better coordinate their activities and to inspire others with the elegance of their models. Models are representations of what we think is going on, what we would like to see going on or, in some cases, models are merely elegant representations of information. Because models are abstract pictures of activities, there are two basic perspectives – the modeler's view of the modeled situation and the observer's attempt to match the model with his or her own personal experience.

When viewing pictorial information, each person has his or her own focus.

Model observers do not only focus on content, they focus on colors, forms, historical relevance and syntactical clarity. What is seen is often unrelated to the intent of the modeler. Appreciation and understanding of models requires more than just clear and concise models, it requires training, experience and effective bi-directional communication between modelers and observers.

Success modeling projects require:

- skilled modelers and observers,
- top level management support,
- sufficient project resources,
- openness within the organization, and
- a tool which concretely presents relevant information in a way which optimizes communication.

If models do not communicate structure and flow information in ways observers understand, observers are unable to give the feed-back necessary to create accurate and useful models. Communication is often inhibited if tools and/or modeling teams are overly influenced by a particular professional group-specific language and/or notational system. Professional languages and notational systems are useful in that they communicate complicated information efficiently but they are also used to maintain professional autonomy and power. For example, system analysts communicate with one another using dataflow diagrams, managers communicate with graphs and pie charts and line workers develop specific informal communication strategies. The ease and effectiveness of communication increases the more homogenous the participants. Communication problems do not begin until a computer specialist shows his dataflow diagram to the sales manager, or until a manager presents her econometric study of departmental efficiency to her secretary or until the billing clerk calls data processing to request an additional change to the material management program.

Organizations also have formal and informal information sharing strategies. Organizational power structures determine the success of individual participants. Individuals who effectively present information using accepted organizational standards are more successful than those who do not. This success is not necessarily correlated to information relevancy or accuracy. Because information flows are often more politically determined, than strategically or rationally decided, tools which selectively support one particular group's information sharing strategy, maintain that group's existing political position within the organization. Tools which are designed to support communication between all members of the organization, threaten existing power structures. The successful implementation of a modeling tool is only possible if upper management clearly supports the modeling tools representation of information and is ready to make decisions based on modeled information.

The ability of a product to support communication is not only one of the most basic uses of modeling and simulations tools, it is also the basis for major product differences. If managers, computer specialists, billing clerks and secretaries are all essential participants in the processes under consideration, representatives from each group should be able to understand and correct models, or in some cases, directly model their group's activities. When considering different tools, it is important to involve all likely participants in tool selection in order to assess model clarity and ease of use. Table 1 is a list of tool characteristics which help both modelers and observers in the preparation and review of models.

2.2 Selection of a Modeling Tool

Most potential tool users have particular modeling goal or they are looking for optimization opportunities which require additional process or organizational information. The more defined the project's goals, the easier it is to assess the advantages and disadvantages of different tools. Problem orientation helps to narrow down the tool choice to those products which concretely provide the means for answering the questions at hand. From the management perspective, tools need to be able to identify areas in need of optimization and to compare various alternative optimization strategies so that minimal resource allocation achieves maximal gain.

Tool manufacturers, recognizing this need, often combine solution components in their tools. Typical associated solutions include reference libraries (with or without benchmarks); specialized niche modeling tools to aid in the design of production systems; specific interfaces to existing applications; or consulting service packages in areas such as Total Quality Management or ISO 9000. Therefore, after ease-of-use, the next major choice in tool selection is to decide if the current project fits an existing solution provided by a tool manufacturer. If the solution fits, and if there are no other associated external organizational process interfaces of importance, and if models can be understood by everyone on the project team, it makes sense to take advantage of the expertise of specialized tools and services. If, on the other hand, process information is not clear, or if there are many complicated interactions between processes and/or organizational entities which are not described, or if the tool language does not fit the existing organizational language, it is dangerous to try to fit the organization to an existing reference model or to a pre-defined alternative structure. Reference model libraries have the tendency to become static business recipes instead of dynamic organizational information repositories. Also, system-defined process terms must be translated into organizational terminology in order to be understood. Because reference models rarely have enough specific details about the organization, model observers also have difficulty in correcting misconceptions or in participating in finding viable alternatives.

The most important advantage in designing models from scratch is that

- limited information in a single model
- integration of existing corporate terminology
- critical information can be selectively shown (e.g. costs, time, user-definable attributes)
- same model data can be preseted in multiple formats
- graphical capabilities
- unique class and instance names
- familiar GUI (e.g. pull-down menus, on-line help, cut and paste, click and drag)
- compatibility with other information types (e.g. bitmaps, documents, videos, sound)
- minimal tool training requirements
- interfaces to other commonly used applications
- intuitive model file sharing strategy
- reusable model objects
- technical model limits (e.g. size limitations, refinements, model directories)
- simulation factors (e.g. simulation run times, model size restrictions, graphics)
- ease of merging multiplc models

Table 1: User Clarity and Ease-of-Use Features

these models require the participation of everyone in the process chain. This communication prepares the organization for change and identifies project shortcomings early in the project. Unique organizational models are created with general support tools. Since general tools support multiple organizational and IS (information system) methodologies, an appropriate methodology must first be selected to maximize modeling productivity. Table 2 lists some common modeling methodological paradigms used with modeling and simulation tools.

Methodologies range in complexity from simple step-by-step instruction guides to highly complex theoretically-based research instruments. Complex methods often require the support of specialized consultants. If consulting services are required, consultants should be included in tool selection. However caution should be used when involving consultants in the tool selection process because the same risks associated with using pre-defined tool solutions may also apply to using consultants with overly structured methodologies.

2.3 Methodologies

Methodologies are created to help to focus activities, offer a step-by-step project guide, and to maximize the internal and external validity of project results. Therefore modeling is most productive when guided by a methodology which best fits the immediate needs of the organization. Additionally, this methodology should fit the knowledge and experience of modeling team members. If a new methodology is to be introduced, extra time must be planned so that all team members are able to receive adequate training in this methodology before the modeling project begins. This early training is necessary because the input of all team members is needed to select the best tool and to prepare a realistic tool implementation strategy.

A method should:

- fit the concreteness and complexity of the project goals (e.g. activity-based costing, ISO 9000, CASE tool data modeling interface)
- take advantage of previous organizational experience
- be more structured if organization success depends on the modeled process knowledge or if this is part of an effort to create a cyber organization
- be less structured if the goal is to identify opportunities or if it is an isolated modeling project
- fit the level of trust in the ability of employees to represent their work
- match the level of procedural control desired from a tool

Even with a methodology in place, due to constant organizational change and risk of getting lost in details, modeling projects are difficult to keep on track. Project success and appropriate planning depends on limiting activities to only those which directly impact project goals as defined by the organization. The easiest way to stay focused is to prepare a list of concrete questions which should be answered by the modeling project. Only those items of information which directly relate to the question list or to the chosen methodology, should be modeled.

- Enterprise Modeling (e.g. TOVE [FCF93], PERA [Wil92])
- Process and Attribute Design
- BPR (Business Process Reengineering) [Ham90]
- Grammatical models [MCLP97])
- SSD (Structured System Design [You89])
- UML (Unified Modeling Language [Rum91])
- OOIE (Object-Oriented Information Engineering [Jac94, Ode94])
- IDEF (Integrated Computer Aided Manufacturing Definition)
- ISD (Instructional Systems Design)
- TQM/CPI (Total Quality Management/ Continuous Process Improvement)

Table 2: Examples of Modeling-Related Methodologies

Throughout the project design and project approval phases, expectations need to be managed. If upper management is not satisfied with project progress or project results, support is likely to be withdrawn. Both tools and methodologies have inherent weaknesses. Models represent a specific period of time and a unique constellation of resources. Models also continually change as organizational units compete for limited resources. Because of the risk of immediate obsolescence, care must be used when interpreting all analysis and simulation results or when making decisions based on this information. If limitations are clear from the beginning, project goals can be better defined and managed. Methodologies and tools can be selected which minimize the most relevant risks. The following is a list of common problems associated with modeling projects:

- A methodology is not used, models are inconsistent and therefore simulation results are not meaningful.
- The modeling methodology does not match project goals.
- Modeling projects are too large to be managed efficiently or they exceed the technical limits of the simulation component.
- Too much information is modeled on a single screen.

- Attribute information for the same object type is entered multiple times.
- Modeling projects are limited to only parts of the organization and they fail to identify critical destructive and synergistic interactions.
- Workers perceive that sharing information will have negative consequences such as job loss or loss of power, and they intentional or unintentional sabotage model accuracy.
- In the desire to create functionally manageable models, models are oversimplified to the point where they no longer provide useful information.
- Modelers do not have adequate modeling skills or modelers are unable to collect or to coordinate the collection of appropriate organizational information.
- The wrong core processes are chosen.
- In restructuring projects good, functional processes are weeded out with bad, dysfunctional processes because of there is no baseline assessment or because of faulty communication.
- Parts of the organization cannot be modeled because they are unique limited structures or events, or because processes are dependent on organizational responses which are made at gut level due to professional experience.
- Tools are so complex that no one in the organization is able to use them.
- Models are so technical that only specialists can understand them or check them for accuracy.

Tools are associated with different characteristics (please refer to Table 3). Of these characteristics, object-orientation is especially useful because it supports reusability through use of class hierarchies and inheritance and polymorphism. Class hierarchies and inheritance allow information to be defined once and polymorphism allows this same object information to be applied in a number of different scenarios. Because modelers do not have to keep defining general object information, they can focus on the specific details of how an object behaves within a process.

3 How does Bonapart work?

Bonapart collects information within diagrams which function as libraries of organizational object classes (please refer to Figure 1). Bonapart reference object classes are categorized as tasks, job titles, people, business entities,

	Bonapart
32-bit Object-Oriented	√
User-Defined Objects and Associations	√
Model Type	complex system
Info dependent modeling	√
Associated Databases	uses OO repositories
Support of Multiple Methodologies	√
Support for Multiple Users	++
Network-wide model viewing	√
Ease of merging multiple models	√
Process View	√
Organizational View	√
Simulation Capabilities	+++
Discrete Event	√
Animation	√
Petri Net	level 3
Hierarchial	√
Timed	√
Graphic,Time Series Data Presentation	√
Speed	+++
Sophisticated Data Analysis	+++
Interfaces to:	+++
Workflow Products	√
SAP Interfaces (e.g. Live Model)	√
Databases	√
CASE Tools	√
Office Software (e.g. MS-Excel, MS-Word)	√
OLE	√
VisualBasic	√
Meta Model Access	√
Reference Model Applications	√
Graphic Capabilities (incl. Bitmaps integration)	√
WEB Model viewer	√
Flexibility of Information Layout	√
Integration of attribute data:	+++
Cost factors	√
Time factors	√
Employee qualifications	√
Processing strategies (e.g. FIFO, FILO)	√
User-defined attributes	√
Information-dependent outputs	√
OO Methods	√
Model consistency checks	√
Automated process documentation and report generator	√
Ease-of-Use	+++
Limited information in a single model	√
Integration of existing corporate terminology	√
Selection of critical object information	√
Presentation of data in multiple formats	√
Familiar GUI	√
Compatibility with other information types	√
Training Requirements	3 days

Table 3: Characteristics of BPR Tools

managers, resources, info containers and information types. Subclasses are created by assigning “is a“ relationships between two classes. Refinements to class objects are created using “consists of“ associations.

Reference diagrams are the repository for organizational knowledge. Each object in a diagram is associated with attribute information (e.g. costs, process times), simulation characteristics and processing rules. Each item of information is described only once. Once described, needed information is available for various lines of retrospective inquiry. If changes need to be made to an object, changes are made within class libraries. Process diagrams using these classes change automatically.

Once object knowledge is defined, objects can be combined in unlimited number of ways within the two integrative process and organizational chart diagrams (please refer to Figures 2 and 3). Process and organizational chart diagrams are scenarios of what is currently happening in the organization or projections of what might happen after optimization. They represent the complex interrelationships between objects and they are used as the basis for analysis and simulation.

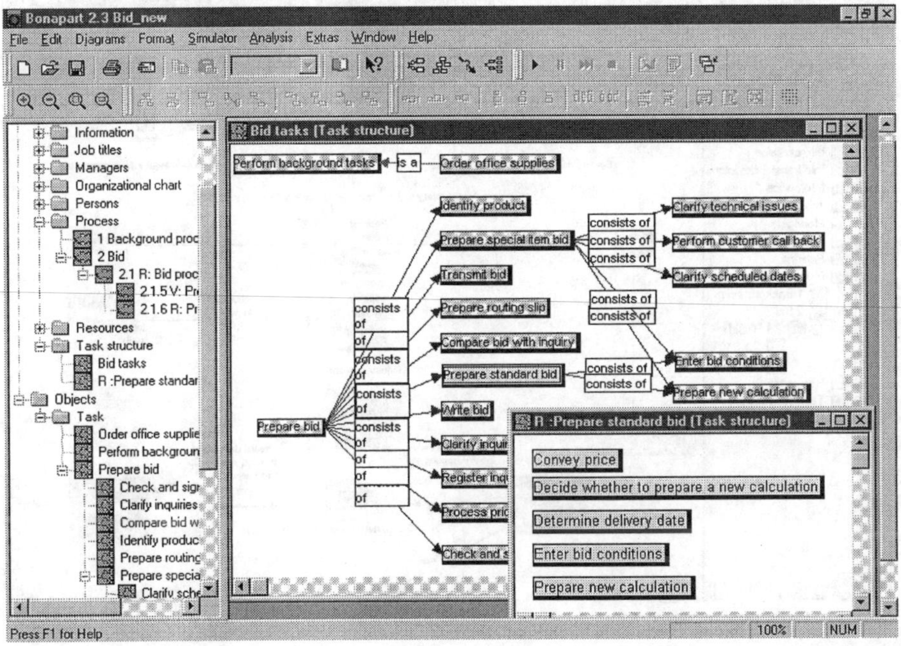

Figure 1: Example of a Bonapart Class Library (Task Diagramm)

In Process and organizational chart diagrams, only instance names and associations between objects need to be assigned, object class choices are made from a list of allowable, previously defined objects. For example, in Figure 1, the task “prepare standard bid“ has a number of subtasks. If a process refinement is created for "prepare standard bid", only the subtasks which were defined in the reference diagram are available for insertion. When inserting human and physical resources, instance names must also be assigned by the user. If a "telephone" is created within a process diagram it must be given an instance name, such as "X4178", to indicate that the telephone being modeled has the extension number "4178".

Bonapart's object-oriented modeling

- supports model consistency,
- creates specialized controlled vocabulary specific to the organization
- allows extension of all system types and
- functions as a general repository for attribute information.

Information is presented in ways people normally view organizations, therefore diagrams are easy to create, refine and modify.

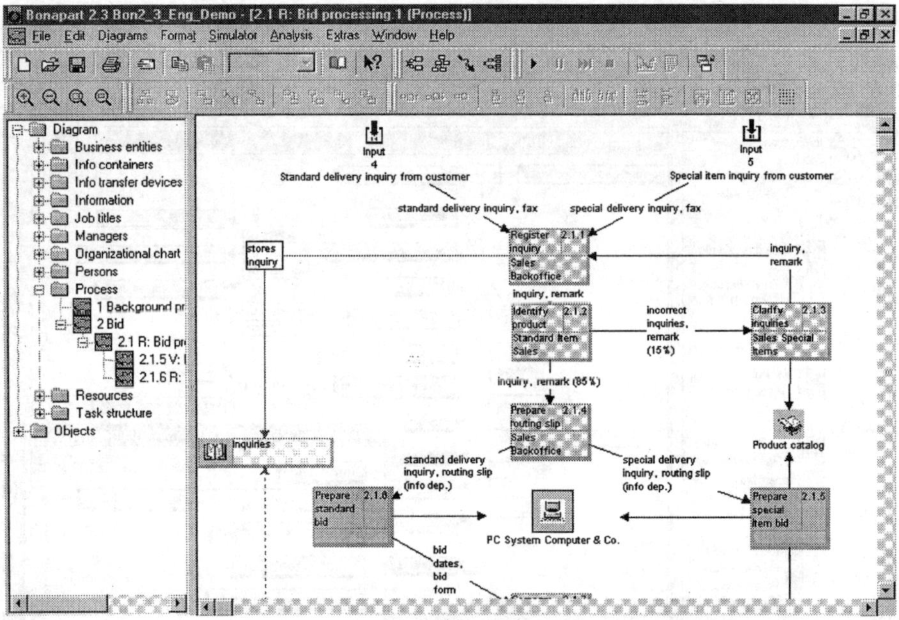

Figure 2: Bonapart Process Diagramm

How do Bonapart models collect and process information?

Figure 2 is a top-level model of a Bid Processing process. The primary components of this process model are:

- Associations

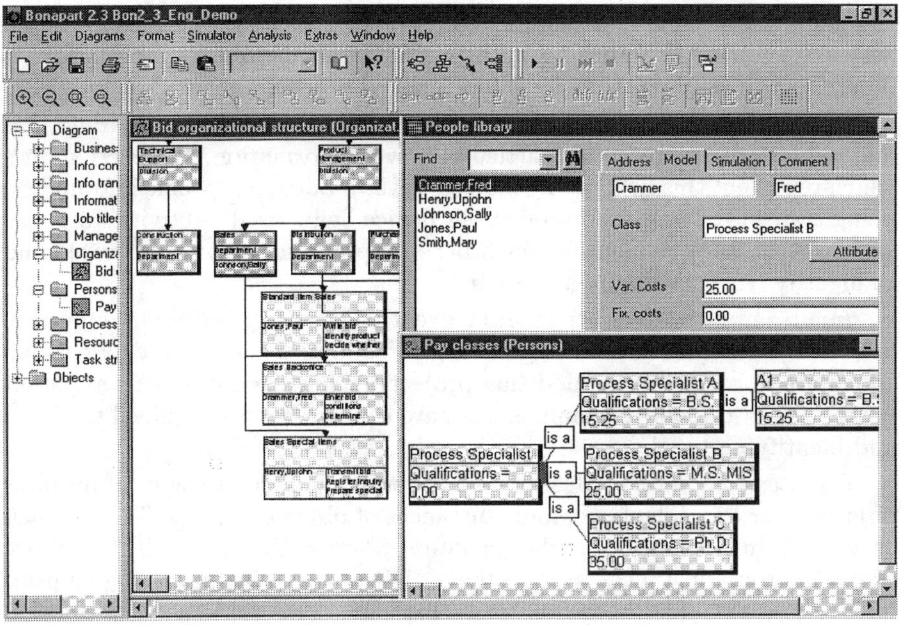

Figure 3: Organizational Chart Diagrams

- Attributes
- Information Flows
- Layout Characteristics
- Instances of Objects
- Operative Person or Group
- Refined Activities

Associations: Associations define object relationship rules. In the above example "uses" and "saves" are associations which define how the activity uses the resource or info container. The "sends info" association is represented in this model with information flow details (e.g. "sends standard bid inquiry with letter").

Attributes: An attribute is a property or characteristic associated with an object class or an instance (e.g. "time to process a task", "cost of a resource per usage").

Icons: Icons are freely definable bitmap pictures which can be imbedded into all Bonapart objects. Based on layout settings, icons can be either supplemental information, as in the above example, or an entire model can be created using only pictures. A typical example would be to use both the employee's name and picture when creating models which will be used as training manuals. Bitmap data, like all other attribute information, is inherited and only needs to be entered into the system once.

Information Flows: The coupling of activities within process diagrams and refinements represents a particular flow of information. Connection lines which represent this flow can be labeled to show both the specific information being transferred and the info transfer device being used. Activities are also given special tags to identify which parts of processes are computerized and to identify when media breaks occur.

Inputs: Inputs are either external event triggers (e.g. customer inquiries, deliveries), internal event triggers (e.g. requests from other departments which are not part of the modeling project) or inherited inputs from parent processes. In the above example, the parent processes are signified by name and identifying number.

Instances of Objects: Classes are a general object descriptions of business objects (e.g. PC, telephone, file). Instances of objects are specific PCs, such as the PC in accounting or the phone on Mary Forbes desk. In the above example object instances include the activities "take inquiries", "give price info", "prepare bid"; resource "price list" list; info container "calculation PC"; operative people "Forbes" and "Heinrich"; info transfer devices "letter" and "original copy"; and information "price inquiry","standard bid inquiry" and "special bid inquiry".

Layout Characteristics: Layout determines what information is shown and in which format. Bonapart allows all nodes and relationships to be color-coded. Bitmap information can be integrated (see Icons). Connections can be labeled generically or with specific information and transfer device information. Each node can present up to 12 associated characteristics. Input/outputs can be labeled as to their origin (inputs) or targets (outputs).

Operative Person or Group: An operative person or group is an employee or group of people (e.g. from above "sales") assigned to perform an activity within a process. Operator assignment is not required as activities may be automatic (e.g. computer performed activities). As with other resources operators have assigned attributes such as associated costs, capacities, unavailability times and processing strategies.

Outputs: Outputs are either outflows of data from a process to an external targets (e.g. customers or another organizational units), outflows to a non-modeled internal organizational unit or outflows to another process (e.g. process refinements). Process refinements automatically inherit the outputs of their parent process.

Refined Activity: A refined activity is further described in other process models. This feature is the functional essence of models. Refined activities are easily recognized because they have a darker frame than the other activities shown. Refinement capabilities allow modelers to zoom in on important processes. In this example the Bid Processing Department has three general activities "take inquiries", "give price info" and "prepare bid". While "take inquiries" and "give price info" were important considerations when simulating the activities of the department, they were straightforward enough that they did not require any additional process descriptions. "Prepare bid", on the other hand, was know to be a problem area. Therefore it was more extensively modeled and further refined to "prepare standard bid" and "prepare special bid". Further and further refinements are possible until the process is represented to the desired level of detail. Refinements keep information manageable without losing the ability to study complex interactions across the organization.

A refinement automatically inherits all related process information from its parent. When modeling a new process refinement, the newly opened diagram already contains inputs, outputs and any resources previously attached to the activity. In the above example, "prepare bid" receives information from input parameters "take inquiries", therefore "take inquiries" automatically inherits the associated objects linked to its parent. All information flows and info transfer devices are also automatically assigned. All the modeler needs to do is to create the new activities and connect them to the appropriate resources or info containers.

Organizational information is combined within Organizational Chart diagrams. Organizational objects (e.g. "job titles", "business entities", "managers" and "operative people or groups") are combined to represent complicated human resources and management control structures. Within object reference libraries, job groupings can be represented and further sub-divided into job titles which are associated with specific tasks. Tasks are then classified according to how they are executed. Job profiles are generated so that rules can be applied regarding the minimum qualifications required to perform a task.

4 Simulation

The most important reason for using both modeling and simulation tools is to show complex, dynamic organizational interactions which cannot be identified or properly understood using other methods. Simulation makes it possible to animate, analyze and validate these complex relationships. This information can then be used to create new alternatives or it can be used to compare multiple alternatives until an optimal solution is found. Most importantly, simulation takes information which was traditionally collected in static reports, and makes this information dynamic. Repository information contained within models grows and changes in tandem with organizational changes.

Bonapart is classified as a "timed, hierarchical, object-related, Level 3 Petri net variant, discrete-event simulation tool with color-coded stochastic graphic flow representation". This definition, which is explained below, contains the technical description which separates Bonapart from other simulation tools.

4.1 What do Simulation Characteristics mean and why are they important?

“Timed“ means that all time variables and time distributions are taken into account during simulation. “Hierarchical“ integrates process refinements into the simulation. “Object-related“ simulates output-dependent information (e.g. sums greater than \$100 flow to activity “A“ and sums less than \$100 flow to activity “B“) automatically instead of having to independently define tokens for each variant. A “Petri net“ is a formal, graphical language which is designed to study concurrent events. “Level three Petri Nets“ contain the most complex token level (level one tokens are boolean and level two tokens are integer) because they allow multiple inputs to enter the same node. “Discrete-event“ simulation is event-driven simulation (as opposed to time-driven simulation). “Color-coded stochastic graphic flow representation“ allows the flow of events to be graphically observed during simulation.

If models are to be simulated, data needs to be consistent or inconsistencies need to be documented so that they can be taken into account during evaluation. Bonapart maintains model consistency through the use of rules, controlled vocabularies and consistency checks.

Simulators vary in the following ways:

- model and analysis complexity,
- the size of models (in bytes) which can be simulated
- amount, type and format of information which must be defined before each simulation,
- the ability to establish user-defined parameters,
- ability to analytically compare two or more simulation runs (including the use of random number generators for multiple simulation runs),
- the ability to independently visualize different problem areas (e.g. resource competition over 24 hours or over a period of days) and
- the type of graphic data available (please refer to Figure 4).

Some of these differentiating features, such as the use of continuous or discrete simulation, are presented as both an advantage and a disadvantage. Since most organizational situations are event-driven (e.g. a customer arrives with an order), discrete simulation is appropriate for most organizational uses. Also, since time variables are included in the analysis, discrete analysis results appear similar to those of continuous simulations.

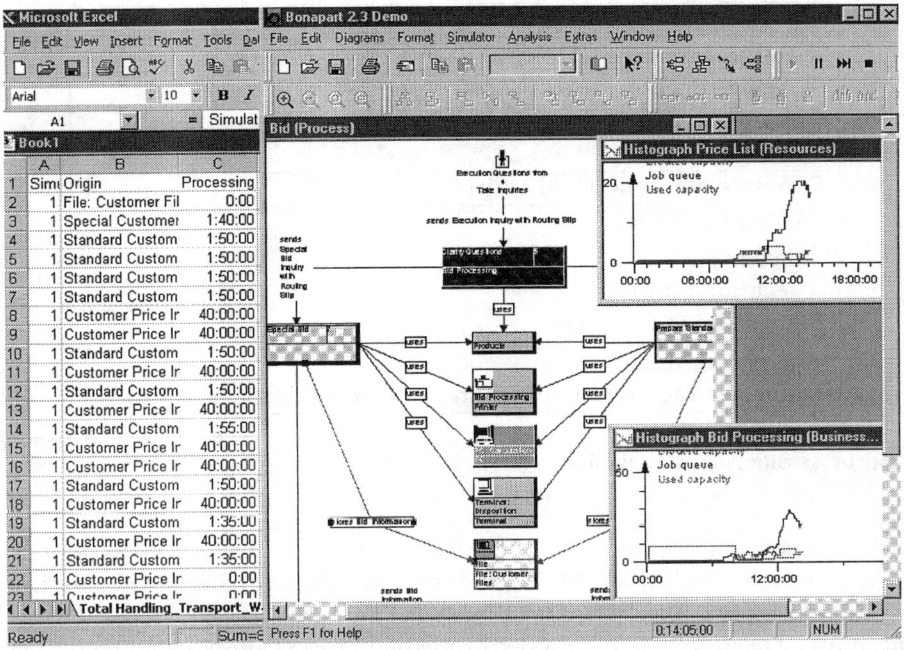

Figure 4: Graphic Simulation Data

One of the most important and most common uses of simulation data is to validate models. It is important to use markers to test model accuracy. This marker should be a variable where there is general agreement among modeling team members. Examples include, the average time it takes to complete a series of related tasks or the costs associated with a particular resource, or a time of day when a department is known to have problems with back-orders. Simulation data should correspond to marker values. For models to be accurate, they must be either consistent or inconsistencies must be documented in such a way so that results can be appropriately qualified.

4.2 How does Bonapart represent an Event?

A Bonapart event is represented by the execution of an activity which is then coordinated using a scheduler and an agenda for each resource. Resources (both physical and human resources) select tasks for execution from their work list using strategies such as FIFO or LIFO. Distribution generators allow users to specify variations in the execution duration, transport duration and in the arrival of external inputs. A post-mortem analysis based on the complete trace of the execution, helps to locate bottlenecks and other weaknesses.

Dynamically updated protocol probes can be created for each involved

Time simulation
-transportation times -waiting times -processing times -throughput time
Simulation of functional entities
-utilization -efficiency -execution strategy
Simulation of resources
-processing resources -transportation resources (charge of communications channels)

Table 4: Simulation Variables

actor, activity, resource or process. These protocols log any event that is related to the watched object. Users then trace the path of a process during simulation so that they can immediately validate whether the process flow is accurate. For example, in an order processing process a user can directly see which actors are involved, which new information is created and where the order gets delayed. In a similar fashion graphical probes visualize workload and work list lengths for the simulated objects. Graphical probes give direct hints on where to detect bottlenecks in the modeled process. Because all probes can be attached or reattached while the simulation is running, the optimization of a business process can be accomplished with Bonapart much faster, and in most cases much better, than is possible with conventional simulation tools.

Because of the high likelihood that models are incomplete or because they may include inaccurate estimations, caution should be used when interpreting simulation results. Whenever simulation data is counter to expected results, check key variables in the model against information obtained from multiple organizational sources. The value of simulation results is only as good as the quality and completeness of the model.

Simulation output and export capabilities vary between products. Bonapart, for example, offers both histographic representation of simulation data (please refer to Figure 4) and a direct OLE to Microsoft EXCEL. Each type of simulator is associated with technical limitations regarding the allowable model size. Due to the technical limitations and because of the need to easily edit and manage models, it is generally better to divide models into sub-models which can be independently tested. These smaller models can then be recombined into larger enterprise models which contain aggregate values of key attribute information. When choosing a simulator it is important to consider the technical capacity of the simulator, the accuracy of the simulation analysis results, the interfaces to necessary analysis tools and the general ease-of-use of the simulator.

5 Analysis

After an organization has been systematically modeled, the depicted corporate model can be examined with the help of the analyzer (statistical analysis component). Using different model views the corporate models are evaluated with regard to particular processes, activities or information flows. Inquiry arguments are graphically selected and freely defined. Examples of task-related analyses include questions related to task structure, function-carrying characteristics, technical and physical resources, costs, process run-times, methodological definitions as well as analyses related to the identification of relevant information and associated information flows. Results can be reported as a list or they can be stored to be processed further.

The goal of the analysis, regardless of whether it is related to a process, functional entity or piece of information, is to attempt to make existing organizational structures transparent so that they can be optimized by eliminating any discovered weaknesses.

6 Conclusion

Modeling and simulation tools offer invaluable process and organizational design support but their ultimate usefulness depends on finding the right project, the right people, the right tool and the right implementation strategy.

When organizational transparency is desired, there are few tools on the market that have Bonapart's ease of use, deeper underlying object-oriented power and its ability to directly incorporate or to interface with critical new technologies. Model observers are also not confronted with more information than desired. Large complex models are easy to selectively view and to organizationally distribute. Because models are easy to create and easy to understand, organizational information can be productively shared between those responsible at the process level and those who must make difficult decisions regarding resource allocation. Organizational potential is continually maximized, customers and employees are more satisfied and resulting flexible organizational structures are better able to respond to changing market conditions.

Bonapart is a registered trademark of the UBIS GmbH.
EXCEL is a registered trademark of the Microsoft Corp.

References

[And96] Andrews, D., Choose the Right Recipe for Success Enterprise Reengineering, http://www.reengineering.com/articles/jun96/nutsbolt.htm, June, 1996

[AF88] Ashforth, B. E., Fried, Y., The Mindlessness of Organizational Behaviors, Human Relations 41, 1988, 305-329

[Bar96] Barrett, R., Chasing the BPR Tool Market Enterprise Reengineering, http://www.reengineering.com/articles/mar96/ March, 1996

[BDMQ95] Bernstein, A., Dellarocas, C., Malone, T. W., Quimby, J., Software tools for a Process Handbook, IEEE Bulletin on Data Engineering 18 (1), 1995, 41-47

[Boo93] Booch, G., Practical objects: Patterns, Object Magazine 3 (2), July-August, 1993

[Boo94] Booch, G., Object-Oriented Analysis and Design with Applications, Addison-Wesley, 1994

[Dav93] Davenport, T. H., Process Innovation: Reengineering Work through Information Technology, Harvard Business School Press, Boston, MA, 1993

[DB95] Davenport, T. H., Beers, M. C., Managing Information about Processes, Journal of Management Information Systems 12 (1), 1995, 57-80

[FCF93] Fox, M., Chionglo, J. F., Fadel, F. G., A Common Sense Model of the Enterprise, Proceedings of the 2nd Industrial Engineering Research Conference , Norcross GA: Institute for Industrial Engineers, 1993, 425-429

[Ham90] Hammer, M., Reengineering Work: Don't Automate, Obliterate, Harvard Business Review, 1990

[Jac94] Jacobsen, I., *et al*, The Object Advantage Business Process Reengineering with Object Technology, Addison Wesley, 1995

[Kin95] King, W. R., Creating a Strategic Capabilities Architecture, Information Systems Management 12 (1), 1995, 67-69

[Kra90] Krallmann, H., *et al*, Die Kommunikationsstrukturanalyse (KSA) zur Konzeption einer betriebswirtschaftlichen Kommunikationsstruktur, Interaktive betriebswirtschaftlichen Informations- und Steuerungssysteme, Berlin, 1990, 289-314

[LCKNCJ94] Levitt, R. E., Cohen, G., Kunz, J. C., Nass, C. I., Christiansen, T., Jin, Y., The Virtual Design, Team: Simulating how organizations structure and information processing tools affect team performance, in: K. M. Carley, M. J. Prietula (eds.), Computational Organization Theory, Erlbaum: N. J. Hillsdale, 1994

[MCLP97] Malone, T. W., Crowston, K., Lee, J., Pentland, B. T., Tools for Inventing Organizations: Towards a Handbook of Organizational Processes, Proceedings of the 2nd IEEE Workshop on Enabling Technologies Infrastructure for Collaborative Enterprises, Morgantown, WV, 1993

[New83] Newmeyer, F. J., Grammatical Theory: Its Limits and Its Possibilities, Chicago, University of Chicago Press, 1983

[Ode94] Odell, J., Six Different Kinds of Composition, Journal of Object-Oriented Programming 6:8, 1994, 10-15

[Pal96] Palmer, N., Business Process Simulation and Modeling, An Introduction and Survey of Tools, Enterprise Reengineering Jan/Feb 1996, http://www.reengineering.com/articles/janfeb96/

[Pen98] Pentland, B. T., Grammatical Models of Organizational Processes, Organization Science, http://ccs.mit.edu/CCSWP176.html, 1998

[Rum91] Rumbaugh, J., *et al*, Object-Oriented Modeling and Design, Prentice Hall, 1991

[Wil92] Williams, T. J., The Purdue Enterprise Reference Architecture, Purdue Laboratory for Applied Industrial Control, Purdue University, West Lafayette, Indiana 47907, USA, March, 1992

[You89] Yourdon, E., Modern Structured Analysis, Englewood Cliffs, NJ, 1989

[Yu89] Yu, E. S. K., Modelling organizations for information systems requirements engineering, Proceedings of the IEEE, 1992

CHAPTER 26

MO^{2}GO

Kai Mertins, Roland Jochem

The planning of information systems requires discussions between different project groups, within the respective project group, and between experts and managers in the enterprise and the project members. Therefore, the modeling of business processes and the related information systems is an essential step in the process of reorganizing enterprises. The software tool MO^{2}GO (method of object oriented business process optimization) supports the modeling process based on the IEM method. Different analysis of a given model are available using the MO^{2}GO tool like the planning of informations systems.

1 Introduction

All methods such as Lean Management, Simultaneous Engineering, Total Quality Management and Continuous Improvement Processes aim at strengthening the competitiveness and productivity of the company by improving the product quality, reducing lead times and optimizing the marginal pricing [AEM93, War92, CH94].

To improve the competitiveness all efforts are traditionally concentrated on optimizing single functions. The traditional way of managing an enterprise is to subdivide it into a number of separate functions which are easier to overview and control. This method results in numerous interface problems regarding the organization and the informations system support at the expense of the manufacturing process and the organization as a whole [JMS96]. When approaching the mentioned targets companies start to concentrate

- on their main business processes,
- on improving the communication by widely sharing information within the processes.

The integration of separated functions, the optimization of the main business processes and the specification of a suitable information flow require a higher degree of transparency within the organization. In consideration of the complex relationships - looking at the manufacturing enterprise as a network of functions - models or modeling methods have to be applied in order to support, to ease and to systematize the planning and integration of functions into business processes and to describe the related information system structure. Such a concept ensures a common understanding of business processes and an understanding of how the required information and the organizational structure needs to be organized [CH94]. In the following, a software sytem called MO^{2}GO (method of object oriented business process optimization) is described which was designed and developed by the Fraunhofer Institute for Production Systems and Design Technology (IPK) Berlin [JMS96]. It supports the modeling process based on the IEM method (Integrated Enterprise Modeling). The description includes an example of a company whose business processes were successfully reorganized with the application of MO^{2}GO. The example shows the modeling, analysis and optimization features of MO^{2}GO.

2 The Tool MO^{2}GO

2.1 Concept and Architecure

Most modelling tools based on traditional approaches to enterprise modeling such as SSA (Structured Systems Analysis), SADT (Structured Analysis and Design Technique) and E/R (Entity/Relationship) complicate the design of business processes. Often, they are dependent on the existing structure. Data and functions can never or only rarely be integrated [BELPR91]. In the course of the process modeling functions are often associated directly with the existing organizational units. Process-organizational alternatives are difficult to describe. The models are not easily accepted in the different departments of the companies. The object-oriented approach including prestructured model constructions facilitates the organization-overlapping analysis and optimization of business processes. Functions are not related to organizational units anymore, but to those objects that are to be processed. Data and Functions are integrated in one model. For example, the enterprise control, resources, the information system support, the manufacturing process as well as their connections may all be represented integrally in one model. The easy to understand and transparent description of the business processes leads to a higher degree of acceptance in the departments concerned.

The tool MO^{2}GO supports the object oriented modeling method of Integrated Enterprise Modeling (IEM). The universally usable tool to describe, analyze and optimize operational structures and business processes enables you to comfortably describe and purposively analyze products, resources, orders and the related business processes. Advantages of the use of the tool include the systematization of the planning and optimization processes and the reusability of the enterprise model for all projects and user views that concern corporate planning, such as information systems, controlling, quality management and organizational development. Restructuring measures and the introduction of new information systems are only sensible if you are familiar with the existing or planned business processes. The tool's systematic organization of corporate objects into the classes 'product', 'order' and 'resource' provides a transparent description of the business processes and their connections. The description in an integrated model is also supported by mechanisms for consistency checks, navigation and model modifications.

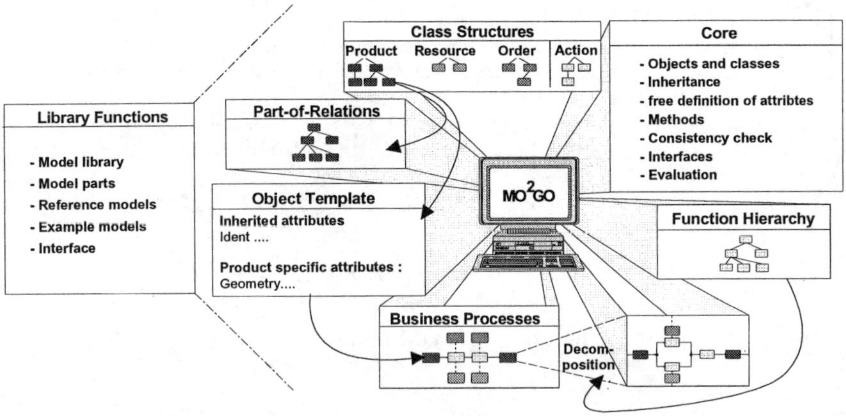

Figure 1: Tool concept

Reengineering requires discussions between different project groups, within the respective project group, and between experts and managers in the enterprise and the project members. Graphic and text-based documents are provided which can serve as basis for communication between the participants of the project. The documents include directories of all modeled functions, objects, their documentation and their graphic representation [JJM94]. To obtain immaculate printouts of the model different printing configurations are supported.

To do justice to the multitude of relevant information and display requirements of individual areas concerned different views on an integrated model of the company may be selected. Business processes and the necessary information is described in a model core. The information and the model structure is stored in the core of the tool (Figure 1) as object classes and instances with their relations. Used views related to the model core include Business Process Description, Class Structures and Object Templates, Part-of-Relations and Function Hierarchies. These views are available in libraries of class structures and models. They are supported by the evaluation functions of the tool. Process-organizational alternatives and changes can described with regard to their changes of control, quality, system support, organizational structure and the qualification profiles of personnel. For example, the

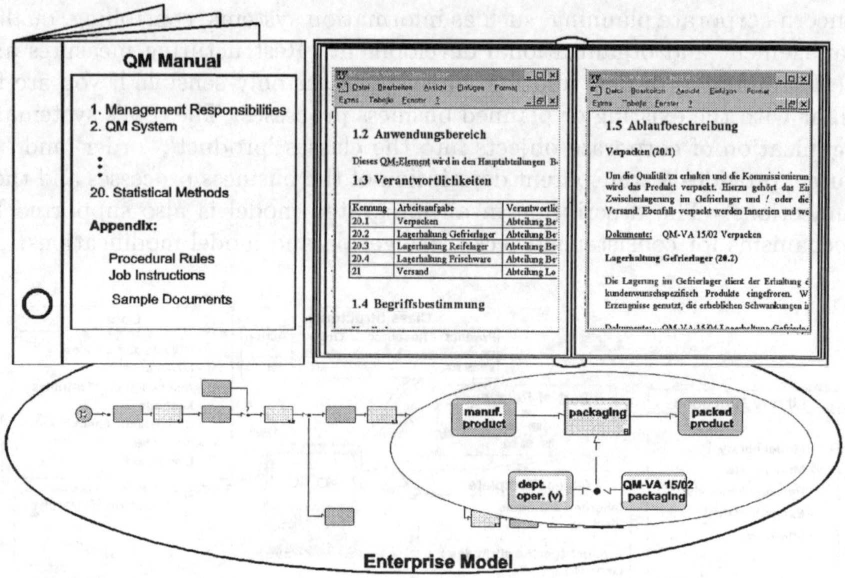

Figure 2: Automated generation of a QM Manual

gradual transition from the actual state to the desired state was pointed out to a medium-sized company of the automobile industry. The transition from a central manufacturing control to a decentralized Kanban-controlled production with immediate customer-supplier-relations was described. For information system planning you require discussion processes, both among the members of a project team and project-overlapping. For this purpose the tool provides graphic and text-based documents as basis for the communication among the participants. The documents contain structured directories of all modeled functions, corporate objects, their documentation and graphic descriptions. In correspondence with the information represented in the IEM model within the tool, informations system specifications and quality manuals, e.g. the structure of ISO9000ff documents, can be generated. The object-oriented approach enables the generation of these specifications and manuals by including additional class sets in an existing model and linking them with the process description. This is supported by the library functionality of the MO^{2}GO tool. It reduces the time for the implementation process of information systems and quality management systems significantly (Figure 2) [GHJM95].

2.2 Functionality and Interfaces

The user interface of the tool enables the simple, interactive design of enterprise models. Business processes and their connections are represented in appropriate windows where they can be refined (Figure 3). Mechanisms to design the models bottom-up or top-down in any combination are implemented. Class editors allow the description of company-specific characteristics of products, orders and resources. The user is enabled to define his own classes and descriptions of the characteristics. The description of the components of an object occurs at the appropriate classes as well, for example to generate bills of material.

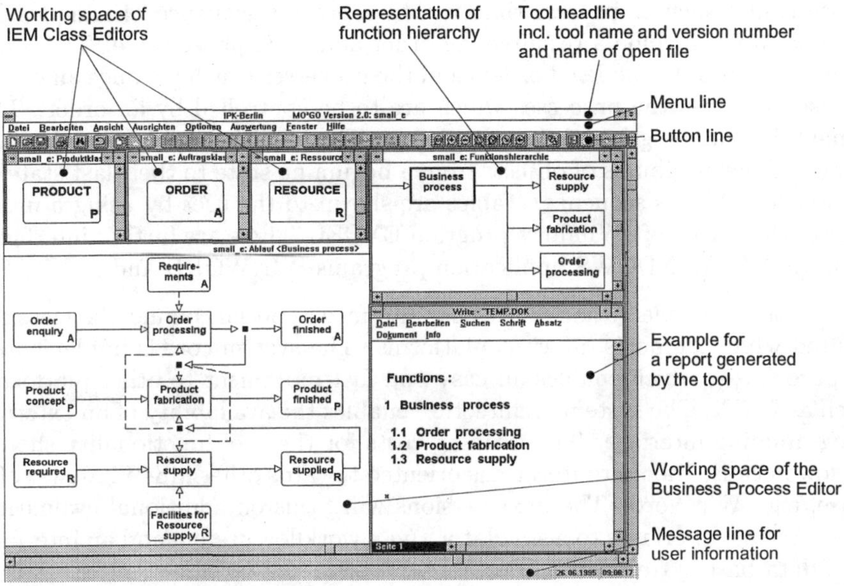

Figure 3: User interface of MO^2GO

The object-oriented approach supports the continuous reusability of partial models as modules of new models and the development of corresponding model libraries [BELPR91]. Reference models and exemplary models for certain applications can be provided. An automatically generated model description language enables the connection of different partial models and the development of interfaces with other tools. Consistency checks support the local consistency of the model.

In the modeling process within the tool it is only necessary to model those things that are in the focus of interest. The user can employ the default structures. For example, it is only necessary to design classes if the user needs them in his approach. He can also use the generic classes product, order and resource directly. During the modeling and analyzing process changes occur every time for both the class and the process structure. The tool supports these changes by navigation and changing functionalities as well as by consistency checks.

IEM enables the modeling of product, order and resource processes within one model. Real models are typically large; the different process sequences and the relations between them could make the model complex. To handle this complexity the tool provides a functionality to fade-out model parts. Therefore, the user can focus on the process sequence of his interest and is also enabled to look at the entire model.

The analysis based on the model is supported by the evaluation functionality of the tool, e.g. the generation of specific tables or the measuring of an attribute such as process time within a process sequence. Examples for specific tables include a resource, an order and a life phase table. The order table describes the modeled orders and the processes which produce an order. It also describes the processes which are to be controlled by an order. The same table can be generated for resources. The life phase table describes the values of the attributes of objects from a beginning state to their last state in a modeled process sequence. Tables are shown to the user by using a interface of the Microsoft-Windows program EXCEL. There are further interfaces with the MS WINDOWS application programs WINWORD and ACCESS.

For the implementation of the user interface a special commercial class set is used which supports different platforms. The system core is implemented in pure C++, which enables an easy and fast movement to other platforms such as UNIX. The system architecture enables the availability of an external programming interface. The training costs for the tool functionality should be low because the user interface is oriented towards other MS-Windows software, e.g. WinWord. The next versions will focus on additional evaluation mechanisms, interfaces to a simulator and a workflow system and an interface to a data base system.

An interface to existing, actual enterprise data is being developed. It should make the process model available to other tools which are used in the entire enterprise. It could, for example, be used for operations scheduling. The use of actual data would reduce the modeling time for analysis and simulation. This would save time for the transfer of parameter values into the model. The interface specification EXPRESS/STEP (ISO 10303) is used to obtain a common interface to different enterprise data and tools. STEP stands for Standard for the Exchange of Product Model Data [AGP93].

The described method and tool is suitable for many planning and structuring tasks in companies (Figure 4). The application includes the design of material flows and information flows. In projects, the systematic and transparent description of business processes as communication base between the departments and between the different hierarchical levels proved to be successful. Among other things, time saving potentials were made clear. The distribution of costs was improved with regard to the respective initiators, the deployment of personnel was improved with regard to qualifications. Method and tool has been employed in various industrial projects of the IPK Berlin and it is also used by customers.

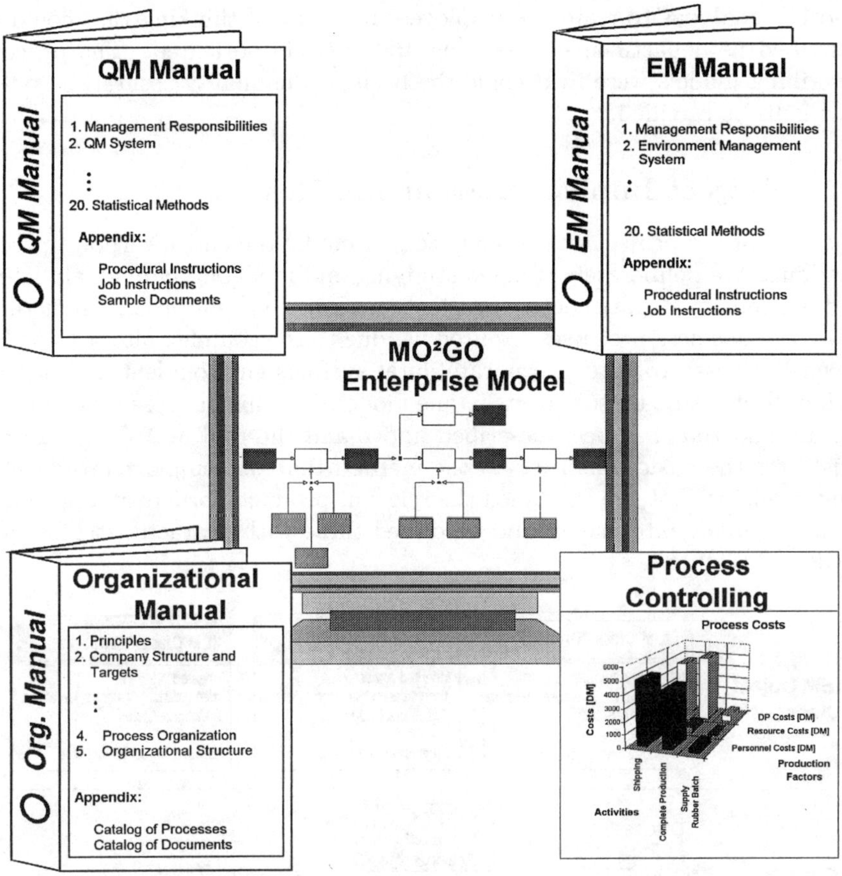

Figure 4: Application areas of MO^2GO

3 Example of Industrial Application

3.1 The Company

As an example, we selected a German machine tool manufacturer that has already had realized significant restructuring measures. The product range had been straightened out, the number of employees was adapted to the new structure of the company and the corporate activities were reduced to core competences. The mechanical production was abandoned. The company now manufactures standard universal lathes and customized engineering and systems analysis machines in small batch production. The objective of the project to optimize the business processes was to improve the customer orientation especially by way of reducing throughput times and improving the performance with regard to quality, compliance with deadlines and costs.

Another goal was to train the employees in a way of thinking that could be described as department-overlapping and customer-oriented. The process-describing models were to become the basis of the quality assurance system that is to be certified.

3.2 Project Implementation and Results

The task of the project was to analyze and model the entire corporate order handling. We deliberately avoided studying and modeling individual, delimited sections or departments. The task of realigning the process structures along the business processes required us, due to the complex interactions between business processes, corporate data, systems environment and organization, to describe these aspects in one model. For this purpose we employed the method that has been described above and the tool MO^{2}GO. Figure 5 illustrates the basic constructs of the method that was employed to develop the model. At first, we combined the relevant products, orders and resources of the company into classes and described these with characteristic features [JM93, JMS92].

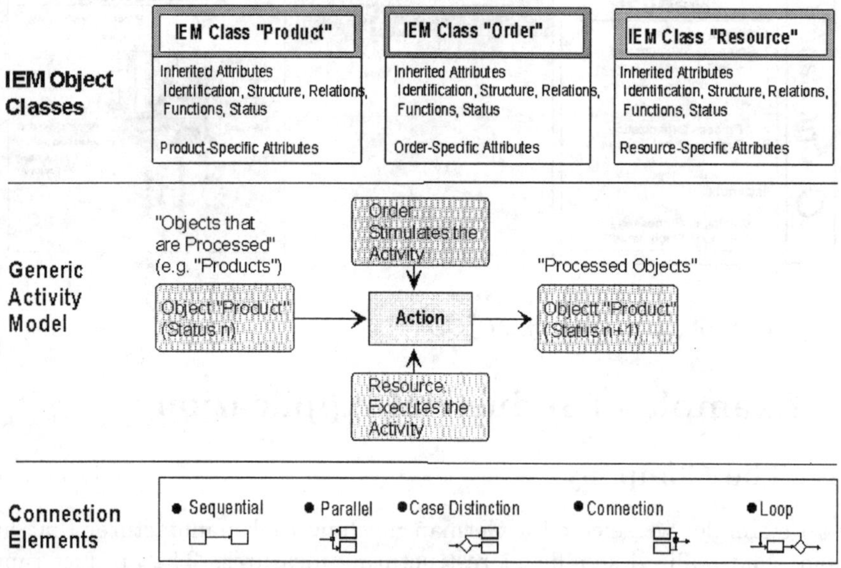

Figure 5: Basic constructs of the model development

The following object classes were studied:

- The orders 'customer inquiry and customer order for standard, engineering and systems analysis machines',
- the products 'entire machine, assembly and single part' and

- the executing resources 'organizational units or departments'.

Considering this, the relevant business processes and their control as well as the resources that are necessary to execute these processes were described. In the course of the project the model was either detailed hierarchically or modified to describe and discuss improvement measures. Supported by the tool MO^{2}GO, the processes, beginning with the inquiry of a customer and ending with the start of the machine, were analyzed. The core of the model consisted of the description of the logical processing sequence of the tasks to accept, schedule and trace the customer order and of the customized construction and assembly of the machines. Supplementary to the process descriptions we also analyzed and modeled the times the execute the tasks as well as their variances. The effective development of the model was guaranteed by mechanisms for consistency checks, navigation and model modifications. Application-oriented, predefined class structures and partial models as well as sample models that were supplied in libraries supported the development and the reusability of models. With regard to customer-oriented order handling the analyses enabled us to identify improvement potentials in the following areas:

- extravagant order scheduling processes, i.e. from the order intake to the order load-in into the PPC system,
- non-participation of the marketing department when preparing an offer,
- delayed entry of customer orders,
- inaccurate schedules of the planned order handling,
- vague procurement cycles for supplied parts and components,
- delayed order release due to unrealistic release dates,
- failures to meet deadlines of special constructions, for example due to unrealistic time allowances or unfavorable order priorities.

Figure 6 illustrates exemplary time and cost potentials. The processes 'design and construction', that are separated in the actual state, determine with a processing time of nine weeks the entire throughput time considerably. The processing time of these processes amounts to 58% of the entire throughput time. This leads to customer dissatisfaction as well as to substantial cost increases. The employment of an appliance construction set and the integration of these processes into the entire production process reduces the throughput time in this area by 50%. The higher investment costs for the construction set pay already off after ten completed production units. Further measures to optimize the process included for example:

- task integration of disposition and procurement

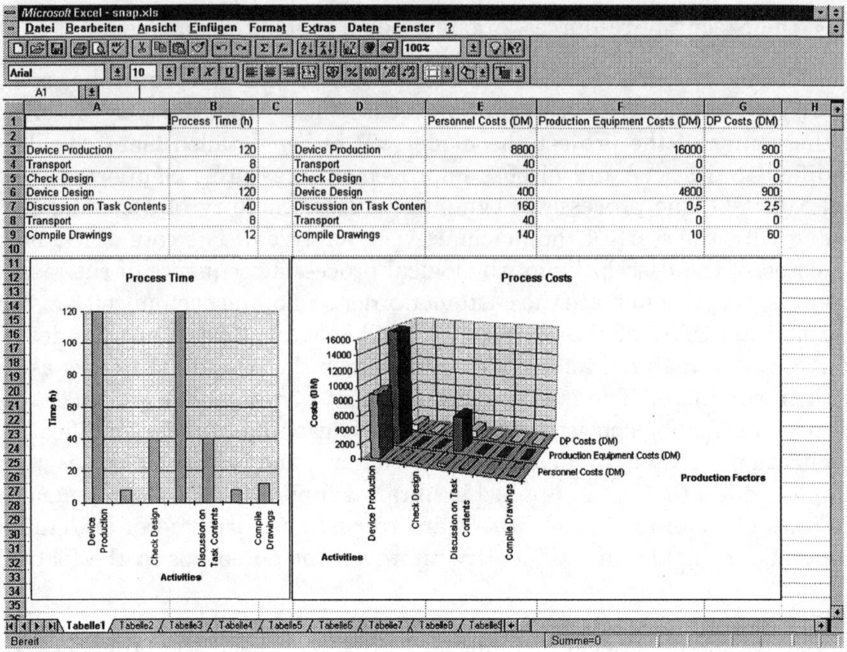

Figure 6: Time and cost evaluation

- development of an order control station with people responsible for product groups beginning with planning and ending with the delivery
- assignment of construction modification tasks to staff members of the respective development team
- the vague replacement times for parts and subassemblies in the PPC system were examined and updated
- orders are released immediately without considering procurement times and release dates.

The measures were documented in a target model and were discussed in the relevant departments with the people concerned. Along the way the tool MO^{2}GO enabled us to create graphic and text-based documents as basis for the discussion. The documents contain structured directories of all modeled business processes and corporate objects. To develop the target model

- redundant and unnecessary processes were eliminated
- needed tasks were summarized within the meaning of functional integration
- new resources were assigned if process responsibilities changed

- processes were concatenated and parallelized with regard to customer orientation.

These measures effected a considerable reduction of throughput times (by ca. 33%) and costs; departmental egotisms were reduced and the orientation of staff members towards the use for the customer was intensified. Furthermore, the QM documents that are necessary for certification were automatically generated from the process models. The quality assurance system is now in the certification phase.

4 Conclusion

The example clearly illustrates that restructuring measures of this scale and with these effects require a methodical approach as well as models. The application of such a tool guarantees the common understanding of the business processes in the company. It creates the prerequisite for assigning the use of design processes as precise improvements of costs, quality or time to the respective business processes and resources. It is therefore the basis for any information system planning process. Based on the model and with the tool support, the requirements specification of the information system support for the business processes can be generated automatically. The company succeeded in reducing the throughput times, improving the process quality, reducing costs and therefore in improving the customer satisfaction and competitiveness decisively.

References

[AEM93] Albrecht, R., Edeler, H., Mertins, K., Manufacturing Philosophy for the New European Factory, IFIP Conference, Athens, Advances in Production Management Systems, Elsevier Science Publishers B. V., North Holland, 1993

[AGP93] Anderl, R., Grabowski, H., Polly, A., Integriertes Produktmodell, Beuth Verlag Ltd., Berlin, Wien, Zürich, 1993

[BELPR91] Blaha, M., Eddy, F., Lorensen, W., Premerlani, W., Rumbaugh, J., Object-Oriented Modeling and Design, New York, 1991

[CH94] Champy, J., Hammer, M., Business Reengineering, Campus Verlag, Frankfurt, New York, 1994

[GHJM95] Gembrys, S., Hermann, J., Jochem, R., Mertins, K., Modellbasierte Erstellung eines Qualitätsmanagement-Handbuches, in: ZwF 90 (1995) 11, Carl Hanser Verlag, München, 1995, 540-543

[JJM94] Jäkel, F.-W., Jochem, R., Mertins, K., Reengineering und Optimierung von Geschäftsprozessen, in: ZwF 89 (1994) 10, Carl Hanser Verlag, München, 1994, 479-481

[JM93] Jochem, R., Mertins, K., Enterprise Modelling: Base for Information System Planning, IFIP Transaction, Elsevier Science Publishers B. V. Amsterdam, London, New York, Tokyo, 1993, 67-76

[JMS92] Jochem, R., Mertins, K., Süssenguth, W., An Object Oriented Method for Integrated Enterprise Modelling as a Basis for Enterprise Coordination, in: C. J. Petrie Jr. (ed.), Enterprise Integration Modelling. Proceedings of the First International Conference, MIT Press, Cambridge, Massachusetts, 1992, 249-258

[JMS96] Jochem, R., Mertins, K., Spur, G., Integrated Enterprise Modelling, Beuth Verlag Ltd., Berlin, Wien, Zürich, 1996

[War92] Warnecke, H.-J., Die Fraktale Fabrik. Revolution der Unternehmenskultur, Springer-Verlag, Berlin, 1992

CHAPTER 27

IBM VisualAge

Alois Hofinger

The following contribution describes the IBM VisualAge product family for object oriented application development. The different offerings constitute an application development environment for object oriented languages like C++, Smalltalk and Java. VisualAge for Smalltalk will be used as an example to describe some of the features of VisualAge in more detail.

1 Visual Programming

Visual programming tools have started to emerge in the market in response to two major requirements:

1. Facilitate the building of advanced user interfaces.
2. Lower the programming skill necessary to assemble and customize applications.

These tools make intensive use of metaphors and icons for computing. Metaphor in computing relates to the usage of visual respresentations that, for implicit comparison or analogy, give the user an immediate understanding of the entity, function, object, or computer processing. The term icon is used to refer to a pictorial representation of an object or a selection choice. Icons can represent objects that users want to work on or actions that users want to perform. A visual programming tool can be defined as a tool that provides users with a means to interactively specifiy programs in a highly graphical fashion. For example, routines, programs, and data have graphical representations, such as metaphors and icons. Relationships among these components are depicted graphically as well. The construction of programs is done graphically; that is, the programmer "writes" programs by manipulating and articulating graphical representations of components in an application (see Figure 1).

Visual programming tools differ significantly from those tools that provide program visualization, in which case programs are still written with traditional techniques and the tool is able to show a graphical view of them. Program visualization tools use graphics only to illustrate either some aspects of a program or its execution. These kinds of tools are commonly used for debugging and teaching.

Visual programming lets individuals take advantage of a larger spectrum of the capacities of the human brain than the one-dimensional textual form of traditional programming. The visual representation of problems is considered closer to people's mental representations of problems. In addition to the graphical construction, visual programming tools usually provide scripts, as a way to describe those functions that cannot be expressed graphically. Scripts often are declared in fourth generation languages, and they come in different varieties. Some of these tools use proprietary languages, while others make use of, or are derived from, standard languages available in the market.

A sample script may look like the following:

```
currentPerson: aAAPerson
"Save the value of current person."
aAAPerson notNil ifTrue: [currentIndex: =
        people indexOf: aAAPerson].
signalEvent: ('current person' asSymbol).
```

This small sample coding is quite straightforward: if the object aAAPerson is not Nil, it is used as an index to position into the people variable. The result is assigned to the variable current Index. The fact that the current person is now different is signaled in the last expression that uses the current person changed event symbol.

Almost all the visual programming tools available in the market offer an object-oriented interface to the user: programs, data, and routines are objects that the user selects and connects. However, not all the tools are based on object-oriented technology and not all of them integrate with an application development platform.

Visual programming tools acquire an even more interesting flavor when they, like *VisualAge* [IBM1], are based on object-oriented technology and integrate with an object-oriented development environment. In this case, the tools provide a comprehensive and consistent approach to application development, in which everything (user interface, business and computing entitites) at every stage is an object, thus avoiding the need to map from the conceptual view of problems to procedural representations.

For example, if we have to implement an invoice and its function using a traditional approach, we have to describe it, with a semantic gap between the conceptual view of the invoice and the procedural way it is enabled by the traditional language. With visual programming tools this gap is eliminated, because the enabling procedures are embedded within the conceptual view.

Several of the visual programming tools available today mainly address end users and focus only on helping them build graphical user interfaces. Often they provide database access for building an interface to a query result. Sometimes they help integrate local applications. Furthermore, the typical development environment addresses single programmers. It is clear from these observations that tools of this kind could hardly be used to implement complete applications that include business logic in a client/server environment.

So the requirement is for client/server programming tools that let you quickly write client/server applications with advanced graphical user interfaces. They also must allow the building of complete, industrial-strength line of business (LOB) applications.

Such a tool meets the requirements for rapidly building user interfaces, customization and assembly of applications without the need of professional programming skills. It also provides a professional-level application development environment with the ability to integrate business logic and client/server kinds of applications and integrated support for team programming.

Characteristics of such a tool may include:

- Visual programming for the construction of the user interface and the assembly of the application.
- Fourth generation scripting language.
- Support for implementing local business logic.
- Support for connecting to databases, preferably from multiple vendors.
- Support for the complete spectrum of client/server application models, using multiple communication protocols.
- Team programming.
- Rapid application development by prototyping.
- Configuration management.
- Packaging.

2 Construction from Parts

Construction from parts is an application development paradigm in which the applications are assembled from reusable and existing software components (parts).

A *part* is a software object that has a number of external features that allow it to be connected to other parts in order to implement application

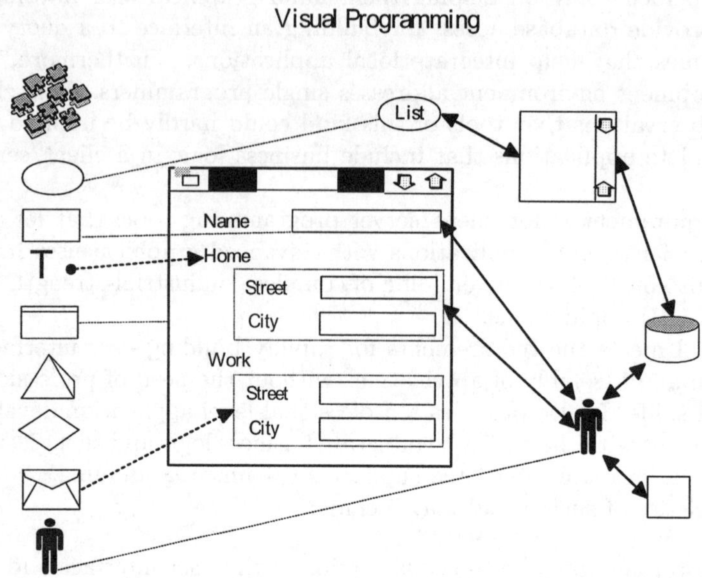

Figure 1: Visual Programming

scenarios. A part is not just an elementary component; it can be composed of multiple interacting subparts. This is refered to as a *composite part*.

The process of building the application consists of:

- Selecting predefined parts that are necessary.
- Using them unmodified or tailoring them for specific requirements.
- Establishing the connections among parts to create the application or a new part.

The process could be performed by writing code; however, visual programming tools are much more suitable for supporting the phases of the construction.

Even though these concepts are rather new to software development, they are not new to the industry and are commonly used in manufacturing. One can draw an analogy between the construction of a personal computer and the construction of an application. For instance, parts correspond to chips, composite parts to cards and the application to the complete personal computer.

To build a new personal computer, who would ever design and construct every singly component from scratch? Who would do so in software to build a new application? Typically, only a few standard subroutines and system services are likely to be reused. Most of the application is developed from scratch and most of the effort is expended in re-writing code that already exists somewhere, often within the same company.

The benefits of the construction from parts paradigm include:

- Reduction of application development costs
  The assembly and the tailoring of parts does not require a professional programmer. Programming will be done by exceptions and the skill of professional programmers can be applied to build innovative components when necessary.

- Enhanced application quality
  The reuse of existing parts reduces the chance of errors. Within a short time, parts will become more and more solid, and almost error free. Based on the obvious idea that if we do not write new code, then we do not introduce new errors, we can conclude that the less new code we have to write for a new application, the fewer errors we will encounter.

- Reduced cycle time with faster and better response to end users' needs
  The rapid development of applications made possible by visual programming tools and existing parts is invaluable to quickly verify user requirements and deliver applications in a short time.

The success of the paradigm in software development depends on various factors. First, interactive tools for visual constructions must be available. The tools must integrate with the development platform to design and build parts and frameworks. Second, interfaces and messaging protocols must be specified and supported by an architecture for interoperability of tools and component parts. Finally, a set of standard parts must be available and the software providers must move towards the building of components.

In VisualAge a *part* is a class with a well-defined public interface, which supports a simple and architected messaging protocol. We use the term subpart to refer to a part taken from the palette and used to build a composite part.

Parts can be very simple or highly sophisticated to provide a wide range of functions. Parts, for instance, can be as simple as a text-entry field or a default window. Often, parts are composed of multiple interacting subparts. Parts can also represent (wrap) programs written in COBOL or C language, thus allowing the reuse of existing code in a construction from parts paradigm.

The public interface of parts refers to the features that are used to connect parts among them. To specify the public interface of parts, the VisualAge introduces three clearly defined features:

1. **Attributes:** Attributes are the logical properties of parts. They are objects that the part can return or set upon request.

2. **Actions:** Actions are the behaviors of the parts, which means the services or operations the part may be requested to perform.

3. **Events:** Events provide a notification mechanism. They are used to signal that something has happened to the part.

Parts can be grouped into two major types: visual parts and nonvisual parts. The major difference between them is the capability of visual parts to present a graphical "view" to the end user at run time.

Visual parts: Have a run-time view, such as a list box, a window, a view of an address or person, and so on.

Nonvisual parts: Usually do not have a run-time view. Examples are business logic objects, such as an address or a person.

There are parts that constitute the basic units from which the other parts are constructed. We call these parts *primitive parts*. Examples are the basic visual parts, such as the text-entry field, the default windows, the push button, etc. When a new primitive part is required, it has to be fabricated using a programming language, and its part interface defined.

In VisualAge a collection of parts that can be managed as a whole is refered to as an *application*. Such an application can be packaged to produce the run-time application that will be distributed to end users.

3 Visual Tools

The VisualAge product family provides three editors that are available within the visual tools. They provide editing facilities to perform the three different steps described previously in construction from parts:

1. Part Composition Editor, used to edit a part built with the Visual Tool.

2. Part Interface Editor, used to edit the interface of parts.

3. Script Editor, used to edit scripts, that are fragments of textual code.

When you edit a part that was built and composed with the visual tools, VisualAge recognizes it and opens on the Composition Editor. If needed, interface and script editors can then be activated with a simple selection. If you edit a part not built with the Composition Editor, such as a primitive part, the visual tools open on the Public Interface Editor. In this case, only the script editor can be selected.

An important advantage is that application builder is also able to handle parts that are not built with application builder itself, and lets you use them to compose your new parts. In fact, any class can be used as a part, after defining its public interface.

A member of the VisualAge product family is VisualAge for Smalltalk [IBM2], which provides a pure object-oriented language. IBM Smalltalk can be used to enhance and extend the applications that are generated through visual programming.

VisualAge is a development environment that provides everything you need to build the client portion of client/server applications in a pure object-oriented development environment:

Visual Tools: VisualAge provides a visual programming tool that allows you to create complete applications non-linearly using construction from parts.

Library of parts: Already-constructed parts that are delivered include support for graphical user interfaces and generic parts for database queries, transactions, remote and local functions.

Graphical User Interface support: The GUI support included in the library of parts enables the development of applications according to the Common User Access (CUA) specifications.

Multimedia exploitation: Multimedia is the construction of animation, sound, video, and other media into interactive computer applications. Multimedia for VisualAge is an addition to the VisualAge development environment, to help developers build applications that will take advantage of this technology.

Client/server and communication support: VisualAge provides comprehensive support for client/server computing that is made possible over multiple protocols and programming interfaces, such as:

- APPC (Advanced Program to Program Communications)
- TCP/IP (Transmission Control Protocol/Internet Protocol)
- NetBIOS (Network Basic Input Output Services)
- ECI (CICS External Call Interface)
- EHLLAPI (Emulator High-Level Language Application Programming Interface)

Relational database support: VisualAge framework includes support for local relational database support and queries. Remote databases can also be accessed transparently through this function. This support is used by VisualAge to provide visual programming parts that enable generic queries.

Enhanced DLL (Dynamic Link Library) support: This feature automates the definitions that are needed to interface a local C or COBOL

DLL by building the necessary objects and behaviors for you. This feature is used by VisualAge to provide the generic DLL visual programming part. The DLL enhancements also provide full multithreading support.

Records to objects mapping: Whenever information must be exchanged between an object-oriented application and an application written with a traditional language, flat record structures must be mapped to objects and vice versa. VisualAge provides a tool that simplifies the buidling of the objects that can provide the mapping.

Team programming: VisualAge provides advanced and comprehensive support for team programming with a central library of parts and classes in a networked development environment.

Configuration management: Besides team programming, VisualAge provides support for version and release control with verification of prerequisites.

VisualAge for Smalltalk enables a user to access a broad range of databases created by IBM and other major database vendors.

- Native DB/2 Support
  This includes support for DB2/2 and via the Distributed Database Connection Services/2 (DDCS/2) access to host databases.
- Access to ORACLE
  This feature provides native access to specific ORACLE functions.
- ODBC Support
  The VisualAge Open Database Connectivity (ODBC) allows the creation of applications, that connect to various data sources. ODBC permits maximum interoperability: a single application can access many different database management systems. This enables an ODBC developer to develop, compile, and ship an application without targeting a specific type of data source. Users can then add the database drivers, which link the application to the database management systems of their choice.

4 Communications/Transactions

The VisualAge for Smalltalk, Communications/Transactions for OS/2, for AIX, and for Windows, enables you to access remote applications across platforms. Its capabilities enable you to:

- Establish communications with remote program logic using visual connections

- Visually define your own network connections
- Provide support for multiple protocols
- Extend your communications design to support protocols other than those available or supported by VisualAge
- Build workstation-based graphical user interfaces (GUIs) that access host applications designed for 3270 terminals.

VisualAge's Communications subsystem supports the following application programming interfaces:

- APPC
- CICS
- CPI-C
- EHLLAPI
- MQSeries
- NetBIOS
- RPC
- TCP/IP

Technically, the communications subsystem is divided into three layers to provide the needed flexibility to implement applications that use network -protocol-independent interfaces for application programs.

The dialog layer provides application programmers with a network-protocol-independent API to communications. A dialog is an implementation of a particular pattern of exchange of messages between two programs.

The system layer provides a complete object-oriented interface to the underlying network subsystem. This interface is designed for application programmers with special needs that cannot be met by existing dialog styles and for implementers of new dialog styles. The system layer handles some of the work necessary to access a network interface and provides a more natural object-oriented view of the concepts of the network protocol.

The system interface layer is the lowest level of interface to an external system such as a networking subsystem. It is composed of the basic Dynamic Link Library (DLL) entry point declaration along with any record types and constants the DLL may require.

The Emulator High-Level Language Application Programming Interface (EHLLAPI) is an interface provided by a terminal emulator that allows a program to behave as an operator sitting at a terminal. You can use VisualAge to build a workstation-based GUI interface that can access host applications designed for 3270 terminals. Rather than requiring users to enter data in a 3270 terminal emulator session, a VisualAge application can interact directly with the host application. EHLLAPI functions are effective for interfacing with business-critical applications, automating repetitive tasks, and performing low-volume transactions.

5 Object Distribution

Object distribution is normally accomplished using one of the Object Request Brokers (ORB's) which are available in the marketplace. In the VisualAge product family VisualAge for Smalltalk as an alternative, offers its own object distribution mechanism. This allows you to easily develop distributed applications with true local/remote transparency across your system environment. You can quickly develop applications that span networks, without having to learn the details of network communications, distributed application programming, or specialized interfaces. The familiar Smalltalk tools such as browers, inspectors, debuggers and workspaces are available in a distributed environment.

Using distributed technology, VisualAge allows you to optimize applications by appropriately partitioning logic across client and server platforms. Distributed objects help developers deal with the complexitiy of heterogenous two and three tier client/server architectures. Letting function and data be freely distributed within a system based on developer decisions enables a high degree of scalability and robustness. Wrappering existing systems behind distributed objects supports an evolution to objects. Developers can reuse existing code stored in major databases on PCs, midrange, LAN, UNIX, and mainframes. They can develop or reuse Online Transaction Process in client/server applications that interface with CICS and IMS.

Distributed objects can send standard Smalltalk messages to one another, regardless of their physical location. They can also freely send other Smalltalk objects as arguments, and receive objects as results. The different parts of an application can be located on any computer in the network that is running with the distributed feature. In addition, you can concurrently execute multiple client requests within a single Smalltalk image.

Using the distributed feature, you can split your applications many ways, to support both client/server and true peer-to-peer design, and dynamically change the distribution throughout the development cycle. You can quickly build portable applications which make the best use of your existing resources. In this way, you can "right-size" your systems to achieve the best use of your existing resources to achieve your business performance, scalability, security, and maintainability objectives.

The distributed feature includes:

- Tools to design, build, debug, optimize and configure distributed applications from a single development environment

- Support for running concurrent client requests in a single image
- Use of industry-standard Generic Security Service API (GSS-API) and currently supports the IBM NetSP Secured Logon Coordinator (SLC) program. Used with NetSP SLC, it provides transparent support for client authentication, message verification, and message encryption.

The distributed object space environment provides:

Messaging: Communication logic is provided, down to the low-level task of passing Smalltalk objects across network.

Distributed garbage collection: Unused memory is freed when it is no longer in use by other local or remote objects.

Activation support: Any remote Smalltalk image can be started as required by the application.

Name server support: You can update object location information without having to change your Smalltalk code.

6 Legacy Integration

A legacy application is an application which exists and actively supports a business in some capacity. Even as legacy applications have become very inflexible over time, they are here to stay. One proven way to deal with legacy systems in an object oriented application environment is the encapsulation of these legacy systems into business objects. Business Objects are application independent, persistent and focus on business rather than on programming. They are abstractions of real-world business concepts, such as product, consumer, vendor, shipment or employee. VisualAge for Smalltalk ships with a feature (CICS/IMS Connection), that allows the integration of existing MVS IMS- or CICS Transactions into object oriented client/server application development without a need for rewrite or restructuring. The existing transactions are "wrapped" into business objects. Business objects developed with the CICS/IMS Connection feature are clearly shielded from any knowledge about the underlying transactions; all the handling of the transactions is done by lower level objects, called the transaction objects. Thus these business objects are protected from changes to the transactions and are also easily adaptable to new requirements , e.g. database access rather than transaction usage. The VisualAge for Smalltalk based CICS/IMS Connection consists of a framework of classes and fully supports the visual programming paradigm. It handles the mapping and navigation problem and is extendible to support communication protocols other than APPC and LU2.

7 Two-Tier or Three-Tier Architecture

In Client/Server computing the basic logical structure of an application consists of presentation and user interaction, processing and access to data. By distributing these components over clients and servers we will get a two-tier model or a three-tier model.

In a two-tier model a client handles user presentation and interaction, as well as the execution of the business logic, while one or more servers take responsibility for data access.

This model has been implemented in most client/server projects in the past and has typically required powerful client stations, also refered to as a fat client.

Even as a two-tier model offers certain advantages, like simple implementation and easy development, it does have some serious disadvantages. Besides the already mentioned resource requirements this architecture is not very flexible. In many cases, evolution of the implemented architecture, whether application or system-related, implies workstation updates and requires extensive administration work. Changes on the client stations have to be validated, and tests have to be performed to determine whether the changes function in the current hardware and software configuration.

These disadvantages lead to a requirement for a three-tier architecture, where a client is responsible for the presentation, the interaction with the user and some limited processing, which do not necessarily have to be executed on servers. One or more servers take care of the logical processes and the third tier constitute one or more data servers.

Business objects would typically be located on the middle-tier of a three-tier or multi-tier architecture, resulting in a lighter (thin) client, since processing code is resident on the servers and a decreased, or completely eliminated technological dependency between clients and servers, increasing the range of choice in terms of operation system and hardware and increasing evolution capacity. Another good example of a three-tier model is the Internet model, where a Web browser resides on the client stations, while data processing and data access is occurring on multiple servers.

8 IBM VisualAge for Java

The latest addition to the IBM VisualAge family constitutes VisualAge for Java [IBM3]. It extends the reach of applications that run in an enterprise today to the web, without writing web applications from scratch.

IBM VisualAge for Java is a powerful suite of application development tools, which builds complete Java-compatible applications, applets and JavaBean components, using the VisualAge Construction from Parts programming paradigm.

Java, a new programming language introduced by Sun Microsystems, is used to create executable microprograms known as applets. A Java applet is delivered over the Internet to a user's Java-enabled browser, where it then runs locally. JavaBeans, by contrast, is the component model for Java. It defines Java components, and how they fit together. By definition, a bean is a reusable software component that can be visually manipulated in builder tools.

VisualAge for Java simplifies the Java development process in four major ways:

1. Simplifies client/server programming in Java through generation of middleware code that connects the Java client to existing transaction, data and application servers.

2. Provides an intelligent development environment that allows the enterprise to build scaleable 100 % pure Java solutions that run on any Virtual Machine or inside any Java enabled Browser.

3. Provides a fully integrated repository-based team environment that allows management of the development process on Java projects.

4. Provides an advanced project-based-development environment which allows programmers to create Java applications/applets or JavaBean components using the Construction from parts programming paradigm.

The Enterprise Access Builder within VisualAge for Java generates components that establish fast connections between the Java client and CICS Transactions Servers, Application Servers and Data Servers. This allows programmers to focus on application logic instead of low level comunications code. VisualAge for Java generates JavaBean components that connect Java Clients to the following server applications:

- CICS Transactions via External Call Interface (ECI)
- Java Servers via Remote Method Invocation (RMI)
- C/C++ Servers via Native Method Call (J2C++ & RMI)
- Relational Databases via JDBC (DB2, Sybase, Oracle)

VisualAge for Java enables enterprises to build more scaleable client/server applications in Java. The components generated by the Enterprise Access Builder allow Enterprise Transaction, Data and Application servers to connect to a thin Java client using faster middleware than current HTTP solutions on the market. The ability to generate Remote Method Invocation and CICS External Call Interface to connect the client and the server, enables data and transaction flow rates that cannot be matched by CGI scripts and single HTTP servers.

VisualAge for Java seamlessly integrates a repository- based team development environment. This repository allows multiple developers to work on a project at any given time while reducing the number of source code collisions that arise when two developers are working on the same source code. As Java development projects scale in size, VisualAge for Java assists in project management by keeping both the client and server aspects of a Java project synchronized.

VisualAge for Java also provides the Visual Builder, which allows the programmer to assemble Java Applets, Java Applications and JavaBeans from pre-selected parts on the visual builder palette. Programmers can drag Java Abstract Windowing Tool Kit (AWT) controls from the palette and visually drop them on the canvas to generate user interface Java code. The programmer then connects the user interface to the business logic JavaBean components generated by the Enterprise Access Builder using the construction from parts programming paradigm.

While in the debug or test phase of a program, programmers often want to add a class, add a method or change a method. VisualAge for Java allow s you to modify the code while in the debug phase. The modified code is compiled and inserted into the application, without the need to exit the debugger and perform a complete compile. This allows programmers to focus on the program logic, without dropping back and waiting for a compile.

References

[IBM1] IBM VisualAge: Concepts and Features, GG24-3946-00, 1994

[IBM2] http://www.software.ibm.com/ad/smalltalk/

[IBM3] http://www.software.ibm.com/ad/vajava/

[IBM4] http://www.software.ibm.com/ad/

PART FOUR

Reference Models

The creation of information systems models is a tedious task, which involves expertise and experience, and therefore expenditure. Modelling started from scratch rarely produces high quality models, at least if the model is of appreciable size. It is therefore necessary for the end user, who wishes to produce a model (for various uses in the life-cycle of the information system), from one or another aspect of the enterprise's information system, to be able to use or re-use models, or parts of models, which have been previously developed and tested. An information system reference model is such a typical, or paradigmatic model, which describes the information system or a well identified part of it. Reference models may be produced on various levels of *genericity* - they can be relevant to any industry, business area or a typical company which belongs to a type of industry.

Reference models can also be produced on various levels of *abstraction*, and so it is possible to talk about policy level reference models (such as the ISO 9000 series of standards), requirements level reference models (this is the most prevalent type of models), and also design level reference models (often found in industry specific standards).

Reference models also enable the information system developer to build implementation models at a lower cost and time than building them from scratch, and also facilitate the development of a marketplace of building blocks, defining products and services typically utilised in information systems. Reference models thus facilitate the classification, evaluation and comparability of models by creating a standard terminology.

The reference model is a tool for an user-oriented configuration of a data processing system or, strictly speaking, for the formal description of a product modelling system. According to the model view, or aspect used, reference models may propose a typical functional model (irrespective of how the functions are implemented in products), a typical structural model (of software, hardware and human resources), a typical data model, etc.

Reference models, if presented as exemplary overall solutions, are not meant to be reused without any change because no enterprise resembles the other exactly. For this reason it has to be possible to subdivide the model into parts which may be individually utilised. The idea can be compared with construction in mechanical engineering: The "whole" consists of components which consist of individual construction elements. E.g. in the area of product modelling when a model of a new product has to be developed which product partly resembles an existing one, whole groups of model components can be reused. If the new product/model does not resemble an existing one, only the "atomic" components (individual construction elements) can be reused, e.g. such low level prefabricated model components of material flow elements can be found in a standard simulator environment. The more complete the catalogue of reference models and the more systematically it is structured the more the construction of a new overall model will be efficient. As a constructor one can use a catalogue of construction elements and components, and if looking for a technical solution for a part-function of the "whole" the model-builder can use a selection of reference models. These offer possible part-models (e.g. running models of different sorter techniques or models of different planning strategies) which can be combined into alternative overall solutions.

This part presents reference models of a great variety. Each of these fit the characterisation of reference model, but as alluded to above, they differ in a number of aspects, such as genericity, level of abstraction, aspect of modelling, and coverage (the whole or part of the information system).

IBM has developed an "Insurance Application Architecture (IAA)" as a reference model for the development of application solutions for the insurance industry. IAA is described in Chapter 28. It works as a reference model for the typical business structures found in insurance companies worldwide.

A similar understanding of reference models is given in Chapter 29 presenting the FhG-Simprolog simulation reference models. Different reference models for various simulation application fields within production and logistics are described together with their typical elements and structures. These models are built on the experience from multiple simulation studies. In addition, ready-to-run simulation building blocks and sample applications to demonstrate aggregation and adoption of the provided constructs to a specific application are given.

Chapter 30 describes a different approach. The reference model describes the business processes which a specific software system (SAP R/3) supports. This reference can be used to compare them to the business processes actually used in an enterprise, before introducing the software. Adaptions have to be made by parametrization of the software. The mechanisms of the event-driven process chain model ensure, that it is possible to make only such selection decisions which are technically feasible in the R/3 system.

The reference model for the German Savings Banks Organization is presented in Chapter 31. It is different from the models mentioned above, as it describes the *data entities* and their relations in high detail and clear structure, but the model does not refer to the processes. This data model, based on the IBM Financial Services Data Model, provides a common terminology and high level data structure without enforcing a particular implementation.

As a joint effort of the international standards bodies ISO and ITU-T (the former CCITT), a generic architecture for the standardization of open distributed processing (ODP) was set up as a meta-model to be used as a common architecture for different concrete models. In Chapter 32, there is a description of ODP and the Object Management Architecture (OMA) developed by the Object Management Group (OMG). The OMA is a framework for a set of standards to support open object-oriented computing in heterogenuous distributed environments. The most well known standard within the OMA, that found a high number of implementations, is the specification of the Common Object Request Broker Architecture (CORBA).

Kai Mertins, Peter Bernus

CHAPTER 28

IAA
The IBM Insurance Application Architecture

Norbert Dick, Jürgen Huschens

The IBM Insurance Application Architecture (IAA) provides an architectural framework for the development of application solutions for the insurance industry. It is based on a general Insurance Business Architecture developed to provide common structures capable of representing the various, different business requirements occurring in the worldwide insurance companies. We will focus on the concepts, the contents and the positioning of the models representing this IAA Insurance Business Architecture. That way the motivation for a Business Architecture as a prerequisite for insurance specific business software components should become evident.

1 Introduction

The insurance industry naturally is very closely related to information processing, since their production process is dealing with an immaterial good, security, that requires information in order to be established. Therefore many application systems in the insurance companies have their origins in the early days of computing and have to be rebuilt in order to follow the current changes in the insurance markets. The challenge often is a fundamental change in the emphasis of the application systems from coexisting, line-of-business-oriented transaction systems to integrated enterprise-wide, information-oriented systems. Moreover, new techniques and technologies (such as workflow management, object technology, Internet) seem to be candidates to realize new business opportunities and to increase competitiveness.

This results in a pressure for a new generation of application systems for the insurance industry. Although there are many offerings for insurance-specific software packages available, insurance companies have difficulties in finding insurance software packages that suite their business needs, but also fit into their interconnected application system environment. The insurance industry express their need for a "mix-and-match"-software market, allowing them to (see e.g. [Wal93, VAA97])

1. buy application software for areas with low competitive relevance
2. share and adopt application systems developed in joint efforts amongst insurance companies or with software vendors
3. have the possibility for in-house developments in areas where either the relevance for competition is high or the necessity of differentiation from the rest of the market is required.

Clearly, such a component-based software market requires open standards for all involved technical dimensions. But experiences in analyzing software package offerings and in-house experiences regarding enterprise modeling led some insurance companies to the conclusion that first of all a general Business Architecture for the insurance industry is needed as a basic structure to ensure that the business requirements and contents can be addressed. This need for a general Insurance Business Architecture articulated by a group of insurance companies to IBM was the beginning of the Insurance Application Architecture (IAA) project by IBM in 1990.

In this paper we intend to discuss the concepts, the contents and the positioning of the IAA Business Architecture. We intentionally exclude the discussion of IAA-based application system models and application software, i.e. the technical and software-infrastructural dimensions of an application architecture, in order to keep a clean focus on the approach of an Insurance Business Architecture.

It will turn out that a Business Architecture can only work out the general structures needed to represent the business requirements, but will not give the business requirements itself. Therefore the IAA Business Architecture is not at the same level as semantically detailed reference models (like for example the SAP-Reference models or project models carrying the business requirements of the project). Only after the step of filling the business requirements into the Business Architecture, the resulting models will be at the same level as usual reference models. By differentiating between the business requirements, which will always be subject to changes introduced by products, organizational decisions, market movements or the business focus of an organization, and their underlying stable structures, i.e. the Business Architecture, it is intended to identify the stable patterns as the basis for development efforts.

This need for differentiating the structures from the requirements populating the structure is crucial to allow various different business views on the same topic as can easily be studied in the field of Party Management Systems of various insurance companies [Hus95]. Recent efforts of the German Association of Insurance Companies (GDV) in establishing business models for specific application areas suffer from neglecting this difference [VAA97, Dic96].

Also in the first efforts of the Object Management Group to standardize Business Objects (also for the insurance industry [OMG96]), there is yet no indication of facing this difference, although the object-oriented modeling approach provides genuine means to address this topic.

2 Overview of the Architecture

The IBM IAA Insurance Business Architecture [IBM95] consists of the following components:

- IAA Data Model
- IAA Function Model
- IAA Function Flow Model
- IAA Business Modeling (IAA Meta Model)
- IAA Business Terms.

This basic structure of the Business Architecture has remained unchanged throughout the publications of the three editions of IAA: Edition 1 in 1992 [IBM92], Edition 2 in 1993 [IBM93] and the Edition 3 in 1995 [IBM95].

While the names of the first four components should give good indication of its contents (discussed later in this contribution), the notion of IAA Business Terms needs some remarks. The "IAA Business Terms" represent a collection of terms used in the insurance business language. These terms are uniquely defined by associating the parts in the IAA Insurance Business Architecture representing the content of the term to the name of the term. This provides a means of a precise definition of insurance business terms without having the fussiness of purely verbal definitions accompanied by examples.

In this way the well-known problem of homonymic and synonym usage of Business Terms occurring inside one insurance company, but also across the whole industry, can be addressed. This provides the chance of establishing a common terminology of Insurance Business Terms, a necessary step for establishing progress in many areas (compare e.g. [IEEE94]). This leads to the remark that the development of an Insurance Business Architecture would have been the natural task of the academic disciplines treating the economy and the business administration of the insurance industry. But since there was no such effort in the academic area (maybe due to a lack of familiarity with modeling techniques in the economic sciences), there was the challenge of establishing an Insurance Business Architecture that should be capable of representing the business requirements of any insurance company, regardless of its market focus (e.g. Health insurance, Car insurance, Reinsurance, etc.) or its geographical market (e.g. US, Japan, Germany). How was this work being done? IBM certainly has never been an insurance

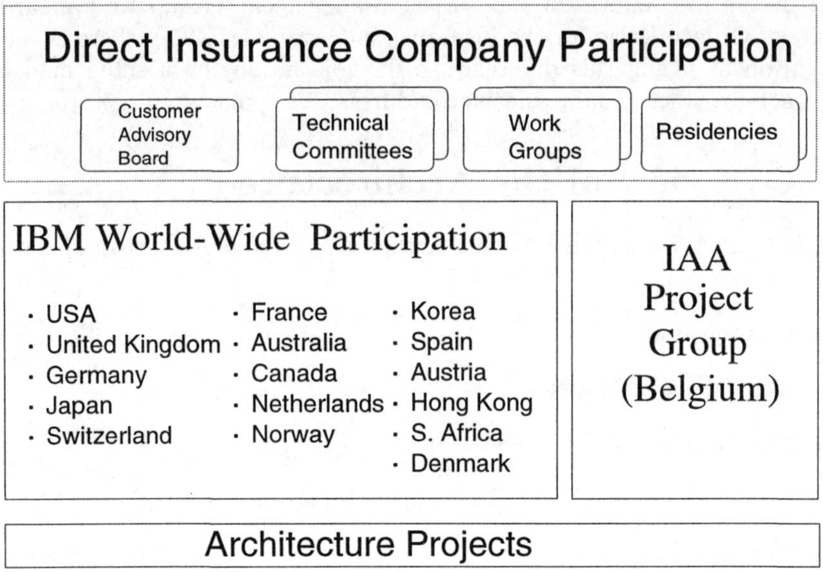

Figure 1: IAA Development

company. Therefore the development of IAA was a joint effort of insurance companies (coming from Europe, the US. and Asia) expressing the need for a common Insurance Business Architecture (compare Section 1) and IBM. IBM provided the project organization, the methodological consultancy and the financial resources for the IAA project, while the actively participating insurance companies (in total about 30 over the project time) drove the development process by sending their business analysts and their business organization specialists into development teams and guided the project plans of IAA.

The development team has been located in La Hulpe, close to Brussels in Belgium. The development was based on "residencies". In such a residency one certain business topic, like Product development, Claims, Life Insurance, Health Insurance, Re-Insurance, was addressed by a project group consisting of the business representatives of the insurance companies (out of the various regions) and IBM. In each residency, the business essence of the chosen topic was discussed and described. In a second phase this input was transformed into model structures (Data-, Function-, Function Flow-models) and consolidated with the structures of the total model. The results have been verified by the insurance business participants. By this iterative process, the scope of the models have been enriched and the final models arose. After the publication of Edition 1 in 1992, also the experiences gained in IAA-based application development projects at specific insurance companies have been fed back into the models.

The step from IAA Edition 1 to Edition 2 was characterized by a general enlargement of the scope and contents, but also by the reworking of the Function Model results in Edition 1, since project use revealed that the Edition 1-Functions really had the qualities of processes. The lesson learned was that a standardization of functional content leads to very fine grid functionality. The step from Edition 2 to Edition 3 basically left the Data Model parts unchanged, except some extensions and minor corrections, but brought methodological enhancements in the Function Flow-area together with an excellent integration with the Data- and Function-Model dimensions.

Interestingly, initial attempts to establish the IAA Insurance Business Architecture by merging already existing models (either partial or enterprise models) of the participating insurance companies failed, since in these models, that have been well suited for their original purposes no distinction between the Business Architecture constructs and the constructs representing the business requirements could be found. This implied that the constructs representing the business requirements (which due to their nature could not be generally accepted) could also not be easily identified and removed. This experience meant that models incorporating also these business requirements could only be valuable in areas with very far reaching standardization of the requirements. This is often the case in an area where the requirements are posted by legal obligations, but diminishes in areas with competitive advantage and strategic interests. Indeed, the clear separation between a Business Architecture level and a level representing the specific business views originated in these experiences. Moreover, by confronting the models carrying the contents with the different cultures of the insurance markets, it was possible to understand, that an enterprise model developed in-house also carries the - maybe retrospective - view of the business that has been correct for that company and its market, but hardly has the chance to come down to the architectural structure, since it lacks the confrontation with different business views on the same topics.

With the publication of IAA Edition 3 in 1995, the IAA Insurance Business Architecture has reached a high level of stability and has proven itself in many application development projects. Since IBM has made an significant investment in IAA, it is treated as licensed material available after paying a license fee and protected as intellectual property of IBM. At the end of 1996 the insurance industry world-wide signed more than 80 IAA-license agreements, resulting in a significant market penetration, since many of these license agreements relate to big international insurance corporations covering a net of associated insurance companies.

In order to visualize the connection of the IAA Insurance Business Architecture to Application Development we want to refer to the "IAA Cube" in Figure 2.

The IAA Insurance Business Architecture is symbolized by the first portion of the cube. It has the three dimensions of Data-, Function-, and Func-

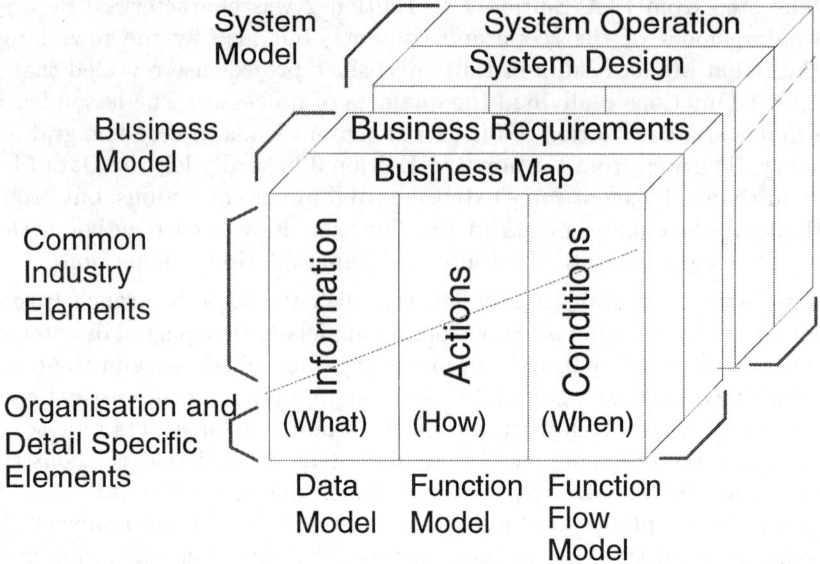

Figure 2: IAA Cube

tion Flow Model. A line indicates how far the standardization of the Architecture will reach in these three dimensions. The experience showed that the scope of standardization in terms of the data structures can be significant, while this deteriorates for the function and function flow dimensions. Before a transformation of the business contents (the first half of the cube) into the System Model for implementation can be done, the business requirements layer has to be completed by the particular insurance organization. This task of adding the specific business requirements of an organization to the IAA Insurance Business Architecture is the point, where the architecture is adopted to a specific company situation. In an IAA-based project all identified business requirements of an insurance company have to be mapped onto the architecture in order to achieve the business content of a model. This way different views on business requirements arising from differences in the business strategies can be represented in the frame of the Business Architecture populated by different "inputs" (compare Section 1).

The main characteristics of the System Model should be driven by the structure in the Business Architecture layer, so that the implementation decisions are mainly dependent on the architectural layer. This results in a degree of independence of the business requirements layer from the System Model layer allowing a "mix and match" on the business contents side of an application.

After the publication of IAA Edition 3 in 1995 the emphasis of the IAA Project was shifted from the IAA Insurance Business Architecture to the

IAA-System Model and to the development of IAA-based application software (see Section 5 for discussions on the Object-Oriented IAA path).

3 Constructs of the Architecture

Since the architecture should provide means to describe the general structures needed to represent the business requirements of specific organizations, it must be constructed accordingly.

3.1 Data Model Constructs

The IAA Insurance Business Architecture Data Model (in the following shortly: IAA Data Model) is built up using an extended Entity-Relationship data model and extensions to address Business Rules in form of data structures ("classification" construct).

Generally, the IAA Data Model represents a high level of abstraction (or generalization). We will give an example to illustrate the level of abstraction. In many insurance companies there is a need to capture the data representing the ownership of a car by a person. In semantic E/R-modelling this could be represented by defining the two entities PERSON and CAR together with the ownership relationship between these two entities (that may be represented by a Relationship Entity). It should be noted that in the following we denote PERSON as entity, not as entity type, since the type notion will be used in a different context. A specific person will be referenced as an occurrence or instance of PERSON, and not as an entity person.

A Data Model with the above level of abstraction corresponds to the semantic models produced within development projects or is used as a reference model. But the development work of IAA showed that a Data Model at this level of abstraction could not serve as an architectural approach because of the following reasons:

First of all, not every insurance company would be interested in these example entities, since they strongly correspond to the business requirements of an insurance organization dealing with car insurance. A health insurance company would have to ignore or even to eliminate the corresponding portion of the model. Moreover, any attempt to describe the insurance business comprehensively at this level of detail would result in extremely large data models that still will lack the possibility of supporting product innovations, since in many cases this will result in additional new data structures. A third observation is the fact, that the interest of the ownership of houses, ships, animals etc. carry related structure and different treatment of same structures has been a cause of difficulty with respect to maintenance effort.

Therefore in the IAA Data Model, an additional step of abstraction is made by recognizing the fact that persons are a certain kind of partners, cars are a certain kind of objects (here object is meant in its physical sense), and the ownership relationship is a certain kind of relationship between partners and objects. The resulting entities PARTY (for partners), OBJECT and PARTY-OBJECT RELATIONSHIP are contained in the model. So, in IAA the modeling content of representing the car ownership of persons will not be found explicitly in the Data Model, rather the general structure of this specific business requirement is provided.

In order to provide the possibility of incorporating the business requirements contents in the general structures, the TYPE-construct is used in IAA. Hence, in addition to the entity PARTY, an entity PARTY TYPE is found in IAA in order to represent the specific different kind of partners needed inside an organization. Therefore by choosing Person as an instance (or occurrence) of PARTY TYPE, Car as an instance of OBJECT TYPE, "is owner of " as an instance of ROLE TYPE accompanied by appropriate specifications, the semantic content of the business requirement "a person is owner of a car" can be represented in the structures provided by the IAA Data Model.

Since the type-instances should align to the rules of mutual exclusivity and completeness, the relation of this construct to the "CLASS"-idea in the object oriented world is evident. The TYPE-construct provides a means to enrich the data structures provided by IAA to incorporate the contents of the specific business requirements. An initiative to standardize the type hierarchies developments by different insurance companies working with IAA, clearly showed that different products and different business strategies resulted in different type settings. The other enrichments needed to represent business requirements in the IAA Data Model consist of the additions of attributes and specifications of relationships. Moreover, this way of modeling "meta-data" inside the data model, proved to be necessary in order to represent the content of insurance products via data structures. Consequently, the IAA Data Model has the quality of a meta-schema, whereas the IAA-based Data Model of a specific insurance company is an instance of the meta-schema.

There are three possibilities to represent business contents in the IAA Data Model. This set of possibilities reflects a very general pattern that corresponds to the way modeling is done. If we take the example of how to model a requirement of "being married", we observe that generally there are at least three possibilities of how to model a business requirement:

- Attribute (fact only view)
- Relationship (limited information scope)
- Type construct (full information scope).

The attribute "married" with the value domain "yes/no" or the attribute "family status" with the value domain "single, married, divorced, ..." correspond to the view that there is only an interest in the fact itself. There is no need for the knowledge of any detail, since this can not be represented in this attribute construct. Accordingly, if there is a business need to also know the spouse, the start date and some detail behind the marriage, a relationship construct like a Party-Party Relationship "is married with" with some attributes of this relationship may be the appropriate choice. The disadvantage of such a relationship construct is the fact that for the establishment of the relationship the second partner has to be known. But if there is significant interest in the details of a marriage, for example because of an insurance product covering the risk of a marriage or a product where a marriage allows for a claim of a benefit, neither of the two variants discussed so far suffice to cover the information related (e.g. to the legal marriage agreement, to the documents proving the marriage, costs for the wedding ceremony etc.). In such a case there is a need for a construct that carries the specifics of the information and allows to use parts of the data model to represent the whole picture of needed information.

In fact, project experience has shown that in different organizations different decisions have been made regarding the scope of information associated to the same notion. Moreover, sometimes different parts of the same organization express different needs! Therefore the business requirement consists of the "notion" and the scope of information associated to that notion. The scope of information is heavily influenced by business strategies and product involvements. This in turn translates to the fact that in semantically complete models decisions have been made on the scope of information that relates to the notion and that this scope must meet the business requirements in order to make the model acceptable.

In the IAA data model either of three possibilities can be represented, since one main achievement of the IAA Data Model is the fact that the basic structure provided is sufficiently rich in order to give suitable entity candidates for the third option without the need of enlarging the data model structure.

After this discussion it should have become evident why IAA intended to deliver an Insurance Business Architecture and why this corresponds to a high level of generalization. We will end the discussion of the data model with some remarks on the "classification" construct used in IAA. The systematic use of the constructs discussed also allowed to express the Business Rules, traditionally contained in program logic, in form of data structures. The IAA Data Model does not provide the collection of the business rules themselves, but it contains the structure that is needed to express these business rules in form of data structures and thereby it provides a way to organize the application systems around a "Product Management System" defined by data contents.

3.2 Function Model Constructs

On the evolution of IAA from Edition 1 to Edition 3, the Function Model has experienced pressure from a strong Data Model and a strong process orientation. As a result, the functionality identified is very fine grained, since early attempts to provide coarse-grid (but meaningful in a business sense) function definitions as an architectural content failed due to the fact that different insurance organizations showed different opinions on what is contained inside such "functionality". Therefore, in order to provide the structures and not decide on the contents, the elements contained in the Function Model consist of basic functions needed to build higher aggregations of functionality that can carry business meaning.

The IAA Function Model consists of

- Business Algorithms
  - Elementary Business Algorithms
  - Calculation Business Algorithms
  - Navigation Business Algorithms
- Elementary Business Functions.

While Elementary Business Functions basically serve for data manipulation, the Business Algorithms provide functionality for logical evaluations. While Elementary Business Algorithms provide the categorization of functions that perform simple logical evaluations (e.g. for obtaining data contents), the Calculation Business Algorithms are capable of performing nested operations. These Calculation Business Algorithms are allowed to contain calculation functionality and Elementary Business Algorithms. For data retrieval generally the Elementary Business Algorithms have to be used. Navigation Business Algorithms are the functionality to provide paths across the data model containing the logic how to navigate through the data structure in order to establish the logical data link needed.

Generally speaking, the categorization given in the IAA Function Model provides a separate data manipulation functionality together with functionality incorporating logical operations ranging from calculations to navigation information.

3.3 Function Flow Model Constructs

The Meta Model constructs of IAA show a strong, well-defined interconnection between the discussed dimensions of Data Model, Function Model and Function Flow Model (which is strongly related to the notion of a Work Flow model [WFCL96]). The IAA structures of Edition 3 satisfactorily cover the data dimension of Function Flows. This allows a strong integration and interaction between the data dimension of workflow and the original business data. The clear separation of the "meta-data" within the model provides the key for the possibility to rigorously define the data dimensions of Function Flows within the model. Moreover, IAA provides significant contributions to the description of flow-dependent functionality.

Since it is commonly accepted that Function Flows are particular for individual organizations and areas of competitive advantage, IAA does not intend to provide standardized business processes or workflows. Therefore the processes documented within IAA are marked as examples demonstrating the interaction and aggregation of all the constructs described. What the function flow related constructs in IAA want to achieve, is an architectural framework of functionality arising in a process that allows for context-independent reuse of parts.

The constructs within the IAA Function Flow Model dimension of the Business Architecture consist of

- Data Condition Functions (DCF)
- Triggering Condition Functions (TCF)
- Flow Control Functions (FCF).

While the Flow Control Functions correspond to the representation of the process description, the Data Condition Functions provide the functionality to check integrity conditions needed to start operations. With the Triggering Condition Functions a join between functionality and the function flow is established that addresses the topic of context independence. DCF and TCF allow a clear description of what kind of function flow is allowed to use a certain kind of general functionality that does not carry any pre-condition information. TCF allow to describe partial processes that may consist of other partial processes, but form a unit of activities, that must be addressed in order to ensure integrity and consistency from a business perspective. This need for emphasizing this special case of workflow was also identified in the VAA-initiative of the German insurance industry [VAA97] giving strong evidence of the importance of this distinction, not explicitly emphasized in the Workflow Coalition models [WFCL96], for the insurance industry.

With the granularity of function flow constructs used in IAA, a very rigorous description of Function Flows can be achieved.

4 Contents of the Architecture

The IAA Data model is made up of the following Business Entity families (where a Business Entity family corresponds to a top-level, or A-level, entity representation of a model)

- Party
- Object (Physical Object)
- Place and Contact Point
- Activity

- Event
- Investment
- Financial Transactions
- Specification (Product)
- Agreement
- Delivery
- Rule.

While the separation of Business Entity families like 'Party', 'Place and Contact Point', 'Investment','Financial Transactions' from the areas 'Agreement' and 'Delivery' is similar to the traditional approaches in the insurance industry (resulting in corresponding central application systems like Party Management Systems, Payment Systems etc.), this clearly is not the case for some others. The separation of the 'Objects' treated in the insurance companies from the areas of 'Agreement' and 'Delivery' is a new approach that strongly corresponds to the idea of 'Specification (Product)'. While until now, separate agreement and delivery administration systems have been built for the various lines of businesses, all of them carrying the product information within the administration systems, the IAA Data Model emphasizes a central 'Specification (Product)' area constructed to hold the product information inside this area via the means of the 'Rule' entities. This focus on 'Product' as the key for organizing the complete interaction between all kinds of application systems is one of the major achievements of IAA. While in many industries this approach has a long tradition, the insurance industry, maybe due to legal regulations and the immaterial character of their goods, only recently started to focus on the product orientation inside their application systems [Woh95]. Indeed, the insurance companies choosing IAA almost always address the product topic and there are first feedback's on how IAA supports this very challenging transition process [LS96].

Because of the fact that all information regarding the insurance product shall be held inside the areas 'Rule' and 'Specification (Product)', the areas 'Agreement' and 'Delivery' only shall hold the generic data content related to the administration of agreements (at its life cycle) and to the processing of requests (like claims) in the area 'Delivery'. Naturally, the necessity of a strong interconnection between Function Flow and Product definition arises, since the static view of the product definition can be addressed by rules and algorithms, while the dynamic aspects have to be described by the Function Flow descriptions applicable for this product. But because of the fact that only the generic data content related to the agreements and requests should encounter the areas 'Agreement' and 'Delivery', product specific information like "what kind of object can be insured" has to move away from these

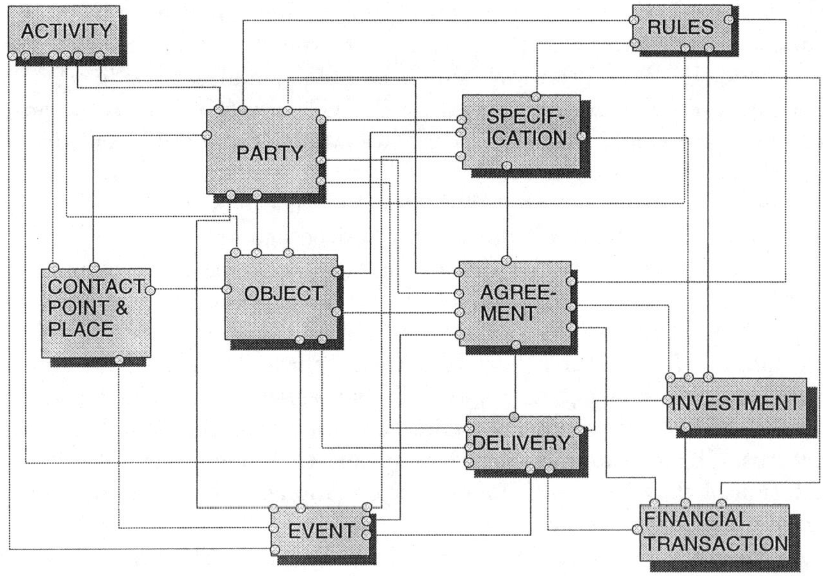

Figure 3: IAA Data Model Overview

areas. So induced by the product approach is the need for a separated area 'Object' that also allows to collect information regarding object dependent risk accumulations or derivations.

The fact that there is need for a new quality of claims processing is reflected in the areas of 'Event' and 'Activity'. The separation of these areas from 'Delivery' allows a fine-grained description of claims causes and the identification of risk centers, independent from its direct effect on the administrative dimension of 'Specification' (product). Rather this information may relate to the product development, the product marketing or the product distribution, since all of them have a special interest on the 'Activity' and 'Events' related to their potential customers.

The content of the Business Entity families, like 'Financial Transactions', 'Investments', 'Place and Contact Point' should be self-explanatory.

In the IAA Data Model documentation these Business Entity families are used to establish views on the whole IAA Data Model. For the Business Entity family 'Party' five different Party Views are used to discuss the IAA Data Model from a Party-centric perspective. For each view, there is a textual discussion about the way the contained entities can address related business topics giving examples how the entities contained in a view interact. The totality of these views represents the whole IAA Data Model, while the totality of the textual discussions of the separate view forms the discussion of the whole IAA Data Model. For each Business Entity Family the views discuss the connection of this family (that might be translated into an application system, e.g. Party system) to the rest of the insurance business. Inside the Party Views we would be able to find entities like PARTY, PARTY-OBJECT-RELATIONSHIP, OBJECT, PARTY TYPE already introduced in Section 3. In the IAA Data Model around 130 entities with 1240 attributes are documented providing the structural pattern of insurance specific data models, but the remarks concerning the construction of IAA (compare Section 3) should be emphasized again.

While the views and their discussions are contained in a volume: "IAA Data Model Reference", the complete entity descriptions are contained in the volume: "IAA Data Model Definitions". In addition to these two volumes, the volume: "IAA Data Model Examples Library" provides an extensive list of examples showing how specific business scenarios, like for example the treatment of an fraudulent claim, translate into the IAA Data Model structures. These example library is meant to provide examples how the population of the IAA Data Model by the mapping of business requirements (or scenarios) may look like.

On the IAA Function Model and IAA Function Flow Model side the covered and analyzed areas consist of the "High-Level Business Functions":

- Plan the business and its resources
- Research and analyze the market
- Develop and maintain insurance products
- Gain, service, and retain client business
- Manage party relationship
- Manage company infrastructure and services
- Manage business operations, finance and cash flow
- Manage investment.

Of course, below this highest level of "High-Level Business Functions" additional sublevels are documented. The substructures of "Gain, service and retain client business" for example consist of:

- Manage client relationship
- Manage promotion
- Manage authorized channel
- Administer insurance agreement
- Manage claim.

These structures are verified by the work documented in VAA [VAA97]. But, as indicated in Section 3, these High-Level Business Functions represent in fact a set of business functionality that clearly incorporates workflow and process character. Hence, a naming convention like "High-Level Business Functionality" would have facilitated the understanding that Function Flows using Functions would provide the content of these "High-Level Business Functions".

In IAA Edition 3 more than 20 Function Flows are completely worked out using the contents of the IAA Function Model and the IAA Function Flow Models, i.e. the elementary Business Functions, the Business Algorithms, the Data Condition Functions and the Trigger Condition Functions related to the Business structures. But each of these documented Function Flows like "Handle Party Information" or "Handle Address Information" is marked as an example, since a specific choice has been made regarding the scope of functionality used and the order in which something is done. These decisions may differ from insurance organization to insurance organization, but all should be composable out of constructs provided by the IAA Function and Function Flow model and the company specific enrichments of the IAA model constructs.

Alike the Data Model contents, the discussion of the Function resp. Function Flow Model contents is provided in the volumes "IAA Function Model Reference" resp. "IAA Function Flow Model Reference". The documentation of the specific contents is provided in the volumes: IAA Function Model Definitions Vol.1 Elementary Business Functions, IAA Function Model Definitions Vol.2 - Business Algorithms, IAA Function Flow Model Definitions Vol.1 - Data Condition Functions, IAA Function Flow Model Definitions Vol.2 - Triggering Condition Functions.

5 IAA and Object Orientation

As discussed in Sections 1 and 4 many characteristics and constructs of IAA are related to OO-approaches. The "TYPE"-construct in IAA Edition 3 corresponds to the Class/Subclass-relationship with single inheritance. Moreover, since the contents in the Function Model of IAA Edition 3 either live within the scope of one entity or belong into the responsibility of one entity, the interpretation of the Function Model elements given in IAA Edition 3 as methods is feasible.

In 1993 the Object-Oriented IAA path was started by building a life insurance prototype in Smalltalk implementing the IAA Edition 3 constructs using an object interpretation. The class library originating from the prototype clearly demonstrated the value of the underlying IAA Business Architecture, since the clear understanding of the business determinants and their interactions allowed the determination of the main business object classes together with a high degree of reuse by enabling inheritance. Therefore even at this early stage of IAA-OO developments some customers have chosen this

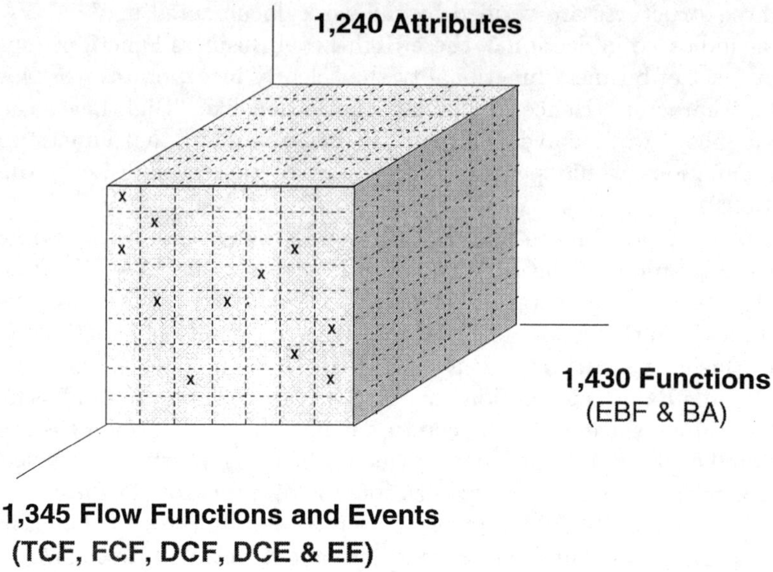

Figure 4: IAA Contents

class library as a basis for their development activities. Other insurance companies used the IAA Business Architecture to develop the structure of their own business object class libraries. So the transformation of the business knowledge contained in the IAA Insurance Business Architecture into class libraries has proven to be feasible.

But regarding the aspects of taking the IAA Insurance Business Architecture along the OO-path to the System Model layer, it has been experienced that work regarding an IAA OO-Meta Model was necessary, since none of the evaluated OO-Meta Models could express all of the needed business model constructs together with the Systems levels considerations.

So the development efforts concentrated on the directions:

- Definitions of the IAA Business Object Model (BOM)
- Defintion of a detailed Object Model for specific topics like "Specification" (AOM)
- Definition of the OO Meta structures
- Definition of the IAA/OT Infrastructure and Platform Architecture.

The IAA Business Object Model is made up of partial Business Object models corresponding to the Business Entity families introduced in Section 4. In the newest version, that is intended to be released as IAA Ed.4 in early 1998,

Business Object Models for all business entity families (compare Section 4) are contained. In these BOMs the structural knowledge of IAA Edition 3 has been transformed into an object model, but also project experiences concerning the business requirements have been fed in. Requirements arising in all projects have been included into the OO-model structures.

Especially in the area of Product/Agreement significant contributions with respect to the contents of Product definition have encountered the Business Object Model. A detailed Object Model of this area has been established as an Analysis Object Model (AOM). The Meta-level constructs are used to organize system boundaries between the different parts of the BOM. In continuation of the IAA development the BOM have been developed in a close relationship with insurance companies doing quality assurance and communicating experiences.

The BOM will serve as the underlying model for industrial strength implementations addressing insurance companies interested in components. With respect to the middleware components, IAA/OT is closely related to the IBM internal projects working in these areas.

6 Observations and Conclusions

Working in the area of IAA for several years, it can be stated that there clearly is a need for an insurance business architecture in order to identify stable structures for the development of the next generation of application systems. The success of IAA all over the world is a clear indication for this.

But it can also be observed that the notion of a Business Architecture brings new topics into the development process that have to be understood and addressed [Scha96]. The fact that the modeling act now consists of the detailing and specializing predefined generic structures instead of the possibility of inventing new structures is a change. Furthermore, the fact that the result of this business analysis is the model containing the business requirements and not necessarily the design for the database structures, is also a topic that has to be addressed with respect to the mass of data and transactions occurring in insurance companies. Therefore working with a business architecture implies the necessity of a design step (and model) dealing with the technical implementation of the business contents into a specific environment. The fact that there is a very clear separation between business content (which is considered to be technology independent) and the actual design (which strongly is technology dependent) introduces the separation of this design step in order to address the fact that a "one-to-one" implementation of the business model often is beyond the capabilities of current technology.

Nevertheless, the activities concerning business process reengineering can be interpreted as the attempt to model the process dimensions of the business by the business people from the business perspective without imposing technology restrictions. A business architecture asks for the additional dimensions of 'what' and 'how'. Both have in common that the business people are asked to express their needs in a formalized manner - an exercise with limited tradition. This means that the success of the usage of a business architecture strongly correlates with the acceptance and usage within the business departments.

Concerning the transformation into application systems, experience has proven that a clear description of the structures carrying the business contents is the key to address the different business needs and hence to produce marketable business software components in areas where no standardization is given. The developments based on Object technology (see Section 5 and [OMG96]) clearly depend on the understanding of the underlying business structures, when the approach of business software class libraries is taken.

Concerning the use of business software class libraries in different industries, this translates to the question how the business architectures for a specific industry like insurance compares to the business architecture ruling the class library. The generosity of the constructs used in IAA gives a good chance for providing the business structures generally occurring inside the general service business.

References

[Dic96] Dick, N., IAA und VAA - Eine ideale Ergänzung, Versicherungsbetriebe, Nr. 3/96, Juli 1996, 6-8

[FM93] Ferguson, C. H., Morris, C. R., How architecture wins technology wars, Harvard Business Review, March-April 1993, 86-96

[Hus95] Huschens, J., Detailierung von IAA am Beispiel Partner, in: Tagungsband, Anwenderkongreß 1995 Versicherungswirtschaft, IBM Deutschland GmbH, 1995

[IBM92] Insurance Application Architecture (IAA), Edition 1, licenced material of IBM Corporation, Copenhagen, 1992

[IBM93] Insurance Application Architecture (IAA), Edition 2, licenced material of IBM Corporation, Copenhagen, 1993

[IBM95] Insurance Application Architecture (IAA), Edition 3, licenced material of IBM Corporation, Copenhagen, 1995

[IEEE94] IEEE, Standard glossary of software engineering technology, IEEE Std 610.12-1990, in: IEEE, IEEE Software Engineering Standards Collection, 1994 Edition, The Institute of Electrical and Electronics Engineers, New York, 1994

[LS96] Leuzinger, R., Schönsleben, P., Innovative Gestaltung von Versicherungsprodukten, Gabler-Verlag, Wiesbaden, 1996

[OMG96] Object Management Group Webpages, http://www.omg.org

[Scha96] Schatzmann, Ch. H., Vorgehensmodell für die Verwendung partieller geschäftlicher CASE-Templates bei der Realisierung von Informationssystemen, Ph.D. Thesis, Universität Zürich, Zürich, 1996

[VAA97] Gesamtverband der deutschen Versicherungswirtschaft (ed.), Versicherungsanwendungsarchitektur, Bonn, 1997

[Wal93] Walter, K. J., Was bedeutet IAA für den Anwender?, in: Tagungsband, Anwenderkongreß 1993 Versicherungswirtschaft, IBM Deutschland GmbH, 1993

[WFCL96] Workflow Coalition, Workflow Model Reference, New York, 1996

[Woh95] Wohlschlager, L., Transformation von Versicherungsprodukten in Datenmodelle - dargestellt am Beispiel der Transformation der Fahrzeugversicherung in das IAA-Datenmodell, Master Thesis, Universität Köln, Köln, 1995

CHAPTER 29

Reference Models of Fraunhofer DZ-SIMPROLOG

Markus Rabe, Kai Mertins

Modeling in the field of application "production and logistics systems" is still based on ad hoc procedures. This contribution describes the development of reference models as well as of supporting methods and guidelines for this field along with design criteria that are applied for the systematic decomposition of this complex area. Modularization and interoperability are the main terms in this discussion. Furthermore, this contribution indicates steps necessary for the development of a simulation integration platform within the Fraunhofer Society. This will allow application-centered working with a set of appropriate model libraries and simulators. An application example demonstrates usage and benefits of the described approach by means of utilizing the reference model "manufacturing systems".

1 Introduction

In order to advance the use of simulation technology in general practice, nine institutes of the Fraunhofer Gesellschaft joined together to set up one research unit called DZ-SIMPROLOG. The individual institutes have expertise in different areas of simulation application, e.g. in the planning of production and assembly systems, in the planning of logistics and of material flows, and in the planning of distribution and personnel organization. Accordingly, a set of different simulation systems were developed, which are best suited to a large number of simulation applications within production and logistics.

Tools like CREATE!, MOSYS, PERFACT!, Persimo, Simple++ or USE! are incorporating know how and experience within these application fields. In addition to adequate tools, simulation experiments require comprehensive technical knowledge in order to model, plan, and evaluate simulation experiments, and in order to interpret the results. The knowledge of how to model production and logistics systems were isufficiently documented before, and experiences were confined to the simulation experts and were frequently no longer available after the respective project ended. The goal of this work is to change this practice, and define a new way of preserving and transmitting this knowledge.

The work done within DZ-SIMPROLOG was divided up into two phases. While the first phase "Exploitation of Distributed Know How and Development of Common Tools" was finished in 1996 the second phase "Development of an Integration Platform for Simulation Systems" was started in 1997.

2 Structure of Reference Models

For larger modeling structures that describe complete systems up to companies, the name "reference model" is often used. So far, there is no clear common definition of the term "Reference Model". Sometimes this term is used as a description of standard business processes, that are supported by a standard software. This type of reference model shows an ideal process that hardly will fit for any existing company. It is used as a guideline for process design and a measure for the process quality. In the joint development project conducted by the Fraunhofer Society, experiences of multiple simulation projects and the last stage of research are used to define standard structures for simulation models. In this project the term "reference model" is used for the complete set of structures together with a description, how these structures apply and how they can be adapted to a given problem. Therefore a reference model is not an ideal solution used as a measure, but a modeling base for a special type of problem. Usually it cannot be used as it is, but has to be adapted [MRK95].

Reference structures can be identified on different levels of abstraction, reaching from the top level where cooperation of companies or company divisions is described down to structures for material and information flow inside a workshop. Also basic structures for personnel employment can be found. These reference models are prefabricated modules for typical problems of application in production and logistics planning. They contain a generalized description of characteristic production or logistics systems, which can be adjusted by the user to the specific conditions of his company. The models describe the interactions between spatial structure, capacity, products and control; they can be executed and used as a basic supporting framework for simulation experiments. A reference model is composed of three main components:

- basic building blocks and structures,
- collection of examples,
- description language which is used for a uniform display, and for exchanging information between the different competence centers.

The basic building blocks and structures contain models of typical machines and transport devices, usual manufacturing structures, control guidelines, typical products, production strategies, and the operation sequence as well as a prepared evaluation of the simulation results. The basic model serves to explain to future simulation users the principles of manufacturing simulation and to ease and speed up the modeling process within the thematic field of the reference model. The collection of examples contains simulation models from industry. It serves to comprehensively explain complex simulation applications. The objectives of simulation projects are described; the attainment is measured against the simulation results.

As the describing language, the Integrated Enterprise Modeling (IEM) is utilized, which is using the modeling constructs of process and enterprise models of ISO TC 184/SC5/WG1 and in ISO TC 184/SC4/WG8.

3 Simulation Model Engineering

A design engineer today will rarely design a new product completely from scratch. In the contrary he will try to use as much existing components as possible to reduce development and production costs. Catalogues of standard parts and subassemblies allow the selection of appropriate solutions. Standardized interfaces and dimensions guarantee that the selected components will fit together.

Unfortunately engineering principles are rarely applied to the construction of simulation models so far. Due to the lack of standardization, the definition and marketing of simulation model components appears not very attractive. As a result, simulation models are still built from scratch every time, consuming valuable resources for the modeling of very similar systems. As an answer to this, Fraunhofer is creating the means to introduce an engineering approach to simulation model construction [MRF96].

Basis of the reference models is a collection of generic model structures, organized in libraries which contain a set of domain specific structures. Every structure comprises a generic description of objects, relations and properties with a well defined interface. These structures are built with the primitives of the simulation language and are therefore more complex. They allow for two different types of usage:

- Black box use, where neither the internal structure nor the parameters of the elements are altered; the structure is used as it is;
- White box use, where the structure is adjusted to specific needs of the task either by adding or deleting elements, changing relations or changing parameters of elements.

As experiences in different application areas show, the degree of abstraction applied to decompose the object domains of the application field is most critical for the usability of the reference model. To allow the application model

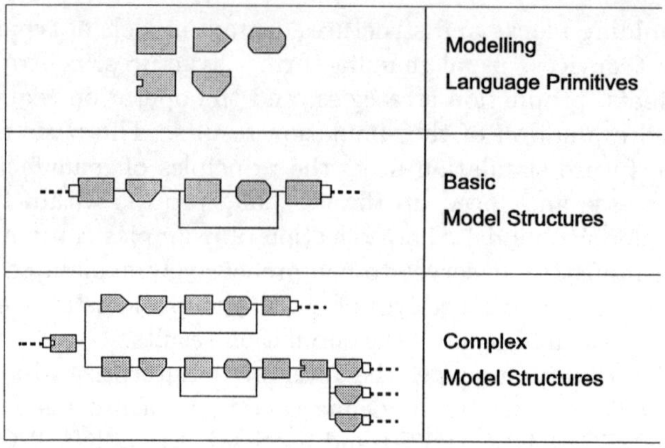

Figure 1: Abstraction levels used in the Reference Model [MRMO97]

builder to choose the appropriate level of detail for his task, the reference model is built hierarchically (Figure 1).

4 Development and Corporate Standards

In addition to documenting and exchanging experiences already available, Fraunhofer has developed new software. This software works with all the simulation tools of the alliance. There are two classes of software:

- Databases to transfer data from industrial clients to Fraunhofer's simulation tools and services. This gives connections to tools like SAP or helps to exchange data between the Fraunhofer institutes.

- Tools to further exploit simulation experiment results. Actually, one tool makes a 3-dimensional animation, that may be photo realistic; another one does a simulation based costing.

To have those tools common for all the different simulation software, corporate standards have been set:

- A process data standard to exchange data like inventory, process plan, production plan,

- A trace standard to exchange event lists for later evaluation.

5 Integration Platform

The integration platform provides the methods and tools for data exchange and synchronization of systems using different time and event models. Data can be exchanged between

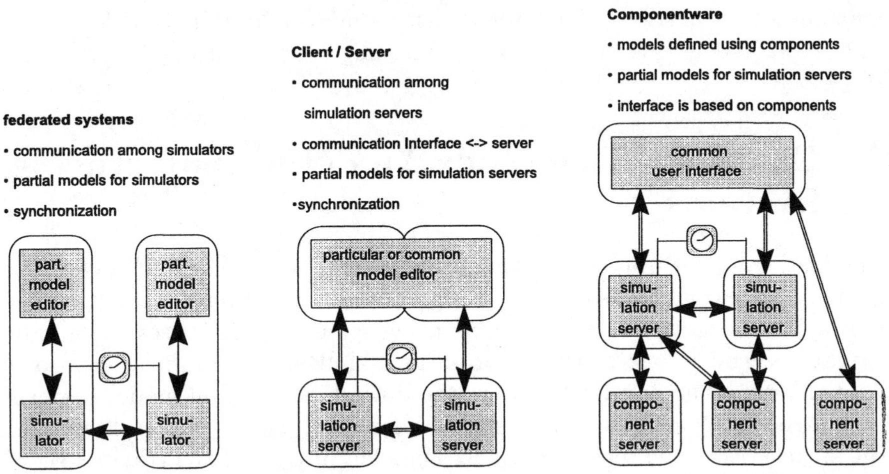

Figure 2: Synchronization of different time and event models (online coupling), Source: FhG-IML

- Any business application like a system for PPC and a simulator,
- Two models running on the same simulation system, or
- Two models running on different simulation systems.

This part of the integration platform supports the so called off-line coupling of different business applications and simulation systems. Off-line means a non-interactive coupling, for example the transmission of data (results of a simulation run) after finishing the first simulation experiment to a second simulation system. The coupling of different business applications and simulation systems in order to realize an interactive exchange of data and algorithms is called online coupling. The main goal for DZ-SIMPROLOG is the coupling of different models running on different simulation systems. In addition to the off-line data exchange there exists the necessity to provide synchronization mechanisms to coordinate the different time and event models. In Figure 2 the symbol for representing this mechanism is a clock.

An example for the application of a distributed simulation network is the semiconductor industry. Different manufacturing systems distributed all over the world are connected in a process chain to produce for example ICs. For each task there are different alternatives (manufacturing systems/organizational units) which can execute the task. For the finding of an optimal plan and the routing through the network the concept of distributed simulation can be used. This includes the online coupling of the different models running on different simulation systems which exist in the nodes of the network. This procedure allows the consideration of the interdependencies among the processes which are executed in each node of the manufacturing network. Therefore this is the only basis for efficiently getting good and evaluated manufacturing plans with realistic time and cost statements.

6 Example: Reference Model Manufacturing Systems

The Institute for Production Systems and Design Technology (IPK) has conducted simulation studies for the design of manufacturing systems for many years. The reference model manufacturing systems summarises the aquired experience and is one of the contributions of IPK to the above mentioned joint project. The approach follows the idea of "simulation model engineering" [MRMO97]. Three main aspects have been considered while building the structures of the reference model manufacturing systems (Figure 3):

- Type of equipment typically used in manufacturing systems,
- Main organizational prinziples used to connect the equipment,
- Influencing factors of the production control system.

The typical equipment for manufacturing systems has been grouped into machine tools, manual workplaces, transportation and testing devices. Additionally a set of structures for modelling of workers, considering different shift models and concepts of multi-machine operation has been defined.

Structures that can be found regularly connect the equipment organizationally. For the integration of organizational prinziples, an analysis of the german market leads to the identification of four basic principles:

- Jop shop production, portraying the task-oriented type of organisation,
- Islands of automation, portraying the product-oriented type of organization without sequential control and sequence of operations,
- Flow production, portraying synchronized work stations that are set up in the order of production sequence, and
- Construction site production, portraying the product-oriented type of organization with machines, tools, material and workers beeing moved to a single location.

It appeared that job shop production still dominates, even though the advantages of islands of automation are well known. But an increasing number of companies uses simulation studies to compare product-oriented to activity-oriented forms of organisation, in order to reorganize their production.

The success of a manufacturing system depends not only on an optimized material flow and balanced capacities, but to a high degree on the information flow and order control [MJR94]. Existing simulation studies often

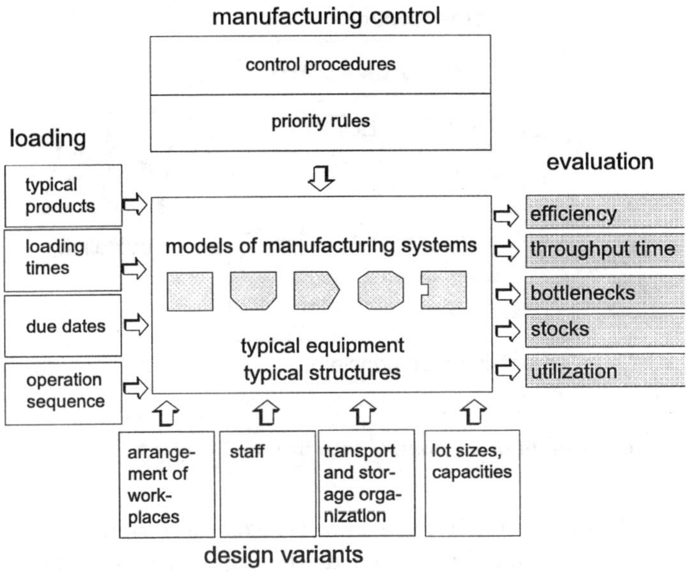

Figure 3: Design of Reference Model "Manufacturing Systems"

concentrate on the physical aspects of the system, neglecting the order control or reducing it to very simple strategies for the selection of the next order on a machine. But numerous influencial factors need to be taken into consideration and the complexity and reciprocal dependencies can hardly ever be controlled with analytical methods. Moreover, if the physical system and the order control are designed independently, mutual dependencies cannot be considered [Rab94]. This leads to an additional, time consuming integration step. For this reason, in the reference model manufacturing systems, the influencing factors of the production control system are considered as an additional feature. They are defined as independent structures for the processing of orders which have well defined interfaces to the structures defining the physical aspects [MRM97].

By combining different structures of order control with a given structure of the physical system, it is now much easier to analyse the impact of different control strategies and select an appropriate strategy.

A manual that describes the modelling, validation and evaluation procedures is a vital part of the reference model manufacturing systems (Figure 4). It contains a guided tour through simulation beginning with data aquisition and ending with possible approaches to solve problems. The usage of the existing structures is demonstrated by examples. A catalogue allows a quick overview over the existing structures and helps the modeller to find and

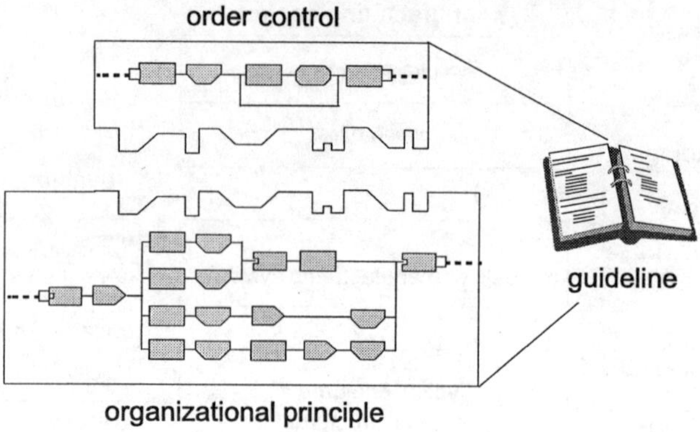

Figure 4: Integration of order control into a model

understand solution alternatives. The interface description of each structure reveals how structures can be combined. If a structure has to be modified, a description of its elements and parameters helps to minimise the effort.

7 Application Example

During a pilot project used to evaluate the basic principles of the reference model a job shop production has been reorganized and the traditional push control has been replaced by a pull control.

In the first step the existing manufacturing system was modeled using the job shop structure available in the reference model. This basic structure was modified according to the number and type of machines and transport devices. These components were selected from the catalogue of predefined equipment and their respective parameters like buffer sizes were adjusted. In the next step, the existing order control system was modeled using the structure for push control available in the reference model. Because the focus in this case was on the manufacturing system only, the control model was restricted to the shop floor control level. Arrival of orders from the PPC-system was modeled as input parameter and derived from an analysis of a past production period. An important aspect of this type of control was the fact that large buffer sizes were necessary to store material while the response from the predecessing manufacturing step was processed in the control system. Only after the release of the order the material could be transported to the next machine. Strategies for reaction on disturbances were little flexible, because the control system was involved in every reaction.

After verification of the model the experimenting phase started. Two alternative combinations were investigated to distinguish the influence of the physical system and the order control system. Thanks to the predefined structures that could be used, it was possible to define the two models very quickly. The first model replaced the job shop production with island of automation, but left the control system nearly unchanged. This resulted in better productivity, because the islands have a certain independency for the scheduling of the work inside the island. But coordination between the islands was left to the central control system and continued to slow the production process. The second alternative investigated the island production with a simplified control system. Now a pull principle between the islands was introduced, eliminating the central control system completely. Coordination was now decentralized and managed with orders exchanged directly between the islands.

The main task turned out to be the adjustment of the buffer size, the minimal stock in the buffer an the effective lot sizes. This process was again supported by the manual, that offers reliable calculation methods for the different parameters. After these parameters had been fine-tuned, a significant rise in productivity could be noticed, compared to the original system.

Indeed the effects demonstrated with this example depend also on the product mix. In the given case, the production times of the different products were close enough together to allow this type of restructuring. But the main purpose of the example, to demonstrate the use of the reference model manufacturing systems, was completely reached. Modelling of alternatives was faster than before and allowed to investigate several alternatives in a shorter period of time.

8 Vision: Simulation Component Ware and Standards

In the past the effectiveness and efficiency of processes in many enterprises were improved through automation and reorganization activities. But in many cases it is possible to achieve further improvements by an integrated design and optimization of the whole process chain. Optimizing the interfaces among different processes and coordinating the execution of the processes requires an integrated view on the material and information flow on one side and the information and communication systems on the other side.

The development to a market and customer driven business leads to strong and not easy to achieve requirements for the quality of planning and control systems. In most cases these requirements are only achievable using the concept of simulation. Simulation allows a dynamic view on the different processes and their interaction and is the basis for optimization, evaluation, and execution of plans. For simulation activities in a network of processes, different models (reference models of DZ-SIMPROLOG, particular models for manufacturing systems etc.) and data out of various systems (systems for PPC, sales and distribution etc.) have to be taken into account.

The vision of DZ-SIMPROLOG is an integrated system including different

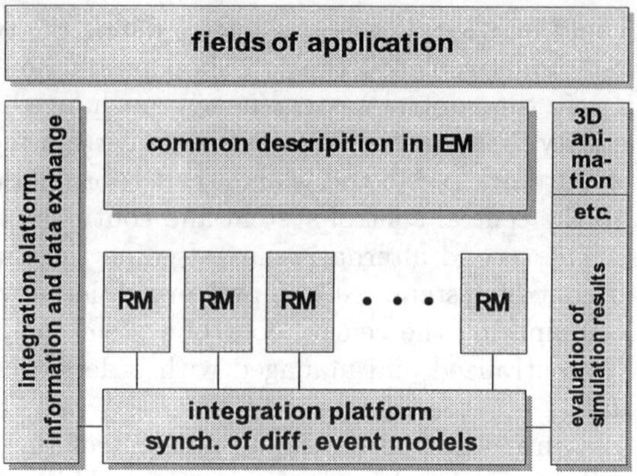

Figure 5: Architecture a future simulation tool box

business applications which are able to efficiently work together by using an integration platform. Figure 5 shows the architecture of a simulation tool box consisting of five main elements:

- Description of the fields of application using a common methodology (IEM),
- Simulator dependent reference models,
- Integration platform for data exchange and synchronization in a distributed simulation environment,
- Integration platform for synchronisation of different executable models,
- Add-on components for animation and evaluation of simulation results.

9 Conclusion

To meet the continuously changing market requirements, companies have to adjust their production constantly. Simulation is an excellent method to evaluate redesign alternatives. Unfortunately, traditional simulation studies require a significant effort for model creation that keeps smaller and medium sized companies from using this technology. Through the usage of reference models the expenses of simulation projects can be reduced.

The reference model manufacturing systems consists of a set of general structures that can be used in specific simulation studies to create models more effectively. The modeller is guided by a modeling manual from the creation of the initial rough model, built from predefined structures, through the adjustment of parameters to the evaluation of the model. The clear distinction of physical aspects of the system and its control leads to easier experiments with control strategies and allows for more alternatives to be investigated. The transparency of the interrelations between technology, organization and production control guarantees reliable decision-making.

References

[MJR94] Mertins, K., Jochem, R., Rabe, M., Factory Planning Using Integrated Information and Material Flow Simulation, in: Proceedings of the European Simulation Symposium, Istanbul (Turkey), 1994, 92-96

[MRK95] Mertins, K., Rabe, M., Könner, S., Reference Models for Simulation in the Plannung of Factories, IMACS Symposium on Systems Analysis and Simulation, Berlin, 1995, 655-658

[MRF96] Mertins, K., Rabe, M., Friedland, R., Referenzmodell Fertigungssysteme - Effiziente Simulation bei größerem Nutzen, 10. Symposium Simulationstechnik, Dresden, 1996, 95-100

[MRMO97] Mertins, K., Rabe, M., Müller, W., Ohle, F., Reference Model Manufacturing Systems: A new Approach for more Efficient Simulation Studies, 14th International Conference on Production Research (ICPR), Osaka (Japan), August 4-8, 1997, Vol. 1, 254-257

[MRM97] Mertins, K., Rabe, M., Müller, W., Reference Models for Process Oriented Manufacturing System Modelling, 32nd International MATADOR Conference, Manchester, Juli 1997, 157-162

[Rab94] Rabe, M., Simulation of Order Processing, in: Proceedings for the Dedicated Conference on Lean/Agile Manufacturing in the Automotive Industries (27th ISATA - International Symposium on Automotive Technology and Automation), Aachen (Germany), 1994, 479-486

CHAPTER 30

Configuring Business Application Systems

Stefan Meinhardt, Karl Popp

In the past few years business process modeling has become established practice in many enterprises. One area where it is used is in implementing standard business application systems. In such projects, reference models provide valuable support to enterprises when they are creating the business process models that describe their enterprise. Reference business process models give an overview of the business processes that are supported by the application system, and in doing so they help select the processes to be applied in an enterprise. However, it has been much more difficult to make use of business process models when you were setting parameters that change the behaviour of a standard business application system accordingly. It is described how the architecture of reference business process models can be extended to support the setting of parameters in a standard business application system. We then provide a practical illustration of the configuration of such a reference model and the setting of parameters in the system concerned.

1 Introduction

Business process models are of great benefit in the implementation of standard business application systems because they explain the functionality of the system, and they are of significant benefit in the creation of models of the enterprise processes to be supported [KM96, Mei95, KP96a]. The scope for using business process models in the configuration of (that is, the setting of parameters in) application systems has so far been very limited. The main reasons for this limitation were the media gap between modeling tool and application system, and the failure to link the actual content of models to the parameters that can be set in the application system. The media gap at least can be bridged by providing open interfaces and integrating navigation and modeling tools in standard business application systems. At SAP much work has been done on linking business process models to the parameters that can be set in the R/3 System. That work has been published

[KMZ94, KP96b, KS96b, Sch96]. This contribution presents an overall conceptual design of an integrated configuration for the business process model and the application system, and illustrates it with a practical example.

2 Business Process Configuration

In response to the requirement that, using the R/3 Reference Model and business criteria, it should be possible to select and analyze R/3 System business processes and subsequently to configure the R/3 System, SAP defined the elements needed and a simple portrayal [KS96b], and determined the following goals:

- to provide a classification of business process models for particular sectors and efficiently present subsets of the overall R/3 Reference Model for specific industries
- to manage variant-richness and improve maintenance of business process models by modularizing the business process models
- to simplify finding, and restrict the variant-richness of, business process models
- to provide mechanisms for linking the business process models to the parameters used in customization of standard application systems.

The elements required to achieve these goals are described in Section 2 and illustrated using a practical case in Section 3.

2.1 Method of Portraying Business Processes as Models

Business process models are made using the event-driven process chain ("EPC") method developed by SAP in the period 1990 to 1992. Business processes are shown simply and clearly [KNS92, KP96a]. The elements that make up an EPC are events, functions, information objects, organization units, relationships between elements (for example, control flows), and logical operators (see Figure 1). An EPC describes the flow of events and tasks (functions) through time and in a logical business sequence. The events to trigger and to complete a chain are defined, and process paths are added to them pointing to any predecessor and successor processes. There is an extensive literature on this method [KNS92, KS96a, KP96a].

2.2 Structure of Business Process Models

The EPC method links tasks to elements of organizational structures, and so it is the cornerstone of business process engineering [Zen94, KM94, PM94,

Name	Symbol	Definition	Example
Event		An event describes the occurrence of a state that causes a certain effect.	Order received
Function		A function describes the transformation from an initial state to a target state.	Check order
Organizational unit	System	Organizational units are used to describe the structure of an enterprise. In the R/3 System, the organizational unit is a system organizational unit.	Sales organization
Information object		Information objects represent, or model, objects in the real world (e.g. business objects, entities).	Sales order Result of check
Process path		The process path shows the connection leading from one process to another	Delivery processing
Logical operator	XOR	Logical operators describe the effects of logically linking together events and functions.	"XOR", "AND", "OR"
Control flow		A control flow indicates the logical or chronological dependencies between events and functions/processes.	
Information and material flows		These flows indicate whether a function writes, reads or makes changes.	
Allocation of resources and organizational units		This describes which organizational unit, employee or resource performs a given function.	

Figure 1: Elements of Event-Driven Process Chains (EPCs)

Pop95b]. For example, when one is analyzing a business process, it is of benefit to see the degree to which a task is automated and the form in which work flows from one task to the next. Another important element of EPCs is the organizational assignment of tasks to owners (organization units). Three kinds of organization units are relevant to implementing a standard application system. The logical organization in the R/3 Systems is described using system organization units (for example, company codes and controlling areas), as well as the enterprise structure that defines departments, positions or roles with their interrelationships [WFBDE95], and the software infrastructure that defines the R/3 Systems working together in an enterprise. These are basic conditions for creating processes that cross organizational boundaries between departments, R/3 Systems or system organization units [MP96]. It is possible to describe distributed systems in terms of the distribution of business processes among departments or among different R/3 Systems [GKG96].

Two hierarchically organized levels of business process models are shown as EPCs in the R/3 Reference Model. At the detailed level there are component business processes. "Customer order processing", "Delivery processing", and "Invoice processing" are examples. Ways in which component processes can be combined are indicated as process paths. At the aggregated level, component processes are portrayed as functions linked together

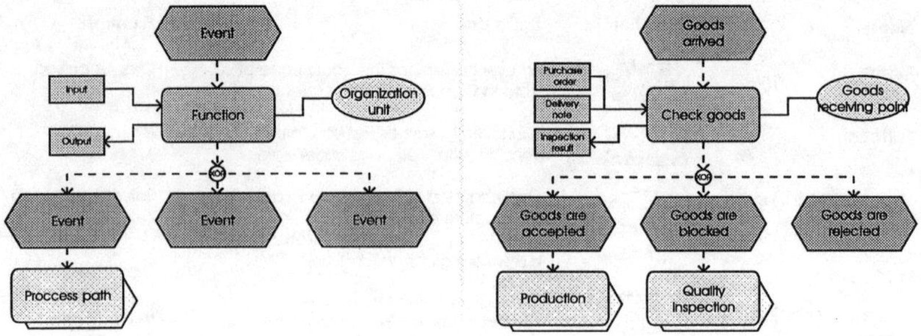

Figure 2: Basic structure of an Event-Driven Process Chain (EPC) with example

in EPCs called scenario processes. Figure 3 shows the "Purchase order processing" component process as a part of the "Procurement handling" scenario process. Scenario processes serve as overview diagrams for combinations of component processes in particular business contexts, such as "Direct sale to industrial consumer" or "Project handling for plant engineering and construction". Scenario processes are themselves combinable: possible combinations are indicated in models as process paths.

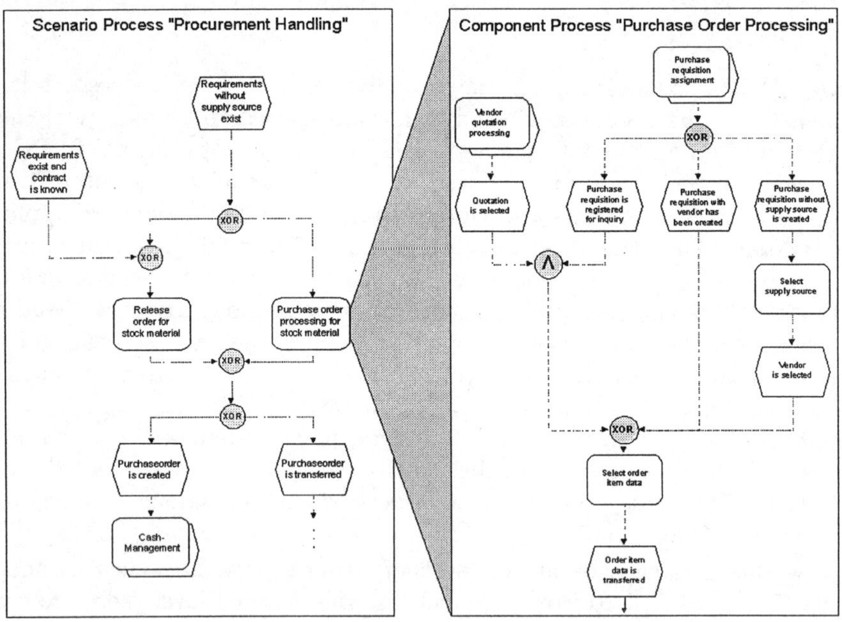

Figure 3: Scenario Processes and Component Processes

The possible combinations that are technically feasible and make business sense are described in the R/3 Reference Model. The eight hundred component processes in the R/3 Reference Model are widely combinable. In addition, a collection of component process combinations specific to particular industries has been prepared, to help enterprises find relevant parts of the R/3 Reference Model easily. Two views of event-driven process chains are useful: looking out and looking in. Looking out you see the possible combinations of the component processes and scenario processes shown as process paths. Looking in you see the scope for varying a component process or scenario processes, for example as optional elements. Although the business process models are arranged in two levels, scenario processes and component processes, it can be difficult for an enterprise to identify the relevant scenario processes and component processes. This is because of the large number of business process models and their variants and because differences occur between corporate and business process model terminology. Such difficulties are typical of large collections of modules [BFP95]. This is why an additional classification structure is used to find the scenario processes needed in a particular sector. The purpose is to create meaningful subsets of the whole content and variant complexity of the business process model. The classification system comprises two levels: the economic sectors and a number of enterprise process areas to which in turn a number of scenario processes are assigned [KS96b]. An economic sector is a factor in the economy. "Manufacturing", "Retail", and "Services" are examples of economic sectors. A number of enterprise process areas, and the scenario processes in them, are assigned to an economic sector. This shows which parts of the R/3 Reference Model are useful in any economic sector. An enterprise process area is a business structure displaying elements of an enterprise that are homogeneous in process-oriented terms. It has defined task areas, which are described in a set of scenario processes. "Product Development and Marketing", "Sales and Distribution Logistics" and "Procurement" are examples of enterprise process areas in the "Manufacturing" economic sector.

Starting from the economic sector in which it is positioned, an enterprise can draw on a manageable set of enterprise process areas and scenario processes. From this set an enterprise can select the required scenario processes and component processes and thus arrive at a specification of its requirements for subsequent use in setting R/3 System parameters. The procedure is described in Section 3 using a practical example.

2.3 Variants of Business Process Models

Business processes can have many variants [Pop95a, Pop96, Rau96]. The "Project handling" scenario process is an example: It has variants for handling make-to-order, investment, and plant engineering/construction projects. These scenario processes may be combinable with variants of other scenario processes for, say, revenue and cost controlling. This simple example shows that a reference business process model must also incorporate mech-

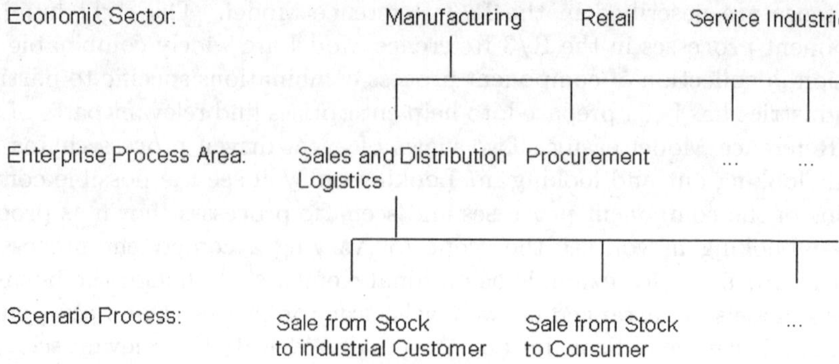

Figure 4: Economic Sectors and Enterprise Process Areas as a classification structure

anisms for managing variant-richness of business processes. Variant-richness of business processes can also arise as the result of differences between enterprises in the organizational ownership or automation of tasks. These variants are not under consideration here. One way of managing variant-richness that is often used is a system of levels. This is used in the R/3 Reference Model, where variants may be created at the scenario process and at the component process levels. The following business process model variants are permitted in the R/3 Reference Model:

- Variants of scenario processes: Looking out, one can produce variants according to the ways scenario processes are allowed to be combined and according to the different flows through a scenario process.
- Variants of component processes:
  - Looking out, variants of component processes reflect the combinations of component processes in different scenario processes.
  - Looking in on component processes there may be both optional functions and function variants (that is, a choice of one or more different practical solutions for particular functions).

The number of variants seen by customers can be considerably reduced by the selection of economic sectors and enterprise process areas. It is useful if the number of scenario process and component process variants presented in the context of any one enterprise process area in an economic sector is not too large. From the developer's perspective, variants of a given component process or function can be created and managed centrally. This improves reusability and maintainability of the models [Pop95a]. The advantage of the variant concept in the R/3 Reference Model is that the context information provided by the economic sectors and enterprise process areas substantially reduces the number of scenario process variants to be considered. Also, only consistent business processes (that is, ones that are useful in business terms and can be executed in the application system) are available to be selected. This makes for efficient selection of models from an extensive reference business process model.

2.4 Linking the Business Process Model to the Application System

The goal is to select a set of required application system components and set their parameters in the system, by restricting the business variability of process models. The following elements are available to be used for linking parameters in the application system with the constituent parts of the business process models:

- Function variants are differing solutions in the R/3 System for functions in component processes. The "Check material availability" function, with function variants for checking availability against stock, against planned stock and against subassembly planning, is an example [KS96a].
- Parameter profiles are ready-to-use sets of parameter values that reflect useful application system settings in a given business context.

The link is made by creating parameter profiles for the function variants in the business process model. Such profiles substantially reduce the number of parameters that have to be set manually in the course of implementation. Parameter profiles make it easier to find and decide on correct and consistent parameter settings. The practical example that follows illustrates the procedure for configuring business processes, and the resulting benefits.

3 Example: Configuring Business Processes

In the course of working on an R/3 implementation project, an enterprise will configure its business processes in levels, from the top down, i. e. from high-level to detailed level [MS96]. The first task is to compare the business areas in the enterprise with the enterprise process areas in the R/3 Reference Model, and so identify the core business processes in the enterprise and the business processes that support them. The main purpose of this is for the R/3 implementation project team to see clearly the business-process-dependent and functional requirements of the enterprise in terms of how they will utilize the R/3 System. The second level is to present possible outline solutions for the core business processes in the R/3 System using the R/3 Reference Model's prepared scenario processes. Then the defined requirements can be compared with the scenario processes, and models configured to reflect the particular needs of the enterprise. The results delivered by this process-based model configuration work effectively to determine the scope and content of the subsequent parameter setting activities that make it possible to run the operative processes in the R/3 System. The following sections demonstrate the main business process configuration and system parameter setting tasks by describing an example of how this work is done.

3.1 Identification and Selection of Scenario Processes

The example discussed is the core sales logistics business process in an enterprise that only sells goods from stock. The goods are serial products made or procured to a sales plan for ex-warehouse delivery to customers. There is thus no direct link between sales orders and procurement. The business process envisions handling sales inquiries and orders entirely within the framework of sales logistics without having to raise design or work order documents. The material requirements planning element addresses only the picking and shipping of finished goods. The emphasis is on shipping product on time by the best route. The product might be, for example:

- white goods (washing machines, refrigerators, coffee machines)
- brown goods (TVs, stereos)
- industrial semifinished products (polymers, tensides)
- industrial electronics products (printed circuit boards)
- components and replacement parts (tires, dynamos)
- groceries.

The R/3 Reference Model includes a group of alternative scenario processes showing implementations of "direct sales" in the R/3 System. The direct sales scenario processes show the handling of sales orders with and without reference to quotations or outline agreements, and of delivery, shipping, and billing. They also contain processes for handling returns and complaints, post-supply credits such as rebates and commissions, and returnables and empties. The various scenario processes are distinguished by customer types (industrials, consumers, retailers). This example assumes the enterprise sells only to consumers, so we need not consider scenarios for direct sales to industrials and retailers in the project. They appear in the set of all scenario processes in the R/3 Reference Model, but we can discard (deselect) them *(Selection and Reduction: Level 1)*.

3.2 Selection and Reduction of Processes

The next level is to analyze the selected scenario process in detail, and to configure it for the particular purposes of the enterprise. This means that

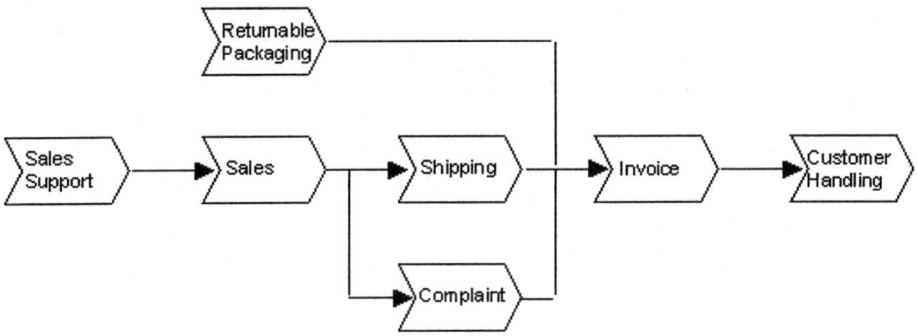

Figure 5: "Direct Sale to Consumer" scenario process (shown as a value chain)

for different forms of direct sales some processes (or parts of processes) can be reduced to a minimum or dispensed with altogether. For example, there may be a "Cash Sales" variant that would not normally include inquiries, quotations, or shipping in its flow, because the customer pays for the goods at the register and takes them away with her. The EPC model of a scenario process shows (through the respective control flows or explicit identification of optional processes) how particular processes are selected or deselected. These mechanisms ensure that it is only possible to make selection decisions that are technically feasible in the R/3 System. *(Selection and Reduction: Level 2)*. Special attention should be paid to process paths, which show the integrating links between the scenario process under consideration and other scenario processes. For example, in the "Direct Sale to Consumer" scenario process, the result of the "Customer Order Processing" process is a completing event, "Sales Requirements are determined", that is linked by a process path to the "Non-Allocated Production" scenario process (in this case to "Repetitive Manufacturing" in the production logistics area).

Once the "Direct Sale to Consumer" scenario process has been adapted to meet the requirements of the enterprise, the next task is to analyze the individual component processes with respect to the functional options they offer. Nonrequired functions are deselected, and where functions have alternative function variants, the ones that are needed in the context of the "Direct Sale to Consumer" scenario process are selected. Processes, with their events and functions, are also shown as EPCs, so the same mechanisms are used to select and deselect events and functions as for processes in scenario processes: alternative control flows and the explicit identification of "optional" functions *(Selection and Reduction: Level 3)*. The following sections analyze the "Customer Order Processing" process more closely. The central functions in the processing of a customer order include determining who placed the order and what items are ordered, pricing, checking availability, determining a date for shipment and a route, and credit control: These are the functions to be carried out in the example. However, the functions to determine article

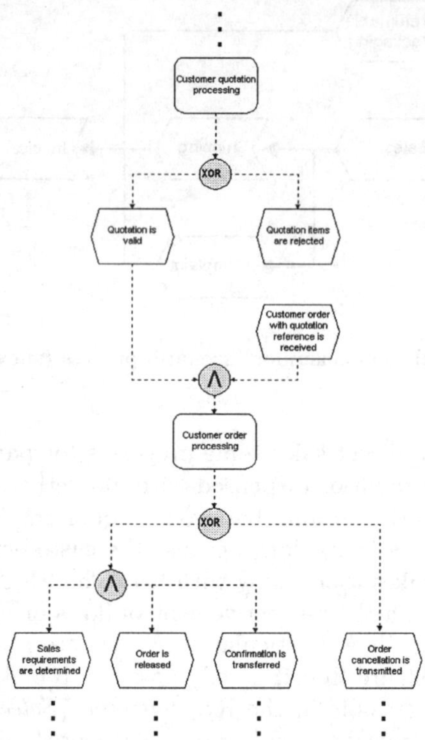

Figure 6: "Direct Sale to Consumer" scenario process

or item variants, batches or serial numbers are not needed for the simple made-to-stock product, so they can be deselected, as can their associated events.

For some of the functions selected, for example the order item availability check and credit control, one can see alternative function variants to identify and select as appropriate for the context of the process under consideration, which is "Customer Order Processing", and variants of the scenario process, which is "Direct Sale to Consumer" *(Selection and Reduction: Level 4)*. An availability check can look at the current stock position for an item, or at planned inward (outstanding purchase order) and outward (outstanding sales order) stock movements. Credit control can be carried out in the R/3 System either in static or dynamic form. These different ways of carrying out functions are expressed as function variants at the process model level, and correspond to parameter profiles at the implementation level. It will be possible to use such profiles and their specific standard parameter settings to greatly reduce the complexity and the amount of work involved in setting system parameters. At the same time, this method achieves automated

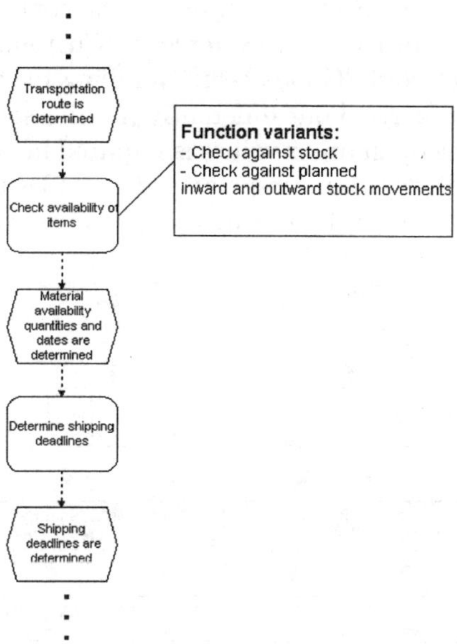

Figure 7: "Customer Order Processing" process (detail), showing function variants

quality assurance in parameter-setting, avoiding consistency errors between interdependent manually maintained values.

4 Setting the System Parameters

Identification, selection and reduction of model elements (scenario processes, processes, functions, and function variants) cause parameter profiles available in the R/3 System to be activated, as seen in Section 3. Only a subset of the parameters can be set automatically. In particular, the parameters that can be set using profiles are those that correspond to different procedures for carrying out functions. The enterprise still has to set the remaining parameters, which are chiefly descriptive, manually, so they reflect the business. However, you can see the whole set of parameters to be set, because the parameters are assigned process model elements. So the parameter values needed to carry out the enterprise business process in the R/3 System can be determined from the business process model.

4.1 Using Profiles to Set Parameters

In this section, the "Credit Control" function is used to illustrate in detail how profiles are used to set system parameters. The "Credit Control" function can be carried out in various processes in the context of the "Direct Sale to Consumer" scenario process, for example in "Customer Order Processing", "Delivery Processing", and "Goods Issue Handling for Stock Material". You can have the function carried out differently in different processes. Dynamic credit control covering open order values is required in "Customer Order Processing", but in "Delivery Handling", and "Goods Issue Handling for Stock Material" static credit control covering open invoiced values is adequate.

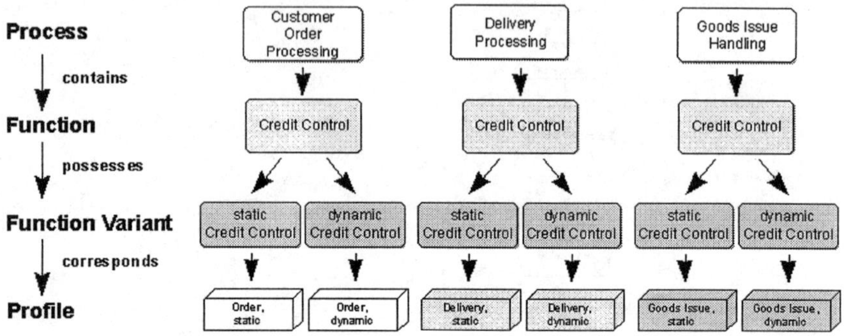

Figure 8: "Credit Control" function with function variants and their parameter profiles

There are six preconfigured parameter profiles in the R/3 System to set parameters that correspond to these various function variants. As they make their decisions in the process model, a part-automated process helps project team members set consistent system parameter values

A parameter profile is fundamentally a set of any number of parameters (values for table fields). All fields that characterize a function variant have appropriate values and are grouped in a profile. Fields that are not relevant for the profile in question are hidden. Dynamically reduced parameter profiles are presented to the implementation team member as regular Customizing views. Fields are "fixed" in system parameter profiles if they are fundamental to the function variant and should not be maintained by the team member. This means there is no danger that any inconsistency between selections made at the process model level are not carried through to the physical values in the system. The enterprise has to verify, and if appropriate change, any standard values for the remaining fields.

Often, selecting a function variant to activate the associated parameter profile does not fill all the fields in the profile with standard values. In particular, profiles often have parameters that depend on organization units the enterprise does not define before the project. This means that at the time the standard values in a parameter profile are verified, appropriate enterprise organization units are assigned. There remains a set of settings that have to be made manually.

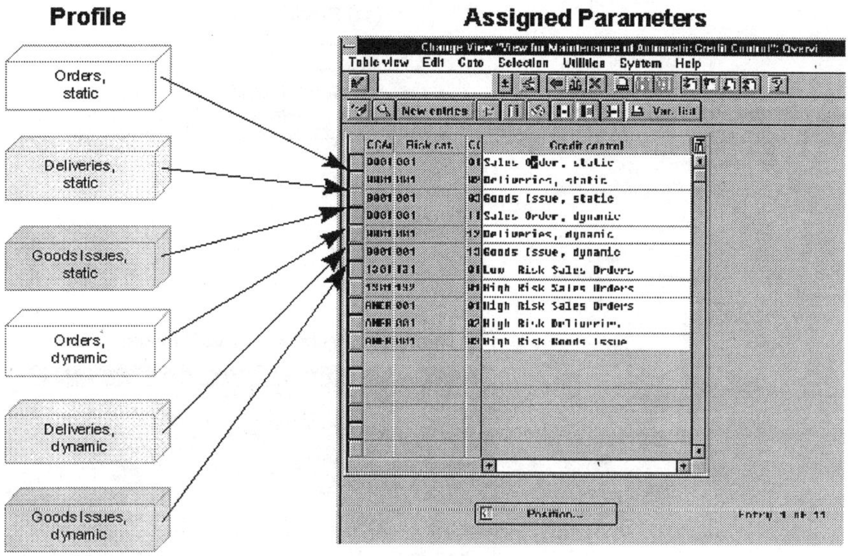

Figure 9: Profiles with assigned parameters in the R/3 System

4.2 Setting the Remaining Parameters Manually

The parameters that cannot be set using prepared profiles are set manually by the enterprise. In future, manual settings work will be process-oriented: This will always be done in the context of the scenario process. For example, for the "Customer Order Processing" process in the "Direct Sale to Consumer" scenario process, enterprise-specific parameter settings have to be made for the "Create Order Header" function, and these parameters are presented to the team member to be individually selected for the business case in question.

Also, the number of parameter settings to be set manually is automatically reduced by deselecting functions, and the project team only sees and works on the settings that are needed to configure the scenario process.

5 Conclusion

This is how the overall conceptual design achieves the goals set out at the beginning of this contribution:

- The structured classification of business process models by economic sector and enterprise process area leads to efficient selection of relevant scenario processes.

- An appropriate variant concept provides control over variant-richness, and improves maintenance of business process models by modularizing them.

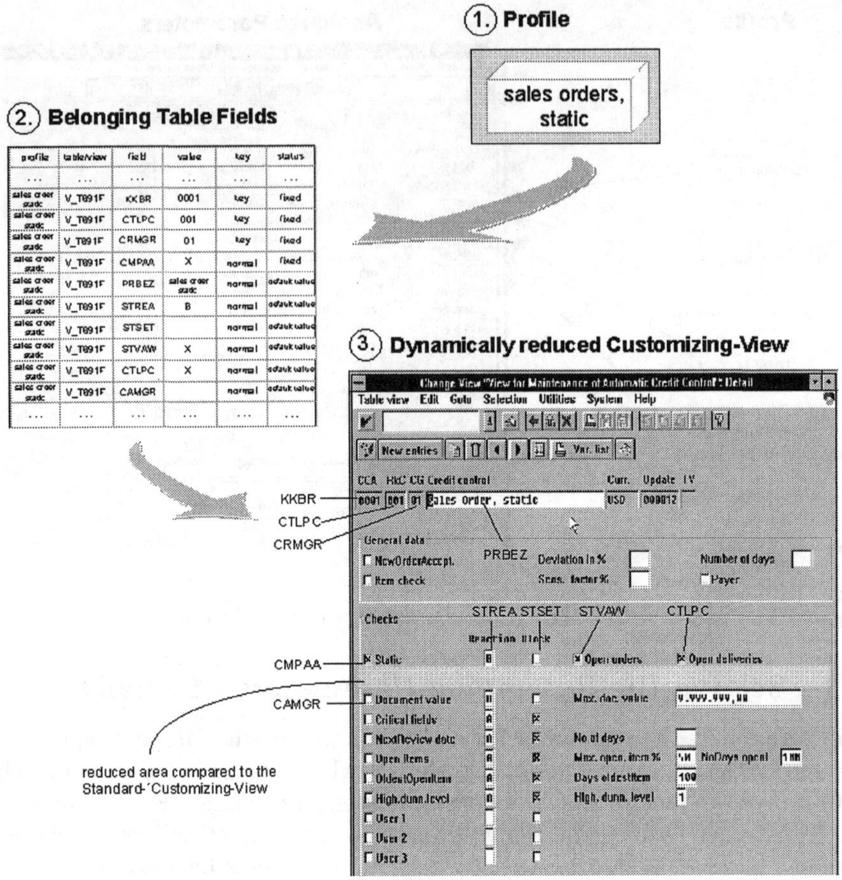

Figure 10: Parameter profile with dynamically reduced view

- The classification structure makes it easier to identify the relevant business process models. Working through layers of context by selecting the economic sector, enterprise process areas and scenario processes progressively reduces the number of variants.

- Using profiles to set R/3 System parameters can considerably reduce the amount of time spent on setting them. At the same time, potential errors can be avoided by defining consistent parameter profiles.

This contribution demonstrated that the envisioned integration of business process model configuration with the system parameter settings level contributes crucially to the customization of enterprise-neutral R/3 System functionality to reflect enterprise specifics. This solution also reduces the amount of work involved in configuring an R/3 System and provides a high level of

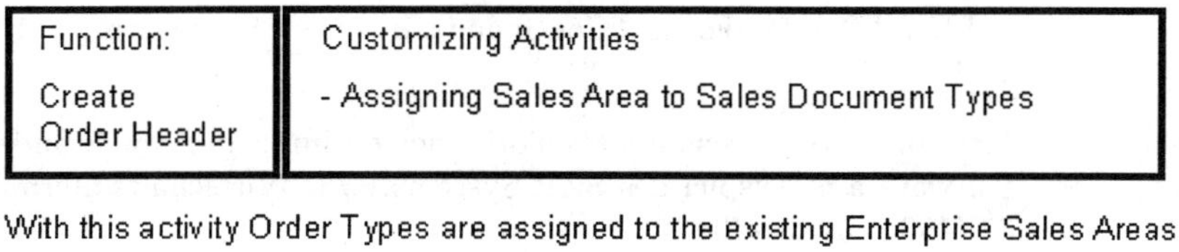

Figure 11: Descriptive customizing activities: example

quality assurance.

References

[BFP95] Bellinzona, R., Fugini, M. G., Pernici, B., Reusing Specifications in OO Applications, IEEE Software, March 1995, 65-75

[GKG96] Gehring, K., Krauss, S., Gruler, S., Strategies for implementing distributed application systems, in: SAP AG (ed.), SAP info, Focus "Continuous Business Engineering", 1996, 56-58

[KNS92] Keller, G., Nüttgens, M., Scheer, A.-W., Semantische Prozeßmodellierung auf der Basis "Ereignisgesteuerter Prozeßketten (EPK)", in: A.-W. Scheer (ed.), Veröffentlichungen des Instituts für Wirtschaftsinformatik, No. 89, Saarbrücken, 1992

[KS96a] Keller, G., Schröder, G., Geschäftsprozeßmodelle: Vergangenheit, Gegenwart, Zukunft, Management and Computer, No. 2, 1996, 77-90

[KS96b] Keller, G., Schröder, G., Konfiguration betriebswirtschaftlicher Anwendungssysteme, in: A.-W. Scheer (ed.), 17. Saarbrücker Arbeitstagung Rechnungswesen und EDV, Heidelberg, 1996, 365-388

[KM94] Keller, G., Meinhardt, S., Business Process Reengineering auf Basis des SAP R/3-Referenzmodells, in: Schriften zur Unternehmensführung, Band 53, Wiesbaden 1994, 35-62

[KM96] Keller, G., Meinhardt, S., DV-gestützte Beratung bei der SAP Softwareeinführung, Handbuch der modernen Datenverarbeitung - Theorie and Praxis der Wirtschaftsinformatik, No. 175, 1996, 74-88

[KMZ94] Keller, G., Meinhardt, S., Zencke, P., Business Process Reengineering im SAP Umfeld, Management & Computer, 2. Jg., No. 4, 1994, 293-305

[KP96a] Keller, G., Popp, K., Referenzmodelle für Geschäftsprozesse, HMD - Theorie and Praxis der Wirtschaftsinformatik, No. 187, 1996, 95-117

[KP96b] Keller G., Popp K., New era in software configuration, in: SAP AG (ed.), SAP info, Focus "Continuous Business Engineering", 1996, 12-17

[Mei95] Meinhardt, S., Geschäftsprozeßorientierte Einführung von Standard-Software am Beispiel des SAP Systems R/3, Wirtschaftsinformatik 37 (1995) 5, 487-499

[MP96] Meinhardt, S., Popp, K., Prozeßorientierte Einführung von R/3, BIT Spezial Systems 1996, 1996, 46-49

[MS96] Meinhardt, S., Sänger, F., R/3-Vorgehensmodell als methodischer Rahmen für einen erfolgreichen Projektverlauf, Handbuch der modernen Datenverarbeitung - Theorie und Praxis der Wirtschaftsinformatik 33 (1996), 193

[PM94] Popp, K., Meinhardt, S., Business Process Reengineering unter Verwendung des R/3-Referenzmodells, in: Informationssystem Architekturen, Rundbrief des GI-Fachausschusses 5.2, No. 2, 1994, 19-21

[Pop95a] Popp, K., Aspekte der fachlichen Wiederverwendung in Geschäftsprozeßmodellen, Informationssystem-Architekturen, No. 1, 1995, 32-41

[Pop95b] Popp, K., Business Process Reengineering using the R/3 Reference Model, in: SAP (ed.), SAP info, Focus "Business Reengineering", 1995, 3-4

[Pop96] Popp, K., Vergleich von Methoden zur Geschäftsprozeßmodellierung in bezug auf Wiederverwendbarkeit - Überblick, Informationssystem-Architekturen, No. 1, 1996, 23-25

[Rau96] Raue, H., Wiederverwendbare betriebliche Anwendungssysteme, Wiesbaden, 1996

[Sch96] Schröder, G., Industry-specific business process modeling, in: SAP AG (ed.), SAP info, Focus "Continuous Business Engineering", 1996, 18-21

[WFBDE95] Wächter, H., Fritz, F. J., Berthold, A., Drittler, B., Eckert, H., Gerstner, R., Götzinger, R., Krane, R., Schaeff, A., Schlögel, C., Weber, R., Modellierung and Ausführung flexibler Geschäftsprozesse mit SAP Business Workflow 3.0(r), in: Proceedings der GI/SI-Jahrestagung, Heidelberg, 1995

[Zen94] Zencke, P., Software-Unterstützung im Business Process Reengineering, Schriften zur Unternehmensführung, Band 53, Wiesbaden, 1994

CHAPTER 31

The SIZ Banking Data Model

Daniela Krahl, Hans-Bernd Kittlaus

The German Savings Banks Organization has established a large enterprise-wide data model as a standard for heterogeneous IT organizations. The basic elements, the architecture of the data model and practical experiences are described which show significant benefits for the organization on several levels.

1 Introduction

In order to understand the purpose and objectives of the SIZ Banking Data Model, one must first understand the structure of the German Savings Banks Organization (GSBO) and the role of SIZ within this organization. This will be explained in this Section before we describe the SIZ Banking Data Model and its development in Section 2. Practical experience with the data model is detailed in Section 3, before we finish with an outlook and conclusion.

1.1 SIZ and the Savings Banks Organization

The GSBO consists of more than 600 savings banks, 13 state banks and a number of associated partners. Each of the savings banks is a legally independent company that is owned by the regional authorities (with a few exceptions). The savings banks have formed associations on a regional level and on the national level. The national association is the DSGV (Deutscher Sparkassen- und Giroverband). The state banks were founded on the regional level, originally with the objective to manage the financial transactions between the savings banks and other banks, but today they operate as wholesale banks. The savings banks are complete retail banks (in contrast to savings banks in the US).

In the world-wide rankings for the finance industry, the GSBO is usually not listed, since it is not one corporation, but an association of banks. However, if the accumulated total balance sheet of all organizations that are part of the GSBO is compared to the industry rankings, the GSBO ranks as the biggest banking organization in the world. In Germany, it has managed to establish a very solid corporate image despite its decentralized structure.

This decentralized structure is reflected on the IT side of the organization. Around 1970, IT centres were formed on the regional level with the objective to provide IT support for the savings banks in their respective regions. The state banks have their own IT departments. In total, there are more than 50 computing centres in the GSBO about half of which develop applications on their own. This situation led to the foundation of SIZ, the computer science centre of the GSBO, in Bonn in 1991. SIZ is an independent company that is owned by the biggest state banks and by regional associations (in some cases their IT centres). Its mission is to make progress in IT available and usable for the GSBO in order to improve productivity and quality. To this end, it is supposed to work towards more conformity and synergy in the IT area, in particular towards the exchange of applications between the IT centres.

SIZ focuses on setting standards for the GSBO in terms of architecture, methodology and products, providing consulting services and co-ordinating joint application development of IT centres (but not developing applications on its own). This is done in close co-operation with the IT centres and the DSGV. According to its mission, SIZ is basically covering all of IT, with special emphasis on new technologies (systems, telecommunication, office), security, application co-ordination and application provision. Application provision includes methodologies and tools for application development, integration and modelling.

2 The SIZ Savings Banks Data Model

A major cornerstone in the SIZ strategy for setting standards in the area of application provision is the SIZ Banking Data Model. The ideas behind this model, its architecture and the innovative and unusual story of its development are covered in this section.

2.1 Purpose

A major opportunity for SIZ to provide more synergy was identified early on in the exchange of applications between IT centres. However, there were a number of obstacles to this in terms of non-compatible system architectures, application architectures, data base designs and even different terminologies. It quickly became evident that an organic, evolutionary approach to these problems was more realistic than to attempt a radical change. Therefore, SIZ chose to focus on standards for new developments that would make the resulting applications more easily exchangeable, without forcing the IT centres into major investments in adapting their legacy applications. In the area of data, this required a focus on a common terminology and logical data model, but not on a common physical data model since the applications would have to run based on the existing non-compatible data bases. This led to the idea of a reference model that would provide a common terminology plus gains in productivity and quality without enforcing a particular implementation. Acceptance in the IT centres could be achieved by a service-oriented approach that centered on productivity and quality gains for each application development project based on the data model (e.g. [SH92]).

The objectives of the project were to create a reference model useful for:

- application development projects with focus on
  - reusability
  - minimization of data redundancy
  - flexible and reliable data structures
- existing database analysis and tracing projects with focus on
  - stable definitions of data from an enterprise perspective
  - understanding existing data bases
  - migration to a maintained and stable model
- quality check of existing data models (e.g. of standard software)

Later on, the data model proved to be very useful in some other constellations, e.g. in the context of object models and when creating a new nomenclature for archive systems.

2.2 Development Approach

The SIZ data model was created and modified over a time of nearly five years. In order to understand the development it is helpful to understand the underlying model architecture which is described later in more detail.

The basic structure of the model is based upon IBM's Financial Services Data Model (FSDM) philosophy and distinguishes three levels called A, B and C (the architectural foundations are described in [Zac87] and [SZ92]). The A level introduces the major data concepts, the so called kernel entities, with their definitions. These kernel entities - in total nine - serve as the major sorting and classification categories for all other banking terms or for all other data concepts.

The B-level contains all data concepts sorted in hierarchies with the A-level kernel entities on top level. Every data item may be integrated in as much detail as necessary to hierarchies structured in super-subtype layers.

The C-level contains all data concepts of the B-level in the same fine granularity. But the representation of the C-level is an entity relationship model and therefore much closer to a conceptual database design.

2.2.1 Customization of FSDM's B-Level

In 1991 IBM offered a general, internationally valid banking data model, intended as a reference model which was to be customized to the national and company-wide rules and specialities. The IBM-Financial Services Data Model (FSDM) was a preliminary, early engineering version and needed thorough and comprehensive quality improvement. The FSDM proposal was made, however, at a time when the SIZ organization was prepared and willing to build such a model from scratch internally.

Both approaches offered different benefits and risks on the road to success. On initial consideration, the idea of buying a comprehensive banking model from IBM seemed to be very attractive, however, the FSDM-option entailed faith in an, as yet, incomplete system. The alternative of building an enterprise model internally would have had the benefit of a tailor-made model for GSBO, but lacked a unifying, central basic structure reflecting the different (and often conflicting) needs of the GSBO members. The use of a model developed internally by one IT-centre would have put too much emphasis on the implemented systems view of that centre and might have had too little regard for future structures and more open, more flexible requirements. Finally, after much internal discussion and consideration, it was decided to purchase and modify IBM's FSDM.

In the first customization project from 1992 to 1993 a large effort was put into the understanding and enrichment of the IBM-FSDM model. The magnitude and complexity of adapting all information items in such a comprehensive model led to an end result where the B-level could only be described as half customized. The structure for the C-level had not been provided by IBM yet. But creating a new structure on the C-level and filling this structure with elements proved to be such a time-consuming exercise that it could only be done on a sample basis, leaving the C-level practically empty for further projects. The customizing top-down process was correctly organized as a joint effort of all IT-centres, however, the absence of specific project requirements and the sheer magnitude of the task at hand only led to theoretical and generic results. The results of the evaluation of this first customized organization-wide data model were disappointing if not discouraging.

The results were too generic. The model required far more detail and a level on which the projects could find their project view with the semantically connected information also connected in structures and the model presentation. The B-level was set as a normative level for naming and data definition alone including a structure that would support a data management view but not a project view. As there was no clear guideline of how to transform the B-level information via C-level to the needed details of data base design, the members of application development projects could not be expected to see the immediate benefits of the B-level model and the not clearly characterized C-level. The IBM C-level that was evaluated later when it became available, seemed to be too generic and unspecific.

The goal, the usage and description of each level of the IBM model architecture and it's C-level was questioned. At this point SIZ was forced to make a decision which would influence the development of GSBO's electronic data systems for decades to come: whether to drop the idea of one common data model across all IT centres or to stick with the further development of the model. While the former option would have meant the abandoning of SIZ's main project and writing off the substantial development costs, the latter option would require a difficult discussion about the architecture of the data model in order to devise an organization-wide data model which would be truly useful.

It was clear that the key success factors for the introduction of an enterprise-wide data model lay in sound decision-making with regard to the architecture and methodological structure combined with a suitable data management organization (e.g. [Dur85, Gil85]). Workshops involving the IT-centres and SIZ were held in order to align both technical and conceptional expectations and possibilities. The creativity, flexibility and vision of the colleagues from different backgrounds with differing practical needs led to a plan which, while ambitious, was felt by all participants to be practical and in the best interests of their individual IT-units.

In this plan, the idea of levels called A, B, C was maintained from the IBM FSDM model. The details, however, had to be fine-tuned and adapted to the requirements we found in our existing organization. It was absolutely necessary that the new plan combined the tools, method, presentation and of course the data items within the data structures itself in a way acceptable for all IT-units. Today, the original IBM-FSDM model and the SIZ data model have grown so far apart that they are hardly comparable any more.

2.2.2 Creation of a Savings Banks-Specific C-Level

The creation of a stable C-level was accompanied by a long debate regarding the purpose and role of the C-level. Basically, the purpose of a reference model in general was questioned. As the different views developed of how the model ought to be used, the modelling techniques also evolved to suit the objectives. Finally, the major success factor for the improvement of the C-level based on bottom-up projects was to reach an agreement on the use of a reference model.

The C-level is a large entity-relationship model (ER-model [Che76], an excellent book is [BCN92]). The creation of the C-level went through three steps. In every step the method, the extension and intention of the ER-model was further developed. As a result the model, called version 1.0, contained 3 organization-wide integrated levels (A, B, C) where every level was regarded as stable enough for being used in projects running in parallel. Before this point, we had two pre-releases.

The three development phases of the C-level:

1. *a sample from the first customization project (free style)*
   In 1993, the first part of the C-level was created in the partition of securities-arrangement. Since there was no quality check against the requirements of a dedicated project or system, the results seemed to be reasonable, but not yet detailed enough (see Figure 1: the prelimary version from 1993 (a)).

2. *a so-called "generic" model after integrating a loan system's model (IBM philosophy)*
   The data interface of a standard loan advisory system was mapped against the B-level. The missing data elements were added to the B-level or changed if necessary. The C-level was created very closely along the classification structures of the B-level following the philosophy of IBM's C-level. As a result, the structures of the loan system had to be split into the dominant classification structures which led to difficulties in locating typical loan information in a particular loan context, especially among the financial (non-IT) staff. Therefore, it was argued that we needed domain views according to major banking concepts such as loan, customer, address etc. A pure reference model seemed to be cryptic for anybody with a practical banking background. The application / banking driven views should be supplementary to the same C-level - not an extra level requiring another encyclopaedia (see Figure 1: the prelimary version from 1994 (b)).

3. *a representative C-level after the complete integration of two controlling application models (SIZ philosophy)*
   The data model required more banking details. Two existing controlling models (large ER models) had major advantages compared to data models of other banking applications: they had been developed and used in a large co-operation between two IT centres and already reflected the required generality and similarity to database design (e.g. [TL82, Dat86]).

   Once again, the information requirements were mapped against the B-level and added or modified if necessary. On the C-level the modelling techniques were analyzed in detail in order to achieve the maximum semantic expression without losing the generic character of a global banking model. For this reason, one of the first results in this integration project was a handbook of the SIZ modelling methodology [SIZ97]. This project was the first one in which we introduced an extra level for project models. The existing controlling models were traced against the C-level. And according to the data management requirements, we built traces from B- to C-level and from model version to model version.

Nevertheless, we decided that the C-level should not be simply a reference model, rather - if required - a base for direct application development. With this C-level the SIZ data model, version 1.0, could be used in various projects.

2.2.3 Project Driven Enhancements through Central Administration

Since completion of version 1.0, the banking model has been enriched bottom-up with the benefit feedback of various projects. We discarded the idea of defining domain clusters on the C-level along major banking concepts. We found that it was not possible to maintain and manage consistent banking domain models which would be compatible with the various, heterogeneous, yet subjectively justified projects views.

Rather, we found that most of the recurring discussions in different projects were questions of semantic principles. For example, in controlling projects a decision about how to model management accounting is required. In the ensuing projects after V. 1.0 we supported three more controlling projects. In order to introduce a unifying view to these overlapping projects we needed a strong argumentation and position to carry through the initial modelling decisions.

We started to define so called "Leitbilder" on all levels which are broad outlines or semantic principles which allowed the central data modelling team to summarize the main decisions on modelling critical concepts such as account or customer. These broad outlines, however, still allow enough variants for specific database designs.

Later, we explain the idea of one "Leitbild": the general decision about how to model "Customer".

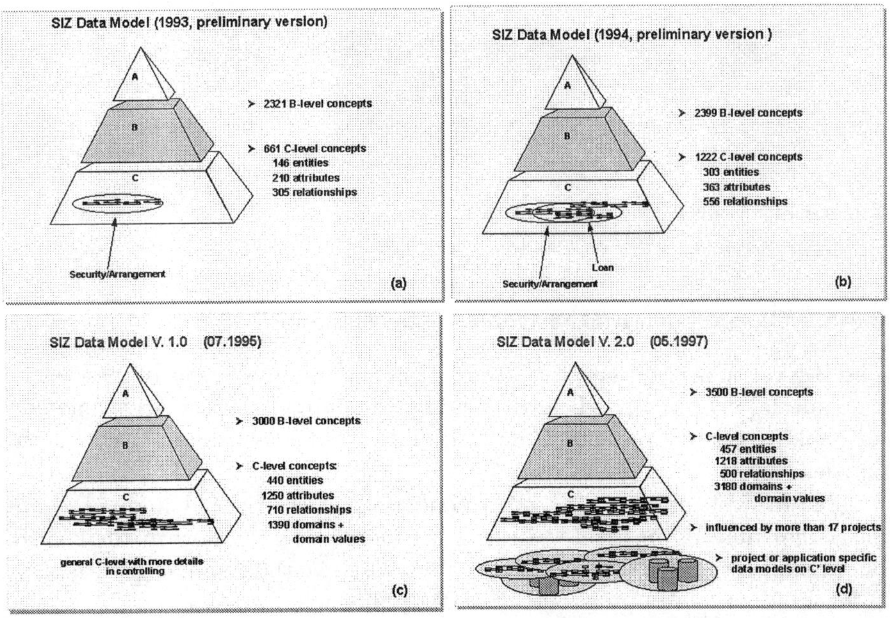

Figure 1: Versions of the SIZ Data Model

2.3 Architecture

2.3.1 A-Level Modelling Concepts, Kernel Entities

On the A-level there are 9 top classification concepts. They serve as a sorting help for all other banking terms or data elements and are equivalent to IBM's main data concepts [Eve96]. We let the definitions go through a fine tuning process which occasionally led to re-definition. The kernel entities are described in Figure 2.

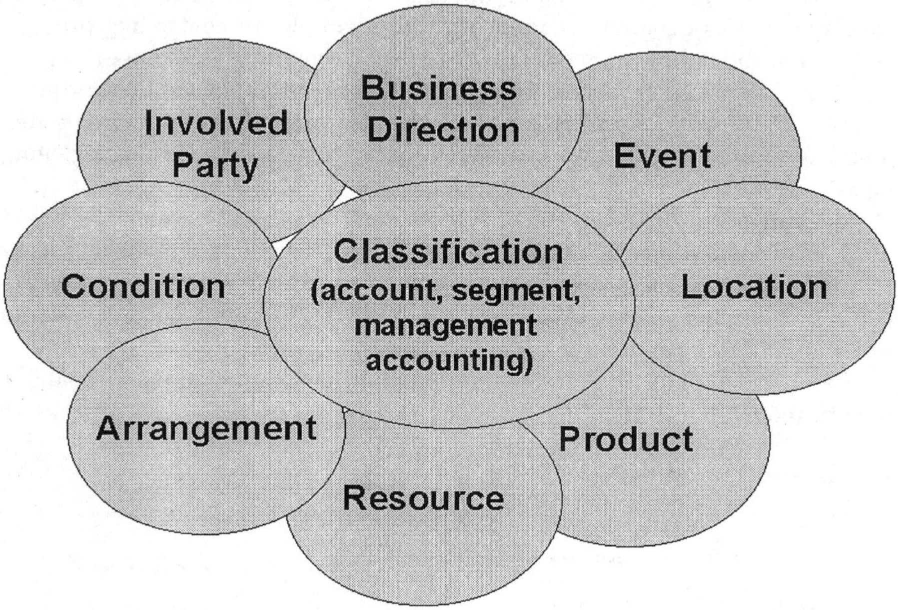

Figure 2: A-level: the kernel entities

2.3.2 Classification Hierarchies: the B-Level

The B-level is used to identify and to select the required scope of information for a special project. The B-level could be compared to a normative language: all banking terms are named, defined and classified by the 9 A-level kernel entities.

The B-level contains a set of concept hierarchies. Every banking business data item may be integrated in as much detail as necessary in the concept hierarchies structured in super-subtype layers. Method and structure of the B-level follow to a large extent the IBM philosophy.

For each kernel entity there are 3 kinds of concept hierarchies: the classification hierarchy, the relationship hierarchy and the description hierarchy.

```
Entity Type: INVOLVED PARTY
:LONG NAME:  Involved Party

:DEFINITION:
 An Involved Party is a natural person, an organization,
 an organizational unit or a group of people about which
 a financial institute wants to collect information in
 order to co-operate in an optimal way.
....
:ALIAS:
      - Business Partner

:EXAMPLES:
      - the natural person "Hans-Bernd K."
      - the organization "Daimler Benz AG"
      - the organization "Norddeutsche Landesbank"
      - the organizational unit "Revision Department Savings"
      - the group of people "Mr and Mrs Krahl"

:COUNTER EXAMPLES:
      - the dog "Hugo zu Wittgenstein" with the right  of
        inheritance
        ....
```

Table 1: Definition of the kernel entity 'Involved Party'

In choosing the most suitable hierarchy for a particular data concept, the following distinctions are helpful:

- A classification hierarchy is the appropriate hierarchy type if the data concept is a subtype of one of the kernel entities. For example the data concept: a bankrupt or solvent company; these are kinds of Involved Party classified by their financial solvency.
- A relationship hierarchy is best suited if a data concept exists only in a relationship between concepts of classification hierarchies. All sorts of roles are concepts that exist when one data concept stands in a certain relationship to another. Cologne is the "home city" of Daniela Krahl. Here "home city" is a concept that exists in the relationship between a concept of the Location classification hierarchy and a concept of the Involved Party classification hierarchy.
- A description hierarchy is appropriate if a data concept gives a further detail to the relevant kernel entity. For example the differentiation between legal names and birth names can be found in the description hierarchy of Involved Party.

It is not always obvious which of the 9 kernel entities or which of the hierarchy types is best suited for a special data item. Often, modelling proved to be a constructive task requiring the analysis of almost equivalent modelling alternatives before choosing the optimal solution. Only some of the modelling decisions can be settled by methods or analytical considerations, for example, when deciding upon the hierarchy type.

But how is a concept hierarchy constructed? The top concept is always one of the kernel entities. When building super/subtype-layers it is helpful to use the subtyping criteria; for example 'Involved Parties' can be classified by their different financial solvency type, their life cycle phase or by their tax status. By means of these criteria, called "schemes", the subtypes or "values" are sorted. A detail of the classification hierarchy 'Involved Party' is given in Figure 3.

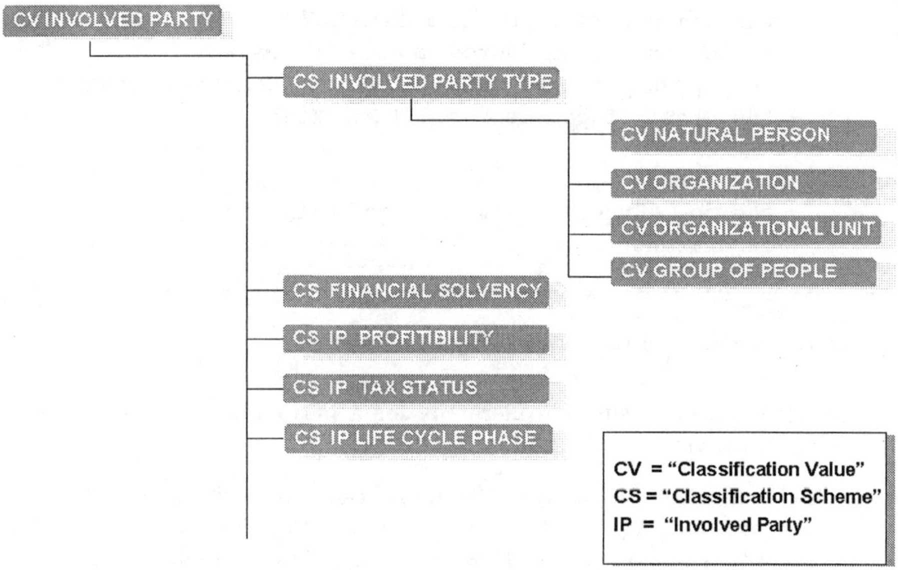

Figure 3: Classification hierarchy 'Involved Party'

A second example for the B-level in Table 2 presents the definition of Customer.

Please note that in Table 2 Customer is defined as a role or as a relationship between two Involved Parties. One of the Involved Parties has an actual or potential business connection to another Involved Party (a bank). This idea forms one "Leitbild". There are some other ways of modelling Customer. Methods or analytical considerations are not relevant at this stage. This definition of Customer leads to a rather flexible and open model.

The detail in Figure 4 showing Customer is taken from the relationship hierarchy of Involved Party.

```
Customer
:LONG NAME:  Customer

:DEFINITION:
 A customer is defined through the relationship between two
 Involved Parties in which the one Involved Party has an
 actual or potential business connection with the other
 Involved Party.
 ....
:ALIAS:
       - Partner

:EXAMPLES:
      - Mr Hitze is private customer of the Savings Bank Bonn
      - Mr Schmidt from Bakery Schmidt is a business customer
        of Hessische Landesbank
```

Table 2: Definition of Customer

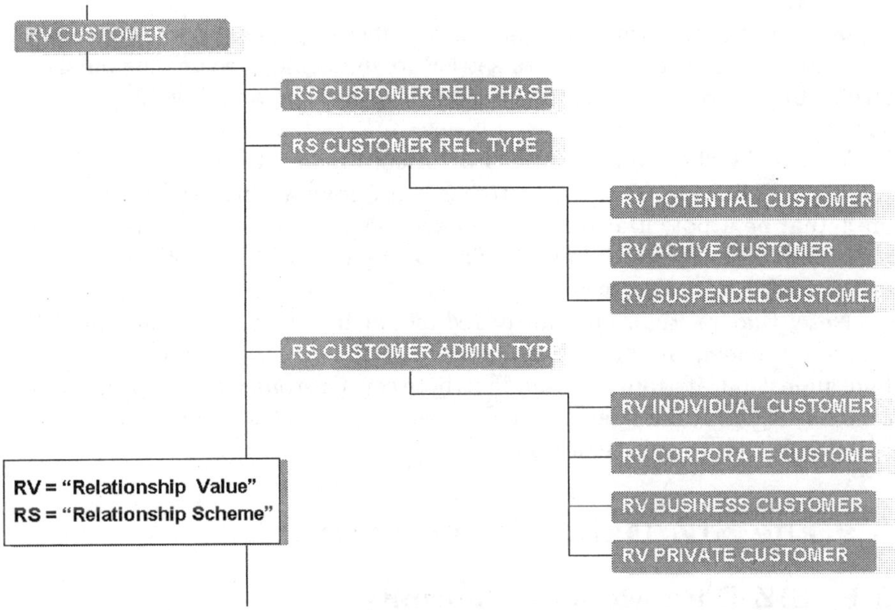

Figure 4: Customer as part of the relationship hierachy Involved Party

2.3.3 Enterprise-/Organizationwide ER Model: the C-Level

The C-level consists of all business data items that can be found on the B-level and that were necessary in one or more projects. The creation of the

C-level is strictly project driven. If no project ever needed to differentiate between a "legal name" and a "birth name" than these data concepts would not be transformed from the B-level to the C-level.

The C-level is structured as a large Entity-Relationship model where only business terms are modelled. It is a conceptual layer without any implementation considerations. Especially noteworthy is the fact that the number of entities is not reduced or limited - this may be done for a good database design in a specific project data model.

Because we assume that most readers are familiar with Entity-Relationship Models we do not explain the main principles: entities, attributes, relationships, attribute domains and domain values. However, we would like to point out some important decisions that were established to meet the requirements in the GSBO. Specifically, the question of how to model relationships and attributes can be seen between two extreme positions. The one position has the interest of expressing as much banking specific content as possible on the ER diagrams in order to be easy to use for projects. The other position has the interest of expressing as much generality and as little specific details as possible in order to support the central data model administration requirements.

We started with the principle: as specific as possible and as generic as necessary. Over time rules were settled for modelling techniques on the C-level. In Figure 5 the representation of Customer and Involved Party is shown.

Why is the "Leitbild" Customer an orientation for further projects? With the given definition (Being a customer is a role of an Involved Party having an actual or a potential business connection with a financial institute) the modelling variations are limited. The example in Figure 6 of the C-level is incompatible with this principle.

Note, that in Figure 6 a lot of redundant information is being modelled due to an inadequate modelling decision. In this counter example you would find almost all attributes redundant between Customer and Non-Customer and consequently between all of their sub-types. This model would not be acceptable due to non-conformity.

3 The SIZ Data Model in Use

3.1 SIZ Data Model Conformity

3.1.1 Definition of Conformity

The definition of conformity is a sensitive point. If the definition of model conformity is too restrictive, some IT-centres of the GSBO would not be able to develop new applications which conform to the definition without unacceptable overhead for connecting their already existing databases. If the definition of model conformity is too loose, then there would not be any benefit from a unified conceptual schema. So we needed to find a balanced way between restrictions and freedom to match the actual needs.

When defining the SIZ model conformity the limited time available in each project for modelling concerns was taken into account. The identification of a project scope on the B- and C-levels, the transformations of this initial scope to a realistic project model together with the final quality checks should be done without long agreement processes involving people not familiar with the project. Moreover, since most projects follow a phase-oriented process the modelling phase requires an official approval at the end, despite the fact that, in a later phase when specifying the functionality and the data base design, changes of the data model are very common.

Therefore the definition of SIZ data model conformity is split into two parts addressing two questions:

1. When does a project data model conform with the SIZ data model?

2. When does an application conform with the SIZ data model?

A *project data model* conforms with the SIZ data model if:

- The following basic requirements are met:
  - Use of terms and definitions given by the SIZ data model

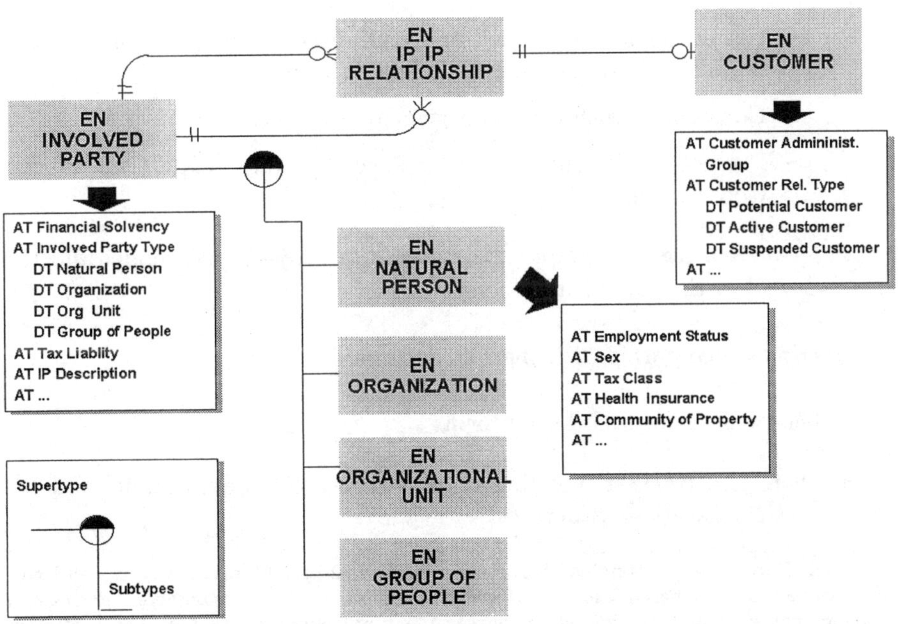

Figure 5: Customer and Involved Party on C-level

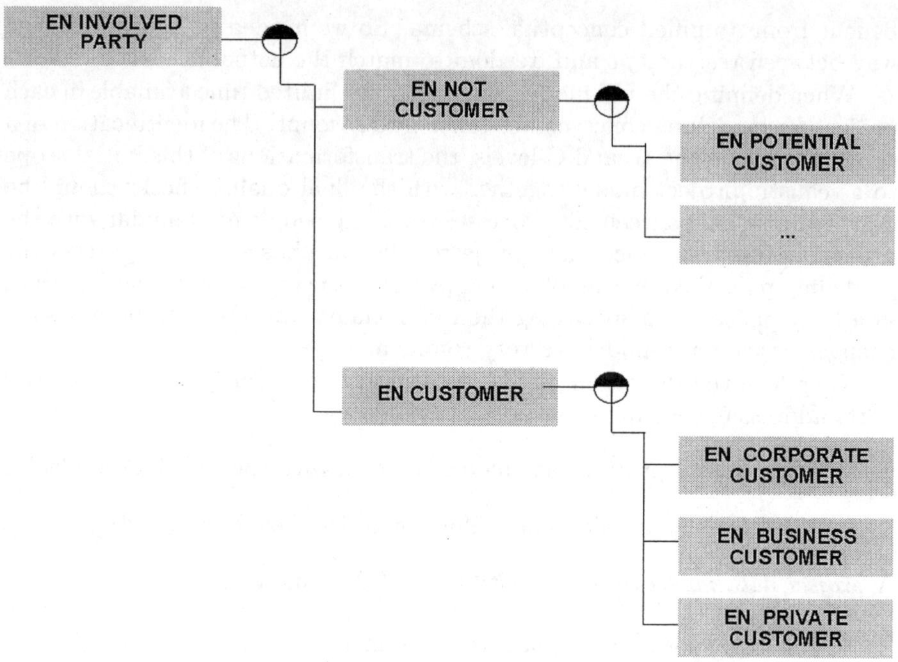

Figure 6: Example for an inadequate modelling decision

- Use of the defined modelling techniques and co-operation with the organization-wide data management team
- Conformity with the main principles ("Leitbilder")
- Project model output is in a special format (export file format Cool:Enterprise)[1]

- There is a trace or mapping between the project data model and the C-level of the SIZ-data model.

An *application* conforms with the SIZ data model if:

- The project data model conforms
- There is a trace or mapping between the project data model and the physical database structures.

[1] Cool: Enterprise (Sterling Software) is a proven OS/2-based tool suite for model-driven development of host-based and client/server applications. It is a complete client/server development environment, generating source code, map definitions, graphical user interface resources, database definitions and network protocol definitions. It is also well-known under the former names: ADW or KEY:Enterprise.

This distinction is also important for introducing 'off-the shelf' software products. In case of a fixed and not modifiable data model or data interface, one can only prove how the given model is covering the reference model (SIZ data model). Quite often, you get no insight how this given data model corresponds to the underlying physical database.

3.1.2 Tracing

A trace documents the dependencies between different model versions or between layers in the SIZ data model. In the latter case, normally the relationship between two adjoining levels is described. But there are exceptions, where the trace is written between the projects models and the B-level. Objects are identified by their unique identifiers which are artificial keys. A typical trace would be the mapping of a project database schema to the C-level of the SIZ data model.

Tracing is an important but time-consuming activity aimed at maintaining a consistent data model of proven quality. Every tool support is helpful, however, tools that are offered on the market never matched our needs exactly. Customization of the tools and organizational support were necessary.

The minimum of information that is required in a trace is the combination of two object keys with some additional information to explain the source of the tracing.

id_object	id_object	trace_comment	trace_date	trace_owner
B0000007	C0000007		28.11.1996	team1
B0000006	C0000030	additional relationship	28.11.1996	team2
B0000003	C0000007	flexibility not required	29.11.1996	team1
B0000010	C0000040		30.11.1996	team2

B-level objects

id_object_b	object_name
B00000001	CV INVOLVED PARTY
B00000002	CS INVOLVED PARTY TYPE
:	
B00000013	CV ORGANIZATION
B00000013	CV ORGANIZATION
B....	CV ACCESS

C-level objects

id_object_c	object_name
C00000001	EN INVOLVED PARTY
C00000002	AT INVOLVED PARTY TYPE
:	
C00000023	DT ORGANIZATION
C00000027	EN ORGANIZATION
C......	EN ACCESS

Figure 7: Example of a B-C-level trace

Note that in Figure 7 the classification value Organization (B-level) is mapped to the entity Organization and the domain type Organization (C-level). This controlled redundancy is accepted when modelling super-/subtype relationships.

We see a strong need for an advanced tool support. The technical environment is being improved this year by the introduction of a repository. The decision was made to use ROCHADE[2], because it offered the most flexible meta model to support the SIZ specific layer structure.

3.2 Application Development Projects

The usefulness of the unified data model and the expected benefits varies depending on the banking context that has to be worked through and the need for freedom to create new structures.

We identified three project types from this respect: new development projects, reverse engineering projects and referencing projects.

3.2.1 New Development Projects

If a project starts from scratch developing a new application, it is most helpful to have an initial, comprehensive data model. In our experience an initial project model can be extracted from B- and C-level in very short time. The better the specific information requirements are known at the outset, the easier it is to identify the required elements on the B-level. If the scope of the B-level is marked accordingly it is very easy to extract the counterpart on the C-level. Here the tool M1[3] offers excellent tracing functionality.

This initial project model will be enriched during the modelling phase and might be modified again after understanding the full functionality of the supported application and creating the database design.

3.2.2 Reverse Engineering of Databases

Reverse engineering projects aim to create a logical view of an underlying database of an already existing application. Eventually, the database may be redesigned. As a result, the data requirement of the application is transparent and comparable to other SIZ conforming applications.

In reverse engineering projects the SIZ data model is important to introduce common terms (unified in the GSBO) and to understand the banking context of the existing database. If serious contradictions to one or more "Leitbilder" are discovered, the drawbacks and benefits of a physical redesign can be considered.

[2]Rochade (by R&O) is a enterprise-scale repository environment implemented in a client/server architecture. It is available on all popular platforms. The Rochade repository is designed to handle an organization's total information management need. It is easy to use, scalable, flexible, extensible, reliable and promotes reuse of the models and components defined by the meta data.

[3]Modelware M1 is a new type of software tool specifically designed by ModelWare to support the Information Framework, IFW (IBM). Functions within M1 include: Navigation of all IFW content models, full support for customizing and extending the models, ability to define countless project views that allow users to select model items relevant to a particular project, model management including model comparison, model merge, audit and security functions.

3.2.3 Referencing Projects

When deploying 'off-the-self' software products it is important to understand the data interface offered by these. Usually, only a non-modifiable data model or data interface is given, from which one may prove how the given underlying model is covering the reference model (SIZ data model).

This analysis may support the decision to purchase and deploy 'off-the-shelf' products. Also, such analysis will help to connect the new software to the existing databases if the underlying database is documented with traces to the SIZ data model.

4 Future Work

In the future, the SIZ data model will serve as a basis for several other strategic projects. In these projects, the data model, in particular the B-level, is the appropriate starting point for different unifying approaches.

4.1 Creation of a Common Nomenclature

All financial institutes in the GSBO use nomenclatures for organizing filing cabinets, archives or record offices. Some of them have introduced electronic archive systems. But everywhere, the manual processes for organizing repositories are still regarded as necessary. For all of these processes -manual or electronic- a structure of the records and a list of keywords is necessary. These lists of keywords form a nomenclature which must be used when an information item is classified in order to archive, and later when the archived information item is being searched for. Unfortunately, there is no such single common nomenclature in the GSBO, but several existing, quite redundant and large nomenclatures. Moreover, none of them include definitions of the keywords. Therefore, the data model's B-level is an ideal basis for mapping the existing nomenclatures.

4.2 Definition of a Target Application Architecture

We plan to develop an application reference model which shows all banking business areas and their connections (e.g. [Sch95]). This requires the identification of the domains of business functions and related flow of information. A further elaboration of such functional architecture should then be the connection with business process models. Process models are developed in parallel. Processes manipulate information that has been modelled on various levels of the SIZ data model and associated project models. This description of a target application architecture is useful for each IT centre individually as well as for co-operations between IT centres especially for data and application interchange.

The SIZ data model can be used for finding the information objects which play an important role for the connection between the business functions. When implementing components in the new application architecture the data model should be used.

4.3 Data Warehouse Model

Data warehouse solutions are based on a logical and a physical architecture. The physical architecture describes the database technologies, the extraction, replication and distribution technologies and end user tools such as On-line Analytical Processing (OLAP) tools or Data Mining tools for different search strategies. The logical architecture describes the end user's information requirements, the data warehouse/data mart data model and the references to the original sources of the data items. Building a comprehensive data warehouse solution means at the same time introducing an enterprise-wide view to information requirements and information management, details of which are beyond the scope of this contribution.

The SIZ data model can be used as a base for defining the data warehouse data model because it already has an enterprise-wide view. Some of the "Leitbilder" and kernel entities are very similar to often required dimensions in a data warehouse. The development of data warehouse schemata, however, needs additional input. We already started to expand the modelling techniques for specific data warehouse approaches (see also [Dev97] or [AM97]).

5 Conclusions

The experience of each project was documented and collected in the central data model administration group. We wanted to learn from the pilot projects in order to understand the drawbacks and project needs. The main focus was put upon six criteria:

1. Expenditure on data modelling
2. Reuse of data structures
3. Method and project proceedings
4. Use of the "Leitbilder"
5. Tool support
6. Generating database structures

5.1 Expenditure on Data Modelling

The evaluation showed modelling with the help of the SIZ data model to be more cost-effective than the previous modelling methods. This assessment was especially apparent and positive when compared to estimates made before the SIZ data model was considered. Not only the modelling itself became more efficient, also the planning of time and of manpower resources became more reliable due to the superior overview of the requirements achieved by mapping the first ideas against the B-level.

5.2 Reuse of Data Structures

But how suitable were the already predefined data structures and the quality of the model description from the projects' view? The feedback from individual projects showed clearly that they were suitable. Only the first two projects had the disadvantage of finding very little business content in the required scope.

Actually, projects with an information requirement comparable to projects already finished, found the reuse of data structures to be very helpful. Even if this assessment does not sound astonishing, it is certainly surprising. Earlier on, the IT centres in the GSBO were convinced that their information requirements and their data structures could not be shared with other IT centres. And since all IT centres are independent and there is no top management giving directions to everybody, only the discernment and insight to the benefits for each of them could convince the whole organization.

5.3 Method and Project Proceedings

The evaluation of the modelling method and project work led to a positive assessment of the entire model. The adequate support of the central data administration group was a key success factor. The data management concept was improved and today offers a good description of the project proceedings and the co-operation with the central data administration group.

5.4 Use of the "Leitbilder"

The semantic principles, "Leitbilder", were proved to be necessary as a basis for compatibility. The ease of application of the "Leitbilder" was dependant on the predominant, already implemented database structures - in some cases the application was uncomplicated where as other projects required longer discussions. However, the overall evaluation was again positive.

5.5 Tool Support

Different modelling tools are used. The central data administration team uses the tool M1 (IBM) in connection with Cool:Enterprise (Sterling Software).

These tools can exchange encyclopaedias via a common export file format. M1 is superior for the B-level and the administration of the traces between B- and C-level. Cool:Enterprise is superior for entity relationship modelling and multi user support. Nevertheless, some traces are maintained with MS Access or other tools. This disadvantage will not disappear until a single repository can be used for large traces and model versions. We have started to extend to use of the repository Rochade, but in some projects other tools are still in use.

The other IT centres may use tools of their own choice as long as the export format is compatible. Here, a toolbus is very helpful. Better tool integration is still a large field with potentials for greater synergy and faster information exchange.

5.6 Generating Database Structures

The first pilot projects did not give feedback to physical database design. In pilot projects databases were designed to service the actual needs, based on the project models that conformed to the SIZ data model. But it is obvious, that the more technical details that are included in the SIZ data model, the more help it offers for this physical DB design. It was not our initial goal to achieve physically unified data structures, but on a conceptual level a unified data model. In the future, we intend to extend work towards a technical level.

5.7 Contribution of the Model to Achieve the SIZ Goals

Since the pilot projects gained many benefits from the data model, its use has recently been declared mandatory for any new application development in the IT centres. This model now represents a cornerstone in SIZ's work towards more synergy in the IT area, in particular towards the exchange of applications between IT centres. By itself, it is not sufficient as a base for exchange, but it is a necessary and valuable prerequisite. Moreover, the common terminology and structure will penetrate the whole GSBO over time and thereby make synergy more easily achievable in far more fields than just logical views of data structures.

References

[AM97] Anahory, S., Murray, D., Data Warehousing in the Real World, Addison-Wesley-Longman, Harlow, England, 1997

[BCN92] Batini, C., Ceri, S., Navathe, S. B., Database Design, An Entity-Relationship-Approach, Redwood City, 1992

[Che76] Chen, P. P., The Entity-Relationship Model - Towards a Unified View of Data, ACM Transactions on Database Systems, vol. 1, no. 1, 1976, 9-36

[Dat86] Date, C. J., An Introduction to Database Systems, vol. 1, Addison-Wesley-Longman, Reading, Massachusetts, 1986

[Dev97] Devlin, B., Data Warehouse - from Architecture to Implementation, Addison-Wesley-Longman, Reading, Massachusetts, 1997

[Dur85] Durell, W., Data Administration - A Practical Guide to Successful Data Management, New York, 1985

[Eve96] Everden, R., The Information Framework, IBM Systems Journal, vol. 35, no.1, 1996, 37-68

[Gil85] Gilleson, M. L., Trends in Data Administration, MIS Quarterly, vol 9, no. 4, 1985, 317-325

[SIZ97] SIZ, Modelling Handbook - Modellierungshandbuch SIZ, Bonn, in German, 1997

[SH92] Scheer, A.-W., Hars, A., Extending data Modeling to Cover the Whole Enterprise, CACM, vol. 35, no.9, 1992, 166-172

[Sch95] Schmalzl, J., Architekturmodelle zur Planung der Informationsverarbeitung von Kreditinstituten, Heidelberg, 1995

[SZ92] Sowa, J. F., Zachman, J. A., Extending and Formalizing the framework for information systems architecture, IBM Systems Journal, vol. 31, no. 3, 1992, 590-616

[TL82] Tsichritzis, D., Lochovsky, F., Data Models, Prentice Hall, Englewood Cliffs, 1982

[Zac87] Zachman, J. A., A Framework for Information System Architecture, IBM Systems Journal, vol. 26, no. 3, 1987, 276-292

CHAPTER 32

ODP and OMA Reference Models

Andy Bond, Keith Duddy, Kerry Raymond

The Reference Model of Open Distributed Processing (RM-ODP) was a joint effort by the international standards bodies ISO and ITU-T to develop a generic architecture for the standardisation of open distributed processing (ODP). The model describes a framework within which support of distribution, interworking, interoperability and portability can be integrated. The Object Management Architecture (OMA) was developed by the Object Management Group (OMG) as a specific architecture based on the generic principles and structures of RM-ODP. The OMA provides a framework for an integrated suite of standards for object-oriented distributed computing.

1 Introduction

Advances in computer networking have allowed computer systems across the world to be interconnected. Despite this, heterogeneity in interaction models prevents interworking between systems. Open distributed processing (ODP) describes systems that support heterogeneous distributed processing both within and between organizations through the use of a common interaction model.

ISO and ITU-T (formerly CCITT) have developed a Reference Model of Open Distributed Processing (RM-ODP) to provide a coordinating framework for the standardisation of ODP by creating an architecture which supports distribution, interworking, interoperability and portability.

The Object Management Group (OMG) has developed an Object Management Architecture (OMA) [Sol95] as a basis for their members to specify a distributed object computing framework which can be independently implemented by any software company. The basic communications mechanism, CORBA, has been stable for several years, and is implemented by dozens of different products.

2 Open Distributed Processing

2.1 The Goals and Deliverables of RM-ODP

RM-ODP aims to achieve:

- portability of applications across heterogeneous platforms
- interworking between ODP systems, i.e. meaningful exchange of information and convenient use of functionality throughout the distributed system
- distribution transparency, i.e. hide the consequences of distribution from both the applications programmer and user.

RM-ODP provides a "big picture" that organises the pieces of an ODP system into a coherent whole. It does not try to standardise the components of the system nor to unnecessarily influence the choice of technology.

There are many challenges in developing a reference model. RM-ODP must be adequate to describe most "reasonable" distributed systems available both today and in the future, so RM-ODP is abstract, but not vague. RM-ODP carefully describes its components without prescribing an implementation.

2.2 Structure of RM-ODP

The RM-ODP standard is known as both ISO International Standard 10746 and ITU-T X.900 Series of Recommendations and consists of four parts:

- Part 1: Overview (ISO 10746-1/ITU-T X.901)[RMODP-1]
- Part 2: Foundations (ISO 10746-2/ITU-T X.902)[RMODP-2]
- Part 3: Architecture (ISO 10746-3/ITU-T X.903)[RMODP-3]
- Part 4: Architectural Semantics (ISO 10746-4/ITU-T X.904)[RMODP-4]

Part 1 contains a motivational overview of ODP and explains the key concepts of the RM-ODP architecture. Part 2 gives precise definitions of the concepts required to specify distributed processing systems. Part 3 prescribes a framework of concepts, structures, rules, and functions required for open distributed processing. Part 4 describes how the modelling concepts of Part 2 can be represented in a number of formal description techniques.

This section focuses on the architecture described in Part 3.

2.3 Viewpoints

Part 3 of RM-ODP prescribes a framework using viewpoints from which to abstract or view ODP systems. A set of concepts, structures, and rules is given for each of the viewpoints, providing a "language" for specifying ODP systems in that viewpoint.

RM-ODP defines the following five viewpoints:

- Enterprise Viewpoint (purpose, scope and policies)
- Information Viewpoint (semantics of information and information processing)
- Computational Viewpoint (functional decomposition)
- Engineering Viewpoint (infrastructure required to support distribution)
- Technology Viewpoint (choices of technology for implementation).

Specifying an ODP system using each of the viewpoint languages allows an otherwise large and complex specification of an ODP system to be separated into manageable pieces, each focused on the issues relevant to different members of the development team. For example, the information analyst works with the information specification while the systems programmer is concerned with the engineering viewpoint. Figure 1 shows how the RM-ODP viewpoints can be related to the software engineering process.

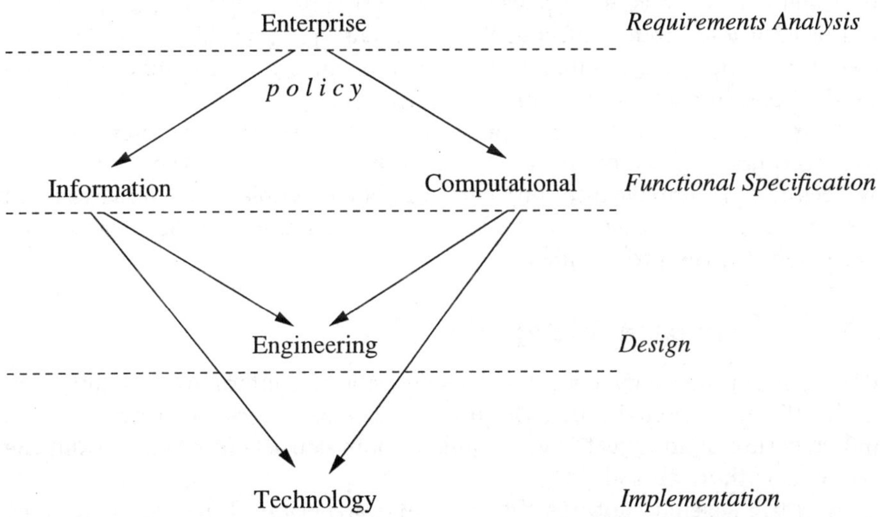

Figure 1: RM-ODP Viewpoints and Software Engineering

2.4 Enterprise Viewpoint

The enterprise viewpoint is used to specify organisational requirements and structure. In the enterprise viewpoint, social and organisational policies can be defined in terms of:

- objects - both "active" objects, e.g. bank managers, tellers, customers, and "passive" objects, e.g. bank accounts, money
- communities - groupings of objects intended to achieve some purpose, e.g. a bank branch consists of a bank manager, some tellers, and some bank accounts; the branch provides banking services to a geographical area
- roles of the objects within communities, expressed in terms of policies:
  - permission - what can be done, e.g. money can be deposited into an open account
  - prohibition - what must not be done, e.g. customers must not withdraw more than $500 per day
  - obligations - what must be done, e.g. the bank manager must advise customers when the interest rate changes.

The enterprise language is specifically concerned with performative actions that change policy, such as creating an obligation or revoking permission. In a bank, the changing of interest rates is a performative action as it creates obligations on the bank manager to inform the customers. However, obtaining an account balance is not a performative action as obligations, permissions, and prohibitions are not affected. Thus, an enterprise specification of a bank need not include the obtaining of account balances; such functionality will be identified in the computational specification.

By preparing an enterprise specification of an ODP application, policies are determined by the organisation rather than imposed on the organisation by technology (implementation) choices. For example, a customer should not be limited to having only one bank account, simply because it was more convenient for the programmer.

2.5 Information Viewpoint

The information viewpoint is used to describe the information required by an ODP application through the use of schemas, which describe the state and structure of an object; e.g., a bank account consists of a balance and the "amount withdrawn today".

A static schema captures the state and structure of an object at some particular instant; e.g., at midnight, the amount-withdrawn-today is $0.

An invariant schema restricts the state and structure of an object at all times; e.g., the amount-withdrawn-today is less than or equal to $500.

A dynamic schema defines a permitted change in the state and structure of an object; e.g. a withdrawal of $X from an account decreases the balance by $X and increases the amount-withdrawn-today by $X. A dynamic schema is always constrained by the invariant schemas. Thus, $400 could be withdrawn in the morning but an additional $200 could not be withdrawn in the afternoon as the amount-withdrawn-today cannot exceed $500.

Schemas can also be used to describe relationships or associations between objects; e.g., the static schema "owns account" could associate each account with a customer.

A schema can be composed from other schemas to describe complex or composite objects; e.g., a bank branch consists of a set of customers, a set of accounts, and the "owns account" relationship.

The information specification of an ODP application could be expressed using a variety of methods, e.g., entity-relationships models, conceptual schemas, or the Z formal description technique.

2.6 Computational Viewpoint

The computational viewpoint is used to specify the functionality of an ODP application in a distribution-transparent manner. RM-ODP's computational viewpoint is object-based, that is:

- objects encapsulate data and processing (i.e. behaviour)
- objects offer interfaces for interaction with other objects
- objects can offer multiple interfaces.

A computational specification defines the objects within an ODP system, the activities within those objects, and the interactions that occur among objects. Most objects in a computational specification describe application functionality, and these objects are linked by bindings through which interactions occur. Binding objects are used to describe complex interaction between objects.

Objects in a computational specification can be application objects (e.g. a bank branch) or ODP infrastructure objects (e.g. a type repository or a trader, see Section 2.9.3). Figure 2 illustrates a bank branch object providing a bank teller interface and a bank manager interface. Both interfaces can be used to deposit and withdraw money, but accounts can be created only through the bank manager interface. Each of the bank branch object's interfaces is bound to a customer object.

2.6.1 Computational Interaction

RM-ODP provides three forms of interaction between objects: operational, stream-oriented, and signal-oriented.

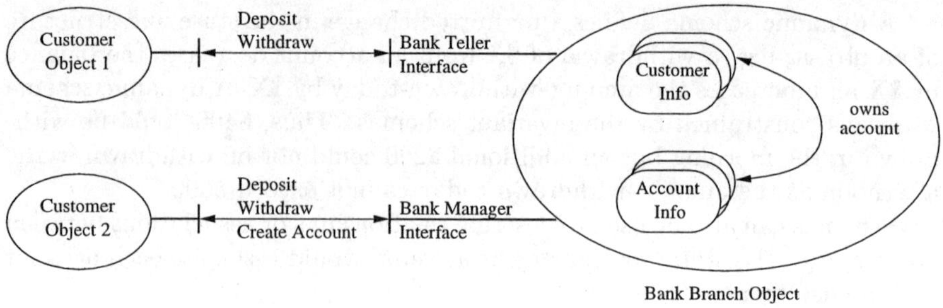

Figure 2: Bank Branch Object with Bank Manager and Bank Teller Interfaces

Operational interfaces provide a client-server model for distributed computing; client objects invoke operations at the interfaces of server objects (i.e. the remote procedure call paradigm). Operational interfaces consist of named operations with parameters, terminations, and results. Operations in RM-ODP can be either interrogations (which return a termination) or announcements (which do not return a termination).

For example, a bank branch object offers a number of BankTeller operational interfaces, whose signature is defined as:

```
BankTeller = Interface Type {

    operation Deposit (c: Customer, a: Account, d: Dollars)
        returns OK (new_balance: Dollars)

    operation Withdraw (c: Customer, a: Account, d: Dollars)
        returns OK (new_balance: Dollars)
        returns NotToday (today: Dollars, limit: Dollars)
}
```

Note that the notation used in the example above is merely illustrative. RM-ODP does not prescribe any particular notation for defining operational interface types. However, it has adopted the use of CORBA IDL for the specification of the operational interfaces to the RM-ODP functions.

Stream interfaces provide (logically) continuous streams of information flowing between producer and consumer objects. Consumer objects connect to the stream interfaces of producer objects or vice-versa, and several streams can be grouped in a single interface, e.g., an audio stream and a video stream. Stream interfaces have been included in RM-ODP to cater for multi-media and telecommunications applications.

Underlying both operational interfaces and stream interfaces are signal interfaces which provide very low-level communications actions. The OSI service primitives (REQUEST, INDICATE, RESPONSE, and CONFIRM) are examples of signals.

2.6.2 Interface Subtyping

The concept of interface type is particularly important in RM-ODP. Interfaces in the computational model are strongly typed and inheritance of an interface type (usually) creates a subtype relationship. Subtypes of an interface type are substitutable for the parent type (or any super-type).

Figure 3 illustrates interface subtyping. The BankManager and LoansOfficer interface types are subtypes of the BankTeller interface (super-)type; either can substitute for a BankTeller as they can perform the Deposit and Withdraw operations expected of a BankTeller. Neither a BankTeller nor a LoansOfficer can replace a BankManager, as neither can provide the CreateAccount operation.

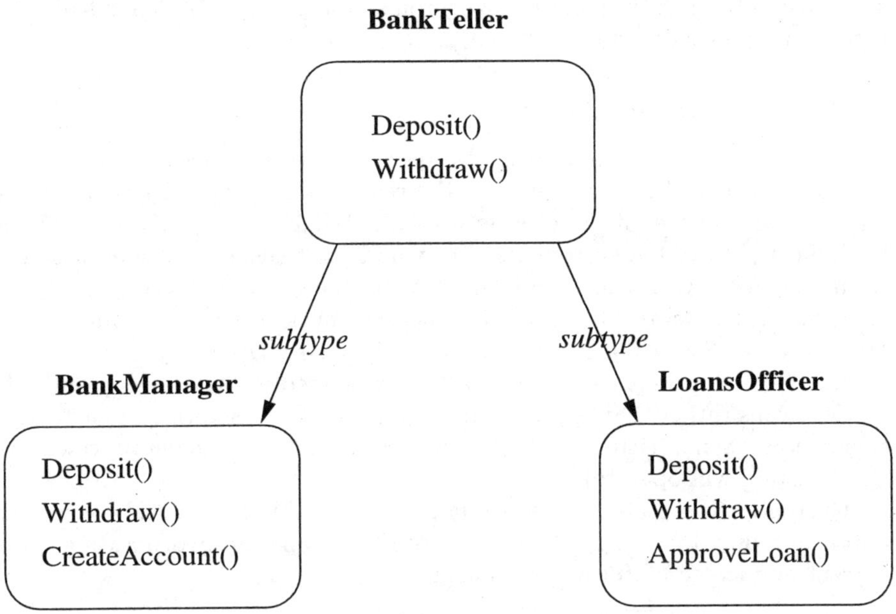

Figure 3: Example of Interface Subtyping

2.6.3 Computational Activity

The computational viewpoint also defines the actions that are possible within a computational object.

These are:

- creating and destroying an object
- creating and destroying an interface

- trading for a interface (see Section 2.9.3)
- binding to an interface
- reading and writing the state of the object
- invoking an operation at an operational interface
- producing/consuming a flow at a stream interface
- initiating or responding to a signal at a signal interface.

These basic actions can be composed in sequence or in parallel. If composed in parallel, the parallel activities can be dependent (the activity is forked and must subsequently join at a synchronisation point) or independent (the activity is spawned and cannot join).

2.6.4 Environment Contracts

The refinement of a computational object and its interfaces might require the specification of requirements on the realization of that object or its interfaces (and, hence, of the objects with which it interacts). For example, a bank must protect the customer's money and must ensure that interaction is secure against a variety of fraudulent activities, e.g. capturing and replaying operations. Therefore, the actual interactions must either be communicated over a secure network or employ end-to-end security checks.

Ideally, environment contracts will be expressed in high-level quality-of-service terms rather than, e.g., specifying a particular network or a particular encryption scheme (either of which presupposes the environment in which the ODP system will operate).

Currently, the state of the art falls short of this ideal. However, it is important that RM-ODP be "future-proof", capable of incorporating both current and expected future technologies.

2.7 Engineering Viewpoint

The engineering viewpoint is used to describe the design of distribution-oriented aspects of an ODP system; it defines a model for distributed systems infrastructure. The engineering viewpoint is not concerned with the semantics of the ODP application, except to determine its requirements for distribution and distribution transparency.

The fundamental entities described in the engineering viewpoint are objects and channels. Objects in the engineering viewpoint can be divided into two categories: basic engineering objects (corresponding to objects in the computational specification) and infrastructure objects (e.g., a protocol object – see below). A channel corresponds to a binding in the computational specification.

2.7.1 Channels

A channel provides the communication mechanism and contains or controls the transparency functions required by the basic engineering objects, as specified in the environment contracts in the computational specification. Figure 4 illustrates the channel between a Customer Object and the Bank Branch object in Figure 2. The shaded area is the channel, composed of stubs, binders, and protocol objects. Stubs and binders are used to provide various distribution transparencies.

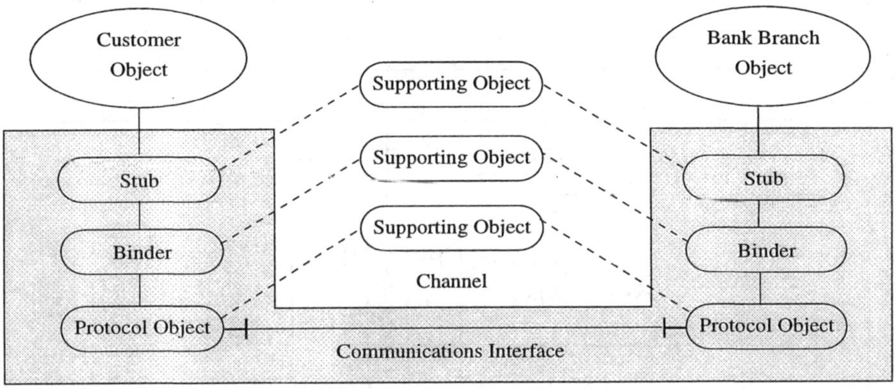

Figure 4: Structure of a Channel

Stubs are created with knowledge of the application interface types. Therefore, transparencies which use knowledge of application interface types must be at least partially implemented using stubs. For example, a stub might be used to maintain an audit trail of operations and their parameters.

Binders are independent of an application's interface types; they merely transport the messages (bit streams). Binders are responsible for managing the binding between the basic engineering objects; e.g., binders could use sequence numbers to foil capture-and-replay attempts.

Protocol objects interact via a communications interface; this models networking.

Outside of the channel, supporting objects assist the stub, binder, and protocol objects within the channel. Typically, supporting objects are repositories of information required by the stubs, binders, and protocol objects. For example, binders register and retrieve interface locations via a supporting object known as the relocator (see Section 2.9.3) in order to achieve location transparency.

2.7.2 Engineering Structures

The RM-ODP engineering viewpoint prescribes the structure of an ODP system. The basic units of structure are:

- cluster - a set of related basic engineering objects that will always be co-located
- capsule - a set of clusters, a cluster manager for each cluster, a capsule manager, and the parts of the channels which connect to their interfaces
- nucleus object - an (extended) operating system supporting ODP
- node - a computer system.

Figure 5 illustrates the structure of a node. Given these definitions, the

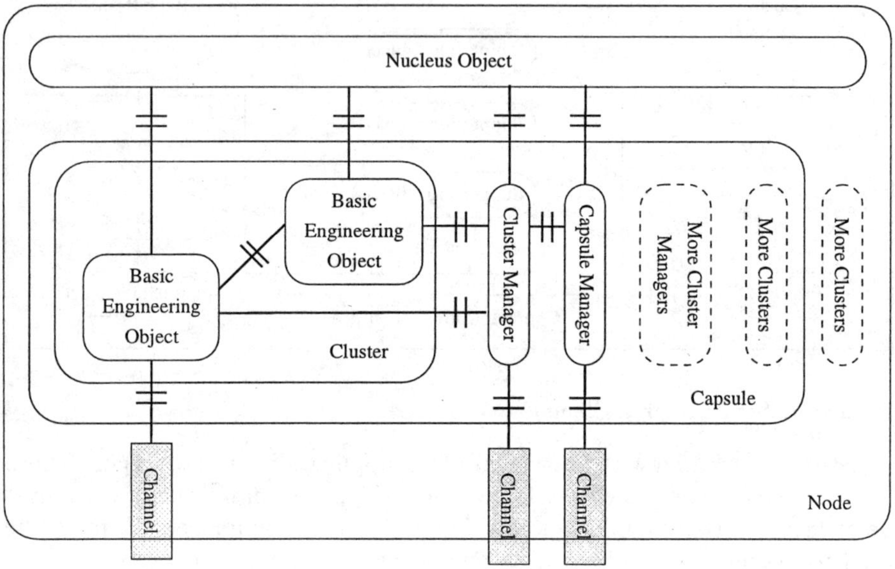

Figure 5: Structure of a Node

following structuring rules are defined:

- a node has a nucleus object
- a nucleus object can support many capsules
- a capsule can contain many clusters
- a cluster can contain many basic engineering objects
- a basic engineering object can contain many activities
- all inter-cluster communication is via channels.

An implementation of an ODP system can choose to constrain the structuring, for example, by allowing:

- only one object per cluster
- only one cluster per capsule.

2.8 Technology Viewpoint

A technology specification of an ODP system describes the implementation of that system and the information required for testing. RM-ODP has very few rules applicable to technology specifications.

2.9 ODP Functions

The ODP functions are a collection of functions expected to be required in ODP systems to support the needs of the computational language (e.g. the trading function) and the engineering language (e.g. the relocator). The following subsections outline the major function groups in RM-ODP; a few of the functions are discussed in more detail to illustrate the scope of RM-ODP.

2.9.1 Management Functions

RM-ODP defines a number of functions to manage the engineering structures, including:

- node management function (provided by the nucleus) for creating capsules and channels
- capsule management function (provided by the capsule manager) for instantiating clusters and checkpointing and deactivating clusters in a capsule
- cluster management function (provided by the cluster manager) for checkpointing, deactivating and migrating clusters
- object management function (provided by the basic engineering object) for checkpointing and deleting basic engineering objects.

2.9.2 Coordination Functions

RM-ODP defines a number of functions aimed at coordinating the actions of a number of objects, clusters, or capsules in order to produce some consistent overall effect.

These include:

- checkpoint and recovery
- deactivation and reactivation
- event notification

- groups and replication
- migration
- transactions.

2.9.3 Repository Functions

In addition to a general storage function and a general relationship repository, RM-ODP defines a number of specific repository functions, concerned with maintaining a database of specialised classes of information. These include:

- service offer repository (trader), which stores information about the services in the ODP system enabling clients to select services on the basis of interface type and other characteristics (e.g. quality of service, ownership)
- interface location repository (relocator), which holds the current location of an interface, enabling a client to rebind to an interface after migration or recovery
- type repository to support type checking during trading and binding.

2.9.4 Security Functions

RM-ODP defines a number of security functions (e.g. access control, authentication, auditing) based on OSI Security Frameworks in Open Systems [ISO-Security].

2.10 Transparencies

Computational specifications are intended to be distribution-transparent, i.e., written without regard to the very real difficulties of implementation within a physically distributed, heterogeneous, multi-organisational environment. The aim of transparencies is to shift the complexities of distributed systems from the applications developers to the supporting infrastructure.

RM-ODP defines a number of commonly required distribution transparencies and describes the computational refinements and use of engineering functions needed to provide these transparencies. The distribution transparencies defined in RM-ODP are:

- access transparency - hides the differences in data representation and procedure calling mechanism to enable interworking between heterogeneous computer systems.
- location transparency - masks the use of physical addresses, including the distinction between local versus remote.

- relocation transparency - hides the relocation of an object and its interfaces from other objects and interfaces bound to it.
- migration transparency - masks the relocation of an object from that object and the objects with which it interacts.
- persistence transparency - masks the deactivation and reactivation of an object.
- failure transparency - masks the failure and possible recovery of objects, to enhance fault tolerance.
- replication transparency - maintains consistency of a group of replica objects with a common interface.
- transaction transparency - hides the coordination required to satisfy the transactional properties of operations.

The transparencies defined in RM-ODP are not intended to be the complete set, merely a starting point of common requirements. Additional transparencies for both general and specific needs could be subsequently standardised. For example, lip-sync transparency could be defined for stream interfaces supporting audio-visual interaction.

3 The Object Management Architecture

The Object Management Architecture (OMA) is a Reference Architecture for the standardisation of the distributed, object-oriented application development framework being developed by the Object Management Group (OMG). The centre-piece of this Architecture is the Object Request Broker (ORB), a distribution-transparent method invocation bus that is specified in the Common Object Request Broker Architecture (CORBA) standard. Industry jargon has come to use the term CORBA to represent the whole of the OMA and all the standards based upon it. The Object Management Architecture Guide [Sol95], which explains the OMA, also contains the Core Object Model, which is a set of foundation concepts used as the basis for CORBA.

3.1 OMA Rationale

The OMA recognises that in order to build distributed systems more is needed than just a remote method invocation mechanism. However, the complete set of additional services and facilities required to support distributed objects could not be predicted when the OMG began standardising CORBA. Therefore, the OMA Reference Model attempts to provide a template for standardisation of infrastructure to support CORBA.

The OMA has evolved since it was first published in the OMA Guide [Sol95]. The Reference Model has always seen the Object Request Broker as the core component that facilitates communication in a distributed application. It states that additional support for the application should be supplied by objects that are identical to application objects in their specification, development and use by the application. The Core Object Model is the basis of the CORBA specification. The Guide also contains a manifesto of the OMG, and explains how the organisation of the OMG closely reflects the structure of the OMA.

3.2 OMA Categories

From its first publication in 1990, until 1995, the OMA contained three categories for object specifications to be populated as requirements became clearer following discussions and developments in the OMG. As illustrated in Figure 6, the categories are:

Application Objects. The parts of a distributed system which provide the application functionality, e.g. the business logic.

Object Services **[OMG96, Trader].** The basic or lower-level services that support applications and the provision of the object-oriented infrastructure. The object services provide configuration and administration needed by all applications, including such services as Naming, Trading and Event transmission.

Common Facilities. These provide common application functionality. This group of services was seen to be higher-level, and directly usable by an application. Common Facilities were subdivided into horizontal facilities (across industry domains) and vertical facilities (specific to an industry domain). Only a small number of Common Facilities were standardised in the first 5 years of the OMG. For example, the Common Document Management Facility, based on OpenDoc.

3.3 The Model Evolves

As it became clear that the OMG required buy-in from end-user communities in order to become a success, the number of special interest groups for various application domains increased rapidly. In 1996, the original Technical Committee of the OMG to which smaller Task Force groups reported was split into two Technical Committees:

Platform Technical Committee (PTC). Specifies objects to be implemented by ORB vendors for the provision of the CORBA infrastructure.

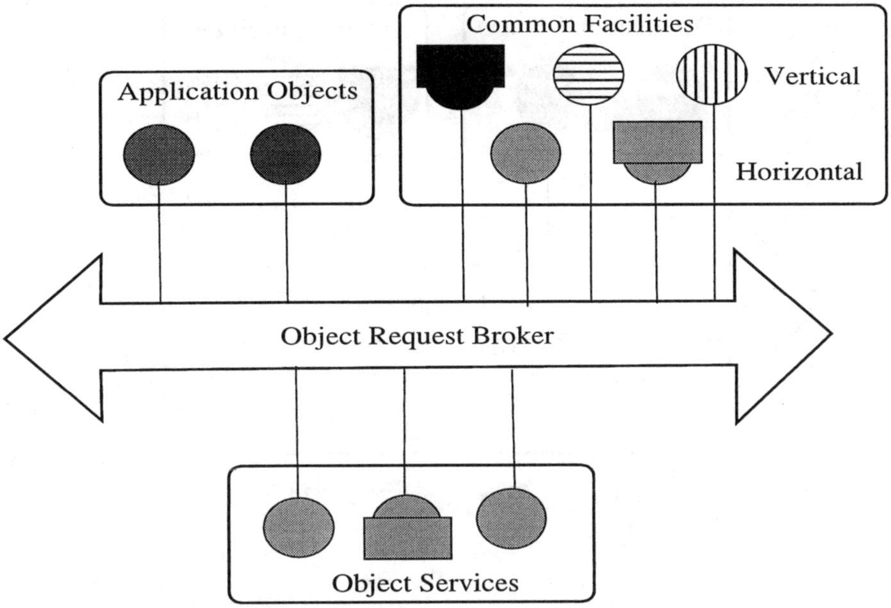

Figure 6: The OMA Reference Model in 1995

Domain Technical Committee (DTC). Specifies objects meeting the needs of specific industry domains.

At the same time, the Common Facilities grouping within the OMA was split, moving the vertical facilities under the control of new Task Forces within the Domain Technical Committee. The Common Facilities Task Force (TF) continued to specify horizontal facilities.

By mid-1997, there were six Task Forces and a number of special interest groups within the DTC, covering such diverse areas as Health-care, Electronic Commerce and Telecommunications. The PTC contained the ORB and Object Services (ORBOS) TF, Common Facilities TF and the Object Analysis and Design (OA&D) TF.

Requirements for particular technologies within certain vertical domains that fulfilled both an industry specific requirement, as well as being horizontally applicable across domains led to confusion over the role of the Common Facilities TF. It was abolished in June 1997. Its continuing work was redistributed to various DTFs and to the two remaining Platform TFs. Although no official updates have been made to the OMA Reference Model, the current de-facto structure appears as in Figure 7.

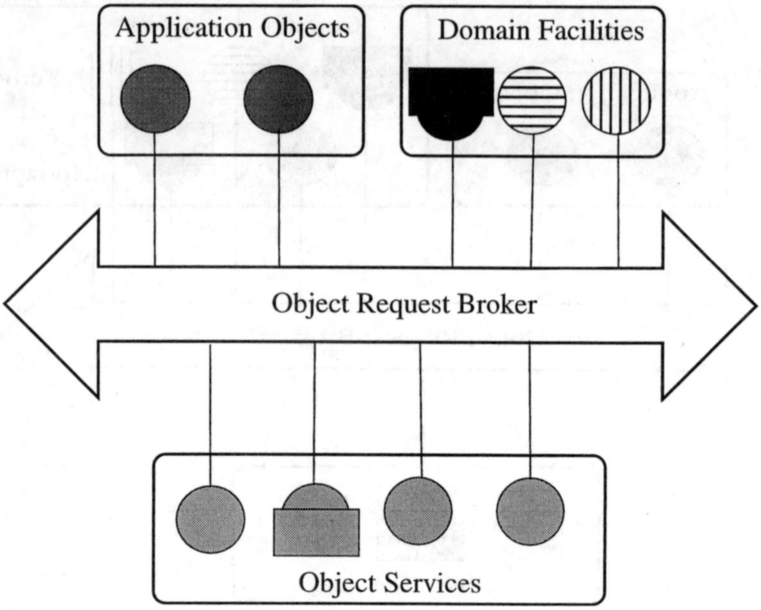

Figure 7: The OMA Reference Model after June 1997

3.4 Core Object Model

The Core Object Model is a concrete basis for the specification of a distributed object system. It is expressed in English, and provides definitions for some fundamental concepts that must be extended to produce any OMA compliant distributed object system. The mechanism for extending the Core is to define *components* that build upon the definitions in the Core, producing what is called a *profile*.

The CORBA specification [OMG95] is an example of a set of components that make the Core concepts usable by real implementations. CORBA's components consist of the Interface Description Language (IDL), Programming Language Mappings, Security, Interoperability Protocols and a number of other functions.

CORBA is the only profile required within the OMG, and it is published with major/minor version numbers that define a current standard to which ORB implementations should conform. However, the Object Database Management Group (ODMG) also uses the OMA Core Object Model and extends it with some CORBA components and some additional components for Database access. This profile is published as the Object Database Standard: ODMG 2.0 [ODS].

3.4.1 Core Object Model Concepts

The key concepts defined in the Core are:

Object. A model of an entity or concept with an identity. Identities are encapsulated in an *object reference.*

Operation. An action offered by an object which is made visible to the outside world by means of its signature. A signature contains a name, parameters and results.

Non-object Types. Other types that can have values which are not references to objects may be defined. None are actually given in the Core definition, but they are a placeholder for things like numbers, strings, records and sequences.

Interface. A collection of operation signatures which can be related to other such collections by inheritance. Inheritance defines a means of identifying subtypes.

Substitutability. Substitution of interfaces can be done according to subtyping. That is, a subtype may be substituted where a super-type is required.

4 Comparison between RM-ODP and OMA

The Reference Model for ODP is a meta-model that is meant to be instantiated by many different concrete models which use its concepts as a framework. The Object Management Architecture, on the other hand, is a concrete set of classifications for components of a distributed system which is gradually being populated by the specifications adopted by the OMG. The OMG Guide [Sol95] explicitly refers to RM-ODP as a basis for the Architecture; however, the mapping between the two is only beginning to be documented by the OMG's Semantics Working Group.

RM-ODP and OMA have definitely impacted on one another, and it is useful to understand how the OMA complies with the RM-ODP framework, and how the OMA is influencing RM-ODP in return.

4.1 Transparencies

The OMA provides specific concepts and technologies that allow the implementation of various transparencies (as specified in Section 2.10). The concept in CORBA of an *object reference* encapsulates and enables access transparency, location transparency, relocation transparency and persistence transparency. In other words, an object reference is used by clients to invoke operations on a CORBA object regardless of which programming language the client and object are implemented in, and regardless of the location and current run-state of the object.

Transaction transparency and migration transparency are provided by the Transaction Service and Life Cycle Service respectively. The ORB also extends access transparency to full programming language transparency, which is provided by the use of an Interface Definition Language (IDL) with mappings to programming languages.

4.2 Viewpoints

The OMA is not specifically expressed in terms of ODP viewpoints, but the use of IDL for object-oriented interface signature specifications of CORBA, Object Services and Domain Interfaces, suggests that most OMG specifications are within the ODP computational viewpoint. OMG specifications that are concerned with programming language mappings and ORB interworking are within the ODP engineering viewpoint. As the OMA explicitly prohibits the use of implementation-specific specifications, the OMG is unlikely to develop specifications in the ODP technology viewpoint.

The efforts being undertaken in the OMG's Object Analysis and Design Task Force are intended to be used as tools of the enterprise viewpoint, which can then be refined to become expressions of computational and information viewpoints. This is closely aligned with the Business Objects Domain Task Force, which aims to provide even higher-level modelling of enterprise requirements, and provide facilities for mapping these (semi-)automatically into lower-level viewpoint artifacts.

4.3 Other Linkages

There has also been some influence in the reverse direction. The OMG's IDL has been adopted in ISO as a standard notation for expressing operational interfaces in the computational viewpoint. In that role, the OMG's IDL has been used in the specification of RM-ODP services and functions.

The recent joint adoption by OMG and ISO of the Object Trading Service/Trading Function Specification [Trader, ODP-Trader] had a long and intertwined history. The work commenced within the ODP group in ISO but was completed by the OMG, and then jointly standardised by both groups. There are intentions to develop further joint standards between the ODP and OMG groups based on their mutual overlap of interests.

References

[ISO-Security] ISO/IEC CD 10181, Security Frameworks in Open Systems

[ODP-Trader] ISO/IEC IS 13235-1, ITU/T Draft Rec X950 - 1, ODP Trading Function - Part 1: Specification, 1997

[ODS] The Object Database Standard: ODMG 2.0, R.G.G. Cattell *et al* (eds.), Morgan Kaufman Publishing, 1997

[OMG95] The Common Object Request Broker: Architecture and Specification, Revision 2.0, OMG, 1995

[OMG96] CORBAservices: Common Object Services Specification, Revised Edition - Updated, OMG, 1996

[RMODP-1] ISO/IEC 10746-1, Open Distributed Processing: Reference Model - Part 1: Overview, 1997

[RMODP-2] ISO/IEC 10746-2, Open Distributed Processing: Reference Model - Part 2: Foundations, 1996

[RMODP-3] ISO/IEC 10746-3, Open Distributed Processing: Reference Model - Part 3: Architecture, 1996

[RMODP-4] ISO/IEC 10746-4, Open Distributed Processing: Reference Model - Part 4: Architectural Semantics, 1997

[Sol95] Soley, R. M., Object Management Architecture Guide, Third Edition, John Wiley & Sons, 1995

[Trader] Trading Object Service, OMG TC Document orbos/96-07-26, 1996

PART FIVE

Selected Topics in Integrating Infrastructures

As a result of the International Conference on Enterprise Modelling Technology (ICEIMT) process in 1992 a reference model for integration has been proposed, with four domains of integration:

- Execution Environment (the information system infrastructure, including humans, computers, communication systems and all hardware and software),
- Application Architecture (the system of application programs that supports business),
- Enterprise Characterisation (models, descriptions of the information in the enterprise),
- Federation Mechanisms (how the above three domains of integration are working together).

This categorisation of the elements of the information system is reported in detail by Ted Goranson in Chapter 33. As it was identified in the subsequent ICEIMT process in 1997, and also widely practiced in the software engineering industry the level of Information Systems integration can be measured with some form of *capability* model that the system achieves through integration. It has been clear that at the end of the 1990's physical systems integration, and much of application integration, are feasible. Physical system integration is achieved through standards (although with a large overhead due to political and historical reasons). Application systems integration techniques are largely based on two techniques: database integration, with enterprises trying to establish enterprise-wide data models and the development of large suites of programs from which tailored interoperable applications can be generated for particular businesses. Examples for both can be found in the fourth part of this Handbook. However, these integration forms do not necessarily lend enough agility and flexibility to the enterprise. Through making the information visible in the enterprise, such as the models of business processes, it becomes possible to implement model based integration, whereupon the execution environment can execute business process models. Richard Weston, Ian Coutts and Paul Clements in Chapter 34 present the technical requirements for this, and also present such a prototype infrastructure.

The most important underlying component of integrating infrastructures is the existence of a distributed processing platform, and Andy Bond, Keith Duddy, Kerry Raymond present in Chapter 35 the essential building blocks. However, higher level, adaptable behaviour of the enterprise necessitates that information integration should not become a completely wired-in facility, or at least that rewiring should be easy, quick, and reliable. It is therefore plausible to assume that truly adaptable and agile systems will themselves have the capability to establish connectivities and decide on joint action, instead of relying on some pre-designed connectivity structure. This of course will need the use of techniques through which relatively independent subsystems, via negotiation protocols, could co-ordinate their activities, including one another's discovery, negotiation and commitment to some shared goal or mission, decision on joint action, and the ensuing delivery of service or production. Mihai Barbuceanu and Rune Teigen present in Chapter 36 techniques that are capable of achieving such a higher level integration.

Peter Bernus

CHAPTER 33

Architectural Requirements of Commercial Products

Ted Goranson

Information architectures only become relevant to most enterprises when they instance in commercially supported products. The mapping of technical appropriateness to commercial appropriateness is not straightforward; it involves a number factors from a larger perspective that act as architectural constraints, often resulting in unintuitive decisions. This contribution reviews those factors. It extends results from a large joint U. S./European precompetitive activity among major information infrastructure suppliers and a recent re-examination. Any such review which relies on specific products as examples is likely to become dated, so in the interest of making these insights more longer-lived, we'll be more general than specific with regard to products.

1 Introduction: The ICEIMT1 Model

1.1 Background

From 1989-91, a special project was sponsored by the major suppliers of information architectures. It was the first and to date only *precompetitive* effort among these firms. It was broadbased in looking at all architectural issues, and very well funded. It got its antitrust protection by being facilitated by the Air Force Manufacturing Technology Directorate (ManTech) and the Defense Advanced Research Projects Agency (DARPA).

The Joint U. S./European *International Conference on Enterprise Integration Modeling Technology* was devised as the relatively low-key public means of reporting some of the results of this work [Pet92]. The sponsoring precompetitive group, the *Suppliers' Working Group* (SWG), was linked to high levels in the participating firms and major strategic shifts in many of those firms resulted following this work.

Among the products of the study were the first complete quantitative assessments of the size, leverage and components of the architectural marketplace. (There were also related national security concerns addressed.) As a significant preparatory effort, detailed proprietary information was pooled from the sponsors concerning 100 international case studies, each of which were revisited under the project.

A workable generic reference model for architectural approaches was devised, and was used to characterize the then strategic directions of each player with the intent of discriminating precompetitive architectural issues from competitive ones.

Because of policy issues in the U. S., the precompetitive program was not continued as such after 1992, but a DARPA/ManTech effort worked to extend and apply the reference model to specific high payoff problems. One of these, information architectures for *agility*, is noted below.

Here, we leverage and extend the results of that initial work, report on results a second ICEIMT which extend this view and provide related perspectives for support of Enterprise Integration.

1.2 Four Major Divisions

The high level of the first ICEIMT reference model is outlined in Figure 1.

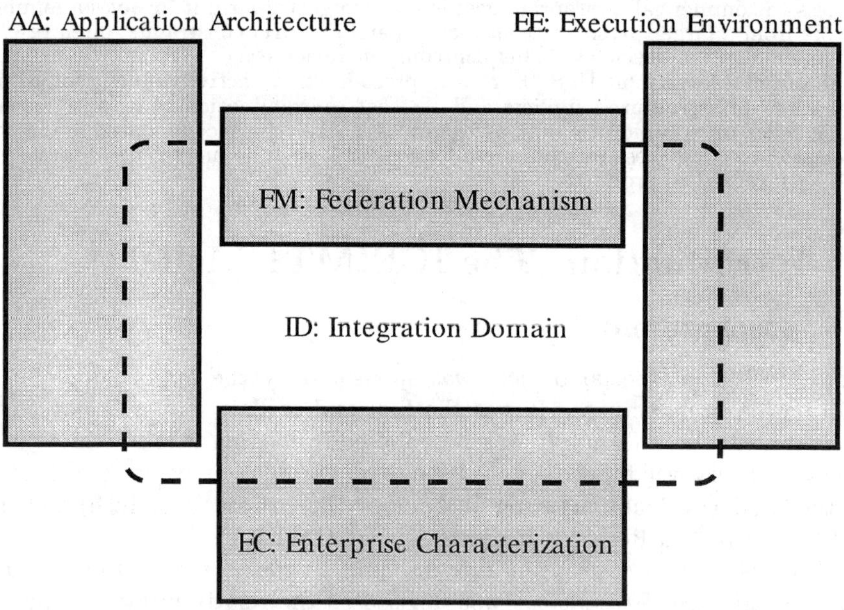

Figure 1: The first ICEIMT reference model

- The box on the left refers to the Application Architecture (AA) which comprises the activity of the enterprise: what it does to conduct its business.

- The box on the right is the Execution Environment (EE). It is constituted from the operating system and communication services used to support the AA functions. In a sense, these are *secondary* services, ones which an enterprise performs only to support those on the left, serving its primary business. The EE includes hardware, but since the model is for *all* information in an enterprise, these services may not all be computer-based.

- The lower box denotes the *information* within the enterprise, which we chose to term Enterprise Characterization (EC); this is both information, such as data and models used by the AA, but also operational information used by the EE.

- Among those three boxes is a fourth *space* denoting the Integration Domain (ID), various strategies used to relate the three areas and provide bases for structuring services within each. These were characterized as the various Federation Mechanisms (FM).

The original work employed an elaboration of this model to define different architectures into which all major product architectures fit. And, as mentioned, we were able to then segregate out technical issues which all shared and could address in a precompetitive space. The purpose of the model was to identify key underlying principles that support EI, and evaluate the strengths and weaknesses of those principles in a *commercial*, rather than purely technical context.

For practical purposes, all of our specific ICEIMT1 *product* parsing is now obsolete as several product cycles have washed through the industry. The speed with which product strategies have shifted should be noted as an indicator of the volatility of current strategies. What we'll do here is review some of the high points of the prior work, and indicate changes and new market trends since then. We shall recast the model in the ICEIMT97 form to help the reader understand the forces at work in shaping architectures, and provide some linkage of architectural characteristics to differing types of enterprises.

Each of these four divisions has internal architectural dynamics which in concert drive considerations of architectures of the whole information system.

1.3 The Application Architecture

The Application Architecture (AA) is the structured collection of processes which support an enterprise's mission. Simple examples are architectures which are *unified* in how they relate to databases, say through SQL; or document architectures which are unified in how they relate to operating system protocol interfaces. The former defines its architecture in the context of the Enterprise Characterization (a database), while the latter is defined in terms of the Execution Environment (for instance Windows).

There are a variety of AA types, which we will not survey here. Major examples are those which inter-relate application processes through a central repository, and those which use an application *framework*: meaning conventions for communication without a centralized reference.

The central repository paradigm is strong; repositories can consist of data (as already noted), or metadata such as object registries or ontological references. It's a costly approach but it suits the management techniques of centrally managed enterprises.

The framework idea is most simply instanced in collections of standards and procedures that are used to *generate* the applications so that they can work together. But more interesting examples are frameworks that have the ability to dynamically adapt to new components as they are introduced with new capabilities.

The Suppliers' Working Group noted three trends concerning the AA:

- Historically, the AA paradigm was determined by suppliers of Execution Environments (IBM, Digital, etc.) and the EE architectures they employed at that level; then they were implemented by third parties such as Computer Associates. That was already changing by the ICEIMT timeframe, driven by the software crisis and the competitive pressures from AA suppliers (who are many, compared to relatively few EE suppliers). The trend now is that EE architectures are expected to support the AA and evolve in response to it.

- There's a circular relationship between *models* and *languages*: each defines the other. All architectures reflect tradeoffs in which of these is eminent, and which domain (AA or EE) defines which. We've seen an evolution over time from:

  - the older paradigm of the model centralized in the AA, subservient to languages in the EE (for example inflexible programming principles guided by languages in the EE which in this case literally are programming languages. The original impetus behind Ada, for instance, represents the height of this thinking.)
  - then a period where the "languages," meaning in this context details of the service calls in the EE, were determined by the application model. The rise of object-oriented application architectures is traced to this reversal, as is the need for object standards and design patterns.

Expected is a future period where the roles are again redefined, the "model" being in the EC with the languages (meaning in this context the different application philosophies) of the AA being defined based on management of that information, which is increasingly being known as intellectual property. But we're getting a little ahead of ourselves with this. We'll revisit it below.

- The third AA-related finding was that the notion of *state* is key to the AA. What happens in the actual enterprise is different that what happens behind the scenes in the silicon and operating services to support those enterprise processes. The processes are fundamentally different in nature and drive basic differences in architecture. (We use *state* here differently than it is used elsewhere in the Handbook. We mean infrastructure support for advanced notions of progress of collaborative processes in the enterprise. We discuss of state more fully later.)

- SWG insights in this area drove several research efforts in manufacturing simulation, since events in manufacturing have feet in both the AA and the EE (the EE including the manufacturing equipment). Also of interest is the asymmetry of the reversible nature of *simulated* states and irreversibility of control states. Control happens in the real world, where time is not reversible; simulations occur in virtual worlds so actions can be undone and alternatives explored but the knowledge gained persists. Different notions of state must be used to support these two functions, and the situation is complex when the same models and infrastructure is intended for both.

Also, while not unique to the SWG, one should reiterate the then much-documented *software crisis*, which is defined as an inability of application within the AAs to meet the needs of businesses. As much as 80% of all software projects (by cost) fail in key respects because of the complexities inherent in AAs. It's generally felt that this is flaw of the architecture, reflected in tools and techniques. By architecture, we mean the capabilities of the AA which are affected by the overall distribution and management of responsibilities among the AA, EE and ID.

1.4 The Execution Environment

We've already jumped the gun on discussing architectural drivers without fully defining the EE. The EE is the *hardware* on which information is processed, together with services that support the hardware. Services include operating, network and other basic software components. Computers and networks are included, as are telephones and message services. Hardware is considered in the large, and also includes the physical architectures of collaborative work/office/shop floor spaces and the equipment and controllers therein. EE *software* is similarly considered in the large roughly including most ubiquitous services.

At one time, the EE was the driver of architectural decisions, and discussions centered on such things as portable UNIX, open communication models, and device plug and play. Clearly, the focus has moved to the AA for three reasons:

- Managers were slow to develop techniques to evaluate costs of technology investment. What they first saw was the cost of capital assets. When the much greater AA-related costs started to become visible in the late eighties, the architectural focus shifted.
- A general management trend developed: "stick to business," and information technologies became more scrutinized for how they could improve the business mission, the domain of the AA. Legions of consultants rose to reinforce this thinking.
- Partly as a result of the above and partly for independent reasons we won't explore here, the AA marketplace revolted against the hegemony of the few hardware suppliers who controlled the EE. The visible shock to IBM was most notable, as a reflection of a sea change in architectures.

We are only superficially touching on the older SWG analyses here, but it should be noted that the EE has a significant non- computerized component which rests on social and cultural "hardware." Efforts in understanding those "soft" architectural issues are emerging in the research community [DR96].

1.5 The Enterprise Characterization and the Integration Domain

Most taxonomies of architectures have something like the AA layered over an EE. The SWG deliberately deviated from this convention in defining a category of information which instead of being in a layer over the AA, interfaced with both the AA and the EE.

This category, the *Enterprise Characterization* (EC), is generally considered as the information in an enterprise. The information constitutes process and business information which the enterprise uses in its mission, in other words, used by the AA; examples are product data models. But some similar information is also used in running the EE infrastructure itself. Information Flow and Resource Models are of this type.

Separating them from both the AA and EE and combining them in a single category sets the stage for examining them relatively independently of AA/EE architectural considerations. The reasons for doing so initially came from some surprising results of the study.

We wanted to know how much was spent on each of the three major categories, and our original look at 100 representative enterprises was initially unhelpful. This was because the value of information isn't normally considered in accounting systems. So we devised some accounting metrics and applied them ourselves, at significant cost to the project.

The findings were that more is spent on information (EC) per year than on AA and EE combined. Moreover, the length of utility was much greater and a substantial percentage had the potential of being sold for reuse.

On examination, the EC information which related to EE in one architectural paradigm could possibly apply to AA in another. So to preserve the architectural independence of the taxonomy, we recognized them as one inseparable item, with its own internal architecture.

Having done so, we realized the intimate relationship between the EC, this structured information, and the strategies which relate the EC, AA and EE through differing connectivity strategies in what we termed the *Integration Domain* (ID).

1.6 Some ICEIMT-Related Strategies

There were a few findings relevant for our current purposes. The SWG predicted that as enterprises strove to understand their information architectures, the trend would be to move more to considerations on how the information is structured (in the EC) than on constraints on how they do their work (in the AA). To understand how powerful this insight was at the time, you need to remember that most members of the SWG were controllers of architecture when EE constraints dominated and were currently occupied with trying to regain positions in the refined focus, the AA.

Great potential leverage for these firms, as well as anticipated benefit to the customer was expected by redefining the focus to the EC. This conclusion resulted in a large number of explorations, including:

- Development of an object oriented application development environment (*Dylan* for Dynamic LANguage) that was well suited to information structuring, while having an architecturally independent foot in each of the AA and EE [Sha96] (More about this below.).
- Development of a multifirm approach to EE services (*Taligent*) that provided for very late binding of those services, depending not on AA constraints, but on those from the EC, structured in clear behavioral categories (people, places and things) [CP95].
- Development (within IBM) of a *System Object Model* for the EE which permanently shifted the language/model relationship noted above so that the EE had a clear model, expressible and manipulatable from the EC.
- Support for the development of an *Object Request Broker* via an industry consortium that would provide (it was hoped) an architecturally neutral way of administratively modeling key state relationships between AA and EE.

The first two of these failed outright, and the second two failed to achieve ambitious goals originally set for reasons reviewed by ICEIMT 97 below.

Having thus set the stage, we can now discuss the more important insights that have been since gained from five years of working with the taxonomy.

These were effected by supplementing internal, proprietary developments. Therefore, while the results are well documented, the process is not.

2 New Trends Since ICEIMT

2.1 MetaStructure

What the SWG developed was an evolutionary roadmap that made sense, solving some key technical problems and providing benefit to the customer of information infrastructure. The prediction was that eventually, information architectures would all be driven by a *metastructure* which is independent of not only equipment and operating systems (the EE) but specific methods of accomplishing work (the AA) as well.

The more advanced contributions in this handbook address possible slants on this metastructure, employing either models or languages as the root of an approach. Incidentally, the feeling of the SWG was that *object orientation* was a useful implementation strategy only, that deliberately was separated from this metastructure. The metastructure, and indeed all of the EC functionality would instead be firmly grounded in the advanced mathematics of logic [Dev91] (but things seem to have gotten stuck in object oriented methods).

We further predicted two commercial trends would emerge:

- that a large and robust economy of reusable information components would emerge, once even a few technical barriers were solved, and
- that knowledge could be managed for *future* rather than *present* needs. This requires some background:
  - currently, enterprises design their information systems around their business processes, the AA. The trend toward *lean and mean* enterprises means that the system is optimized for those processes. The possible metastructure of the EC isn't ordinarily considered because all that matters is narrow optimization.
  - But most critical business problems arise because the enterprise is ill-equipped to respond to *unexpected change.* If the information architecture was designed as metastructure at the EC level, then different AA processes could be much more easily substituted or evolved. This need for *agility* and the promise of metastructure was the rational for DARPA and Air Force ManTech to make substantial research investments in information systems for *agile manufacturing* [Gor97a].

However, the world did not rush from AA-oriented architectural paradigms to EC-oriented metastructure. Indeed, most commercial energy is currently focused on new AA strategies (Java and other component architectural enablers) and even new EE strategies (the "open" standards-based Internet). Why is this? What commercial forces are at work?

The key factor is the way that the marketplace for architectures is supported by market forces and investor scrutiny, and these have not mapped to the technical drivers we envisioned. The other key factor is the largely independent way that those suppliers now define architecture as a strategic weapon. We'll briefly outline these two factors in this and the next section, then apply them to a new model of the marketplace.

2.2 Investor Analysis and Internationalization

An important turning point came with SEMATECH, the U. S.-based multi-billion dollar semiconductor manufacturing research consortium, which spawned the SWG (Details of the SEMATECH adventure and failure at its information systems-driven mission are at [Gor97a].). Before that point a case could be made for relating infrastructure suppliers to national destinies, in particular the hardware/operating systems/network suppliers with U. S. national and defense interests.

In the early nineties, all that changed. Three revolutions occurred simultaneously:

- As noted above, the world shifted from EE to more AA-oriented architectural philosophies, and also as noted the AA locus became more model-oriented rather than language-oriented.
- The suppliers of infrastructure became more truly internationalized (as opposed to just selling internationally). This resulted from:
  - The aforementioned shift in focus from platform- determined (EE) architectures to business-process oriented (AA) architectures. And of course more parties became involved as the cost of entry dropped. The result was more localized solutions as well as more localized and niche suppliers.
  - National governments quietly forced the multinationals to locate basic research and product development laboratories in their countries. (The SEMATECH experience played a role in this.) And much to everyone's surprise, this has worked well as the big firms discover relative national strengths to leverage.
  - With the end of the cold war, special benefits that followed from research sponsored by the U. S. military evaporated allowing development to leave the U. S.
- These two major changes spawned a third, deeper revolution. It used to be that the investment community simply trusted the technologists

to be wise concerning architectural decisions. This was the case for investors in both the supplier end and the user end. Those days are well past.

- Now, the investment community closely scrutinizes every decision. A well-known story is how Boeing determined its computer-aided design strategy for the 777 not for product excellence or lower cost, but to lower investor concerns of the technical risk (thus greatly reducing the cost of the project since the cost of money was lowered).
- The bad news is that investors haven't simultaneously improved their technical sophistication. Near-sighted strategies, buzz-word dominance, and sweeping fads have become more common. Complex tradeoffs often get boiled down into simple, high concept descriptions.

2.3 Architecture as Strategic Weapon

A second type of revolution has swept through the information infrastructure community.

It used to be that firms were in business to make money. Toward the sixties, as professional sports became televised, a new sports-oriented business metaphor came into common usage. Fed first by consultants, and later by concerned politicians, business became seen as a zero-sum game, with winners and losers. The goal became to crush the competition.

This idea took hold particularly strongly in the information technology world because the pace of change is so fast and new markets are constantly being defined. The first to snuff out all competitors owns the playing field.

We owe this unhappy state of affairs to Microsoft. They've set a tone for competitiveness which has completely permeated the developer world. And the fact that Microsoft is successful monetarily, both the firm and the founders, has attracted the support of the investment community for this carnivorous stance.

Microsoft products are not designed to be technically best, thereby attracting customers the old-fashioned way. Nor do they use more modern business techniques of identifying niches and opportunities. Their products are designed primarily as strategic weapons in the continuing war with their competitors. There's something to be said for the fact that Windows95 took $200 million to develop (essentially copying a competitor) and $300 million to promote.

These non-technical, commercial factors of investor-driven high concept, and supplier jostling in a world of constant change make the world a dangerous place for businesses who depend on commercial information infrastructure. They were what was missing from the SWG reference taxonomy.

3 ICEIMT97: A Revisiting

After five years, the ICEIMT experience was revived to take a fresh look at EI, to look at new pressure points for research investment by updating the prior work. The same work model was supported: a number of focused workshops by invited experts on both sides of the Atlantic. In this latter case, we had the National Institute of Standards and Technology (NIST) as the U. S. sponsor, DARPA having been legislated out of the manufacturing infrastructure area. ESPRIT remained the European sponsor.

3.1 The Capability Model

A Capability Model was developed, shown in Figure 2. Level 1 is the lowest level, *Fragmented Islands of Automation.* Level 2, *Rigid*, adds to fragmented the ability to coordinate processes across the entire system. Level 3, which we called *Visible*, adds the ability for each process to understand the actions of its peers so that it can optimize itself in the system context.

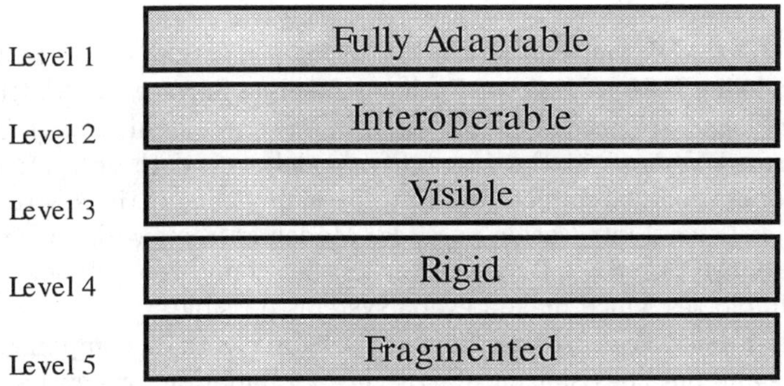

Figure 2: Capability Model

Interoperable, or Level 4, adds the ability for each process to trigger control points in peer processes to optimize operation in the systems context. And Level 5 adds the ability for each process to reconfigure control mechanisms in other processes for system optimization. We called that *Fully Adaptable* EI.

This model was developed to help understand the basic technical needs. A dimension is added to the levels to create a technology food chain (Figure 3). At the top of this dimension is the business of the enterprise. This layer is decomposed according to the management philosophy of the enterprise. Each of those work components are supported by numerous systems, shown by an underlying layer. Each of *these* systems is supported by numerous technologies which we assign it's own layer, a third.

For example, consider an engineering department which is integrated to Level 3. One of the key *systems* which supports integrated engineering pro-

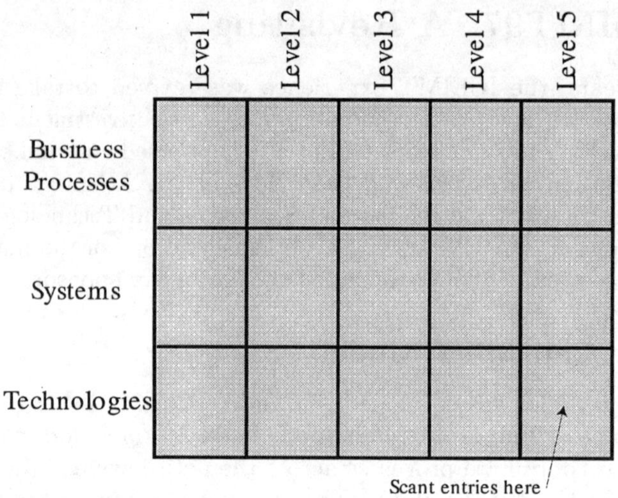

Figure 3: Layer and levels

cesses is 3D CAD. And one of the key *technologies* that supports 3D CAD solids modeling is Non Uniform Rational B-spline Surfaces or NURBS.

Technologies are needed to support infrastructure architectures (for what we've termed *systems* in the capability model). And those systems make possible operational architectures. Enterprise modeling is the key technology that makes Level 2 integration possible. Modeling frameworks (for instance, GERAM, CIMOSA, SAP, Baan) and others noted in this handbook are (tools and) technologies which make Level 3 systems possible.

Levels 4 and 5 are currently beyond us. Some work on component- based semantics and ontology sharing start to lay a foundation for Level 4. But the Level 5 technology cell is blank, in terms of fieldable candidates.

3.2 Limits of Object Orientation

In 1990-92, implementing Level 3 EI was the goal, and it was hoped that any tools and technologies brought to bear could apply to the higher level problem. All of the SWG initiatives and their outcomes *(CORBA, Java, design patterns)* are object oriented (OO). This has made scaleable Level 3 EI feasible, and there is some movement toward the envisioned $100B EI market. But it appears that object orientation may be a barrier to higher levels of EI.

The reason is that market forces have been such that only AA-based solutions seemed to be profitably productized. OO allows the AA, EE and EC to work harmoniously in a scaleable manner, but it does so by imposing AA sensibilities on the EC. One of the key tenets of OO is encapsulation; only the external behavior of objects is visible.

But if process dynamics, the actual physics of how they work, are hidden within objects then clearly the visibility of Level 3 is defeated. OO is fine when designing software and systems other than EI systems, systems where *control* is not complex issue. But in cases where you have different state spaces, like our EE, AA and EC, the state paradigm must allow the system to see its own dynamics.

An example is in order. An airline reservation system can have a simple layered architecture (Figure 4). The state space of the reservation-related information can be abstracted/translated into a collection of database/application services. Those applications utilize underlying computer and communication services. The state of a given reservation is simply related to the state of certain data at our rudimentary AA level. And that is simply related to the status and activity of for instance communication packets at the simple EE level.

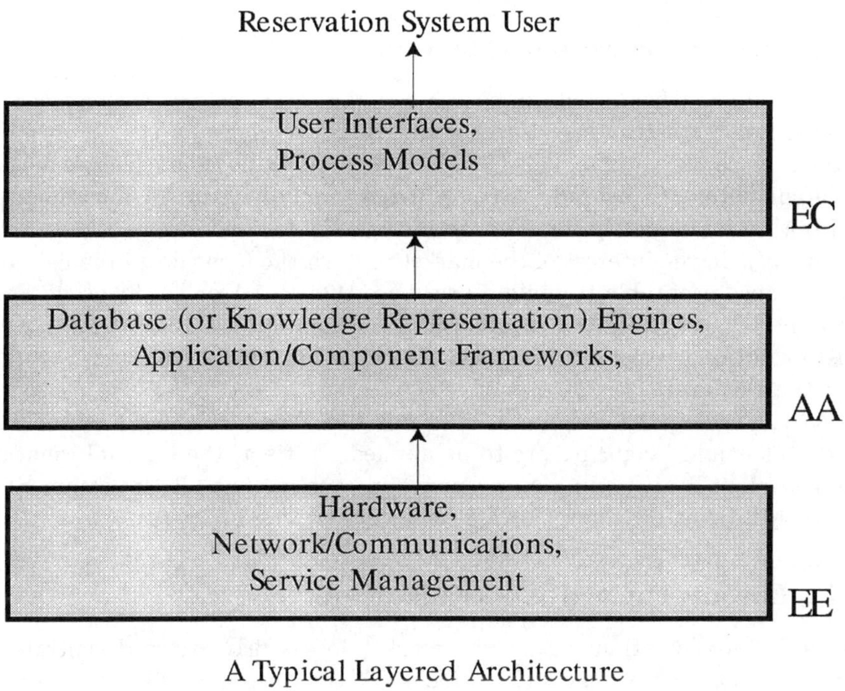

Figure 4: Example

But an EI environment is more complex. Managing the enterprise includes managing its EI resources, which is to say the EE (which includes manufacturing resources and people) as well as the AA. A change in state in any of the components can fundamentally alter the internal mechanics of the other. For instance: a process trigger (AA) may cause a machine tool (EE) to go off-line, which changes the model of available resources of the enterprise

(EC) which might trigger a reconfiguration of the scheduler (AA) bringing latent tooling assets (EE) on-line.

Without developing the argument formally, the reader should begin to see how complex the state and causality relationships are because EI systems include themselves. It's not straightforward like the reservation system is. There encapsulation is your friend; in EI with aspirations, it becomes your enemy as it prevents *introspection.*

What's needed is an EI strategy that relies on an introspective EC, while allowing the AA folks to leverage OO within their own scope.

3.3 New Commercial Forces at Work

Combined with the insight of Levels, and the problems of OO, some non-technical marketing forces were noted.

3.3.1 Forces Toward Lower Services

What would benefit the enterprise user would be architectures with a focus on EC-oriented metastructure, as just noted. This would insulate the investment in the architecture and models from how they might be used. There's a clear hierarchy here: EC-focused systems are more friendly than AA-focused ones, and both are manifestly more powerful than EE-focused ones.

But it is in the interest of the market to push the focus down the list. It's simply more profitable to build a user base that is AA or EE focused. Consider the biggest perceived revolution in information systems: the *Internet.* It is revolutionary in that it is not a centrally controlled architecture. But it is at the EE level.

As you review the contributions of this Handbook, consider how the various models and languages are to be applied. If it's at the pure information (EC) level, it'll give you a more powerful system, but all the commercial energy will be at the "lower" AA level in integrating processes.

3.4 Forces Toward Centralization

We've already mentioned that the market forces drive toward centralized systems, regardless of the axis of focus. Many customers like this as well because it suits common top-down management styles.

But there's a technical reason as well: centralization helps mitigate the problems of complexity that vex any interesting enterprise. A less centralized solution has more power; it

- allows different groups or functions to innovate rather than having to swallow the lowest common denominator,
- sets a stage for some self-organizing, and adaptive behavior,

- increases the number and types of goals for which the system can economically optimize, and
- perhaps provides for the long-sought holy grail of integrating the diverse planning models with those of even greater diversity used for control.

But you will not see a market rush from consolidated SAP and Oracle paradigms. As you review the Handbook's contributions, consider which can allow you the power of federated diversity balanced against the (non-technical) commercial and managerial benefits of consolidation.

3.4.1 Forces Toward "Hardness"

Most of the important dynamics in an enterprise are *soft*, that is, resulting from human collaboration. There are no Maxwell's equations for the elusive physics behind these interactions. Solving the problem of how to model soft dynamics in a logical information science context is the next grand challenge.

One type of soft information is information which is tacit. Empirical studies show that the greatest part of all models have tacit components: important information that each party assumes. This is soft information that can be made hard, or explicit, with some effort.

But there's a more difficult type of softness, that deals with the nature of communication. The SWG study reported that more than well over half of all business or project failures that can be attributed to information systems are because of the system's inability to comprehend soft relationships, that incidentally to humans are usually just common sense.

As you consider the approaches described above, ask yourself if there is accommodation of this reality. Consider whether its entry into commercial products (if not already) would attract vendors who would innovate in this area. We'll revisit this below.

3.4.2 Multiple Entries by All Players

A new dynamic has entered the marketplace. Architectural assumptions are being challenged. It's clear that some changes are underway, and will be for some time. Since technical appropriateness is eclipsed by commercial factors, no one can predict the "winners." The result is that anyone who can, bets on multiple approaches.

This further destabilizes the situation. Settling on any one approach would damp the hysteresis, allow convergence on a starting point and begin technically-driven evolution. But since everyone backs every horse, this cannot occur. It's the reason, by the way that DARPA initially got involved, because the effect is a compromised defense industrial base.

A focus on EC modeling can allow an enterprise to avoid being buffeted by this thrash, switching from one AA/EE architecture to another promiscuously. Which of the approaches described above allows this? Who will you buy your tools from to support it?

4 A Level 5 EC-Based Federation Mechanism

ICEIMT97 identified two major technical barriers to Level 5 EI. They are siblings; each could be seen as a subset of the other. It was felt that if commercial infrastructure products addressed these barriers, they could:

- provide a basis for Level 5 EI;
- likely overcome the non-technical barriers noted above;
- merge OO advantages for AA development and EE services while supporting a non-OO EC metastructure; and,
- be robustly supportable by market forces.

4.1 Problems

4.1.1 System-Level Engineering of Distributed Control

Level 5 EI has its clearest benefits in the *Virtual Enterprise* (VE) situation. VEs bring two benefits:

- access to an essentially infinite portfolio of core competencies, and
- greater speed and quality associated with decentralized control.

This latter advantage brings problems to the enterprise engineer; EI has as it's primary goal the ability to understand and optimize at the system level. However, existing techniques (that is, Level 3 techniques) assume some system level view of control states, and a high degree of determinism over those control states. The VE as well as the very definition of Level 5 defeats this.

Therefore in order to support Level 5, we need the ability to model and engineer distributed state and *causality.* These notions are supported at all levels in the infrastructure, including the EE, and is understood as the *late-binding* problem. The state of any element in the enterprise cannot be predicted (or engineered) by top down methods, because the causal linkages that generate state change are made at the last moment.

We need a way of representing and controlling state and causality abstractions such that:

- we can get the advantages of system-level engineering without the disadvantages of top-down control and determinism, and

- those abstractions convey across the AA, which is the usual realm for such things, but also the EE and the emerging EC metastructure.

This latter can only be addressed by commercial infrastructure suppliers and supplier partnerships who include EE services in their offerings.

4.1.2 Soft Modeling

There is a superset of the state and causality issues which have been identified by ICEIMT97 which collectively have been termed *soft issues.* Support of softness is the core of an expanded Level 5 requirements list. Soft issues include the ability to represent, understand and reason about:

- unexpected events or unforeseen conditions (external holes in the models),
- deviations from the model because of human autonomy (internal holes),
- ontological mismatches between processes and agents,
- misreadings of tacit knowledge requirements,
- the fact that processes are intended to be optimized at the system level, but no interesting system can be modeled at the same level of resolution as a typical system (layered formalism and zooming), and
- the fact that no explicit models of human collaboration have the same *physics* as harder models, yet we want to analyze them as if they do. (We call this the *supersoft or ssoft problem.*)

These are all problems of the same type: we need to represent elements of models or situations about which we know little and conduct logical analyses over those representations. Existing techniques are all unsatisfactory for general use:

- modal logics (complexity and exceptions are too costly),
- probabilities (doesn't reveal internal causality), and
- constraint modeling (which is the theory of reverse modeling: what can the process not do - which has the same limit as above).

4.2 Needs

So far as commercial products, we need capabilities in two areas: (EC) modeling and (AA/EE) infrastructure.

4.2.1 Soft and Distributed Models

Both the soft and distributed problems require:

- that there be a mathematically formal logical basis for the representation,
- that there be the ability to have as first class members of the logic entities that represent the soft items noted above: items whose constitution or behavior is not fully known.

This goes deeper than usual when modeling methodologies are designed. Consideration of the underlying language and logical issues are required. Models are required which are physics-based: they *represent behavior by representing how the behavior results.*

4.2.2 Integrated Late Binding AA/EE Infrastructure

Assuming we have the above, those models need to be related to the infrastructure in a particularly intimate fashion, a requirement that non-manufacturing enterprises do not encounter. The requirement is that elements that are soft in the model change to become hard under certain conditions, for example:

- your analysis shows that certain features need to be made more explicit, so you do,
- you discover the underlying cause of a process or effect by executing that process, and
- some nondeterministic event occurs that allows what follows to be more deterministic.

Those are situations where the AA/EE affects the EC. But because we assume that the same (or related) models are used to both analyze and control, it works the other way as well. For instance, statements of control events may be evaluated (made sufficiently hard for the desired action to take place) only at the last minute.

Abstractions of state and causality need to be passed back and forth in the modeling language (and method) to the services environment. The state of the enterprise (as it evolves) needs to explicitly represented in the same space as the state of the model (as it similarly evolves to and from softness).

4.3 Example: Dylan/Rhapsody and Situation Theory

As an example, we'll discuss a specific environment being considered for ICEIMT97-related work.

4.3.1 NeXT

Some time ago, the notion of state abstraction in the EE matured, with designers understanding the benefits of segregating state information into a kernel, an inner microkernel and surrounding EE services. State information needs to be passed among the layers of course, but more difficult is the distribution of state information among peers: microkernel to microkernel in a distributed processing environment, for instance.

Recognizing this need, DARPA sponsored research into state managing. The result was the Mach microkernel. Mach subsequently became a basis for the NeXT Operating System (EE).

NeXT went further by introducing state passing between the AA and EE. They wanted an object oriented AA to support modern notions of programming, and engineered a linkage between the states of the AA (in features and classes of *Objective C*) and the EE. The novelty here was it allowed tight integration of the AA/EE with the effect that state elements could be soft in the sense of being initialized as soft in the AA and evaluated at runtime by the EE. This is a particularly useful implementation of the notion of *late binding*.

It would be of use to our problem if we used the older notions of ICEIMT1: AA-centered with an object oriented philosophy. But we need to go further, to EC, meaning model-based, and to a metastructure oriented philosophy. It serves as probably the best basis for Level 5 engineering.

NeXT has since been acquired by Apple who is adding substantially more EE services and a collection of multimedia, user interface and Java elements to the AA.

4.3.2 Dylan

Apple, with perhaps some invisible partners, invested in research to bridge the gap between EC-type abstraction, specifically functional dynamism and AA-type requirements, specifically the advantages of OO abstraction. This project started as Ralph but became known as Dylan. It's an OO *dynamic* language; with the main goal to greatly shorten the software development process (within microprocessor parameters).

This is essentially a marriage of Lisp-based EC abstraction strengths with Smalltalk and C++ AA conventions. Being able to introspectively pass state information among the EC, AA and EE would allow developers to work on code while it is executing, with extraordinary benefits.

While not its primary goal, this would have also allowed an enterprise engineer to introspectively engineer control states for optimization, using the same models for EI design, control and operating optimization. But instead of enterprises, Dylan tried to speak to a development community addressing small, standalone shrinkwrapped PC applications.

This is a problematic community, and for uninteresting reasons Apple dropped the project after developing an impressive demonstration version (which is available to the public). DARPA sponsors a Dylan project called *Gwydion*, but this focuses more on easing the abstraction-to-code problem. And Harlequin has a product, *DylanWorks.* But that integrates with Windows, a particularly blunt environment with respect to state introspection.

Much of the capability of AppleDylan could be handled in modern Lisp environments, but the decision was made to not extend MacCommonLisp (MCL) because it was considered too RAM-hungry and too hard to learn for their target environment: commercial PC applications and their developers. But MCL has greatly improved with respect to RAM, which has become a non-issue with lowered chip prices. And in any case, it's not a driver in the enterprise domain.

Apple has transferred the Dylan technology to DigiTool, and the relevant parts are being incorporated into MCL.

5 Conclusion

An ideal future commercial infrastructure would allow the modeler to:

- build models according to an EC metastructure of first order logic, mixed soft and hard entities involving state information, and mixed representations of processes (activity models) and actions (agents),
- express these in OO classes and agent applets for EE management, and
- have them both represent for engineering and operate the EE, the enterprise and its information processing equipment.

And to have state and causality information migrate among these domains. At least one commercial environment may be capable of Level 5 EI support. We can assume that market forces will probably sustain this model, and a number of similar environments will populate the space if Level 5 capability (and the competitive advantages for the enterprise) is demonstrated.

References

[CP95] Cotter, M., Potter, M., Inside Taligent Technology, Addison-Wesley, 1995

[DR96] Devlin, K., Rosenberg, D., Language at Work, CSLI Publications, Stanford, 1996

[Dev91] Devlin, K., Logic and Information, Cambridge University, 1991

[Gor92a] Goranson, H. T., The Integration Domain and the Enterprise Characterization, in: [Pet92], 1992, 23-34

[Gor92b] Goranson, H. T., The Integration Domain and the Application Architecture, in: [Pet92], 1992, 47-55

[Gor92c] Goranson, H. T., The Integration Domain and the Execution Environment, in: [Pet92], 1992, 56-66

[Gor92d] Goranson, H. T., Metrics and Models, in: [Pet92], 1992, 78- 84

[Gor92e] Goranson, H. T., Dimensions of Enterprise Integration, in: [Pet92], 1992, 101-113

[Gor92f] Goranson, H. T., The Suppliers' Working Group Enterprise Integration Reference Taxonomy, in: [Pet92], 1992, 114-130

[Gor92g] Goranson, H. T., The CIMOSA Approach as an Enterprise Integration Strategy, in: [Pet92], 1992, 167-178

[Gor92h] Goranson, H. T., Services in the Sirius-Beta Inter-Integration Domain, in: [Pet92], 1992, 341-355

[Gor92i] Goranson, H. T., Metrics in the Sirius-Beta Integration Domain, in: [Pet92], 1992, 430-444

[Gor97a] Goranson, H. T., Agility Measures: Engineering Agile Systems, http://www.agilityforum.org/Ex_Proj/MAVE/mave.html, 1997

[Gor97b] Goranson, H. T., workgroup reports, in: Proceedings of the Second International Conference on Enterprise Integration Modeling Technology, Springer-Verlag, 1997

[Pet92] Petrie, C., (ed.), Enterprise Integration Modeling, Proceedings of the Second International Conference on Enterprise Integration Modeling Technology, MIT Press, 1992

[Sha96] Shalit, A., The Dylan Reference Manual, Addison-Wesley, 1996

Chapter 34

Integration Infrastructures for Agile Manufacturing Systems

Richard Weston, Ian Coutts, Paul Clements

Requirements of general purpose integration infrastructures are analysed in the context of realising more agile manufacturing systems. The analysis provides a framework for characterising generic capabilities of existing integration infrastructures. The framework is used to highlight the role of the CIM-BIOSYS integration infrastructure and its associated software tools. Also classified are necessary future developments before integration infrastructures can underpin evolutionary behaviour in distributed systems.

1 Introduction - A Context for Integration Infrastructure Development

In a climate of increasing global competition and continuous (often unexpected) change, todays businesses need constantly to be reformed, possibly as an integral part of a virtual enterprise with processes and systems distributed around the globe. When operating in such a climate all companies will need continuously to assess, model, analyse, define and implement change to their core business processes. Essentially this can be viewed as a requirement to conduct Business Process Analysis and Business Processs Re-engineering (i.e. BPA and BPR) via a series of Enterprise Engineering Projects on an ongoing basis. The result may be a need to form new company partnerships and business units and define and implement a radical realignment of existing unit operations. Species of business capable of responding rapidly and effectively should thrive in an environment characterised by change, or at the very least they should have the capability to survive.

In practice it is extremely difficult to implement radical change on a wide scale. Change on an enterprise-wide scale may simultaneously require change to existing organisation structures, company cultures and IT systems; each

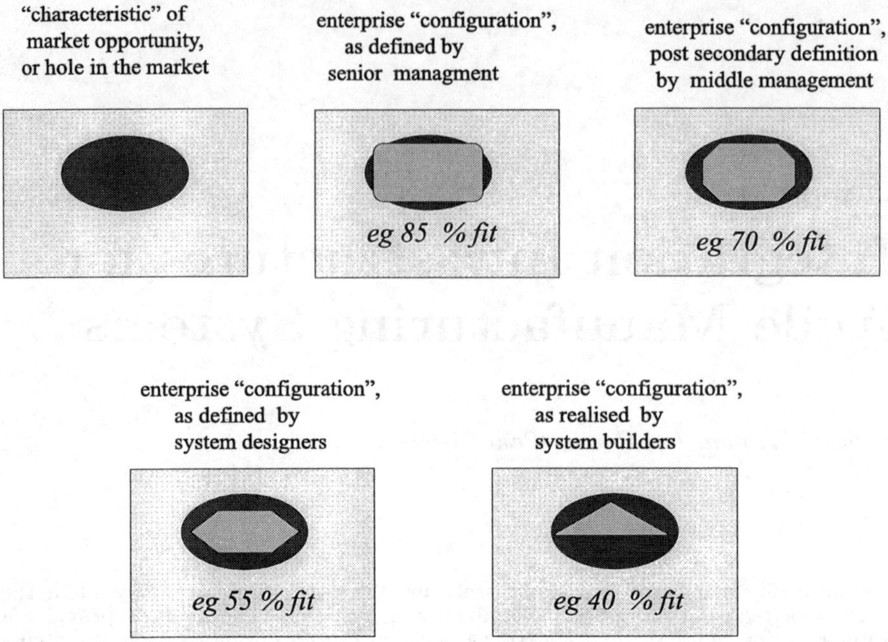

Figure 1: BPA/BPR practice in the UK

of which will be complex in its own right and possess characteristic properties which resist change. Associated with wide-scale change will be difficulties in defining, communicating and adopting a sufficiently meaningful consensus view of new requirements. Figure 1 was constructed to illustrate this point following a government funded study of BPA/BPR practice in the UK [BJWG96]. This exemplifies key problems when formulating a holistic view of IT system requirements. Although research world-wide on enterprise modelling seeks to support the development of a holistic view of wide-scale complex systems, as explained in other contributions of this handbook there is still much to achieve. Furthermore, even where a consensus view can be translated into a well defined requirements specification it is evident that the time frame of major scale IT projects will be of the order of 6 months to 3 years [BW97]. Such projects also require very high levels of capital investment [GZW97]. Major complications arise as the timescales and cost involved in changing or extending pre-existing large scale IT systems may be much greater than those involved in engineering a replacement. Hence, in many cases the stripping out of (so called existing legacy) software is the only viable option.

Figure 2 has been constructed to highlight the effect of deficiencies of existing approaches to creating software systems. Essentially current approaches either involve the design and development of a specific software sys-

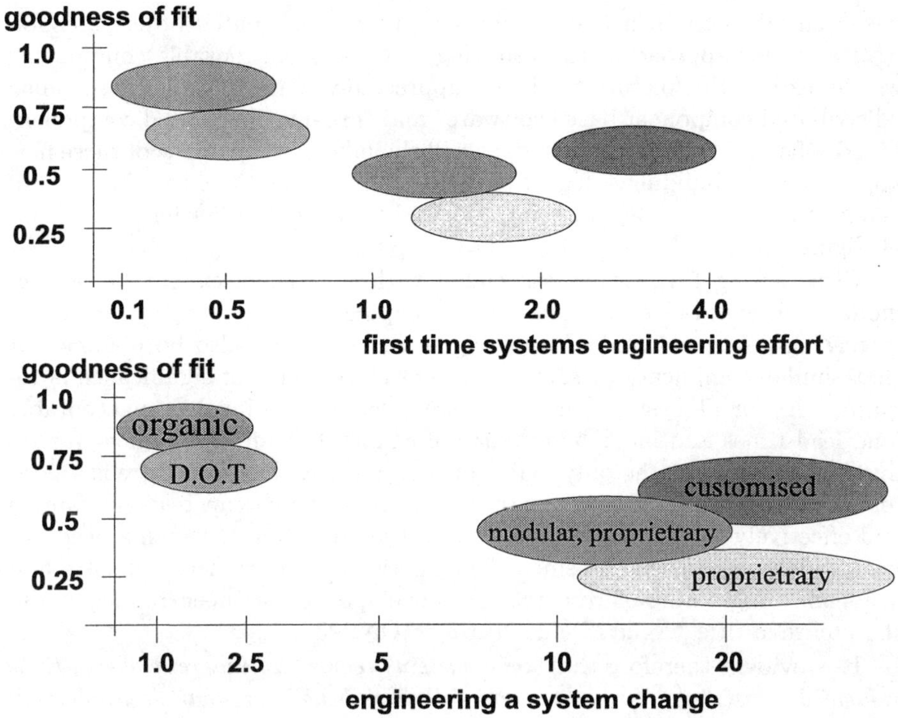

Figure 2: Deficiencies of approaches to creating software systems

tem for an end user (which is referred to here as "custom designed monolithic software") or are based on the use of general purpose software designed to be configured to meet common end user requirements. In Figure 2 the second approach is characterised by the use of two terms, namely: "proprietary general purpose monolithic software" or "modular proprietary general purpose monolithic software," the latter class of software system being distinguished from the former by an increased (albeit limited) level of configurability (this being provided through a modular packaging of the functional elements of a larger software system by its manufacturer/supplier). Invariably to-date either approach to building large and medium scale software systems has resulted in a so called "monolithic" solution, in which function, presentation, information, communication and distribution issues are mixed together in a "tangled web" [Pri96].

The result continues to be solutions which are difficult to build and implement and generally even more difficult to modify and extend. Hence generally speaking current generation software systems will lie in the bottom right-hand quadrant of Figure 2. Whereas, as explained in this contribution, with the advent of integration infrastructure technology (which itself is based on advances in network, information and distributed object technology) and new approaches to producing software from reusable components we can expect this picture to change appreciably. Later the role of so called "distributed component based software" and "organic distributed component based software" will be explained, as will the inherent capability of these new approaches (to building software systems) to move solutions to a "region" of "good fit, reduced (re)engineering effort," i.e. to the top left-hand quadrant of Figure 2).

Clearly long time scales associated with IT change cannot be accommodated in world-class manufacturing companies where change is becoming increasingly frequent and of widening scale. It should also be pointed out that similar complications arise where cultural change of significance is required. As for IT systems, human system change can involve unacceptably long lead-times and incur high cost; unfortunately staff replacement (or redundancies) may be the only viable option. Clearly therefore there is a need for more agile business and production systems which can respond rapidly and effectively to changing needs. Indeed the importance of such a need has been widely recognised and since 1992 a major US government, industry and academic programme of research and development has been funded under the umbrella title "Agile Manufacturing" [GNP95].

It is evident therefore that *agile systems require an inherent ability to be reformed so that the individual and collective behaviour of their component elements can rapidly be realigned to meet changing needs.*

This implies the need for suitable resources (i.e. system building blocks "or components") from which high performance systems can be built quickly and readily. In turn this implies the need for mechanisms to establish flexible linkages between components, so that an ability to facilitate system reconfiguration and reengineering[1] is an inherent property of resultant systems. Also implied is a need for means of supporting the rapid definition and redefinition of system behaviour, in a form which helps specify, implement, control and change the individual and collective operation of components.

In this context Figure 3(a) illustrates generic elements of a system built from reusable components. In seeking to promote the widespread realisation manufacturing systems from reusable components we need to address outstanding research issues such as:

1. What generic classes of system component can (individually and collectively) realise generic functions required by, and hence can be reused

[1] The terms *reconfiguration* and *reengineering* both concern the realisation of changes in a system. However the former relates to change which can be realised via relatively minor physical modification to a system and its functional capabilities; rather *reconfiguration* will normally be realised by establishing new logical relationships between physical components. Whereas typically *reengineering* will involve a more radical redesign and require the physical replacement of system components so as to modify the functional capabilities of the system as a whole.

in, different businesses? What should be the "grain size" of these components, their "target domains," the nature of their "interfaces," the way in which they should be organised and controlled, and so on so that generic and changing end user requirements can be met and technical performance targets and commercial benefits readily achieved? What are the commercial and practical implications of using reusable components, what change will be required to existing IT system and component supply chains and how can attendant difficulties be overcome?

2. What generic classes of integration service are required and need to be widely supported to facilitate interoperation[2] in a flexible way between reusable system components? How can these services build upon emerging standards? How can suitable organisational structures and control architectures be chosen and implemented to meet specialist requirements of different applications and component configurations? Are new standards required to cover different business domains and realise interoperation between distributed components of enterprises which may physically span various parts of the globe?

3. What new tools will be required to support the life-cycle engineering of agile systems built from reusable components? How can tools more readily support the definition and implementation of individual and collective behaviour of components, their use of integration services and the adoption of suitable organisational structures and control hierarchies? How can these tools build upon currently available *software engineering and enterprise modelling* methods and tools? What new tools will be required to facilitate the rapid development of software and the rapid prototyping of associated system elements?

Implicit in a consideration of the issues raised above (and particularly with respect to (1) and (2)) is the need to define and provide appropriate *infrastructural services* and *infrastructural functions.* As illustrated by Figure 3(b), *infrastructural services* will be considered to be general purpose facilities which underpin and thereby enable the operation and interoperation of system components. They will not themselves realise domain specific functionality but will essentially play a "passive" role in accomplishing user defined tasks. However their use as a "catalyst" may lead to enhanced functionality and can lead to significant simplification and rationalisation in resultant systems; particularly in systems comprising many components requiring one or more similar facilities. Indeed section 6 of this contribution will illustrate general technical and practical benefits arising from the use of an integrating infrastructure. However, if *unnecessary infrastructural services* are included

[2]The term *interoperation* is defined later (in section 3) of this contribution.

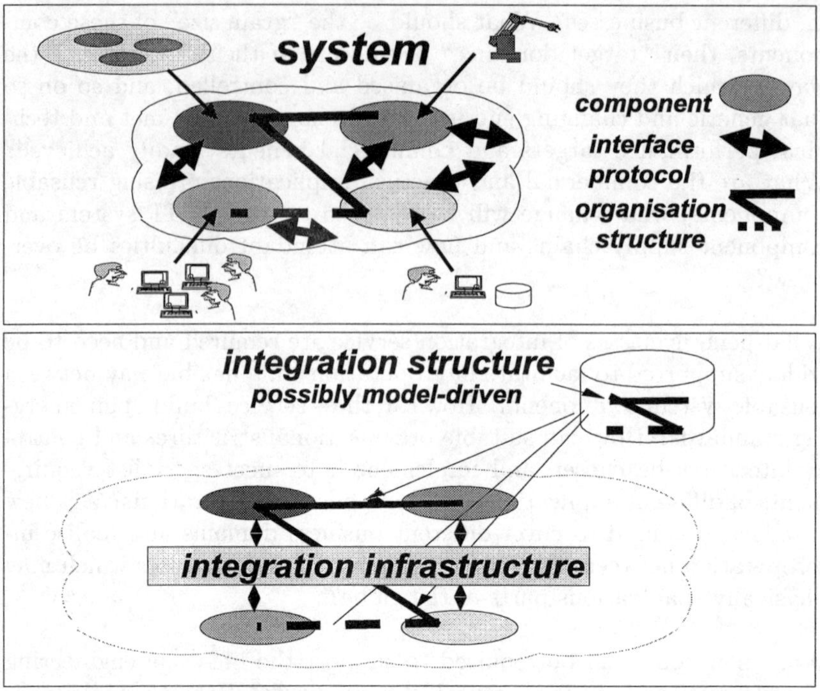

Figure 3: Generic elements of a system and infrastructural services

this can raise the base level entry cost of systems[3]. There will be a similar trade off involved when deciding what *infrastructural functions* to provide; which will be considered here to be common facilities which play an "active" role in realising functionality in a given domain and thereby offer general support functions to system components.

Also implicit in the research issues raised above is a consideration of appropriate *integration structures.* The purpose of *integration structures* will be to organise and control component interoperation in systems, so that their collective behaviour can be targeted at specific system-wide goals. Certain forms of *integration structure* can be viewed as being "passive" in nature, such as an organisational structure or framework which defines responsibilities and roles for individual components. Alternatively *integration structures* may be "active" in nature, such as control hierarchy which actively functions (possibly embedded within one or more systems components) to control the behaviour of a group of components. Thus *integration structures* restrain and

[3]Note, however often in wide-scale systems the actual need for infrastructural facilities may not be known and can be expected to change. Hence it may be appropriate to provide a more extensive infrastructural capability than initially considered to be necessary provided that the implied capital cost is not inordinately high (as the cost of change and lost opportunity costs may be much higher).

focus system behaviour, whereas *integration infrastructures* enable and support system behaviour. However both *integration structures* and *integration infrastructures* may comprise both "passive and "active" elements.

It is important to bear in mind that the way in which *integration infrastructure* and *integration structure* is realised can have a significant impact on characteristic properties of resultant systems, in terms of their "agility," "performance" and "ease of use." Theoretically various options exist. For example potentially *integration infrastructure* and *integration structure* elements in a system can be separated from each other and from specific system functionality required in any given application. However in practice contemporary IT systems used industrially have been implemented as a tangled web of interconnected generic (infrastructure and structure) and application specific elements. Previously this may have been because of a lack of understanding of the issues involved and associated disbenefits, or because of technological constraints or simply pragmatism. However, particularly in the case of wide scale systems the result has been high cost systems, long lead-times and solutions which may only fit their purpose acceptably well for short periods of times (as earlier exemplified by Figure 2).

In the context of supporting the development of agile manufacturing systems this contribution will focus on the provision of *infrastructural services* and *infrastructural functions* as part of an integration infrastructure. It will consider certain standards initiatives in the area and describe examples of *infrastructure technology.* Necessarily the development and application of *infrastructure technology* is intimately linked to requirements of and developments in *component technology* and *modelling technology.* Technological developments in such areas promise means of producing general purpose infrastructures (comprising *infrastructural services* which support "syntactic plug and play")[4] [Ful96].

2 Integration Infrastructure Requirements

Theoretically there are an infinite number of possible infrastructures which can underpin the operation of business and manufacturing systems. These may take the form of complex, domain specific functions and services, such as that provided by a finance, human resource or engineering department or more general purpose services and utilities, such as the provision of factory air, electrical power or a computer network. In this section we focus on the

[4]The term "syntactic plug and play" was defined by Fulton as meaning "an architecture in which the relationships among the data manipulated by various applications are managed through the models that define the data and the operations performed upon it." ... "Semantic plug and play" promises that different applications can exchange specific types of objects, each with specific roles in each of several applications, without excessive dependency on the user's knowledge of how that specific data functions in those other applications." Whereas "syntactic plug and play" relates more directly to hardware and possibly object compatibility between simple system components.

provision of general purpose computational infrastructures which build upon technological advances in networking and computer science.

It is evident that many contemporary components of businesses and manufacturing systems comprise suitable combinations of human, computational and electromechanical elements. One way of viewing these components is that they are resource elements which have the capability to *act* and *interact* in a variety of ways to realise business and manufacturing processes; in so doing collectively they can operate to accomplish business goals.

Increasingly common is the use of embedded computational capabilities within such components. When computer processing facilities are not formally embedded into components often it is practical and desirable to facilitate the activities of people and machines by assigning them computational support. Hence in this context it is appropriate to seek to provide integration infrastructures which via computational mechanisms support interaction between business and manufacturing components, where potentially such components may be distributed around a factory, or globally.

Business and manufacturing components can take numerous forms and are required to interact in many different ways. Arguably therefore it is inappropriate to seek to optimise the design of a special purpose integration infrastructure for each manufacturing situation. On the other hand it may be equally difficult to specify a set of general purpose infrastructural services which can, in an effective way, underpin the operation of all types of business and the components they deploy. Nonetheless, a number of integration infrastructures have been produced which provide a compromise between these extremes. Furthermore these infrastructures are already being used with great benefit.

In seeking to provide a generic framework suitable for drawing comparisons between the capabilities and scope of emerging integration infrastructures the authors refer back to the previous section which identified the need to:

1. support the life-cycle engineering of systems,
2. support problem decomposition, and thereby appropriate system architectures and perspectives,
3. cater for advances in enabling technology.

They also point to an evident need to:

1. conform where possible to the use of existing standards,
2. realise encapsulation (separation of the "what" from the "how") so that component interoperation and system operation can be modelled in an abstract manner which is independent of the details of the physical mechanisms deployed,

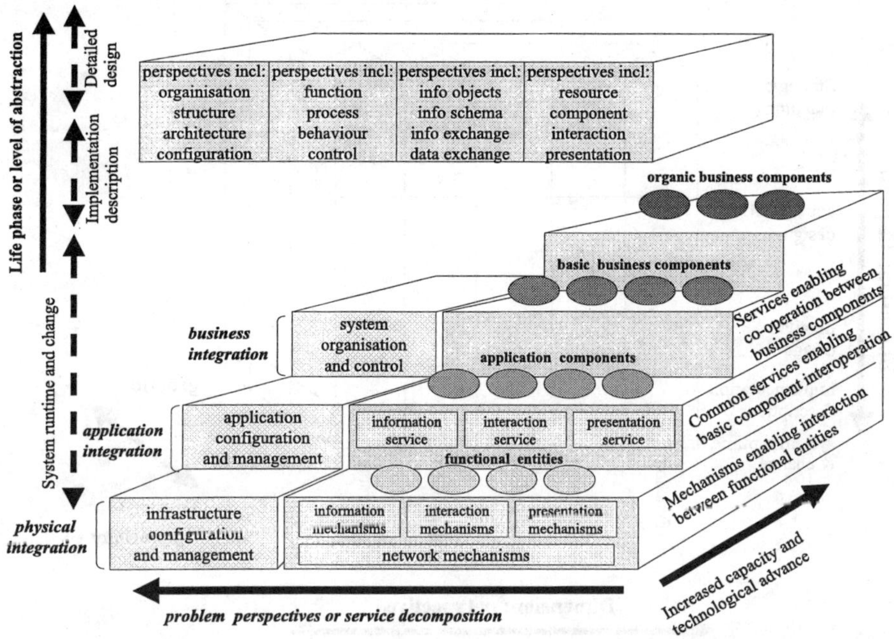

Figure 4: Integration infrastructure development

3. be structured according to modern systems theory and enterprise modelling ideas, and thereby support generally used problem decompositions (or modelling perspectives) and architectures,

4. separate out infrastructure provision from the specific system functionality required in any given application,

5. separate out *infrastructure service* provision from the provision of *infrastructural functions*, where the former provide simpler domain independent underpinning services and the latter add functional capability into a given domain.

Figure 4 has been constructed to illustrate in conceptual form various notions and assumptions related to integration infrastructure development.

This figure should be viewed as the lower part of Figure 5, which itself has been constructed as an abstract representation of the GERAM cube [BN95] which has been used to help unify previous separate understandings and developments in the area of enterprise modelling and integration. During the detailed design stage of engineering integrated systems previous experience of the authors has emphasised the need to describe systems (i.e. model them) from four major viewpoints, namely:

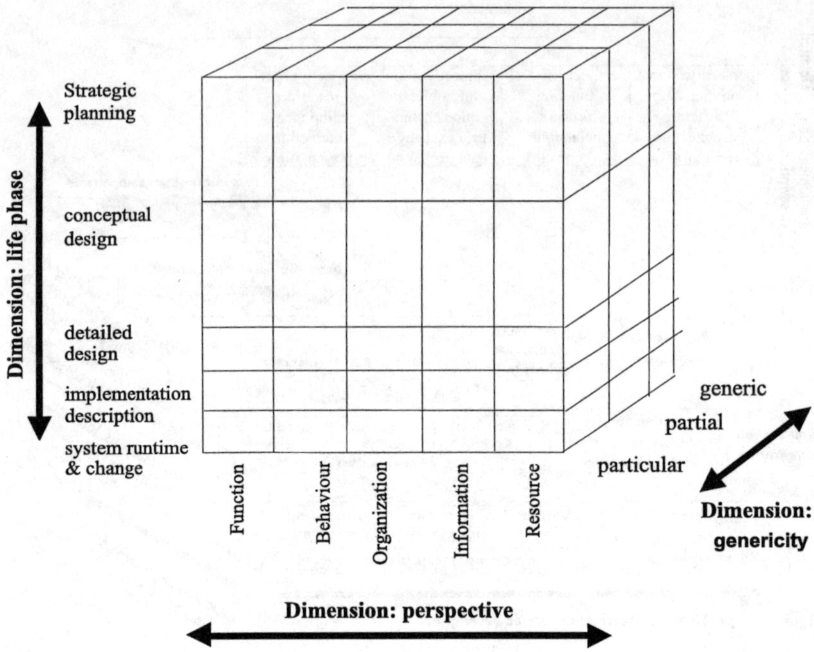

Figure 5: Abstract representation of the GERAM cube

1. structure viewpoint: which relates to the configuration of a system which in turn may concern organisational and architectural relationships and issues connected with system components,

2. application viewpoint: which concerns system functions and controls expressed in terms of the behaviour and interactions between components, possibly to realise a defined process, procedure or set of events,

3. information viewpoint: which concerns the way in which shared information is represented, translated, accessed, updated and stored within a system,

4. component viewpoint: which describes the resource elements deployed in a given system such as in terms of their interface and interaction protocol and information sharing and presentational requirements.

Figure 4 distinguishes between *organic* and *basic* components, *infrastructure functions* and *infrastructure services*; and *abstract service descriptions* from *integration mechanisms*. Clearly following international and *de facto* standardisation processes world-wide, general purpose and standard computational mechanisms exist to realise data transmission, data interchange, messaging and data distribution, as well as data retrieval, update and storage. However if it is to be used with relative ease, a general purpose integration infrastructure needs to offer a more abstract set of integration services, described in terms which indicate "what" service they provide rather than "how" the service is achieved (i.e. by some low level standard network or computational mechanism, like MMS, RPC, RS232 protocols, etc). Indeed previous experience of the authors has shown the need for abstracted (encapsulated) descriptions of general purpose configuration, application, information and presentation services, which may be implemented via alternative network and computational mechanisms. It is also possible to realise formal mappings between abstract descriptions of these services and the four modelling viewpoints (described above) which need to be supported during the detailed design of engineering systems. As discussed later this can help facilitate rapid prototyping, reconfiguration and reengineering of systems built from reusable components which operate over an integration infrastructure.

Technological advances have already been made which support the development of and interoperation between reusable components of systems. Generally we will see that some classes of component may best be served by infrastructure services which operate at a greater level of abstraction than that required to support lower level interaction (and so called "syntactic plug and play") between other generally simpler classes of component. We will see that this may be viewed as providing "semantic plug and play" infrastructural facilities for so called *business components*, i.e. providing them with appropriate support capabilities which allow them to co-operate with other components in a very flexible manner. We may conclude that a cost of increased flexibility and support will be a need for a "clever" infrastructure which may only function fully in a more restricted application domain, i.e. it will need to contain infrastructural functions as well as infrastructural services.

Although not explicitly illustrated by Figure 4 it is also important to consider the capability of infrastructural services to execute "models," which may well have been captured during the detailed design of a specific system or indeed a system of similar type. Potentially such a capability can much enhance the ability to realise rapid system change (including rapid application development and rapid prototyping of systems) in such a way that subsequent actions and interactions carried out by a system are well aligned to higher level (i.e. more abstract) requirements and goals, as defined for example by an enterprise engineering toolset. We will return to the issue of model enactment in sections 5 and 6.

3 Infrastructural Support and Different Levels of Interaction

It is evident therefore that business and manufacturing systems will continue to be distributed around the globe and comprise autonomous components (i.e. business units and their underpinning component resources) which need to interact[5] with each other to realise global goals, in addition to accomplishing their own local goals. As classified by CIMOSA [KK90] and illustrated by Figure 6, conceptually we may consider interaction between system components to occur at three different levels of abstraction, namely "business," "application" and "physical" levels. In such a schema:

1. *Business Interaction* is required to realise *cooperation* between business functions. To facilitate ***business interaction*** high level (abstract) integration functions and services will be required to underpin the control, monitoring and management of business processes. The Business Integration layer of Figure 6 illustrates examples of high level integration functions and services needed to underpin the interworking of business functions (which will be termed ***business components***). With respect to the conceptual framework of Figure 4 essentially cooperation between business components will require infrastructural support services from a class of infrastructural functions which correspond to the layer of *semantically rich infrastructure functions*, albeit that their own operation will rely on the use of *general purpose infrastructural services*,
2. *Application Interaction* concerns integration at the level of software applications and associated system components. This will involve *interoperation* at a medium level of abstraction between *application components* with concentration on *what* needs to be integrated in a system (e.g. organisation, control, information exchange and presentation issues) ideally without concern for how it will be realised or where information and specific software processes physically reside. The middle (Application Integration) layer of Figure 6 shows typical examples of *infrastructural services* required to support *component interoperation.* These services correspond to the layer of *general purpose infrastructural services* depicted in Figure 4, and essentially will be a medium level abstraction of general purpose services which physically are realised by a lower level set of (network and computational) mechanisms,
3. *Physical Interaction* concerns physical structures, mechanisms and controls to realise *interaction* between *functional* entities which provide

[5] Until now the term *interaction* has been used in a general sense to imply that components "act collectively" to realise system-wide goals. Of course they will also "act" individually to realise local goals. *Interaction* between components requires use of *common* structures, mechanisms and controls so that collective goals can be realised; generally this will involve common event synchronisation and resource sharing (such as the sharing of information of common interest).

atomic building blocks of components. It is concerned with how integration is practically achieved and by which physical mechanism. It therefore corresponds to the lowest level of abstraction when characterising integration services.

Typical examples of mechanisms which realise Physical Systems Integration are also illustrated by Figure 6 and correspond to a *set of physical mechanisms* which form the generic integration services of Figure 4.

Clearly medium and high level interactions, which subsequently will be referred to as *interoperation* and *co-operation* respectively, only exist conceptually. In practice they will be realised by an organised set of low level integration mechanisms. However, the use of abstractions is vital in simplifying the use and characterising and guiding the development of general purpose *interoperation* and *co-operation* structures and infrastructures.

4 Properties of Components

Normally a *business component* will comprise a set of *application components*. Whereas an *application component* will consist of a lower level *set of functional entities* (or primitive software building blocks). Naturally therefore we will expect *business components* to have a greater range of functional capabilities than the constituent *application components* they inherit. Likewise *application components* can be expected to possess functional capabilities in advance of the primitive building blocks of functionality from which they are built.

Hence one way in which system components can be classified is in respect to the scope and range of functional and business process capabilities they can deliver. Clearly the need to support the various types and scale of these functions will impact on the infrastructural services which need to be provided.

A second way of classifying system components is in respect of their inherent ability to act "intelligently" when they are left to operate as part of a host system. In this respect *basic components* (be they *business components, application components* or primitive *functional entities*) may be expected to provide application specific functionality which can be reused in different systems and operating scenarios. However they will not be required to negotiate or self optimise the way in which they work with other components, with a view to optimising the performance of a system as a whole. Nonetheless to facilitate reuse these *basic components* will require well defined internal properties (i.e. be described in the form of a model, possibly at various levels of abstraction) and should utilise "standard" (within domains where they are to be used) interaction capabilities. In this context the minimum set of capabilities needed by *basic* (reusable system) *components* is that they should positively facilitate their rapid inclusion within systems, and their subsequent reconfiguration and re-engineering in the event of changing needs. However

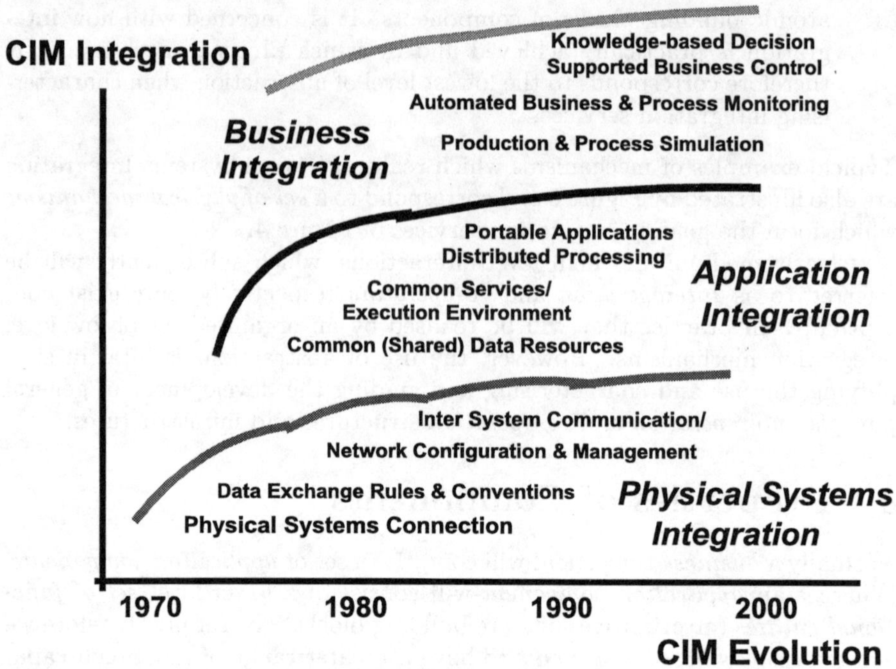

Figure 6: Interaction between system components

basic components will not be expected to operate organically and thereby automatically develop their own role in a given system. The use of well defined models of *basic components* (at different levels of abstraction) should facilitate the life-cycle engineering of new component generations as well as that of the systems in which they are used. For example component abstractions can be used to guide the development of bigger and better components, their implementation using different hardware and software platforms, and their maintenance in the field. It is evident that the advent of distributed object technology, fuelled by the recent availability of infrastructural services supporting object distribution and interaction, will provide important concepts and mechanisms on which to build to produce families of *basic component* and thence building blocks of next generation businesses.

With a growing emphasis on agile systems we also anticipate the need for clever *organic components*, i.e. a class of components which have sufficient knowledge of themselves and their environment (or have the capability to access such knowledge) for them to be able to modify their own role and behaviour whilst functioning (i.e. during system runtime) as an integral part of a host system. By producing systems from organic components the result would be systems which can also demonstrate organic behaviour. Such a clever class of *organic component* may require less detailed information and intervention from system designers and builders, thereby potentially much reducing the time and effort involved in first off system development and even reducing to zero effort involved in subsequent system change. However, inevitably *organic components* will require greater capability within each component as well as more comprehensive infrastructural services and functions to underpin interoperation and cooperation in an organic way. Clearly various possible "grades" or organic behaviour could be realised individually and collectively by *organic components*, thereby systems could be designed to realise various behavioural properties which will provide them with an evolutionary capability required by next generation agile systems. In many such situations it may be expected to be necessary to constrain behavioural change and system evolution so that associated people and machine systems components could function in harmony and safety, whilst meeting business goals. Hence allied advances in the development and use of *integration structures* will be necessary to promote the successful deployment of next generation organic systems.

In this context it may also be appropriate to classify the role of "intelligent" components of the kind commonly deployed within human computer interface systems, such as those based on the use of "intelligent autonomous agents". Here distinction is drawn between intelligent components which during system runtime can adapt and/or evolve their behaviour so that they competitively realise local (to an individual component) goals from intelligent components which at system run adapt and/or evolve their behaviour so that they competitively realise global (i.e. system wide) goals. On categorising their inherent systems integration capabilities in a given systems context the former class of intelligent component will be viewed as *basic components* and the latter as *organic components*.

The two dimensional component classification described above (i.e. *business/application/function entity* versus *organic/basic*) is illustrated graphically by Figure 7. This classification has been developed further in Table 1 which draws distinctions between the infrastructural and structural services required to support interaction between each component class (this being designated by a cell number in Figure 7).

NB: The odd numbered entries concern infrastructure services whereas even numbered entries concern structural services.

This highlights a fairly obvious conclusion that whether or not *basic components* have local intelligence their infrastructural requirements will be the same. Indeed only where organic behaviour is required between a collection of components so that the system itself can behave organically will it be necessary to provide infrastructural capabilities which underpin the use of knowledge about a component grouping. Hence distinction is drawn between: components which act individually in an intelligent way and a collection of components which interact intelligently to facilitate the evolutionary

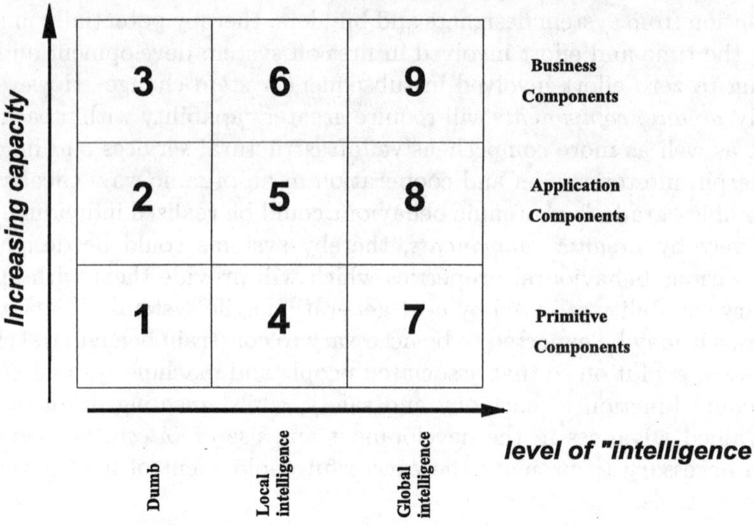

Figure 7: A two-dimensional component classification

behaviour of a system which may include emergent behaviour[6].

5 CIM-BIOSYS: A Research Integration Infrastructure

This section will seek to emphasise many of the concepts and classifications introduced earlier in this contribution by referring to the capabilities and example application areas of the Computer Integrated Manufacturing - Building Integrated Open SYStems (CIM-BIOSYS) integration infrastructure. The origin of CIM-BIOSYS concepts and first generation software tools were in the mid 1980s. Since that time the concepts and their implementation have been the subject of ongoing development by researchers in the MSI Research Institute.

5.1 The Basic Set of CIM-BIOSYS Infrastructure Services

By the late 80s early 90s a basic set of CIM-BIOSYS infrastructural services had been advanced into a sufficiently complete and robust form to enable their use in (a) selected industrial application domains and (b) to underpin

[6]The term *emergent behaviour* is used in this context to imply that synergy between components may lead to new behavioural properties and phenomena not present in individual components.

For Cell 1 and Cell 4
(1) relatively simple, general purpose and distinct physical mechanisms to underpin the distribution of components and their functional interaction and data exchange.
(2) mechanisms which support the use of a suitable organisational structure, such as an architecture or application framework which structures and helps configure components.
For Cells 2 and 5
(3) a logical abstraction of (1) to provide a set of "standard" infrastructural service mechanisms which support component distribution, interaction and data exchange.
(4) a logical abstraction of (2) to support system management (i.e. configuration, modification and extension).
For Cells 3 and 6
(5) abstract, semantically rich mechanisms (with embedded distribution, functional interaction and information interchange capabilities) which underpin the co-operative working of components in a given domain.
(6) as for (4) but system management capabilities are likely to be at a more abstract, user friendly level which is tailored for use in a target domain.
For Cell 7
(7) as for (1) but in addition physical mechanisms will be required to enable components to access and store knowledge (e.g. behavioural rules) about their environment.
(8) as for (2) but additional mechanisms required to support the management of environmental knowledge.
For Cell 9
(9) as for (5) but in addition, abstract, semantically rich mechanisms will be needed to access and store environmental knowledge in a way which underpins decision making leading to adaptive behaviour and evolutionary change.
(10) as for (6) but in addition the need to facilitate automatic system configuration capabilities, based on performance oriented decision making.

Table 1: Nature of infrastructure and structural services required for each class of component

the operation of numerous laboratory based proof-of-concept systems (both in MSI and by other research groups internationally).

This basic set of CIM-BIOSYS infrastructural services is depicted in Figure 8. Essentially they were designed to underpin the interoperation of component types 1, 2, 4 and 5, according to the classifications of Figure 7.

This early version of the CIM-BIOSYS integrating infrastructure can be considered to comprise a number of functional blocks which are described briefly in the following.

The service manager provides a consistent set of interaction mechanism for all integration services provided by CIM-BIOSYS, thereby providing applications with a consistent set of access mechanisms. Example services supported to date include establishing a communication data link with another application, sending data to an application, opening a remote file, etc. These services have built on and incorporated various emerging international and *de facto* standards.

The runtime manager controls all external processes (manufacturing applications and device drivers) and monitors any error conditions that occur within the CIM-BIOSYS integrating infrastructure. As part of the system, engineering, administration and operator interfaces are also provided which enable full manual control of applications and a window into the system such that the operator can see the state of processes within the system. This provides facilities for debugging and maintaining the operation of integrated systems.

The configuration manager maintains all internal system configuration data and external configuration files. The administration interface offers one means of enabling manipulation of system configuration data.

The driver manager allows a variety of device drivers to access CIM-BIOSYS using its consistent set of interaction mechanisms. Device drivers are required to hide/cater for differences between, and within, the various classes of resources which require to be integrated into a manufacturing system. Examples of system resources supported in this way include shop-floor machines, proprietary databases, CAD/CAM and MRP packages, human interface systems, etc. These mechanisms and an associated methodology for creating device drivers provide the means whereby an installed base of subsystems can be included within soft (or highly flexible) integrated systems; thereby offering a graceful migration towards fully conformant open systems.

5.2 European Standards Specification for Infrastructural Services (EMEIS) – CEN TC 310: A Requirements Specification for Integrating Infrastructures

To aid the reader's understanding and appraise the suitability of the design concepts and integration services included within CIM-BIOSYS here we refer to the European Standards Specification for Infrastructural Services, which is known as EMEIS. EMEIS was specified during the period early to mid 1990s by Working Group one (WG1) of CEN TC310[7].

[7]CEN: Communaute European de Normes (European Standards Community)

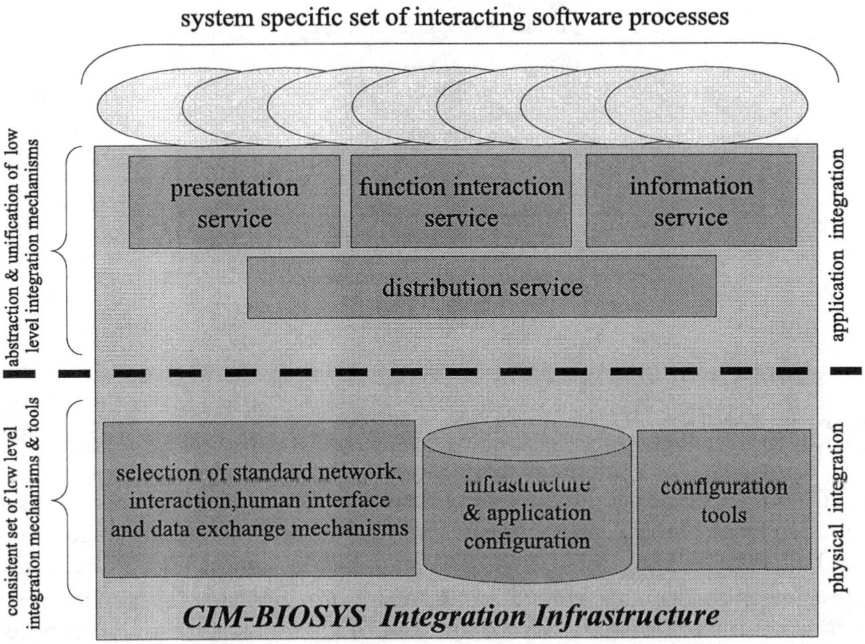

Figure 8: The basic set of CIM-BIOSYS infrastructural services

As illustrated by Figure 9, this specification defined requirements of a generic set of IT systems integration services (GenIS) which:

- facilitate distribution transparency and interworking between open systems
- provide protocol to achieve data exchange
- make maximum use of available standards, i.e. protocols and services
- are decoupled from underlying technology, such as via the use of a client / server architecture
- contain an abstraction of service mechanisms which support encapsulation, i.e. describe "what" not "how"
- utilise an application programming interface to provide transparency of service provision and application portability
- are structured according to systems theory, so that system interoperation can be enabled rapidly and effectively

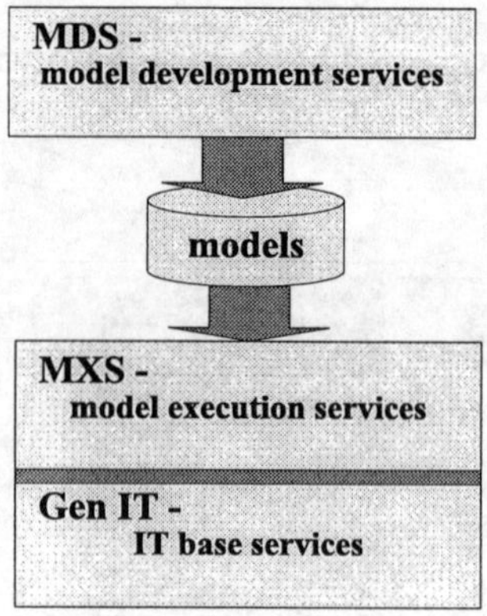

Figure 9: EMEIS

The EMEIS specification also defined the need for appropriate model execution services (MXS) which should be "open" to different modelling approaches. The purpose of the MXS is to structure and semi-automate the realisation of systems by embedding a model into EMEIS, thereby converting it into an executable entity. Hence the MXS should provide all services required to execute models, including an ability to support three types of modelled component, namely: compiled, interpreted, and parameter driven.

Thirdly EMEIS specifies the need for model development services (MDS) to enable models to be developed and tested before release. Key requirements which straddle model development and model execution services (i.e. MDS and MXS) were:

- common mechanisms to describe modelled components, using different languages available from alternative suppliers,
- common mechanisms to support interaction, primarily messaging between MDS and MXS. standard ways of describing model behaviour,
- common set of semantics to model the states of components and to achieve signalling those states,
- common procedures for declaring, registering and withdrawing modelled components.

5.3 Assessment of the Basic Set of CIM-BIOSYS Services with Reference to EMEIS

Although they were realised before the EMEIS specification was developed, essentially the basic set of CIM- BIOSYS integration services (depicted by Figure 8) meet each of the requirements specified for the GenIS of EMEIS.

This is illustrated by Table 2. However, as the EMEIS specification is focused on generic functional requirements and general design principles, in practice EMEIS conformance can be realised in different ways; therefore Table 2 explains how CIM-BIOSYS meets EMEIS design criteria and functional requirements.

Requirement	**Means of achieving requirement in CIM-BIOSYS**
facilitate distribution transparency	network configuration hidden from applications, this being supported by configuration tools
facilitate interworking	interaction and connection service provision
facilitate data exchange	information service provision
maximise use of standard/available protocol and services	provides an abstraction of service protocols, thereby acilitating the use of commonly used standards like RPC, SQL, MMS, RS232
means of decoupling services from underlying technology	neutral data exchange mechanisms for service invocation
abstraction mechanisms used and means of realising encapsulation	generalised service provision
use of application programming interface	APIs provided for each service
structuring of solutions according to systems theory	promotes an organised, reusable and scaleable decomposition of application processes to support their (re)engineering and (re)configuration

Table 2: How the basic set of CIM-BIOSYS services meets EMEIS design criteria and functional requirements

5.4 The Provision of EMEIS Conformant MDS and MXS Capabilities

Since the early 1990s MSI researchers have focused significant research and development effort on producing MDS and MXS capabilities. In most cases model execution has been targeted on the CIM-BIOSYS infrastructure. However the work has provided proof-of-concept facilities which can readily be retargeted at other infrastructural forms. Hence facilities have been developed which conform to MDS and MXS requirements of the EMEIS specification. Most of these developments were realised between 1992 and 95 as part of a UK Government funded project known as "Model Driven CIM"; the results of which are reported in greater detail elsewhere [WEH95]. However, MSI research in this area is ongoing, as outlined in section 7 of this contribution.

Two threads of related research within the Model Driven CIM project led to (a) general purpose MXS facilities and (b) a high level of abstraction of general purpose infrastructure facilities. The level of abstraction was chosen with the purpose of decoupling MXS operation from details of the infrastructural services which it is required to use. This was considered to be important, particularly as commercially available alternatives to CIM-BIOSYS began to emerge (e.g. CORBA [CORBA95], NEWI [SSA96] and WWW products and services). Another thread of related research within the Model Driven CIM project developed a number of alternative modelling environments which satisfy the MDS requirements of EMEIS. Here meta CASE tool technology has been deployed to produce a complementary set of workbenches which facilitate enterprise modelling. Two such workbenches respectively support "process oriented" and "object oriented" modelling of systems during various life phases and from different perspectives. Both workbenches support the capture and development of models and their transformation and release to model execution services which are capable of executing the models over an integrating infrastructure. More complete descriptions of these alternative modelling environments can be found in [WEH95, WG95b, Wes97].

Table 3 has been constructed to summarise key aspects of MSI research related to the development of MDS and MXS facilities. However it should be re-emphasised that many MSI researchers have been working in this arena and other perspectives on such issues are reported elsewhere in the literature.

Potentially enormous benefit can be realised from an ability to execute models over an integrating infrastructure, particularly if this can be achieved in a standard and flexible way. Under laboratory conditions MSI researchers have shown in various application domains that combinations of MDS, MS and GenIS facilities can naturally:

1. generate multi-perspective computer processible models of components and systems which can be transformed and used in different ways,

2. support the decomposition of existing and future systems into reusable objects (i.e. components and resources) and their organisation within object classes, object frameworks, object libraries, and so on,

3. utilise "flexible" and "standard" integration mechanisms (such as those provided by a GenIS) to realise different system behaviour via various object interactions, in a reusable, reconfigurable, extendible and scaleable manner. What is more, the interoperating objects can be "modelled components" or "real components," or combinations of them.

MDS and MXS requirement	**Example approaches supported by MSI workbenches and tools** (used in conjunction with CIM-BIOSYS)
common mechanisms for describing modelled components	Various process oriented and object oriented modelling constructs, made available as an integral part of enterprise modelling and software engineering tools. These include CIMOSA, IDEF, EXPRESS, STEP, Booch, STL, PetriNet and Estelle modelling constructs
common mechanisms to support interaction between MDS and MXS	CIMOSA IIS conformant service mechanisms, MSI derived Binary Transition Language, EXPRESS and STEP Translators, Parsers and Configuration Tools, Estelle and STL process description mechanisms
standard way of describing model behaviour	Timebased Stochastic, Coloured and Modular Petri Nets, Harrel State Charts, MSI's Binary Transition Language
common set of semantics	No underlying ontology
common procedures for declaring, registering and withdrawing components	Management functions for start, terminate, connect, select, status

Table 3: Means of Realising MDS and MXS Requirements

We may confidently expect property (3) above to have a major impact on current practice when engineering and configuring agile systems from components which have embedded software processes. Indeed naturally this property can facilitate:

1. system analysis based on simulation to help realise better system designs, such as via the selection of suitable candidate models, real components and integration schemata,

2. system implementation and extension based on emulation. When the operation of modelled components is proven they can be replaced incrementally by real components, i.e. thereby providing an ability to add, delete, modify or change behaviour and functionality,

3. model driven system operation as a precursor to model driven configuration, real-time data processing and visualisation, model capture and automatic validation and model based system adaptation and evolutionary behaviour.

6 Case Study Examples

6.1 Flexible Integration and the Control of Shop Floor Systems

Early versions of the CIM-BIOSYS integration infrastructure were engineered by MSI researchers[8] to solve generic problems of co-ordinating and controlling the operation of heterogeneous manufacturing machines. Figure 10 illustrates example flexibly integrated manufacturing systems in which the interoperation of various classes of manufacturing component was achieved by enabling structured and configurable access to CIM- BIOSYS integration services.

Figure 10(a) illustrates conceptually a relatively simple integrated system produced (in early 1990) in this way for a major UK manufacturer of printed circuit boards. In this case the original requirement was to control in a flexible way the operation of a surface mount technology (SMT) production line comprising different types and makes of computer controlled machine. Individual machines deployed different computational platforms and interface protocol; required different styles of interface mechanism to achieve interaction with machine operators; and had different local application software support capabilities. The original systems specification determined the need for a cell control system capable of: (1) co-ordinating the collective operation of machines deployed by a production line; (2) supporting individual machine operation and set up by providing database access to machine programmes and printed circuit board data; (3) monitoring the operation of machines; (4) supporting machine operators, via common "look and feel" interfaces. Also implicit was a need to enable modification and extension on a system-wide basis, as it was evident that: (i) there were also opportunities to improve the performance of other printed circuit board production lines within the company; (ii) it would be necessary to replace SMT machines with more advanced machinery as it became available (possibly within months rather than years) and (iii) the functional capabilities required from any given production line could be expected to extend (with resultant increase in system complexity) as pressures for increased productivity levels and reduced lead-times continued.

The successful installation in the company of the CIM-BIOSYS based system depicted by Figure 10(a) followed an unsuccessful attempt by an external IT subcontractor to use conventional system design and construction techniques[9] to meet the identified need. The relative success of the CIM-BIOSYS

[8]Much of the early CIM-BIOSYS work was the brainchild of Jack Gascoigne.

[9]The sub-contractor involved deployed well proven methods of building custom designed

approach stemmed directly from the availability of common infrastructural services. This led naturally to a separation of *distribution, interaction, information sharing and presentation* issues, and a further separation of issues concerned with *application functionality* and *system management and configuration.* Thus use of the CIM-BIOSYS Integration Infrastructure led to a natural problem decomposition and thereby provided a means of handling complexity. Evidently, however, whether or not systems are structured and supported via an infrastructure there remain complex systems integration problems to solve.

One generic integration problem, illustrated by the case study example of Figure 8(a), is that of coping with "legacy" components and systems. For the case study, the SMT machines offered only rudimentary and custom designed digital data link capabilities to upload and download data and to remotely invoke and monitor machine operation. This situation is a very common one with respect to shop floor machinery used in many industries. Hence a structured approach to handling legacy machines was developed in MSI based on the use of so called "alien application handlers," which essentially function as a configurable "gateway" for non-CIM-BIOSYS conformant system elements. These handlers provide a structured and reprogrammable way of facilitating protocol conversion between heterogeneous protocols (deployed by specific machines or groups of them) and the "standard protocol" required to access the services of CIM-BIOSYS. In this way flexible linkage can be established with "alien" machines to facilitate remote control of their operation; albeit that typically (1) the capabilities of such a link will be constrained by the interface and interaction capabilities provided by the machine builder and (2) it is necessary to develop an "alien application handler" for any machine not previously supported. Although in respect to (2) generic alien application handlers have been produced by MSI researchers which much simplify this process and once a machine handler has been produced it can be reused many times over.

A second generic integration problem illustrated by the case study concerns the configuration and management of systems. On their own the basic set of CIM-BIOSYS infrastructural services do not realise systems engineering and reconfiguration, rather they structure and support this requirement. Hence MSI researchers also produced a set of generic software tools which support the configuration of CIM-BIOSYS application processes and thereby facilitate system reconfiguration (and hence system modification and extension). The case study industrial use of CIM-BIOSYS determined a need to provide different styles of interface to these tools which suit generic requirements of system managers, builders and maintenance personnel. Although each of these needs were satisfied it became evident that conceptual

computer links between computer systems and their underlying processes. Although these links were established using well proven methods the approaches used failed to provide a sufficiently well structured and robust way of building a system in which complex interaction processes are involved.

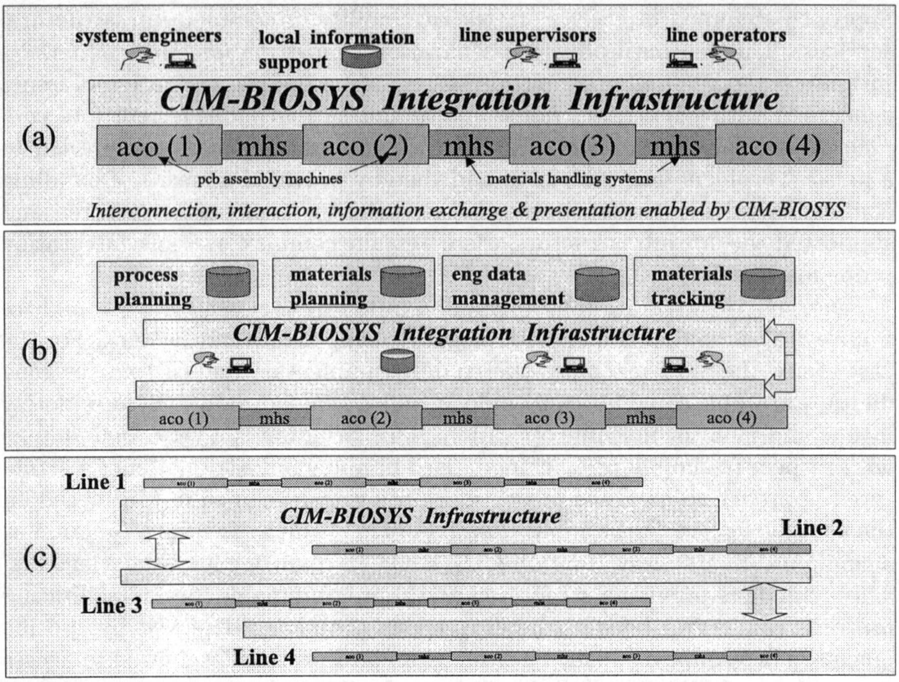

Figure 10: Flexibly integrated manufacturing systems

design decisions had to be made concerning the inclusion of domain specific functionality into systems configuration tools intended for generic use. Hence for example the basic system configuration capabilities included into the CIM-BIOSYS infrastructure support different styles of user interface but only directly facilitate the processes of forming associations between application processes and establishing their distribution. To maintain a general approach therefore formal architectural structures linking CIM-BIOSYS application processes (i.e. *integration structures*) are implemented and maintained by one or more other CIM-BIOSYS application processes, whereas the configuration services only support the engineering of such architectures.

A third class of generic systems integration problems illustrated by this case study was highlighted following subsequent needs of the company to extend and enhance its SMT lines. In particular this exemplified difficulties involved in choosing an appropriate decomposition of application functionality and mapping that decomposition onto a suitable set of application processes which can interoperate effectively over an integration infrastructure. Clearly this area of need is vast in its scope as it raises issues such as: how can the operation of the application processes in a system be aligned to high level business needs? can a particular application decomposition be realised effectively and changed readily? and so on. Hence significant research effort in MSI has been focused of finding ways of realising appropriate application decomposition rapidly and effectively. Here enterprise modelling and software engineering tools have been utilised and advanced. A primary area of study has been centred on developing MDS and MXS capabilities which support the mapping of abstract models of system functions, system behaviour, and information flows onto application processes executed over an integrating infrastructure.

A fourth generic system integration problem illustrated by the case study application concerned a company requirement to provide common classes of interface to machine operators, shopfloor supervisors, maintenance personnel and systems engineers. The interfaces required need to be largely independent of specific human interface requirements of proprietary machines as this can improve the efficiency with which different classes of user fulfil their role and reduce training requirements and system implementation time frames. Once again MSI researchers deliberately separated the use of the basic CIM-BIOSYS infrastructural services from abstract representations of human presentational requirements and the support of these requirements by off-the-shelf software tools. In this way specifics of company methods and developments can be separated away from technology developments in human computer interface (HCI) techniques and from specifics of the software processes involved. Indeed this thread of study led onto more generic research in MSI on modelling and profiling users of manufacturing systems by deploying MDS, MSX and GenIS facilities as reported by Monfared [MWWH96]

Shortly after commissioning the system depicted by Figure 10(a) (i.e. in mid 1990) it became necessary to support new integration requirements. Certain of these new requirements emerged for business reasons, others emerged as it became evident to the company that the approach of using an integrating infrastructure could be beneficially applied on other SMT production lines in the company. The inherent flexibility of the CIM-BIOSYS approach and the reusability of software processes, human interface systems and alien application handlers allowed changes depicted by Figure 10(b) to be accommodated with orders of magnitude saving in both engineering effort and lead-times when compared with conventional approaches to systems engineering. The most challenging changes in requirement concerned the need to realise remote access to proprietary software systems (used to support materials requirements planning, computer aided process planning, engineering data management and materials, inventory and quality tracking) as depicted by Figure 10(c). At the time the approach taken was similar to that adopted for machines; where an alien application handler was specified and implemented primarily to realise protocol conversion (as appropriate via "screen scrapping") between abstracted CIM-BIOSYS service protocol and the programmatic and/or human interfaces utilised by specific software packages. In this case remote terminal access to such packages was already available, but the natural abstraction of the integration services realised by deploying an

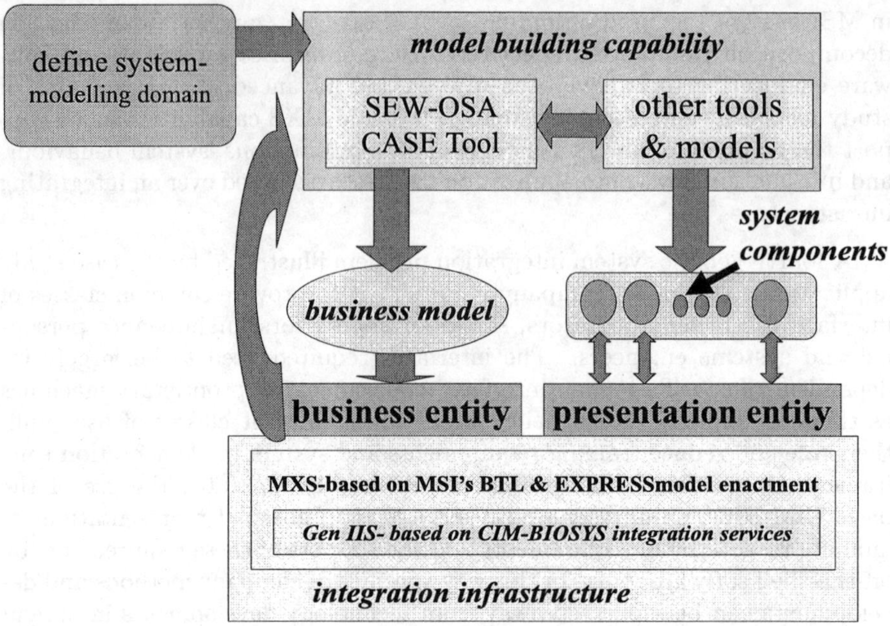

Figure 11: Support of the integration of software components

integration infrastructure proved to be highly beneficial as the company employed a variety of networks and protocols. Indeed this line of study served as a forerunner to a number of follow up research projects which have studied alternative means of accessing legacy software and more futuristically utilising MDS, MHX and GenIS facilities to investigate how contemporary monolithic software systems can be broken down into smaller grained, reusable software components [EHW97].

6.2 The Provision of Generic Integration Services for Enterprise Engineering Workbenches: A Surrogate CIMOSA IIS

During the early 1990s the basic set of CIM-BIOSYS infrastructural tools were used in a variety of application areas. Probably the most innovative of these has been its use to provide the basis of a runtime execution environment for a number of enterprise engineering workbenches. As mentioned earlier, much of this work is reported elsewhere in the literature. However to illustrate the principles involved here we consider a case where the CIM-BIOSYS toolset was extended to enable it to execute CIMOSA conformant models [Agu95].

Figure 11 illustrates how the CIM-BIOSYS integrating infrastructure has been used to support the interoperation of software components in accordance with the requirements of the Business Entity of CIMOSA. By so doing the Business Entity provides an MXS facility for executing models of system behaviour expressed both in Petri Net forms and by using a behavioural description language (BTL) defined and developed by MSI researchers. This approach has proven to be very powerful in facilitating system analysis and visualisation leading on consistently to the co-ordination and control of real and model components, which function collectively by accessing the common CIM-BIOSYS infrastructural services. Thus models created, tested and released by a CIMOSA conformant modelling tool (in this case MSIs SEWOSA enterprise engineering tool which functions as a MDS) can be used to structure and drive the operation of real systems in a way which flexibly maps integration structure onto concurrently operating application processes. The so called business model (used as input to the Business Entity) can be modified rapidly and if required the effect of such modifications can be assessed via use of a simulation tool before the new executable model is released. In this way cooperation, interoperation and interaction between modelled and real components of various systems can be changed rapidly and effectively. Such changes can be invoked having followed rigid system design processes and procedures, whereas alternatively they could be invoked on-line, either under human supervision or automatically, e.g. in response to predefined commands, environmental stimuli or changed system goals. In such cases CIM-BIOSYS can readily support the incremental addition of software processes including processes which control and/or adapt and evolve the behaviour of groups of processes.

7 Next Generation Agile Systems

Thus we have seen that modelling, component and infrastructure technologies are emerging which promise a step change in practice leading to better systems, more quickly and cheaply. On the not too distant horizon are self adapting systems in which components interact not only flexibly but intelligently so that resultant systems can be considered to demonstrate organic behaviour.

Ongoing research in the MSI Research Institute seeks to promote the development of integration infrastructures and model driven integration structures which promise to promote the realisation of a new generation of agile manufacturing systems. Ongoing studies are investigating such developments along both dimensions of the component classification matrix illustrated by Figure 7. Along the vertical axis being considered are alternative basic component decompositions and their interaction, interoperation and cooperation needs with a view to meeting sometimes conflicting needs of IT component and system providers and the manufacturing end user communities they serve. Whereas along the horizontal axis of Figure 7 an area of current study seeks to identify generic requirements of organic components, and their impact on integration structures & infrastructures, so that systems can be realised which are capable of rapidly responding to change without the need for human intervention. The types of change being considered include the addition/removal of components into/from a system, the modification of structures used to organise and control the system, and the resultant impact on quality of service. This work has confirmed that additional infrastructure services and functions are required to underpin interaction, interoperation and cooperation between organic components which are over and above those required by basic components.

Indeed to date the work has identified additional infrastructure requirements which include:

- a capability to register the capabilities of each component in a system, so that other components can select and utilise those capabilities, this being analogous to advertising capabilities on yellow pages of a telephone directory,
- a capability for the infrastructure to support the negotiation process between components, as new or modified relationships are developed,
- a capability for the infrastructure to have (or have means of accessing) knowledge of system structures, so that the components of a system collectively function in alignment with system-wide goals,
- a capability for the infrastructure to report its state and activities to external entities.

To realise the infrastructural capabilities listed above MSI researchers are investigating the use of various mechanisms and standards including: KQML [FMFM94], the Business Object Facility proposed within OMG [OMG96] and Newi negotiation protocols.

8 Conclusions

This contribution has highlighted key barriers which must be overcome before we can produce complex systems, comprising distributed software processes. Currently the timeframes involved in developing large scale software systems are orders of magnitude too long. Also difficulties involved in systems reengineering place undue constraints on business processes. In this context this contribution has illustrated the important enabling role that network and associated computational infrastructural services will play in building better systems, more quickly and cheaply.

It is evident however that many parallel technical and commercial developments will be necessary before the potential of infrastructure technology can be fully realised. In some areas tools based on Internet are already dramatically impacting practice. However to more generally enable the development of business processes this contribution has shown how it will also be necessary to:

1. develop and agree upon appropriate problem decompositions to handle the complexity involved. This leading to descriptions of reusable components and systems, and possibly business processes,
2. develop and agree upon more abstract, user friendly and comprehensive general purpose integration services, which can support the flexible and effective integration of the decompositions identified under (1),
3. develop and unify the use of enterprise (including software) engineering toolsets. This providing means of creating better specialist enterprises and systems and of supporting developments under (1) and (2).

Already researchers and system developers have advanced systems integration technology to a point where larger scale solutions can be handled better than before, at least in proof-of-concept form. Hence the challenge is to accelerate this trend and more widely bring industry and commerce on board.

References

[Agu95] Aguiar, M. W. C., Executing manufacturing models of open systems, PhD Thesis, Loughborough University, 1995

[BJWG96] Barber, M. I., Jennis, S., Weston, R. H., Gascoigne, J. D., A Study of Business Process Re-engineering Practice in the UK, MSI Pub., Loughborough University, 1996

[BN95] Bernus, P., Nemes, L., A Framework to Define a Generic Enterprise Reference Architecture and Methodology (GERAM), Div. Rep. No. MTM 366 CSIRO Div. of Manuf. Tech., Preston, 1995

[BW97] Barber, M. I., Weston, R. H., Scoping study on business process reengineering: towards successful IT application, in: International Journal of Production Research, 1997

[CORBA95] The Common Object Request Broker: Architecture and Spezification, Revision 2.0, OMG, July 1995

[EHW97] Edwards, J. M., Hodgson, A., Weston, R. H., Manufacturing Software Interoperability: Steps Towards Interoperating Distributed Objects, Second Review Report to EPSRC/CDP, Loughborough University, 1997

[FMFM94] Finin, T., McKay, D., Fritzson, R., McEntire, R., KQML: An Information and Knowledge Exchange Protocol, in: K. Fuchi, T. Yokoi (eds.), Knowledge Building and knowledge sharing, Ohshama, and IOS Press, 1994

[Ful96] Fulton, J. A., Semantic Plug and Play - Model-Driven Interoperable Information Systems, in: J. G. Nell (ed.), Proceedings of Joint Workshop on Standards for the Use of Models that Define the Data and Processes of Information Systems, NIST, Ga., USA, 1996

[GNP95] Goldman, S. L., Nagel, R. N., Preiss, K., Agile Competitors and Virtual Organisations, Van Nostrand Reinhold Pub., New York, 1995

[GZW97] Gascoigne, J. D., Zhang, B. L., Weston, R. H., A Report on the UK Cell Control Marketplace, in: Integrated Manufacturing Systems, Vol. 8, No. 2, 1997

[KK90] Kosanke, K., Klevers, T., CIMOSA: Architecture for Enterprise Integration, Journal of Computer Integrated Manufacturing Systems Vol.3, No.1, 1990, 317-332

[MWWH96] Monfared, R. P., Waine, P., West, A. A., Hodgson, A., A Common User Interface for CIM, Intelligent and Cognitive Systems Conference 96, Tehran, Iran, Sept 1996, Ed. Caro Lucas, Pub. IPM (Institute for studies in theoretical Physics and Mathematics), Tehran, 1996, 310-316

[OMG96] OMG96, Common Business Objects and Business Object Facility (cf/96-01-4), Object Management Group, Framingham, MA, US, 1996

[Pri96] Prins, R., Developing Business Objects - A framework driven approach, McGraw Hill, 1996

[SSA96] SSA96, New World Infrastructure (Newi), SSA Object Technology, Newbury, UK, 1996

[WEH95] Weston, R. H., Edwards, J. M., Hodgson, A., Model Driven CIM: A framework and toolset for the design, implementation and management of open CIM systems, Final Project Report to EPSRC, Loughborough University, 1995

[WG95b] Weston, R. H., Gilders, P. J., Enterprise engineering methods and tools which facilitate simulation, emulation and enactment via formal models, in: P. Bernus, L. Nemes (eds.), Working Conf. on Models and Methodologies for Enterprise Integration (E195), IFIP TC5 Special Interest Group on Architectures for Enterprise Integration, Heron Island, Australia, Chapman and Hall, London, 1996, 1-16

[Wes97] Weston, R. H., A suite of software tools for rapid prototyping of flexible and extendible manufacturing systems, International Journal of Production Research, 1997

Chapter 35

Distributed Processing DCE, CORBA, and Java

Andy Bond, Keith Duddy, Kerry Raymond

DCE and CORBA are two distributed processing technologies that provide remote procedure calls in a location-transparent manner between heterogeneous platforms. Java is not a distributed processing technology, but a programming language that can be executed remotely using Web browsers. There are advantages and disadvantages to the use of each of these technologies, and there are some benefits in combining them.

1 Introduction

Distributed processing involves the construction of an application from multiple components which are physically distributed over a number of computers. The challenges of distributed processing include:

- enabling communication and synchronisation between the components
- overcoming the heterogeneity of the hardware, operating systems, and programming languages used by the components
- finding the components wherever they are located in the current configuration.

DCE and CORBA are superficially similar technologies for constructing distributed applications. Both DCE and CORBA provide remote procedure calls in a location-transparent manner between heterogeneous platforms. However, the goals of DCE and CORBA and the approach to their standardisation were significantly different, resulting in two technologies with an almost disjoint set of strengths and weaknesses.

Java is widely touted as the "new direction" for distributed applications. Unfortunately many commentators mistakenly believe that Java is a distributed processing technology. On the contrary, Java is not a distributed processing technology, but a programming language that can be executed remotely using Web browsers, giving the illusion of distributed processing. In this review, the goals and history of DCE, CORBA, and Java are explored, and the major components of each technology described. An outline is given on how to develop a distributed application using the various technologies, and the underlying infrastructure of each technology is explained. Based on this information, the technologies can be compared and their future predicted.

2 Distributed Computing Environment – DCE

The Open Software Foundation's (OSF)[1] Distributed Computing Environment (DCE) emerged in 1990 following a request for technology issued in 1989 [FKR92]. The request called for a single software technology that would provide vendor transparency and the sharing of resources. A snapshot of DCE was released in 1990 incorporating technologies from organizations such as Digital, Hewlett Packard, MIT, Siemens-Nixdorf, and Transarc. The selected technologies were mostly individually mature and the contribution of DCE was their integration into a single toolset.

DCE is licensed as source to vendors. Several reference platforms are provided to verify further ports to vendor platforms. As a consequence of this common code base, DCE products offered by different vendors are highly interoperable.

2.1 Components

DCE supports the development, use and maintenance of distributed applications based on the client/server interaction model. The environment is provided through a layered architecture as presented in Figure 1. It is a middleware or enabling technology designed to provide distributed system services layered above the basic operating system and network services. DCE was primarily designed for use by C programmers.

Services within DCE are strongly integrated. Each relies on the others for essential distributed systems support. In addition, DCE is an extremely adaptable environment allowing the programmer to modify the behaviour of these services by the setting of attributes and by selecting between alternative mechanisms.

2.1.1 Threads

Threads provide multiple execution paths within a single program while sharing common program data. Private data is maintained within each thread

[1]The OSF is now part of The Open Group.

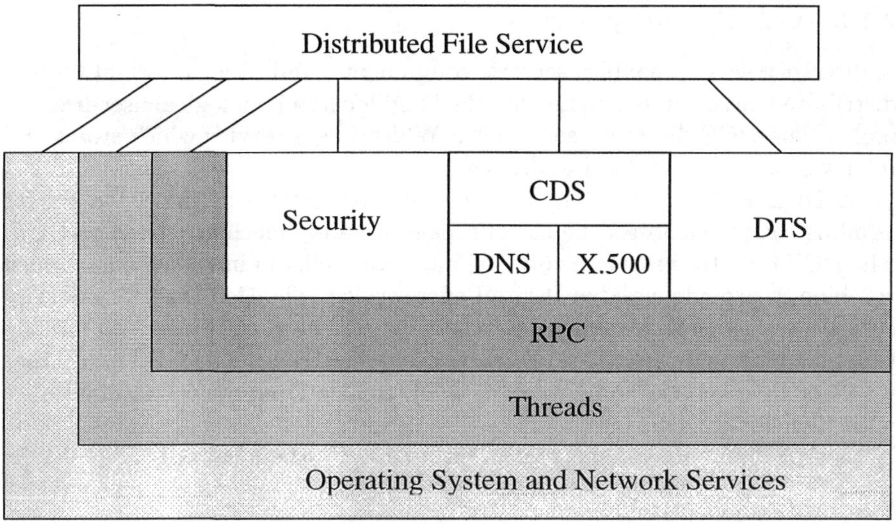

Figure 1: The Distributed Computing Environment components

stack. Threads are not a fundamental requirement for a distributed environment, but threads provide a more sophisticated programming model suited to the more complex needs of distributed applications. For example, a multi-threaded process can prevent deadlock caused by cycles of interactions which occur when a number of services make use of one another.

DCE threads use the Posix 1003.4a threading interface known as *Pthreads* for thread management, synchronisation, and mutual exclusion. All DCE Services are fundamentally thread-aware allowing support for simultaneous access to resources.

2.1.2 Remote Procedure Call

The Remote Procedure Call (RPC) is a syntactic model for process interaction which supports a client/server communication model. The RPC is the backbone of DCE as a distributed system. The DCE run-time supports:

- the selection and location of an appropriate server for the client
- the allocation and maintenance of a communication path between the client and server
- the transmission of messages between the client and server to implement the RPC
- the marshalling and unmarshalling of data transmitted between the client and server.

2.1.3 Cell Directory Service

A directory service enables servers, components, and other information of a distributed environment to be identified and located by a logical user-friendly name. The DCE directory service is a White Pages service which stores and retrieves names, types and addresses.

A DCE *cell* is a set of nodes, grouped together as a single domain for administrative purposes; the use of cells is a scaling mechanism within DCE. The DCE directory service is divided into inter-cell and intra-cell parts which combine to provide a global White Pages service. The Cell Directory Service (CDS) uses a hierarchical naming scheme within each cell. Inter-cell naming is handled through the Global Directory Service (GDS). The GDS uses either X.500 or the Domain Name Service (DNS) to locate remote cells and interact with their local CDS.

A CDS name uses a shortcut prefix to specify the local cell

```
/.:/servers/addition
```

while GDS names include either a DNS or X.500 component to specify the cell of origin. An example of a DNS-based name is:

```
/.../paladine.dstc.edu.au/server/addition
```

while an example of a X.500-based name is:

```
/.../C=AU/O=DSTC/OU=Architecture/server/addition
```

2.1.4 Security Service

Security is an important aspect of distributed computing, and DCE's interoperable security infrastructure [Hu95] is one of its strengths. DCE's authentication is based upon MIT's Kerberos authentication service which uses private key technology to verify the identity of resources and allocate tickets based on that identification. DCE has extended this technology to include access control through a privilege service. This uses access control lists (ACL) to specify resource access for both local users (within a cell) and also foreign users (from other cells). The ACL data structure used by DCE is a superset of POSIX 1003.6 [Posix-10036, Posix-10036a]. Servers use an ACL manager to determine whether an authenticated client has permission to access the named resource. DCE can protect the on-the-wire communications between client and server by using private-key encryption. Future releases of DCE will incorporate public key technology.

2.1.5 Time Service

Synchronised time is critical for the DCE's security service to ensure non-repudiation and valid access management. DCE's distributed time service provides synchronised time to each node within a DCE cell. The synchronisation algorithm sets the system clocks of the nodes of the cell based on the average time computed by a quorum of reliable time keepers within the cell and (optionally) external time providers. DCE's Time Service supports both local area networks and time management across wide area networks within the same cell.

2.1.6 Distributed File Service

DCE's Distributed File Service (DFS) provides a single, consistent, global namespace for all file access, both within a cell and beyond to other cells. An example of a fully qualified DFS file name is:

```
/.../paladine.dstc.edu.au/fs/home/kerry/foo.c
```

while the local reference for the same file would be:

```
/:/home/kerry/foo.c
```

DFS is not part of the core DCE services; instead, it is an additional service relying on a DCE environment for its distributed system services. File replication is supported in addition to full Unix file semantics, such as file and record locking. Access control is integrated with the security service providing consistent access control similar to that provided for all DCE applications. Administration is also a strong feature of DFS. The file system is logged to provide efficient failure recovery, and backups can be taken as the system is being used. Since DFS is implemented using DCE services, it benefits from the portability and interoperability features for which DCE is known.

2.2 Application Development

The first step in developing a DCE application is to design the interfaces of the server processes.

2.2.1 Interface Definition Language (IDL)

Interfaces in DCE are defined using DCE IDL. This is a C-like notation for defining interface signatures. Figure 2 shows a bank teller interface with three operations to obtain the balance, deposit money, and withdraw money from a customer account.

The primitive data types supported by DCE cover at least the set available in C. The basic data types include:

- `boolean`
- `byte`, `char`, `ISO_LATIN_1`, `ISO_UCS`, `ISO_MULTI_LINGUAL`

- integers: small (8 bits), short (16 bits), long (32 bits), hyper (64 bits), signed by default, but optionally unsigned
- float (32 bits), double (64 bits)
- void, void *
- handle_t.

```
[
  uuid(15b11683-01b3-11d1-bf88-08002bbceeee),
  version(1.0)
]interface BankTeller
{
  import types.idl

  Result Balance ([in]Customer c, [in]Account a,
                  [out] Dollars balance, [out] text error);

  Result Deposit([in]Customer c, [in]Account a, [in]Dollars d,
                 [out]Dollars new_balance, [out]text error);

  Result Withdraw([in]Customer c, [in]Account a, [in]Dollars d,
                  [out]Dollars new_balance, [out]text reason);
}
```

Figure 2: The interface definition for a bank teller service

ISO_LATIN_1, ISO_UCS, and ISO_MULTI_LINGUAL are the internationalised character types. void is used when no return types is required by an operation while void * is used to pass arbitrary pointers. handle_t is a binding handle, which is used for specifying a particular server.

DCE includes a number of type constructors:

- *Arrays.* These can be of *fixed* size or of *varying* length. In addition slices of arrays can be specified and are referred to as *conformant* arrays. An operation can have only one conformant array parameter, and it must be the last parameter of the operation.
- *Enumerated types.*
- *Structures.*
- *Discriminated unions.* The typed discriminator selects the current data type used in the union. This differs from the C use where no explicit discriminator type is provided. The discriminator is required for type safety.

- *Pipes.* A pipe delivers an arbitrary-length stream of typed data. Pipes are defined as being either input pipes or output pipes. Programmers provide functions to generate and consume data depending on the direction of the data stream of the pipe. All input pipe processing must be completed before output pipe processing begins.

Attributes are used in IDL to define additional semantics for operations, parameters, or the interface as a whole. The attributes on IDL types include:

- `full` and `reference` pointers
- `string`
- `size_is`, `max_is` (for varying-length arrays)
- `first_is`, `length_is`, `last_is` (for conformant arrays).

DCE distinguishes itself amongst other distributed environments by providing full pointer support allowing complex pointer-linked structures such as recursive linked lists to be used as operation parameters. While `full` pointers implement normal C-semantics for pointers, there is a heavy overhead for their use. Reference pointers incur less overhead than full pointers, but are subject to a number of simplifying restrictions. Reference pointers can never be `NULL`, cannot change in value during an RPC call, and are assumed to reference separate memory from other pointer parameters in the same RPC call.

The `string` attribute is used to indicate a `NULL`-terminated string as distinct from a pointer to a single character, `char *` or `char []`. The C language does not make this important distinction, essential for type safety.

The flexibility of DCE as a distributed programming environment is illustrated by the range of attributes that can be applied to IDL descriptions to customise interaction semantics. For example, DCE IDL attributes provide idempotent, broadcast, and one-way announcement RPCs as well as pre- and post- marshalling of parameter values.

Operation parameters can be input only, output only or both input and output. Operations can return a result type; or `void` when no result is required. Operations are synchronous unless a `maybe` attribute is included and the return value is `void`. Timeouts on synchronous RPCs are selectable through ten stages between a minimum value favouring response time over correctness and an infinite timeout which will attempt to communicate forever.

DCE provides some support for exception handling. There are two kinds of exceptions, communication errors arising during the RPC (`comm_status`) and exceptions generated by the server code (`fault_status`). These are optionally returned as output parameters, but are not visible in the IDL.

DCE supports a limited form of subtyping between interface definitions based on the use of version numbers. However, this mechanism depends on the careful decision of the application programmer, and is not checked to determine if the interfaces are actually subtypes based on their definitions.

2.2.2 Building the Application

The IDL file is compiled using the IDL compiler to produce a header file and client and server stub files. The header file defines types for use by client and server applications while the stub files are responsible for the marshalling and unmarshalling of data as well as the maintenance of the communication connection.

In order for a client to invoke the operations of a server, the client must establish a binding to the server. A server makes itself available for binding by exporting one or more of its interfaces to the name service (CDS). Clients can access the server interfaces after binding to the service. The client may choose one of three binding mechanisms.

- *Automatic* binding is the default and is provided by the client stub. The client names the required server through the environment variable `RPC_DEFAULT_ENTRY`, and the stub uses the CDS to find and bind to a correspondingly-named server. If the connection to that server is lost, then another server with the same name is automatically selected for subsequent interaction.
- *Implicit* binding requires the client programmer to specify a server binding. All client RPC calls will be directed to that server until another server is specified. In this case, the programmer is responsible for re-establishing a lost server connection.
- *Explicit* binding allows the programmer to bind to many servers simultaneously by specifying a binding handle at each RPC call. This provides both the most flexibility but also the most work for the programmer.

The client/server infrastructure defines an extensive application programming interface (API) covering all aspects of application interaction and management [HS94, Loc94]. Some work has been done to extend the C API to work in the C++ and Java worlds to provide an object-oriented interface to the DCE run-time to minimize the complex steps required to register a service interface. These extensions have not gained widespread popularity; DCE continues to be primarily used in C programming environments.

2.3 Infrastructure

The priority for DCE has been interoperability of mature technology. As a consequence, DCE components provide an API-based infrastructure rather than using the more popular object/interface based approach. DCE servers can be considered as objects, since a server encapsulates its state and makes it accessible only through well-defined interfaces. However, DCE does not support the features generally expected of an object-oriented system (e.g. inheritance). DCE is better described as an object-based system.

DCE is available on a wide range of platforms, e.g. Unix, PC, and several mainframe systems including MVS and VMS. As a product, DCE consists of three parts.

- The DCE run-time is required on each computer running DCE applications.
- The DCE development environment (primarily the IDL compiler) is required only on computers used for DCE applications development.
- DCE services (e.g. Security, Naming, and Time) need only be installed on one computer per DCE cell, unless replication is required for greater availability and reliability.

Note that some vendors supply the DCE run-time as part of their standard operating system.

All DCE implementations support TCP and UDP transport protocols, while some also support additional proprietary protocols, e.g. DECnet. The common code base used to develop DCE products ensures that DCE is highly interoperable, even between such disparate platforms as PCs and mainframes.

The promise of distributed systems is transparent access to resources, both local and remote. In DCE, IDL-generated stubs mask the difference in data representations between systems, while the CDS masks the need to be aware of the location of resources. DFS makes the location and replication of data transparent to the application programmer.

DCE is a robust distributed environment. Components are tightly coupled, and critical services employ caching and replication to ensure availability. The security service is pervasively used in the DCE infrastructure, thus ensuring secure access to the administrative interfaces of DCE services. Errors in remote invocation are handled through exceptions which are ultimately managed by the calling process.

The cell as a grouping of nodes provides a strong basis for scalability. Cells partition a possibly worldwide set of nodes into manageable groups. Cells are usually created to reflect administrative and/or geographical domains. Within each cell, security and name services provide essential distributed system functionality. A cell can be subdivided into smaller cells, but, in practice, it is often more effective to replicate the DCE services within a single cell than to create a hierarchy of cells.

2.4 Administration

Administration covers the planning, installation, configuration, maintenance, and evolution of a distributed environment. The cell defines the administrative domain for DCE. Users within that cell are given privileges (through

ACL managers) to administer components of the DCE run-time and services. Installation and configuration of a DCE cell must initiate the required services (naming, security, and time), register the users, and assign privileges for those users.

Ongoing maintenance will adjust DCE performance through the system APIs and management utilities. Typical maintenance tasks include modifying the acceptable inter-node time difference, adjusting the frequency of security replica updates, or flushing the caches of the directory service. DCE is highly configurable, and users typically require some training to become proficient in its administration.

2.5 Summary

OSF DCE is a layered distributed environment supporting the development and management of distributed applications. The environment is tailored toward C with an object-based architecture rather than an object-oriented application development framework. It provides several distributed system services including naming, security, and time. Key contributions from DCE include a proven scalability architecture based on administrative cells, interoperable private key security through Kerberos, and support for threaded applications.

3 CORBA

The Object Management Group (OMG) [OMG] was formed in 1989 to provide a common development environment for distributed object-oriented applications. Its aim was to provide open specifications in a programming-language neutral notation that could be implemented independently by its members. The OMG had over 700 members at the beginning of 1997, making it the largest computer industry consortium in the world.

CORBA [CORBA95] is the acronym for Common Object Request Broker Architecture. This is the central "communication bus" for distributed object-oriented method invocations within the Object Management Architecture (OMA) [Sol95]. However, CORBA is the name commonly used to denote the whole family of specifications produced by the OMG.

The OMA, as depicted in Figure 3, reflects the Technical Committee organization [OMG-TC] within the OMG. There are two Technical Committees: the Platform Technical Committee (PTC) and the Domain Technical Committee (DTC). The PTC specifies common infrastructure standards. In terms of the OMA, this consists of the ORB itself, the Object Services, and the Object Modelling methodology. The DTC specifies Domain Interfaces that are for use in particular vertical industry domains, e.g. Transport, Health-care, Telecommunications and Finance. The Application Interfaces are specified by ORB users according to the needs of their application; these are not subject

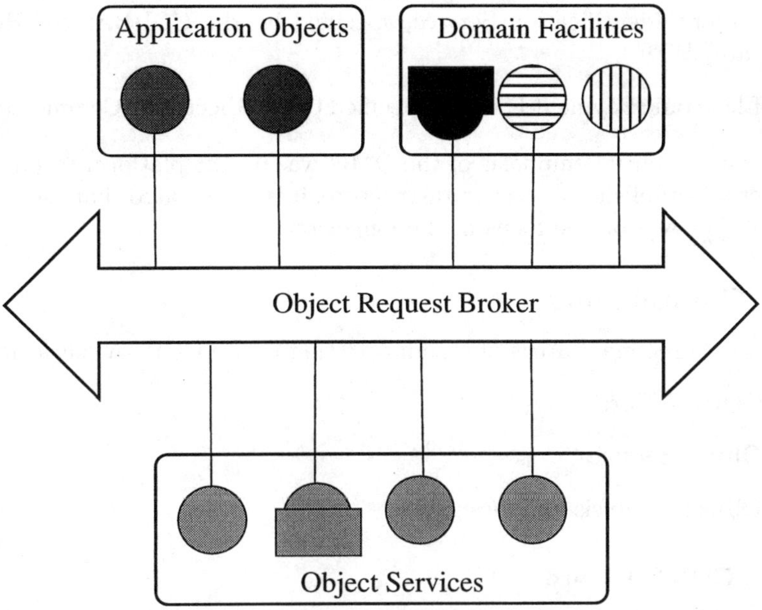

Figure 3: The Object Management Architecture

to standardisation by the OMG.

Working groups within the Technical Committees called Task Forces issue Requests for Proposals (RFPs), that solicit specifications of technology. OMG member companies submit specifications that satisfy the particular requirements identified in the RFP. The Task Force provides feedback to submitters on the merits of their proposals, and often this results in a merger of the original proposals to combine their best features. After revised submissions are presented, registered Task Force members vote to select a proposal to recommend to the OMG as a whole. The final stage is an adoption vote to confirm that the recommended technology is acceptable to the majority of OMG members. The submitters of an adopted proposal are expected to produce commercial implementations of their specification within 12 months of adoption.

3.1 Domain Technology

The DTC has many Task Forces that focus on specifying interfaces to objects for use in their particular domain. Some examples of Domain Technology Specifications include:

- Control of Audio/Visual Streams, specified by the Telecommunications DTF

- Patient Identification Service, specified by the CORBAmed (Healthcare) DTF
- Electronic Payment Facility, specified by the Electronic Commerce DTF.

Although the initial emphasis of the OMG was on the platform technologies in order to establish the basic infrastructure, it is anticipated that the domain technologies will be the focus in the longer term.

3.2 Components

There are three main areas of standardisation in the CORBA platform:

- CORBA Core
- Object Services
- Object Analysis and Design.

3.2.1 CORBA Core

The Object Request Broker is essentially a mechanism for the location-transparent invocation of object methods. *Object references* are opaque data types that encapsulate a CORBA object's type and location information. Object references can refer to objects in the same process, in another process, or in a process on a remote machine. Object references can be used as if they were pointers to local objects. They can be passed as parameters, and can be used to invoke methods on objects regardless of their location or state of activation. The ORB performs all binding, network connection maintenance, and activation of servers transparently to the client using the object reference.

The OMG Interface Definition Language (IDL) is used to define the CORBA object types. As the IDL is designed to be architecture-neutral, CORBA programming can be supported in many different programming languages and machine environments. The OMG defines standard mappings between types in IDL and types in programming languages including C, C++, Ada, Smalltalk, Java and even COBOL. Many more non-standard mappings exist for other languages.

IDL compilers generate *stub code* (for use in clients) and *skeleton code* (for use in servers) that marshall the programming language parameter values into network packets and convey them as a *request* to the server object which replies with results, as illustrated in Figure 4. Typically, objects playing a "server" role will also act as clients to other objects, making the system truly peer-to-peer.

Because ORBs are developed by many companies, using many implementation techniques, they require a common protocol to ensure that objects developed for one ORB can interoperate with objects developed for another

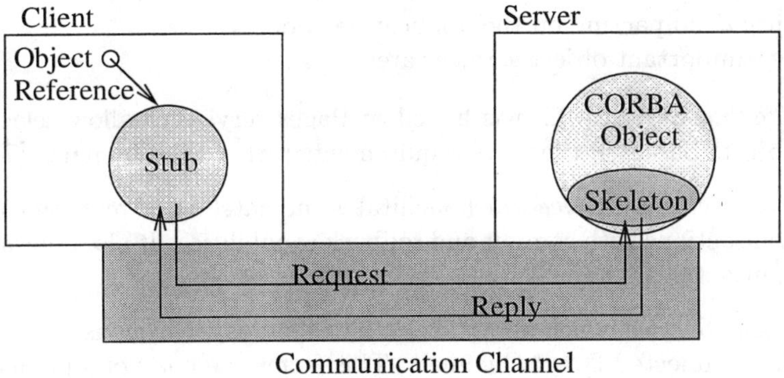

Figure 4: A CORBA Operation Invocation

ORB. The OMG has specified a General Inter-ORB Protocol (GIOP) which specifies the layout of messages for CORBA types, regardless of the network protocol used to convey them. The OMG's Internet Inter-ORB Protocol (IIOP) uses GIOP over TCP/IP, and all conformant CORBA systems must support IIOP. ORBs can also support other inter-ORB protocols. One that is currently standardised by the OMG is the DCE Common Interoperability Protocol. This uses the DCE RPC wire format to make CORBA operation invocations.

3.2.2 Object Services

Object Services provide the basic services commonly required in most applications. The OMG has produced many Object Service specifications, but not all ORB vendors offer all of them in their product suites. Some object services have become widely available, others are available only from specific vendors, while a few may never be commercially available. The specifications are collectively known by the brand name *CORBAservices*. These are published as [CORBA96], with regularly issued additional chapters for new services. All the services described below are found in this document, unless other citations are given.

Naming and Security can be viewed as the most fundamental object services. The Naming Service is a simple context-relative hierarchical naming service that allows applications to identify objects by human-readable names, rather than by object references (which print as a very long sequence of digits).

The Security Service [CORBAsecur] allows a large range of security policies to be implemented to ensure that authentication, access restriction and auditing can be tailored to the needs of most environments. The interfaces to administer these policies are separate from the security mechanism itself, allowing a range of public and private key security implementations to be used without impacting on the application code.

Other important object services are:

- *Trading Service* which is a Yellow Pages service to allow selection of objects based on type and requirements rather than by name [TOS96].
- *Transactions Service* which facilitates the batching of method calls into transactions with commit and rollback capabilities. It also allows nested transactions.
- *Event Service* which allows objects to send asynchronous messages via interconnected Event Channels. This forms the basis of a publish/subscribe event service known as the Notification Service.
- *Query Service* which enables standardised queries to be made on heterogeneous databases and a standardised way to return the results of those queries.
- *Property Service* which manages sets of name/value pairs.
- *Life Cycle Service* which provides standard interfaces to create, move, copy and destroy objects. This service is really a template or pattern for applications to employ when implementing object life cycle management.

3.2.3 Object Analysis and Design

Current work within the Object Analysis and Design Task Force hopes to achieve a convergence of the major object modelling languages and techniques that have emerged since the mid 1980s, including Booch, OMT and OOSE. The outcome will become the OMG standard for Object Modelling.

3.3 Application Development

ORB vendors provide a range of tools and environments for development of CORBA-based applications. These vary from fully integrated environments including IDL and language compilers with visual debuggers, profiling tools and many CORBAservices to simple tool suites containing only an IDL compiler, a run-time agent/daemon and simple server administration tools.

3.3.1 Interface Definition Language (IDL)

Developers start by defining interfaces to the CORBA objects they will use in their application using CORBA IDL. IDL supports a rich set of data types, loosely based on C++, which do not include any implementation constructs such as pointers. Figure 5 shows the CORBA IDL for a bank account interface with two operations to deposit money and withdraw money, and a read only attribute to obtain the balance.

```
#include "types.idl"

module Banking {
    interface Account {

        exception InsufficientFunds {
            Dollars available_balance;
        };

        readonly attribute Dollars Balance;

        void Deposit (in Dollars d, out Dollars new_balance);

        void Withdraw (in Dollars d,  out Dollars new_balance)
            raises (InsufficientFunds);
    }
}
```

Figure 5: The interface definition for a bank account object

The basic types include `long` and `short` integers, floating and fixed point numbers, octets, characters, strings, enumerations and a container type called `any`. "Anys" can contain any CORBA value and are tagged with a type description, known as a `TypeCode` to ensure type safety.

CORBA IDL provides a `struct` type, a discriminated `union`, fixed-length `arrays`, and variable length `sequences`. Named `modules` provide a means of grouping IDL definitions in a new name scope, thereby providing structure and reducing name clashes.

IDL uses the `interface` for object-oriented encapsulation of data type declarations, operations and `attributes`. An operation is similar to a C++ method. Any data types or interface types can be used as parameters or results of operations. Operation parameters are always tagged as `in`, `out`, or `inout` to indicate whether the arguments will be supplied by the client, or returned by the server (or both). IDL specifies the user-defined `exceptions` that can be raised by each operation. An `attribute` is shorthand for a pair of operations, one to access a value in the object's state, and another to set the value.

Normally, CORBA operations require the client to wait for either a valid reply or a raised exception. However, `oneway` operations can immediately return to the caller without waiting. One way operations cannot return any information. Therefore, they must must have a `void` return type, they must have no `inout` or `out` parameters, and they must have no user-defined exceptions.

An interface type can inherit from existing interface types. Inheritance allows the derived interface to add new types, operations and attributes, but not to overload or override existing declarations in the base interfaces. However, programming language mechanisms for overriding methods may be employed in implementations of these interfaces. If interface type X inherits from interface type Y, then X is said to be a sub-type of Y. Subtyping of interface types enables polymorphism, in which an object reference of a derived interface type[2] may be used where the base interface type is required. That is, an object reference of type X may be passed wherever one of type Y is required. The semantics are those of dynamic late-binding. That is, the implementation of X will always be used when an X reference is passed, even when it is being used as a Y.

IDL definitions are compiled by an IDL compiler, which implements the language mappings supported by the ORB. For object-oriented language mappings, the IDL compiler generates a number of skeleton and stub classes which perform the network connection management and marshalling from programming language data types into network packets and back again. Non-object-oriented languages are at some disadvantage, as they have no obvious mappings for some of CORBA's object-oriented concepts. This can result in very inelegant stub and skeleton code, combined with greater reliance on programmers to handle issues such as object reference management and exception handling. Most stubs and skeletons also require the linking of libraries into the application to support standard CORBA types, marshalling, and communication with the ORB run-time environment.

3.3.2 Building an Application

Having completed the IDL definitions, the developer implements the application semantics of the server objects by writing the methods (or functions) using the data types and invocation mechanisms defined in the mapping of CORBA IDL to the particular programming language. These method implementations are associated with the generated skeleton class either by inheritance or by delegation (commonly known as the "tie" mechanism). Developers must also implement the `main` routine for a server that will create its initial object instances, and notify the ORB of the readiness of the server and its objects for CORBA interaction.

Servers are registered with an *Implementation Repository*, which allows the ORB to activate server processes on demand when the references to their objects are used by a CORBA client. Clients can obtain object references in many ways. Object references can be obtained by querying a Naming Service with a name, or from a Trader Service by specifying the interface type and desired characteristics. Object references can be returned as the result of other invocations, or might be stored in a file in a string format. Some ORBs provide additional proprietary mechanisms for obtaining object references.

[2]Confusingly, the type of an object reference is an interface type. Unfortunately, the OMG does not always clearly distinguish between the concepts of "object" and "interface".

Finally, the developer creates the client programs. A simple CORBA client does not contain any CORBA object implementations, but rather uses object references and stub code to invoke operations on server objects. However, many CORBA clients are themselves CORBA servers, and do contain CORBA object implementations.

3.4 Infrastructure

The abstract infrastructure components shown in Figure 6 are supported by all compliant CORBA implementations. The ORB Core is the basic protocol engine that supports the interaction between clients and server objects. The OMG mandates that the ORB Core supports at least the IIOP protocol.

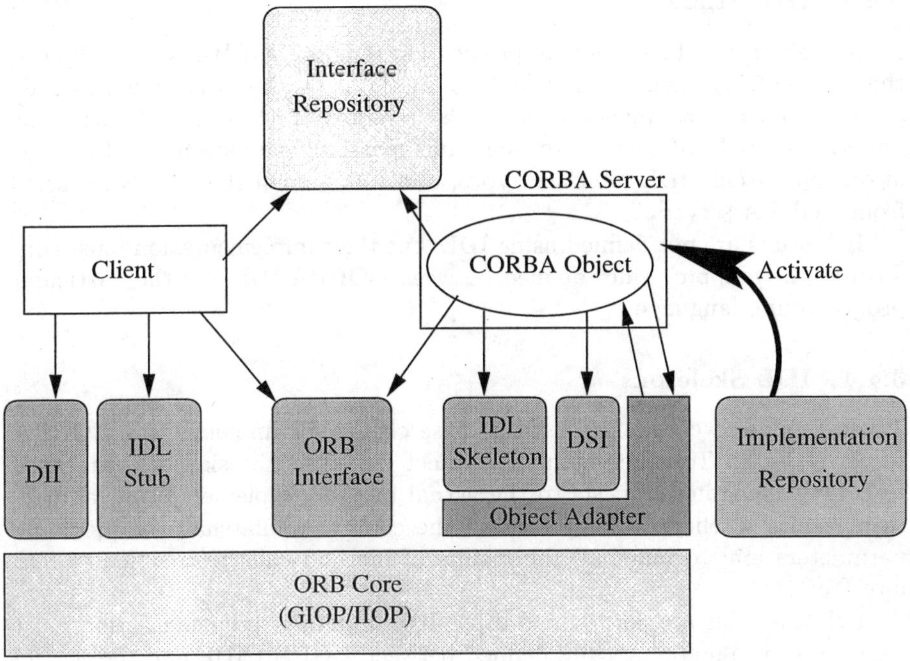

Figure 6: The Components of the Object Request Broker

3.4.1 ORB Interface

The ORB interface is used by CORBA applications to obtain bootstrap object references and manage object references. The functionality of the ORB is typically implemented through a combination of library code linked into applications and run-time agents (often known as daemons). The ORB interface is standardised by the OMG and expressed in IDL.

3.4.2 Object Adapter

The Object Adapter allows servers to manage the lifecycle of objects and their references. CORBA 2.0 defined an under-specified Basic Object Adapter (BOA) which has been implemented differently by all ORBs. In 1997, the Portable Object Adapter (POA) specification was adopted, allowing server code to be written portably for all ORBs. The POA allows servers to map object references to actual implementation instances in a flexible, scalable and policy-driven manner. Object Adapters are also responsible for activating and deactivating servers, which they do in cooperation with the Implementation Repository (see section 3.4.5). The Object Adapter is defined using IDL.

3.4.3 IDL Stubs

These generated classes act as proxies for remote CORBA server objects, thereby allowing clients to invoke local methods on the proxies, which then perform the remote invocations on the remote server objects. Using the underlying ORB infrastructure, the stubs marshall the parameters for operations on specific IDL interface types, and unmarshall the results returned from CORBA servers.

IDL stubs are not defined using IDL, but their implementation must conform to the mapping rules defined between CORBA IDL and the particular programming language.

3.4.4 IDL Skeletons

These generated classes are used as base classes for implementing CORBA server objects. Together with the Object Adapter, the skeletons are used to convey incoming requests to the actual method implementations and return results to clients. They contain the code to unmarshall the incoming parameters and to marshall the results of method calls for particular IDL interfaces.

IDL skeletons are not defined using IDL, but their implementation must conform to the mapping rules defined between CORBA IDL and the particular programming language.

3.4.5 Implementation Repository

The function of the Implementation Repository is to name servers (as opposed to server objects) and to activate a server (if required) when a client attempts to interact with one of the server's objects. The Implementation Repository is typically a registry of executable code for each server (usually maintained by the programmers or system administrators) and a registry of currently running servers (maintained through interaction with the Object Adapter of the servers).

Although the purpose of the Implementation Repository is well-defined in CORBA, no specific interfaces or semantics are prescribed by the OMG, to enable a wide variety of implementations.

3.5 Infrastructure for Dynamic Clients and Servers

Some clients must invoke operations of interfaces not known to the client program at compile-time, e.g. a generic browser. Therefore, such client programs cannot use the stubs generated by the IDL compiler.

Similarly, some servers must provide interfaces of a type not known to the server program at compile-time, e.g. object wrappers and bridges between ORBs and/or other middleware. Therefore, such server programs cannot use the skeletons generated by the IDL compiler.

Such clients and servers require "dynamic" mechanisms for making and handling invocations at run-time.

3.5.1 Interface Repository

The Interface Repository is a registry of CORBA type information, which can be used to support "dynamic" clients and servers. CORBA types can always be described using IDL. However, the textual form of IDL is not well-suited to run-time processing. Instead, the Interface Repository stores type information as a set of linked objects, which can be more easily queried and navigated at run-time. For example, from a nominated interface, the Interface Repository can reveal the operations of that interface. From an operation, the names, types, and direction of its parameters can be determined. Note that IDL and the Interface Repository contain the same information; it is simply in a different format.

All object references support a built-in operation that returns an object reference within the Interface Repository, which acts as a starting point for learning about the interface type of that object reference.

Dynamic clients and servers use the Interface Repository to learn about interface types not known to them at compile-time.

3.5.2 Dynamic Invocation Interface (DII)

The DII allows CORBA clients to construct and issue an invocation without the use of a stub.

Having learnt about the interface type (via the Interface Repository or some other mechanism), the client can use the operations of the DII to construct a `Request` containing the name of the operation and the values of the `in` and `inout` parameters (held inside "any" types). The DII can be used to invoke that Request at a nominated object reference, and to receive the values returned.

The DII is specified using IDL, and is implemented by library code which is linked into the dynamic client application.

Note that a server is not aware whether an invocation has been made via a stub or via the DII.

3.5.3 Dynamic Skeleton Interface (DSI)

The DSI allows a server to process invocations for any interface type without the use of a skeleton for that interface type.

Again, the server learns about the interface type (via the Interface Repository or some other mechanism). Using the operations of the DSI, the dynamic server can receive the invocation, access the operation name and supplied parameter values, and return the outgoing parameters and return value.

Again, a client is not aware whether its invocations are being handled via a skeleton or via the DSI. Both client and server are free to use dynamic mechanisms without affecting the other.

3.6 Administration

The administration of CORBA applications can be considered at three levels:

- administering the ORB and its object services
- administering the IDL and other type information
- administering the application implementation.

Each ORB product has its own administration requirements, and usually includes a set of proprietary tools for ORB administration. These range from simple installation and removal scripts to suites of GUI utilities. The OMG does not standardize an interface for administering an ORB.

Some object services have IDL interfaces to support their administration, e.g. the Trader Service has administrative interfaces which enable both the configuration and tuning of both an individual trader and of a federation of cooperating traders. Other object services depend entirely on proprietary solutions for their administration.

Even when the OMG provides a standard interface for administration, ORB vendors provide very different user tools to access those interfaces, e.g. command-line tools versus GUI tools.

The administration of IDL types primarily involves the population of Interface Repositories with type information. This task is typically done as a by-product of the IDL compiler. The OMG does standardise the IDL for the Interface Repository to create and retrieve type information, but does not provide any IDL for administrative functions such as maintaining consistency between a number of Interface Repositories. Other aspects of type administration include the registration of Trader service types, Object Analysis and Design classes, and Naming Service conventions. During 1997, the OMG is standardising the Meta-Object Facility, which is a framework for defining repositories for types and other meta-data to provide a more complete and pervasive management of type information.

Typically the administration of applications will involve:

- registering servers in the Implementation Repository
- registering the server's object references in the Naming Service
- registering the server's object references in the Trader Service.

The OMG does not standardise the means by which servers are registered in the Implementation Repository.

By registering with the Naming Service, a server's object references can be obtained using some logical name. The Naming Service provides operations defined in IDL to link cooperating Naming Services together. In 1998, the OMG is expected to define standard naming conventions to further assist in the administration of a group of cooperating Naming Services.

By registering with the Trader Service, object references can be retrieved using their interface type and characteristics. While the Trader Service provides administrative interfaces defined in IDL, it may take some experimentation to determine the most appropriate policy choices and thresholds for optimal performance in a particular environment.

3.7 Summary

CORBA is a term used to collectively describe technology based on the Object Management Architecture and standardised by the OMG. The main components of CORBA are:

- CORBA Core
- Object Services
- Object Analysis and Design
- Vertical Industry Domain Facilities.

CORBA IDL is an architecture-neutral and object-oriented notation for defining data types and interface signatures. It is syntactically similar to C++, but supports only simple multiple inheritance, and ignores pointers and other programming level constructs. CORBA IDL and its many mappings to different programming languages allow object-oriented distributed applications to be developed despite the heterogeneity of programming languages and hardware platforms involved.

CORBA applications, the CORBA infrastructure and the CORBA services all appear as distributed objects, whose interfaces are specified using CORBA IDL.

4 Java

Java [GM95, JavaOverview, AG96] is a new object-oriented language from Sun which has being popularised through its use in creating dynamic information content for pages on the World Wide Web (WWW). The Java language is similar in flavour to C++ but has additional features such as garbage collection and multi-threading. Some aspects such as pointers and operator overloading were removed to make Java a safer language for programmers to use.

Java has had a diverse past. Originally called Oak, it was first used in an experimental SGML editor. Later Java moved into the domain of consumer electronics, and was used for a set-top box operating system for pay television. Finally, Java found its niche in the WWW with the creation of the first HotJava browser [GM96, HotJava].

This rich history has cemented some interesting features in the Java language. It is

- object-oriented
- architecture-neutral
- type-safe
- garbage-collected and
- multi-threaded.

Java is designed to enable easier development of bug-free code by eliminating many of the "unsafe" features of C++. Java permits only single-inheritance for implementations. Memory management is controlled by the Java language run-time system and not by the programmer. The removal of pointers is a major contributor to type-safety. As a consequence, the use of the Java language enhances the security [SecureJava] and reliability of applications.

Java programs are usually interpreted, making them highly portable, as only the interpreter itself has to be ported to each new platform. As interpreted programs usually run more slowly than native-compiled code, there might be a trend towards compilation for production versions of large Java applications (and now the use of Java chips for native silicon execution).

Java is *not* a distributed environment in itself, but it is a language whose characteristics make it attractive for distributed system development. Its marriage with the WWW has highlighted the benefits of an adaptable, portable and safe distributed systems language.

4.1 Components

The Java environment consists of two main components, the Java pre-compiler and the Java interpreter.

4.1.1 Java Pre-Compiler

Java source code is first pre-compiled into an intermediate form called *Java bytecodes*. These Java bytecodes are then interpreted by the Java interpreter [3].

Figure 7: Compiling Java source to bytecodes

The Java compiler (Figure 7) acts as the first step in the multi-stage security infrastructure [FM97] supported by the Java language. The compiler checks for illegal operations such as pointer arithmetic and forged access through casts.

4.1.2 Java Interpreter

The Java language definition defines a *Java Virtual Machine* (JVM) [LY97] which provides a platform-independent software architecture for executing Java compiled applications (Figure 8).

Java bytecodes are JVM instructions, and pre-compilation produces the same bytecodes, irrespective of the platform on which the Java source was compiled.

As the Java interpreter executes the bytecodes, it may find references to other Java classes. The interpreter loads the bytecodes for the additional classes and continues execution. Typically, the interpreter loads only those classes needed for the specific execution of the Java application.

4.2 Java Applets

It is the WWW and, in particular, Web browsers that have promoted the use of Java.

Java *Applets* are a restricted form of Java applications. They limit the allowable functionality so that the programs can be confidently provided by an untrusted party and executed in a local interpreter. This local execution "sandbox" ensures limited file and network access so that rogue applets cannot abuse the local resources.

[3] It is possible to compile other languages into Java bytecodes and this is being actively undertaken by many research and commercial groups. For example, see [AppletMagic] using ADA-95 to generate Java bytecodes.

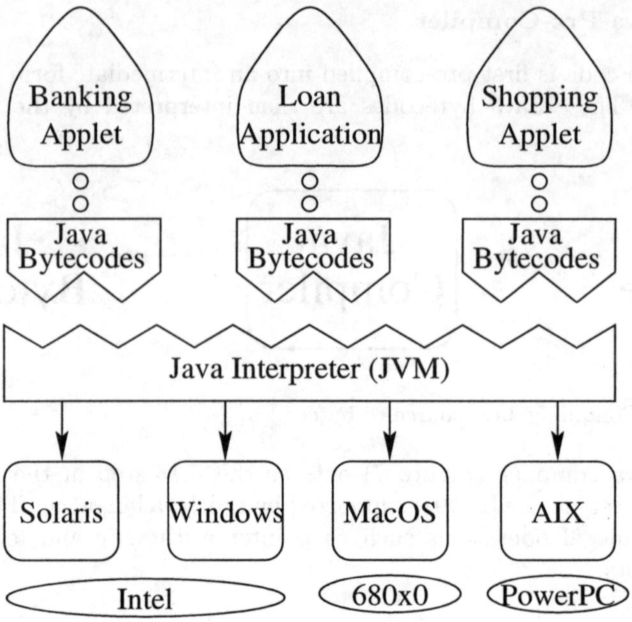

Figure 8: The Java Virtual Machine

The majority of Web browsers now include a restricted Java bytecode interpreter as depicted in Figure 9. When an applet is downloaded to a Web browser (as part of a WWW page), a bytecode verifier performs another stage of security checking. The verifier checks that the applet conforms to the Java language specification as well as looking for illegal data type casts and memory management violations such as stack underflows or overflows. It is necessary for the verifier to redo some checks performed by the Java compiler since there is no guarantee that the bytecodes were generated by a conforming compiler. The bytecodes are then interpreted and results displayed within a browser environment.

Applets load classes on demand at run-time. If the required class is not one of the natively supported Java classes, the class will be requested from the source of the applet (i.e. the Web server). A *class loader* checks for namespace violations and prevents the masquerading of built-in classes. Figure 10 shows a simple applet loaded over HTTP obtaining an additional Java class at run-time. Digital signatures can be attached to classes to authenticate the provider of a class. Java Archives (JARs) include a digital signature based on the contents of the JAR and give the software user confidence as to the provider of the entire archive.

Java applets are a mechanism to execute a remotely stored program on a local computer. However, the Java applet is not a distributed application.

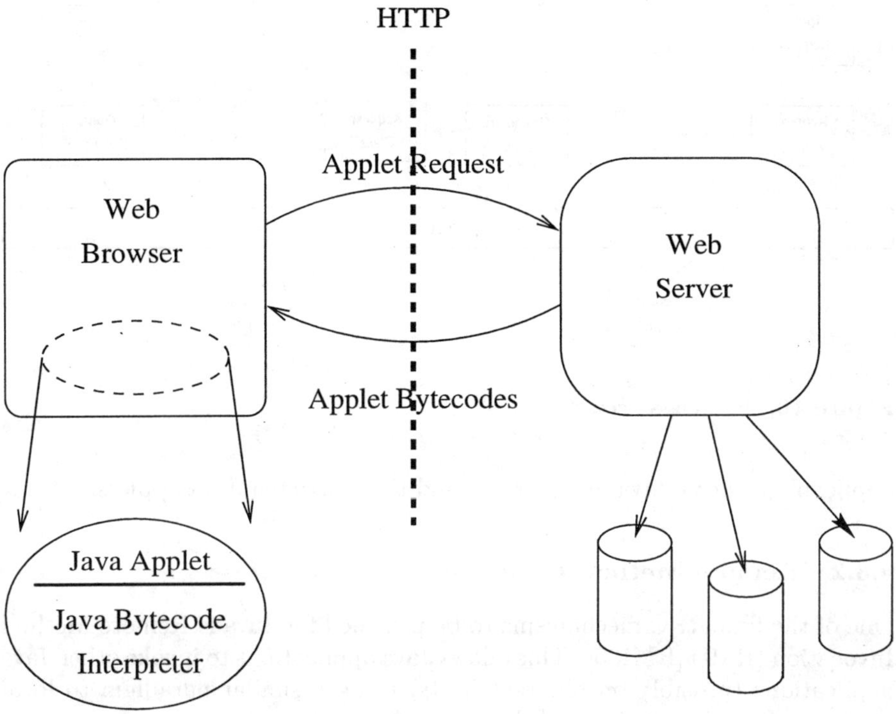

Figure 9: Java and the World Wide Web

It is a single program executing on a single local computer. Java must be used in conjunction with some distributed systems infrastructure to build true distributed applications.

4.3 Infrastructure

There are a number of distributed systems mechanisms which can be used by Java programmers to build distributed applications.

4.3.1 Sockets

Sockets are a traditional building blocks of distributed systems, and are available to Java programmers through a socket library. Sockets provide a simple stream interface to deliver data to and from a remote process. Sockets are a very low-level mechanism, and any large application will justify the use of more sophisticated distributed systems mechanisms, such as remote procedure calls.

The following sections consider a number of ways in which remote procedure calls can be used in Java programs. Note that these mechanisms are

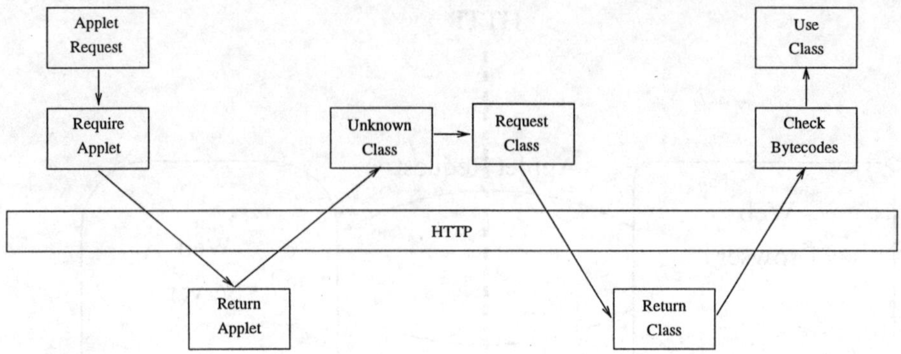

Figure 10: Java class access

applicable to both Java applications and the restricted Java applets.

4.3.2 Remote Method Invocation

One of the first RPC mechanisms to be provided for Java is Remote Method Invocation (RMI) [RMI96]. This allows Java applications to invoke other Java applications (possibly on different hosts) using a similar paradigm to local object method invocations. A local proxy object is responsible for passing the method invocation to the remote object. The parameters of the remote invocation can be any Java type that is serialisable (i.e. can be marshalled into a sequential bit stream).

```
public interface BankAccount
       extends remote
{

   public Dollars balance;

   public void Deposit(Dollars d)
          throws java.rmi.RemoteException;

   public void Withdraw(Dollars d)
          throws InsufficientFunds, java.rmi.RemoteException;

}
```

Figure 11: The interface definition for a bank account

Figure 11 shows a simple banking account interface. It appears very similar to a local interface definition except for the additional exceptions that must be handled on a remote method call (and of course the extension of the Java remote class).

A simple bootstrap name server is provided to bind to remote objects. This is URL-based (Uniform Resource Locator) and the naming class provides methods to bind, unbind, and lookup names. It is expected that the majority of remote object references will be obtained as a return value in a method call.

4.3.3 Java and CORBA

The OMG has adopted a language mapping for Java [Java-Map], and several products are available that implement this mapping. Java is perhaps the most straightforward of the mappings from IDL, as Java has the concept of interfaces that simply specify the abstract signatures of object classes. The Java data types and standard language classes also correspond closely to IDL types.

Seen only as a programming language, Java is simply another object-oriented programming language that can be used to develop CORBA applications [DV97]. However, the use of Applets in conjunction with CORBA produces an interesting hybrid. The typical scenario involves an applet providing a graphical user interface with minimal application semantics, which acts as a CORBA client to a number of CORBA servers, which perform computation intensive tasks and access data stores. The applet is downloaded to the user's Web browser and runs on the user's workstation.

There are a number of benefits to this approach. The computational load of running the GUI is handled locally by the applet. The network traffic is restricted to the application interactions defined in CORBA IDL and not the more numerous GUI updates. As the CORBA servers are not downloaded to the user's site, the server code cannot be stolen through reverse engineering at the user's site. The data accessed by the server is accessible only to the extent permitted by the server.

The combination of Java applets and CORBA is so attractive that most Web browsers now include the Java classes needed by CORBA applets. Making these classes locally available avoids the need to down-load these classes over the WWW for each CORBA applet. Problems that have arisen due to the restrictions placed on applets running in Web browser "sand boxes", such as only making network connections to the machine from whence they were loaded, are being overcome by firewall software at the applet provider that redirects CORBA requests to other machines.

4.3.4 Java and DCE

The Java language does not readily integrate with DCE. DCE is primarily designed for C programmers, although DCE version 1.2.1 has included a C++ interface. This provides class encapsulation of various components from DCE as well as extending the IDL to provide support for C++ concepts such as references.

No native Java mapping for DCE exists but there are products to gateway between Java and DCE (for example see [DCE-Java]). The gateway exports a simplified distributed computing interface accessed through a number of Java classes. The gateway then acts as an intermediary constructing calls to the selected DCE server and filtering results back to the Java application.

In theory, the use of DCE in Java applets should have similar benefits to the use of CORBA. CORBA's more object-oriented approach makes it a more natural choice for combining with Java. However, developers with existing DCE applications should consider the advantages of creating Java clients to encourage Web-based use of their applications.

4.4 Summary

The Java programming language has emerged from its start in embedded systems to provide a portable language for distributed system programming. Java as a language does not provide true distributed processing but offers an attractive environment for distributed computing when combined with a distributed infrastructure such as CORBA or Remote Method Invocation (RMI).

Language safety is an important trait of the language and is exploited in a marriage with the World Wide Web and the provision of Java Applets. These programs use a restricted Java subset designed to provide trusted sharing of programs on the untrustworthy Internet. The Java Virtual Machine (JVM) incorporated in Web browsers interprets the Java subset and provides a portable application environment across multiple platforms. The niche for Java in the distributed systems world is the provision of a "safe" language and a widely available virtual machine.

5 Comparing DCE, CORBA, and Java

DCE is the oldest and most mature of the three technologies. DCE exhibits a high degree of interoperability between products, arising from its common code base. Its disadvantage is its close-coupling with the C programming language, the consequent lack of support for object-orientation, and difficulty of supporting fine-grained objects. However, it is the only one of the three technologies that currently has a truly interoperable security mechanism across multiple platforms, and that will continue to be its strongest selling point until other technologies achieve a comparable level of security. In addition, DCE has a very scalable architecture based around the administration cell which is used as the basis for scalability throughout the environment. DCE has been stable for some time, and there do not appear to be any plans for a significant extension of DCE's scope in the near future. For that reason alone, CORBA is likely to overtake DCE, once the CORBA products achieve a similar level of maturity.

CORBA set itself a much more ambitious scope than DCE, and gave initial emphasis to the provision of an object-oriented infrastructure using multiple programming languages on multiple platforms. The result was a more elegant approach than DCE, and capable of supporting finer-grained objects than DCE. However, issues such as interoperability between ORBs and security infrastructure were addressed relatively late in the OMG standardisation process. As a result, many ORB products today do not fully interoperate and many do not implement the OMG security infrastructure, leading to doubts about CORBA's readiness for industrial-strength applications. However, there is significant user and vendor impetus behind CORBA which should result in superior products in the near future with a wider range of services available compared with DCE.

Java is a safe and easy-to-use programming language with the attraction of being downloadable into Web browsers for execution. To build distributed applications, Java needs to be married with another technology to provide the interaction between the components of a distributed application. Java Remote Method Invocation is likely to be popular for simple distributed applications, but more complex applications will need a more extensive infrastructure making Java-with-CORBA the more appropriate choice. There are near-term proposals to integrate Java and CORBA more closely. Such an integration will only strengthen the benefits of combining these technologies, making their combination ideally positioned to be the technology best placed to exploit the Internet phenomenon.

References

[AG96] Arnold, K., Gosling, J., The Java Programming Language, Addison-Wesley, 1996

[AppletMagic] http://www.appletmagic.com, Intermetrics

[CORBA95] The Common Object Request Broker: Architecture and Specification, Revision 2.0, OMG, 1995

[CORBA96] CORBAservices: Common Object Services Specification, Revised Edition - Updated, OMG, 1996

[CORBAsecur] Security Service Specification, Version 1.0, OMG Documents 97-07-23 and 97-07-24, November 1996

[DCE-Java] Transarc DCE Encina Lightweight Client, http://www.transarc.com/afs/transarc.com/public/www/Public/ProdServ/Product/DELight/index.html

[DV97] Duddy, K., Vogel, A., Java Programming with CORBA, John Wiley & Sons Inc., 1997

[FKR92] Fisher, G., Kenny, D., Rosenberry, W., Understanding DCE, O'Reilly & Associates Inc., 1992

[FM97] Fritzinger, J. S., Müller, M., Java Security, http://java.sun.com/security/whitepaper.ps, Sun Microsystems, 1997

[GM95] Gosling, J., McGilton, H., The Java Language Overview: A White Paper, Sun Microsystems Technical Report, 1995

[GM96] Gosling, J., McGilton, H., The Java Language Environment: A White Paper, http://java.sun.com/docs/white/langenv/, Sun Microsystems, 1996

[HotJava] HotJava Browser, http://java.sun.com/products/hotjava/, Sun Microsystems

[HS94] Hu, W., Shirley, J., Guide to Writing DCE Applications (Second Edition), O'Reilly & Associates Inc., 1994

[Hu95] Hu, W., DCE Security Programming, O'Reilly & Associates Inc., 1995

[Java-Map] IDL/Java Language Mapping, OMG TC Document orbos/97-03-01, 1997

[JavaOverview] The Java Language: An Overview, http://java.sun.com/docs/overviews/java/java-overview-1.html, Sun Microsystems

[Loc94] Lockhart, H. W., OSF DCE: Guide to Developing Distributed Applications, McGraw Hill, 1994

[LY97] Lindholm, T., Yellin, F., The Java Virtual Machine Specification, Addison-Wesley, 1997

[OMG] Object Management Group, http://www.omg.org

[OMG-TC] OMG - Technical Committee Work in Progress, http://www.omg.org/schedule/

[Posix-10036] IEEE Std 1003.1-1990 Standard for Information Technology - Portable Operating System Interface (POSIX) - Part 1: System Application Programming Interface (API)

[Posix-10036a] P1003.1a Draft Revision to Information Technology - POSIX Part 1: System Application Program Interface (API) [C Language]

[RMI96] Remote Method Invocation Specification, http://www.javasoft.com:80/products/jdk/1.1/docs/guide/rmi/spec/rmiTOC.doc.html

[SecureJava] Secure Computing With Java: Now and the Future, http://java.sun.com/marketing/collateral/security.html, Sun

[Sol95] Soley, R. M., Object Management Architecture Guide, Third Edition, John Wiley & Sons, 1995

[TOS96] Trading Object Service, OMG TC Document orbos/96-07-26, 1996

CHAPTER 36

System Integration through Agent Coordination

Mihai Barbuceanu, Rune Teigen

Agents are software components that support the construction of distributed information systems as collections of autonomous entities that interact according to complex and dynamic patterns of behavior. A major problem of multi-agent structured information systems is the coordination of these interactions and behaviors to achieve the goals of the participants and coherence of the system as a whole. This paper articulates a precise conceptual model of coordination based on a representation of coordination knowledge as plans described in a special planning language enhanced with communicative actions. The execution of these plans by agents results in multiple structured 'conversations' taking place among agents. The model is extended to a complete language design that provides objects and control structures that substantiate its concepts and allow the construction of real multi-agent systems in industrial domains. To support incremental, in context acquisition and debugging of coordination knowledge we provide an extension of the basic representation and a visual tool allowing users to capture coordination knowledge as it dynamically emerges from the actual interactions. The plan-action organization exhibited by the coordination language departs in several ways from the standard object orientation of computational languages and is, we argue, more appropriate to modeling coordination. The language has been fully implemented and successfully used in several industrial applications, the most important being the integration of multi-agent supply chains for manufacturing enterprises. This application is used throughout the paper to illustrate the introduced concepts and language constructs.

1 Introduction

1.1 What's in an Agent?

Traditionally, computing has been viewed as 'data processing', essentially transforming data from some form into another. The increasing complexity, the globalization and the acceleration of business and social processes together with the wide availability of networking and communication infrastructures at all levels of society is quickly changing this perception. More and more what we are interested in is not the mere transformation of data, but rather the integrated support for complex patterns of interaction and behavior among autonomous, proactive, goal oriented entities. Software agents are the main technology behind this shift. Although the notion of agent is still debated [MWJ97], there exist clear aspects that distinguish agents from other current models of software systems.

- First, agents encapsulate complex and dynamic patterns of behavior, interaction and communication that increasingly characterize businesses and social processes in general. The state-of-the-art object oriented organization is more preoccupied with structural representations of static or steady state domains, where consistent and repetitive processing of structured data is more important than dynamic interactions and behavior.
- Agents promote autonomous action and decision making. This requires peer-to-peer interaction, while the object oriented organization still supports a client-server model where servers only respond to client requests.
- Because of their autonomous and interactionist behavior, agents are best described and understood using notions like beliefs, goals and plans. Object models on the other hand are best described and understood in structural terms like attributes, relations, generalizations, etc.
- Finally, the highly interactionist nature of agents has also led to more powerful models of communication and interaction. Agent communication languages (ACL-s) for example [Fin92] are based on well-defined, small sets of 'communicative actions' that are ammendable to declarative semantics. Object communicate through unrestricted and idiosyncratic messages with *ad-hoc* semantics. This creates communication barriers and increases communication costs by requiring multiple semantic translations. Moreover, based on ACL-s, several higher level coordination languages have been developed that are able to describe abstract coordination protocols that encompass distributed problem solving knowledge allowing agents to efficiently cooperate for solving complex tasks. One such language forms the subject of this paper.

Focusing on the agent level of system (de)composition brings to attention a number of specific issues that are not adequately dealt with at other levels of system organization. Some of these are:

- *Agent interaction:* How do agents communicate? How do agents coordinate in joint work, such as to achieve the individual and joint goals of the participants? How are problems stemming from dynamically occuring events and partial knowledge about the environment handled during coordinated behavior? How do we model the patterns of interaction and interoperation that characterize coordinated behavior? How do capture these patterns during the on-line operation of the system?

- *Representation:* How do agents represent their local views of the domain? How is the local view updated or maintained as a consequence of interaction? How are the semantic problems related to conflicting or different meanings of the exchanged terms solved? How do agents revise their beliefs due to exchanged information? How do agents share models and how does the shared model change? How do agents model each other in a cooperative community? How are common-sense issues, e.g. time, action, causality, handled?

- *Reasoning:* How do the requirements for communication and coordination impact the internal reasoning of agents? How do agents handle contradictory information, and how is consistency maintained across agents that may have diffeirent goals, views, preferences?

- *Legacy integration:* How can pre-existing (legacy) applications be integrated into agents and thus used in agent communities?

From the practical standpoint, any solutions to the above issues must provide the ability to *reuse* descriptions of coordination mechanisms, system components, services and knowledge bases. Based on this recognition we have developed a multi-agent coordination language that, without addressing the above issues in totality, provides a number of reusable constructs and services for agent construction and interaction, relieving developers from the effort of building agent systems from scratch and guaranteeing that essential interoperation, communication and cooperation services will always be there to support applications.

1.2 Coordination

Coordination has been defined as the process of *managing dependencies between activities* [MC91]. An agent that operates in an environment holds some beliefs about the environment and can use a number of actions to affect the environment. Coordination problems arise when (i) there are *alternative actions* the agent can choose from, each choice affecting the environment and the agent and resulting in different states of affairs and/or (ii) the *order and time of executing actions* affects the environment and the agent, resulting in different states of affairs. The coordination problem is made more difficult as agents usually have incomplete knowledge of the environment and of the consequences of their actions and the environment changes dynamically making it more difficult to evaluate the current situation and the possible outcomes of actions. In a multi-agent system, the environment is populated by other agents, each pursuing their own goals and each endowed with their own capabilities for action. In this case, the actions performed by one agent constrain and are constrained by the actions of other agents. To achieve their goals, agents will have to manage these constraints by coordination.

In this paper we adhere to the view that the coordination problem can be tackled by recognizing and explicitely representing the *knowledge about the interaction processes* taking place among agents. As such, Fox [Fox87] has proposed that it be studied as an "organization level" and applied Organization Theory concepts to characterize this level. More recently, Jennings [Jen92] has coined the term "cooperation knowledge level" to separate the social interaction know-how of agents from their individual problem-solving know-how and to help focus efforts on coming with principles, theories and tools for dealing with social interactions for problem solving. We also believe that principles and theories must be put to work in real applications, and a major and often neglected way of doing this is by consolidating them into usable languages and tools.

Our contribution in this sense is the articulation of a model of "agent interactions" as execution by the interacting agents of *coordination knowledge intensive plans*. As plans contain specifications of communicative actions to be performed at different stages of the interaction process, plan execution results in structured conversations carried out amongst agents. This model has been consolidated into a practical language design and implementation. A visual knowledge acquisition tool supports users in incrementally acquiring and modifying coordination knowledge as it dynamically emerges from interactions. We argue that the plan-action orientation of this language differs in important respects from the standard object orientation and is more appropriate for modeling coordination. The language, named COOL (from COOrdination Language), has been used in several industrial multi-agent systems, the most important of which is suppply chain integration, thoroughly used in this paper to illustrate the concepts and constructs of our system.

2 Background on Coordination Knowledge

Previous work in Distributed Artificial Intelligence (DAI) [Huh87] can be seen as investigating various facets of this level of knowledge. One direction is concerned with devising useful structures for cooperative problem solving. Thus, the Contract Net protocol [Smi80] provided a way of coordinating agents without global control, by means of a contracting model comprising dynamic task decomposition, negotiation of subtask assignments among agents and the commitment of agents to their assigned subtasks. In the Partial Global Planning method (PGP) [DL91] and its Generalized PGP form [DL95], agents maintain their own subjective views of the tasks, task dependencies and the responsibilities of agents. Various coordination mechanisms (like exchanging private views of tasks, communicating results, handling various types coordination relationships) enable agents to modify their subjective view of the task structure and their commitments to tasks in the task structure, ultimately improving performance. The Joint Responsibility model [JM92] prescribes when and how agents should form teams and how team members should behave during joint action. The code of conduct imposed by Joint Responibility ensures that the group will operate in a coordinated and efficient manner and that it is robust in face of changing circumstances.

Given the diversity of such cooperation structures, how can we identify, analize and formalize the essential elements cooperation structures are composed of? This is the focus of a second major direction of work in DAI. We make several distinctions here. The first is between what happens inside an agent when it coordinates with other agents and what happens between agents when cooperative behavior occurs. The second is between explaining how human agents behave and how programmed agents behave. Although in this paper we are solely concerned with artificial agents, insights into human agenthood will help us build agents that are understandable and thus easier to integrate as partners for human users.

Talking about what happens inside human agents, many researchers believe that mental states, like intentions and commitments are the central notion here. Intentions and commitments have been studied for example in [CL90, Bra87, Sea91]. These studies uncovered a number of essential properties of intentions. Intentions must be consistent with each other and with the beliefs of the agent, the latter meaning that if the intended actions are executed and the agent's beliefs hold in the world, then the desired state of affairs should follow. Also, intentions should have a degree of stability, however without being totally inflexible. Agents should not spend all their time considering and reconsidering intentions. At the same time, they should be able to drop intentions if changes in the situation makes it impossible or undesirable to achieve the intended state of affairs. The reexamination of agents' intentions should be "regulated" by known policies or conventions [Jen93] stating under what circumstances intentions should be reconsiderd. In the Cohen and Levesque [CL90] model for example, an agent should reconsider its commitment to a goal G if any of the following happens: G is already satisfied, G will never be satisfied, the motivation for G does not exist any more.

The above approach has been extended to the modeling of inter-agent phenomena. Levesque, Cohen and Nunez [LCN90] have proposed for example necessary and sufficient conditions for having Joint Persistent Goals that would allow agents to form teams: (i) agents mutually believe G is currently not true, (ii) they mutually believe they all want G to become true (iii) until they all come to mutually believe either that G is true, that G will never be true or that the motivation for G is false, they will continue to mutually believe that they each have G as a weak achievement goal (roughly either a normal goal, or a goal whose achievement status has to be mutually believed by all team members). The last condition allows agents to undertake actions knowing that if a problem with goal satisfaction occurs, the agents detecting it will inform the others. In order to act cooperatively, a number of other conditions have been discussed, including the mutual desire of agents to co-operate [CL91] (otherwise agents may for example compete) and the need for a common plan to achieve the goal that will determine the contributions of participants (otherwise inconsistent action may result even if there is a common goal). The latter issue has been dealt with by distributed or multi-agent planning research, including for example [Dur88, Geo84]. Monitoring the execution of joint action has been investigated as a way of determining what to do when things go wrong or unexpectedly [Jen95]. Another approach to coordinating multiple agents is to restrict their activities in a way that enables them to achieve their goals without interfering with each other. Shoham and Tennenholtz [Sho95] have proposed social laws as the means to specify these restrictions and have studied how such laws can be designed to guarantee certain behaviors from the multi-agent system.

From a sociological perspective, Castelfranchi [Cas95] has shown that internal commitments of agents (commitments of individual agents to certain actions) are not enough to explain social phenomena. He discusses social commitments as basic relations between two or more agents with respect to executing some actions. This is different from having several agents sharing the same internal commitment. This notion uncovers the dependence and power relations among people that form the objective basis of social interaction and has important normative consequences, like obligations and expectations, that pertain to the notions of Group and Organization.

Given work like the above, how do we brigde the gap between the logical, sociological and psychological analysis and the engineering of practical multi-agent systems, performing in real environments and bringing real services to people? There aren't too many answers to this question, but a few of them deserve mentioning. A first answer is represented by the applicative work of Jennings [Jen95] who started with the Cohen and Levesque model for joint intentions, extended it to better fit the need for a common plan and then implemented it with state of the art AI technologies. The result was an industrially applied multi-agent system that comprised the results of theoretical work on joint intentions.

The second answer lies in developing generic agent architectures that integrate the results of theoretical investigations into practical languages and tools. This is the path taken by Agent Oriented Programming [Sho93] where a generic notion of agent was proposed, using speech-act based communication, rule-based behavior and encapsulation into object-like structures. This approach talks about an agentification process in which real systems are casted in terms of mental states and the other concepts provided by the approach. Other work in the same direction focuses on specific aspects that are perceived as important when developing practical systems. The ARPA sponsored Knowledge Sharing Effort [PFPKFGN92] attempts to build technologies for inter-agent communication by proposing a language for content communication based on logic, KIF [GF92], and a language for intention communication, based on communication acts, KQML [Fin92]. Together, these form an Agent Communication Language (ACL), and approaches like Genesereth's define an agent as anything that communicates using the ACL [GK94].

As far as our approach to coordination is concerned, we take the above investigations as revealing the nature of the knowledge that is involved in social behavior and interactions. Our aim is to provide generic tools for the capture, representation and use of this knowledge in multi-agent systems. As previously noted by Jennings [Jen95], the evolution of applicative DAI systems follows the evolution of applicative knowledge based AI systems in the following sense. Initially, knowledge based systems were encoded in more or less ad-hoc ways, such that a lot of relevant knowledge about e.g. the task structure and problem solving methods were buried into the code once systems were implemented, hence could not be explicitely analyzed and reasoned about. This created growing problems with explanation, reusability and maintainability. In response to these problems, emphasis has later shifted onto explicitely characterizing the problem solving task at a higher level, for example in terms of generic problem solving methods [Der88] like heuristic classification [Cla85] or distinguishing between the various types of knowledge used to model the domain, the inferences, the task structures and the higher order strategies for resolving impasses [WSB92]. With this emphasis came a new generation of tools that are now able to explicitely represent such higher level types of knowledge and assist users in building systems in more principled and accountable ways.

In an essential way we are trying to do the same for the coordination knowledge agents must posess to interact successfully. In other words we are trying to come up with higher level constructs for describing coordination processes and to fully support these constructs in a programming environment for building multi-agent systems. The insights into the nature of social interaction, from sociological or psychological sources, described semantically in logic systems, give us principles and background knowledge for understanding and modeling interactions. Together with domain and application knowledge, they are used by developers to design the coordination structures that would be actually used by applications. These coordination structures, encoded into our coordination language, then guide the interactions among agents. Even if structures of human social interaction may be a source of inspiration for some agent coordination structures, note that *they are not our object of study and we do not aim in any way at building programs that behave similarly.* Our goal is to build clear, understandable, reusable models of interaction for artificial multi-agent systems and to support their engineering as far as we can.

3 Integrating the Supply Chain

Before presenting our approach in detail, it is useful to review the application context in which this research is taking place, by presenting a brief characterization of the supply chain.

The supply chain of a modern enterprise is a world-wide network of suppliers, factories, warehouses, distribution centres and retailers through which raw materials are acquired, transformed into products, delivered to customers, serviced and enhanced. In order to operate efficiently, supply chain functions must work in a tightly coordinated manner. But the dynamics of the enterprise and of the world market make this difficult: customers change or cancel orders, materials do not arrive on time, production facilities fail, workers are ill, etc. causing deviations from plan. In many cases, these events can not be dealt with locally, i.e. within the scope of a single supply chain "agent", requiring several agents to coordinate in order to revise plans, schedules or decisions. In the supply chain, our ability to enable timely dissemination of information, accurate coordination of decisions and management of actions among people and systems is what ultimately determines the efficient achievement of enterprise goals and the viability of the enterprise on the world market.

We address these coordination problems by organizing the supply chain as a network of cooperating agents, each performing one or more supply chain functions, and each coordinating their actions with other agents. Figure 1 shows a multi-level supply chain. At the enterprise level, the Logistics agent interacts with the Customer about an order. To achieve the Customer's order, Logistics has to decompose it into activities (including for example manufacturing, assembly, transportation, etc.). Then, it will negotiate with the available plants, suppliers and transportation companies the execution of these activities. If an execution plan is agreed on, the selected participants will commit themselves to carry out their part. If some agents fail to satisfy their commitment, Logistics will try to find a replacement agent or to negotiate a different contract with the Customer. At the plant level, a selected plant will similarly plan its activities including purchasing materials, using existing inventory, scheduling machines on the shop floor, etc. Unexpected events and breakdowns are dealt with through information dissemination and solution negotiation among the interested parties.

In the recent virtual organization framework, systems like the supply chain exhibit features that impose even more difficult requirements to the coordination capability. Virtual organizations are temporary consortiums where members have associated to pursue some common opportunity, and will normally disband when the opportunity ceases to exist. In such an organization, participants retain a high degree of autonomy and reveal less or more selective information about themselves. This increases the level of uncertainty and the stochastic nature of interactions that will have to be coordinated.

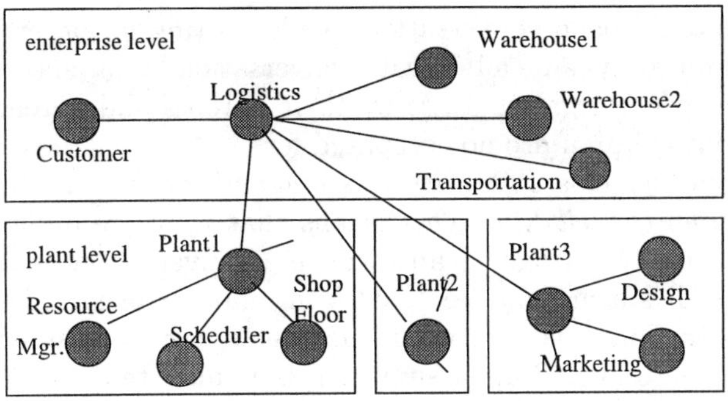

Figure 1: Multi-level supply chain

4 Assumptions and Basic Ideas

While coordination can be defined as before, without making assumptions about the ways to achieve it, building a practical language for representing coordination can not be done without clearly stating such assumptions as its foundation. The assumptions on which our language is built are as follows.

1. Autonomous agents have their own plans according to which they pursue their goals.

2. Being aware of the multi-agent environment they are in, agents plans explicitely represent interactions with other agents. Without loss of generality, we assume that this interaction takes place by exchanging messages and that all messages consist of communicative actions.

3. Agents can not predict the exact behavior of other agents, but they can delimitate classes of alternative behaviors that can be expected. As a consequence, agents plans are conditional over possible actions/reactions of other agents.

4. Agents plans may be incomplete or inaccurate and the knowledge to extend or correct them may become available only during execution. For this reason, agents are able to extend and modify their plans during execution.

The most important construct of the language is the *conversation plan.* Conversation plans are general plan descriptions that specify states and associated rules that receive messages, check local conditions, transmit messages and update the local status. Each COOL agent may posess several conversation plans which can be instantiated simultaneously to drive interactions with other agents. Instances of conversation plans, called *conversations*, hold the state of execution with respect to the plan. Agents can have several active conversations in the same time and control mechanisms are provided that allow agents to suspend conversations while waiting for others to reach certain stages and to dynamically create conversation hierarchies in which child conversations are delegated issues by their parents and parents will handle situations that children are not prepared for.

Multi-agent systems built with this language operate on the assumption of *mutual comprehensibility*. This means that they are designed in such a way that, normally, an agent can retrieve a conversation or a conversation plan that handles a message received from another agent. This guarantees that, normally, conversations would not get stuck because agents can not understand a message. This assumption is weaker than the assumption of cooperative systems, because it does not presuppose any intentional stance of the agents. On the other hand, we are aware of the limitations of this assumption and we provide mechanisms that allow agents to continue even when mutual comprehensibility is not satisfied. These come as recovery rules (which can modify the execution status or the plan) and much more importantly, as support for direct, in context, user guidance which is used for debugging and knowledge acquisition.

5 The Coordination Language

5.1 Communication

COOL has a communication component that uses an extended version of the KQML language [Fin92]. Essentially, we keep the KQML format for messages, but we leave freedom to developers with respect to the allowed vocabulary of communicative action types. Also, we do not impose any content language. This makes our approach practically independent of KQML (any message language with communicative actions would do), although a standard would be a marked advantage. The following example illustrates the form of extended KQML we are working with.

```
(propose                      ;; new communicative action
   :sender A
   :receiver B
   :language list
   :content (or (produce 200 widgets)
                (produce 400 widgets))
   :conversation C1           ;; two new slots
   :intent (explore fabrication possibility))
```

5.2 Agents and Environments

An *agent* is a programmable entity that can exchange messages within structured conversations with other agents, change state and perform actions. A

COOL agent is defined by giving it a name, specifying the conversation plan for its *initial conversation* and specifying the variables that form its local persistent data base:

```
(def-agent 'customer
   :initial-conversation-plan 'initial-conversation-plan).
```

When an agent is created, its initial conversation starts running and while it runs, the agent is "alive". Any other conversation is created as a descendant of this conversation. Agents are run as lightweight processes inside *environments* that execute on local or remote sites. TCP/IP is used at the transport level.

5.3 Conversation Plans

Conversation plans are rule based descriptions of how an agent acts and reacts in certain situations. COOL provides ways to associate conversation plans to agents, thus defining what sorts of interactions each agent can handle. A conversation plan specifies the available conversation rules, their control mechanism and the local data-base that maintains the state of the conversation. The latter consists of a set of variables whose persistent values (maintained for the entire duration of the conversation) are manipulated by conversation rules. Conversation rules are indexed on the values of a special variable, the *current-state*. Because of that, conversation plans and actual conversations admit a graph representation where nodes represent states and arcs transitions amongst states.

Figure 2 shows the conversation plan governing the Customer's conversation with Logistics in our supply chain application. Figure 3 shows the associated graph of this conversation plan. Arcs indicate the existence of rules that will move the conversation from one state to another. As it will became clear immediately, conversation plans are general plan specifications not restricted in any way to exclusively describing interactions amongst agents by message exchange. They can equally describe any local behavior of the agent that does not involve interaction with other agents. In our applications we also use conversation plans to describe local decision making, for example based on using local solvers (e.g. constraint based schedulers) or other decision making tools available to agents.

Error recovery rules are another component of conversation plans (not illustrated in Figure 2). They specify how incompatibilities among the state of a conversation and the incoming messages are handled. Such incompatibilities can be caused by both planning and execution flaws. Error recovery rules are applied when conversation rules can not handle the current situation. They can address the problem either by modifying the execution state (e.g. by discarding inputs, changing the conversation current-state or just reporting an error) or by executing new plans or modifying the current one (e.g. initiating a new clarification conversation with the interlocutor).

```
(def-conversation-plan 'customer-conversation
    :content-language 'list
    :speech-act-language 'kqml
    :initial-state 'start
    :final-states '(rejected failed satisfied)
    :control 'interactive-choice-control-ka
    :rules '((start cc-1)
             (proposed cc-13 cc-2)
             (working cc-5 cc-4 cc-3)
             (counterp cc-9 cc-8 cc-7 cc-6)
             (asked cc-10)
             (accepted cc-12 cc-11)))
```

Figure 2: Customer-conversation

Actual conversations instantiate conversation plans and are created whenever agents engage in communication. An actual conversation maintains the current-state of the conversation, the actual values of the conversation's variables and various historical information accumulated during conversation execution.

Each conversation plan describes an interaction from the viewpoint of an individual agent (in Figure 2 the Customer). For two or several agents to "talk", the executed conversation plan of each agent must generate sequences of messages that the others' conversation plans can process (according to the mutual comprehensibility assumption). This raises two problems. The first is how an agent that received the first message in a new conversation can select the appropriate conversation plan that will handle this and the next messages in the conversation. We adopt the convention that the first message in a new conversation has to have attached a specification of the purpose of the conversation. The receiver will then use this specification to find a conversation plan that can sustain a conversation with that purpose. This is done by having in each conversation plan a predicate that determines if the stated purpose matches the current conversation plan. This shows that plan selection is dynamic and that agents that carry out an actual conversation `C` will instantiate specific and different conversation plans internally (neither being aware of what plan the other has selected). The second problem is a naming one. When a message for a conversation `C` is sent, internally the conversations will have unique names (e.g. `Customer-C` for a conversation `C` with the `Customer` agent) inside each agent, allowing the system to direct messages appropriately.

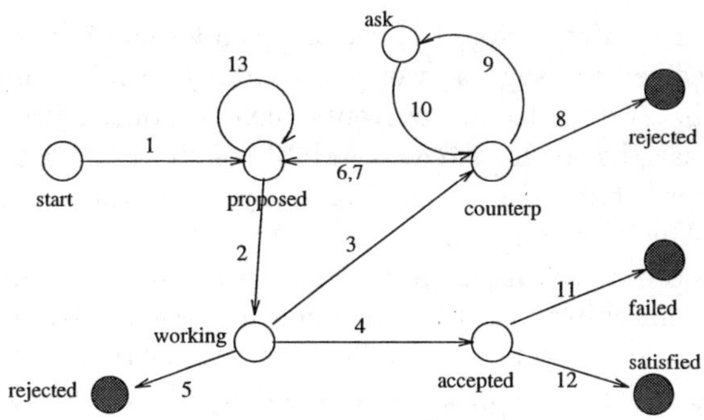

Figure 3: Graph representation of customer-conversation

5.4 Conversation Rules

Conversation rules describe the actions that can be performed when the conversation is in a given state. In Figure 2 for example, when the conversation is in the `working` state, rules `cc-5`, `cc-4` and `cc-3` are the only rules that can be executed. Which of them actually gets executed and how depends on the matching and application strategy of the conversation's control mechanism (the `:control` slot). Typically, we execute the first matching rule in the definition order, but this is easy to change as rule control interpreters are pluggable functions that users can modify at will. Figure 4 illustrates a conversation rule from the conversation class that Logistics uses when talking to Customer about orders.

```
(def-conversation-rule 'lep-1
   :current-state 'start
   :received '(propose :sender customer
                       :content(customer-order
                                 :has-line-item ?li))
   :next-state 'order-received
   :transmit '(tell :sender ?agent
                    :receiver customer
                    :content '(working on it)
                    :conversation ?convn)
   :do '(update-var ?conv '?order ?message))
```

Figure 4: Conversation rule

Essentially, this rule states that when Logistics, in state `start`, receives a proposal for an order (described as a sequence of line-items), it should inform the sender (Customer) that it has started working on the proposal and go to state `order-received`. Note the use of variables like `?li` to bind information from the received message as well as standard variables like `?convn` always bound by the system to the current conversation. Also note a side-effect action that assigns to the `?order` variable of the Logistics' conversation the received order. This will be used later by Logistics to reason about order execution. Among possibilities not illustrated, we mention arbitrary predicates over the received message and the local and environment variables to control rule matching and the checking and transmission several messages in the same rule. Also note that both the `:received` and `:transmit` slots are optional, which means that local behavior that does not involve message passing is equally representable in the language.

Our typology of rules also includes *timeout*, *on-entry* and *on-exit* rules. Timeout rules have a `:timeout` slot filled with a value representing a number of time units. These rules are tried after the specified number of time units has passed after entering the current state. Such rules enable agents to operate in real time, for example by controlling the time spent waiting for a message or by ensuring actions are executed at well determined time points. On-entry and on-exit rules are always executed when a conversation enters (exits) a state. They are useful for both mundane things like set-ups, clean-ups or instrumentations and non-mundane activities like strategic reasoning. In a next section we will illustrate their use to evaluate the current state of plan execution and dynamically determine new criteria for which execution is to be optimized.

5.5 The Initial Conversation

When an agent is created, its initial conversation starts running. As long as this conversation is not terminated, the agent is alive and active. All incoming messages are dispatched by the initial conversation. Sometimes they are dispatched to existing conversations, sometimes new conversations are created to handle them (for example we define an `:intent` slot of messages to help identify the conversation plans that can handle messages with given intents). The initial conversation is the ancestor of any conversation in the system. As new conversations are created, they can later create their own child conversations, incrementally building trees of conversations. The message dispatch mechanism allows direct dispatch to known conversations, or various forms of top-down or bottom-up forwarding of the message (possibly with annotations added along the way) to several conversations. This can emulate Brooks-like or hierarchical architectures. Figure 5 illustrates one rule from one initial conversation plan. This rule checks if there exists a conversation (immediately) runnable or waiting for messages and, if so, forwards it the messages addressed to it and then executes it.

```
(def-conversation-rule 'icc1-1
  :current-state 'process
  :such-that '(exists-runnable-or-waiting ?agent ?conv)
  :next-state 'process
  :do '(progn
         (move-msgs-to-addressee-conv ?conv ?runnable)
         (execute-conversation ?runnable)))
```

Figure 5: Conversation rule of the initial conversation

5.6 Synchronized Conversation Execution

Normally, a conversation may spawn another one and they will continue in parallel. When we need to synchronize their execution, we can do that by freezing the execution of one conversation until several others reach certain states. This is important in situations where an agent can not continue along one path of interaction unless some conditions are achieved. In such cases, the conversation that can not be continued is suspended, the conversations that can bring about the desired state of affairs are created or continued, and the system ensures that the suspended conversation will be resumed as soon as the condition it is waiting for becomes true. The specification of this condition is as an arbitrary predicate over the state of other conversations.

6 Situated Acquisition and Debugging of Coordination Knowledge

Coordination structures for applications like supply chain integration are generally very complex, hard to specify completely at any time and very likely to change even dramatically during the lifespan of the application. Moreover, due to the social nature of the knowledge contained, they are better acquired and improved in an emergent fashion, during and as part of the interaction process itself rather than by off-line interviewing of users, which for widely distributed systems will be hard to locate and co-locate anyway. Because of this the coordination tool must support (i) *incremental modifications* of the structure of interactions e.g. by adding or modifying knowledge expressed in rules and conversation objects, (ii) system operation with *incompletely specified interaction structures*, in a manner allowing users to intervene and take any action they consider appropriate (iii) system operation in a *user controlled mode* in which the user can inspect the state of the interaction and take alternative actions.

We are satisfying these requirements by providing a subsystem that supports in context acquisition and debugging of coordination knowledge. Using

```
(def-conversation-rule 'cc-13
   :current-state 'proposed
   :received '(ask :sender logistics)
   :next-state 'proposed
   :transmit '(tell :receiver logistics
                    :sender ?agent
                    :conversation ?convn)
   :incomplete t)
```

Figure 6: Incomplete conversation rule

this system execution takes place in a mixed-initiative mode in which the human user can decide to make choices, execute actions and edit rules and conversation objects. The effect of any user action is immediate, hence the future course of the interaction can be controlled in this manner.

Essentially, we allow conversation rules to be *incomplete*. An incomplete rule is one that does not contain complete specifications of conditions and actions. Since the condition part may be incomplete we don't really know whether the rule matches or not, hence the system does not try to match the rule itself. Since the action part may be incomplete, the system can not apply the rule either. All that can be done is to let the user handle the situation. Interaction specifications may contain both complete and incomplete rules in the same time. Assuming the usual strategy of applying the first matching rule in the definition order, we can have two situations. The first is when a complete rule matches. In this case it is executed in the normal way. The second is when an incomplete rule is encountered (hence no previous complete rule matched). In this case the acquisition/debugging regime is triggered, with the user in control over what to do in the respective situation, as explained further on.

Figure 6 shows an example incomplete rule from the *customer-conversation* that allows a user interacting with the Customer agent to answer (indeterminate) questions from the Logistics agent.

The rule is incomplete in that it does not specify how to answer a question - the `:transmit` part only contains the generic part of the response message. It is designed to work under the assumption that once a question is received, the user will formulate the answer interactively, using the graphical interface provided by the acquisition tool. When the knowledge acquisition interface is popped up, the user will have access to the received message containing the actual question. Using whatever tools are available, the user can determine the answer. Then, the user can create a copy of the rule and edit the transmitted message to include the answer. This rule can be executed (thus answering the question) and then discarded. Alternatively, if the new

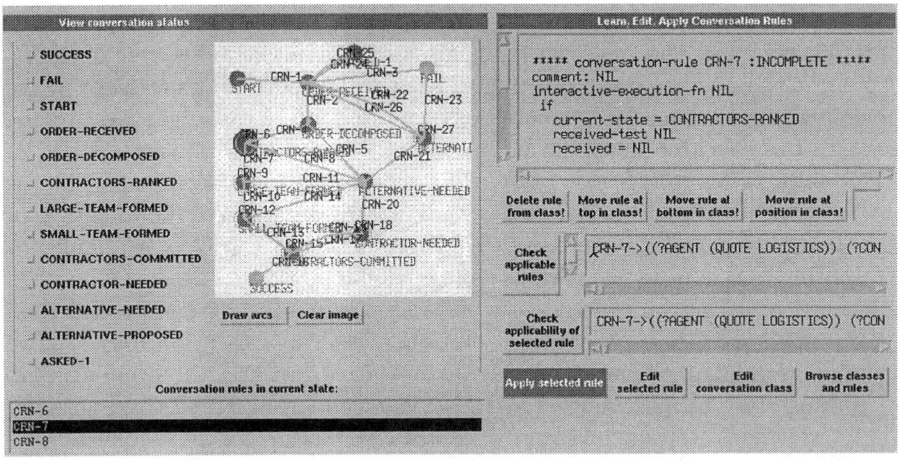

Figure 7: Inspecting, editing and applying rules

rule contains reusable knowledge, it can be retained, marked as complete and hence made available for automated application (without bothering the user) next time.

The facilities provided by this service can be illustrated with examples from its graphical interface. To view the status of the conversation at the time an incomplete rule was encountered, the acquisition service shows the graph representation (like in Figure 7). Here we have an instance of the logistics execution process as seen by the Logistics agent. A textual presentation of the conversation and a browser for the conversation variables are also available.

Another aspect of the conversation context is formed by the available rules. This is also shown in Figure 7. The browser for conversation rules allows the user to inspect the rules indexed on the current state (drawn as a larger circle). Rules can be checked for applicability in the current context, with the resulting variable bindings shown so that the user can better assess the impact of each rule. The interface allows the user to perform a number of corrective actions like moving a rule to a different position or removing it from the conversation class. It is also possible to invoke the rule editor, the conversation class editor or the browser for classes and rules allowing the user to inspect other classes and rules in the system. The effect of any of these modifications will be immediate. Finally, the user can leave the interface and continue execution by applying a specified rule.

When the user needs more information about the history of conversation execution, especially with respect to message exchange, the interface also provides appropriate presentation and interaction facilities. First, the history of the conversation can be traced by viewing the sequence of past states and the actions performed in each state (received messages, rule triggered, transmitted message). Second, the messages received (and not yet processed) by the conversation are also displayed. Again, here we provide means for corrective actions, assuming that message transmission is an important source of errors. Amongst them we mention deleting messages and reordering messages in the conversation queue. To better access the content of messages we provide pattern based search mechanisms.

Finally, when the action part of an existing rule is not complete or is not what the user needs, the service allows the interactive modification of the action part before executing it. First, a set of forms is available for presenting and editing the various slots of the action part. They can be filled automatically from a selected rule. The user can edit these slots and then execute them either separatedly or together. As rule execution may remove messages from the conversation queue, messages shown in the previous part of the interface can be marked as to be removed (or accepted) and actually removed when desired. Arbitrary conditions testing for any conversation variables can be also evaluated in this context to obtain more information. Finally, the modifications performed to the action part can be saved into a new rule that can be "learned" by the system, replacing the original one.

7 Perturbation in the Supply Chain

Let us now apply this agent coordination technology to the integration of a supply chain where unexpected events take place. We have designed a fictious yet realistic enterprise manufacturing personal computers and we wish to simulate its supply chain, measure and evaluate performance and improve behavior in face of unexpected events taking place. The agent based design of the supply chain is represented in COOL, and all simulation is equally done in COOL using the above described mechanisms.

7.1 Enterprise Structure

The Perfect Minicomputer Corporation (PMC) (Figure 8) is a small manufacturer of mother boards and personal computers situated in Toronto, Canada. The minicomputers are sold to customers in two markets, Canada/USA and Germany/Austria. To satisfy the different standards of keyboard and power supply in the two markets, the computers need to be slightly differentiated, and are regarded as two distinct products. The mother board is PMC's third product sold to the computer industry of the Canada/USA market.

Plants and Production. PMC is a vertically integrated company. In addition to the assembly of the finished computer systems (computer, monitor and keyboard), they assemble the motherboard and the computer boxes (without power supply) themselves in separate plants in Toronto. Each plant has a `Planning`, a `Materials`, a `Production`, and a `Dispatching` agent. The `Planning` agent is responsible for production planning. The `Materials` agent handles raw product inventory (RPI), the on-order data base for raw

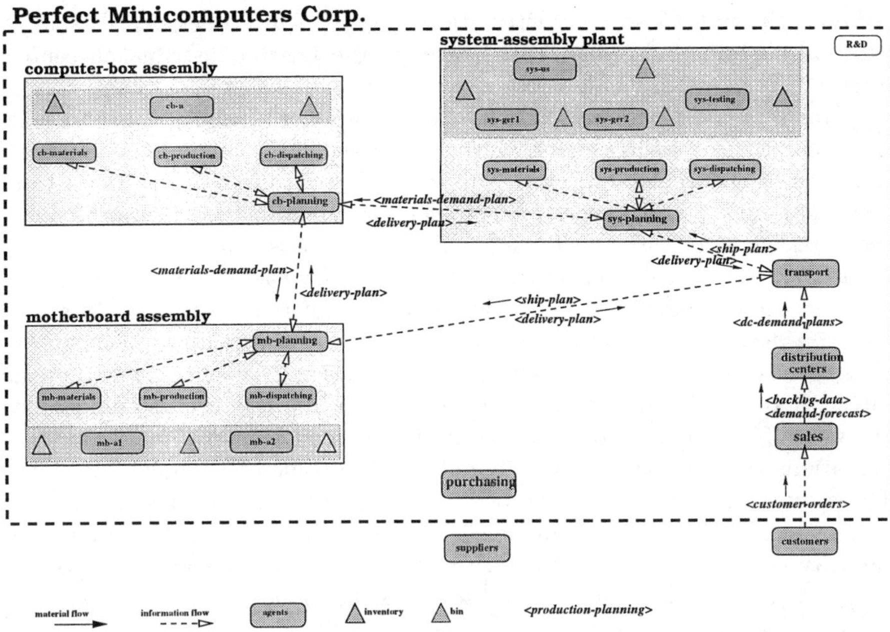

Figure 8: The Perfect Minicomputer Corporation

products, and all reception of raw products. The `Production` agent handles production and the work in progress inventory, and has knowledge of the plant architecture. The `Dispatching` agent handles the finished goods inventory (FGI) and all shipments from the plant. In each plant we also have a set of workstations, bins, and stocks. The workstations are production units with a set number of lines giving the number of units that can be processed simultaneously, a scrap rate (in percent), and a production time for each unit of a given product. The production capacity of the workstation will be given by the number of lines times throughput rate (1 / production time) minus scrap. Each workstation is modeled as an agent. The storage areas between workstations are modeled as *bins*. Each bin has a maximum inventory level, which is the inventory level where the bin is full, hence no further products can be entered. There is a single bin agent in each plant, which is responsible for all bins in the plant. Each plant has two stocks areas, the RPI for incoming components or raw materials, and the FGI on the other end of production. Production is modelled as strictly pull production, where workstations finish products as long as the output bin is not full, and start products as long as the input bin is not empty. Production ceases when weekly production goals are achieved.

Markets and Distribution Centers. PMC also owns and operates their two distribution centers, one in Detroit for the Canada/USA market (`dc-us`), and one in Hamburg for Germany/Austria (`dc-ger`). All computers are distributed through these two distribution centers. All mother boards sold to external customers are distributed through the Detroit distribution center. Each DC is modeled as an agent.

Suppliers and Customers. Each external supplier is modeled as an agent. PMC has a `Purchasing` agent which is responsible for communication with suppliers. The `Purchasing` agent has knowledge of which parts to order from which suppliers. Three types of customers are identified for each product in each market, a, b, and c-customers, with a-customers being most important. Customers are modeled in one `Customer` agent for each market. The `Sales` agent in the company is responsible for communication with customers.

Transportation. A `Transport` agent is defined to handle transportation. This agent has knowledge of transportation times and capacities, and damage rates where applicable. It also keeps logs on tranports currently underway. Deliveries from plant to distribution centers is modeled with uncertain tranportations times (normally distributed), and in some cases limited capacity. Three types of carriers are used; boat, truck, and plane. Internal transportation from plant to plant is modeled as instantaneous, and with unlimited capacity. All transports from external suppliers are the responsibility of the suppliers and are therefore not addressed in the model.

7.2 Coordination Processes

Production Planning. Production is planned through lists of goals for this week and a number of future weeks. These plans propagate upstream through the internal supply chain, and come back downstream as plans of delivery. On the way upstream each agent contributes with its own knowledge.

To examplify the use of conversation plans and rules, let's look at the issuing of demand-forecasts, which start production planning. (The demand-forecast gives the expected number of units ordered for this and coming weeks.) The `Sales` agent has a conversation plan for distributing demand-forecasts to the distribution centers. When a *demand-forecast-conversation* is created, the first rule of the conversation plan applies a specific method to compute the demand-forecast. The next rule of the plan prepares the data for sending, and rule `dfc-3` (Figure 9) sends the message. The ?next-dc-forecast variable contains the demand-forecast for the market of the DC agent that is bound to the ?next-dc variable.

A demand-forecast message from `Sales` creates a *demand-plan-conversation* in the DC's. The rules of these *demand-plan-conversation*-s use knowledge of the DC's inventory levels. *DC-demand-plans*, defining the targetted quantity of each product arriving at the DC at the end of this and coming weeks, are made and sent to the `Transport` agent (and similarly creates a corresponding conversation in the `Tranport` agent). `Transport` knows how much is onway to the DC, and can therefore make *ship-plans*, defining the quantity of each product that should be shipped from a plant to a given DC at the end of this week and a number of future weeks. The *ship-plans* are

```
(def-conversation-rule 'dfc-3
 :current-state 'sending-forecasts
 :such-that '(and (get-conv-var ?conv '?dc-left)
                  (get-conv-var ?conv '?ready-to-send))
 :transmit '(tell :sender ?agent
                  :receiver ?next-dc
                  :content (:demand-forecast ?next-dc-forecast)
                  :conversation ?convn)
 :do-after '(progn (put-conv-var ?conv '?dc-left
                      (rest (get-conv-var ?conv '?dc-left)))
                   (put-conv-var ?conv '?ready-to-send nil))
 :next-state 'sending-forecasts)
```

Figure 9: Sending Forecasts Conversation Rule

sent to the planning agents of the plants concerned.

The aim of a plant's `Planning` agent is to convert the incoming *ship-plan* (if it has external customers) and *materials-demand-plans* from the next downstream plants (if it has internal customers) to the plant's own *materials-demand-plan*-s for all internally supplied parts. These are sent to the next plants upstream. A *materials-demand-plan* defines the number of units of a given product the plant needs this week and a number of future weeks. To calculate the *materials-demand-plan*-s the `Planning` agent will use data from the other agents in the plant.

The *materials-demand-plan*-s will move upstream till they meet a last planning agent in the internal supply-chain. This agent will make *delivery-plan*-s for each customer (next plants downstream, or transport for deliveries to DC-s), defining the number of units the plant will deliver this week and a number of future weeks. This is of course the total demand limited by part availibilities and production capacities. Upon receiving *delivery-plan*-s from upstream internal suppliers, a planning agent has the knowledge it needs to decide the *actual-build-plan* of the plant, i.e. the production goals for this and coming weeks. Thereby it will also make its own *delivery-plan*-s, and these plans will flow down-stream to the end of the supply chain.

Materials Ordering, Delivery, and Reception. From the *actual-build-plan*, via the BOM, the materials agent can calculate a *materials-order-plan* for externally supplied parts. The plans are sent to the purchasing agent, who transforms them to part orders for the suppliers. The supplier agents will send acknowledgment messages to the materials-agents. The materials agents update their on-order data base. Materials-shipments arriving at the plants are modeled as a messages sent by the suppliers to the materials agents. The materials agents update inventory and on-order.

Products Dispatching, Transportation, and Reception. Product tranportation from plant to DC is started through messages from dispatching agents to the `Transport` agent. Arrivals at DC are done by messages from `Tranport` to the DC agent.

7.3 Dealing with Unexpected Events

Each agent within the corporation records its own relevant data every week, building a data base that will be communicated to a `Simulation` agent at the end of the simulation and saved for later analysis. We measure parameters related to inventory levels and customer satisfaction. Examples include the values of all inventories, the company backlog, the incoming orders, the shipments from plants to DC-s, the average time from order arrival till product delivery, the percentage of shipments delivered on-time. We are especially interested in understanding the value of various coordination structures when unexpected disruptions occur in the supply chain and how coordination can be used to reduce the negative consequences of these disruptions. A typical situation is a machine breakdown during normal operation. Such an event tends to increase the level of raw product inventory in the plant where the breakdown occurs because the plant's ability to consume inventory is diminished. The carried inventories of the upstream and downstream plants are also affected and specific coordination is needed to atenuate these effects. Accumulation of inventory is very costly which explains why many manufacturing strategies focus on reducing the level of carried inventories.

To see how coordination can be used to deal with this problem, we have performed a series of experiments involving breakdowns of workstations in several plants and using various coordination mechanisms for dealing with them. There are two levels at which we use coordination to atenuate the disruptions produced by breakdowns. First we increase coordination inside the plant where the breakdown occurs by notifying the plant's planning agent of the breakdown. Knowing of the reduced capacity of its plant, the planning agent will order less materials from its suppliers. Second, we need more interplant coordination to allow all plants to react to this event. We remember that production planning takes place by a process in which first demand flows upstream (from sales to DC-s, then to transport, then to the plants) and then committed delivery plans flow downstream (from the motherboard plant to the computer box assembly plant, then to the system assembly and test plant, and then to transport). When disruptions do not occur delivery plans normaly satisfy the demand. But when disruptions like machine breakdowns occur, some plants will deliver less than demanded and the downstream flow of delivery plans will be used to propagate information about the consequences of the disruptions. To analize these possibilities we simulate breakdowns in various plants and then run the system with the four possible combinations of internal notification and delivery plans: (1) no delivery plans, no notification, (2) no delivery plans, notification (3) delivery plans, no notification and (4) delivery plans, notification. In all cases we assume the breakdown occurs in week 35 and takes 12 weeks to repair. Also, the severity of the breakdown is high, 80% of the plant's capacity being lost.

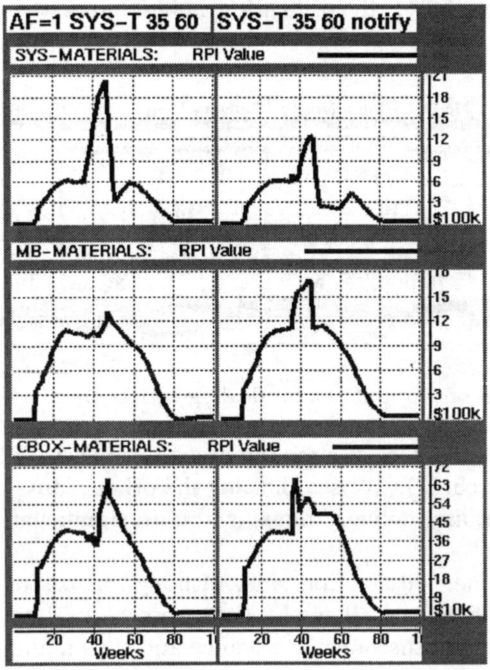

Figure 10: Effect of system test plant breakdown notifications over inventory levels

Some results of these simulations are shown in Figures 10, 11, and 12. In Figure 10 we assume that the breakdown occurs in the system test and assembly plant (the last plant in the chain) and we show the change in the RPI level in cases (3) and (4) above. The results show that the simple notification introduced reduces the average value of the raw product inventory at the system test plant (where the breakdown occured) with 26%. It also shows that for the upstream plants there is a noticeable increase of the same inventory, because they have to keep more inventory in their own stocks. Globally however, the total inventory decreases with about 4% in average. The most important consequence is avoiding the sudden take-off of the system test plant's stock. In the non-notification case the stock is more than tripled in the ten week period following the breakdown. The notification reduces the magnitude of the peek by almost half.

In Figure 11 the breakdown occurs in the computer box assembly plant (second in the chain) and we show the inventories in all four cases above for the next plant downstream (system assembly and test). First, we notice that the local notification has virtually no effect when delivery plans are not sent downstream. This was to be expected, since in this case the breakdown knowledge is not shared with downstream planning agents. However, when delivery plans are used, even without notification, there is a clear gain in RPI reduction of about 16%. If notification is also used, the gain is as high as 26%.

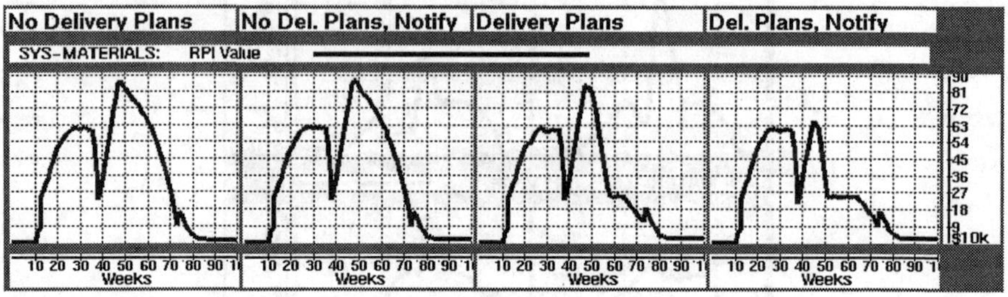

Figure 11: Effects of coordination for dealing with computer box plant breakdown

Finally, in Figure 12 we assume the breakdown occurs in the motherboard plant (first in the chain). We see that for the other plants only the combined use of notification and delivery plans is able to significantly reduce the level of inventories.

On the customer satisfaction side, although a loss of production is inevitable, the notifications allow the enterprise to update the delivery time quotations sent to the customer in advance and thus maintain the customer's trust.

7.4 Evaluation

The above supply chain system has 40 agents and just about the same number of conversation plans. The entire specification takes about 7,500 lines of COOL code, plus about 2,000 lines for GUI-s. A typical simulation run over 100 weeks generates thousands of message exchanges and takes less than 1 hour to complete (no optimizations attempted, and the system runs in an interpreted mode). The system was writen by one author, who hasn't a computer science background, in less than 3 months. Learning the underlying agent and coordination technology was done in another 2 months, during which time a simpler supply chain was built. (Some limited code sharing between these systems occured). We take these data as early indications that the agent coordination model is natural, understandable and adequate to modeling distributed agent systems like the supply chain. We are aware that such evidence, collected from a reduced number of applications, is only partial. Since we are dealing with evaluating a computer language, more compelling evidence requires much more experimentation and many more users than we could afford. We believe however that incomplete as they are, our results show promise that our plan-action oriented coordination language

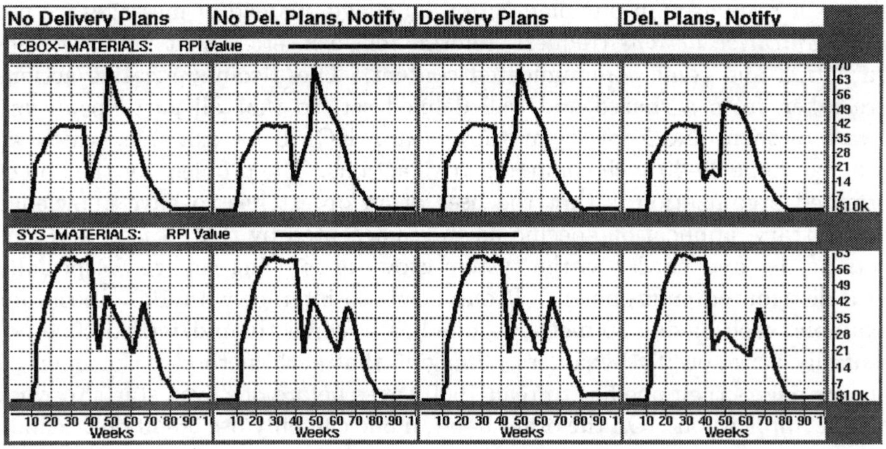

Figure 12: Effects of coordination for dealing with motherboard plant breakdown

addresses the problem of multi-agent coordination in a practically relevant manner.

In terms of how far we have gone with the understanding of coordination as a way to cope with disruptions in a dynamic supply chain system, the answer is that we are in an early stage. Although we have an appropriate experimental setup for studying coordination in face of unexpected events, we have only modelled very simple situations of this kind. We expect to go deeper into the problem once we integrate in our setup more powerful scheduling solvers that agents would use to plan production locally. These would allow agents to develop a precise understanding of the options they have when responding to an unexpected event, and of the consequences of these options. Globally, agents would be in a position to manage change by negotiating about the actions and objectives of each of them.

8 Plan-Action Versus Object Oriented Organizations

A main conclusion we draw from this work is that object oriented languages may not provide the most appropriate organization for modelling coordination. Instead, we belive that a plan-action, process oriented language of the type described is better. There are two main reasons for this. The first has to do with the local and idiosyncratic meaning of communication in object oriented systems. Object oriented languages allow syntactically and semantically arbitrary messages to be exchanged. The structure and meaning of messages are neither declaratively stated nor shared. Instead, meaning is procedurally determined by the code (method) the receiving object will activate in response. In our plan-action language, instead of messages we use *communicative actions* (request, inform, tell, ask, etc.) that bind together an action and some communicated content. These communicative actions are taken from a shared and well defined set, so that all participants are aware of them and know what they mean. KQML for example, which we use, has some 30-40 such communicative actions. The problem for the object oriented organization is that the user of an object has to have knowledge of arbitrary, application specific messages accepted by that object, and this gets harder and harder as the system grows or is being changed, especially in a distributed environment. If one needs to interact with 100 objects for example, each having 10 methods, one has to correctly understand 1000 potentially very specific behaviors. (Imagine that each method is documented on one page - then one has to read 1000 pages before one even starts to work on one application). On the other hand, if one can only use 30-40 well defined message types (communicative actions) no matter how many agents there are and who wrote them, all there is to do is initially learning this small language. Also note that writing translators and interface definition languages in the object oriented case does not address the cause of the problem, but rather its symptoms.

The second reason has to do with the reactive, server model of objects as opposed to the active and reactive model of plans. In the standard organization, objects only respond to messages from clients and can not trigger action at their own initiative. This is in contrast to our coordination enhanced plans that describe long running interactions which can trigger agent action at any time deemed appropriate. This confers autonomy to agents and supports peer to peer as opposed to client-server interaction. Our model of an agent executing symultaneously many plans that drive interactions with many other agents, in each interaction the agent being allowed to behave both proactively and reactively, goes beyond standard object oriented capabilities.

9 Conclusion

We believe we have contributed in several ways to the goal of constructing models and tools enabling multiagent systems to carry out coordinated work in real world applications. First, we have contributed a model of the new type of coordination knowledge as complex, coordination enhanced plans involving interactions by communicative action. The execution by agents of these plans results in multiple structured conversations taking place amongst agents. These ideas have been substantiated into a practical, application independent coordination language that provides constructs for specifying the coordination enhanced plans as well as the interpreter supporting their execution. Our interpreter supports multiple conversation management, a diverse rule typology that, amongst others, provides for handling exceptional or unexpected situations, conversation synchronization, conversation initiation, as well as optimization of plan execution by decision-theoretic mechanisms.

Second, we have provided methods and interfaces for acquiring coordination models in an asynchronous, situated manner. Our knowledge acquisition method is suited to autonomous agents that operate without central control, as it supports capturing knowledge as it dynamically emerges in the context of each agent's interactions. Together, these two enable developers both to reuse coordination structures and to efficiently build new ones.

Third, in cooperation with industry partners, we have applied these models and tools to industrially relevant problems, in order to keep our work in touch with reality and "falsify" our solutions as early as possible based on feedback from reality.

With respect to the coordination model, previous work has investigated related state based representations [Mar92] but has not consolidated the theoretical notions into usable language constructs, making it hard to use their ideas into applications. Formalizations of mental state notions related to agency (like [CL90]) have provided semantic models that clarify a number of issues, but operate under limiting assumptions that similarly make practical use and consolidation difficult. Some conversational concepts have been used by [KTBB92, SMK90, MWFF92] in the context of collaborative and workflow applications. We have extended and modified them for use in multi-agent settings and added knowledge acquisition and sophisticated control that led to a more generic, application independent language. Agent oriented programming [Sho93] similarly uses communicative action, rules and agent representations. Our language differs from AOP in the explicit provision of plans and conversations, the more powerful control structures that emerge from them and the more powerful programming environment including the support for knowledge acquisition.

The coordination language has been now evaluated on several problems, including supply chain coordination projects carried out in cooperation with industry. Although the number of applications we have built as well as the number of users of our system are both limited, the evidence we have so far shows that our approach is promising in terms of naturalness of the coordination model, effectiveness of representation and power and usability of the provided programming tools. In all situations, the coordination language enabled us to quickly prototype the system and build running versions demonstrating the required behavior. Often, an initial (incomplete) version of the system has been built in a few hours or days, enabling us to immediately demonstrate its functionality. Moreover, we have found the approach and the acquisition tool explainable to and usable by industrial engineers who don't necessarily have a computer science background. We credit the knowledge acquisition approach and tool with this. Users can very quickly prototype an application, e.g. by copy and paste from other applications. The new system can be very incomplete (all rules can be empty) but will still run, immediately giving users a sense of what's going on and putting them in control of their work. Due to the active exploration allowed by the KA tool users can *in the same time* learn the system and prototype their application, so they do not loose time in a lenghty learning curve before doing what they are really interested in.

Finally, we believe that the coordination language is a representative of a class of languages which we call plan-action oriented. We have shown that the plan-action orientation, significantly different from the standard object orientation, brings in new capabilities that are required for modeling and executing coordinated behavior among distributed agents. Thus it may be considered as a useful approach for addressing the new issues raised by building systems for the Internet.

Acknowledgments: This research is supported, in part, by the Manufacturing Research Corporation of Ontario, Natural Science and Engineering Research Council, Digital Equipment Corp., Micro Electronics and Computer Research Corp., Spar Aerospace, Carnegie Group and Quintus Corp.

References

[Bra87] Bratman, M., Intentions, Plans and Practical Reason, Harvard University Press, 1987

[Cas95] Castelfranchi, C., Commitments: From Individual Intentions to Groups and Organizations, in: Proceedings of First International Conference on Multi-Agent Systems, AAAI Press/The MIT Press, 1995, 41-48

[Cla85] Clancey, W. J., Heuristic Classification, Artificial Intelligence 27, 1985, 289-350

[CL90] Cohen, P. R., Levesque, H., Intention is Choice with Commitment, Artificial Intelligence 42, 1990, 213-261

[CL91] Cohen, P. R., Levesque, H., Teamwork, Nous 15, 1991, 487-512

[DL91] Durfee, E. H., Lesser, V., Partial Global Planning: A Coordination Framework for Distributed Hypothesis Formation, IEEE Trans. on Systems, Man and Cybernetics 21 (6), 1991, 1363-1378

[DL95] Decker, K. S., Lesser, V., Designing a Family of Coordination Algorithms. in: Proceedings of First International Conference on Multi-Agent Systems, San Francisco, AAAI Press/The MIT Press, 1995, 73-80

[Dur88] Durfee, E. H., Coordination of Distributed Problem Solvers, Kluwer Academic Press, 1988

[Fin92] Finin, T., *et al*, Specification of the KQML Agent Communication Language, The DARPA Knowledge Sharing Initiative, External Interfaces Working Group, 1992

[Fox87] Fox, M. S., Beyond the Knowledge Level, in: L. Kerschberg (ed.), Expert Database Systems, Benjamin/Cummings Publishing Company, 1987, 455-463

[Geo84] Geogeff, M. P., A Theory of Action for Multi-Agent Planning, in: Proceedings of National Conference on AI, Austin, 1984, 125-129

[GF92] Genesereth, M. R., Fikes, R. E., Knowledge Interchange Format, Version 3.0, Reference Manual, Computer Science Department, Stanford University, Technical Report Logic-92-1, 1992

[GK94] Genesereth, M. R., Ketchpel, S., Software Agents, Communications of the ACM 37 (7), 1994, 100-105

[Huh87] Huhns, M. N., (ed.), Distributed Artificial Intelligence, Pitman Publishing, London, 1987

[Jen92] Jennings, N. R., Towards a Cooperation Knowledge Level for Collaborative Problem Solving, in: Proceedings 10-th European Conference on AI, Vienna, Austria, 1992, 224-228

[Jen93] Jennings, N. R., Commitments and Conventions: The Foundation of Coordination in Multi-Agent Systems, The Knowledge Engineering Review 8 (3), 1993, 223-250

[Jen95] Jennings, N. R., Controlling Cooperative Problem Solving in Industrial Multi-Agent Systems Using Joint Intentions, Artificial Intelligence 75 (2), 1995, 195-240

[JM92] Jennings, N. R., Mamdani, E., Using Joint Responsibility to Coordinate Collaborative Problem Solving in Dynamic Environments, in: Proceedings of 10-th National Conference on AI, San Jose, CA, 1992, 269-275

[KTBB92] Kaplan, S. M., Tolone, W. J., Bogia, D. P., Bignoli, C., Flexible, Active Support for Collaborative Work with Conversation Builder, in: CSCW 92 Proceedings, 1992, 378-385

[KGWTGO93] Kuokka, D., McGuire, J., Weber, J., Tenenbaum, J., Gruber, T., Olsen, G., SHADE: Knowledge Based Technology for the Reengineering Problem, Technical Report, Lockheed Artificial Intelligence Center, 1993

[LCN90] Levesque, H. J., Cohen, P. R., Nunes, J. H., On Acting Together, in: Proceedings of 8-th National Conference on AI, Boston, 1990, 94-99

[MC91] Malone, T. W., Crowston, K., Toward an Interdisciplinary Theory of Coordination, Center for Coordination Science Technical Report 120, MIT Sloan School, 1991

[Mar92] Martial., F. von, Coordinating Plans of Autonomous Agents, Lecture Notes in Artificial Intelligence 610, Springer Verlag Berlin Heidelberg, 1992

[Der88] McDermott, J., A Taxonomy of Problem solving Methods, in: S. Marcus (ed.), Automating Knowledge Acquisition for Expert Systems, Kluwer Academic Press, 1988, 225-226

[MWFF92] Medina-Mora, R., Winograd, T., Flores, R., Flores, F., The Action Workflow Approach to Workflow Management Technology, in: CSCW 92 Proceedings, 1992, 281-288

[MWJ97] Muller, J. P., Wooldridge, M. J. Jennings, N. R., (eds.), Intelligent Agents III: Agent Theories, Architectures and Languages, Lecture Notes in Artificial Intelligence 1193, Springer Verlag, 1997

[PFPKFGN92] Patil, R., Fikes, R., Patel-Schneider, P., McKay, D., Finin, T., Gruber, T., Neches, R., The ARPA Knowledge Sharing Effort: Progress report, in: B. Nebel, C. Rich, W. Swartout (eds.), Principles of Knowledge Representation and Reasoning: Proceedings of the Third International Conference (KR'92), San Mateo, CA, Nov. 1992

[Sea91] Searle, J., Collective Intentions and Actions, in: P. R. Coehn, J. Morgan, M. E. Pollak (eds.), Intentions in Communication, MIT Press, 1991, 401-416

[Sho93] Shoham, Y., Agent-Oriented Programming, Artificial Intelligence 60, 1993, 51-92

[Sho95] Shoham, Y., Tennenholtz, M., On Social Laws for Artificial Agent Societies: Off-line Design, Artificial Intelligence 73 (1-2), 1995, 231-252

[Smi80] Smith, R. S., The Contract Net Protocol: High Level Communication and Control in a Distributed Problem Solver, IEEE Transactions on Computers 29 (12), 1980, 1104-1113

[SMK90] Shepherd, A., Mayer, N., Kuchinsky, A., Strudel - An Extensible Electronic Conversation Toolkit, in: CSCW 90 Proceedings, 1990, 93-104

[WSB92] Wielinga, B. J., Schreiber, A. Th., Breuker, J. A., KADS: A Modeling Approach to Knowledge Acquisition, Knowledge Acquisition 4 (1), 1992

List of Contributors

- ***Reiner Anderl***
DiK
TU Darmstadt
Petersenstr. 30
D-64287 Darmstadt
Germany

- ***Mihai Barbuceanu***
Enterprise Integration Laboratory
University of Toronto
4 Taddle Creek Rd
Toronto M5S 3G9
Canada

- ***Peter Bernus***
School of Computing and Information Technology
Griffith University
Nathan (Brisbane)
Queensland 4111
Australia

- ***Andy Bond***
CRC for Distributed Technology
Level 7, Gehrmann Laboratories
The University of Queensland
Brisbane, Queensland, 4072
Australia

- ***David Chen***
GRAI/LAP
Université de Bordeaux
351, Cours de la Libération
F-33405 Talance Cedex
France

- ***Paul Clements***
Department of Manufacturing Engineering
Loughborough University
Loughborough
Leics. LE11 3TU
England

- ***Ian Coutts***
Department of Manufacturing Engineering
Loughborough University
Loughborough
Leics. LE11 3TU
England

- ***Wes Crump***
Knowledge Based Systems, Inc.
One KBSI Place
1500 University Drive East
College Station, TX 77840-2335
USA

- ***Jules Desharnais***
Département d'informatique
Université Laval
Québec, QC G1K 7P4
Canada

- ***Norbert Dick***
IBM Deutschland Informationssysteme GmbH
Gustav-Heinemann-Ufer 120-122
D-50968 Köln
Germany

- ***Guy Doumeingts***
GRAI/LAP
Université de Bordeaux
351, Cours de la Libération
F-33405 Talance Cedex
France

- ***Keith Duddy***
CRC for Distributed Technology
Level 7, Gehrmann Laboratories
The University of Queensland
Brisbane, Queensland, 4072
Australia

- ***Otto K. Ferstl***
Universität Bamberg
Feldkirchstr. 21
D-96052 Bamberg
Germany

- ***Clive Finkelstein***
Information Engineering Services Pty Ltd
P.O. Box 84
Caulfield South, Vic 3162
Australia

- ***Marc Frappier***
Département de mathématiques et d'informatique
Université de Sherbrooke
Sherbrooke,
QC J1K 2R1
Canada

- ***Ted Goranson***
Sirius Beta
1976 Munden Pt
Va Beach VA 23457-1227
USA

- ***Michael Gruninger***
Enterprise Integration Labatory
Department of Industrial Engineering
University of Toronto
Toronto, M5S 1A4
Canada

- ***Terry Halpin***
Visio Corporation
520 Pike Street, Suite 1800
Seattle WA 98101
USA

- ***Alfred Helmerich***
FAST e.V.
Arabellastr. 17
D-81925 München
Germany

- ***Brian Henderson-Sellers***
Swinburne University of Technology
John Street, PO BOX 218
Hawthorn, Victoria 3122
Australia

- ***Alois Hofinger***
  IBM Deutschland GmbH
  Anzingerstr. 29
  D-81671 München
  Germany

- ***Jürgen Huschens***
  IBM Deutschland GmbH
  Gustav-Heinemann-Ufer 120-122
  D-50968 Köln
  Germany

- ***Matthias Jarke***
  Lehrstuhl Informatik V
  RWTH Aachen
  Ahornstr. 55
  D-52056 Aachen
  Germany

- ***Manfred A. Jeusfeld***
  Infolab
  KUB Tilburg University
  Warandelaan 2
  Postbus 90153
  5000 LE Tilburg
  The Netherlands

- ***Yan Jin***
  Denney Research Building
  Suite 101, 1042 W. 36th Place, University Park
  Los Angeles,
  CA90089-1111
  USA

- ***Roland Jochem***
  Fraunhofer Institute for Production and Design Technology
  Pascalstr. 8-9
  D-10587 Berlin
  Germany

- ***Harald John***
  DiK
  TU Darmstadt
  Petersenstr. 30
  D-64287 Darmstadt
  Germany

- ***Hans-Bernd Kittlaus***
  SIZ Informatikzentrum der Sparkassenorganisation GmbH
  Königswinterer Str. 552
  D-53227 Bonn
  Germany

- ***Wojtek Kozaczynski***
  SSA R&D Labs
  Chicago, IL 60661
  USA

- ***Daniela Krahl***
  SIZ Informatikzentrum der Sparkassenorganisation GmbH
  Königswinterer Str. 552
  D-53227 Bonn
  Germany

- ***Herrmann Krallmann***
  Informatik
  TU Berlin
  Franklinstr. 28/29
  D-10587 Berlin
  Germany

- ***Jintae Lee***
  Department of Decision Sciences
  University of Hawaii
  2404 Maile Way
  Honolulu, HI 96825
  USA

- ***Volker Levering***
  GPS Prof. Schuh Komplexitätsmanagement GmbH
  Monnetstr. 9
  D-52146 Würselen
  Germany

- ***Thomas Malone***
  MIT
  Center for Coordination Science
  1. Amherst St.
  Cambridge, MA 02139
  USA

- ***Richard J. Mayer***
  Texas A&M University
  College Station, TX 77840-2335
  USA

- ***Stefan Meinhardt***
  SAP AG
  Postfach 1461
  D-69185 Walldorf
  Germany

- ***Jim Melton***
  Sybase Inc.
  1930 Viscounti Drive
  Sandy, UT 84093-1063
  USA

- ***Christopher Menzel***
  Texas A&M University
  College Station, TX 77840-2335
  USA

- ***Kai Mertins***
  Fraunhofer Institute for Production and Design Technology
  Pascalstr. 8-9
  D-10587 Berlin
  Germany

- ***Ali Mili***
  Institute for Software Research
  1000 Technology Drive
  Fairmont, WV 26554
  USA

- ***John Mylopoulos***
  Department of Computer Science
  University of Toronto
  6 King's College Road
  Toronto M55 1A4
  Canada

- ***Hans W. Nissen***
  Lehrstuhl Informatik V
  RWTH Aachen
  Ahornstr. 55
  D-52056 Aachen
  Germany

- ***Karl Popp***
  SAP AG
  Postfach 1461
  D-69185 Walldorf
  Germany

- ***Jean-Marie Proth***
  INRIA Lorraine
  Technopôle Metz
  4, rue Marconi
  F-57070 Metz
  France

- ***Christian Pütter***
  DiK
  TU Darmstadt
  Petersenstr. 30
  D-64287 Darmstadt
  Germany

- ***Markus Rabe***
  Fraunhofer Institute for Production and Design Technology
  Pascalstr. 8-9
  D-10587 Berlin
  Germany

- ***Kerry Raymond***
  CRC for Distributed Technology
  Level 7, Gehrmann Laboratories
  The University of Queensland
  Brisbane, Queensland, 4072
  Australia

- ***Walter Rupietta***
  Siemens Nixdorf Informationssysteme AG
  Heinz-Nixdorf-Ring 1
  D-33094 Paderborn
  Germany

- ***August-Wilhelm Scheer***
  IWi
  Universität des Saarlandes
  Postfach 15 11 50
  D-66041 Saarbrücken
  Germany

- ***Günter Schmidt***
  ITM
  Universität des Saarlandes
  Postfach 15 11 50
  D-66041 Saarbrücken
  Germany

- ***Günther Schuh***
  University of St. Gallen
  Dufourstr. 50
  CH-9000 St. Gallen
  Switzerland

- ***Elmar Sinz***
  Universität Bamberg
  Feldkirchstr. 21
  D-96052 Bamberg
  Germany

- ***Thomas Siepmann***
  GPS Prof. Schuh Komplexitätsmanagment GmbH
  Monnetstr. 9
  D-52146 Würselen
  Germany

- ***John F. Sowa***
  21 Palmer Avenue
  Croton-on-Hudson
  NY 10520
  USA

- ***Martin Staudt***
  Swiss Life
  Information Systems Research, CH/IFUE
  P.O.Box
  CH-8022 Zürich
  Switzerland

- ***Austin Tate***
  Artificial Intelligence Application Institute
  The University of Edinburgh
  80 South Bridge
  Edinburgh EH1 1HN
  UK

- ***Rune Teigen***
  Enterprise Integration Laboratory
  University of Toronto
  4 Taddle Creek Rd, Rosebrugh Building
  Toronto M5S 3G9
  Canada

- ***Florence Tissot***
  Knowledge Based Systems, Inc.
  One KBSI Place
  1500 University Drive East
  College Station, TX 77840-2335
  USA

- ***Bruno Vallespir***
  GRAI/LAP
  Université de Bordeaux
  351, Cours de la Libération
  F-33405 Talance Cedex
  France

- ***Francois Vernadat***
  LGIPM - Fac. des Sciences
  Université de Metz
  Ile du Saulcy
  F-57012 Metz Cedex 1
  France

- ***Gottfried Vossen***
  Lehrstuhl für Informatik
  Universität Münster
  Steinfurter Straße 107
  D-48149 Münster
  Germany

- ***Mathias Weske***
  Lehrstuhl für Informatik
  Universität Münster
  Steinfurter Straße 107
  D-48149 Münster
  Germany

- ***Richard Weston***
  Department of Manufacturing Engineering
  Loughborough University
  Loughborough
  Leics. LE11 3TU
  England

- ***Gay Wood***
  UBIS GmbH
  Alt-Moabit 98
  D-10559 Berlin
  Germany

- ***Gregg Yost***
  Ellora Software, Inc.
  7 Bean St., Bldg. 2602
  Devens, MA 01432
  USA

Index

Druck: Strauss Offsetdruck, Mörlenbach
Verarbeitung: Schäffer, Grünstadt